Reconfigurations

Reconfigurations

Critical Theory and General Economy

Arkady Plotnitsky

University Press of Florida

Gainesville   Tallahassee   Tampa   Boca Raton   Pensacola   Orlando   Miami   Jacksonville

An earlier version of Chapter 2 was published in *Studies in XXth Century Literature* 12, no. 2 (Summer 1988): 199–228.

University Press of Florida is the scholarly publishing agency for the State University System of Florida, comprised of Florida A&M University (Tallahassee), Florida Atlantic University (Boca Raton), Florida International University (Miami), Florida State University (Tallahassee), University of Central Florida (Orlando), University of Florida (Gainesville), University of North Florida (Jacksonville), University of South Florida (Tampa), University of West Florida (Pensacola).

Library of Congress Cataloging in Publication Data

Plotnitsky, Arkady.
Reconfigurations: critical theory and general economy / Arkady Plotnitsky.
   p. cm.
Includes bibliographical references and index.
ISBN 0-8130-1172-8. — ISBN 0-8130-1173-6 (pbk.)
1. Critical theory. 2. Postmodernism. 3. Bataille, Georges, 1897–1962. 4. Derrida, Jacques. 5. Nietzsche, Friedrich Wilhelm, 1844–1900. 6. Aesthetics.
I. Title.
B831.2.P55 1993
190' .9'04—dc20

92-22271
CIP

University Press of Florida
15 Northwest 15th Street
Gainesville, FL 32611

Contents

Acknowledgments

I thank my students for many years of extraordinarily productive and rewarding intellectual exchange. The present study is a product of this exchange and a contribution to it.

I owe a debt of gratitude to friends and colleagues who have supported my work throughout many years and made important contributions to this study by their encouragement, suggestions, and criticism. I am especially grateful to Barbara Herrnstein Smith for the attention she has given my writing, her generous help, and many invaluable discussions. Special thanks also to Stuart Curran and Gerald Prince for their continuous support of my work and intellectual pursuits. My thanks to Jean Alter, Claudia Brodsky, Marjorie Levinson, Vicki Mahaffey, John McCarthy, Warren Motte, Elliott Mossman, Michèle Richman, Frank Trommler, Gregory Ulmer, Joseph Valente, Constance Walker, and Samuel Weber.

I am grateful to Silke Weineck and Gwen Wells for their invaluable help with German and French sources and for many productive discussions. My particular thanks also to Paula Geyh for her help and suggestions. Irene Fizer, Patrick Hartigan, and Jeanne Gurley were instrumental in preparing the manuscript. My thanks to Jeanne Ruppert, from Florida State University, for her interest in my work and her support of the project, and to Walda Metcalf and the staff of the University Press of Florida for seeing the manuscript through its production and publication. I am grateful to Sharon Ann Jaeger for her care and skills in copyediting the manuscript.

Finally, my very special thanks to Nina and Marsha.

Preface

The essays comprising this study deal with transformations—reconfigurations—of critical theory associated by this study's argument with Georges Bataille's idea of general economy and the general economic dimensions of Jacques Derrida's discourse. These transformations, however, may be seen as beginning with Nietzsche. Coincidentally, they reach their culmination in the closing decade of this century (around 1990), as Nietzsche's works, which date to 1889, did at the close of the previous one. The critical theory of my title thus refers primarily to this conjunction, via the idea of general economy, of Nietzsche and theory in the wake of poststructuralism, most particularly in Bataille and Derrida. It does retain other possibilities as its frames of reference, some more immediate and others more mediated: critique in the Kantian or a post-Kantian sense; critical economies in Marx and Nietzsche; critical theory as understood by the Frankfurt School; or more recent critical economies (in addition to Derrida and deconstruction) in Heidegger, Lacan, Althusser, Deleuze, Foucault, Lyotard, and their extension in literary criticism and theory.

The developments at issue cannot be uniquely grounded in Nietzsche. First, such a unique grounding is impossible for general theoretical reasons because the reconfigurations these developments produce allow and indeed force us to suspend all unique or unconditional grounding. Second, such a grounding is also impossible for specific historical reasons since some of these developments precede Nietzsche or evolve along historico-theoretical trajectories that are different from those suggested by the present study, and thus mark different evolutionary and revolutionary points. Some of these alternative trajectories have been explored in recent literature, variously engaging the major figures and themes discussed in this study, or else pursuing still different routes. Furthermore, the reconfigurations considered here depend on radical *rereadings* of Nietzsche, specifically on the French scene, beginning with Gilles Deleuze's *Nietzsche and Philosophy* (1962). Bataille's, Heidegger's, and several other thinkers' earlier encounters with Nietzsche were major forces on this scene as well; and the subsequent rereadings of Nietzsche often operate specifically against the background of their work. Nevertheless, Nietzsche remains a momentous, perhaps unique, revolutionary event in this history.

Nietzsche himself speaks in *Daybreak* [*Morgenröte*] of the "tremendous consequences [die ungeheuren Folgen]" of the new things—and the new reasons for old things—that he has discovered. Perhaps the most radical consequences as yet will be new transformations, the new possibilities of theory and the new constraints on theory, including impossibilities, that emerge as a result. In any development, revolutionary or evolutionary, there is a double economy of possibilities and constraints. Once *new* configurations become possible, some *old* configurations become impossible—theoretically, psychologically, or politically. The psychology and politics of such transformations are always complex since, depending on the conditions, some of us find the changes to be for the better, others for the worse. The very complexity of demarcations between the old and the new must be kept in mind. Nor do transformations always make things easier. In the case of theory, the most revolutionary transformations may well make things more difficult: they lead to more complex problems and questions, and the questions and problems that used to be difficult and complex become simple or even trivial as a result.

Nietzsche understood this process very well; indeed, the saying is attributed to him that, as science gets better, the questions become stranger. The very opposition between simple and complex itself becomes increasingly more problematic and demands reconfiguration, a process that will be considered in this study. By the same token, it is rarely *simply* a question of choice or of *simple* choice between things old and new, or complex and simple, or conversely, *simply* a question of necessity, whether theoretical or political, or both at once. Choices are possibilities, but they are never unconstrained; and often one is not given the possibility of a choice at all, so that, as Derrida points out, the very category of choice—and, one must add, the category of necessity—become trivial.

In great measure, the present study is an analysis of Derrida and of the relations—the affinities and the differences—between Nietzsche and Derrida, with Bataille as a key mediating figure. Bataille's work is crucial because it introduces and develops the matrix of the general economy—the economy that takes into account, or rather relates to, the irreducible loss in representation and meaning, but that cannot be *restricted* to an economy of loss only. This matrix constitutes the main theoretical instrument of the present study; and the question and the metaphor of economy constitute its major point of entry onto the poststructuralist scene. Equally importantly, the general economy offers an extraordinarily effective possibility of accounting for the textual practices of Nietzsche, Bataille, Derrida, and other practitioners of the plural or, as I shall call it, the complementary style.

The notion of the plural style was introduced by Derrida, via Nietzsche, in order to account for the simultaneous operation of a given text or group of texts inside and outside the register of philosophy. The plural style is necessitated by the general economy: it is always general economic, although one should not identify it with the general economy. I shall further extend the notion of plural style—and by implication the notion of general economy—so as to approach more multiple registers, most specifically of theory, although these notions are applicable to a great deal more than theory. This extension proceeds via complementarity as a model for a critical practice that can work out of a general economy.

The principle of complementarity is drawn from Niels Bohr's interpretation of quantum mechanics, where it is developed in order to account for the indeterminacy of quantum systems and to describe—simultaneously, but without classical synthesis—their conflicting aspects. The principle is expanded by this study so as mutually to enrich and develop both ideas—general economy and complementarity—within a comprehensive theoretical and historical framework. The resulting framework enables the book to consider and engage diverse discursive practices—literary, critical, theoretical, historical, and political—and to show how the general economy operates in and transforms the contemporary theoretical landscape.

Derrida's theoretical matrix and his style as plural style define themselves as general economic. I shall argue that Nietzsche's discourse also conforms to a general economy and is one of Bataille's main sources in this respect. By the same token, all three economies and styles are plural or, again, complementary. One must also rigorously differentiate between different general or restricted economies, even though, by definition and in opposition to restricted economies, there cannot be one single general economy, even in a given text: this is one of the reasons for the necessity of plural or complementary styles. But such styles are themselves different, as in Nietzsche, Bataille, and Derrida; and the practice of plural style, particularly in the extended sense of this analysis, is not confined to these figures.

This study concerns itself more with exploring the theoretical configurations and reconfigurations emerging in and resulting from the works at issue than with offering a reading or interpretation of them. 'Readings,' in various senses of this now very complex term, must inevitably be engaged, even assuming that one could finally separate theory and reading or theory and history or reading and history. All these, however, must always be engaged according to complementarity and general economy. There is always a difference in emphasis and in balance, or imbalance, of gains and losses in reading, theory, history, theory, or politics. But then, given the ineluctably general economy of the process, one can never fully calculate in advance, maintain, or ensure for the future one's balances or one's losses and gains.

The first chapter, "Exchanges, the Play of Forces, and General Economy," considers the significance of the matrix of the general economy and its place on the scene of poststructuralism or postmodernism. The chapter introduces complementarity by conjoining Bohr's idea, understood as a metaphorical model, with the general economy, and then uses this joint framework in its analytical mapping of the historical, theoretical, critical, and political features of the poststructuralist landscape, a landscape that is itself plural and complementary. The chapter also offers a discussion of a number of recent commentaries on the major figures and themes at issue.

Chapter 2 considers the relations among Kant, Bataille, and Derrida and, in this context, the *reconfiguration* of the relations between art and philosophy and of theoretical style in general. As I discuss in Chapter 1, the significance of Kant in recent theoretical discussions, particularly in relation to the thematics of economy, has been momentous. *The Critique of Judgement* has played a major role in the poststructuralist debate, particularly in the works of Deleuze, Derrida, Jean-François Lyotard, Jean-Luc Nancy, and Paul de Man. Hegel's role was, of course, no less momentous, with respect both to the question of history and, more recently, to the question of aesthetics. Like Kant, Hegel shapes both modern intellectual history and the poststructuralist scene. Thus the poststructuralist scene also features a reconfiguration of Kant and Hegel, the juncture that had dominated modern, or let us say post-Hegelian, intellectual history. Along with Bataille's encounters with Nietzsche, his confrontation with Hegel has played an important role in recent theoretical discussions. The question of the general economy is a major product of this confrontation, proceeding through Marx and the Marxist readings of Hegel, specifically by Alexander Kojève. As I suggest in Chapter 2, however, the question of Kant may be of greater importance in Bataille than is immediately apparent.

In theoretical terms, Chapter 2 explores a multiple reconfiguration of philosophical, political, aesthetic, and artistic economies as restricted and as general systems. I conclude this analysis with a discussion of the question of plural style on the modern theoretico-political scene. Whether it aspires to be such or not, a theoretical style can never be *only* theoretical. Conversely, neither can there be an absolutely or unconditionally nontheoretical style, although the very denomination "theoretical" itself becomes stratified and problematized, both inside and outside any theoretical field, particularly in philosophy. In this context the question of plural style becomes extended and reconfigured quite differently from the figure of plural style introduced by Derrida. In Derrida, plural style refers to a simultaneous operation inside and outside the philosophical register, in order to enact a radical critique of philosophy, to make its concepts tremble. This economy of plural style is a part of the economy of the closure of philosophy introduced by Derrida. As I shall suggest, however, through an analysis of Nietzsche's and Bataille's styles in Chapter 2 and later in Chapter 4, this configuration of plural style and of closure may be further pluralized and extended in relation to the economy of transformation of a given closure or configuration of closures.

Proceeding by way of Nietzsche and deconstruction, Chapter 3 further explores the stylistic transformation of philosophical discourse. It also considers the poststructuralist reconfigurations of narrative and the theory of narrative. The question of narrative has been raised throughout the recent history of theory, indeed by many of the authors at issue in this study. This question has many important implications for modern literary and critical theory, and historical studies, reaching far beyond the thematics of narrative itself. The present analysis, however, is specifically concerned with the notion of play and with the relations between play and narrative. Emerging early in Nietzsche, the (general) economy of play anticipates and announces his massive theoretical revolution—a radical reconfiguration of interpretation and theory or, to use his own phrase, a "reevaluation of all values."

Chapter 4 considers the significance of Nietzsche in relation both to the reconfigurations of theory at issue in this book and to Derrida and deconstruction. This analysis proceeds by engaging both certain historico-political concerns of theory and the question of art and aesthetics. The division of the chapter reflects the different degrees of emphasis in each area. As I have previously noted, however, these issues necessarily interpenetrate each other and must often be engaged simultaneously. The chapter concludes with an analysis of the questions of closure and of interminable analysis, and the difference between Nietzsche and Derrida along these lines. Throughout, however, it considers more general relations between philosophy and other forms or economies, restricted and general, of theoretical practice. In many ways, this analysis is the theoretical center of this study.

The first three chapters constitute the first part of the project, describing the major transformations of theory. The second part deals with the major consequences and implications of these transformations, first in relation to the question of theory in Chapter 5, and then to the question of history in Chapter 6. The background configurations of Chapter 6 are the recent Marxist conceptions of history, specifically those of Louis Althusser and Fredric Jameson, juxtaposed to what may be seen as a deconstructive, or postdeconstructive, economy—a general economy—of history. The reconfiguration that emerges as a result is thus a general economy of history, together with the new shapes of historical, critical, and theoretical projects that such a general economy suggests and demands.

The last chapter deals, via Nietzsche, Heidegger, Bataille, and Derrida, with the question of science and technology, specifically with respect to the various concepts and metaphors of economy that emerge in this context. The more general problematic of science and technology in the poststructuralist context is also considered, such as the questions and metaphors of undecidability (via Kurt Gödel's incompleteness theorem, on the one hand, and deconstruction, on the other), Niels Bohr's theory of complementarity, and the question of matter. By way of theoretical or experimental findings and the metaphorical models that these findings offer, modern science and technology are crucial to all the texts considered in this study, beginning with Kant and Hegel, and continuing through Nietzsche, Heidegger, Bataille, and Derrida.

Thus, proceeding via Nietzsche, Freud, Bataille, and Derrida—all thinkers of the unconscious—the book begins with the Kantian problematic of taste and ends with the Hegelian problematic of history and Heidegger's question concerning technology. This, in a way, is a logical progression in a study that is also an exploration of the relations between consciousness and the unconscious in the practice of theory and the new technologies of theoretical style.

Part I
Transformations

Chapter 1

Exchanges, the Play of Forces, and General Economy

The main goal of this chapter is to consider the role of the thematics of economy and general economy in contemporary theory. The "exchanges" and the "play of forces" of my title refer both to two major economic themes or metaphors engaged by general economy as a theoretical or a historico-theoretical matrix, and to the exchanges and forces operating in the intellectual history and current discussions at issue in this study. More generally, the historico-theoretical configuration considered by the present study demands a general economic description and analysis. The history, or the history-theory, of general economy is itself general economic. The framework, however, implies a general economic efficacy of any historical or theoretical representation or analysis. The direction of the present study is more theoretical than historical; but some historical treatment is helpful, even aside from the fact that it is impossible, under the conditions of general economy, to have an absolute separation, or an absolute unification, of forces and fields—such as theory, history, criticism, and literature.

From this perspective, while the principal approach offered by the book is more critico-theoretical than historical, much of this analysis is also a form of historical analysis responsive to the limits of *historical* analysis under the conditions of general economy. This chapter and several other portions of the study are, conversely, more historical than the rest of the book. But, reversing the perspective, one may suggest that this historical analysis offers a form of theoretical analysis that is responsive to the limits of *theoretical* analysis under the conditions of general economy. Similar propositions can be advanced concerning the relationships between criticism and theory, or criticism and history, or criticism and politics.

Such interactions may be described by way of what I shall call, by analogy with Niels Bohr's complementarity principle in quantum mechanics, complementary interactions. I shall offer specific definitions and elaborations presently. In the context at issue at the moment, complementarity implies that one's analysis may, and at times must, be pursued via interaction among theoretical, critical, historical, or political forms of inquiry; but without claiming—indeed, prohibiting, in practice and in principle—their classical and specifically Hegelian synthesis. Such inter- or cross-disciplinary complementary interactions both characterize general economic textual practice and are necessary in order to describe the historico-theoretical configuration within which such a practice has emerged.

The general economy itself, as understood by Bataille, relates the configurations it considers to the loss of meaning—a loss that it regards as ineluctable within any given system. According to Bataille, "the *general economy* makes apparent that *excesses of energy are produced, and these excesses cannot be utilized. The excessive energy can only be lost without the slightest aim, consequently without any meaning.*" The general economy, as it is practiced by Nietzsche, Bataille, and Derrida, is juxtaposed to classical theoretical systems or *restricted economies*, such as Hegel's philosophy or Marx's political economy. Such classical theories configure their objects and the relationships between those objects as always meaningful and claim that the systems that they present avoid the unproductive expenditure of energy, containing within their bounds multiplicity and indeterminacy. The general economy exposes all such claims as finally untenable; it demands—and enacts—a different form of theoretical practice. This practice, I shall argue, also demands plurality and, in the present terms, complementarity of textual and strategic engagement; and complementarity, as developed by the present study, is consonant with and, in effect, correlative to the general economy.

The idea of complementarity is drawn from Bohr's interpretation of quantum mechanics. Complementarity was developed by Bohr in order to account for the indeterminacy of quantum systems and to describe—simultaneously, but without classical synthesis—their different and at times conflicting aspects, such as continuity and discontinuity, particles and waves, coordination and causality. Bohr speaks in this context of features of description that are mutually exclusive but *complementary* insofar as both are necessary for a comprehensive description and understanding of a given process. Thus we need both the particle-picture and the wave-picture of quantum processes, although we cannot use them both simultaneously and neither one is by itself sufficient for a comprehensive description and analysis. It is clear that complementarity can be defined in very general terms, well beyond physics, as Bohr himself already had suggested. The present study offers, however, a much broader and more radical expansion of the complementary mode of theorizing. I shall generalize Bohr's definition, first, by engaging multiple as well as double complementary clusters, and second, by engaging, simultaneously, but again without a full synthesis, more diversely interacting, rather than only mutually exclusive, configurations.

Conjoining general economy and complementarity allows one to enrich and develop both ideas within a comprehensive theoretical and historical framework. This juncture can be rigorously supported both in theoretical and historical terms. For along with Gödel's findings on incompleteness in mathematics, quantum physics and specifically uncertainty relations have figured prominently in the poststructuralist debate, and particularly in Bataille and Derrida.[1] More generally, these discoveries are among the greatest transformations of scientific and indeed all theoretical thinking in this century; and as such, they play a role analogous to Newton's calculus and physics in the preceding intellectual history.

The framework joining complementarity and general economy developed by the present study is its main contribution to contemporary theory. It enables the book to consider and engage diverse discursive practices—literary, critical, theoretical, historical, and political—and to show how the general economy operates in and transforms the theoretical landscape of modernity and postmodernity. This framework offers extraordinarily effective possibilities for reading Nietzsche, Bataille, and Derrida, and accounting for their discursive practices and the interrelations of their texts. I consider their works extensively throughout the present study while also discussing works by other major figures that define the scene of contemporary theory—Kant, Hegel, Marx, Freud, Heidegger, Bataille, Althusser, Deleuze, Lyotard, Jameson—as well as recent commentaries on all these authors. The task of the present chapter is to enable the book consistently to relate its terms and argument to the terms and arguments shaping the current theoretical debates about deconstruction, poststructuralism, postmodernism, and contemporary Marxist and psychoanalytic discourse. The chapter thus also offers an overview of contemporary theory, organized around the idea of general economy.

The first section, "Complementarities," discusses the principle of complementarity as it applies to the conjunction or intersection of various forms of analytical and discursive practice—theoretical, critical, historical, or political.

The second section, "Economies," considers the metaphor of economy as the main entrance to the scene of contemporary theory and the principal transition to the thematics of general economy. The third section, "General Economies," analyzes the notion of general economy as introduced by Bataille and its extensions in Derrida and Nietzsche.

The fourth section, "On Some Postmodernisms," considers the intersection between the thematics of general economy and the thematics of the postmodern in the debates on contemporary theory.

The fifth section, "Reconnections: Theory, Politics, Practice," extends this discussion to the political dimensions and implications of contemporary theory.

Complementarities

Complementarity, as concept and then framework, was developed in quantum physics, where Bohr introduced it to account for, and interpret, via *complementarity*, the wave-particle *duality*, the difficulties of simultaneous determination of coordination and causality in quantum interactions, and related problems. For Bohr, complementarity was an attempt to understand the physical—and *meta*-physical—meaning of quantum processes and to offer an overall interpretation of these phenomena. Its most fundamental impact is arguably quantum mechanical indeterminacy, expressed mathematically by Heisenberg's uncertainty relations. In Bohr, this indeterminacy becomes the *complementarity* of coordination and causality, leading to a radical reconsideration of the concepts of observation, experiment, and related notions. According to Bohr, "the space-time coordination and the claim of causality, the union of which characterizes the classical theories, [become] *complementary* but exclusive features of the description, symbolizing the idealization of observation and definition respectively" (*Atomic Theory and the Description of Nature*, 54–55; emphasis added).[2] Complementarity allows one to account for the indeterminacy of quantum systems and to describe—comprehensively, but without classical synthesis—their conflicting aspects. Bohr's notion and the matrix as a whole are thus correlative to Heisenberg's uncertainty relations, which are a rigorous mathematical expression of the limits on the possibility of *simultaneous* exact measurement of such complementary variables as position and momentum, or time and energy. Both complementarity and uncertainty relations were developed simultaneously in

1927, in collaboration, or cooperation and mutual influence, between Bohr and Werner Heisenberg.

Uncertainty relations may be seen as inhibiting information about some components of a given system, if one wants to increase information about other components, such as time against energy or position against momentum, thus leading to a mutual inhibition between causality and coordination. To offer a helpful and instructive analogy, all historical accounts must oscillate between a comprehensive description of a given configuration of events—or differences and forces involved—and causal or efficacious relations between them. The attempt to describe both or to analyze them comprehensively would inhibit each. Such descriptions are further complicated and inhibited, but never fully created, by the *historical* position—whether psychological, technological, theoretical, ideological, cultural, political, politico-economic, and so forth—of a given *historian* as a historiographer and analyst. This situation is analogous to, although much more complicated than, the position of the observer inhibiting, but again not creating, the quantum mechanical process and results of observation and measurement in quantum mechanics. The relationship between the observer and the observed has been persistently cited in modern intellectual history, specifically in historical investigations or investigations into the nature of history. One can reverse the metaphor and suggest that a quantum mechanic description is also a history of a quantum mechanic event or sequence of events, where the inhibition at issue leads to the uncertainty relations and, in Bohr's overall interpretation, to complementarity.

It is important to keep in mind the metaphorical status of this parallel, a status that implies certain limits of applicability and an inherent complexity of stratification. To be specific, the differences must be taken into account between *more immediate* records of observations, such as scientific reports of experiments or historical records, and the *more mediated* records of historical analysis. In the end, both sorts, being *records*, must be seen as *writing* in a Derridean sense, so that the opposition between types, as an unconditional opposition, cannot be unequivocally maintained, invariably proving itself deconstructable. Even in the case of so-called immediate observation, in quantum mechanics, only mediated records are available. One only "observes" photographs or, at best, traces left in cloud chambers by "elementary particles," that is, by what is constructed—metaphorically, conceptually, technologically, and mathematically—as elementary particles. The fact that one never deals with the particles themselves makes the very concept of the particles themselves problematic and finally untenable, just as Kant, as Nietzsche pointed out, has no right to speak of things-in-themselves. As Heisenberg writes: "There was not a real path of the electron in the cloud chamber. There was a sequence of water droplets" ("Remarks on the Origin of the Relations of Uncertainty," *The Uncertainty Principle and the Foundation of Quantum Mechanics*, 8). One is dealing with only traces or traces of traces and the complex networks of differential substitutions they entail. This *general* economy problematizes and deconstructs the opposition between the immediately observable and the mediated, whether by way of examination of records, theory, technology, or otherwise; and it equally problematizes and deconstructs these last categories, but without dispensing with them. In classical physics one deals with the observable data more immediately, or so it appears; in quantum mechanics, too, one still *observes classically* by "reading"—in terms of classical physics—measuring devices. Quantum mechanics, specifically Bohr's complementarity, is an interpretation of the complexities arising in such classical readings with respect to quantum events. These complexities, it may be argued, demand a general economy, and Bohr's understanding can be seen as general economic.

In a general economy, then, the immediate must always be recomprehended as an effect of mediation. The irreducibility of mediation was Hegel's great discovery. The radical mediation demanded by a general economy is, however, also a deconstruction, if not a destruction, of Hegelian mediation. Given the history of the term 'mediation' and its metaphysical and specifically Hegelian appurtenance, which always entails a certain immediacy and presence of the mediated, that term may not be applicable to the processes demanding general economies. Such processes produce and dislocate both the classical immediacy or presence and the classical mediation, but they cannot themselves be represented or analyzed classically.

Nietzsche's historical analysis and theoretical elaborations offer the necessary ingredients for such an economy of interpretation and history. As will be discussed in Chapter 7, Nietzsche shares some common sources with quantum mechanics, given his interest in and metaphorical and theoretical dependence on thermodynamics and other developments in contemporary science. Physics itself is a different matter, although the difference is not simple or unequivocal; but one should rigorously adhere to the limits of such analogies and metaphoric transfers between various fields. Following the inception of quantum mechanics, the complementary-inhibiting economy has been extended, with varying degrees of effectiveness, to various interpretive processes, individual and collective. Some extensions of that type have been offered by physicists themselves, specifically by Bohr.[3] C. G. Jung invokes complementarity on several occasions. Wolfgang Pauli, one of the founders of quantum mechanics, was analyzed by Jung, with whom he also corresponded, specifically on complementarity.

Bohr's complementarity principle itself refers to the relationships between, on the one hand, waves and particles and on the other, between "the space-time coordination and the claim of causality, the union of which characterizes the classical theory," seen as "complementary but exclusive features of the description, symbolizing the idealization of observation and definition respectively." On the one hand, the quantum mechanical "events" always require, as it were, a complex plot—a conjunction of a particle-plot and a wave-plot. Actually, two complementarities emerge thereby—the wave-particle complementarity and the continuity-discontinuity complementarity—exhibiting complex, *complementary*, conceptual and metaphoric relationships with each other. On the other hand, the relationships between two other plots involved—that of coordination and that of causality—can be determined only within certain limits. The two, or three, sets of relationships at issue in quantum mechanics—waves and particles, continuity and discontinuity, and coordination and causality—are themselves multiply related. They are complementary.

We may expand Bohr's term "classical theories" to all metaphysical theories, those theories based on unity, on absolute wholeness, on synthesis without loss, on presence—whether as being or becoming, or on history, as in Hegel. I shall further expand the very term *complementarity* as well, beyond its relation only "to *mutually exclusive* features" of a given configuration. In practice, this expansion also characterizes the application of Bohr's principle in quantum physics. For, within given limits, specifically the limits of classical theory, both descriptions may apply simultaneously. Classical theories are not discounted in the process; they retain their values and necessity within their refigured limits. In quantum mechanics the necessity of the relationships between classical and quantum theory leads to another major principle introduced by Bohr—the correspondence principle. Establishing and critically analyzing such limits becomes one of the aims of theory.

Taken in these terms, complementary relations are neither simply mutually exclusive nor simply subjected to a full synthesis, as in Hegel, but are interactively heterogeneous and heterogeneously interactive: at times one; at times another; at times jointly, including in various modes of synthesis; at times in conflict, acting against and inhibiting each other; at times, separately or jointly, entering other relations—other complementarities—or at certain points yielding description or analysis to different complementarities, or to other modes altogether. Such complementarities, moreover, need not only be paired but also can be multiple, as may be the case with different and multiply related complementary pairs in quantum mechanics—such as waves and particles, continuity and discontinuity, or coordination and causality.

Complementarity thus understood can be extended to any conjunction or clustering, double or multiple, of terms and concepts or structures such as Derrida's *différance*, which is "neither a concept nor a word [ni un concept ni un mot]" (*Margins of Philosophy*, 11; *Marges de la philosophie*, 11). Most complementarities discussed by this study cannot be seen or named as concepts in any of the classical senses of this term, such as in Hegel or Saussure. Complementarity thus is itself a trope that often proceeds by way of complementarities and complementarities of complementarities. The modern, poststructuralist understanding of metaphor, as the relation of both similarity and difference between its constituents, suggests the potential of complementarity, in metaphor itself and in the constructing of new metaphors. The principle of complementarity may, and in fact must, be extended to the complementarities of whole theoretical matrices, engaging intersecting matrices. In general, any given term, concept, or cluster of terms and concepts cannot exist other than within a given conceptual chain or matrix, and indeed always within a network of chains or matrices or fields that are themselves intersecting or complementary. Thus, the principle of complementarity may be applied to the classical paired oppositions of philosophy, such as consciousness and the unconscious, mind and matter, in conjunction with their deconstruction or not; or to less standard pairings and clusterings, such as history and the unconscious; or to different fields such as philosophy and literature, or criticism.

In some cases such complementary relations may emerge as finally undecidable, thus also making it possible to deconstruct a relevant text or configuration. Ultimately, these relations may never be decidable; and they are never decidable once and for all. But there are possible and necessary local determinations, some by way of complementarity. To some degree, the project of deconstruction may be seen as an exploration of such undecidability. 'Undecidability' is one of Derrida's most important terms, introduced by analogy to Gödel's theorem. To borrow Roger Penrose's description, "What Gödel showed was that any . . . precise ('formal') mathematical system of axiom and rules of procedure whatever, provided that it is broad enough to contain description of simple arithmetical propositions . . . and provided that it is free from contradiction, must contain some statements which are neither provable nor disprovable by means allowed within the system. The truth of such statements is thus 'undecidable' by the approved procedures. In fact, Gödel was able to show that the very statement of the consistency of the axiom system itself, when coded into the form of a suitable arithmetical proposition, must be one such 'undecidable' proposition" (*The Emperor's New Mind*, 102).

The difference between "deconstruction" and "complementarity" may be defined by way of their relations to the two notions in modern mathematics and physics: the *undecidability* of Gödel's theorem and the *complementarity* of quantum physics—in the latter case under the condition of and in relation to the *indeterminacy* of interpretation. In a given case, particularly in a metaphorically extrapolated matrix, such indeterminacy may imply or be linked to various forms of undecidability between descriptive terms. Undecidability deals with the question of the truth and (in)completeness of the systems of formal logic and metaphorically *analogous* configurations in the field of philosophy. Complementarity, as defined here, deals with the production and the operation of theoretical matrices under the conditions of indeterminacy and of complementarity itself.

Derrida addressed Gödelian thematics starting with his earliest work on Husserl. Most directly, undecidability is played out in *Dissemination*, first via Mallarmé in "The Double Session [La Double séance]" and then, in a kind of "arithmetic" in Derrida's "cooperative reading [lecture en quelque sorte co-orératrice] of Sollers' *Nombres*" in *Dissemination* (*Positions*, 61; *Positions*, 44). In introducing undecidability there, Derrida gives it an anti-Hegelian twist: "An undecidable proposition (Gödel demonstrated such a possibility in 1931) is a proposition which, given a system of axioms governing a multiplicity, is neither an analytical nor a deductive consequence of those axioms, nor in contradiction with them, neither true nor false with respect to those axioms. *Tertium datur*, without synthesis" (*Dissemination*, 219; *La Dissémination*, 248; translation modified).

The thematics of indeterminacy and of quantum physics have affected Derrida's framework, in part through Bataille, for whom the conceptions of quantum mechanics, specifically the uncertainty relations or, as they may also be called, "the unknowability relations," remain a major source (Pais, *Inward Bound*, 262). In my assessment, however, a preference for undecidability fundamentally reflects the character, or style, of Derrida's project. Deconstruction is thus *oriented* toward, but is not reducible to, the analysis of undecidable or aporetic configurations, at times by way of complementarities structured around the thematics of undecidability, such as

Derrida's *supplementary* relations or Paul de Man's aporias. Derrida's inscription of *dissemination* in "The Double Session" and "Dissemination" may be seen, metaphorically or analogically, as an analysis of undecidability and the construction of undecidable propositions, and overall as a kind of incompleteness theorem of philosophy and its closure.

New theoretical matrices, it should be stressed, are generated as well, alongside and *by means of* exposing the undecidability of the theses of philosophy, above all the thesis of thesis itself, within what Derrida calls the movement of a-thesis.[4] This movement locates the space or the interval of undecidability as *différance* and *dissemination, but is not restricted to it.* Thus the process also locates and introduces, specifically as *writing*, new economies of interpretation, history, or literature. The *logic* and the exploration of undecidability, however, decisively mark Derrida's writing, in either sense of the term, and much of deconstruction, even when the production of new structures is at stake.

The general economy, as I understand it, may be characterized by the conjunction or complementarity of two configurations: the economy of loss in (re)presentation, which, as will be seen in detail shortly, defines the general economy in Bataille and Derrida, and the complementary matrices of theoretical articulations and inscription, insofar as they can be offered. One needs both simultaneously: a more radical general economy of *différance*, with its accompanying structures, such as *dissemination, trace, supplement*, or still others, and a complementary configuration, double or multiple. Nietzsche's practice conforms perhaps most closely to this double economy, with greater emphasis on complementarity than on the economy of loss or undecidability. In Derrida the balance is shifted in the opposite direction: undecidability, resulting from the general economic loss, dominates the complementarity of inscription. Conversely, however, the loss in presentation remains an irreducible condition of all *complementary* descriptions in *general economy* as well; and it is this loss that *always* demands complementarity in the first place. In quantum mechanics, too, complementarity is conditioned by the uncertainty relations, signaling the irreducible *loss* in representation of all the processes involved.

Extending this economy, I suggest that there are always complementary and inhibiting relations between various aspects of analysis and description—interpretive, critical, theoretical, historical, or political. This complementarity imposes structural limitations upon one's analysis; in practice, it forces one to oscillate between different modes, even within any given mode. To add another variation on the economic theme, one must manage a complex economy, a diversified portfolio of investments and divestitures. In this sense, a certain plurality of style is inevitable, although very few manage to play it out with the power and effectiveness of its best and most deliberate practitioners, such as Nietzsche. The ineluctability of the plural—and complementary—style forces one to reconsider the economy of possibilities and necessities of denominations such as history, theory, or criticism, but without simply suspending or eliminating them in one's practice. Practice, too, is a denomination that is always functioning in one complementary chain or another.

It is impossible, however, to have a complete picture, or rather we must reconfigure—and refigure, remetaphorize—the very notion of a complete picture. Such was Bohr's position in his famous debate with Einstein concerning quantum mechanics. Quantum mechanical descriptions are, in this sense, *complete* descriptions of whatever they describe, even though, and indeed because, in Bohr's own phrase, "such kinds of information cannot be combined into a single picture by means of ordinary concepts" (*Atomic Physics and Human Knowledge*, 26). I am hesitant to say that they are descriptions of "nature" or "matter," given the general economy of matter, which will be considered in Chapters 6 and 7. *It is as complete as it can be under the available conditions*—experimental, historical, technological, theoretical, and even political—all of which are involved in any quantum experiment and the field as a whole. As used by Bohr and in general, the very word *complementarity* suggests both a degree of completeness of description, and, *at certain points*, a necessary mutual exclusiveness of the features involved.

This completeness of complementarity does not mean that there are no limits upon what a comprehensive description or theory can offer—the limits established within and between the fields can always be transformed or exceeded by new theories. Moreover, the fields at issue in the present study, under the currently available conditions of their operation, have more complex and more undetermined limits of operation and demarcation than does physics. Bohr's point is the *radical* incompleteness of all possible descriptions. They cannot be complete in the classical sense of causality, coordination, wholeness, coherence, logic, demanding a rigorous suspension and redefinition—reconfiguration—of all these concepts. In all its subsequent developments, up to the most recent, modern physics remains constrained by uncertainty relations; and many of these developments have been radical, leading to far more "complete," or comprehensive, descriptions and theories. Uncertainty relations themselves have proved to be very productive constraints, generating positive propositions in the field of physics. An analogous, but not identical, incompleteness characterizes Gödelian mathematics—that is, all of modern mathematics, more or less.[5] It is worth pointing out that quantum physics does not consist of uncertainty relations alone. Nor do some of the recent developments, such as deconstruction, or a great deal in Nietzsche's texts, consist of negative possibilities alone, although both have often been unrigorously construed as such.[6] The general economy, whose inception in Bataille was influenced by modern science and specifically by quantum physics, must relate to a structural incompleteness, a structural, irreducible loss in all (re)presentation and theory. Under these ineluctable conditions, general economic theories are as complete as theories can be; they are certainly more complete than their classical counterparts—restricted economies.

Economies

'Economy,' from the Greek *oikonomia* (household), is a conjunction of management-organization relations, exchange relations, and energy relations. These relations are interactive, or interactively heterogeneous and heterogeneously interactive—in short, complementary. One of the results of this complementary interplay is the emergence of the notion of economy as theory or science, such as the political economy of Adam Smith and later that of Marx, which constitutes a crucial dimension of the functioning of the term 'economy' in Bataille. The general economy is defined by Bataille as theory—science—even though it is difficult and finally impossible to separate the various levels of its functioning, in particular, that which studies and that which is being studied.

On the one hand, then, 'economy' implies the exchange-management cluster, thus engaging the history of political economy in the widest sense, from Greek 'households' to Smith and Ricardo, and then to Marx and beyond. On the other hand, 'economy' also suggests a metaphor of energy and, more thermodynamically, of the expenditure of energy. Thus economy-energy is also the play of forces—"das Spiel der Kräfte." The matrix of general economy, however, while engaging and depending on such metaphors and productive of their interaction, is not reducible to any single metaphor or to any given form of such interaction. As Derrida shows in the case of the general economy of *différance*, a general economy can never be reduced to being governed by any given name, concept, or theoretical or political configuration, including its own. The metaphorics of the play of forces and of differences are suggestive of this *dissemination* of descriptions; as such, they operate against the metaphorics of exchange and interest. Hence they acquire a certain, but not absolute, strategic priority in Nietzsche, Bataille, and Derrida. Much can be achieved within the limits of restricted economy. Moreover, as will be seen, any general economy depends on restricted economies for its functioning.

The phrase "the play of forces [das Spiel der Kräfte]" is reminiscent more of Nietzsche than of anyone else. Indeed, Nietzsche gave it its most radical—most forceful and most playful—meaning in both its aspects—play and force. The phrase, however, is actually Hegel's. It occurs at two crucial moments of the *Phenomenology*. Hegel uses it first in his great elaborations on the "inverted world [verkehrte Welt]" (*Hegel's Phenomenology of Spirit*, 89; *Phänomenologie des Geistes, Werke in 20 Bänden* 3:116). There it also appears to be related to the Newtonian thematics or metaphorics. The title of this section of the *Phenomenology* is "Force and the Understanding [Kraft und Verstand]." It contains concepts crucial to the history at issue in this study—from Nietzsche, to Saussure, to Freud, to Heidegger, to Lacan, to Deleuze, to Derrida; concepts such as difference, force (Kraft), play (Spiel), the play of forces, and solicitation (Sollizitieren). Then Hegel powerfully utilizes his notion of the play of forces in the dialectic of master and slave in "Self-consciousness."[7] There this notion is combined with the metaphorical configurations just considered—the play of forces, the economy of exchange, and the management economy (*oikonomia*). This part of the *Phenomenology* is crucial for Bataille, who transfers the problematic beyond the question of the political economy to the economy of meaning. The latter economy is powerfully explored by Derrida's reading of Bataille. The transfer at issue does not suspend the political economy; it necessitates and complicates the interaction of both.

Thus, both through the question of the political economy and otherwise, Hegel engages different dimensions of economic problematics and metaphorics. Although the degrees and specifics of this engagement can be debated, as they have been throughout the history of reading Hegel, the significance of the question of the political economy in Hegel's thinking, especially as developed by Adam Smith, is undeniable, particularly during the years leading to the writing of the *Phenomenology*. The importance of the question of political economy and labor in Hegel was a major point of departure for Marx, and then for the Marxist Hegelians, such as Georg Lukács, Kojève, and Jean Hyppolite. Marx states without hesitation that "Hegel's standpoint is that of modern political economy [Hegel steht auf dem Standpunkt der modernen Nationalökonomie]"

("Economic and Philosophical Manuscripts of 1844," *The Marx-Engels Reader*, 112; "*Ökonomisch-philosophische Manuskripte (1844)*," *Marx/Engels Gesamtausgabe, Erste Abteilung* 3:157). In Marx's own texts, from his earliest work to *Capital* and beyond, the interplay of various economic metaphors is rich and complex. It should not be forgotten that labor, too, is defined by the *investment* of *energy*, along with the investment of capital. What I wish to stress here, however, is that Hegel, while not without important predecessors, is the major *force* and *value*, overt and hidden, in these historical and theoretical *exchanges* and, further, that these exchanges and forces can themselves be productively explored by way of a general economy.

Much of Kantian problematics, specifically in *The Critique of Judgement*, is also conditioned by the metaphorics of play, force, and the play of forces. Newton's physics plays a major role in Kant, as it does in Hegel, particularly as concerns causality, the core issue in Bohr's complementarity—a very different question, but still an economy and play of forces. Here, as Nietzsche points out, Kant poses a "tremendous question mark" between "*Leibniz'* incomparable insight [*Leibnitzens* unvergleichliche Einsicht]" on the accidental nature of consciousness and "the astonishing grasp of *Hegel* [den erstaunlichen Griff *Hegels*]," his grasp of the historicity of concepts: "Let us recall, secondly, *Kant's* tremendous question mark that he placed after the concept of 'causality'—without, like Hume, doubting its legitimacy altogether. Rather, Kant began cautiously to delimit the realm within which this concept makes any sense at all (and to this day we are not done with the fixing of these limits)" (*The Gay Science*, sec. 357, p. 305; *Die fröhliche Wissenschaft*, in *Sämtliche Werke* [hereafter *KSA*] 3:598; translation modified).

In his analysis of "Force and the Understanding" in his lectures on the *Phenomenology*, Heidegger sees Hegel's move from force to the play of forces as a major *force* of Hegel's response to Kant, specifically *The Critique of Pure Reason* (*Hegel's Phenomenology of Spirit*, 116–17; *Hegels Phänomenologie des Geistes*). One might agree to a certain extent with Lyotard's suggestion that Heidegger does not sufficiently take into account *The Critique of Judgement*, where the play of forces, to use Heidegger's own phrasing, unfolds more richly. Like Heideggerian play itself, however, Kant's is conceived so that "the more richly it unfolds, the more strictly it is held(within the domain governed) by a hidden rule [Regel] [je reicher es sich entfaltet, um so strenger in einer verborgenen Regel gehalten bleibt]" and thus remains a restricted economy (*The Question of Being*, 105; Zur Seinsfrage;

translation modified). Lyotard "see[s] a much earlier modulation of Nietzschean perspectivism in the Kantian theme of the sublime" ("Answering the Question: What is Post-Modernism?" in *The Postmodern Condition: A Report on Knowledge*, 77; "Réponse à la question: qu'est-ce que le postmoderne?" 363).

I am not suggesting that this unfolding of play in the third critique is sufficient to supplant Hegel's magnificent achievement in the *Phenomenology*,[8] or the Heideggerian play of differences and transformations, let alone the Nietzschean play. Kant, one might say, misses a great *chance* in his analysis of the sublime; and so does Hegel, as he pursues to the limits the conditions, which from the perspective of the general economy are impossible, of overcoming both the radical loss in presentation and the radical plurality of interpretation and history. Whether Kant or Hegel, in truth, really had a chance to "discover" the unconscious is a complex question. I doubt that such a chance, if any, could have been very great. The Kantian economy of aesthetic judgment and taste, however, as a theoretical or a political economy, may be seen as suspended between 'economy' as exchange and 'economy' as a play of forces. 'Economy' as management and 'household' amalgamates Kant's economic configuration as well, as it does Hegel's or the later Heidegger's, whose economic thinking, proceeding via "early Greek thinking" and concepts of economy (*oikos*), is perhaps closer to Kant's, although powerfully overshadowed by both Hegel and Nietzsche. It is quite possible that, although it remains a restricted economy, the third critique, particularly concerning "The Analytic of the Sublime," offers a better model of practical or political reason than, for example, the second critique. The aesthetic itself, for many reasons, is also political, of course, as well as ideological. As Geoffrey Bennington comments in his reading of Lyotard: "The aesthetic is political not just because in this case [the demand for a presentation of what cannot be presented] it involves judgement on a political referent, but because any aesthetic judgement, in Kant's description, demands universalization, anticipates a *sensus communis*, a community, a consensus" (*Lyotard: Writing the Event*, 167).[9]

One easily recognizes here the contours of the general economic configurations and reconfigurations of the political; and in my view, the first, more general economic aspect of the political at issue here—"the demand for a presentation of what cannot be presented"—is more important than the second—"a *sensus communis*"—both in the context of Kant and in general. It is this demand that, at the limits, (re)defines both the political and

17

the social as general economic. To the extent, however, that one could remain within Kantian terms and divisions, one would need the general economy of multiple complementarity and ultimately undecidability among pure reason, practical reason, judgment, and other "faculties" invoked by Kant. One would not deny the rigor of Kant's distinctions; the second critique and related writing on ethics, morality, and politics offer a complex, interpenetrating conceptual and textual economy. These interpenetrations demand rigorous differentiations of various denominations and the understanding of the conditions of their possibility and necessity in Kant, or elsewhere.

From this perspective, Nietzsche's lifelong encounter with Kant may be seen as a movement "from restricted to general economy," similar to Bataille's encounter with Hegel. Nietzsche, of course, has crucial relationships with Hegel as well. As I suggest in Chapter 2, Kant may also have a greater significance for Bataille than may first appear. Perhaps "the Kantian theme of the sublime" represents powerful "earlier modulations" of what Bataille calls "inner experience," especially insofar as at issue in both cases are experiences without an object of experience. Derrida's encounters and exchanges with Kant, as with Hegel, also proceed by way of the question of general economy. The question of Kant plays a major role in, besides Lyotard and Derrida, Deleuze, de Man, Nancy, and of course Heidegger, whose "uncircumventable meditation [l'incontournable méditation heideggerienne]" overshadows the poststructuralist scene (*Margins*, 22; *Marges*, 22).[10]

In the history of the exploration of the economy of meaning, and often functioning alongside the metaphors of economy, the metaphors of the play of differences and the differences of forces have been decisive, from Nietzsche to Freud, Heidegger, Bataille, Lacan, Althusser, Deleuze, Lyotard, and Derrida. The role of various economic themes and metaphors in both Lacan and Freud is enormous, and it has been widely explored in recent history. Also, as in Saussure, the problematics of political economy may well have been much more important in Lacan and Freud than is immediately apparent, and not only by way of more or less obvious theoretical and metaphoric links or transfers. Althusser's analysis of Marxist theory used such metaphoric transfers powerfully; but his analysis also suggests that one can effectively engage a massive reverse traffic, from Marx to Freud, Lacan, or Saussure.

Saussure's linguistics has been a major mediating force in this respect, in great degree defining the poststructuralist scene and the structuralist scene before it. Saussure's definition and economy of the sign, and his linguistics as a whole also actively engage *economic* metaphors, such as the metaphor of exchange economy. This engagement is clearly conditioned by Marx and by his predecessors, the creators of the science of political economy.[11] It can be easily shown, however, in part by way of Nietzsche's "linguistics," beginning with "Über Wahrheit und Lüge in aussermoralischen Sinne [On Truth and Lie in the Extra-Moral Sense]" and Derrida's many analyses, that Saussure fundamentally engages the play of forces and differences of forces, and of differences to begin with. The word "force" (*force*) itself plays an important role, both in his conceptual economy and in shaping, at times imperceptibly for and against Saussure himself, the rhetoric of the *Course*.[12] In part along both these metaphoric lines—exchange economy and the play of forces—there emerge fundamental relationships between Saussure's and Hegel's "semiology," as Derrida shows in "The Pit and the Pyramid: An Introduction to Hegelian Semiology" (in *Margins*).

Various economic metaphors acquire a major role in Derrida. Derrida proceeds via Saussure, as in "White Mythology" (in *Margins*), Freud and Lacan, who has already powerfully explored the juncture of Freud and Saussure, and other theoretical and metaphoric trajectories, engaging along the way various political thematics suggested by these economic metaphors. Throughout Derrida's texts, the metaphor of exchange-economy operates alongside the metaphor of energy-economy as play of forces, allowing Derrida to engage their mutual interplay and, whenever necessary, a deconstruction of related forms of metaphysics induced by privileging either metaphor or by forgetting the metaphoric status of all such models. Derrida's early essay "Force et signification" (1963), whose title alludes to Hegel's "Force and Understanding," is a critique and deconstruction of structuralism and thus, at least by implication, of Saussure. It juxtaposes, via Nietzsche, meaning and structure to force and the play of forces. The more famous, and more important, "Structure, Sign and Play in the Discourse of the Human Sciences"[13] and subsequent works explore these thematics with great *force* and *understanding*, and with great *significance* for poststructuralist or postmodernist problematics and debate. Defined by a movement from restricted to general economy, Derrida's discourse is thus also a multiple general economic juncture of the various economic thematics, proceeding via the authors just discussed. More generally, however, the modern scene of theory may be characterized by its relation to the question of economy and the general economy, although this question does not quite define it; no single relation can fully define this, or any other, scene.

General Economies

The *general economy*, as Bataille defines it, relates to the material or intellectual production of excesses that cannot be utilized—*in principle*, rather than only in practice. Such losses in practice would be recognized within many classical or philosophical frameworks—*restricted economies*—specifically in Hegel and Marx, to which Bataille juxtaposes the *general economy*:

> The science of relating the object of thought to sovereign moments, in fact is only a *general economy* which envisages the meaning of these objects in relation to each other and finally in relation to the loss of meaning. The question of this *general economy* is situated on the level of *political economy*, but the science designated by this name is only a restricted economy (restricted to commercial values). In question is the essential problem for the science dealing with the use of wealth. The *general economy*, in the first place, makes apparent that *excesses of energy are produced, which by definition, cannot be utilized. The excessive energy can only be lost without the slightest aim, consequently without any meaning.* This useless, senseless loss *is* sovereignty.

> [La science rapportant les objets de pensée aux moments souverains n'est en fait qu'une *économie générale*, envisageant le sens de ces objets les uns par rapport aux autres, finalement par rapport à la perte de sens. La question de cette *économie générale* se situe sur le plan de l'*économie politique*, mais la science désignée sous ce nom n'est qu'une *économie restreinte* [aux valeurs marchandes]. Il s'agit du problème essentiel à la science traitant de l'usage des richesses. L'*économie générale* met en évidence en premier lieu que des excédents d'énergie se produisent qui, par définition ne peuvent être utilisés. L'énergie excédante ne peut être que perdue sans le moindre but, en conséquence sans aucun sens. C'est cette perte inutile, insensée, qu'*est* la souveraineté.] (*L'Expérience intérieure*, 282–83 n.; emphasis added)[14]

The matrix of the general economy has many dimensions and implications—historical, political, theoretical, aesthetic, or artistic—and significantly affects our understanding of the relationships between these fields, specifically by making them complementary. Bataille does not always fully perceive the consequences of the general economy, and Derrida's expansion of Bataille's matrix offers powerful new theoretical possibilities. Derrida's essay on Bataille, "From Restricted to General Economy: A Hegelianism without Reserve" (*Writing and Difference*), may be most relevant here, but the notion itself is crucial throughout Derrida's works. As the title of Derrida's essay suggests, one can approach the general economy, as Bataille and Derrida do, by way of a certain reading of Hegel and a displacement of dialectic and the *Aufhebung*. This displacement is, according to Derrida, infinitesimal and radical at once; as such, it defines the general economy of *différance* in Derrida. Derrida points out that the general economy cannot be rigorously compatible with *Aufhebung* in Hegel (*Writing and Difference*, 274–76), even though Bataille himself, at certain moments, claims otherwise: "It is useless to insist upon the Hegelian character of this operation [the contradictory experience of prohibition and transgression], which correspond to the moment of dialectic expressed by the untranslatable German word *Aufheben* (to surpass while maintaining)" (*Erotism: Death and Sensuality*, 36 n. 1; *L'Erotisme*, 42 n.; *Writing and Difference*, 275).[15] On that occasion, as Derrida indicates, Bataille speaks of a transgression without "return to nature," which in part explains his appeal to the *Aufhebung*, though it may not necessarily justify it. The movement "from restricted to general economy," however, is not a return to some pre-Hegelian, particularly ahistorical, theoretical or political economy. In Bataille, Marx is as decisive as Hegel, and in both Nietzsche and Derrida many other deconstructions are simultaneously engaged.

For both Bataille and Derrida, as for Nietzsche, the loss in question is always related to a certain irreducible—structural—unconscious. Via Nietzsche, Freud, and Bataille, and against Hegel, Derrida describes this economy—the general economy of *différance*—at "the point of the greatest obscurity, . . . the very enigma of *différance*":

> A certain alterity—to which Freud gives the metaphysical name of the unconscious—is definitively exempt from every process of presentation by means of which we would call upon it to show itself in person. In this context, and beneath this guise, the unconscious is not, as we know, a hidden, virtual, or potential self-presence. It differs from, and defers, itself; which doubtless means that it is woven of differences, and also that it sends out delegates, representatives, proxies; but without any chance that the giver of proxies might 'exist,' might be present, be 'itself' somewhere, and with even less chance that it might become conscious. (*Margins*, 20–21; *Marges*, 21)

The movement from a restricted to a general economy is thus always a movement from consciousness to the unconscious, as the latter is in turn refigured according to the general economy. The general economy, while productive of all economic metaphors at issue here, must relate to that which is not economic in any given sense. As a result, while it is rigorously theoretical, even *scientific*, and while it must utilize and is productive of restricted economies, strategically and textually it must engage a very different style.

The general economy also can relate theory and politics more richly than a restricted economy. It is worth stressing that the Hegelian restricted economy of self-consciousness—*Geist*—is always historical and therefore always a political economy. In Marx, it is reconfigured by way of a materialist political economy. Both Hegel and Marx have a common source in Adam Smith's political economy. Drawing on both Hegel and Marx, "the *question* of this *general economy* is situated on the level of *political economy*" (emphasis added). Therefore, one must proceed by way of complex—complementary—interactions, rather than by way of unequivocal separations between them, although the general economy remains a precomprehending matrix with respect to both. In a prelogical or pretheoretical sense, as distinguished from a preontological sense, a general economy precedes any restricted economy; but it does not simply suspend the latter. As opposed to restricted economies—political, conceptual, or other—the general economy must relate to losses, unreserved expenditures. But it is not solely the economy of losses or expenditures, whether calculable or incalculable, reserved or unreserved. By the same token, the interplay of conservation, or accumulation, and expenditure in a general economy is not simply conflictual and oppositional but, again, multiply complementary.

The precomprehending character of the general economy is a crucial point for Derrida, both in his reading of Bataille and in general, as the matrix is transferred or translated into the general economy of *différance*. The latter, analogously, precedes or precomprehends restricted economies such as that of Hegelian *Aufhebung*, although it depends on restricted economies in a textual production of the general economy, by way of which one can relate, obliquely, to such structures as *différance*. In this sense, *différance* replaces sovereignty in Bataille.

It is true that "the *general economy*, in the first place, makes apparent that *excesses of energy are produced, and these excesses cannot be utilized. The excessive energy can only be lost without the slightest aim, consequently without any meaning.*" That the *excessive* energy is lost does not mean, however, that some energies *cannot be* utilized, via the production of meaning or value—conceptual, politico-economic, aesthetic, or other. One can even *utilize* losses, write them off, as it were, including in Derrida's sense of writing and within its general economy. Bataille is careful to maintain that there is no more absolutely productive expenditure than absolutely unproductive expenditure, no more absolute losses than there are absolute gains, no matter how actively one wants to engage either losses or gains.

The suspension of either sort of expenditure, productive or unproductive, is problematic; and, as will be seen, such suspensions remain persistent even in some very recent discussions, both those critical of and those sympathetic to the ideas at issue. A suspension often functions as what Derrida terms the 'unproblematized reversal,' a configuration that has been much discussed in and after deconstruction. It is a reversal that leaves the metaphysical base untouched. For example, it may lead to the metaphysics, or the politico-economic utopias, of expenditure, difference, plurality, otherness, and so forth. But restricted economies can take other forms as well, even within attempts to avoid the unproblematized reversal. One is best off seeing the general economy as the economy of interaction, or as a complementarity of losses and gains, which figures the diversity of their interplay. The inscription of loss, waste, expenditure without reserve, however, where classical theories—restricted economies—"see" gain, conservation, or investment, remains Bataille's great contribution to modern intellectual history. It radically transforms and expands theoretical and metaphorical horizons of modern theory. Throughout this study, I understand the "general economy" to relate to the complementary interplay of production, conservation, and expenditure. It enacts a kind of translation and displacement, or a rigorous suspension, radical but not absolute, of Hegelian *Aufhebung*, which negates, conserves, and supersedes *simultaneously*, which is another notion to be deconstructed in the process.[16] The joint functioning of restricted and general economies is decisive in both Bataille and Derrida, and a similar interplay characterizes Nietzschean economy as well.

In his discussion of Bataille in *Philosophy Beside Itself: On Deconstruction and Modernism*, Stephen W. Melville is correct in saying that "[restricted economies] are necessarily inscribed in and dependent on the larger general economy—whether they acknowledge that dependence or not. But at the same time, there is no sense in which one can speak of a 'general economy' apart from its effects on or its refractions through the projects of growth and conservation given within the restricted economy—just as the notion of 'sovereignty' is bound wholly to the 'restricted' dialectic of master and slave whose disruption and (im)possibility it is. . . . what . . . Hegel ha[s] seen and fled, . . . ha[s] (visibly) annulled with his system, is the fact that the progress of Spirit depends on the necessity of pure and irrecoverable loss" (80). It is crucial, however, that, conversely, while one cannot avoid restricted economies in practicing a general economy, "the sovereign operation," as Derrida points out, "cannot be inscribed in discourse, except by crossing out our predicates or by practicing a contradictory superimpression that then exceeds the logic of philosophy" (*Writing and Difference*, 259; *L'Écriture et la différence*, 380). Nor are restricted economies *restricted* to "the projects of growth and conservation." The projects of absolute or unconditional decay and waste would be equally restricted. One must always engage a complex interplay of conservation or accumulation and expenditure, an interplay of many restricted and many general economies, as any general economy is always—"always already"— more than one.

Melville, I think, draws too close a proximity between Bataille and Hegel, even though, as I have indicated, to a degree, Bataille at times suggests so himself. In this sense, "interpret[ing] Bataille against Bataille, or rather . . . one stratum of his work from another," Derrida is correct in arguing that "Bataille is even less Hegelian than he thinks" (*Writing and Difference*, 275; *L'Écriture et la différence*, 404–5).[17] Melville claims that "Bataille lacks any guiding disciplinary matrix to pose this issue [of communication]. Instead, his writing tends to fall into either the 'science' of *La Part maudite* or the 'mysticism' of *La Somme athéologique*, and the problem of communication likewise falls into two *complementary* forms" (*Philosophy Beside Itself*, 81; emphasis added). Melville's assessment here is correct—indeed, that type of problem invariably invokes complementarity—but in the sense of the term as developed in this study. The "project" demands an *interactive* complementarity of various fields and genres, both locally, within a given text, and globally, between different texts. One should not necessarily or simply identify all Bataille's own practices of writing with the practice of the general economy, major forms of writing, and other textual strategies and operations he analyzes and engages. Richer complementarities are at stake, and one must be careful in this respect. By definition, however, under the conditions of the general economy, no framework or rubric, including the general economy itself, can fully contain any given case of writing. Dividing, or uniting, or complementarizing different projects and styles, Bataille's task and text, in classical terms, are "necessary" and "impossible," as, with some important differences, are Derrida's or Nietzsche's.[18]

The word "mysticism" in Bataille also requires much more analysis and qualification than Melville offers. "*Hegel, la mort et le sacrifice*," which is the principal focus of Melville's analysis, is particularly important in this respect; and 'mysticism,' or indeed 'science,' is a complex term to apply, even in quotation marks, to the works—*Inner Experience, Guilty, Sur Nietzsche*—constituting *La Somme athéologique*, unless one qualifies it greatly, as Melville does not do. Derrida warns that, like all Bataille's notions, the term and concept of the mystical is radically atheologically—and "a-mystically"—displaced and must be read accordingly. Referring, in particular, to "*Hegel, la mort*," Derrida points out, "That which *indicates itself* as mysticism, in order to shake the security of discursive knowledge, refers beyond the opposition of the mystic and the rational. Bataille above all is not a new mystic" (*Writing and Difference*, 272; *L'Écriture et la Différence*, 399–400). Derrida also offers an effective analysis of continuum and communication in Bataille in "From Restricted to General Economy" (262–64), suggesting a complex interaction of different components of Bataille's discourse. Similar considerations will apply to Derrida's own and, differently, to de Man's works.

Bataille's massive insistence on waste and expenditure can be and at times has been seen as problematic, despite the numerous qualifications he makes. As will be seen, this emphasis, often much greater and far more problematic than anything else in Bataille, characterizes many recent approaches to Bataille or, following Bataille's ideas, others, especially Nietzsche; and it is a complex question whether, while retaining the significance of the political and, at the same time, (con)figuring the general economy as an economy of waste and expenditure, Bataille avoids a certain idealization of *waste*. This question especially concerns the practice of "sovereignty" in Bataille as distinguished from Bataille's theory of "sovereignty," that is, the general economy. For the moment, I use the term "general economy" strictly in Bataille's sense, which might be seen as somewhat different from its functioning in the present analysis, where it is related to a cluster of general economies, such as those in Nietzsche, Bataille, and Derrida. Throughout this study, when I speak, without further qualifications, of *the* general economy, I refer to the common traits within this cluster. Bataille's text—or at least enough of it—may be "saved," I think, even if in following the labyrinthine complexity of his concepts. As I indicated, Bataille directly points out the impossibility, in "real life," of either "purely productive" or "purely unproductive expenditure" at the outset of *The Accursed Share*, his main text on general economy: "But real life, composed of all sorts of expenditures, knows nothing of purely productive expenditure; in actuality, it knows nothing of purely nonproductive expenditure. Hence [in a general economy] a first rudimentary classification will have to be replaced by a methodical description of every aspect of life." Indeed, it is even "regrettable that the notions of 'productive expenditure' and 'nonproductive expenditure' have a basic value in all the developments of my book" (*The Accursed Share*, 1:12; *La Part maudite*, 52).

The question, then, becomes whether, even given the interaction between both economies, the difference between restricted and general economy does not retain a trace of absolute difference, or whether this trace is not sufficiently erased and comprehended by Bataille. The issue may concern not only an unconditional priority of expenditure over consumption but also the difference and relative priorities between an exchange economy and an economy of nonexchange, whether that of consumption, as in Kant or Hegel, or that of waste, as in Bataille. The most important issue, however, is an unconditional privileging of general economy itself, however configured, or indeed an unconditional privileging of any given economy over any other. Suspending all such unconditional privileging enables us to practice a different theory, which as a general economy will be radically different from any restricted economy, philosophical or other. At issue may be the question of taste or art, or the question of meaning, consciousness, conceptuality, in Descartes, Kant, or Hegel, among others; or it may be the question of political economy, Marxist or other. Within such a general economy, one cannot unconditionally establish the difference between restricted and general economies involved; between that which accounts and that which is being accounted for; or other unequivocally conceived and metaphysically claimed differences of that type.

In this sense, the questions such as that of the possible privileging of waste are important only with respect to the question of situating Bataille's "own" text. Under the conditions of general economy as understood in this study, no economy of any kind can be unconditionally privileged. We must operate under this ineluctable constraint—the constraint of the conditional.

By the same token, however, we cannot unconditionally separate the question of theory and the question of Bataille, and the question of situating Bataille's text historically. Thus, the qualifications just given cannot resolve this issue once and for all, or contain or decide upon the reading of Bataille. In reconstituting in this specific way the chain of Bataille's conceptions, I am in agreement with Derrida in seeing Bataille's matrix as a *displacement*, even a radical trembling of the *Aufhebung* and Hegel, or philosophy in general. This displacement would similarly affect other— Hegelian, Kantian, Marxist, or otherwise classical—propositions of Bataille's discourse. These relations might be reversed by a more Hegelian reading of Bataille, displacing toward Hegel his more critical or deconstructive propositions.[19] The very possibility of such a reading of Bataille remains important in the question of Bataille and would have to be accounted for in the context of this question. Also, such a "Bataille" may have had significant historical effects in extending Hegel's domination over the modern scene. Furthermore, the very conflict between these two readings and these two chains "within" Bataille's text can never be simply inside, nor simply outside any given text. Such interpretations and their possible combinations have a complex functioning within potential totalities—reconstituted longer chains—or, conversely, heterogeneities of Bataille's text.

"Here, we must interpret Bataille against Bataille, or rather, must interpret one stratum of his work from another stratum [Il nous faut ici interpréter Bataille contre Bataille, ou plutôt une strate de son écriture depuis une autre strate]" (*Writing and Difference*, 275; *L'Écriture et la différence*, 404). But which Bataille against which, and which stratum from which, and where, at what point, and which "we"? "The equivocality" that Derrida speaks about "can [be] dispel[led]" considerably through a rigorous working of the chain of Bataille's displaced and displacing concepts, even though it cannot be reduced absolutely in Bataille and even though, in general, there are no undisplaced concepts.

Critical and metaphysical propositions of Bataille's discourse can be reread as affecting each other in a direction opposite to any given reading. The propositions and sliding concepts in Bataille to which Derrida refers can already be so reread and reinscribed, since once they can slide, they cannot form immutable atomic units. All concepts and all discourses must slide in this sense, and it is always the question how radically they displace the classical concepts and make them "tremble." Some of Derrida's inferences from Bataille's propositions may not be altogether convincing. Unquestionably, however, Bataille's propositions do inscribe the configurations of general economy: radical loss of meaning, disruption, the unconscious in the deconstructed field, and others that are *not* inscribed or dismissed by the text of philosophy, "of Kant, of Hegel" (*Inner Experience*, 27; *L'Expérience intérieure*, 40). These "unconscious," "meaningless," "non-present" structures become the efficacity of the meaning, consciousness, and presence of philosophy, such as in Kant or Hegel. This efficacity enables Bataille's concepts to slide and to make classical concepts tremble, and makes it difficult, if not impossible to return, "against Bataille," his text to Hegel.

To be sure, even such displacing propositions and (non- or anti-) concepts can still be reread "against Bataille." But such a rereading has to be produced against a more critical or deconstructive, such as Nietzschean or Derridean, Bataille; and it would not, I think, be easy to do it. I am not aware of any such reading, that is, of a reading of these *displacing* propositions as against more overtly problematic propositions of Bataille's stratified text. By this statement I mean, once again, a reading that would *relate* by a chain or network both, or various, types of propositions of Bataille's text instead of suspending either productive or unproductive expenditure, or acquisition, of the general economy, as do some of the readings referred to in this study. Bataille's displacement is enacted within and by way of such chains; and once one configures them, the "metaphysical" Bataille becomes difficult to construct.

Such textual rigor may be seen as a requirement of reading; and it is true that Bataille's often elliptical text may present a particular complexity in this respect, perhaps more so than even Nietzsche's, and certainly more than Derrida's text, which is hardly elliptical.[20] Beyond such a demand, it is also a question of the theoretical effectiveness of such extension, or conversely truncation, of the chain of a given text. For one often—in truth, always—in practice truncates and extracts propositions from the chain, with different degrees of implied congruence with respect to *broader* chains or networks; and there can be no full chains or networks. Bataille does so with respect to Hegel; and more self-consciously, Derrida does so with respect to Bataille, even though both are well aware of and warn against extracting the propositions from their chains.

At issue, thus, is the *relation* or re-relation of different propositions or those that appear as different within truncated chains in a given reading— propositions that are more or less critical or more or less metaphysical. Since my goal is the *displacement* of the classical configurations, these are the critical and deconstructive effects of Bataille's text that are most crucial for me; and the same is the case in regard to Nietzsche, or Derrida. The effects of and dependence on Bataille in the text of modern theory, and specifically in Derrida, are irreducible. Whatever his proximity to Hegel, what is crucial is what Bataille, unlike Hegel, *does not* claim—above all, *consciousness*. Much closer to Nietzsche's and Freud's than to Hegel's, Bataille's is undoubtedly the economy of the unconscious. A general economy is always, by definition, the economy of the unconscious, itself reconfigured general economically. I shall therefore pursue this reading of Bataille, without making a stronger claim for, or against, Bataille. If this reading is, finally, a projection upon Bataille's text of other theoretical matrices or a "prejudiced selection" of corresponding textual elements, it is unfortunate. For I do believe in and, throughout this study, shall insist on the significance of rigorous discrimination in this respect; and I shall attempt to maintain it in Bataille's case as well. My main concern, however, is the effectiveness of the resulting theoretical conclusions for the critique and re-configuration of the classical theories; and Bataille's contribution to this transgression and this transgressive recomprehension is decisive.

It is equally important that, as both Bataille and Derrida insist, the general economy as theoretical practice remains a rigorous science or theory, however much it undermines the classical theories and however much it extends or complementarizes itself by way of other forms of writing, such as literature, criticism, history, or politics. For Nietzsche, Bataille, Derrida, and other major authors relevant here, theoretical, historical, or critical rigor is a crucial dimension of their work and style. The point of scientific—or historical and critical—rigor, specifically in Bataille and in general, is stressed by Derrida throughout and is equally important with respect to his own practices.

In this sense, the general economy and the plural style as understood here are very different from several recent antitheoretical agendas, such as the one advanced by Richard Rorty, from *The Consequences of Pragmatism* (1982) on, to his most recent and, I anticipate, forthcoming essays and collections,[21] or "the complacent notion of *pensiero diebolo* introduced by Vattimo and Rovatti," to borrow a characterization from Lacoue-Labarthe (*Heidegger, Art and Politics*, 6 n. 1).

In general, the antitheoretical ideology has been extraordinarily prominent in recent discussions, partly in relation to what may be seen as a Foucauldian—*not Foucault's*—agenda that has dominated much of the last decade. In part, this ideology is a reaction to powerful and problematic theoretical or, in de Man's terms, aesthetic ideologies; but it carries equally severe problems—at least from the *theoretical* point of view. In turn, of course, one can question the necessity of insisting on theory or rigor. This question cannot be addressed here, although some arguments will be offered throughout this study. The latter itself does operate in the theoretical register; but the main point at issue here is the general economy and the practices, positions, and claims of its practitioners, such as Nietzsche, Bataille, or Derrida, and possible misconceptions that can arise and have arisen in this respect. The insistence on theoretical rigor is pronounced in Bataille, Lacan, Deleuze, Foucault, Derrida, or de Man.

While praising the Yale critics, especially Geoffrey Hartman, for their move toward literature and criticism, as against philosophy—as so seen by Rorty, but not by Hartman and certainly not by de Man—Rorty ignores, or suspends without a theoretically, historically, or textually *rigorous* consideration, the insistence of these critics on the necessity of textual, critical, and theoretical, and indeed philosophical rigor. Such suspension is possible and may be argued, as in fact Rorty does, as a kind of alternative to rigorous theory. I do not think such arguments are effective. Moreover, Rorty speaks of important political and theoretical problems that should be thus antitheoretically addressed. I simply do not think they can be.

The problem of philosophy in this respect may be the insufficiency, rather than the excess of rigor. In this sense, an association, rather too unequivocal, of rigor, specifically in Derrida, with philosophy in Rodolphe Gasché's *The Tain of The Mirror: Derrida and the Philosophy of Reflection*, appears to me problematic, even though some of Gasché's targets are well taken and his motives are understandable.[22] I shall comment further on Gasché's book later in this study. My point at the moment is that a move toward the general economy is not a suspension of rigor but an enhancement of it under the conditions of a more plural and general economically defined style.

Nietzsche equally insists on the necessity of both theoretical rigor and textual rigor in reading, in the latter case even to the point of insisting on "philology," although his reasons and argument are subtle. His own style of reading, when it is engaged, would, I think, be very different from *readers*, such as Derrida, de Man, or indeed Heidegger, or other authors or commentators that could be mentioned here. Nietzsche, however, is often more rigorous in this respect than he is given credit for; and as his many elaborations would suggest, his "philological" demands upon his readers are not always inconsistent with the theories and practices of reading developed by these authors. The case demands extremely complex and nuanced stratifications of texts and positions.[23]

Nietzsche's theoretical rigor is exquisite under all conditions. I would strongly maintain this claim, whatever the differences between his theoretical style and that of Derrida, or Bataille. From very early on, however, Nietzsche understood the severe limitations of the philosophical analysis and of all philosophy hitherto, often precisely for the type of problems philosophy wants to address. The most powerful point made by Nietzsche—by his theories and by his practice—may even be that the problem of philosophy is that it is not rigorous, not *scientific* enough, even though, and because, it is also not playful enough. The general economy is the economy and complementarity of play and rigor. Nietzsche's critique may not always be sufficiently rigorous in some specific cases, such as Hegel's, for example. In fairness to Nietzsche himself, however, he gives enough credit in this and other respects to most of his great enemies, indeed particularly to his great enemies—Socrates, Kant, and Hegel—especially *as* his great enemies. From his earliest writings on, he suggests powerfully that rigor often lies elsewhere, including, but not exclusively, in art or modern natural and exact sciences, both of which he often in turn criticizes. He also understood that a very different form of rigor is often necessary and that in all cases of rigor or logic one always encounters its limits. The main point, however, is that the insufficiency of theoretical rigor is not only the problem of a given philosopher, but also the problem of the rigor of philosophy as ontotheology or the metaphysics of presence, to use Heidegger's and Derrida's terms.[24] This understanding also tells us that theory, or history, must be complementary to that to which it often opposes itself. The latter point has been effectively explored during the last two decades of studies of the role of metaphor, rhetoric, narrative, politics, and other "external" forces with respect to just about every field conceivable—philosophy, history, psychoanalysis, social sciences, or natural and exact sciences. By the same token, the nontheory may and, under certain conditions must, be theoretical, often against itself.

General economically understood, theory is itself a plural—*disseminating*—term, transforming its meaning, or force, and functioning by way of different complementary clusters, double or multiple. But as such theory may still be seen as connoting a component of great—I do not say absolute or everywhere irreducible—stability across very large historical intervals. Its distribution, however, may and must transform, for example, in relation to philosophy and its history—*as a specific body of texts and institutions.*

The latter qualification is crucial, and it applies and is presupposed throughout the present study. At issue in the question of the exterior and margins of philosophy is also the question of the sufficiently specific, although perhaps never strictly defined, texts and institutions, their history and their politics. The claims made here and throughout this study, however, need not imply that a different, for example, possibly a radically deconstructive, specific project cannot be pursued from the "inside" of philosophy. Rather the effects of such institutional appurtenance—"belonging," "properly" and not "properly," or not "belonging"—must be considered in all cases, for example, Nietzsche or Derrida, or such authors as Bataille, Blanchot, or Benjamin, or conversely Heidegger or Wittgenstein.[25]

"The end or death of philosophy" announced by such figures as Nietzsche and Bataille or, differently, Marx—to the extent that one can speak in these terms even in their cases, let alone in those of Heidegger, Levinas, or Derrida—is never simply an appeal, for example, to some atheoretical, specifically literary, mode, however important such a move may be in subverting or deconstructing the classical logic of philosophy. As shall be seen in more detail later, terms such as "literary" in turn have a complex structure and are multiply complementarized by both Nietzsche and Bataille, or by such authors as Blanchot and Benjamin, and differently, by Derrida. In Derrida, under the rubric of the closure of metaphysics, this economy specifically functions simultaneously against the uncritical suspension—the end or death—of theory or philosophy, or against the very rhetoric of the end, and against the death of philosophy announced within philosophy itself and constituting in fact a crucial dimension of its modern project, at the very least, from Hegel on.[26] If not philosophy itself, the closure of philosophy, according to Derrida, remains irreducible.

Perhaps, however, and with these qualifications in mind, against Derrida's economy of the closure of *philosophy* or *metaphysics*, such as the metaphysics of *presence*, one might speak of a certain common, but transforming, theoretical closure. The latter will function, on the one hand, alongside and as the effect of even more powerful interpretive closures, such as the closure of *presence* or the closure of *difference*, rather than the closure of the *metaphysics* of presence or difference, and on the other hand, the closure of metaphysics or philosophy, differently delimited as a result. The latter closure in Derrida has a sufficient, indeed a great, complexity and heterogeneity—"a more twisted structure [une structure plus retorse]," as Derrida describes it in the context of Heidegger, who is crucial here.[27] This complexity, however, does not suspend its functioning as the closure in this respect; and Derrida never speaks either of multiple closures or of transformation of closure, but rather of transformations that "may continue indefinitely" of "what is held within the delimited closure [Ce qui est pris dans la clôture dé-limitée peut continuer indéfiniment]" (*Positions*, 13; *Positions*, 23; translation modified). The issue is complex, and I shall consider it in more detail in Chapter 4. From Nietzsche on, however, the general economy offers extraordinary *theoretical* possibilities, as both Bataille's and Derrida's works demonstrate, and is suggested by other relevant texts, such as Lacan's, Deleuze's, and Foucault's. In these cases, too, beyond Hegel, Marx, and Heidegger, all of whom are crucial connections, Nietzsche's impact is immense and the importance of Bataille is much greater than may seem apparent.[28]

While, then, the preeminence of Marx's contribution, both theoretical and political, cannot be denied wherever the question of economy is concerned, it may well be that, by enacting a general economy, it was Nietzsche who made the most radical use of various economic thematics and metaphors: economy itself, value, energy, the play of forces and differences of forces, exchanges and the impossibility of exchange, the interplay of losses and gains or, to begin with, the notion of play. Nietzsche's general economy is a part of the ensemble that defines or conditions what, in the wake of Derrida's analysis, may be best defined as Nietzsche's plural or, again, complementary style and that, in its various aspects, has been explored, beyond Derrida's own reading in *Spurs: Nietzsche's Styles* (*Éperons: Les Styles de Nietzsche*) in a number of recent works, Continental and Anglo-American, including, importantly, feminist readings of and encounters with Nietzsche.[29] I shall address the question of Nietzsche's style more specifically in Chapters 2 and 4. Here I shall comment only on the general economic dimensions of Nietzsche's text and their broader general economic implications.

The general economic considerations at issue apply both to Nietzsche's own creative economy and to Nietzsche's understanding of the process—his major terms and concepts involved here and elsewhere. Wherever it operates—in nature, culture, art, politics (grosse Politik), tragedy, or his own style—Nietzsche's, as he calls it, "grand economy [grosse Ökonomie]" is, I maintain, already a general economy as the interplay, or complementarity, of multiply defined expenditures and profits (*The Will to Power*, sec. 291, p. 164; "Nachgelassene Fragmente," in *KSA* 13:372).[30] Nietzsche announces an economy of the active process of appropriation, or active interpretation or evaluation—value positing—that differentiates itself more freely at times as accumulation, conservation, at times as expenditure, wasteful or in turn productive. This multifaceted process characterizes Nietzsche's own creative economy, society and culture, or nature, or in Nietzsche's own terms, life. This process is far from free of conflict, for example, the conflict between what is, according to Nietzsche, noble or active and what is not noble or reactive, although one simplifies the case somewhat by identifying noble with active, but the nuances would in fact further support the general point at issue. These conflicts, including potentially problematic dimensions of Nietzsche's text, but in particular Nietzsche's main ideas and strategies—his styles—are, I think, most effectively understood in general economic terms.[31]

In this sense, and for these reasons, Nietzsche becomes Bataille's "closest" text and (re)source. Bataille's own readings of Nietzsche, however elliptical and at times displaced, are extremely powerful, particularly in drawing the radical implications of Nietzsche's theories and insights. So is Bataille's understanding of the most complex Nietzschean issues, such as the question of (non)dialectic of master and slave, the economy of pity, or love, sacrifice and its relation to death. Thus, for example, "pity" has been the subject of much controversy throughout the history of reading

Nietzsche, and is indeed a difficult problem, as both Nietzsche and Bataille understood. The gigantic figure of Rousseau, Nietzsche's grand enemy, inevitably appears on the horizon of the problem of pity. To a great degree, however, the problem of pity delimits the whole history of Christian morality, or morality in general, or philosophy. According to Nietzsche, the history of one is the history of another. The issue here is not only, or perhaps finally not so much, Nietzsche's devastating critique. For while Nietzsche does not have much pity or patience for Christian or Rousseauvian pity and morality, Nietzsche does recognize, for example, in *Zarathustra*, pity's "deepest abyss [der tiefste Abgrund]" (*Thus Spoke Zarathustra*, in *Portable Nietzsche*, vol. 3, pt. 2, 269; *KSA* 4:199).[32] As such, however, it may require an analysis that is even more general economic than others of Nietzsche's main concepts or targets.

The question of general economy may not seem to be directly involved in these issues. In fact, however, it may be particularly necessary here. This necessity is suggested by some of Derrida's elaborations and juxtapositions occurring at very important junctures, such as Nietzsche and Rousseau, via Lévi-Strauss at the end of "Structure, Sign, and Play," leading to a *différance* and thus a general economy of "two interpretations of interpretations" (*Writing and Difference*, 292–93), or, in the context of Nietzsche's plural style, to the difference between the superior man and the superman in the end of "The Ends of Man." I shall discuss it in more detail in Chapter 2 in the context of the question of style. What is important here is that both Nietzsche and Derrida invoke "a last movement of pity [un dernier mouvement de pitié]" (*Margins*, 135; *Marges*, 164); and it is unquestionable that the problem of pity and its general economy is also at issue. Both Nietzsche and Derrida very likely, indeed inevitably, also allude to Rousseau. Following, and displacing Hegel, for whom, too, or for Kant, Rousseau is an uncircumventable figure, the general economy is also an economy of death, or to split the metaphor, an economy—"science"—of the economy of death.[33] It transforms all aspects of the psychoanalytic, or political, machinery involved, for example, the economy of mourning and melancholy, or pity and nostalgia, or love, or justice. All these must be seen in Nietzsche through the optics of the tragic affirmation of life—the affirmation of life even under conditions of the greatest tragedy. This is not a perspective, or perspectival evaluation, that is customarily assumed; and, as I shall discuss in Chapter 4, this attitude is neither easy nor always unproblematic.

All these questions, however, have a profound relation to the question of general economy in Bataille and Derrida, a relation that further suggests, on the one hand, the operation of general economy in Nietzsche and, on the other, the effectiveness of the matrix of general economy in approaching Nietzsche's theories, text, strategies, and style in their complementary interplay. Bataille may not be free from his own reappropriation or displacements of Nietzsche's concepts. My point here, however, is a general economic character of Nietzsche's theories and practices—styles; and in this sense Bataille's extrapolations are more crucial than his displacements.

Derrida's understanding of Nietzsche's plural style as operating simultaneously inside and outside the philosophical or restricted economic register is cogent in this respect. In short, this approach is general economic, both in the sense of Derrida's own and in relation to Nietzsche's plural styles, and yet at the same time suggesting or allowing one to establish the differences between them.[34] Derrida does not equate the "complement" of the philosophical register with either Nietzsche's grand economy or Bataille's general economy. Instead, the joint economy of operation in both "the inside" and "the outside" of philosophy should be seen as a general economy and complementarity in the present sense, as opposed to only conflict, opposition, or dialectic. It must be considered in terms of the closure of philosophy, leading to a still more diverse economy of the plural and a different form of difference between Nietzsche and Derrida.

My main concern in this study is the radical theoretical implications of Nietzsche's various economies. But also, as far as Nietzsche's text is concerned, a reading would, I think, be amplified and made more effective by being more general economic, more plural, and more play-ful in this sense, the conjunction that defines Nietzsche's style. There is, of course, much else in Nietzsche, beyond general economy, plural style, or play. Both on the basis of Nietzsche's texts and attitudes and on general grounds, one cannot reduce Nietzsche's texts to any particular aspect or give a unique significance to anything there. Such a reduction cannot be performed even by way of complementary pairs or clusters—such as play and theory, play and history, play and narrative, or other paired or multiple clusters—all of which are engaged by Nietzsche in this complementary fashion. Still, one might say that Nietzsche loses nearly everything once play is suspended; and all too often play has indeed been suspended, even in recent studies of Nietzsche, including many of those cited here, particularly on the Anglo-American scene. The conjunction of play and general economy, however, defines Nietzsche's, Bataille's, and Derrida's theoretical frameworks and their plural, complementary styles.

I do not mean to imply here that Nietzsche is free from problematic positions and propositions. Nor do I suggest that Nietzsche always fully controls his text in this respect, as I shall discuss in Chapters 4 and 7. Such problems are better understood, however, if one assumes the general economic and plural style of Nietzsche's writing. A general economic matrix enables both a more effective positioning of Nietzsche's text—his theories, strategies, style—and a more effective analysis of the problematic dimensions of this text. Whether what is at issue is his own textual practice or his understanding of the world, in Nietzsche an economy without a general economy will not suffice, whether historically, politically, or economically, psychologically, or theoretically. Nor, therefore, can an economy without a general economy suffice in our reading of Nietzsche and in our understanding of the world—at least for some of "us," and at least for now.

On Some Postmodernisms

The rubric of the postmodern must be applied with considerable caution, particularly at this point in history. In *Heidegger, Art and Politics*, Philippe Lacoue-Labarthe correctly warns against "the obliging catchall category of the 'post-modern'" [. . . cet accueillant fourre-tout qu'est le "postmoderne"] (6 n. 1; *La Fiction du politique*, 19 n.). The problem, of course, is not confined to the postmodern. Deconstruction and, perhaps to a lesser degree, poststructuralism pose similar problems. Taking as point of departure Lyotard's understanding of the postmodern, I shall remain within the limits contained, first, by the poststructuralist landscape, and second, by the thematics of general economy. My goal is not to analyze the postmodern itself, but to use it in order to illustrate the significance of these thematics and of the major figures considered by the present study. One would certainly be hesitant to apply the rubric of the postmodern to Nietzsche, Heidegger, or Bataille, however decisive their role in the work of many poststructuralist authors, or even their importance to such authors as Lacan, Barthes, or Foucault. But then, of course, much depends on how one locates, historically and geographically, the beginning, or the end, of modernism, or postmodernism, or poststructuralism, or other many recent "isms."[35]

The importance of all such rubrics and genealogies, though relative, is not discountable. Who among these authors comes *before* or *after* whom is often decisive, although not always easily decidable, and at times is undecidable. Much also depends on where the readers come from, historically or geographically. It is not my intention to offer a map, partially decidable or partially undecidable, of postmodernism or poststructuralism. Some mapping, however, is unavoidable and may even be helpful. To use a fashionable postmodernist metaphor, postmodernism may also be *mapped* as the postmodernism of maps, whose historical or geographical decidability or even possibility, particularly as totalizing possibility, many, *but not all,* recent postmodernisms, put into question.[36] The maps of postmodernism themselves conform to the general economy of maps. Geographically or cartographically, it is the economy of the complementary (inter)play of decidable and undecidable maps, and then, of maps and nonmaps; historically, it is the economy of continuities and discontinuities, random encounters and necessary connections.

Lyotard's definition of the postmodern in "Answering the Question: What is Post-Modernism?" proceeds via Kant and "an aesthetics of the sublime": "I think in particular that it is in the aesthetics of the sublime that modern art (including literature) finds its impetus and the logic of avant-gardes finds its axioms" (*The Postmodern Condition*, 77; "Réponse," 363). It is further modulated by way of Wittgenstein's language games and other, by now standard, postmodernist icons. The definition itself, however, is finally analogous, even isomorphic, to the definition of the radical loss of general economy in Bataille and Derrida, if supplemented by the programmatic twist, a kind of ideological agenda of the postmodern: "The postmodern would be that which, in the modern, puts forward the unrepresentable in presentation itself; that which denies itself the solace of good forms, the consensus of a taste which would make it possible to share collectively the nostalgia for the unattainable; that which searches for new presentations, not in order to enjoy them but in order to impart a stronger sense of the unpresentable" (*The Postmodern Condition*, 81; "Réponse," 366–67).

One must adhere, of course, to the differences both in the specific context of Lyotard's definition, at this particular juncture applied to the postmodern in art, and in the general functioning of the respective economies. Lyotard's approaches to the issue disseminate the name and concept considerably.[37] *The Postmodern Condition*, we recall, introduces the theme of the postmodern by way of the question of narrative and metanarrative, and offers a much discussed definition of the "postmodern as incredulity toward metanarrative" (xiv). All these approaches, however, do manifest major traits suggested or implied by the definition just given and by the present discussion as a whole, including, as will be seen in Chapter 3, in the context of the question of narrative. In particular, the aesthetic and the political are deeply interconnected in Lyotard's matrix or economy, partly but not exclusively via Kant. The economic problematic itself is massively engaged by Lyotard, often directly, as one of his major titles, *Économie libidinale*, suggests, the book itself engaging in one way or another all major figures at issue here: Marx, Nietzsche, Freud, Bataille, Lacan, Deleuze, and Derrida.

The general economy, we recall, equally relates its discourse to the loss of meaning—a loss that it regards as ineluctable; and following Nietzsche, one must conceive of and practice this loss and this excess, in Derrida's words, "without nostalgia, that is, outside the myth of a purely maternal or paternal language, a lost native country of thought. On the contrary, we must *affirm* [this loss], in the sense in which Nietzsche puts affirmation into play, in a certain laughter, and a certain step of the dance" (*Margins*, 27; *Marges*, 29). This last aspect of *modern* theory—the abandonment of *nostalgia*, the abandonment of nostalgia without nostalgia—can, as Lyotard's formulation suggest, be seen as fundamentally *post*modern, indeed as defining the postmodern, and defining it well beyond the space of theory. In Lyotard and elsewhere this economy extends to the political, the cultural, the technological, and so forth, indeed across the (post)modern geography; it remaps, re-writes (also in Derrida's sense), re-figures and reconfigures all our landscapes and households (*oikonomia*). The modern would then be defined not so much by the nostalgia for a lost native country of thought, but rather by the nostalgia for the place that modernism knows has never existed and is impossible. The postmodern, then, merely abandons that which has never existed; but that abandonment does not make the task any easier, but rather more difficult, for the nostalgia for the nonexistent is quite real and very powerful.

By locating "the postmodern" *in* "the modern," Lyotard's definition relates the two corresponding economies of representation—and of the unrepresentable—along the historical, ideological, theoretical, and political trajectories of "modernity," and particularly those of the question of general economy. Lyotard's positioning of Kant may in fact be seen as part of his debt to some of the more classical ideologies of modernism, such as, to borrow de Man's title phrase, "literary history and literary modernity."[38] As Deleuze and many others do, for example, Bataille and Derrida,[39] Lyotard sees Proust and Joyce are central paradigmatic literary examples of, *for Lyotard*, respectively the modern and the postmodern: "The work of Proust and that of Joyce both allude to something which does not allow itself to be made present" (*The Postmodern Condition*, 80, "Réponse," 366). The impact of Bataille, as well as of Derrida and Nietzsche, and in some measure Althusser, is unmistakable here. The formulation itself, "something which does not allow itself to be made present," is by no means sufficient for making an economy—whether of interpretation, literature, history, politics, or theory—a general economy. This formulation may refer both to Kant and to Hegel. Various "modulations" of the postmodern range from Kant, to Hegel, to Marx, to Nietzsche, to Freud, to Heidegger, to Bataille, to Lacan, to Deleuze, to Derrida, or Lyotard. They do not always constitute a movement "from restricted to general economy," and the question of differences and proximities among these figures is complex. Lyotard's matrix itself is not unproblematic, being unable in the end to exceed the limits of restricted economy; and analogous problems arise in the cases of Lacan, Deleuze, and Foucault.

Lyotard, however, is correct to relate the radical loss in (re)presentation to a radical plurality or heterogeneity—dissemination. A general economy is always the economy of the heterogeneous or is what Bataille calls *heterology*;[40] and a relation to the radical loss in representation, defining the general economy, is a relation to and of the heterogeneous, although, again, not all economies of heterogeneity are general economies. Irreducible multiplicity and heterogeneity do, however, become a crucial part of the postmodern and its reconfigurations. The exploration and the implications—and the applications—of this structural multiplicity possibly even allow one to move beyond the limits of the postmodern, or poststructuralist, although we are as yet far from exhausting the possibilities they offer.

In Nietzsche, this necessity of dissemination leads to perspectivism, specifically by way of the unconscious within a given "subject"—the term and concept that Nietzsche subjects to a radical critique and finally suspends. That suspension is rigorous: it situates and recomprehends subjectivity, rather than simply dispensing with it, as is the case later in Derrida, although Nietzsche's renunciation of the value of the concept itself, and of most other classical concepts, is more radical than Derrida's. In Bataille, the same necessity produces the heterogeneous and a *heterology*, which implies the general economy, but should not be simply identified with it. In Derrida, it irreducibly relates *différance* and *dissemination*.

Deleuze's contribution to the history of the heterogeneous has been decisive, from *Nietzsche and Philosophy* to, with Félix Guattari, *Anti-Oedipus* and *A Thousand Plateaus*, the book invoked by Lyotard at the opening of his essay, by way of reading, among others, Kant and Spinoza.[41] Throughout his career, Deleuze pursues the economy of radical fragmentation, of partial objects without a whole, or rather without one whole, without a full totalization. The chapter "Many Politics" in *Dialogues* may be invoked here, in view of its proximity and perhaps influence on Lyotard's propositions on the postmodern and his matrix of the postmodern in general. Some more limited manifestations or "modulations" of this economy may be found, as will be seen, in Lacan and, in part via Lacan, in Althusser or Theodor Adorno, and indeed in various degrees in Hegel and Kant. Lyotard's elaboration of the thematics of postmodernism in *The Postmodern Condition* and other works exhibits a number of proximities to Deleuze and Guattari's analysis, in both its positive and its problematic aspects.[42] It is also greatly indebted to Bataille's ideas. As "a modulation of Nietzsche's perspectivism," radical plurality defining the postmodern is at the core of Lyotard's confrontation with Jürgen Habermas. The opening section, "A Demand," of Lyotard's essay defines the terms of this debate:

> Jürgen Habermas . . . thinks that if modernity has failed, it is in allowing the totality of life to be splintered into independent specialties which are left to the narrow competence of experts, while the concrete individual experiences "desublimated meaning" and "destructured form," not as a liberation but in the mode of that immense *ennui* which Baudelaire described over a century ago.
>
> . . . What Habermas requires from the arts and the experiences they provide is, in short, to bridge the gap between cognitive, ethical, and political discourses, thus opening the way to a unity of experience.
>
> My question is to determine what sort of unity Habermas has in mind. Is the aim of the project of modernity the constitution of sociocultural unity within which all the elements of daily life and of thought would take their places as in an organic whole? Or does the passage that has to be charted between heterogeneous language games—those of cognition, of ethics, of politics—belong to a different order from that? And if so, would it be capable of effecting a real synthesis between them?
>
> The first hypothesis, of a Hegelian inspiration, does not challenge the notion of a dialectically totalizing *experience*; the second is closer to the spirit of Kant's *Critique of Judgement*; but must be submitted, like the *Critique*, to that severe reexamination which postmodernity imposes on the thought of the Enlightenment, on the idea of the unitary end of history and of a subject. (*The Postmodern Condition*, 72–73; "Réponse," 358–59)

The terms and issues of this debate have been much discussed during the last decade. In great measure, the debate has been overshadowed by Kant and Hegel. The confrontation between them, the grand philosophical confrontation of modernity and perhaps even of postmodernity, crucially affects the contemporary terms of the debate. Some postmodernisms, perhaps all postmodernisms so far, may still be Hegelianisms or Kantianisms, or both at once, to too great an extent.[43] The spirit—*Geist* or ghost—of this confrontation is clearly felt in the above passage as well.[44] One may recall that for Hegel the experience, or that which deserves the name—a very problematic name—of experience[45] is always the experience of consciousness and indeed of self-consciousness, which, as announced from the outset of the *Phenomenology*, is the truth of consciousness. In this sense, Lyotard is not wrong in juxtaposing it to Kant's economy of the sublime, where Kant comes closest to the unconscious and to Freud.[46] As Hegel does along different lines, Kant, thus, does at times approach the economy of the heterogeneous, although never its most radical, most Nietzschean aspects, which, and particularly the perspectival or plural character—*dissemination*—of interpretation and history, define the general economy *as* general.[47] Nor, as I have suggested, does in fact Lyotard come close enough to this economy, and his desire, or necessity, to remodulate Nietzsche by way of Kant confirms this point. In the end, the spirit (esprit) of Kant may well be the spirit—*Geist* and ghost—of Hegel—before, for example, in Kant, and after Hegel—rather than of Nietzsche.

Bataille customarily joins, rather than juxtaposes, Kant and Hegel. He juxtaposes both to Nietzsche, although he finds, as to a degree does Nietzsche himself, more of a "spirit" of Nietzsche—the spirit of affirmation—in Hegel than in Kant. While Nietzsche is not without his spirits— his *Geister* and ghosts—his remains perhaps the greatest and most powerful attempt to exceed the force of this determination of interpretation and history by way of Kant and Hegel. There have been numerous (pro)claimed overcomings; and we are amply warned by Heidegger, Bataille, and Derrida, or indeed Hegel himself, against all too easy ways of leaving Hegel, or Kant, behind. Yet in Nietzsche's case the departure appears to be quite radical, although not absolute; absolute departure may never be radical enough. Derrida's deconstruction, while often no less radical a critique of philosophy than Nietzsche's, proceeds and, to a degree, defines itself by a closer, even infinitesimal proximity to philosophy, even when it exhibits a radical difference from philosophy. This double relation of simultaneously infinitesimal proximity and radical difference may be seen as a defining relation between deconstruction and philosophy, reinforced through the economy of the closure of philosophy as the metaphysics of presence.

In Lyotard, the proximity is even closer and the difference less radical than in Derrida. Beyond the degree of proximity and distance involved, in Lyotard the very economy of the interaction with the text of philosophy is different. I cannot take up here the question of this difference between Lyotard and Derrida. It can be said, however, that Lyotard's engagement with the text of philosophy is *less* deconstructive, insofar as this term is used in

Derrida's sense or to describe Derrida's engagement with philosophy.[48] Lyotard also operates more within or from within, rather than simultaneously inside and outside, or on the margins of, philosophy, as Derrida does.

The Differend can serve as an interesting example in this respect, and as an important point or frame of reference for the present discussion. The book may be seen as an attempt to pose, and in some degree to solve, a set of problems by means of classical philosophy, whereas, to follow Nietzsche, these problems are most effectively *posed* radically, but again not absolutely, outside or on the margin of philosophy. Often, technically, in the margins of the text of *The Differend*, the text of philosophy is overwhelming and quite central in the book; in this sense the book, while postmodernist in form, is classical, or if you wish, modernist in substance. A comparison with many of Maurice Blanchot's texts, such Derridean texts as "Tympan" in *Margins of Philosophy*, "Living On: Border Lines," "Parergon," or *Glas*, Luce Irigaray's writing, and work by several other recent authors, readily invites itself. Often in *The Differend*, a lifetime of engagements with philosophy is brought to bear, where, to oversimplify, any one of Nietzsche's texts—let us say, *Beyond Good and Evil* or *On the Genealogy of Morals*—would do. I am not saying that philosophy, including Lyotard himself and specifically *The Differend*, has nothing to offer us in this or other respects, for example, against and in order to deconstruct itself. Nor do I think that Nietzsche, radical as he is in this sense, would quite say so; and certainly neither Bataille or Derrida would, with Hegel as perhaps the central case for both. Whether it can offer enough at this point of history is a different matter. For example, Lyotard's description of his "philosophical" mode is a juxtaposition to what he defines as the "theoretical" mode:

> The book's mode is philosophic, reflective. The A.'s [author's] only rule here is to examine cases of differend and to find the rules for the heterogeneous genres of discourse that bring about these cases. Unlike a theoretician, he does not presuppose the rules of his own discourse, but only that this discourse too must obey rules. The mode of the book is philosophical, and not theoretical (or anything else) to the extent that its stakes are in discovering its rules rather than in supposing their knowledge as a principle. In this very way, it denies itself the possibility of settling, on the basis of its own rules, the differends it examines (contrary to the speculative genre, for instance, or the analytics). The mode is that of a metalanguage in the linguist's sense (phrases are its object) but not in the logician's sense (it does not constitute the grammar of an object language). (*The Differend*, xiv; *Le Différend*, 12)

The "theoretical" mode appears in fact to be close to the classical view of philosophy itself.[49] I leave aside the potential problem of the opposition

at issue as Lyotard defines it, particularly via the insufficiently critical opposition between language and metalanguage. Lyotard's goals are com-
pelling enough. The question is whether these goals are best achieved by
the actual practice of his text, massively engaging and relying upon the
texts, the modes, the tropes, and ideas of the classical philosophy. A more
general issue, to be addressed throughout the present study, is that of positioning, and the positions of, the general economy inside, outside, and in
the margins of philosophy and its closure. From the perspective of the present study, and with Nietzsche and Bataille in view, I would rather speak
of the rigorously theoretical but nonphilosophical mode or again style.
But, as will be seen, such a style is also radically plural, a notion that, interestingly, is absent from Lyotard's notion of the mode, style, or genre and,
in its radical form, from his practice. Indeed, as he says here, his "mode is
philosophical, and not theoretical (*or anything else*) [Le mode (du livre) est
philosophique, et non théorique (ou autre) . . .]" (emphasis added)—an
important parenthesis. The plural style, while not discounting anything,
transgresses more decisively both in *form* and *substance*, or in new mixtures
of both, to the extent that one can apply such classical terms. One can ascertain the difference in this respect between Lyotard's style and more radically critical or deconstructive and plural modes or styles, such as in
Nietzsche, Bataille, and Derrida.

Lyotard acutely senses the problem of the philosophical appurtenance
of his text, for example, in his brief engagement with Derrida on Aristotle
(74). Even more self-reflexive and revealing is the only reference to
Nietzsche in *The Differend*. It is also an excellent warning to every project
or antiproject—literary, theoretical, critical, or political. Nietzsche enters
the scene, the landscape or here rather a seascape, in parentheses after a
long discussion of Kant, via some geographical rubrics—"archipelago,"
even "goulag archipelago," "passages," "navigating between islands" (*The
Differend*, 135)—and alongside some mourning and melancholia, and "the
hope that is born with it [l'espérance qui naît avec lui]," Freud's or Heidegger's hope, or both.[50]

> Is this the sense in which we are not modern? Incommensurability, het-
> erogeneity, the differend, the persistence of proper names, the absence of
> a supreme tribunal? Or, on the other hand, is this the continuation of ro-
> manticism, the nostalgia that accompanies the retreat of . . . , etc.? Ni-
> hilism? A well-executed work of mourning for Being? And the hope that is
> born with it? Which is still the hope of redemption? With all of this still
> remaining inscribed within the thought of a redemptive future? Could it
> be that "we" are no longer telling ourselves anything? Are "we" not
> telling, whether bitterly or gladly, the great narrative of the end of great

narratives? For thought to remain modern, doesn't it suffice that it thinks in terms of the end of some history? Or, is postmodernity the pastime of an old man who scrounges in the garbage-heap of finality looking for leftovers, who brandishes unconsciousnesses, lapses, limits, confines, goulags, parataxes, non-senses, or paradoxes, and who turns this into the glory of his novelty, into his promise of change? But this too is a goal for a certain humanity. A genre. (A bad parody of Nietzsche [Mauvais pastiche de Nietzsche]. Why?) (Sec. 182, pp. 135–36; *Le Différend*, 197)

Nietzsche is a point of tranquillity in the eye of the storm, perceived or unnoticed, or both at once, around which everything—all the galleons, or even archipelagoes, of philosophy, and of much else—is in danger of collapsing. New passages may be opened, however, new paths broken.[51]

The problematic dimensions of Lyotard's works allow various critics to establish a proximity between Lyotard and Habermas. Jameson does so in his foreword to *The Postmodern Condition*, as does Richard Rorty in "Habermas and Lyotard on Postmodernity" (161–75). While, in my view, the differences between Lyotard and Habermas are of much greater significance, problematic aspects of Lyotard's texts cannot be ignored. This is one of the reasons why the present analysis proceeds by way of the general economy and the Nietzsche-Bataille-Derrida axis rather than that of Lyotard, Deleuze, or Foucault, or several other authors whose works might be related to the questions at issue.[52]

The confrontations between Habermas and Lyotard, and between Habermas and deconstruction, have been much discussed in recent literature. From the perspective of the present analysis, virtually all of Habermas' theoretical positions in this debate appear to be untenable. Whatever their own problems may be, Lyotard's and, even more, Derrida's deconstruction can be employed much more effectively against Habermas than the other way around. An analysis of these relationships cannot be fully pursued here. The difference—the *differend*—of the positions appears, at this point, to be sufficiently pronounced and irreducible, including concerning the question of the very possibility of positions, and of taking or not taking positions—or choosing both options simultaneously. *Understanding* these differences and the impossibility of reducing them and their *differends*, "their phrases in dispute," is far from finished. I shall comment only on this debate in relation to the historico-theoretical landscape, or again seascape, of this study.

Beyond Marx, Freud, Nietzsche, Heidegger, and Bataille, all of whom have had a powerful impact on the scene, the confrontation between Lyotard and Habermas is part of a more complex economy of relationships between poststructuralist theories, most specifically between deconstruction and thinkers such as Adorno and Walter Benjamin. Both are extremely important in the general context of postmodernism or poststructuralism, and specifically in the context of deconstruction, particularly what may be seen as late deconstruction.[53] As Lyotard writes: "It is this critique [which postmodernity imposes on the thought of the Enlightenment] which not only Wittgenstein and Adorno have initiated, but also a few other thinkers (French or other) who do not have the honor to be read by Professor Habermas—which at least saves them from getting a poor grade for their neoconservatism" (*The Postmodern Condition*, 73; "Réponse," 359).

Habermas' more recent writing may be seen as a reply to the challenge posed by Lyotard and deconstruction, in its attempt to address major precursors such as Nietzsche, Heidegger, and Bataille; deconstruction, most specifically Derrida's; and Foucault. Habermas' *The Philosophical Discourses of Modernity*, published in 1985, is perhaps his most representative treatment of the ensemble at issue, proceeding from Hegel to Nietzsche, to Heidegger, to Adorno and Max Horkheimer, to the recent developments on the French scene. While it is with a very different assessment from the one offered here, Habermas, too, sees Nietzsche as a radical critic, along the two major lines of modernity and "the entry into Postmodernity":

> Nietzsche's critique of modernity has been continued along both paths. The skeptical scholar who wants to unmask the perversion of the will to power, the revolt of reactionary forces, and the emergence of a subject-centered reason by using anthropological, psychological and historical methods has successors in Bataille, Lacan, and Foucault; the initiate-critic of metaphysics who lays claims to a unique kind of knowledge and pursues the rise of the philosophy of the subject back to its pre-Socratic beginnings has successors in Heidegger and Derrida. (*The Philosophical Discourse of Modernity*, 97; *Der philosophische Diskurs der Moderne: Zwölf Vorlesungen*, 120; translation modified)

Even leaving aside for the moment the question of the textual or critical rigor of Habermas' assessment and claims here and throughout this and other texts,[54] his demarcation is textually problematic and theoretically ineffective. One certainly can offer, as many recent studies have done, much more effective genealogies of these interactions.

It is true that Nietzsche decisively affects all of these texts—and Freud can be added to the list; that one cannot avoid relating Lacan to psychological, or more precisely, psychoanalytic, dimensions of postmodernity; that one should not miss, indeed often in contrast to Heidegger, the anthropological dimensions of Bataille's work; and that one may see Foucault's discourse as a postmodern re(con)figuring of the historical. Bataille, of course, is crucial for Foucault, but, then, equally so for Derrida, or for the French, let us say, post-Heideggerian scene in general; and, as the latter denomination suggests, Heidegger affects everything there as well. The textual configuration in the cases of Lacan, Bataille, and Foucault is thus infinitely more complex and multiple in its registers—philosophical, historical, anthropological, literary, psychological and psychoanalytic, linguistic and, of course, political. Both Lacan's and Foucault's dependence on Heidegger is equally uncircumventable. Foucault unequivocally states so himself, saying that "for [him] Heidegger has always been the essential philosopher" and that his "entire philosophical development was determined by [his] reading of Heidegger"—in conjunction with Nietzsche, as has been the case for most figures at issue here.[55] Such a statement by itself is not necessarily of fundamental significance. In this case, however, Foucault's self-assessment is correct; in addition, it suggests, whether intentionally or not, an important general point concerning the whole Foucauldian project, or a cluster of projects engaged by Foucault himself and his many followers. Many dimensions of Foucault's project, or his various projects, can be traced to Heidegger, specifically to *Being and Time*. Bataille's relation to Heidegger is more complex.[56] Partly given that Bataille's own comments suggest a stronger sense of difference than proximity between himself and Heidegger, the juxtaposition of their enterprises may be effective, even necessary. But Habermas does not offer such a productive juxtaposition. The overriding point is that in all these relations, one needs a complex interplay of proximities and distances, rather than a simple demarcation along any given set of lines, even if such lines, within a network, must be drawn and can be very effective.[57] While one may not always engage this complexity, one cannot uncritically suspend it to the degree Habermas does, particularly when it affects the relations under consideration and assessment here, and even more so when, as in Habermas, a negative assessment is offered.[58]

It is also true that between Derrida's text and the text of philosophy, specifically Heidegger's, there is, *together with a radical displacement*, a much closer, even an infinitesimal proximity, indeed much closer than Habermas is able to show. Also in Derrida's more recent works, while he continues to maintain a distance from Heidegger, a still closer proximity to, or affinity with, Heidegger emerges, in contrast to the way Nietzsche is situated in Derrida's earlier texts. From his earliest works, however, the relationship of Derrida and Heidegger has always been complex, suspended between proximities and distances from infinitesimal to radical.[59] Analogously to Derrida's encounter with Hegel, these relations also manifest Derrida's somewhat Heideggerian attitude to the history of philosophy and his mode of relating to this history.

The move closer toward Heidegger is actually characteristic of a number of recent studies;[60] and it is cogent with respect to Derrida's more recent work, particularly on Heidegger, although differences remain and Derrida always points them out. These texts, however, do indeed shorten the distances somewhat.

It may be said, in general, that given the enormity of Heidegger's actual text, some of which has become available only recently, and the scope and complexity of his analysis, the departures become more difficult the more one gets engaged. As with other major thinkers, one discovers that many arguments have been anticipated by Heidegger, as one establishes different levels and layers of even already familiar texts, such as *Being and Time*, for example. The departures are not impossible; and the complexity, variety and transformations of Heidegger's ideas and positions do not erase but at times reinforce the sustained trajectories of ideas and positions, from his earlier to his later texts.

Clearly, however, the analysis of Derrida's encounter with Heidegger would further foreground the problems inherent in Habermas' views of Derrida, or for that matter, of Heidegger, with important implications for the debate surrounding deconstruction and its impact upon different fields, including philosophy, literary criticism and theory, and historical studies. Beyond offering powerful direct arguments against Habermas, even more philosophically inclined commentators argue—*from within the philosophical register of analysis*—that Derrida's exploration does proceed in the "margins of *philosophy*," within and outside its register, and by way of exploring its closure. Against Habermas' demarcations, Derrida's enterprise cannot be assessed effectively outside the framework of the unconscious, via Nietzsche, Freud, Lacan, and particularly Bataille and the framework of general economy, to which Derrida consistently refers throughout his texts, often at crucial junctures. Also, whether in relation to the general economic thematic or in general and whether seen in theoretical or in textual terms, Derrida's encounter with Freud is irreducible; and it is altogether, albeit predictably, missing from Habermas' critique. In addition, the proximity of Derrida to Lacan, via Saussure, remains crucial in Derrida. These dimensions of Derrida's text and deconstruction constitute a decisive "*margin* of philosophy," much more radically so than in Heidegger. To this configuration or economy of "margins" Habermas does not pay much, if any, attention, either, while the configuration makes containing Derrida within a philosophical register an extremely complex and problematic issue, to the degree that such a containment is possible at all. One needs very different terms for this relation, and they will certainly have to be very different from the terms of Habermas' analysis. Even more importantly, they will reconfigure the parerga of philosophy and its margins, which constitute one of the central questions posed and explored by deconstruction. This reconfiguration is what is at stake here, rather than Habermas' critique as such, more interesting for what it misses than for what it has to offer.

In Heidegger's case, it is, conversely, Heidegger's proximity to Nietzsche, or rather Nietzsche's to Heidegger, as suggested by Habermas, that is problematic. The radical, but again not absolute, distance between Nietzsche and philosophy is a major issue and a major theme of the present study, to be considered in detail in Chapter 4. It is clear from Bataille's, Deleuze's, Foucault's, and Derrida's writing, that what is at stake throughout the scene at issue is also the difference from Heidegger's reading of Nietzsche. The latter positions Nietzsche within metaphysics. It may well be one of the major sources for Habermas' assessment; but it is much more important as a general feature of the modern intellectual scene.

The point at issue at the moment is by no means diminished, rather reinforced, by the fact that Derrida incessantly explores and, whenever necessary, deconstructs the operation of metaphysics in texts on the margins of philosophy as much as in the texts of philosophy, or what is conventionally so seen. I am not suggesting that the proximity between Derrida and philosophy, and the resulting differences in the attitude to and critique of philosophy, specifically as against both Bataille and Nietzsche, should not be taken into account. Quite the contrary, as must be clear from the preceding analysis; nevertheless, along with proximities, one must explore the differences between the margin and the excess *of philosophy* in Derrida, and the *margin* and the *excess* of philosophy in Nietzsche. One cannot suspend either this margin or the general economy in Derrida's text, however, emerging by way of Nietzsche, Freud, Lacan, and Bataille, alongside and inscribing the difference from Hegel, Husserl, and Heidegger. The question of the relationship between deconstruction and literature, or literary criticism and theory, is another important aspect of this economy and of the poststructuralist configuration in general. It is particularly crucial in the context of plural or complementary style—the style of writing in and in the margins of different registers: literary, philosophical, psychological or psychoanalytic, critical, historical, or political. These issues, too, are hardly addressed by Habermas, except in the familiar forms of uncritical separation or, conversely, unification of different fields, such as, specifically, literature and philosophy.

The issue is more general and more complex, of course. Gasché's *The Tain of the Mirror* poses a similar problem, and Gasché offers a treatment incomparably more rigorous and more sophisticated than Habermas'. Both in relation to Heidegger and at a more general level, the problems, as I have indicated, is easily detectable in Herman Rapaport's *Heidegger and Derrida*. It is equally apparent in Henry Staten's *Wittgenstein and Derrida*. The importance of Gasché's book, along with these studies other recent treatments of the question of Derrida and philosophy, is that it rigorously pursues the irreducible philosophical dimensions of Derrida's text. As I have argued, one can ignore neither Derrida's specific positioning of his texts and projects in relation to the text and history of philosophy, nor the philosophical appurtenance of his texts and projects. Nor, therefore, can one ignore the differences—or, conversely, the proximities—in this respect between Derrida and Nietzsche, or among all figures who can be seen as operating on or in relation to the margins of philosophy, such as Bataille, Blanchot, and Benjamin, or in the more philosophical register, Heidegger, Levinas, Althusser, or Wittgenstein.[61] Suspending the matrix of the general economy and of the—general economic—unconscious severely diminishes the critical and theoretical potential of Derrida's discourse.[62]

The assertion is not that Derrida's matrix must be rendered most specifically in these terms or *only* in these terms. The latter form of containment would be equally problematic. Instead, the assertion is that certain dimensions and effects of Derrida's matrix cannot be suspended either in terms of their theoretical effectiveness or in terms of textual rigor. These dimensions can be addressed effectively and are addressed by Derrida himself in terms of general economy. In addition, the perspective of the general economy enables one to understand much better the proximities and differences among the different figures at issue, such as Nietzsche, Heidegger, Bataille, Derrida, and Lyotard.[63] In terms of textual rigor, the suspension of the general economy and the unconscious, is problematic as well, as part of the general problem of containing Derrida's deconstruction within the register of philosophy.

Neither Gasché nor several other commentators that are pertinent here[64] deny the significance of, or always fully suspend, the exterior of philosophy in Derrida's text, although such a suspension or repression is by no means always absent and has powerful effects. A more interesting and important problem, however, is that of what can be called the "local containment" of Derrida's text and style of writing in a double register, simultaneously inside and outside, or on the margin of, philosophy. Even *locally, at each point* of Derrida's text, its nonphilosophical dimensions cannot be suspended; "the *tain* of the mirror[s]" involved does not allow one to do so. These dimensions must be rigorously taken into account in following Derrida's matrix of *différance, dissemination, writing,* and so on—in short, the general economy or general economies of his texts. Obviously, the balances vary; and the more directly "deconstructive" strata of Derrida's texts, such as his readings of Husserl and Heidegger, in particular, are more philosophical in this sense. The closure of philosophy itself is distributed heterogeneously. Still, the loss of the nonphilosophical, the loss of the general economy—the loss of the economy of loss—is too big a price to pay, even in Gasché's book, which is one of the most extensive and sustained American commentaries on Derrida.[65] The situation actually *mirrors* the standard economy of deconstruction, as exemplified most graphically in Derrida's analysis of Husserl in *Speech and Phenomena.* No matter how strenuously and rigorously Husserl tries to suspend or bracket the nonphilosophical, including the unconscious, inhibitions of signification and meaning, *rigorously,* it cannot be done.[66]

All such interpretive and theoretical choices and necessities acquire a much more complex economy—a general economy. It must thus relate to losses that cannot be utilized, theoretically or politically, even though one must still keep in mind that the general economy is not only or unconditionally the economy of loss. Furthermore, there is no reason, in principle, why one cannot *sacrifice* any given general economy;[67] and under certain conditions one indeed must do so. The locality of such conditions is itself complex and is often sufficiently extended or sufficiently global. Such is certainly the case in relation to the question of the philosophical appurtenance of all the texts at issue here, particularly Derrida's. The loss—sacrifice—of the general economy itself becomes problematic, however, in view both of the textual rigor of such an analysis and the possibilities or again constraints of the theoretical, historical, and perhaps political matrices that emerge. At the same time, I am not suggesting that such a sacrifice uniformly takes place across the spectrum of reading Derrida or the commentary on deconstruction and related issues. Also, while the rubrics and metaphors do count, of course, the relevant questions need not necessarily be directly addressed in any given set of terms; they may be implicitly taken into account. These are certain necessary effects that are at issue; and, conversely, merely speaking in these terms or taking Bataille's analysis into consideration does not in itself guarantee a general economy.[68] I do think, however, that the problematic has remained somewhat marginal, both in the commentaries on Derrida and in general; while it offers extraordinary theoretical and critical resources.

The more philosophically oriented works at issue respond to the marginalizing of the philosophical register in Derrida's text, particularly in the earlier stages of deconstruction, and to some extent, particularly in Gasché, to the question of the necessity of theoretical rigor. They also respond to the hostility to Derrida and deconstruction, or related developments in France, including Lyotard and Deleuze, as philosophical enterprise on the part of the institutionalized philosophy, particularly Anglo-American philosophy. The latter is part of a broader configuration of relationships between the American, and somewhat differently the British, institutions of philosophy and those of Continental philosophy, including Kant, Hegel, and Heidegger. It is worth recalling, in this context, that most of the French authors associated with deconstruction and postmodernism can be seen as operating from within or on the margins of the institution of philosophy, and in some measure psychoanalysis, particularly along the lines of feminist theory. Such is not the case in the United States, where during the last decade or so most of these issues and much of Continental philosophy have been pursued within the institutions of literary criticism and theory.[69] Indeed, the very possibility of doing so within literary studies is one of the most interesting and remarkable of recent developments, given the resistance to deconstruction, philosophy, or theory in general on the part of the institutions of literary studies, again particularly at the earlier stages of deconstruction. In this sense, the role of the Yale critics and particularly of de Man was decisive.[70] During recent years the configuration has changed on the philosophical side of the debate, although in a rather limited fashion and within a limited scholarly circle—and not without posing new problems of its own. Such problems may well be inevitable, from both sides of the issue—literary-critical or philosophical—and both in turn engage the socio-political or the psychological and psychoanalytic thematics. All these registers can operate against each other, including deconstructively; or jointly, but without full synthesis, whether Hegelian or other. They are, in short, complementary; and their economy is a general economy.

Within this general economy, Derrida's proximity to philosophy and specifically to Heidegger and Hegel, may also be appoached and criticized differently, namely, by way of the closure of metaphysics.[71] This approach would allow one to pose the question without discarding the radical margin and the excess of philosophy enacted in Derrida's text. The writing, also in Derrida's sense, of the authors at issue here, beginning with and following Nietzsche, requires a general economy and plural style in relation to philosophy and its closure, or a still more heterogeneous economy of closure. This approach contrasts with that of demarcation suggested by the authors under discussion, even those closer to deconstruction. It is structured by three configurations—general economy, closure, and plural or complementary style—which jointly constitute the major subject and the main matrix of the present study.[72] Such a matrix would demand a more complex relation between literature and theory, or criticism. It may also allow us to move beyond poststructuralist or postmodernist thematics.

Following the movement from the restricted to the general economy, one can reconfigure the play of forces and the exchanges in the landscape after poststructuralism, or after postmodernism, where theoretical—or historical and political—discussion can be effectively positioned along different intervals of the spectrum of such a movement. To indicate some of the major critical and theoretico-political or ideological forces of this spectrum, one might mention Marxist criticism and theory, Foucauldian criticism, specifically New Historicism; what may be called sociologically oriented criticism;[73] deconstruction, including institutional deconstruction; race and colonial and postcolonial studies; many developments in feminist theory and gender studies; and recently, gay studies.

Feminist criticism and theory, and gender studies constitute a decisive development in the shaping of this scene. I want to stress this point, because at issue is arguably the most radical transformation in modern—at least this century's—intellectual and political history. In most of the major texts in this field, starting with Simone de Beauvoir, the matrix of economy in all its aspects plays an important role. Such feminist theories often suggest the necessity of moving from a restricted to a general economy, or to use a recent metaphor, a general ecology of gender, although, as a rule, this transition is enacted quite differently than that in Bataille or Nietzsche. They are often, such as in Irigaray, Hélène Cixous, and Sarah Kofman, much closer to Derrida. One finds interesting proximities to Deleuze, however, specifically via Nietzsche, in both Irigaray and Cixous, although on occasion Irigaray offers critical assessments of the Deleuzean matrix. Against the background of Freud and Lacan, this proximity to Deleuze may be defined via the economy of desire, a problematic that Derrida does not engage, at least not as massively and radically as does Deleuze, who may be seen as the philosopher of desire. In this sense, Derrida, in closer proximity to Freud, may be seen as the philosopher of re-

pression. Along with his many important deconstructions of psychoanalysis, Derrida radically problematizes the concept of repression itself,
while Deleuze, in contrast, does not always take in sufficiently critical
fashion the concept of desire, particularly in his later works written with
Guattari. In addition, even the classical, precritical or undeconstructed—
restricted—economy of repression, not to speak of its deconstructed—
general—economy, has proved its powerful critical or deconstructive
potential in Nietzsche, Freud, Lacan, Derrida, and elsewhere. As such, this
economy of repression may, to a degree, be contrasted to the often more
problematic, particularly utopian, matrices of desire, specifically in Deleuze
and Guattari, or Irigaray and Cixous.

The feminist encounters, overt and implicit, with all these figures—
Nietzsche, Freud, Heidegger, Bataille, Lacan, Derrida; or Kant and Hegel;
or indeed Socrates and Plato—occur in the margins of philosophy, even
more radically exceeding its registers. Cixous' and Irigaray's works are the
most powerful examples that massively engage—reconfigure and refigure—the modern and possibly, or potentially, postmodern historico-
theoretical configuration. The spectrum of feminist theory, criticism, and
politics, however, has by now reconfigured a very long history. The history of feminist and gender analysis—and, to use this term against Hegel,
the synthesis, or in terms of this study, complementary anti-synthesis—
cannot be restricted to the French scene, of course, however important the
latter may be; and the list of powerful and important texts and authors is,
by now, very long. This history has been a decisive development—a decisive difference, a decisive force, a decisive economy—on the scene of theoretical and political economy, a decisive reconfiguration of all that these
economies encompass. This reconfiguration, quite possibly, moves beyond
any *economy*, even a general economy; and suggests the potential limitations
of this, or any, matrix, however capacious it may be.

New possibilities of theory, history, politics, or of rubrics, thematics,
or metaphorics may emerge at any point. There is nothing *sacred*, to use
Bataille's already displaced term, in general economy. Since things can
always be sacrificed, provided that more interesting and effective possibilities emerge or present themselves from the exterior of such exploration,
thus, if Hegel does not sacrifice science, or consciousness and meaning altogether, to the naïvete of sacrifice, even though Bataille thinks that he
does in the end of the *Phenomenology*, we can and must sacrifice them as the
grounding economy, which is also the economy of the ground and thus a
restricted economy. Yet we also must refigure its limits, both insofar as we
want to understand such a possibility and necessity for Hegel, and insofar

as we still must rely on Hegelian logic within the reconfigured limits of general economy. Such configurations are complex, perhaps more complex than those emerging by way of general economy itself. But they are not unapproachable; no unapproachable configuration is any longer complex enough.

Reconnections: Theory, Politics, Practice

The richness of the configurations and reconfigurations—the connections and reconnections—considered by the preceding analysis makes it difficult to accept the claims of many critics that the practitioners of general economy and related modes of criticism and theory, specifically deconstructive or postdeconstructive, are not or until recently have not been "politically" engaged. Quite the contrary: they have often been so engaged. This engagement is immediately demonstrated by the very point of the general economy and the significance of Bataille, and thus of Marx, in Derrida. Marx admittedly is present in a more mediated and oblique fashion in Derrida. The relationship to the political is pronounced, however, even in Derrida's early works, in *Of Grammatology*, and certainly in *Positions* and *Dissemination*. Whether one speaks of the politics of the university or politics at large, that relationship is featured prominently in many of his subsequent works, more politically oriented and more position-taking. Nietzsche may be a different case in this respect; but, as shall be seen in Chapter 4, his case does not contradict the present assessment, but, giving it a further complexity, will reinforce it.[74]

The matrix of the general economy is a politico-theoretical matrix, although its scope and effectiveness cannot be reduced to political considerations. The practice of general economy itself is not only theoretical, but also political; and even in Nietzsche, this matrix is different from, if interactive with, the Marxist matrix, or in later developments, Foucault's and Deleuze's matrices. In Bataille and Derrida, or in deconstruction in general, the relationships between theory and practice have always played a crucial role. Theory and practice, political or other, are indissociable, but importantly, they are not identical. These, once again, are relations with a tremendous complexity and richness of stratification, involving multiple double binds, undecidables, aporias, indeterminacies, and complementarities. They require careful analysis and discrimination, both theoretical and political, with respect to the authors involved. The degrees of political involvement and the modes of political engagements in the texts of these authors are quite different. One should therefore pose such questions in rigorous terms in relation to given texts, such as those of Nietzsche, Heidegger, Bataille, Derrida, and others; and without uncritically unifying theory and practice, or uncritically suspending either. There are always politics of theory, but there are also theories of politics, and theories sufficiently removed from *any given political configuration*, although, once again, not from politics altogether. One must respect the richness of these stratifications. One should certainly be hesitant simply to relate theory to the political choice, as, among others, Foucault, hardly a nonpolitical thinker, warned us.[75]

In approaching these issues, one can in fact effectively utilize the framework of the general economy and the difference between restricted and general economies of these relationships between theory and practice or politics. Thus Marx's, Heidegger's, Deleuze's, and Foucault's must all be seen as restricted economies. Dialectic in Marx and indeed in Hegel remains a differential play but, as will be seen later, a controlled one; or as developed, in its perhaps greatest generality, by Heidegger in *The Question of Being*, the play of transformations that the more richly it unfolds, is the more strictly governed. Marx's change of the Hegelian base of dialectic— a *transformation* assigning a material base to "transformations"—does not change the economy, in whatever sense of the term, in this respect. The latter may be a well-known and relatively obvious point by now; and in itself it does not seem to be denied, wherever one's theoretical or political preferences are in this respect. Even if one assumes, however, that most pronounced metaphysical dimensions can be usefully suspended or more subtly and productively reinscribed in reading Marx or some modified forms of Marxism, many other manifestations and implications of the restricted economy will be found there. Many of these manifestations will be found theoretically, let alone politically, necessary within a Marxist framework and will be seen as theoretical and political alternatives to Nietzsche, Freud, Bataille, and Derrida, among others. *Some* of the implications, such as various materialist aspects, will be used, conversely, to bridge both types of framework, a function that characterizes more recent approaches of that type, particularly to Derrida and deconstruction. In most recent analyses, however, one actually finds a mixture, at times quite complex, of both strategies, without, for the most part, transforming one's ideological and political beliefs.

This force of politico-ideological determination is predictable, indeed unavoidable. As Kierkegaard grasped in his *Concluding Unscientific Postscript*, and as Nietzsche understood very well, one's beliefs have a highly complex and indirect, or to use Hegel's term against Hegel, a *mediated* relation to any form of theorizing, whether specifically on, or against, the subject of such beliefs, or in general. This mediation has enormous capacity for reinforcement, including by way of incorporating the elements of new theories—or histories—no matter how theoretically problematic such incorporation may be from the perspective of such new theories and histories.[76] One knows very well by now that *différance* is not dialectic, or dialogue, as in Mikhail Bakhtin; or at least it is clear that such a distinction must be made, at least initially, and one's politico-theoretical discussion adjusted accordingly. The adjustment, however, is not always easy and far from always careful; and confusion and misunderstanding are not uncommon even now. The relevant articles and books would form a long list.

The complexity of the configuration is amply justified by the complex economy of differences and proximities among all the figures involved and, it might be added, made still more complicated by the introduction into the picture of Foucault, Deleuze, Bakhtin, as well as feminist theory and politics, often via Lacan and Derrida. Certainly there are powerful elements of critical Marxism, let us say, in Bataille, who always maintains, via Kojève, some affinities with Marxism, in part via Bataille, in Derrida, or even in Nietzsche, although the anti-Marxism of Nietzsche's text is obviously far more pronounced. Conversely, as shall be seen in Chapter 6, some of the major ideas and strategies of Derrida and deconstruction have their trajectories in Marxism, specifically in Althusser.

The very denomination of Marxism becomes problematic as a result, given the powerful impact of both Derrida and deconstruction and of a Foucauldian theoretical, or particularly political, agenda in many recent studies. Many other factors must be taken into account, specifically Freud and Nietzsche, whose impact on the history of Marxism has a much longer history. Suspending for the moment, however, the difficult question of political alternatives, theoretically, Marx's political economy and, I think, just about all Marxist political economies so far, remain restricted economies in Bataille's sense or, if the term must be differentiated from Bataille, in the sense of the present analysis.[77] A similar problem arises with respect to some Foucauldian critics. The affinities and interactions between the frameworks at issue are, let me stress, possible and indeed inevitable. The general economy, however, imposes powerful constraints, as do, conversely, other frameworks at issue. Among Marx, Nietzsche, Freud, Bataille, Foucault, and Derrida, or Heidegger, who never can quite be left aside, there are—and to different authors and readers differently—"Such welcome and unwelcome things at once / 'Tis hard to reconcile" (*Macbeth* IV.iii.138–39), or even to balance without a reconciliation. Political and ideological agendas powerfully affect the configuration, no matter how subtle the relations between politics and theory may be.

That is not to say that there are no valid questions to be posed and debates engaged in concerning the question of deconstruction and politics, whatever politics is at issue. Such debates have often been productively engaged, along various lines and with respect to other figures and general frameworks of criticism, history, or theory. Our understanding of both politics and deconstruction has been enriched as a result; and to begin with, neither can be considered uncritically—outside, for example, the politics of deconstruction or the deconstruction of politics. While the general point concerning political engagement has often been missed at the earlier stages of the poststructuralist, specifically deconstructive, debate and continues to be debated, it need not be belabored in view of many recent studies. The number of such studies has been growing, particularly in the wake of the case of de Man's war journalism; and, even more than Derrida, de Man has been at the center of institutional and political debates concerning deconstruction. The discussion of this issue may exhibit various degrees of rigor and success in treating the authors at issue, as well as very different political agendas—Foucauldian, Marxist, or other, or various combinations of these. In addition, a number of these analyses are problematic, specifically in relating the factors of theoretical rigor, the rigor of reading, and the political agenda. Still, the question of deconstruction and politics, and specifically Marxism, has played a major role in recent debates in this country, whether specifically in relation to Derrida or de Man or in general; it has been addressed by many studies and commentaries cited here.[78] Misunderstandings remain, although there have been some major changes in this respect in recent years, alongside with some marked changes, let us say, from right to left, in viewing the political possibilities offered by Derrida's texts and deconstruction more generally. Whether one speaks of the politics of the academic institutions or broader political configurations, including geopolitics—from apartheid and colonialism to nuclear politics—such changes have affected both the theoretical developments and the political positions and strategies of the authors associated with deconstruction, particularly in speaking on the political issues.

Against more critical earlier readings, deconstruction or even Nietzsche, or certain strata of their texts and theories, are often seen as conducive to positive social change. In a number of recent approaches, the transformations emerge as directed—toward positive social changes, for example—in the absence of direct political control or enforcement, proceeding in the right direction under the condition of play, such as—or so it is claimed—the general economy of *différance* in Derrida.

The resulting economy itself often has other models, including some indicated earlier, for example, in Foucault, Deleuze, or Bakhtin, or other authors, and the play of substitutions of proper names in this respect may be practiced in a very subtle manner. The possibility or necessity of relating such agendas to Derrida or Nietzsche is a separate issue. *Certain* strata of Nietzsche's, Bataille's, and Derrida's texts may indeed so operate, "for other reasons than hitherto"; and there are affinities between corresponding political or moral positions. The problems, as I indicated a bit earlier, emerge insofar as one must confront a theory—an economy—of the conditions of possibility of such political changes and other strata in Derrida's, Bataille's, and particularly Nietzsche's matrices as general economies that problematize such possibilities and point out the complexity of these conditions. Whether in stratifications of theory or relationships between theory and politics, the suspension of such strata in a general economy may take subtle although never rigorously workable forms. The more or less utopian frameworks that emerge are always problematic from the perspective of the general economy. The democratizations of deconstruction in particular are not easy; democratizing Nietzsche is virtually impossible.

One of the recurring problems of that type is the insistence on the ethical subject, or the subject, to begin with.[79] It is true that Derrida's analysis does not simply destroy the subject, but situates and resituates or reinscribes it—to the extent, finally very limited, that subjectivity can be retained, outside of the necessity of accounting for its functioning elsewhere.[80] That *deconstruction* does not simply destroy the subject was perhaps the main point used in the appropriation—the domestication and democratization—of deconstruction by way of ethical subjectivity, which is often not attentive enough to this point. Derrida's analysis and certainly Nietzsche's, are radical critiques of subjectivity.[81] Such a critique would, I think, apply to many forms of ethicized or historicized subjectivity as well; the latter remains a metaphysical subjectivity, in the name of historicity and difference. In this sense, while the economy of Being itself must be deconstructed, Heidegger's critique of subjectivity, is very important, specifically for Derrida, or Foucault. In general, this type of the return to the subject and indeed to the ethical subject has been a persistent gesture; it usually occurs by way of a detour and, in my assessment, is accompanied by a "democratization" of deconstruction—or other theoretical and historical frameworks—to suit a given ethical or political agenda. It can be encountered even with respect to Nietzsche, although the latter is a much more difficult case for such an appropriation. The strategy is in part a response to attacks on deconstruction on the counts of political nihilism, the reactionary character of its project, or similar allegations—the attacks often being equally problematic.[82]

These considerations, to repeat, do not mean that deconstruction or indeed Nietzsche forbids various convictions, positions, or actions, that may be construed as socially progressive, democratic, and so on. Neither deconstruction nor Nietzsche forbids anything in practice, except, of course, the uncritical application of corresponding theories that, for example, relate as fully to the possibility of political difference—"democratization"—as to a repression of such differences. The effectiveness of these theories, and specifically of Nietzsche's, is that they account, historically and theoretically, for very different genealogies of morals.[83] Derrida's *différance* is clearly as much an efficacity of identities and similarities as of differences and alterities, and therefore an efficacity of a repression of difference; of course, there always exist simultaneously the possibility and the impossibility that repression will succeed. Politically, therefore, these theories suggest a substantial dose of skepticism as to how most utopian programs would be implemented, while not discounting the political or the theoretical value of utopian visions or models.

Recent political discussions, however, have in turn affected developments in such areas as deconstruction. The whole theoretico-political landscape has been configured quite differently, with respect to the relationships among such figures as Bataille, Blanchot, Althusser, Foucault, Deleuze, Levinas, Lacan, Lyotard, and Derrida, partly because of a very different history of reading both Hegel and Heidegger. The shift to a politico-ideological problematic characterizes the more recent scene, particularly that of the previous decade. This shift also characterizes related developments in deconstruction. In France, too, the focus of the theoretical and intellectual debate during the last decade has shifted toward political questions, including in the works of the authors customarily associated with deconstruction. Part of this shift has been motivated by the case of Heidegger, specifically, but not exclusively, his involvement with National Socialism, similarly to the recent discussion in this country of de Man's case, often along with Heidegger's. While Heidegger's case is important, however, and while, as I have pointed out earlier in other connections, Heidegger's prominence has increased, if anything, in recent discussions, it is still a relatively small part of the general concern with the question of politics, institutions, or interactively the questions of science and technology, which is another prominent issue on the scene of postmodernism. The emphasis on the political has always been pronounced in such major postmodernists as Lyotard, Deleuze, or Foucault.

The Foucauldian agenda, joined more recently by the Deleuzean, has long held undeniable prominence in this country, both in its own terms and alongside various Marxist or post-Marxist agendas. Much recent critical idiom may be seen as largely deconstructive, or perceived as such, given its history—*in the United States*, as opposed to France. A great deal of the recent agenda—critical, theoretical, and political—is Foucauldian or Marxist, or often both interactively, with deconstructive or, we can now say, more traditionally deconstructive thematics and analysis moving toward Heidegger, as discussed earlier. Hence Deleuze's work has become increasingly significant, a particularly interesting development given that Deleuze is arguably the most anti-Heideggerian figure on the modern or postmodern scene. Nevertheless, while the power and the impact of Deleuze's and Foucault's analyses are undeniable, affecting the major questions at issue in this study, they remain, as do most Marxist analyses, within the limits of a restricted economy.

Yet their work also shows how much can be done within the limits of a restricted economy, or outside the matrix of general and restricted economy, in relation to deconstruction. While Derrida's critique of early Foucault appears to be extremely effective, one would have in addition to consider the later, more Nietzschean, Foucault, whose case in this respect would demand a separate analysis. In addition, the historico-theoretical configuration itself has been affected by the changes in deconstruction, specifically through the expansion of the role of political problematics; or conversely by the introduction of deconstructive elements, along with Marxist and psychoanalytic ones, into the Foucauldian theoretical, historical, and political agenda. These interactions have always been complex, of course, in part because of the significance of such figures as Marx, Nietzsche, Freud, Saussure, or Heidegger, or indeed of Hegel and Kant, to the works involved. But the transformation of the historico-theoretico-political horizon is undeniable, given also such developments as gender studies, race studies, postcolonial studies, gay and lesbian studies, and other investigations of previously marginalized—or even exiled—theoretical, historical, and political fields.

In general, one is by no means unconditionally constrained to place either Foucault's or Deleuze's, or any other texts, including Nietzsche's—

or historical, theoretical, or political analyses—within the matrix of general economy. This matrix may be, or may appear to be, powerful and capacious; yet it cannot be unique, all-encompassing, or total. It cannot calculate all variables, not even by calculating them as incalculable. It is designed, among other things, to operate against all such economies, by definition restricted ones. Nor would such a suspension—actual or potential, possible or necessary—be prohibited by the openness of the matrix of general economy from differentiation or dissemination, inside and outside the domains or intervals of its functioning, or from putting into play all such boundaries and demarcations. The matrix, of course, does constrain, for many complex reasons, the choices and necessities of this study, which will argue for the significance of general economies and their extensions to the current, and possibly the future, intellectual and political scene.

Chapter 2

The Maze of Taste:
On Bataille, Derrida, and Kant

Ma chambre donne sur un salon délabré, où des meubles du début
de l'autre siècle achèvent de tomber en poussière. Dans le fracas du ciel,
il me sembla entendre un bruit d'éternuement. Je me levai pour aller
éteindre la lumière, j'étais nu et je m'arrêtai avant d'ouvrir . . .

. . . J'avais la certitude de trouver Emmanuel Kant, il m'attendait
derrière la porte. Il n'avait pas le visage diaphane qui le distingua de son
vivant: il avait la mine hirsute d'un jeune homme décoiffé sous un
tricorne. J'ouvris et, à ma surprise, je me trouvai devant le vide. J'étais
seul, j'étais nu dans les plus vastes écroulements de foudre que j'eusse
encore entendues.

Je me dis gentiment à moi-même:

— Tu es un pitre!

J'éteignis la lumière et je retournai vers mon lit, lentement, à la
lueur décevante des éclairs.[1]

—Georges Bataille, *L'Abbé C.*

In Parentheses

Following Bataille's own views, Bataille's confrontation with Hegel is customarily, and often productively, seen as central to his thought and
writing. Kant seems to function mostly as one of the "signs," or "signifiers," of philosophy in general, often appearing alongside Hegel, although
Bataille was clearly familiar with Kant's major texts, to which he refers.
Thus, Bataille juxtaposes Kant and Hegel with Nietzsche in *Inner Experience*: "Nietzsche was only a burning solitary man, without relief from too

much strength, with a rare balance between intelligence and unreasoned life. The balance is not very conducive to the developed exercise of the intellectual faculties (which require calm, as in the existence of Kant, of Hegel). He proceeded by insights, putting into play forces in all directions, not being linked to anything, starting again, not building stone by stone" (*Inner Experience*, 27; *L'Expérience intérieure*, 51).

Nietzsche's multidirectional play of forces is indeed quite different from Hegel's play of forces (das Spiel der Kräfte), or from Kant's play (Spiel)—a concept of great importance in Kant, especially in the third critique. Given what Bataille has to say on Hegel elsewhere, or Hegel's own statements in this respect, "calm" is hardly the right word here, particularly applied to the period when Hegel, writing the *Phenomenology*, seemed to believe he was going mad, on which Bataille himself comments on several occasions. Even more pointedly, as Bataille knew, the difference of play between Hegel and Nietzsche, which is also the play of difference, will not be contained by the differences and forces that Bataille invokes. Kant is perhaps what defines the contrast suggested by Bataille, together with, by metonymic proximity, a certain *Kantian* Hegel. For Nietzsche, as Bataille undoubtedly knew, Kant serves as a focus of an attack on philosophy and morality (and philosophy as morality), possibly conditioning Bataille's parenthesis in the passage from *Inner Experience* just cited. The Nietzschean margin, then, may extend the Kantian parenthesis in Bataille's text. Moreover, as my epigraph suggests, Kant may play a much greater role in Bataille's thinking than is immediately apparent, even if his face has been transformed into the "hirsute mien of a bushy-haired man wearing a three-cornered hat." Unlike Robert C., we may not expect "to find Immanuel Kant waiting for [us] behind the door[s]" in the corridors or labyrinths of Bataille's text, where we proceed by "guiding [ourselves] by the duplicitous light of the flashes of lightning." To our surprise, however, we might in fact come upon him there, even if the sign on the door proclaims "Hegel" or "Nietzsche." It is not inconceivable that Bataille's passage itself has its source, deliberate or repressed, in Kant's example in "Was heißt: sich in Denken orientieren?":

> In the dark I orient myself in a familiar room if I can only seize on a single object whose position I can remember. Nothing, however, apparently helps me here except the capacity of determining positions by a *subjective* ground of distinction. For I do not see the objects whose position I should find, and if somebody had played a joke on me by putting on the left what was previously on the right while still preserving the relative

order of the things [in the room], I could not find my way [I would not be able to find myself] in a room with otherwise completely equal walls [so würde ich mich in einem Zimmer, wo sonst alle Wände ganz gleich wären gar nicht finden können]. Thus, however, I quickly orient myself through the mere feeling of a difference between my two sides, the right one and the left one. ("On Orientation in Thinking," *Critique of Practical Reason*, 295; "Was heißt: sich in Denken orientieren?" *Sämmtliche Werke* 46b:150; translation modified)

From the body to writing to politics, from left to right and from right to left, the potential implications of this passage for Bataille, in *L'Abbé C.* and in general, may be many, giving still more space to Kant in Bataille.[2] While not the first proper name, which is Nietzsche, Kant is the first parenthesis of *Inner Experience*, a parenthesis to the opposite of inner experience and of Nietzsche and Bataille—"inner hypocrisy [l'hypocrisie intérieure], . . . solemn distant exigencies (such as the morality in Kant) . . ." (*Inner Experience*, xxxii; *L'Expérience intérieure*, 10).

I shall not argue for the significance of Kant in Bataille in specific terms of textual influence. Rather, I want to explore what can be seen as a Kantian *moment* in Bataille that emerges via the economic thematics in the third critique. I focus on two major implications of this interface as seen from the perspective of the relations between the restricted economy and the general economy.

The first one is a dislocation of the *restricted* economy of consumption, particularly that of pleasurable consumption, that controls all Kant's conceptual, aesthetic, and political economies—all forms of understanding and reason, pure or applied (practical), and judgment in Kant.

The second one is the transformation of the theoretical, and by implication literary and political, practice or style into the heterogeneous—*plural* and *complementary*—style under the conditions of general economy.

The radical loss defining the general economic conditions demands heterogeneity. This loss is more an effect of the richness than of the poverty of the system; or, better, it signals a complex complementary interaction of poverty and riches, losses and gains, consumption and expenditure, conservation and waste. The interface at issue reflects, in part, the historical and conceptual closure that, according to Derrida, defines Western philosophical discourse, or theoretical discourse, or discourse in general.[3] At the same time, this analysis of this interface leads to the question of the transformation of this closure—to the point of the necessity, a more Nietzschean mode, of "starting again, not building stone by stone."[4]

Thus one might want to look, with Nietzsche, for stones or building blocks elsewhere, outside the castle or cathedral of philosophy—"of Kant, of Hegel."

The significance of Kant in this respect is perhaps best illustrated by Bataille's passing remark, again joining Kant and Hegel, in "The 'Old Mole' and the Prefix *Sur* in the Words *Surhomme* [Superman] and *Surrealist*": "It was necessary at any cost to endow antinomies in general with a mechanical and abstract character, as in Kant and Hegel" (*Visions of Excess*, 35; "La 'Vieille taupe' et le préfixe *sur* dans les mots *surhomme* et *surréaliste*," *Oeuvres complètes* 2:97). The coupling of Kant and Hegel is, of course, familiar to the point of triviality. It is far less trivial and far more significant, however, that Bataille conceives of this coupling in terms of a historical and conceptual closure of philosophy—perhaps in the wake of Heidegger. Our discourse, at least up to a point, must depend on this closure, even when it is aimed at undermining the power of metaphysics and philosophy. The phrase immediately preceding the one just cited analogously defines the philosophical closure of language: ". . . for human vocabulary continues everywhere to maintain throughout a faithful memory of fundamental categories [. . . car le vocabulaire continue sans explication à conserver une mémoire fidèle de catégories fondamentales dans l'humanité entière]" (*Visions*, 35; *Oeuvres complètes* 2:97). With the exception of Derrida, one can hardly think of a better invocation of the philosophical closure: however much "philosophical usages themselves are in question [. . . les usages philosophiques eux-mêmes sont en cause . . .]" (*Visions*, 35; *Oeuvres complètes* 2:97) and however transformed they might become, metaphysical remnants, in part left by the history of such questioning, are ineluctable in our language. This economy of closure is central to Derrida and is powerfully explored throughout his texts. The notion of closure so conceived is one of Derrida's most significant contributions to modern theoretical thought and intellectual history.[5]

The closure at issue does not begin with Kant since the concept or category *of* category invoked by Bataille is as Aristotelian as it is Kantian. But it does not begin with Aristotle either, or Plato and Socrates. Bataille's essay, through its title and its epigraph from Marx, metaphorically defining historical materialism—"In history as in nature decay is the laboratory of life" (*Visions*, 32)—already announces this closure and the proper names that demarcate it in terms of more modern intellectual history: Marx, Nietzsche, Freud, and, indirectly, several others. In so doing, Bataille's text defines and enters the modern, and postmodern, historico-theoretical configuration. Simultaneously, however, he frames this configuration—configuring and reconfiguring its parergon—between the communist and surrealist manifestos, and thus also between art and political economy. The term 'parergon' functions in this sense of the deconstruction and the reinscription of the classical notion of framing, boundaries, and margins in Derrida's analysis of Kant in "The Parergon" in *The Truth in Painting* (*La Vérité en peinture*) and "Economimesis."[6] The word *parergon* itself initially occurs in section 14 of *The Critique of Judgement*, defining "that which does not belong to the complete representation of the object internally as an element, but only externally as a complement [(Selbst was man *Zieraten* [*parerga*] nennt,) d.i. dasjenige, was nicht in die ganze Vorstellung des Gegenstandes als Bestandstück innerlich, sondern nur äußerlich als Zutat gehört]" (*Critique of Judgement*, 61; *Kritik der Urteilskraft* [hereafter *KdU*], *Werkausgabe in 12 Bänden* 10:142; translation modified).[7] The proposition clearly invites a deconstruction of the whole Kantian scheme of taste. The question of the parergon between Marxism and surrealism in Bataille proceeds via the question of restricted and general economy. As will be seen, the question of parergon in Kant, as Derrida shows in "Economimesis," is also the question of political economy.

These parergonal structures still await an analysis at the level that their complexity demands. Such an analysis will undoubtedly involve a reconfiguration of everything these structures engage, whether they are viewed in a wider theoretico-political context or, specifically, as the locus of Bataille's discourse between Breton and Aragon—in the Breton-Aragon parergon, as it were. The latter juncture might still be a reconfiguration of the Kant-Marx and thus the Kant-Hegel parergon, since Hegel and, in a certain way, Marx declare the death of art. Hegel proclaims in his *Aesthetics* that art is no longer the highest way in which truth manifests itself—the truth of *Geist* for Hegel, or the truth of capital for Marx. It is not that this context or intertext can exhaust the parergon of Bataille's discourse. Indeed, no parergon, as Derrida shows, can be exhausted or saturated. It can be neither uniquely originated nor unequivocally closed. Consequently, these parergonal effects cannot be subsumed under the rubric of context, particularly the *conscious* context.[8] One of my goals here will be to follow the *complexity* of the parergonal in the context, or parergon, of Bataille's and Derrida's texts.

If the shadow of Hegel looms large over all these reconfigurations—refigurations, remetaphorizations, or re- or de-parergonizations—whether in Marx, Nietzsche, Heidegger, Bataille, or Derrida, it is accompanied—adumbrated—by the shadow of Kant. There are many shadows cast in these chiaroscuro-like interactions of aesthetic, political, sexual, and other "economies" that inhibit and transform each other, disseminating beyond the possibility of containing and controlling their interplay. But, as I indicated at the outset of this study, Hegel and Kant cast perhaps the longest shadows. If, as Derrida comments on Bataille, "Hegel is always right as soon as one opens one's mouth in order to articulate meaning [(A) Hegel (qui) a toujours raison dès qu'on ouvre la bouche pour articuler le sens]" (*Writing and Difference*, 263; *L'Écriture et la différence*, 386), he cannot be right without Kant. This Kantian margin—or perhaps the center, or one of the centers—of this play is what I want to explore here by way of Bataille and Derrida. Throughout this discussion, however, Nietzsche remains a crucial margin or parenthesis.

My text—my "Kant"—will be a small but an extraordinarily interesting and important portion of the third critique taken from section 51, "Of the Division of the Beautiful Arts." As in Bataille, the question of the philosophical will be situated in Kant between the question of the aesthetic, which is analogous, but not identical, to the question of surrealism in Bataille, and the political. In the interplay of the artistic and the political, a certain "left" margin of philosophy emerges. This margin will be my subject here, first more—or more or less—along its political dimensions and then more—or more or less—along its artistic dimensions. Both, however, must be seen and analyzed as interactive throughout. As Bataille's "sur" suggests, this "margin"—that which is minimized within the text of philosophy—will *exceed* the "center" in the power of its efficacy and will be reconfigured as one of the conditions of the possibility of all centers. In this sense, "sur" is also a kind of bridge between Nietzsche and Derrida. The role of this "margin" is crucial, yet it cannot be absolutely or unconditionally central, either.

This decentering play opens an extraordinarily complex and multidirectional traffic of centers and margins; and it should always be kept in mind, that this play is as de-marginalizing as it is decentering. To a degree, but only to a degree, Kant may already have known that such "left" margins, both aesthetic or political, may not be fully marginalized—only repressed—or he was afraid to know it, suppressing, or repressing, the *excess* of knowledge that makes knowledge, and philosophy, possible in the first place. As Derrida says, unquestionably alluding to Kant, but possibly also with Bataille's (un)concept of "un-knowledge" in mind, "we know this . . . only *now*, and with a knowledge that is not a knowledge at all [. . . nous savons *a priori*, mais seulement *maintenant*, et d'un savoir qui n'en est pas un]" (*Of Grammatology*, 164; *De la grammatologie*, 234; emphasis added).

My major concern is what Bataille manages to do with this "(un)knowledge," if the term is still possible here.

Politics

When Kant establishes first a division and later a hierarchy among the beautiful arts, he writes of the arts of speech, of which poetry will then be assigned "the first rank":

> The *orator*, then, announces [a serious] business and conducts it as if it were a mere *play* with ideas in order to entertain his audience. The *poet* merely announces an entertaining play with ideas, and yet the results provide so much for the understanding that it is as if he had only intended to carry on its business. The combination and harmony of both cognitive faculties, sensibility and understanding, which cannot dispense with each other but which yet cannot well be united without force and mutual disparagement, must be intended and must appear to have come about as it is by by itself; otherwise it is not *beautiful* art. Hence, all that is deliberate [Gesuchte: artificial, far-fetched] and anxious must be avoided in it, for beautiful art must be free art in a double sense: so that it is not a work like a mercenary employment, the greatness of which can be judged, enforced, or paid for according to a definite standard; and also so that the mind [Gemüt] feels itself occupied, but at the same time without looking to any other purpose (independently of reward) feels contented and awakened.
>
> The orator therefore gives something which he does not promise, viz. an entertaining play of the imagination; but he also falls short of supplying what he did promise, which is indeed his announced business, viz. the purposive occupation of the understanding. On the other hand, the poet promises little and announces a mere play with ideas; but he achieves something which is worth occupying ourselves with, namely, in providing in this play food for the understanding and, by the aid of imagination, giving life to its concepts. Thus the orator at bottom gives less, the poet more, than he promises. (165–66)[9]

In part, the connection with Bataille's problematic emerging in this and the surrounding passages in Kant is an effect of the historical closure of philosophy as indicated earlier. This closure operates in Kant and Bataille alike, even though it might be seen as transformed by subsequent developments, most specifically Nietzsche, and then *by* Bataille's discourse itself. Radical transformations, to which Kant's concepts must be subjected, result from Bataille's profound understanding, in the wake of Nietzsche and anticipating Derrida, that the text of philosophy is produced within an economy very different from that which is articulated by the text of philosophy—the *general* economy as against the *restricted* economy. Philosophy as a restricted economy does not "see" this general economy, but its text is produced by it and, against itself—unconsciously, as it were—manifests it continuously.

To begin with, Kant's passage poses the question of "economy" in its more or less conventional sense. Beautiful art is first conceived as free art. One might, and perhaps must, see this question of the relationships between independent—free—and dependent art as the question of *political* economy. In the context of Bataille, it is hardly useful—"productive"—to speak of an *economy* that would not be political, even though Bataille subjects the science of political economy and its concepts to a radical critique as a *restricted* economy. Beautiful art in Kant, then, "is not a work like a mercenary employment [Lohngeschäft], the greatness of which can be judged, enforced or paid for according to a definite standard" (165). It is, or is claimed to be, outside the economy and economics of labor, and thus outside political economy. But given its structure *as* an economy, specifically as an economy without loss, it cannot be a general economy, either. A general economy always exceeds the restricted political economy radically, although it cannot exceed it absolutely. To theorize excess as *absolute*, whether in a Kantian, Hegelian, or other fashion, is not radical enough.

Derrida has powerfully explored these "political economic" connections in Kant in "The Parergon" and "Economimesis." He proceeds by exposing the politico-economic grounding of the question of genius in Kant, specifically in its relation to the question of imitation. As an *economimesis*, the imitative work of genius is an imitation of economy as a *process*, or as a play of forces, not an imitation of the product. The genius, through his creation—his *production*—imitates *how* Nature—or, possibly, God—produces, rather than *what* is produced. Given the specificity of this economy in Kant, one can use the term and the notion of *mimesis*, even as *economimesis*, only with caution. Kant himself seems to avoid it. These nuances are important, but they will not undermine the conclusions of Derrida's analysis. Economic metaphors, including those of political economy, still permeate the *philosophical* account of this "economy." Kant expands the difference between beautiful art and a material—"hard"—economic process—"a work like a mercenary employment"—to a difference in the *occupation* of the mind: ". . . the mind feels itself occupied [employed: das Gemüt sich zwar beschäftigt], but at the same time, without looking to any other purpose [Zweck] (independently of reward [unabhängig vom Lohne]), feels itself contented and awakened" (165).

Kant's *borrowing*, whether negative or positive, of economic terms and metaphors does not in itself constitute a problem. First of all, the discourse of political economy, beginning with Adam Smith, might itself be seen as *borrowing* from Kant, although it would be *unproductive*, and in fact impossible, to see Kant's discourse as original in this respect. Kant must have borrowed his "economic" metaphors from earlier forms of economic and political economic discourse. There can no more be an originary metaphor here than anywhere else. Second, as was considered in the preceding chapter, the history of theory from Kant to Hegel, Marx, Nietzsche, Freud, Bataille, and many others demonstrates that the metaphors of economy have proved to be as theoretically *productive* as they are unavoidable. As Bataille's analysis shows, it is the insistence on consumption within theoretical economies at multiple and often interacting levels—economic, political, conceptual—that is problematic. Theories that privilege consumption must confront the metaphoric loss of the economy of loss, and thus the loss of a general economy on which they are founded. As we have seen, consumption and the pleasure of consumption do play a role in general economic accounts. To reverse the configuration absolutely and to privilege expenditure unconditionally is equally untenable, as Derrida's more general analysis of such reversals demonstrates.

Similarly to Hegel's dialectic, as the economy of *Aufhebung* as a negating-conserving synthesis,[10] the Kantian economy is an economy of *consumption* and thus must be seen as a restricted economy. It is the (restricted-economic) science of the operation of mastery in Hegel's sense (Herrschaft) rather than the general economy of sovereignty (souveraineté) in Bataille, which economy, while remaining rigorously theoretical, requires a very different form or style of writing. A considerable portion of the third critique might be seen as Kant's attempt at a science of a noneconomic economy of genius, represented best by the genius of poetry, which "of all the arts . . . maintains the first rank." Or, closer to Bataille's terms, one might speak of economy as the science of this operation of genius, analogous to, but also different from, the sovereign operation in Bataille.

"General economy" or "restricted economy" in Bataille's sense designates, we recall, a science—a rigorous theory. In Derrida's reading of Kant, "economy" and "economimesis" designate an operation, an activity of genius. The unequivocal separation between such economic operations and the economic theories inscribing and processing them is impossible under the conditions of general economy; and the metaphorical interpenetrations between both types of economies are as productive as they are in-evitable. For one thing, our theoretical economies produce the economies or operations for which we want to account. Under the conditions, and indeed constraints, of general economy, however, there can be no ab-solute, or Hegelian, fusion between an account or dis-count, or accounts-discounts (if such names can still apply) and processes that are accounted for. The difference between them can never be fully reduced in a general economy, whereas such a reduction is possible and indeed often necessary in a restricted economy, specifically the Hegelian economy. The latter might well offer the general calculus of that type.

Nor, conversely, can there be in a general economy an absolute differ-ence between an account and that which is being accounted for. Once dif-ference is absolute, it is not radical enough for a general economic calculus. An absolute difference of that type would always lead to a restricted economy, repressing the radical—but again never absolute—general eco-nomic difference. This type of repression characterizes the Kantian economy of "things-in-themselves," or as shall be seen below, related con-figurations in the Kantian economy of taste. The Kantian economy appears to provide a kind of general calculus or logic of absolute difference, just as the Hegelian economy offers the general calculus of the opposite type.

The Kantian logic of absolute difference, in effect, opens the way to the Hegelian economy of difference. For once philosophy can *conceive* of a difference that is absolute, once it can conceive of the possibility of philos-ophy's absolute other, there follows Hegel's *logic* that there can be a subject (*Geist*) that overcomes this difference by way of a self-conscious *historical* process. The logic of this overcoming is Hegelian logic, developed throughout his works, specifically in the first, greater *Logic, The Science of Logic*, and then in the second *Logic* that opens the *Encyclopedia*. This subject is necessarily, *logically*, superhuman, even though it is indissociable from humanity and accomplishes its work by way of human *history* as the objec-tive form of its existence. The overcoming of difference is, crucially, con-ceived by Hegel as the play of difference and transformation—history coupled with consciousness and indeed self-consciousness. By the same token, however, this play is always controlled, indeed consciously and self-consciously controlled, making the resulting theoretical economy re-stricted.

Thus, whether by way of a Kantian or a Hegelian economy, difference is retained within and demanded by a philosophical and a political economy, which always interpenetrate each other. Such an economy, however, always conceives of and theorizes—philosophizes—difference as a controlled difference, however richly the play of difference or transformation unfolds. One needs instead a (general) economy of difference, which is neither Hegelian nor Kantian, even though one still relates to such a difference by way of the double closure defined by "Kant" and "Hegel," to name here the two types of calculus just considered. In the process, the relationships between that which accounts and that which is being accounted for becomes *complementary* in the present sense: heterogeneously interactive, interactively heterogeneous.[11]

It is worth reiterating that the theoretical frameworks of that type (jointly general economic and complementary) do not imply that our accounting will be able to comprehend everything—"to take everything into account"—in the the labyrinths of our theoretical household or economy (*oikonomia*). Such a conclusion, or hope, would still be an illusion, however comfortable—a Kantian or Hegelian corridor, however subtle, not yet the labyrinth of the general economy. Any total accounting is a restricted economy, whether political, as in Marx, or conscious or conceptual in the general—absolute—sense, as in Hegel; and it inevitably misses the difference of general economy. We may think of the word "difference" here in either sense, or as designating a complementary (general) economy of both: a difference between two economies, restricted and general, and that between an economy and an operation—like a sovereign operation—which one wants to account for. The radical difference announced by Bataille by way of general economy, and the one in Derrida's general economy of *différance* have to do with problematizing the possibility of an account and economy—as science or theory—*however conceived.*[12] This double—at least double—difference, or *différance*, will affect enormously the shape of all our "accounting" and all our calculations and movements, the movements in the labyrinths. One must *employ* a calculus —a kind of complementary accounting-discounting—of the interminable and the indeterminable, permeated by inhibitions, contaminations, and double binds, which I shall discuss in more detail in Chapter 5. The labyrinth may well be too classical a structure or economy, still too restricted. For it is still built by a master, a Daedalus of one kind or another; one can still get out, or fly out of it, *figure* it out, or configure or reconfigure it.

Kant's economic considerations imply a fundamental asymmetry between the two economic operations. One, "a mercenary employment," is an economy of exchange, actual or potential, including, but not exclusively, monetary exchange. We might call it an "economic" economy. Another "noneconomic" economy, the economy of beautiful art and genius, is configured through a radical prohibition of exchange. To be rigorous, one should speak of at least three economies here, since Kant's formulations, and indeed already the Introduction (24), also suggest a possibility of a kind of exchange-reward economy, or at least a purpose economy, in the domain of understanding as the *occupation*—employment—of the mind. This economy would not be operative in the case of aesthetic judgment, or creation and experience of the beautiful arts. Undoubtedly, a philosopher's employment cannot be mercenary; it must be independent of "reward," one suspects, perhaps in a very similar if not identical manner to the beautiful arts. However, logic and concepts are the rewards—pure and high rewards—of philosophy and its work, its econo-logic, which, too, must be juxtaposed to any mercenary employment, but must in turn be distinguished from the economimesis of the beautiful arts.[13]

The asymmetries at issue are of fundamental significance in Kant, although this distinction cannot be sustained on Kant's grounds, as absolute or fundamental. It is not only that the economy of beautiful art cannot be fully liberated from an exchange or reward of some sort. The latter must also be factored in, whether the economy of the beautiful or the economy of beautiful art is at issue. It might include, for example, an exchange and reward for "the mind . . . occupied" by the play of imagination and feeling "itself contented and awakened" "without looking to any other purpose (independently of reward)." As I have indicated, however, an *unconditional* insistence on this form of pleasurable consumption must be seen in turn as problematic. *Conditionally*, this consumption and this exchange must be taken into account.

More significant is the impossibility of an "absolute" reduction of a mercenary or "economic" economy and employment to a definite standard or a paid reward, as Kant implied. As Bataille's analysis of expenditure suggests, no economy of any kind can be unconditionally, or once and for all, reduced to either an exchange economy or an economy absolutely free of exchange. Such economies have constantly to be engaged jointly, or in present terms, complementarily, often simultaneously along many lines. "The Notion of Expenditure," for example, powerfully reconfigures, as against the classical configuration, the structural and *structuring* supplement of exchange (*Visions*, 116–29). Simultaneously, however, by insisting, in proximity to Nietzsche, on the *exuberance* of "exchange" and expenditure or, better perhaps, on the exchange *of* expenditures, Bataille radically problematizes the concepts of expenditure and waste, along with those of highest value—absolute consumption—and an exchange-transaction economy. The operations involved there are not only always more than consumption or exchange, but they are also always more than simply expenditure or waste.

This point does not mean that such reductions—or purifications, as it were—*in either direction*, are not found in theoretical practice. As I have suggested, such a reduction may occur in Bataille, who tends at certain moments to subordinate the effects of exchange and consumption to the effects of exchange. Some of this subordination, of course, is strategic; and most importantly, Bataille makes no definitive claims concerning the efficacity of either type of effects. What Bataille's analysis demands, however, even if at times against itself, is a different *economy* of the economic and its efficacity. As was discussed earlier, neither the structures of reward, including at the level of monetary or political economy, nor differences among these various economies would disappear as a result. Instead, they must be configured otherwise, in effect, with an increased rigor, which is necessary precisely in order to account for the multiplicity and richness of these differences. For in the enlarged difference or *différance* of this general economy, one would no longer be able to speak either of *one* operation or *categorically*, parcel out operations in a demarcated, accountable set, including, as Kant does, through *categories*.

This is not the place to consider Marx's general analysis of the concept of value, most specifically in the opening section of *Capital*, which is a crucial text insofar as the question of the exchange economy—as restricted and as general economy—is concerned. It is important to understand, however, that "value" and "values," of whichever type within Marx's pointed stratification, are inscribed by Marx in a complex "space"—or perhaps "time"—and in a *complex* "economy" of transformations, mediation, or, according to Marx himself, dialectic, as an always—"always already"—profoundly *historical* process.[14] One might speak in this sense of neither "space" nor "time," but of a differential play—a "difference." This play of difference will engage similarities and their efficacities as well.

One must maintain most rigorously, however, the difference between *différance* and dialectic, here specifically Marx's—or more broadly, Marxist —and the difference or again *différance*, which includes the commonalities, between the two economies and the laws of transformation they necessitate. In this sense, as both Bataille and Marx understood, there are profound connections—conceptual, metaphorical, and political—between economy, in the sense of "exchange" and "commodities," and broader "management" (*oikonomia:* household). These connections are conceptualized and metaphorized, on the one hand, via the economy as becoming, transformations, history, "play of forces," and on the other hand, by way of other forms of the metaphor of energy. Every analysis of Marx must take into account the "fact" that Marx inscribes value under these conditions. These are the conditions of dialectic, indeed of Hegel's dialectic, although put back from its head onto its feet, on its material base. Yet, like *all dialectic* produced so far, this economy of transformations will remain a restricted economy, with respect to the structures that govern and control these transformations and the ways in which they are controlled.[15]

For Bataille, we recall, political economy *is* "the level on which the *question* of general economy situates itself." This formulation is decisive. First of all, it irreducibly relates restricted and general economies and announces their difference. Second and most crucially, it announces the irreducibly "unconscious" character of general economy as theory. Bataille's text and style are fundamentally political throughout. For the "revolutionary" Bataille, the general economy is the economy—"science"—of *political* action, of the acts of "sovereignty." Alongside, and interacting with, political action, a creative act, such as a literary or theoretical act, will also be conceived via sovereign operation. This complementary interplay demands the plurality of style and genre that shapes his general economic vision and his own practice as always, complementarily, theoretical, artistic, and political.

As we have seen, for Bataille, "the science designated by this name [political economy] is only a restricted economy (*restricted to commercial value*)." As an economy of commercial value, it is an economy of transaction and exchange value. Thus it is an economy privileging exchange, or this cluster as a whole, multiple perhaps but still contained within and controlled by this "exchange" cluster as theoretical economy. Insofar as an economy—of value, or other—remains an economy of exchange, it will remain a restricted economy, no matter how it is modified or how far it is shifted from traditional economics, such as the economics of the commercial or monetary exchange. It can be shown, for example, by reading the first chapter of *Capital*, that Marx is in effect unable to maintain the possibility of political economy as an economy of exchange value. A restricted economy at any level *cannot* be maintained, above all as dialectic, whether in Marx's or in Hegel's sense, on which Marx always depends. One always needs a general economy in order to maintain at least a minimal rigor of theoretical articulation of these issues.[16]

It is not enough for a theorist of exchange, profit, interest, or value of "the exchange economy" to recognize the relativity, or even a relative relativity, of this point of view or metaphorization. Nor would it be enough to point out that, for a variety of theoretical, cultural, and personal reasons, including "emotional" or political ones, other perspectives and positions may refuse to accept this view. This observation is obvious enough; or rather, it would be obvious were it not for the necessity of counteracting the opposite tendency and desire—the tendency and desire to repress the exchange economy of value in favor of the highest, absolute, or transcendental value, or that which is above value and could be positioned outside any exchange economy. This tendency has been hardly any less prevalent, and indeed more so, throughout the history of these issues. In this sense, the critical as well as the positive—theoretically productive—*value* of an exchange value economy may be considerable: no *absolute* value or any other absolute so opposed to exchange economies, relativity of interests and values, can *ever* be acceptable from the standpoint and within the matrix of general economy.

That standpoint, of course, excludes those who accept such absolutes or who develop such conceptions. They do not operate from the standpoint or within the matrix of general economy. Their standpoint is that of a restricted economy of one kind or another, such as the standpoint of political economy in Marx and in most Marxism, often as much in those amalgamated with it by deconstruction as those juxtaposed to it.

Thus, conversely, one would have to utilize whatever one could, including at times the absolute and transcendental excesses of exchange economies—*as a starting point*—to undermine and deconstruct the privileging of exchange. Here, as elsewhere, a mutual juxtaposition and counterdeconstructive interplay of different textual and conceptual layers are often in order. *The main point* is that, from the perspective of and within the matrix of general economy, no matrix, no given theory or metaphor, will be sufficient. That statement includes the exchange-interest-profit matrix, particularly in the absence of an inscription and a reinscription in the deconstructed field of the unconscious, of the "effects" of the "unconscious"—of, again reconfigured, "*Freudian effects.*"

The necessity of inscribing a radical—*structural*, irreducible—unconscious seems to have been a crucial, defining point for Bataille. It may have forced him, although unnecessarily from the present standpoint, to retain some of the Hegelian capital against *Das Kapital*. While accounting or relating to the efficacity that is productive of all such economic effects, this efficacity cannot be restricted to them. Conversely, however, it cannot be conceived of as absolutely different from more restricted economic effects of efficacity, or more generally as an absolute difference of any kind.

Thus it is not so much the relativity of value that is at issue as the *complementarity* of value as defined earlier. It is an economy, but a general economy, of values—whether economic, cultural, political, aesthetic, or other—that at times are relative or even radically relative, while at times are quite—indeed, radically, but never absolutely—global.[17]

The maintaining of any unique or absolute grounding, such as fundamental meaning, consciousness, or presence, will lead to a restricted economy. "Exchange economies," however, and perhaps even value, remain an important specific case. Nietzsche, who insists on "value," does not so much see "value" in terms of exchange. His "value" might be seen as being close, specifically by way of "the unconscious," to Bataille's "unreserved expenditure." Or rather, it is the latter that is a condition of the general economy as opposed to Marx's political economy of value. An interesting question arises of the economy of hierarchy and of the relations, within the general economy, between hierarchization and exchange. Exchanges may affect and, under certain conditions, structure hierarchies, or vice versa; and one cannot in general demarcate once and for all the domain of their application.

Neither can one say, however, that there is *always* an exchange or always a hierarchy, let alone a given unique form of either—*the* exchange or *the* hierarchy. The economy of constraints, which must be configured as a general economy, clearly plays a major role in these interactions yet by no means can fully govern all economies. Constraints do not determine everything. These considerations are crucial both in the case of Nietzsche, who insists on value, and in the case of Bataille, who is "against" value. This question cannot be fully addressed here. It will not, in my view, affect the difference between restricted and general economies at issue in this study. This question must be posed *in relation to* this difference.[18]

Incorporating and indeed announcing the unconscious, including through value, remains one of Nietzsche's greatest achievements. By contrast, the Hegelian residual of consciousness, self-consciousness, and dialectic in Marx's science of political economy makes the latter, irreducibly, a restricted economy. One of my major points throughout the present study is that without the unconscious, without "accounting" for or, better, playing out Freudian—or Freudian-Nietzschean—effects, any theory of value—economic, cultural, aesthetic, or other—indeed, any theory at all, would remain only a restricted economy. That is not to say, of course, that such restricted economies have no theoretical or other significance, including political, *value, interest,* or local hierarchical priority. Freud often uses and depends, conceptually and metaphorically, on exchange and transaction economy in his analysis, in whatever sense of theory or practice—the analysis of the unconscious.

The unconscious, let me reiterate, must in turn be reconfigured in a general economy, a requirement that implies that there can be no uninhibited unconscious, either. It may, for example, be inhibited or contaminated by various forms of "consciousness." I shall consider these issues in more detail later. It should be pointed out in the present context that the economy of value in Nietzsche, including *as* truth-*value*, or thought-*value*—"*coin of the spirit* [*das Geld des Geistes*]"[19]—as opposed to *truth*-value and *thought*-value, is also conditioned by the theory and metaphors of modern political economy as developed in, among others, Smith, Hegel, and Marx. As we have seen, it is equally significant in Saussure and Derrida, or Freud and Lacan, thus broadly affecting the axis of the general economy, even beyond its role in Bataille. But one needs a general economy of all values and all economies of values.

We might recall that Derrida speaks of "themes in Nietzsche's work that are linked to the symptomatology that always diagnoses the detour or ruse of an agency disguised in its *différance*; or further, to the entire thematic of active interpretation, which substitutes incessant deciphering for the un-veiling of truth as the presentation of the thing itself in its presence, etc. Figures without truth, or at least a system of figures not dominated by the value of truth, which then becomes only an included, inscribed, circum-scribed function" (*Margins*, 17–18; *Marges*, 19). Metaphorically, Derrida clearly combines "Nietzsche" and "Freud"—not without reason, given Nietzsche's cases across the history of philosophy, most elaborately Socrates and Kant. I do not think, however, that *Nietzsche*'s "active inter-pretation" always "substitutes *incessant* deciphering." "Active interpreta-tion," for example, can be a fiction of presence, taken by a philosopher for truth. Indeed, all interpretation is "active" in this sense. But there can be different "*interpretations* of interpretation" and different practices of inter-pretation, such as Freudian therapy, as practice, and whatever is modeled on it, for example, to a degree, Derrida's practice of deconstruction. The latter admittedly remains very effective in Derrida. I doubt greatly, how-ever, that such incessant deciphering is Nietzsche's theoretical practice. It would not be Dionysian enough for Nietzsche. In a certain sense, Nietzsche's practice might be seen as strangely political in the directness of its *theoretical* impact, although this practice remains worlds apart from most other practices that present themselves under the name of politics. Still, there are many politics, and many politics of politics. By contrast, Derrida's last proposition in the statement cited, "Figures without truth, . . ." holds in very general terms. This proposition is decidedly Nietzschean, in gen-eral and specifically with respect to the metaphor of value employed by Derrida; and it holds under different conditions and different modes of the-oretical or political practice, such as in Nietzsche and Derrida.

One must take all the necessary precautions, however, against a "prof-itable" interpretation or metaphorization of loss. Such a metaphorization is only one of a number of possibilities; and the motif of profit in general, even through loss, could be the least acceptable, for example, to Bataille. One of the issues may be a critical analysis and—*re-comprehending*—deconstruction of the concept of profit, as well as the metaphysical concept of economy. Everything depends on *how* all such concepts are inscribed in the chains of a given text. As I suggested earlier, the concepts of profit and interest have often fundamentally depended on the framework of consciousness, however hidden, throughout its history. We cannot simply *discount*, as this very term implies, the concept of profit, either, however critical one wants to be toward it. Nor should we, since it can be extraordinarily effective under certain conditions. A general economy, as the economy of irreducible inhibition, must expose and argue as much against the "repression" of "market" metaphors as against privileging it on the "marketplace" of theory.[20] It must replay all these concepts—profit, interest, exchange, and many others—in its complex and diverse, and inhibiting, play,[21] just as it must replay there the concepts of consciousness and, in particular, presence, whose closure remains very powerful.

Lacan makes the point brilliantly in the famous "excommunication" lecture (1964), and it is important for any theorist of the unconscious to keep this point in mind: "No doubt, to be used in negotiation is not a rare situation for a human subject, contrary to all the verbiage about human dignity and, indeed, the Rights of Man. Each of us, at any moment and on every level, is negotiable, for the notion of exchange is the source of all serious insights into the social structure" ("L'Excommunication" (1964), reprinted in *Le Séminaire*, 11:10; "Excommunication," in *The Four Fundamental Concepts of Psycho-Analysis*, 5; translation modified).[22]

Derrida, in closing *The Post Card*, characteristically disseminates this *economy*. He speaks of his "published" writing, as he qualifies it, as "an offer on the scene in which the attempts to occupy the place of the *Sa* (that is, the place of the *Savoir absolu* stenographed in *Glas*) are multiplying, that is, simultaneously all the places, those of the seller, the buyer, and the auctioneer" (*The Post Card*, 521; *La Carte postale*, 549). They are in fact multiplying well beyond the capacity of this or any metaphor. We do not always sell, buy, or auction—or are sold, bought, or auctioned. And it is not only profit, or interest that determines our relations—which are therefore not always necessarily "exchanges," either—on this or any other scene, landscape, or theater. Further, this scene may not always be a scene, in whichever sense of the term.

"Exchange," "interest," "profit," then, must be *critically* comprehended. In the case of the question of meaning, they must be comprehended by "referring" in one way or another "to an entire configuration of meaning." "For the economic character of *différance* in no way implies that the deferred presence can always be found again, that we have here only an investment that provisionally and without loss delays the presentation of presence, the perception of its profit or the profit of its perception. Contrary to the metaphysical, dialectical 'Hegelian' interpretation of the economic movement of *différance*, we must conceive of the play in which whoever loses wins, and in which one loses and wins on every turn" ("Différance," in *Margins*, 20; *Marges*, 21; translation modified). As will be seen in Chapter 3, the logic and "the game theory" of this play is thus a complex one; for, conversely, against this tax-exempt strategy, one cannot fully calculate all profits and losses in advance. It is almost, but never altogether, a blind strategy. The question of the "style" that is always plural and that enables this play is a question of extraordinary complexity. It is, however, also a question of an equally extraordinary necessity, as much in the matter of taste and its many economies—political, theoretical, and other—as in all matters and reconfigurations at issue in the present study. It is an irreducible question. But then, to repeat this irreducible proposition, style is always irreducible, too.

Poetics

The richness of the unfolding of differential and transformational play is a crucial aspect of Kant's various economies, and the same is the case in Hegel and many other classical theories or restricted economies; and this richness cannot be ignored. But the double structure of simultaneously unfolding and controlling the play of differences and transformations, defining all these theories, always makes them into restricted economies. Heidegger's work, both earlier and later, may be seen as a culmination of this double economy, which, as we have seen, was so formalized by Heidegger himself in a beautiful passage in *The Question of Being*. This passage, which I shall cite only partially here, reaches perhaps the limits of classical thinking. To a degree, the latter statement characterizes the Heideggerian meditation as a whole; and in this sense this meditation may indeed be "uncircumventable [incontournable]," as Derrida says. Classical thinking can go no further—classical, but not necessarily post-classical—post-Nietzschean—or general economic. Which is not to say, of course—quite the contrary—that general economic thinking will not one day reach its limits and, in this sense, will—and perhaps already has—in turn become classical. As Heidegger writes:

The meaning-fulness [Mehrdeutigkeit: literally, the "more-meaning-ness," both in the sense of the fullness of the meaning and plurality and (controlled) ambiguity of meaning] of what is said [die Sage] by no means consists in a mere accumulation of meanings [Bedeutungen] emerging haphazardly. This meaning-fulness is based on a play which, the more richly it unfolds, the more strictly it is held (within the domain governed) by a hidden rule [Regel]. Through (the presence of) this rule, this meaning-fulness plays within the balance(d), whose oscillation we seldom experience. That is why what is said remains "bound into" the highest law [Gesetz]. That [this being bound into the highest law] is the freedom that "frees into" the all-playing structure [Gefüge: juncture] of never-resting transformation [Verwandlung].

[Die Mehrdeutigkeit der Sage besteht keineswegs in einer bloßen An-häufung beliebig auftauchender Bedeutungen. Sie beruht in einem Spiel, das, je reicher es sich entfaltet, um so strenger in einer verborgenen Regel gehalten bleibt. Durch diese spielt die Merhdeutigkeit im Ausge-wogenen, dessen Schwingung wir selten erfahren. Darum bleibt die Sage ins höchste Gesetz gebunden. Das ist die Freiheit, die in das allspielende Gefüge, der nie ruhenden Verwandlung befreit.] (*The Question of Being*, 104–5; translation modified)

The Kantian difference always obeys and in many ways announces such a "highest" law, from the first to the last critique. It may be argued that this law connects all three critiques—in a very specific Kantian way, but also in conforming to the very general law at issue here. To begin with, the economies of difference which Kant conceives of always remain the economies of *consumption*. The point is suggested most graphically by Kant's overarching metaphor—*taste*—in *The Critique of Judgement*, but "consumption" in one form or another controls Kant's logic throughout. Whether as conceptual, metaphorical, political, or extending to still other domains and denominations, this grounding in consumption would al-ready delimit all Kant's economies as restricted economies.

According to Bataille, such is also the case in Hegel. As Derrida points out in "From Restricted to General Economy," Bataille's "inner experi-ence," in contrast to Hegelian mediation, "does not pleasurably consume [jouit: enjoy] an absolutely close presence [elle ne jouit pas d'une présence absolument proche]" (*Writing and Difference*, 273; *L'Écriture et la différence*, 402). Alan Bass's rendering of "jouit" as "pleasurably consumes" is inter-esting and justified, although it may *repress* somewhat the sexual connota-tions of the French word. One may in fact suggest that the "jouit" of Bataille's inner experience also engages or implies a general economy of sexuality, no longer based only on pleasurable consumption, proximity, presence, although not dispensing with them either. It is not "based," to begin with.

A similar economy was also developed, in the wake of Bataille, in French feminist theory, specifically in Irigaray and Cixous. As the deconstruction of the metaphysics of proximity and consumption, this economy can also be related to the Nietzschean economy of the feminine as the economy of distance, considered by Derrida in *Spurs*, if at certain points against Nietzsche himself and, again differently, against Irigaray and Cixous.[23] There is also, of course, the obverse metaphysics of absolute distance, at times functioning simultaneously with the metaphysics of proximity; and it must be deconstructed in turn. The determination, finally irreducible, by way of "consumption" and, codefinitionally, consumption of presence suggests a crucial link between Kant, specifically in the third critique, and Hegel. It also manifests the profound connections between the first and the third critique, and in truth the second critique as well. Kant's practical reason is also a "consuming reason." "The Critique of Consuming Reason" could serve as the title for all three of Kant's critiques.

The economy of the sublime might appear to offer a potential exception in this respect, and in some measure it does. Governed by the "negative pleasure [negative Lust]" (sec. 23, p. 83) of its "consumption," the sublime leads to an economy that attracts and repels at once without ever being quite able to frame, via a parergon, consume, or indeed create its object, unlike the beautiful object within the economy of the beautiful. It is thus an economy of proximity-distance, as are, let me stress, many Hegelian economies; but, finally, it is a restricted economy and an economy of consumption. The economy of the sublime, furthermore, engages pain and desire, and therefore a complex economy of the interplay of pleasure and pain, or rather un-pleasure or dis-pleasure (Unlust), including "a pleasure, which is only possible through the medium of a dis-pleasure [einer Lust . . . , die nur vermittelst einer Unlust möglich ist]" (99).[24] Thus, the sublime presents certain attractive—or to Kant perhaps repelling—theoretical complications. These complexities have had powerful implications for modern, though not only modern, criticism and theory, on which I shall comment further later.

It becomes immediately apparent, however, that these complications will not be enough to undermine the restricted, and specifically consumptive, character of the Kantian economy of taste and art. Indeed, the restricted nature of the economy of the sublime is apparent from the outset of Kant's analysis of the sublime. Kant does assert that there "are remarkable differences between the two [the beautiful and the sublime]. The beautiful in nature concerns the form of the object, which exists within boundaries [in der Begrenzung besteht]. The sublime, on the other hand, is also to be found in a formless object, so far as in it or by occasion of it *boundlessness [Unbegrenztheit]* is represented . . ." (82; translation modified). These elaborations, however, do not close Kant's clause on the sublime, for he adds, characteristically, as perhaps a philosopher always must, "and yet the totality of its boundlessness is added [summed up] in *thought* [und doch Totalität derselben hinzugedacht wird]" (83; emphasis added, translation modified).[25] Or, one might suggest, this totality is present to and consumed by thought; and as Derrida's analysis of Kant in "Economimesis" and *The Truth of Painting* shows, Kant is in fact unable to maintain the unequivocal difference between the beautiful and the sublime. These propositions and surrounding elaborations on "the idea of absolute whole" again suggest an important connection to Hegel and Absolute Knowledge. Absolute Knowledge is the condition of the totality of *Geist* summed up, present and *self*-present to thought. As Absolute Knowledge, *Geist*'s totality becomes fully self-present to its own thinking—in the *conceptual* and *historical* as opposed to the aesthetic experience, of course. Absolute Knowledge is the self-conscious historical sublime; it is the self-consuming sublime. These are then, by definition, restricted economies, notwithstanding all the differences between Kant and Hegel. These differences cannot, of course, be discounted in other respects. It may be suggested that both economies play their role in Bataille, who is able to utilize the empty form of the Kantian sublime as much as "the *empty* form of the [Hegelian] *Aufhebung* [la forme *vide* de l'*Aufhebung*]," displacing both concepts, making them tremble, "*as was never done before [ce qui ne s'était jamais fait]*" (*Writing and Difference*, 275; *L'Écriture et la différence*, 406).

The critical potential of Kant's economy of the sublime and the other destabilizing configurations that emerge in the third critique, combined with their influence in subsequent history, cannot be ignored. These roles and influences have been powerful in Schiller, Hegel, Nietzsche, and Freud, particularly on "the uncanny [das Unheimliche]," among others, as well as in much of contemporary theory.[26] As we have seen, "Kant on the sublime" is a crucial margin, or perhaps the center, of Lyotard's position, and is one of the central topics of his work in general.[27] The sublime is perhaps the closest that Kant comes to the unconscious and Freud,[28] and, as was indicated earlier, this part of the third critique offers the most interesting and important earlier modulations of postmodern themes. Kant, in fact, must have the unconscious, but, as he—and philosophy—perhaps also must, he refuses to give it an entrance to the economy of taste, understanding, reason, or art. Philosophy, as such, is thus compelled to remain a restricted economy, or rather, within the history of Western philosophy as ontotheology or the metaphysics of presence, a spectrum of restricted economies—economies without the unconscious. Such is the law of philosophy, although philosophy is not the only form of a restricted economy, whether what is at issue is the question of taste or art, of theory, or of political economy.

The influence of the Kantian sublime and the discussions in "The Analytic of the Sublime" may be found, as I have indicated, in Bataille's concepts, too. If one can speak of a Kantian aspect in Bataille and the question of general economy in general, it would have to relate to the economy of the sublime. With the exception of Nietzsche, the economy of the sublime may be the closest approach to what Bataille calls "inner experience," as experience without object. Particularly important in this respect is the configuration and the economy of difference between the interior and the—absolute—exterior of the system of consumption.[29] In this sense, the economy of the sublime is closer, as it must be, to the economy of reason (Vernunft) than to understanding (Verstand). Kant makes this connection or analogy at the outset of the "Analytic of the Sublime," elaborating on propositions cited earlier: "Thus the beautiful seems to be regarded as the presentation of an indefinite concept of understanding, the sublime, however, as that of a like concept of reason [so daß das Schöne für die Darstellung eines unbestimmten Verstandesbegriffs, das Erhabene aber eines dergleichen Vernunftbegriffs genommen zu werden scheint]" (82; *KdU*, 165).

Still, however, the nonobject of the sublime again appears as *"present to thought"—present*. For Hegel, too, reason (Vernunft) is a crucial moment and the condition of possibility of the *presence* of difference—and exteriority—and the reduction of difference in *presence*. As he says in the *Phenomenology*: "Now that self-consciousness is reason, its hitherto negative relationship [Verhältnis] to the otherness [Anderssein] turns over into a positive relation [Damit, daß das Selbstbewußtsein Vernunft ist, schlägt sein bisher negatives Verhältnis zu dem Anderssein in ein positives um]" (*The Phenomenology of Spirit*, 139; *Phänomenologie des Geistes*, *Werke* 3:178). Hegelian Reason is therefore a decisive step on the road to Absolute Knowledge, in *Geist*'s overcoming of difference and exteriority.

Indeed, from the first critique on, the experience of Reason, for Kant, is something like the sublime. It creates anxiety—great, colossal,[30] or sublime, that is, "absolutely great"—anxiety; but, in its uncanny nature, it has no object, all the efforts of the philosopher notwithstanding. The art of understanding—or reasoning out—Reason itself (*Vernunft*), becomes for Kant a kind of aesthetic—*sublime*—experience. Such an experience can be recreated in a reading of his text. That text, though it also creates anxiety, may have no object, thus further violating many of Kant's or philosophy's parerga. Kant's is not the only sublime text, of course. But even if, under now unavoidable theoretical constraints, there can no longer be an object-text, even for a beautiful text, not every text creates anxiety or is beautiful or sublime. But, equally, no text can always be sublime for everyone, which further violates the demarcations—parerga—that philosophy wants to or must introduce and that it attempts to maintain.

In the case of beautiful art, the Kantian economy also emerges as an economy of the consumption of meaning, as is, of course, the economy of understanding or, with some further qualifications, reason in Kant or Hegel. For, as we recall, the poet "provid[es] in this play [of ideas] food for the understanding" (165). This is one of the reasons why one must rigorously insist on the difference between Kant's economy of the beautiful and Kant's economy of beautiful art. The latter relates to the former, but it also exceeds the aesthetic economy of beautiful feeling by a philosophical dimension of understanding, although still *understood*—or *consumed*—through the economy of consumption. According to Kant, "for beautiful art, therefore, *imagination, understanding, spirit,* and *taste* are requisite" [Zur schönen Kunst würden also *Einbildungskraft, Verstand, Geist* und *Geschmack* erforderlich sein]" (164; *KdU*, 257; Kant's emphasis). That Kant does not mention reason and the sublime here may be significant. The very name "beautiful art" is important, implying an art *framed*—dependent and determined by a parergon as a structure and an economy of framing. A corresponding—restricted—economy of art as the art of the sublime or sublime art can be constructed, as has been done many times in the history of post-Kantian aesthetics, beginning with Schiller.

Kant follows the tradition initiated by Aristotle in which, after art is initially demarcated by its difference from philosophy, specifically in affecting feeling and the feeling of pleasure, the value of art is established on the basis of philosophical criteria of one type or another. Poetry may be more philosophical than history, as in Aristotle, or it may be more philosophical than rhetoric, as in Kant. An account of this difference still remains within the domain and power of philosophical explanation. Claiming, in either sense, poetry as "more philosophical" may even be necessary in order to maintain this parergon, to maintain it by locating the difference that establishes the boundaries of philosophy. Neither Aristotle nor Kant, however, is able to sustain the boundaries and parerga at issue. From within their own discourse, poetry and art can exceed the containment of the philosophical account.

For Kant, then, as for Aristotle and many others between and before and after them, the proper and best art is never altogether nonphilosophical. Art is actually more philosophical than almost anything else, except, though still not always, philosophy. In Hegel, of course, art is finally never philosophical enough. On the other hand, particularly in the later Hegel, by virtue of the *Aufhebung*, as "the unity of Art and Religion [die Einheit der Kunst und Religion]," philosophy is art enough no longer to require any art (*Encyclopedia*, sec. 572; *Enzyklopädie der philosophischen Wissenschaften im Grundrisse, Gesammelte Werke* 19:404). In the *Phenomenology*, such an *Aufhebung* of art and religion, while still necessary, is a more radical departure from art and religion alike. Poetry is more philosophical than history, Aristotle famously argues in chapter 9 of the *Poetics*, because it deals with universal things rather than with particulars, as history does. Aristotle never claims that poetry as philosophy will ever exceed philosophy as philosophy; and in this point he remains forever indebted to Plato, or Socrates.

The scheme, which can be pursued interminably, culminates in Heidegger, who responds to and oscillates between Kant and Hegel. Contrary to Heidegger's earlier ontological project, in his later work the central conception becomes that of thinking as poetizing—advanced via the Greeks, specifically the Pre-Socratics, and Hölderlin, who is also conceived of by Heidegger as a Greek and a Pre-Socratic. Heidegger does maintain a subtle, though still a controlled difference and distribution of roles between the poet and the philosopher.[31] In this sense, Heideggerian "thinking-poetizing" on the truth of Being is also a *restricted* economy, whether one speaks of the interpretation or, of course, the creation of poetry, philosophy, or history, including the history of art and philosophy. Hegel, then, is somewhat of an exception, and Heidegger's remarks on Hegel's *Aesthetics* in the "Epilogue" to "The Origin of the Work of Art" are of great interest in this context:

> "Art no longer counts for us as the highest manner in which truth obtains existence for itself."
>
> "One may well hope that art will continue to rise and perfect itself, but its form has ceased to be the highest need of the spirit [*Geist*]."
>
> "In all these relationships art is and remains for us, according to the side of its highest vocation, something past."

The judgment that Hegel passes in these statements cannot be evaded by pointing out that since Hegel's lectures in aesthetics were given for the last time during the winter of 1828–29 at the University of Berlin, we have seen the emergence of many new art works and new art movements. Hegel never meant to deny this possibility. (*Poetry, Language, Thought,* 80; "Der Ursprung des Kunstwerks," in *Holzwege, Gesamtausgabe* 5:68; translation modified)

Heidegger places the "decision" on the truth of Hegel's judgment—"the decision . . . [that] has not yet been decided [Die Entscheidung über Hegels Spruch ist noch nicht gefallen]" (*Poetry,* 80; *Holzwege,* 68; translation modified)—within the restricted economy of the ultimate control of historical transformations considered earlier.

This economy, of course, is different from Hegel's in regard to the role of art, specifically poetry. "The Origin of the Work of Art" is in many ways an application of this conception to the question of art and its history, and thus is indissociable from the history of thinking as "poetizing" on the truth of Being. The final paragraph of the "Epilogue" is Heidegger's subtle variation on the theme of "Truth *is* beauty, beauty truth"—it is and it is not, not quite, almost, and so forth: "Truth is the truth of Being. Beauty does not occur alongside [and apart from] this truth [Die Wahrheit ist die Wahrheit des Seins. Die Schönheit kommt nicht neben dieser Wahrheit vor]" (*Poetry,* 81; *Holzwege,* 69). But it is also a succinct summary of this history of truth—and beauty—offered, I think, in response to Nietzsche's "The History of an Error" in *Twilight of the Idols*; and thus, via Nietzsche, in response to Hegel. Nietzsche affirms and celebrates "the *briefest* shadow" and the "end of the longest error" as Zarathustra begins, "*INCIPIT ZARATHUSTRA.*" [Mittag; Augenblick des kürzesten Schattens; Ende des längsten Irrtums; Höhepunkt der Menschheit; INCIPIT ZARATHUSTRA.]" ("Wie die 'wahre Welt' endlich zur Fabel wurde. Geschichte eines Irrtums . . ." [*Portable Nietzsche,* 486; *KSA* 6:81]). But Nietzsche's shadow over Heidegger is long.

Hegel's statement reflects the general indeterminacy of a given moment of history, be it in 1807, the year of the *Phenomenology,* or 1829, the year of the lectures. The question of art does have a specific significance, however, given the whole post-Hegelian, and some pre-Hegelian, history of the question of the relationship between philosophy and art, specifically literature, and the more recent post-Heideggerian interest in Hegel's *Aesthetics,* particularly in and concerning de Man. For de Man, the question of reflexivity constitutes in turn a crucial, defining, dimension of the question of literature, of the literariness of literature.[32] The elaborations on art toward the end of the *Phenomenology* (in "Religion") and in the conclusion of the *Encyclopedia* are of particular interest and importance in this respect. They also relate the question of language and, as it were, of genre, such as "poetry" or "literature," as opposed to the "prose" of philosophy, and the question of Romantic genre as the Literary Absolute, as found in the Schlegels and the whole Jena scene.[33] These considerations, as is well known, have played a major role in the contemporary post-Hegelian landscape, specifically in Nietzsche, Heidegger, Bataille, and Derrida. In the wake of Nietzsche, Bataille's "deconstruction" of Hegel is enacted by reading—or writing, reinscribing—Hegel's text as a forgetting of the *comedy* of the *Aufhebung*, as against its tragedy, or against the seriousness of its prose.[34] Prose is the language born of the slave, "from right to left or from left to right"; to it, Bataille juxtaposes major —"poetic"—form or writing, sovereignty, and general economy. For both Bataille and Derrida play, chance, and laughter are crucial, central, margins of Hegel and philosophy, its Nietzschean margins. It is possible that, in the end, the influence of Hegel's *historical* thinking outweighs the influence of his thinking about art and aesthetics. Art and aesthetics, in any event, are subjugated by Hegel to his historico-philosophical teleology—a restricted economic procedure, notwithstanding the complexity of the process in Hegel. The question of Hegel's aesthetics remains important, however. The very question of the possibility and, for Hegel, the necessity of the subjugation of art to philosophy certainly needs to be considered. The influence of Hegel's *ideology* in this respect, to a degree in opposition to Kant, has been enormous, in particular in Marx and Marxism.[35]

Kant's projection or inscription of the philosophical into the poetic is nontrivial enough. It should also be recalled that Kant's opposition to the philosophical, and a certain excess of the philosophical that it implies, are set between the orator and the poet rather than between the philosopher and the poet. The former juxtaposition establishes the philosophical nature of aesthetic value in Kant. If the poet gives more than he promises, that "more" *is* philosophy—"food for understanding." The orator, of course, also gives more than he promises: "the orator therefore gives something that he does not promise, viz. an entertaining play of imagination." The difference, however, is crucial: the orator "also falls short of supplying what he did promise, which is indeed his announced business, viz. the purposive occupation of the understanding" (165). That purposive occupation, according to Kant's division of intellectual labor, will be supplied by the philosopher, or by the activity for which philosophy is the best model. The orator thus fails because he in fact entertains, rather than conducting "an announced [serious] business." The results of the poet's announced entertainment, in contrast, "provide so much for the understanding, as if he had only intended to carry on its business" (165), its serious philosophical, or almost philosophical, business.

As I have said, the Kantian scheme of beautiful art thus opens the way to Hegel, and within the Hegelian but not the Kantian scheme, teleologically to "the death of art." Kant's "food for *understanding*" is very much a Hegelian transformation, or reappropriation, of art into the restricted economy of philosophical consumption. Hegel's Absolute Knowledge and, by proximity, the advanced stages of philosophy, might be seen as a sublation (*Aufhebung*) of this experience. It is a full integration of art—or what is good and proper, authentic (eigentlich) in art—into the consciousness of philosophical production, where the economy of play and the economy of labor of understanding may be reorganized so as to eliminate the need for art. Philosophy becomes a most logical extension of art, since it is *as* "the food for *understanding*" that the superior value of artistic consumption and artistic production is determined. This value is determined by its philosophical potential and the degree of its adjustment to *philosophical* consumption—a philosophical consumerism. Philosophy alone would suffice by virtue of its close proximity to *Geist*, closer than art has ever been or can ever be, as *Geist* itself *approaches*—enters the immediate proximity to—Absolute Knowledge.[36] If *Geist* is (*the*) *Artist* [*Künstler*], as Hegel contends in the *Phenomenology* ("The Artificer [Der Werkmeister]," 424), it can never be a nonphilosopher. At different stages of history, Religion and Art were in an analogous position of proximity to *Geist*, but never as close to *Geist* as philosophy is at these most advanced stages of History. This progression or this *progress* and this economy of proximity defines History in Hegel. Philosophical production would still remain an uninterrupted, uninhibited, and fully conscious process that generates new knowledge at each point: a grand utopia of theoretical life.

Given the general logic governing all formal and transcendental logic of philosophy, Kant's division of the beautiful arts is inevitable. Inevitably, too, this division gives poetry priority over rhetoric, even though both are arts of speech that are related to the mouth, the organ of both taste and speech. This priority of voice and the hierarchies of arts and senses it entails are analyzed by Derrida in "Economimesis." The activity of the poet, as discussed in the passage at issue, and that of the genius of beautiful art in the third critique in general are configured so as, in the end, to efface the phonetic substance—to make it disappear in fully internalized play. Facilitating, as against *writing*, this effacement of phonetic substance, the immediate proximity—*presence*—of "voice" to "mind" allows one to dwell in the absolute or—and they are, structurally, the same thing—the immediate proximate presence of mind and ideas. The "speech" and the "voice" of poetry thus become "the art of mind," similar to the internal self-present speech of Husserl's transcendental phenomenology, considered by Derrida in *Speech and Phenomena* (*La Voix et le phénomène*) as, among other things, part of his general project of deconstruction and of the general economy of *différance, dissemination, writing,* and so forth. As Husserl writes in one of his very rare specific references to art:

It is naturally important, on the other hand (once again as in geometry, which has recently and not in vain been attaching great value to collections of models and the like), to make rich use of fancy in that service of the perfect clarification demanded here, to use it in the free transformation of the data of fancy, but previously also to fructify it through the richest and best observations possible in primordial intuition; noting, of course, that this fructifying does not imply that the function of experience as such is to ground validity. We can draw an extraordinary amount of profit from what history has to offer us, and in still richer measure from the gifts of art and particularly of poetry. These are indeed imaginings [Einbildungen], but in respect of the originality of new formations, of the abundance of detailed features, and of the consistency [Lückenlosigkeit] of motivation, they greatly excel the achievements of our own fancy, and moreover, given the understanding grasp, pass through the suggestive power of the media of artistic presentation with quite special ease into perfectly clear fancies [Phantasien].

Hence, if anyone loves a paradox, he can really say, and say with strict truth if he understands the ambiguity of meaning, that "fiction" is the *element* which *makes up the life of phenomenology as of all eidetical science,* that fiction is the source whence the knowledge of "eternal truths" draws its sustenance. (*Ideas*, 184; *Ideen zu einer reinen Phänomenologie und phänomenologischen Philosophie, Werke* 3:163; translation modified)

The presence of Kant here is powerful. The insistence on poetry "particularly" is particularly revealing, even though, as I have just indicated, it is also necessary given the privileged role of voice and phonetic substance in their immediate proximity to mind—the "voice that keeps silence"—in Husserl. What is most interesting, however, is the question of profit or even extraordinary profit in Husserl's formulation. The philosopher "can draw extraordinary profit from what history has to offer [him], and in still richer measure from the gifts of art and particularly of poetry." The philosopher's desire to consume and to take full economic advantage from both history and art, particularly poetry, is irrepressible. Here Husserl "improves" a bit on Aristotle. In Husserl, too, however, as in Aristotle and

Kant, poetry is more philosophical than history. It is the most philosophical of the arts. Nor does Aristotle quite say that history is not philosophical; it is only less so than poetry. The consumptive desire—the appetite—of the philosopher demands the philosophical from art in order to make it ready for philosophical consumption.

Here we might expect a burst of laughter from Bataille. To begin with, Bataille would laugh at the possibility of pleasure and of the pleasure of consumption without displeasure or even without disgust—taste without distaste, *goût sans dégoût*. As Derrida shows in "Economimesis", it is not that the economy of dis-gust goes unnoticed or is dis*counted*. It is accounted for by philosophy, but as that which does not belong, is not *proper*—in every sense of the word—to the economy of taste. In singularly bad theoretical taste, it is accounted for precisely as dis-gust, dis-taste, as what does not belong.

A more significant issue, however, in the context of general economy is the overall conceptual and metaphoric structure of Kantian economimesis as economy and mimesis of consumption. It is this, whether in Kant or Hegel, that would be unacceptable or laughable to Bataille. "Waste and taste" may occupy separate compartments in the corridors of dialectic or philosophy in general, but they are ultimately and intimately related in the mazes of the general economy, for example, the general economy of Bataille's own life. Bataille himself multiply relates various forms of production—philosophical, sociological, artistic, or other—to the economy of waste. One might even think of the difference, or *différance*, between *consummation* and *consumption* and relate this difference to the unreserved expenditure of tuberculosis, Bataille's disease, *consomption*, which consumes—*wastes*—"without the slightest aim, consequently without any meaning." It enacts all defining expenditures of the general economy—unreserved expenditure, loss, waste, and finally death.

Either in Bataille or Derrida, or Nietzsche, however, the general economy of taste—as the economy of expenditure without reserve, loss, waste, or death—and the operations for which it aims to account cannot be reduced to the economy of disgust exemplified by Derrida's analysis in "Economimesis" of "disgust" and "vomiting" in Kant. The loss and expenditure of Bataille's sovereign operation and the general economy as the science of sovereignty are enormously rich and complex. They involve a formidable array of conceptions that Bataille considers, in his nonphilosophical mode, with great rigor and precision, for example, the conceptions of "gift"[37] and, in particular, "sacrifice," one of Bataille's central concepts.

In the overall context of general economy, however, the economy of "vomiting" has, of course, its place in Bataille, too, a very definite place in a memorable quotation from de Sade in a significant essay entitled, quite pertinently, "The Use Value of D.A.F. de Sade: Open Letter to My Current Comrades." Bataille writes: "The process of simple appropriation is normally presented within the composite process of excretion, insofar as it is necessary for the production of an alternating rhythm, for example, in the following passage from Sade: 'Verneuil makes someone shit, he eats the turd, and then he demands that someone eats his. The one who eats his shit vomits; he devours her puke'" (*Visions*, 95; *Oeuvres complètes* 2:590).

The pleasure—or pain—and the taste—or disgust—that take place here might be, or might be seen as, monstrous and singular enough, but they must be accounted for as what Derrida calls in "Signature Event Context" "a *structural possibility*," even if they occurred only once—and they have certainly occurred more than once. In a certain sense, they occur all the time; not necessarily in the specific shape described by de Sade, but as analogous effects of a *general* economy of "taste" that must incorporate "dis-taste" and "dis-gust" as its ineluctable constituents. It thus follows again that a general economy cannot be seen as only an economy of loss, waste, unreserved expenditure, or death. Nor, again, can it ever be unconditionally separated from a restricted economy of one kind or another. Both "taste" and "disgust" are still restricted effects of their general economy. Bataille, in the essay at issue, brilliantly relates de Sade's passage to the question of sacrifice, communion, gift, and the general economy of expenditure, thus establishing the effects of disgust as a manifestation, however extreme, of the general, rather than of the exclusive, as philosophy would want to do.

"Vomiting" thus is an exemplification of absolute dis-gust, something that cannot be consumed, has to be "thrown up." Or must it be? Certainly by definition, it cannot be included, consumed, by Kant's economy of taste. This is one of Derrida's major points in "Economimesis." In general, however, in the *general economy*, things are not so simple or restricted, or *proper*. The general economy thus threatens the whole Kantian, and the whole philosophical, scheme of taste. In every sense conceivable, it makes the economy of taste into a maze populated with all sorts of monsters, of which philosophy wants to purge its consciousness. The unconscious, as we have seen, must be purged by philosophy altogether. Even leaving aside that the unconscious is the site and the origin of all other monsters, the unconscious itself as structure and economy is already monstrous enough for philosophy. It is, as Derrida shows, only in the Kantian economy of taste as an economy of pleasurable consumption that the question of vomiting and disgust must acquire and be philosophically accounted for as having a *unique* position, from which the whole scheme might thus be deconstructed. It is this special position that allows and invites this deconstruction. Once such a deconstruction is performed and the economy of taste is reconfigured as a general economy, "vomiting" and "disgust" become regular effects of this enriched economy, although under certain conditions, they might have asymmetrical relations and be subordinated by the effects of taste and consumption.

Expenditure must be brought into the foreground because philosophy and other classical theories, being restricted economies, have throughout their history suppressed and repressed the economy of expenditure,[38] particularly of unreserved expenditure, and not because the economy of expenditure has absolute privilege over the economy of consumption. The latter economy, as a theory, must now be made general as well. This economy must take into account the possibility of consumption and production as effects of expenditure and unreserved expenditure, much as work, exchange, or profit need at times to be related to and reconfigured along with play, nonexchange, excess, and loss. Any unique form of efficacacity, however—be it consumption or expenditure, profit and conservation, or loss and waste, work or play, or whatever—will be prohibited thereby.

Since the restricted economy manifests itself, above all, at the level of the political economy, these consequences and implications *are* the value—and it can no longer quite be called the use-value—of D.A.F. de Sade, the value brilliantly exposed in Bataille's "Open Letter to My Current Comrades" ("La Valeur d'usage de D.A.F. de Sade [I] [Lettre ouverte à mes camarades actuels]," *Oeuvres complètes* 2:54–69). A general economy as the economy of the political must take into consideration—put in play or put to work—the effects emerging in (the text of) de Sade. Conversely, a general economy of the sexual must take into account the effects and the very economy of the political. The relations between these two economies should not be seen as always necessarily symmetrical. There are, to begin with, more than two economies involved here. The assumption that such economies form a *countable* set is, as Derrida shows, untenable in a general economy. There will be, of course, multiple "set-effects" in our economic calculations and accounts of, and in our encounters by way of general economy, with the unaccountable.

These interactions, in general, may again proceed—politically, theoretically, or artistically—"from left to right or right to left, as a reactionary movement or as a revolutionary movement, or both at once" (*Writing and Difference*, 276; *L'Écriture et la différence*, 406–7). Bataille's conceptions are hardly "reactionary" insofar as they operate in the sphere of the classical political economy, although, as Derrida suggests in the same sentence, "they can read" in either direction. At times they need to be read from left to right or in directions that cannot be subsumed by this rubric, whether itself read "from left to right or from right to left" and whether in a classical fashion or in a critical or deconstructive fashion.

A general economy can and must operate more broadly and mediate between indissociable, but never fully identical, political and nonpolitical spheres. For example, theoretical or literary domains "between literatures and revolutions, such as Bataille conceived of them in the course of his explication with Surrealism" (*Writing and Difference*, 261; *L'Écriture et la différence*, 384), and the complex political stratifications within and between them are among Bataille's major concerns.

There is as much a temptation to take a general economy outside the political economy—toward literary revolutions, for example—as there is to reduce it to the question of revolutionary politics, although both strategies may at times be necessary. Bataille's "positions" on these issues are complex and resist either move. Derrida correctly points out the revolutionary, even the "absolutely revolutionary," character of Bataille's sovereignty, which, we recall, itself *is not* the general economy. The latter is the "science" of sovereignty. When Derrida comments on Bataille's defining propositions on the *production* of the excesses of energy that cannot be *consumed*, he connects economic and philosophical—"meaning-ful"—consumption:

> One would commit a gross error in interpreting these propositions in a "reactionary" sense. The consumption of the excess of energy by a determined class is not a destructive consuming of meaning, but a significative reappropriation of a surplus value within the space of restricted economy. From this point of view, sovereignty is absolutely revolutionary. But it is also revolutionary as concerns a revolution which would only reorganize the world of work and would redistribute values within the space of meaning, that is to say, still within restricted economy. This last movement—only slightly perceived, here and there, by Bataille (for example, in *La Part maudite*, when he invokes the "radicalism of Marx" and the "revolutionary sense that Marx formulated in a sovereign way")—and most often muddled by conjectural approximations (for example in the fifth part of *La Part maudite*)—is rigorously necessary, but as a phase within the strategy of general economy. (*Writing and Difference*, 337 n. 33; *L'Écriture et la différence*, 397 n. 1)

Bataille's conceptions play a major role in Derrida, in this case in Derrida's sense of both "literatures" and "revolutions"—of a kind that "as yet have no model," which is to say, all, or just about all, literatures and revolutions.[39] There will therefore never be *one* model, *the* model. While the borderlines between various political and poetic, or theoretical, economies constantly shift, one must be extremely careful in relating the theoretical implications of the general economy to the possibility of any political program, whether one proceeds from left to right or from right to left. Yet "sovereignty" is "absolutely revolutionary," even as against all revolutions, including those which emerge in Marxism. Marxism would certainly "reorganize the world of work . . . and redistribute value within the space of meaning . . . within *restricted* economy."

The practice of sovereignty would not seem to have anything to do with *slave* labor, even only as a stage or a phase, whether in literature and revolution or in philosophy or theory. Bataille himself always engages a plural textual and political practice, a plural style of practice. Hence the necessity of a radical break from philosophy in the general economy of sacrifice in Bataille, on which he insists and which he even attributes, untenably, to Hegel's *Aufhebung*. Therefore, unlike in Marx, the move to the exuberance of sovereignty is not a reversal of Hegel within "the world of work" and thus is not the economy of dialectic, theoretical or political, materialist or idealist, from right to left or from left to right. Sovereignty, thus, has a very different relation to Hegel's mastery (Herrschaft).

One would not trust Bataille, or Nietzsche—"I do not know any other way of associating with great tasks than *play* [Ich kenne keine andre Art, mit grossen Aufgaben zu verkehrten als das *Spiel*]" ("Why I Am So Clever," in *Ecce Homo*, 258; *Ecce Homo*, KSA 6:297; Nietzsche's emphasis)—insofar as the *work* of either is concerned. A great, immense labor, quite on the Hegelian scale, is involved in their tasks, although not without play, which is necessary, even in Hegel. Bataille's remarks in *Guilty* (7) suggest a very complex economy, a *general* economy, of relationships between play and labor. More crucial are the general—theoretical—constraints that must be imposed. Without understanding labor, even slave labor, and without a restricted economy, no general economy can be *comprehensive* enough. It cannot be comprehensive enough as a "science" or theory that relates to the moment of sovereign operation, and to the sovereign moments of its own operations. For example, all such operations would always involve work, *perhaps* mostly, but not exclusively, in a form different from slave work, assuming that latter economy of work is rigorously defined. Such a definition is just as difficult and problematic as defining, once and for all, a master's play or work. The general economy puts into question all of these as un-critical or pre-critical—philosophical—concepts, "of Kant, of Hegel."

A radical reconsideration and reconfiguration of the relations between work and play are at stake. Under certain conditions, play is also work, and conversely work is play, although the range and richness of the asymmetries between them may be immense. Children's games are an important case in this respect, on which I shall comment further in Chapter 3. In this context, in Kant's restricted economy, the play of beautiful art, as against the experience of the beautiful, and the economimesis of the genius of beautiful art as play also imply an ability to perform—and whenever necessary to *work* through—more difficult tasks. Such tasks would be unsurmountable for other—"lesser"—minds and types or "a work like mercenary employment." Against Kant, and Hegel, however, all these relations must be reconfigured, *in both directions*, within a general economy.

Derrida seems to detect in Bataille a form or a degree of the privileging of sovereignty or revolution as sovereignty. The latter is not, or at least not sufficiently, configured in Bataille as only a phase, only *one* strategy, whether that of reversal, as against work, or other. "Strategy" is itself a term with powerful and rich political dimensions of great relevance in the present context: many a political strategy of the French landscape is referred to and is at stake in Derrida's own essay. To some extent, Derrida follows Sartre here, to whom he refers (*Writing and Difference*, 336 nn. 30, 31; *L'Écriture et la différence*, 399 n. 1, 395–96 n. 1). Perhaps such is the case; perhaps, as I discussed earlier, Bataille offers a more complex and more comprehensive relation. He himself certainly works, and knows that he works, although indeed not as a slave; and slave work here, needless to say, is not a question of effort and expenditure of energy. His own work and his relation to his own work play a tremendous role in his "general" conceptions. This role is particularly apparent in the opening of *Inner Experience*, where Bataille differentiates hierarchically among forms of his own writing.

Work, then, cannot be reduced absolutely. Nor can meaning, produced by the work of concepts, specifically philosophical concepts. But then what is at issue is always, always already, work-play. Foucault, we recall, defines "madness" as "the absence of work." Foucault, it is true, is not Bataille; but Bataille's balances—accounts and dis-counts—are, once again, complex enough, too, at all levels of his theory and his practice; no less so, perhaps even more so, are Nietzsche's balances—the (dis)equilibria of the Dionysian. It is of considerable significance that Hölderlin is one of the crucial contexts of Foucault's statement. That reference, or that frame of reference, would further engage the question of Nietzsche's madness, along multiple lines or planes of the French and German landscape, or complementarily both. Derrida comments on these issues in *Writing and Difference*, both in his essay on Foucault, "Cogito and the History of Madness," and in his first essay on Antonin Artaud, "La Parole soufflée." Artaud is, of course, another "exemplary case," although Derrida's remarks there concern mainly Hölderlin and Foucault on Hölderlin.

Another immediate connection here would be Heidegger's discussions of both Hölderlin and Nietzsche, connecting, not always unproblematically, their madness and the limits of their thinking, and indeed the limits of thinking in general. Nietzsche's remarks on the limits of logic in *The Birth of Tragedy* (sec. 15, pp. 97–98; *KSA* 1:101) remain a governing context. This passage is, I think, also a significant context for Bataille's idea of "inner experience," which has crucial connections to the issue of Hegel's proximity to madness in writing the *Phenomenology*, as well as to Nietzsche. One would be well warned, however, against establishing any simple link between the question of the limits of logic and any specific case of madness, such as Hölderlin's or Nietzsche's. In my view, Heidegger's comments to that effect are problematic. But, then, these are questions of extraordinary complexity.

Along with the question of literature and revolution, the question of sexuality and revolution remains, as we have seen, pivotal for Bataille. It powerfully affects Bataille's explorations of the limits of the possible in sexuality, literature—or religion and philosophy—and revolutions in *Inner Experience* and other major works. To a degree, the major proper names of *Inner Experience*, such as Descartes, Sade, Hegel, Nietzsche, Rimbaud, Proust, those of religious mystics or indeed God (102–15), designate these limits. Both essays mentioned earlier are also of great significance in the context of sexuality and revolution. "The 'Old Mole' and the Prefix *Sur* in the Words *Surhomme* and *Surrealist*," opening with the epigraph from Marx, is suspended, as it were, and moves from right to left and from left to right, between the Surrealist and the Communist manifestoes, in the Breton-Aragon parergon. "The Use Value of D.A.F. de Sade: An Open Letter to My Current Comrades" establishes another powerful axis, from right to left and from left to right, from de Sade, or Rousseau, to Marx, to Freud. All these connections proceed via Nietzsche, anticipating much of the current scene of theory—after-Marx, after-Nietzsche, after-Freud, as *perhaps* against Kant, against Hegel.

In his analysis of Bataille, Derrida may also be suggesting that sovereignty, as Bataille conceives of it, does not quite conform to the operations or at least the possibilities of what Bataille offers as a general economy. Derrida is careful to maintain throughout the difference between sovereignty and general economy in Bataille. In any event, what we need is a comprehensive general economy, even if in the end it cannot be attributed to Bataille, or to Derrida, or to Nietzsche. These, it must not be forgotten, are different general economies.

A general economy, let me reiterate, by definition cannot exist in general. It also exposes the fact that nothing can exist in general. Nothing is outside an economy in which it is produced, whether that economy is general or restricted. Any such restricted economy must be recomprehended by a general economy. There cannot be one, single or unitary, general economy even in the case of a given general economy, such as Nietzsche's, Bataille's, and Derrida's. A *general* economy must perhaps "know" that it can never be one; whether or not it does know that, however, it never is "one." A restricted economy, of course, can never be one economy, either; it just aims to be. There are also economies, including many of those that have emerged "after deconstruction," that are restricted in spite of their aims and claims to be plural. The "texts" and "styles" of restricted and general economies are different, in addition, whatever the "knowledge" and "aims" in any given case. The styles of general economy must always be plural, radically plural; and such is the case in Nietzsche, Bataille, and Derrida. But there are also differently plural economies and styles.

Styles

Derrida's analysis of Kant in "Economimesis" fundamentally relates to and depends on Bataille's matrix; and as I have suggested from the outset, the same can be said of Derrida's matrix in general. The economy of *différance* is by definition a general economy, specifically in its juxtaposition to—or simultaneously an infinitesimal proximity to and a radical displacement of—Hegel's dialectic and the *Aufhebung* (*Margins*, 14; *Positions*, 44). Derrida's reading of Bataille in "From Restricted to General Economy: A Hegelianism without Reserve" is central, both in relation to Derrida's own matrix and in the recent history of reading of Bataille. In "Différance" the question of Bataille and general economy emerges, in proximity to Freud and Nietzsche and the question of the unconscious, at "the point of greatest obscurity, . . . the very enigma of *différance* [le point de la plus grande obscurité . . . l'énigme même de la différance]" (*Margins*, 19; *Marges*, 20). The question of (the *différance* of) matter is also posed by way of Bataille and general economy (*Positions*, 64), dislocating the metaphysical materialism and the restricted historical and political economies defined by it. In *Glas* Bataille is a major presence throughout, mediating between Genet and Hegel, as well as Kant; and Kant's importance in *Glas* is in turn considerable, in juxtaposition to Hegel and in general.[40] The analysis of Kant in "The Parergon," in many ways a necessary companion to "Economimesis," proceeds, overtly, outside the framework of general economy.[41]

In "Economimesis," however, this framework is decisive. Derrida offers, first, a brief introductory statement relating the Kantian restricted economy of "pure judgments of taste [des jugements de goût pur]" where "under the cover of a controlled indeterminacy, pure morality and empirical culturalism are allied" to a political economy ("Economimesis," 3; *Mimesis*, 57). "A politics, therefore, although it never occupies the center of the stage, acts upon this discourse. It ought to be possible to read it" ("Economimesis," 3; *Mimesis*, 57). The rigorous Kantian specificity of "such an implication" must be rigorously maintained, even though, and indeed because, "politics and political economy, to be sure, are implicated in every discourse on art and on the beautiful." The "sorting out and measuring lengths," between Plato or Aristotle and Kant alone, for example, "will not suffice."

> Once inserted into another network, the "same" philosopheme is no longer the same, and besides it never had an identity external to its functioning. Simultaneously, "unique and original" ["inédits"] philosophemes, if there are any, as soon as they enter into articulated composition with inherited philosophemes, are affected by that composition over the whole of their surface and under every angle. We are nowhere near disposing of rigorous criteria for judging philosophical specificity, the precise limits framing a corpus or what properly belongs [le propre] to a system. The very project of such a delimitation itself already belongs to a set of conditions [un ensemble] that remains to be thought. In turn even the concept of belonging [to a set] is open to elaboration, that is dislocation, by the structure of the *parergon*." (3; *Mimesis*, 57–58)

Derrida opens the main text by introducing "economimesis" in the context of the relationships between restricted and general economies:

> It would appear that *mimesis* and *oikonomia* could have nothing to do with one another. The point is to demonstrate the contrary, to exhibit the systematic link between the two; but not between some particular political economy and *mimesis,* for the latter can accommodate itself to political

systems that are different, even opposed to one another. And we are not yet defining economy as an economy of circulation (a restricted economy) or a general economy, for the whole difficulty is narrowed down here as soon as—that is the hypothesis—there is no possible *opposition* between these two economies. Their relation must be one neither of identity nor of contradiction but must be other. (3–4; *Mimesis*, 58)

The two sections into which Derrida divides his essay, "Production as Mimesis" and "Examplorality," might be seen as demarcating, "more or less," the problems involved along the two lines or rubrics considered earlier. The first section explores the nature or the structure of the operation, inscribing the economy of mimesis as a mimesis of economy. The second offers a critique of the Kantian or, more generally, philosophical account as the restricted economy of the beautiful or the sublime and the economy of beautiful art. As always, however, the two—"operation" and "its science"—remain within a complex, *general*, economy of interaction. I have discussed the structure of the economic operation and the role of the difference between consumption and expenditure in accounting for—or *producing*—such operations earlier. I shall conclude this chapter by considering the theoretical *text* and theoretical *style* that emerge under the conditions of general economy. In short, I shall address the question of general economy as "science" and "style." Jointly, the expenditure without reserve and its general economy, and the plural, or complementary, style demanded by this type of discourse may well be the most decisive reconfiguration of the modern theoretical, cultural, and possibly political, landscape.

In his deconstruction of Kant in "Economimesis," Derrida stresses the "desire" of the system of taste to account for dis-gust—absolute dis-gust. The sublime, as we have seen, introduces interesting complexities but does not change the economy itself. Clearly, the issue is more general; in fact, it affects the very core of the Kantian configuration—the "thing in itself," in either sense. It is the question of the other of the system, and of accounting for that other, that, in general, is pursued by Derrida throughout his texts. Thus he writes in *Dissemination*, in the context of Hegel but with very general implications, and with some echoes of Kant: "The breakthrough toward radical otherness (with respect to the philosophical concept—of the concept) always takes, *within philosophy*, the *form* of an a posteriority or an empiricism. But this is an effect of the specular nature of philosophical reflection, philosophy being incapable of inscribing (comprehending) what is outside it otherwise than through the appropriating assimilation of a negative image of it, and dissemination is written on the back—the *tain*—of that mirror" (*Dissemination*, 33; *La Dissémination*, 39). "The other"—the term and concept of the other—is, of course, already an account of the other, but in Kant's analysis, "vomit" takes a specific, privileged role. As Derrida writes, concluding "Economimesis":

> Disgust is not the symmetrical inverse of taste, the negative key to the system, except insofar as some interest sustains its excellence, like that of the mouth itself—the chemistry of the word—and prohibits the substitution of any non-oral *analo*gue. The system therefore is interested in determining the other as *its* other, that is, as literally disgusting.
>
> What is absolutely foreclosed is not vomit, but the possibility of a vicariousness of vomit, of its replacement by anything else—by some other unrepresentable, unnameable, unintelligible, insensible, unassimilable, obscene other which forces enjoyment and whose irrepressible violence would undo the hierarchizing authority of logocentric analogy—its power of *identification*. . . .
>
> The word vomit arrests the vicariousness of disgust; it puts the thing in the mouth; it substitutes; but only, for example, oral for anal. It is determined by the system of the beautiful, "the symbol of morality," as its other. *It* is then for philosophy, still, an elixir, even in the very quintessence of its bad taste. ("Economimesis," 25; *Mimesis*, 92–93; emphasis added)

Both Bataille and Derrida make apparent the folly and "naivete" of this powerful and irrepressible desire to exclude. The latter is itself a gesture of rejection and not consumption. A rejected—repressed—rejection, however, makes its powerful return—the return of the repressed into the structure of the philosophical consumptive account. The Lacanian notion of "foreclosure" is also suggested by Derrida, in the context and metaphor of radical "therapy"—a kind of short session, induced by a strong medicine. Can philosophy succeed, then, in foreclosing "the possibility of a vicariousness of vomit"? Derrida inserts in the passage just cited:

> Vicariousness would in turn be reassuring only if it substituted an identifiable term for an unrepresentable one, if it allowed one to step aside from the abyss in the direction of another place, if it were interested in some other go-around [interesse à quelque manège]. But for that it would have to be *itself* and represent itself as such. Whereas it is starting from that impossibility that economimesis is constrained in its processes.
>
> This impossibility cannot be said to be some thing, something sensible or intelligible, that could fall under one or the other senses or under some concept. One cannot name it within the logocentric system —within the name—which in turn can only vomit it and vomit itself in it. One cannot even say: what is it? That would be to begin to eat it, or —what is no longer absolutely different—to vomit it. The question *what*

is? already parleys [arraisonne] like a *parergon,* it constructs a framework which captures the energy of what is complete inassimilable and absolutely repressed. Any philosophical question already determines, concerning this other, a paregoric *parergon.* A paregoric remedy softens with speech; it consoles, it exhorts with the word. As its name indicates. ("Economimesis," 25; *Mimesis,* 92–93)

This restricted economy of exclusion is, thus, one of the powerful subsystems of the logic of philosophy, for it also ensures the work of the logic of consumption, the point of Bataille's famous laughter. Bataille would undoubtedly laugh no less looking at the naïvete of the philosopher accounting for beautiful art, or the beautiful, or even the "sublime." Un-framed, deprived of the parergon, the sublime would still not be, not even nearly, un-framed enough for Bataille. Philosophical accounts and the *science* of philosophy are all, by definition, consumptive, and thus remain *restricted* economies. Whatever the philosophers—beginning with Socrates or perhaps Anaximander—claim to the contrary, such a restricted philosophical economy would remain a *pleasurable* consumption of presence; and its accounts are based on various forms of the calculus of presence—being-presence or becoming-presence.

General economies, let me stress, do not deny the role of or simply suspend either presence or pleasure, including, as against the claims of restricted economies, in the theoretical process itself. One must always rigorously situate and, against restricted economies, resituate both presence and pleasure. As Derrida shows throughout his analysis, the latter concept of presence is never given up by philosophy, however much it may be, and in fact, had mostly been the philosophy of difference. Such is in fact the "difference" between the two economies—restricted and general: the restricted economy of difference is always, finally, *governed* by presence, being-presence or becoming-presence, and the general economy that does neither simply dispenses with nor privileges either, but reconfigures both differently.

The philosopher, it is true, often "forgets" this, at times quite sublime, pleasure of consumption and mastery. This "forgetting" may take the form of either unconscious repressing or conscious concealment—or various combinations of both—of the knowledge of this pleasure. It has powerfully shaped the history of philosophy ever since Socrates founded the difference between and opposition of philosophy and literature on the difference and opposition between truth and pleasure.

In Kant, a difference of pleasures of that type is configured—framed and reframed—with great complexity and ingenuity,[42] without, however, his ever quite succeeding in maintaining all the parerga that his economy aims for. Once the philosophical discourse *pleasurably consumes*, however, would not the framing—the parergon—that divides the philosophical and the literary or artistic, be threatened in its very core? This parergon also fundamentally divides, separates—or claims to separate, at least in principle—that which produces such accounts, namely philosophy, from the experience of the beautiful, or sublime, and beautiful art, or rather what is seen as such by philosophy. Derrida's analysis of Kant in "Economimesis" and "The Parergon," and the analysis throughout *The Truth in Painting*, suggests at least that much. Cannot, then, for example, the third critique, an account that pleasurably consumes, be itself read as an aesthetic experience or as a work of beautiful art? Derrida certainly plays—and works—quite extensively, with treating it in this fashion. As I have suggested, Kant's own interaction with the beautiful, art, or reason, also may be replayed and reworked along these lines. As one of the defining parerga, the parergon of art and philosophy is already—always already—to one degree or another violated in Kant's own text, as it is in Aristotle's, by establishing the fundamentally philosophical value of the beautiful art of highest rank—poetry. The parergonal violation and divisions, within and without, deparergonizations, announced in the questions just asked are more radical, more violent and, in theoretical terms, more fundamental.

First, as we have seen, according to both Bataille and Derrida, the economy of such an account must exceed the economy of consumption as a restricted economy to which both philosophy and beautiful art conform in Kant. It is philosophy's belief—its "naive" or, to use another of Bataille's characterizations, "vulgar" (common) belief—in the possibility of the utilization of all intellectual energy which Bataille laughs at. For a philosopher can only believe or claim to take everything into his account or into his dis-count, but cannot "actually" do so. The economy of every account—literary, philosophical, or other—is always already a general economy or is precomprehended by a general economy; or, better, it can always be and often must be re-configured in a general economy that relates to what is "lost without the slightest aim or meaning" and what therefore cannot be taken into account, or into dis-count.

More significant, however, is the question of the law or, better, the style of a discourse in the general economy, or, in Derrida's terms writing—"major writing"[43]—that, simultaneously, relates to the loss of meaning and extends into the heterogeneous. It would be naive or again vulgar to reverse the configuration, to reverse the parergon, and replace philosophy or theory, and to make literature or "beautiful art" into a unique or ultimate genre of general economy. The latter, we recall, still remains a science, a theory, although, to be sure, in neither the Hegelian nor a positivist sense; it is not a "positive science." Nevertheless, it must retain a scientific rigor in its discourse. These problematics of unproblematized reversal, having been exhaustively analyzed by Derrida, have become by now another commonplace of deconstruction, although by no means a discountable commonplace. Such reversals are still practiced in various forms, including in the name of deconstruction. Under the constraints of general economy, reversal or overturning is often a necessary but rarely a sufficient move.

Much as Nietzsche did, Bataille practiced a plural style and a plural genre in his own discourse, within and between given works, thus making his discourse, and at times simultaneously, theoretical, in his essays, and literary, in his novels or poetry, or critical; and all these generic characterizations can apply only in a provisional fashion.[44] *Inner Experience*, in particular, combines all these elements and fields, and several other modes, genres, and models; furthermore, it depends on a variety of literary and theoretical models. The book would obviously qualify as postmodern in Lyotard's sense as discussed earlier; and the style of Joyce's *Ulysses* may well have been one of its models, alongside Nietzsche's works, most notably *The Gay Science*. A minor point at the moment, this possibility suggests that a great deal more might be at stake in such postmodernist texts—in Joyce, Bataille, and others—than only putting forward the unrepresentable in representation itself, to bring in Lyotard's definition of postmodern art.

Bataille, however, also attempted something more in his activities related to the Collège de Sociologie. One must then speak of at least three genres that are necessary, for Bataille, to enact a general economy of discourse and a major form of writing. Undoubtedly, one must be rather cautious in relating general economy and a major form of writing, on which Derrida comments. The issue is complex, however, all the more so given the difference indicated earlier in the economic thematics and styles in Derrida and Bataille. In short, these relations, too, must proceed by way of intersecting matrices of complementary interactions. Bataille was, in addition, a librarian and the founder and editor of the journal *Critique*. In all of these "genres" or "styles," social or political economies, as general economies, are actively engaged.

Thus, what is most at stake (en jeu) in the question of general economy is the law and the multiple style and a multiple genre of the *social* and *institutional* forms of our text and practice. But this law, this style, and this genre *cannot*, nor should they, be established once and for all, although, of course, the claim can be made that they have been established.

"Referring to the entire French landscape" (in 1968), Bataille's presence is inescapable, Derrida writes: "What we need, perhaps, as Nietzsche said, is a change of 'style'; and if there is style, Nietzsche reminded us, it must be *plural*" (*Margins*, 135; *Marges*, 163).

The configuration or the *general* economy of the plural style that I suggest here may be different from the plural style in Derrida's sense, although still related to it. Derrida's denomination of plural style, at least in his own practice but perhaps also as a general theoretical necessity, a kind of constraint, appears to refer to the simultaneous operation inside and outside "the terrain" or register of philosophy. This thematics of the inside and the outside of the terrain and text of philosophy is central to Derrida's theories and practice. It is clearly suggested in the end of "The Ends of Man" just before the invocation of style appears, concluding the second of the three "rubrics": "2. The strategic bet."[45]

On the one hand, there is *continuity*: "a. To attempt an exit and a deconstruction without changing terrain, by repeating what is implicit in the founding concepts and the original problematic, by using against the edifice the instruments or stones available in the house [*oikos* and *oikonomia*—economy], that is, equally, in language."

And on the other, there is *break*: "b. To decide to change terrain, in a discontinuous and irruptive fashion, by brutally placing oneself outside, and by affirming an absolute break and difference."

Derrida qualifies immediately: "It goes without saying that these effects do not suffice to annul the necessity for a 'change of terrain.' It also goes without saying that the choice between these two forms of deconstruction cannot be simple and unique" (*Margins*, 135; *Marges*, 162–63). As Derrida points out, correctly, either of these transformational or de(con)structive strategies entails the considerable risk of confirming metaphysics, specifically in Heidegger in the first case and Lévi-Strauss or structuralism in general, in the second. Hence "a new writing *must* weave and interlace these two motifs [of deconstruction]" (*Margins*, 135; *Marges*, 163; emphasis added).

This project is possible; in any event, the balance of this relationship of continuity and break with philosophy does count. It appears to be quite different in different general economies and different plural styles, such as in Nietzsche, Bataille, and Derrida. There is, of course, a relation to philosophy in Bataille and Nietzsche as well, as to a degree there must be; and the relationships between the plural style in Derrida's sense and the plurality of styles and genres in the present sense may finally be irreducible. At issue, as will be discussed more extensively later, is the balance of such relationships within and between different fields. There must be, therefore, moments of dislocating philosophy, and much else that is shaped by philosophy, by "using against the edifice the instruments or stones available in the house"—concepts, language, and strategies. Derrida, in fact, powerfully locates such moments in both Nietzsche and Bataille.[46] But one can also proceed by creating and operating in the new terrains and territories, along with, to use Deleuze's term, many deterritorializations. To a degree, one must always do so, by deterritorializing and exterritorializing even within the house. For both, Nietzsche and Bataille, more powerful resources may well be those found "outside" rather than "inside" of the house of philosophy.

Such may be the case in Derrida as well, although in his case the balance is different and is *shifted* toward philosophy and the first strategy of deconstruction—"mostly that of the Heideggerian questions [celui (le style) des questions heideggeriennes]" (*Margins*, 135; *Marges*, 163). Derrida's strategies cannot be reduced to the latter, either. Derrida's style is not Heidegger's style, and the difference between the two is itself an issue of great significance that emerges throughout Derrida's text. For, as Derrida says, "a radical trembling can only come from the *outside* [Un ébranlement radical ne peut venir que du *dehors*]" (*Margins*, 134; *Marges*, 162).

Heideggerian trembling or, as Heidegger himself calls it, the "destruction [Destruktion]" of metaphysics is never radical enough. As Derrida shows, finally, it always reinstates and affirms metaphysics, in its own "instance of the logos and truth."[47] That is assuming, of course, that one wants philosophy to tremble radically. If one wants a successful theory—of taste, for example, or art, or language, or of just about anything—perhaps one must want exactly that, though maybe more than Derrida suggests and certainly far more than Heidegger does. Such a theory can perhaps no longer be philosophy, especially after Nietzsche. This may well be Heidegger's problem, too—after Nietzsche it is too late for Being, its presence, its difference, its truth.

Exterior resources themselves—"stones and instruments"—must have sources, of course. They cannot come out of nothing or fall from the skies any more than any other differences can. There are, therefore, always other chains—continuities—or networks—territories—that enable one to break with philosophy. It is not a question of an absolute break, for, as I have stressed all along, a radical break, a break that is radical enough, may never be absolute. However, a more radical break than Derrida indicates and more radical than the one his own practice enacts on the margins of philosophy may be at issue.

The plurality of styles, genres, and practices to which I refer here, particularly in the case of Bataille, in addition to multiplying theoretical strategies and adventures, also relates the possibility of a different balance of relations to the house—the always restricted economy of philosophy. It enables an exploration of theoretical, or political, chains *exterior* to philosophy. These chains may not be absolutely exterior, and certainly will not be so at all points; yet they may be exterior enough, perhaps even more radically exterior than Derrida's practice and theory of style would suggest.

Also, some common enough closures may still exist, such as the closure of presence, or difference. As I shall discuss later, the closure of philosophy may be dislocated more radically than Derrida seems to allow, even though both concepts—presence and difference—cannot be absolutely dissociated, in all rigor, from the history of philosophy. Conversely, neither can they be contained there. At issue is the general economy, or perhaps still more radical theory, of *transformations* of theoretical closure(s), the economy Derrida never invokes, even though he inscribes closure heterogeneously. The latter, however, remains a kind of economy of the everywhere dense—irreducible—force of *philosophy*, as a field or discipline, which might be questioned in this form.

Bataille might well be more anti-Hegelian and anti-philosophical in this respect, perhaps more so than he himself thinks, or more than Derrida suggests in saying that "Bataille is even less Hegelian than he thinks [(Ce par quoi) Bataille est encore moins hegelien qu'il ne croit]" (*Writing and Difference*, 275; *L'Écriture et la différence*, 405), and more so than Derrida himself. In the case of Nietzsche's plural style, the departure from philosophy might be still more radical.

No one strategy or set of strategies, no single style or balance can guarantee success once and for all. One cannot decide on such a strategy or set of strategies once and for all, so that it may be deliberately practiced and thus enable one to calculate the undecidable, including as any given form of undecidability. Much depends on who is pursuing strategies, genres, or styles, and when and how one does so. Derrida's style has been extraordinarily successful. Yet it is possible that today, two decades after the statement by Derrida under scrutiny, a different ensemble of styles, a different plural style, might be necessary. Given Nietzsche's and Bataille's practice, taking place well before this statement, such ensembles may have already been necessary and operative, and before and after their practice, this necessity has produced and shaped, at least in part, other—for example, more Derridean—forms of plural style.

Derrida does not quite *end* "The End of Man" with "today" (1968), but rather with Nietzsche—Nietzsche and the *end* of *Zarathustra*—that is, both with yesterday and perhaps tomorrow. His last rubric and last difference is related to "the strategic bet" of deconstruction just considered, but is a different one:

> 3. *The difference between the superior man and the superman.* Beneath this rubric is signaled both the increasingly insistent and increasingly rigorous recourse to Nietzsche in France, and the division that is announced, perhaps, between two *relèves* of man. We know now, at the end of *Zarathustra*, at the moment of the "sign," when *das Zeichen kommt*, Nietzsche distinguishes, in the greatest proximity, in a strange resemblance and an ultimate complicity, at the eve of the last separation, of the great Noontime, between the superior man (*höhere Mensch*) and the superman (*Übermensch*). The first is abandoned to his distress in a last movement of pity. The latter—who is not the last man—awakens and leaves, without turning back to what he leaves behind him. He burns his text and erases the traces of his steps. His laughter then will burst out, directed toward a return which no longer will have the form of the metaphysical repetition of humanism, nor, doubtless, "beyond" metaphysics [as in Heidegger], the form of memorial or a guarding of the meaning of Being, the form of the house and of the truth of Being. He will dance, outside the house, the *aktive Vergesslichkeit*, the "active forgetting" and the cruel (*grausam*) feast of which the *Genealogy of Morals* speaks. No doubt that Nietzsche called for an active forgetting of Being: it would not have the metaphysical form imputed to it by Heidegger.
>
> Must one read Nietzsche, with Heidegger, as the last of the great metaphysicians? Or, on the contrary, are we to take the question of the truth of Being as the last sleeping shudder of the superior man? Are we to understand the eve as the guard mounted around the house or as the awakening to the day that is coming, at whose eve we are? Is there an economy of the eve?
>
> Perhaps we are between these two eves, which are also two ends of man. But who, we? (*Margins*, 135–36; *Marges*, 163–64)

I am less certain about "proximity" and "resemblance," however strange, and "complicity," particularly "ultimate complicity" between the höhere Mensch and the Übermensch; and the juncture at issue signals perhaps rather distance than proximity between Nietzsche and Derrida. "Who are we, then?" This is Nietzsche's question, too, one of his great "question marks" (*The Gay Science*, sec. 346, p. 285). Nietzsche does not seem to have much faith in the power and potential of the philosophical project in approaching his question marks. He continues to insist on theoretical rigor, however, even though it may take radically new forms that philosophy does not anticipate.

There is always more than one position in between, for example, philosophy and Nietzsche; there are also positions on the other, nonphilosophical, side of Nietzsche. Bataille, let us recall, "considered himself closer to Nietzsche than anyone else, than to anyone else, to the point of identification with him [plus que tout autre, plus que de tout autre, jusqu'à l'identification, il [Bataille] se voulut proche de Nietzsche]" (*Writing and Difference*, 251; *L'Écriture et la différence*, 369). Perhaps this proximity is greatest in the force of the impact, in the radical transformation of "theoretical" or "literary" style, in making this style *plural*. It is the maze of style and the style of a maze. "NIETZSCHE'S DOCTRINE CANNOT BE ENSLAVED. It can only be followed [LA DOCTRINE DE NIETZSCHE NE PEUT PAS ÊTRE ASSERVIE. Elle peut seulement être suivie]" (*Visions*, 184; "Nietzsche et les fascistes," *Oeuvres complètes* 1:450).

It is a thought and style—*writing*—that must be entered like a labyrinth. In a brilliant little—Nietzsche-style—chapter of "The Obelisk," "Nietzsche/Theseus," an essay on Hegel and Nietzsche that can be seen as in many ways a companion piece to "The Labyrinth," Bataille invokes "a derisive and enigmatic figure placed at the entrance to a labyrinth [une figure dérisoire et énigmatique placée à l'entrée du labyrinthe]." Then, anticipating much of deconstruction, he speaks of "the *foundation* of things that has fallen into a bottomless void. And what is fearlessly conquered—no longer in a duel where the death of the hero is risked against that of the monster, in exchange for an indifferent duration—is not an isolated creature; it is the very void and vertiginous fall, it is TIME [(Car) ce qui est tombé dans un vide sans fond est l'*assise* des choses. Et ce qui est proposé à une conquête impavide—non plus à un duel où se joue la mort du héros contre celle du monstre, en échange d'une durée indifférente—ce n'est plus une créature isolée, c'est le vide même et la chute vertigineuse, c'est le TEMPS]" (*Visions*, 222; "L'Obélisque," *Oeuvres complètes* 1:513).

No wonder that Kant, in *contemplating* the beautiful, would oppose tulips in the garden to the vertiginous and even nauseating experience of the labyrinth. In all fairness to Kant, he approaches some of this vertiginous experience in his analysis of the sublime, and thus can be seen as a precursor of both Nietzsche and Bataille in this respect. But then one would have to renounce the ground upon which the opposition between the beautiful—the one that is framed, is in a parergon—and the sublime—the one that is "absolutely great" and that exceeds all parerga—can be established unequivocally, and once and for all. This and all such grounds crumble and finally collapse. This collapse is also a collapse of philosophical style.

It is not that in so recognizing Bataille's enormous contribution one would want to claim for Bataille, or Nietzsche, or indeed for anyone, a unique significance in this transformation of the theoretical field. Rather, in an *account* that, in the absence of a better term, might be termed complementarily "historico-theoretical," one would want to explore, in a stratified ensemble—from Kant and Hegel to Nietzsche, and beyond—that which has made and still makes possible radical transformations of the field—the transformations that make the field, and style, *plural*.

In thinking of the theorists and practitioners of the *plural style*, such as Nietzsche, Bataille, or Derrida, one will have to refer to a landscape that can no longer be demarcated as either French or German, however important these two *land*scapes might be. It would have to include many a *no man's* land, and not only geographically speaking. One can specifically think of the names, from Simone de Beauvoir on, defining the scene of modern feminist theory—crucial proper names in the context of plural style and genre, in Derrida's sense of relation to philosophy or in terms of many other pluralities that may be invoked, between philosophy and literature, genre and gender, gender politics and sexual politics, between—and reconfiguring—the field of work and the field of play. These names, together with the many other proper names, histories, and geographies that they imply, signal yet another reconfiguration in all fields at issue in this study: the (re)configurations of gender difference. These reconfigurations will be, and have already been, perhaps more radical than any that have been effected since that ensemble of reconfigurations designated by the names of Darwin, Marx, Nietzsche, Freud, that defines this century. It is difficult to predict whether and to what extent these transformations and reconfigurations—the gender and feminist revolution(s)—will be determined by or related to the reconfigurations, styles, and landscapes at issue in the present study. In recent history, after *The Second Sex*, they have been part of them and have been played against them, particularly on the scene of French feminism, but not exclusively on that scene which is not one. Certainly, in Luce Irigaray's and Hélène Cixous's works, the significance of these landscapes was crucial, posing, in the wake of Nietzsche and "on the eve and aftermath of philosophy," the tremendous question of the Dionysian and, also possibly against, gender difference.[48]

The originality and complexity—and the plurality of style—in the texts of modern feminism have been a major contribution to modern intellectual history. Undeniably, after philosophy and after Nietzsche, these texts have also transformed the scene—the landscape, the theater, the style—of modern culture, theory, or politics, and they demonstrate, perhaps more radically than ever before, that if there are styles and landscapes, they must be *plural*.

Chapter 3

Rich and Strange: Of Giving Gifts, Counting Numbers, Drawing Lines, Telling Stories, and Playing Games

Numbers

> Vouchsafe to those that have not read the story,
> That I may prompt them; and of such as have,
> I humbly pray them to admit th'excuse
> Of time, of numbers, and due course of things,
> Which cannot in their huge and proper life
> Be here presented.
> —Shakespeare, *Henry V* 5, Prologue, 1–6

Storytelling is not found among Prometheus' gifts to mankind, the gifts that "made them to have sense and be endowed with reason," at least not according to Aeschylus' version of the events. Aeschylus' account, however, is given *as* a story, told by Prometheus himself:

But listen to the miseries among mortals, how I made them—who were formerly senseless—able to use their intelligence, and rational [skilled in mind]. . . . First of all, though they could see, they looked in vain, though they could listen, they did not hear, but like the shapes of dreams they jumbled up everything willy-nilly throughout their long life; and they neither knew [how to make] brick houses that faced the sun, nor [did they know] woodworking, but they lived under the ground like swarming [*lit.*: light as wind] ants in the sunless corners of caves. They had no sure sign [*lit.*: witness, testimony] of winter or of flowery spring, or fruit-bearing summer; but they did everything without judgment, until [I came along and] showed them the risings of the stars, and their settings, which are difficult to discern. And I also discovered for them

113

number, that most excellent of intellectual inventions, the combining of letters, [with which one has] memory of everything, that worker who is mother of the Muses. And I was the first one to bring beasts under the yoke to serve the harness, so that they might become the recipients for mortals of the greatest burdens. And I led rein-loving horses beneath the chariot, as an ornament of exceeding luxury. And no one other than I discovered linen-winged vessels of ships that wandered on the sea. Inventions such as these I (miserable wretch that I am) discovered for mankind, though I have myself no cleverness with which to extricate myself from my present suffering. (Aeschylus, *Prometheus Bound* 1:254–57; translation modified)[1]

That storytelling is absent among Prometheus' gifts is not without interest, particularly given how much in Aeschylus and Greek tragedy depends on one's ability or inability to tell a story, and further, one's ability to tell a *good* story. Once "numbers" (*arithmon*)—"the *chiefest* of all discoveries"—are "invented," however, sequential—for example, temporal—arrangements become possible, and narratives along with them. It is, of course, also possible, even likely, that numbers *as* numbers emerged, at least in part, from the possibility of telling stories and thus from sequences embedded in or derived from narratives, although it is impossible to ascertain any given origin or a single story line in this genealogy, to use Nietzsche's term. The story is much *longer*, in temporal and structural terms, than the one that Aeschylus tells us here. For one thing, he does not tell us *how* Prometheus invented numbers.

If narrative can, or must, be related to temporality, then the questioning of classical models of temporality, or interactively, of history, that characterizes much of modern intellectual history must have a profound effect on the question of narrative. By "classical" I mean here temporality, or historicity, *based* on "presence," even if in the form of, or controlling the economy of, difference, exteriority, transformation, becoming—the configurations analyzed by Derrida under the rubric of the metaphysics of presence. Both Husserl's and Heidegger's analyses have been momentous steps in this questioning. In its most radical form, however, this questioning may be seen as beginning with Nietzsche, and from Nietzsche on, proceeding along the lines of the unconscious—among others, in Freud, Bataille, Lacan, Deleuze, and Derrida. The cases of Husserl and Heidegger, or Levinas, who should be mentioned here, are quite different. The unconscious and, by extension, the general economy, rather than being engaged in their texts, are repressed; and if the questioning of metaphysics in Heidegger and Levinas becomes a reinstatement of metaphysics, it is due, at least in part, to this repression of the unconscious.

In this respect, Husserl, Heidegger, and Levinas follow Hegel, the great philosopher of consciousness. In general, once the unconscious takes center stage, the emerging economy of the temporal and historical leads to a radical undermining of Hegel, where both time and history are indissociable from consciousness. This confrontation with Hegel takes a direct form in Bataille and Derrida, although Nietzsche and Lacan make some decisive moves. Hegel, the great Heraclitean, remains a great philosopher of classical temporality and, in particular, history, and the economies of narrative based on them. Hegel is also a great master of the narrative, particularly narratives about time, history, and consciousness, including philosophy. Although many other targets are at stake, Nietzsche's famous great narrative or, complementarily, narrative-antinarrative, in "How the 'True World' Finally Became a Fable: History of an Error," is also constructed against Hegel, as a parody—a very serious one—of Hegel's many long histories and stories.

The metaphysics of presence, restricted economy, in general and specifically as a theory of temporality, enacts a repression of the unconscious, and thus a repression of "repression" itself, insofar as repression constitutes a major part of the economy of the unconscious. The structure of this repression is by no means simple; and the very concept of repression, if it is a concept, is extraordinarily complex. Understanding it demands no less, perhaps more, than *différance* and its general economy.[2] Also, importantly, some general economic effects may be produced differently than by directly engaging the unconscious, as, among others, Heidegger's, or Levinas', or indeed Hegel's case would demonstrate.

It is equally important that a general economy also demands a deconstruction of all restricted economies of the unconscious, beginning, let us say, with Schopenhauer, perhaps Nietzsche's most immediate antithetical precursor. One must continuously engage complementary and mutually inhibiting—interactively heterogeneous and heterogeneously interactive—configurations, such as presence and absence, identity and difference, *the* conscious and the unconscious, continuity and discontinuity, temporality and a-temporality, history and nonhistories, narrative and nonnarrative, and indeed already different complementary interactions within each rubric, as well as more multiple clusters. With these qualifications in mind, however, repression, specifically the repression of *writing*, as Derrida demonstrates exhaustively, has played a major role in the production of the text of philosophy. While the philosophical register of their texts must always be taken into account, *insofar as one's goal is a general economy*, one should be careful to avoid unrigorously displacing Nietzsche's, Derrida's, or Bataille's general economic approaches into the philosophical register. Without the unconscious—or more precisely, without accounting for the effects of the unconscious—a radical "temporality," if such can be the term, cannot be inscribed.

This temporality is in fact so radical that it cannot be inscribed, let alone re-*presented*, including inscribed or represented as (absolutely) *un*representable. For, by virtue of its "unconsciousness," it is related and indeed equivalent to the radical, but again never absolute, general economic loss in representation. One can, therefore, approach this temporality only *obliquely* and within a constraining economy of closure. The latter proposition, furthermore, itself needs a general economic network of inscription; for an analogous, but not identical, proposition can be produced within a restricted economy, specifically a Heideggerian one. A general economy of this temporality would be simultaneously anti-Kantian—prohibiting an absolute difference or exteriority—and anti-Hegelian—prohibiting a reduction of difference in full presence, either being-presence or becoming-presence—while the inscriptions or *textualizations* themselves may be constrained by the closure of both, or other closures of that type.

Derrida, in this context, speaks in "Différance" of "a certain alterity—to which Freud gives the metaphysical name of the unconscious—[and which] is definitively exempt from every process of presentation by means of which we would call upon it to show itself in person" (*Margins*, 20; *Marges*, 21).[3] The formulation occurs in the context of Bataille and general economy, and "at the point of greatest obscurity, . . . the very enigma of *différance*" (*Margins*, 19; *Marges*, 20). The resulting general economy has far-reaching consequences for the question of temporality. Already in Bataille these consequences manifest themselves in such—displaced—concepts as "instance" and "continuum." As Derrida points out in "From Restricted to General Economy," "instance" is not really "instantaneous" any more than "continuum" is really continuous. The general economy of Bataille's "inner experience," in relation to which Bataille specifically discusses "continuum" and "instance," enacts the most radical dislocation of classical temporality, whether Aristotelian, Kantian, Hegelian, Husserlian, or Heideggerian, with the possible exception of Derrida's analysis, where it plays a major role in this context, together with Freud and Heidegger.[4]

In *Of Grammatology*, Derrida argues that "the absolute past," perhaps the only past finally to be discovered "*à la recherche du temps perdu*,"[5] is itself incompatible with the *concept* of presence, while it must replace and comprehend all sign production, and thus all *presence*. Derrida then makes the following bold, but inevitable conclusion: "It is the problem of the deferred [nachträglich] effects of which Freud speaks. The temporality to which he refers cannot be that which lends itself to a phenomenology of consciousness or of presence and one may indeed wonder by what right all that is in question here should still be called time, now, anterior present, delay, etc." (*Of Grammatology*, 67; *De la grammatologie*, 98) The statement, made in the context of Husserl, reflects the profound relations between the unconscious and temporality. Derrida explores these relations in his analysis of Husserl and throughout his discourse. Perhaps the most crucial of Derrida's insights emerges as a conclusion of "*Ousia* and *Grammē*." The essay offers a powerful critique of Heidegger, but it is equally indispensable for Derrida's inscription of *différance*. Derrida writes:

> There may be a difference still more unthought than the difference be-
> tween Being and beings. We certainly can go further toward naming it
> in our language. Beyond Being and beings, this difference, ceaselessly
> differing from and deferring (itself), would trace (itself) (by itself)—this
> *différance* would be the first or last trace if one still could speak, here, of
> origin and end.
>
> Such a *différance* would at once, again, give us to think a writing
> without presence and without absence, without history, without cause,
> without *archia*, without *telos*, a writing that absolutely upsets all dialectics,
> all theology, all teleology, all ontology. A writing exceeding everything
> that the history of metaphysics has comprehended in the form of Aris-
> totelian *grammē*, in its point, in its line, in its circle, in its time, and in its
> space. (*Margins*, 67; *Marges*, 77–78)

Such a *différance* would *give us to think* writing in Derrida's sense, against Heidegger's concept of *thinking*, either in the earlier or in the later works. Here and throughout the essay, Derrida multiply alludes to Heidegger's concepts and language—such as "give us to think (es gibt denken)," gift (Gabe), and related notions—in the process of deconstructing and *rigorously suspending* them, that is, utilizing their deconstructed economy.[6] Hei-degger's "un-thought"—of "what is unthought in what is thought"—re-mains an important move, however, specifically in juxtaposition to Hegel. As Heidegger says: "Our concern is to experience unconcealment as clearing. That is what is unthought in what is thought in the whole history of thought. In Hegel, the need consisted in the satisfaction of thought. For us, on the contrary, the plight of what is unthought in what is thought reigns" (*Heraclitus Seminar*, 162; *Heraklit: Seminar Wintersemester 1966/ 1967*, 260). As decisive and possibly "uncircumventable" as Heidegger's "meditation" is to Derrida, one of Derrida's main conclusions is that there will never be one name, such as Being, or one unnameable, or one un-thought for this difference, not even *différance* itself ("Différance," in *Margins*, 26–27), hence, necessarily, the very *dissemination* of names and concepts—"neither names nor concepts"—in Derrida's own texts.[7]

Can such a difference be *thought*, then, in terms of narrative? Can we do without narrative in *inscribing* this difference? Or, conversely, should we see the latter "as absolutely upsetting all narratology" as well?

The *"Huge* life . . . of things" that Shakespeare invokes so powerfully can *never* be *presented* by a narrative or by anything, not even a play, not even Shakespeare's. In addition, under the conditions of *différance*—which Derrida also describes: "the history of *life* . . . as the *history* of the *grammē* [l'histoire de la vie . . . comme histoire du grammē" (*Of Grammatology*, 84; *De la grammatologie*, 125; emphasis added)—this life can never be "proper" and there can never be an unconditionally due sequence of anything, including "time," "numbers," or "things." Instead, in these transformations "nothing of [life] that doth fade, / But doth suffer a sea change / Into something rich and strange" (*Tempest* I.ii.402–4).

One could also think here of Alfred Hitchcock's movie of the same title, *Rich and Strange*, Hitchcock's own favorite. A great master of narrative, Hitchcock is no less a master of what cannot be narrative, even what upsets narrative radically—which, again, is more radical than upsetting it absolutely—and yet at the same time also that which makes specific narratives possible. In effect, complementary relationships between narrative and nonnarrative might be particularly pronounced in film and its temporal organization. Film narratives are always "rich and strange"; they continuously "suffer a sea change."

It can in fact be suggested that in Hitchcock's economy a similar deconstruction and complementary organization takes place even with respect to the visual and the nonvisual, such as narrative, aspects of film, or other—perhaps all—pairs or clusters through which our engagement with film can be described. In this sense Hitchcock's, let us say, film-writing enacts a radical and radically deconstructive general economy, akin to that of the general economy of writing in Derrida. This economy and its deconstructive cinematic reinscriptions or refigurations—"cinema-scriptions"—dislocates in advance, always already, classical figurations and configurations, even as it *produces* and *complementarizes* them. This productive and complementarizing work, or play, of writing, Derrida's or Hitchcock's, is no less, perhaps more crucial that its dislocating and deconstructive operation. As in Derrida's economy, Hitchcock's film-writing relates to and participates in that (*différance*) that "produces what it forbids, makes possible the very thing that it makes impossible" (*Of Grammatology*, 143; *De la grammatologie*, 206).

Such dislocations, or again productions-dislocations, may take place by splitting and dislocating a given configuration or by complementarizing classical configurations, paired or multiply clustered, and playing them out against each other in mutual deconstructions. The process may engage more specifically cinematic economies or economies operative elsewhere. It may well be that Shakespeare, in many ways "the Hitchcock of the Renaissance," and his "rich and strange" writing machine, self-describing or self-inscribing itself in the passage at issue, remain the best literary example of that type, even given more obvious and much discussed modern or postmodern examples, such as Joyce's writing machines.[8] The profound affinity between Nietzsche and Shakespeare may also be approached from this perspective, which is in fact the perspective of play, general economy, *différance*, writing, complementarity.[9]

While it cannot perhaps be "thought" in narrative terms, the *différance* invoked by Derrida upsets narratology less than it upsets "all dialectics, all theology, all teleology, all ontology." In fact, some narratology assists in upsetting the metaphysics of presence, specifically the metaphysics of history. Narratology, historically speaking, has helped the emergence of the difference at issue in Derrida's statement. One could also suggest that narratology, or a kind of general economic narratology, as theory, might yet tell us a great deal about the sequentiality of time and numbers, particularly once all absolute origins—or terminations—are suspended and the propositions of narratology are in turn suitably modified.[10]

The question of narrative and narratology is already implicated in Derrida's propositions once "the origin" and "the end" are at issue. In accord with the mode and the model of linear temporality that characterizes, indeed defines, all subsequent metaphysics of presence, "the end," along with "the middle," defines "plot" in Aristotle's *Poetics*, the first narratological structure of the first narratologist. The question of narrative is no less implied and no less implicated by the question of history, including teleology, if teleology can be seen as separate from the origin and the end, that is, from the archaeology and teleology of our interpretative and narrative practices. Finally, the question of the line (grammē) always already calls up a plotline of one kind or another. These "plots" or "lines" suggest a rather broad, and in fact, insaturable, historico-political margin of all points and lines of philosophy, in either sense of these words—"geometrical"—presence and continuum—or "logical"—deduction. Geometry, too, as David Hilbert first rigorously demonstrated in *Grundlagen der Geometrie* (1899), is the formal logic of points and lines, and their relations, in which the argument of formal logic can be rigorously presented but, as became clear later (1931), only under the conditions of Gödel's incompleteness theorem.

Thus at issue in Derrida's deconstruction is also the question of linearity and linearization in its broadest sense. In many ways, this deconstruction begins with Derrida's introduction to Husserl's "The Origins of

Geometry" (1962). According to Derrida in *Of Grammatology*, "the 'line' represents only a particular model, whatever might be its privilege. This model *has become* a model and, as a model, it remains inaccessible. If one allows that the linearity of language entails this vulgar and mundane concept of temporality (homogeneous, dominated by the form of the now and the ideal continuous movement, straight or circular), which Heidegger shows to be the intrinsic determining concept of all ontology from Aristotle and Hegel, the meditation upon writing [i.e., also as delinearization] and the deconstruction of the history of philosophy become inseparable" (*Of Grammatology*, 86; *De la grammatologie*, 128). That deconstruction, as we have seen, must also apply to Heidegger's temporality. The latter, finally, is no less, but also no more, vulgar or mundane than Aristotle's or Hegel's; this fact, however, does not exclude the differences and stratifications within the ensemble of the metaphysics of presence.

The undermining of metaphysics and ontology, or of classical historicity and classical narrativity, is thus also a radical undermining of all linearity, from Aristotle, or even before him, up to Heidegger. The first poetics as the first narratology must have been given by Prometheus; at least to Aristotle, this master linearist, along with numbers that can be arranged, as points, along a line—*the* line. They were given along with and by their arithmetics—their rhythms, *rhythmos*[11]—and their geometry or topology. The latter may allow further complications, by way of complex plots in Aristotle, for example, but only within the limits that can still be controlled by the classical linearity, possibly multidimensional, or decidability, or controlled undecidability. For Derrida, the emerging economy has, therefore, a natural relation to writing—which is, among other things, also the drawing of *lines*—and its opposition to the living presence of speech or thought, to which speech is more proximate; and thus to grammatology as a "science" of writing. These relationships—between numbers and writing, writing and memory, writing and art—have been explored by Derrida, beginning in *Of Grammatology*; and they can be played out in the passage from *Prometheus Bound* with which I began here.[12]

Derrida's own ventures into the problematics of the narrative, most specifically in his readings of Maurice Blanchot,[13] explore the complexities arising from this radical questioning of linearity and sequentiality, or more generally what might be called "narrative decidability." "The [undecidable] law of genre" is also the possibility—or what Derrida calls elsewhere "a structural possibility"—of undecidable narratives.[14] Narrative decidability can, or even must, be related to its mathematical—Gödelian—prototype, if only "by analogy" and metaphorically. "Undecidables," as we have seen, are introduced "by analogy" with Gödel in Derrida's reading of Mallarmé in *Dissemination*. One could extend this analogy to the sequential "arithmetics" or, more accurately perhaps, "topology"—a kind of narratological equivalent of the knot theory in topology—of the narrative in Blanchot's texts such as *L'Arrêt de mort* and *La Folie du jour*, which are central to Derrida's analysis.

One might be hesitant to call these texts narratives, or other relevant denominations, including Blanchot's own, such as *récit*, or to assign them any of these rubrics, even *écrit*, and yet keep them all in mind. Blanchot's, Derrida's analysis suggests, *are* "undecidable narratives"—narratives that cannot be "resolved" into linear sequences. The play of their events, to a degree that one can divide them into "events," cannot be presented as transformations of ordered, linear sequences. One can speak of their theory as "gramma-narratology."

They are, let me stress, *radically* undecidable, much as are Gödel's propositions in mathematics. Inside or outside their frames, they cannot be resolved by any intertextuality, rich as it may be, or by any intertext or hypertext, which has been presented lately as a fashionable version of the intertextual. Naturally, the undecidability of even their more or less immediate framing by way of overt or assigned genre denominations, the history of writing, publication of different versions, and so on, is already important enough. This undecidability plays a crucial role in Derrida's analysis, mapping Blanchot's topology of "double-invagination."[15] This undecidability, however, is not the only or the most crucial one, or the most radically undecidable, to the extent that one can contain this seemingly immediate economy of framing. They, too, are, simultaneously, both effects and conditions of a radical, general economic *différance* and undecidability that are at issue here.

Beyond making this and related points directly, if as much by way of a-thesis—as a kind of textual drift—as by way of theses,[16] the very framing of Derrida's own discussions, particularly in "Living On: Border Lines," pursues this "rich and strange" general economy of the undecidable. In part Derrida does so by a complex quasimimesis, a kind of economimesis, of Blanchot's economy of play, although such different aspects of Derrida's analysis may in turn be separated only provisionally. The undecidability of these parerga will not be determined only by the impossibility of their saturation, owing to a more or less linear intertextual expansion, which may easily and quickly approach infinity, although in practice can never reach it. Much more intricate narrative "knots" are at stake, along with the undecidable logic of narrative.[17]

The topology, often extremely complex, of the expanded intertext or hypertext is certainly implicated here; but the economy of narrative undecidability cannot be contained by it. Or rather, it might force us to complicate even further the economy of the intertext and hypertext.[18] Narratology is, no doubt, rich enough for undecidability since it contains the numbers—by virtue of Prometheus' gift, as it were. It is "rich and strange," as is arithmetic. Some, perhaps most, of the structures of narratology—its plots—cannot be decided. This "rich and strange"-ness of narrative undecidability is powerfully explored in Blanchot's plots or antiplots, or however one might or must name them in view of the history of narratology and the profusion of names and concepts, or neither names nor concepts, that it produces.

Aristotle might not have liked such plots, even though, according to his own terms, a good plot is a complex plot. Simple or complex, however, Aristotle's plot is always decidable, particularly with respect to the difference between simple and complex. Aristotelian temporality and Aristotelian narratology are thus connected within the metaphysics of presence. Both are based on the model of the line; and the concepts this model produces, "the concepts of *present, past, and future*, everything in the concepts of time and history [or narrative] which implies evidence of them—the metaphysical concept of time in general—cannot adequately describe the structure of trace" (*Of Grammatology*, 67; *De la grammatologie*, 97). As we have seen, much more radical "complications" are at stake than those that can be offered by any "complex plots" of Aristotelian metaphysics of temporality, or any other metaphysics of temporality, from Plato to Husserl and Heidegger—or by implication, by Aristotelian or other corresponding narrativity. Finally deciding upon it, finally resolving it, is part of the pleasure of tragedy—for the author, the viewer, and the philosopher alike. Derrida's readings of Blanchot may be seen as a joint deconstruction of both Aristotelian narrativity and Aristotelian temporality.[19]

Blanchot's, in his "narratives," is a different "poetics." It is a poetics in which one, as a writer, reader, and theorist, may want in the end to "decide" on undecidables, although one often cannot "decide" between decidability and undecidability. Very radical suspensions are at work, or in play, which offer many new possibilities, not confined only to the *lines*— or plots—of undecidability. In this sense, I suggest, they offer something beyond Blanchot's own, more Heideggerian, theories of narrative or temporality; and the resulting general economy of narrativity may be juxtaposed to it. It may be suggested that in some of Blanchot's later works, perhaps influenced by Derrida and related poststructuralist developments, more radical economies emerge;[20] but they are not, I think, radical enough. In this sense, Derrida, in commenting on Blanchot's theory of narrative in *L'Entretien infini*, displaces and radicalizes it and makes it more general economic ("Living On: Border Lines," 104–7).

By making this claim, one risks sliding into a customary strategy of juxtaposing a more radical Blanchot-writer and a less radical Blanchot-theorist and, more generally, separating theory and practice. Although as often unconscious or subliminal as deliberate, this strategy is among the most persistent ones. It is found in, among others, several of Derrida's approaches to the literary figures—or the literary counterpart in the writings of such figures—and is consistent with his customary practice of using literary texts, rather than deconstructing them, in order to exemplify—play out—the play of *différance, dissemination, writing,* and so forth. In this particular case, however, the approach is, I think, justified, even though the fact that one deals with the same writer increases the complexity of the issue. But then, as with any other "sameness," the same writer is one of a kind of *différance*, for example, *différance* of literature and theory, and their general economy. In this case, the distinction between them, while in some measure provisional and always complex—complementary and general economic—is not only possible but, I maintain, also necessary. The same case obtains with theory and practice, which can be neither unconditionally separated nor unconditionally unified. Blanchot's "literature"—or "theory"—or Derrida's reading of Blanchot's narratives, or Derrida's own matrices, earlier or later, can of course be read otherwise, specifically on the axis of Nietzsche, Heidegger, Bataille, and Derrida. In addition, the very notions or positions with respect to what is more or less radical, or the necessity of the radical, and the relative priority of these thinkers, can differ from infinitesimal to radical. All sorts of agendas, overt or subliminal, operate in "saving the texts of theory," and specifically of philosophy, such as Blanchot's or Heidegger's. For the moment at least, I suggest that Derrida's readings of Blanchot's narratives expose a radical, general economic undecidability and *différance* of narrative.[21]

Obviously, once any theoretical structure or configuration is introduced, a writer can always *play* on it. The author can play with narrative: dislocating and twisting its structure and possibility, or producing undecidable effects. Or the author can further twist a narrative by *playfully* injecting the announced or implicit narratives with elements that cannot be incorporated into a given narrative. Or the author can play, as it were, "beyond" narrative, exploring in the narrative that which is not narrative and undermines the narrative. These possibilities have by now become a standard topic—*play*ground—of both narrative production and narratology. The latter two terms are not easily distinguishable, of course, at least in one direction: modern narratives, such Blanchot's, are themselves explorations of the problematics of narrative. To be fair, the arguments of narratologists are often—in a certain sense always—stories, narratives about the narrative; but, to be perhaps a bit unfair, this aspect is rarely their strongest feature. At its best, modern narratology is an exploration of the conditions of the possibility of narrative, rather than only of the "logic" of narrative. This narrative logic is by no means suspended; it remains an important field, acquiring new possibilities and dimensions as a result of further theoretical exploration.

Blanchot's constructions, his *undecidables*, are brilliant achievements. Such non- or antinarratives open up a theoretically general exploration into what makes undecidable narratives possible, and they are extremely difficult to construct. It is also difficult to construct undecidable propositions of logic or to prove existing propositions to be undecidable. What makes undecidable narratives possible, moreover, is often what makes all narratives possible. Thus, such explorations of narrative undecidability as Blanchot's, or the undermining or "upsetting" of narrative, history, and temporality characterizing recent history, inject narratology with new force, rather than destroy its theoretical base. This expansion has been amply demonstrated during the last decade, including in the field of historical studies.[22]

The undermining or upsetting at issue here is indissociable from the social and political efficacity of narrative, or of all interpretation. The psychological, or psychoanalytic, dimensions of *différance* are essential to its "logic." These are hardly apolitical, either—a line can be drawn between Marx and Freud in either direction, from the Oedipal politics of classical psychoanalysis to the political unconscious of class struggles. It might yet be the political that best exemplifies the new logic at issue, impossible and playful at once. "An unthought-of difference" is also the logic of the political. For example, it can be considered in the context of Lyotard's work, which has pursued over the years the complexity of relationships between the question of difference and the question of the political. It may be suggested, however, that particularly in *The Postmodern Condition* or even in *The Differend*, the economy of the political that is developed via the multiplicity of the narrativizations and the deconstruction of grand narratives and metanarratives, falls short of providing a kind of engagement of undecidable narratives or the complements of the narrative, for example, which would lead to a general economy.[23] Can one comprehend the problematics of narrative without them? From the perspective of the present analysis, the political or social theories of narrative would be deficient insofar as they bypass the problematics at issue.

Narratives will not disappear. Often we cannot do without them. Otherwise, narratives not would be possible in the first place. Nor can one prohibit the use of narratives in theory, such as narratology, or in practice, including political practice; narratives, used well, are powerful and attractive instruments. Nevertheless, at times we *must* do without them, both without narratives and without the concept or category of narrative; for we always seem to need something besides narrative. Narrative always possesses an irreducible nonnarrative supplement. Under these conditions, narrative cannot be *the*, or even *a*, fundamental category. No category can be fundamental, of course. Under the same conditions, however, the narrative might be as fundamental, as possible and necessary *a* category, as any category can be. Perhaps the category of 'category' itself, assuming there is one, is less fundamental, less necessary, than the category of 'narrative.' Both categories, however, are often, perhaps always, mutually implicated; this mutual implication is certainly found in Aristotle, the father of both. Or, as Nietzsche pointed out in relation to Kant, all such categories, in the end, are impossible (*Beyond Good and Evil*, 19). One would have to ask instead, why and when, and how, they are, *conditionally*, possible or necessary; what constitutes fundamentality or categorization; and what would enable narrative to be comprehended under the condition of this general economy. Thus, a different—more differential, more transformational—structure must be put into play.

Play-Game

> "The play's the thing"
> —Shakespeare, *Hamlet* II.ii.605

But what would such a structure be, particularly given that it cannot be a single, unitary structure and that it may not even be a 'structure'? What would be its relation to the interminably disseminating array of Derrida's "neither terms nor concepts" such as *différance*, *dissemination*, and so on, already designed to approach this radical difference—"the unthought of difference"? Among the multiple dimensions of the general economy of this difference, I want to consider those related, via Nietzsche, to the idea of play. As I suggested at the outset, the Nietzschean, or post-Nietzschean, reconfigurations at issue in this study may be seen as a conjunction of the economy of play and the general economy. "Play" is a crucial aspect of Bataille's matrix: *Inner Experience* opens with Nietzsche and play. It is equally irreducible in Derrida's general economy, which, again via Nietzsche, defines play as follows: "One could call *play* [*jeu*] the absence of the transcendental signified as limitlessness of play, that is to say as the trembling [or unhinging: *ébranlement*] of onto-theology and metaphysics of presence" (*Of Grammatology*, 50; *De la grammatologie*, 73; translation modified).

It is not only play that enables Derrida's approach toward *différance*. Nothing is assured—or *insured*—in the economics of *différance*. For Nietzsche, there can never be a *"sure play"*; one must "play without security." Thus it cannot be *only* play, or any single name or concept—play, —*différance*, or whatever. First, then, one must enact a destruction or deconstruction of the previous systems and regimes. There is much to destroy, even if one thinks more in terms of Heideggerian or Derridean "style" than in terms of more radical Nietzschean style, or Bataille's "trembling" positioned perhaps closer to Nietzsche. Second, however, whether by way of recomprehension alongside deconstruction or after de(con)struction, one must also approach . . . What? Such is the question. Play, difference, "the unthought of"? There will be no unique or single name. These structures may not be unique, either; they are in fact always *not*—never quite and altogether—what they are. And in the first place, they are *not*; and this erasure of "being" must be different from Heidegger's putting Being under erasure.

Play nevertheless remains indispensable to the economy of *différance*; and it has historically been crucial, at least since Nietzsche,[24] to nearly all that is at stake here and on the scene of modern theory in general. The history of the idea of play is much longer, however, perhaps as long as any history, human or maybe not only human. Indeed, one might suggest, with caution but with sufficient justification, that we have played ever since and indeed before we have been human; and one would be reluctant to claim any unconditional demarcation. We may not always have had a *conception* of play. But as Nietzsche brilliantly grasped, play has been put into play at least since Heraclitus. Whether it is play or "limitlessness"— that is, the absence of the transcendental signified or signifier—that is more crucial to Derrida's co-definition of play, the critical and deconstructive resources of the idea of play are immense, leading, among other things, to a general economy of play relating to the (de)formations such as *différance*, conceived as neither term nor concept.[25]

From this perspective, too, the question of play may well be crucial to the juxtaposition, proceeding via Nietzsche, of deconstruction and metaphysics, including, finally, in Heidegger. As we have seen, in reference to Heidegger one can speak of the juxtaposition of two deconstructions. Beginning with *Being and Time*, the thematics of play continues to reemerge in the margins of Heidegger's text. Derrida invokes it throughout his readings of Heidegger, particularly in his most recent writings, specifically in *Of Spirit*.[26] In *Of Grammatology*, Derrida concludes his paragraph on play as follows: "It is therefore *the game of the world* [Nietzsche] that must be first thought; before attempting to understand all the forms of the play in the world" (*Of Grammatology*, 50; *De la grammatologie*, 73). He also suggests that these themes in Heidegger's meditation must refer back to Nietzsche (*Of Grammatology*, 326 n. 14; *De la grammatologie*, 73). "The game of the world" is the same "unthought of" play that appears in the end of "*Ousia* and *Grammē*." As we have seen, this play—*différance*—is also "thought" of there *as* "unthought of" by Heidegger. The (general) economy of this play and this "unthought of" is therefore radically different from the "unthought of" in Heidegger—one of Heidegger's favorite "thoughts" on which Derrida *plays*. The word *jeu*—play and game—is thus twice underlined by Derrida in this passage. As elsewhere in *Of Grammatology* and related early texts, Heideggerian and Nietzschean themes are related here through the deconstruction *and* the comprehension of Heidegger by way of Nietzsche.

By the same token, all of these references already imply or implicate the thematic of the difference between the human and the animal world (*Welt*). Derrida's main reference, here as well as in *Of Spirit*, is Heidegger's essay "The Thing [Das Ding]." To a great extent, the analysis in *Of Spirit* may also be seen as an elaboration of this question of "the game of the world." Indeed, Derrida relates the very question of the erasure of Being in Heidegger to the question of the animal world (*Welt*). From the opening paragraph of "On Truth and Lie in the Extra-moral Sense" and throughout his writing, Nietzsche playfully, yet also very seriously, deploys the opposition of the human and the animal, which has been crucial to the history of metaphysics and philosophy. This opposition figures in the relations among the spirit (*esprit*) of play and the play of spirit—*esprit* and *Geist*; the world of spirit, particularly *Geist*, and the spirit of the world (*Welt*); the world of play and the play of the world. Bataille's discourse remains a decisive reference in this context as well, particularly the opening of

Inner Experience, Bataille's elaborations of these themes often proceeding via Nietzsche. Not surprisingly, the concept of play plays an equally decisive role throughout Derrida's reading of Bataille in "From Restricted to General Economy" and in most elaborations around the general economy, including on Kant in "Economimesis."

It also follows, however, that not just any play would suffice. Throughout the history of philosophy, the idea of play has been utilized, often against the radical play at issue here, specifically in Kant, Hegel, and Heidegger. In Heidegger's case, it is, as we have seen, "the play of transformations" that "the more richly it unfolds, the more strictly it is held (within the domain governed) by a hidden rule," which is also "the highest law" (*The Question of Being*, 104–5). "The Thing" (in *Poetry, Language, Thought*) would in fact suggest that the thing in Heidegger's sense is this play or that this play is the thing. Shakespeare's usage is different, of course, although Heidegger would not necessarily see it thus. The issue is how such a play is governed, controlled—"played out"—how the law of the economy of this play is conceived. "The highest law" and "the hidden rule" are what one needs to undermine or deconstruct, but also to recomprehend by way of a more radical economy, difference, and play as indicated by the word "limitlessness" in Derrida's formulation.

Such an economy enacts a juxtaposition of *controlled* play of philosophy as the metaphysics of presence and *limitless* Nietzschean play and of the two laws of difference and transformation they respectively offer. Possibly reaching the limits of the classical vision in general, Heidegger's conception can be seen as a culmination of controlled play, although both Kant's and Hegel's notions, as well as Schiller's, are extraordinary examples of play. Hegel's dialectic is play—the play of differences, the play of transformations, theoretical and political play. But the play at stake in the question of general economy cannot be dialectic. Radical play may and often must be related, constructively or de(con)structively, to dialectic and particularly to Hegel, more so in Derrida and Bataille than in Nietzsche. In all these cases, however, the *general* economy of play radically undermines dialectic and *Aufhebung*. Further articulating the general economy of play as Nietzschean, Derrida writes on Lévi-Strauss:

> Turned toward the lost or impossible presence of the absent origin, this structuralist thematic of broken immediacy is therefore the saddened, *negative*, nostalgic, guilty, Rousseauistic side of the thinking of play whose other side would be the Nietzschean *affirmation*, that is, the joyous affirmation of the play of the world and of the innocence of becoming, the affirmation of a world of signs without fault, without truth, and without

origin which is offered to an active interpretation. *This affirmation then determines the noncenter otherwise than as loss of the center.* And it plays without security. For there is a *sure* play: that which is limited to the *substitution* of *given* and *existing, present,* pieces. In absolute chance, affirmation also surrenders itself to *genetic* indetermination, to the *seminal* adventure of the trace. (*Writing and Difference*, 292; *L'Écriture et la différence*, 427)[27]

The structuralist thematic at issue here is, or is functionally analogous or isomorphic to, the thematic of classical narratology as well. Derrida's statement, let us keep in mind, dates to about 1967; in narratology, although perhaps not in structuralism, much has happened since. If "in [the] delineation of *différance* everything is strategic and adventurous," then the play enacting and enacted by these strategies in turn enacts a radical transformation of the *concept* of play. Derrida writes:

Strategic because no transcendent truth present outside the field of writing can govern theologically the totality of the field. Adventurous because this strategy is not a simple strategy in the sense that strategy orients tactics according to a final goal, a *telos*' or theme of domination, a mastery and ultimate reappropriation of the development of the field. Finally, a strategy without finality, what might be called blind tactics, or empirical wandering if the value of empiricism did not itself acquire its entire meaning in its opposition to philosophical responsibility. If there is a certain wandering in the tracing of *différance*, it no more follows the lines of philosophical-logical discourse than that of its symmetrical and integral inverse, empirical-logical discourse. The concept of *play* keeps itself beyond this opposition, announcing, on the eve of philosophy and beyond it, the unity of chance and necessity in calculations without end. (*Margins*, 7; *Marges*, 7)

The juxtaposition of two sets of strategies should not lead to a *simple* or unequivocal dismissal of the classical strategies, or even of the *absolute* principles, grounds, origins, or centers to which Derrida refers, perhaps with Hegel's Absolute Knowledge as the most important reference. These absolute principles must be reconfigured as *local*—conditional—formations, and thereby *comprehended* along with the inscription of *différance*. They are also to be utilized wherever necessary, including in the undermining of their own claims, functioning, and power. Radical as they may be, Derrida's "new" concept or "neither a term nor a concept" of *différance* and the ensuing (re)configuration of play-game must depend on the old concepts of play. Derrida sees in *différance*, which is "neither a *word* nor a *concept*," "the juncture—rather than the summation—of what has been most decisively inscribed in the thought of . . . our 'epoch' ("Différance," in *Speech and Phenomena*, 130; "La 'Différance,' *Bulletin de la Société Française de la Philosophie*, 74).[28] Derrida refers here to, among others, Nietzsche, Saussure, Freud, Levinas, and Heidegger. Thus, *différance* is also a "story" or a textual play in Derrida's sense of *writing*, in which a part of the history of modern philosophy is reinscribed and recomprehended. But conversely, *différance, writing, play*, and so on could not be inscribed or conceptually articulated without these discourses and the "old" philosophemes, although they, too, depend on other histories, different from philosophy. "The play of chance and necessity" could thus be traced, via Lucretius and Epicurus, to Democritus, and "calculation without end" to Freud's concept of interminable analysis. All these names, along with Heidegger and Lacan, are brought together—by chance and by necessity—and *played* out, between necessity and chance, in Derrida's "My Chances/*Mes Chances*: A Rendezvous with Some Epicurean Stereophonies" (in *Taking Chances*).

The problems that are at issue invite a more complex logic, however: the logic of theory *as* the logic of play. This logic—which, with Nietzsche, one can call Heraclitean or Dionysian—may be more *playful*, but it is also in the end more serious. For, as Nietzsche would say, it is only then, alongside this playfulness, that "*great seriousness [der grosse Ernst]*" begins—and "*tragedy begins*" as well (*The Gay Science*, sec. 382, p. 347).[29] Only by looking "at life through the optics of play" does a real seriousness begin for Nietzsche. Laughter, however, cannot be excluded from this logic, as logic as play, the logic of laughter and play against the logic of dialectic. Nietzsche's and Bataille's laughter, at Socrates and Hegel, or Kant—in short at philosophy, from Socrates to Heidegger and beyond—is also a juxtaposition of laughter and play to dialectic and philosophy, or rather a complex complementarity that contains enough classical logic, perhaps more than philosophy does. A more radical difference at issue here demands a conception of play-game that will offer a different "logic." According to Nietzsche, such a "logic" cannot be *logically* arrived at; but it can be "guessed," in Heraclitean fashion, "artistically."[30] Such a conception should eventually enable one to avoid the metaphysical logic, be it formal or transcendental, that is based on absolute truth, origin, center, and so on—the metaphysics of presence, in however complex and hidden a manner the latter might appear.

The difference between the economy of play in Nietzsche and in Kant's *The Critique of Judgement* becomes particularly important in this context. As we have seen, Kant allocates the concept of play a significant place. Among other things, play demarcates and formalizes the concept of the beautiful, the beautiful arts, or even the economy of the Kantian sublime, which is closer to a general economy and which may, as I indicated, be particularly important in the context of the question of narrative. Kant's demarcation includes the crucial *separation* of aesthetic—*disinterested*—play both from practical, including political, reason and from conceptual and philosophical *reason.*

As opposed to this Kantian "suspension" of life under the conditions of play, Nietzschean play and affirmation remain indissociable from the play—and affirmation—of life. Nietzsche writes in the later "Attempt at a Self-Criticism": "—before a much older, a hundred times more demanding, but by no means colder eye which also has not become a stranger to the very task which this audacious book [*The Birth of Tragedy*] dared to tackle for the first time: *to look at science through the optics of the artist, but at art in that of life"* (*The Birth of Tragedy and The Case of Wagner*, 19; *Die Geburt der Tragödie, KSA* 1:14; translation modified, Nietzsche's emphasis).

For Nietzsche there is nothing disinterested in the play of life; and there is no suspension of life in play, least of all in art.[31] Under all conditions, however, Nietzschean play is the play of the *affirmation* of life even in its serious and indeed most tragic aspects. For Nietzsche, as we have just seen, play is also *limitless* play, as opposed to Kant, for whom play always remains a *proper*, in every sense of the term, and properly controlled play. It is, in fact, precisely *the* proper play controlled by the highest law—or at least the proper play that should always attempt to conform to the highest law—and the metaphysics of the proper it enacts that are defined in Heidegger, as considered earlier.[32]

In a characteristically Nietzschean reversal, the economy of play emerges as exterior to both philosophy and the practical or political reason of philosophy and is returned to *life* and the *practice* of life, psychological and political—"*to look at science through the optics of the artist, but at art in that of life.*" "Moral" would not be a Nietzschean term. The moral and the ethical—"the genealogy of morals"—are instead reconfigured in this reversal, an issue I shall discuss in the next chapter.

The situation is somewhat more complicated in Kant, although, as I suggested in Chapter 2, in principle it obeys this law of separation and Nietzsche certainly saw it as doing so. What I say here might be seen as referring mostly to the analysis of the beautiful as formal, disinterested, and so on, to which Nietzsche refers in *On the Genealogy of Morals*, where, after juxtaposing Kant, and then Schopenhauer, and Stendhal—"a genuine [true] 'spectator' and artist— . . . who once called the beautiful *une promesse de bonheur* [a promise of happiness] [ein wirklicher 'Zuschauer' und Artist gemacht hat—Stendhal, der dass Schöne einmal une promesse de bonheur nennt]," Nietzsche offers one of his extraordinary perceptions:

> If our aestheticians are never weary of asserting in Kant's favor that, under the spell of beauty, one can *even* view undraped female statues "without interest," one may well laugh a little at their expense: the experiences of *artists* on this tricky point are more "interesting," and Pygmalion was in any event *not* necessarily an "unaesthetic man." Let us think the more highly of the innocence of our aestheticians which is reflected in such arguments; let us, for example, credit it to honor of Kant that he has to teach on the subject of peculiar properties of the sense of touch with the naïveté of a country parson! (*On the Genealogy of Morals and Ecce Homo*, 104; *KSA* 5:347; translation modified)[33]

The uncontrolled—interminable and indeterminate, *limitless*—play is seen by Nietzsche as comprehending the controlled transformations and indeterminacies of philosophy. Such play cannot be controlled by Nietzsche's texts, either. No more than any other text can his calculate the undecidable, or decode or encode the uncodifiable; nor does it want to. It also knows that it cannot do so, although it does not know fully either what it knows and does not know.[34] As always, Nietzsche's reversal is much more than a reversal. Art, particularly that of the Greeks and Shakespeare, becomes a celebration, an affirmation, of *life*—"of the play of the world and of the innocence of becoming"—even under the conditions of the greatest tragedy. As a result, the Heraclitean idea of play enables Nietzsche to offer a powerful critique of both Aristotle's and Kant's aesthetics.

In order to demonstrate how the idea of play in Nietzsche functions, I shall turn now to one of Nietzsche's early and less discussed works, his lectures on *Philosophy in the Tragic Age of the Greeks*—extraordinary in its own right, but also consistent with many of the later, and the best, of Nietzsche's texts. It is Heraclitus who appears in Nietzsche's works, proclaiming "the affirmation of the play of the world and of the innocence of becoming" invoked by Derrida. For "what he [Heraclitus] saw, the teaching of *law in becoming* and of *play in necessity*, must be seen from now on in all eternity. He raised the curtain on this greatest of all dramas [Das, was er schaute, *die Lehre vom Gesetz im Werden und vom Spiel in der Nothwendigkeit*, muß von jetzt ab ewig geschaut werden: er hat von diesem größten Schauspiel den Vorhang aufgezogen]" (sec. 8, p. 68; "Die Philosophie im tragischen Zeitalter der Griechen," *KSA* 1:835). Somewhere between the drama—play—and the story, Heraclitean play and becoming must emerge. One is compelled to recall at this point that the Greek meaning of *theoria* is also 'spectacle,' the etymology that Nietzsche appears to have in mind and to play upon consistently.

Although, as is clear from the preceding analysis, much more is at stake in the question of play, it seems fitting to invoke Nietzsche's early insights in the context of the question of narrative. At issue in Nietzsche's discussion of Anaxagoras is also the origin, which is the central problem, as it must be in the context, and the evolution of the world—the universe. At issue is ultimate history—how one can, and cannot, tell the story of this and thus any history, perhaps also how one can—and cannot—tell any story. Nietzsche concludes his analysis of Anaxagoras by locating the inevitable "blind spot" and returning everything to Heraclitus, or perhaps to himself. He certainly returns everything to the idea of "play-game," to "just gaming":

> At this point we might well ask what notion back then so suddenly befell the *nous* to impel a random material particle, chosen from that enormous number of points and to revolve it in a whirling dance, and why this notion did not befall it earlier! To this, Anaxagoras would say, *Nous* has the privilege of free random choice [Willkür]; it may once start at random; it depends on itself, whereas all other things are determined from the outside. *Nous* has no duty and hence no purpose or goal which it would be forced to pursue. Having once started with that motion, and having set itself a goal, that was nothing but . . . the answer is difficult. Heraclitus would supplement ". . . a *game* [*ein Spiel*]." (Sec. 19, p. 112; *KSA* 1:869; translation modified)

"The answer is difficult . . . "—it is "a game." Who begins it? Who plays? "What differs? Who differs? What is *différance*? [Qu'est-ce qui diffère? Qui diffère? Qu'est-ce que la *différance*?]"—Derrida will ask in "Différance" (*Margins*, 14; *Marges*, 15). Derrida's answer will also in effect be "It is a game," referring via Nietzsche and Heidegger to Heraclitus (*Margins*, 22). Indeed, as Derrida says elsewhere: "It is to Heraclitus that I refer myself in the last analysis."[35] It is nonetheless a very serious game, often more serious than the high seriousness of philosophy. Once these questions are posed, one's "logic" demands the "play" defined by Derrida "as the absence of the transcendental signified." Nietzsche announces this kind of play here perhaps for the first time; and he develops it ever more forcefully and ever more playfully in his later works.

For Nietzsche, then, Heraclitean play responds to or defines the Greeks' and the philosophers' problem. Under these conditions and within this closure, Heraclitus' "It is a game" is the best that the Greeks could do.

It may well be, however, that this is also the best that we can do, insofar as this formulation suggests to us the logic of radical difference and radical multiplicity. It also suggests complementarity between all notions involved, such as chance and necessity, or play and narrative. Nietzsche ends—almost ends—his analysis as follows: "This [a game] seems to me to have always been the final solution or answer, hovering on the lips of the Greeks" (sec. 19, p. 112; *KSA* 1:869; translation modified).

Nietzsche's actual conclusion is in praise of Anaxagoras and is also well worth citing: "Anaxagoras assumed an arbitrary [willkürlich] *nous*, dependent on itself alone. What he especially esteemed in it was its quality of randomness, hence its ability to operate unconditionally, undeterminatedly, guided by neither causes nor goals" (sec. 19, p. 117; *KSA* 1:872; translation modified).

Nietzsche's propositions introduce structures that, while powerfully enabling theoretical production, also constrain it. Along the way, a certain transformation of our conceptual closure is enacted, particularly insofar as these propositions are read, as to a degree they must be, as Nietzsche's own, here and especially in his subsequent works. This transformation need not, and does not, mean an absolute departure from the old closures; nevertheless, it is a radical enough departure. This transformation is also dependent on theories and histories exterior—at times radically exterior—to philosophy, but not absolutely discontinuous from it. Here also absolute departures are not radical enough.

One of the major aspects of this transformed closure would be the fundamental deferral of the first "origin," which eventually leads to the introduction of *trace* and *différance* in Derrida. As a *structure*, this deferral is clearly of major importance to the question of narrative. Derrida's analysis of narrative might in fact be seen as a further elaboration of this thematics of the necessary, or *structural*, suspension of absolute origin. As a rigorous suspension, such a suspension does not eliminate origins, but instead articulates and constrains the whole thematics differently. Against—and re-delimiting—the "old" closure of origin, a "new" *double* closure emerges: the closure of the necessity of origins and the closure prohibiting absolute origins. Once we want to speak about origins, and we cannot avoid speaking about them and in their terms, we *always* have to suspend the first origin. Of course, at times we do not need to speak about origins or must actively repress, forget, or evade the thematics of origin. To an extent, this active forgetfulness may play a role in the inscription of nonoriginary *différance*, which, as we recall, is also never one thing, and is always already *dissemination*, including of "itself." Nor is it ever "it-self," either. Whether one speaks of the origin of language, as in Rousseau, of the origin of geometry, as in Husserl, which are two great cases specifically analyzed by Derrida, or of any other origin, the suspension of the first origin is rigorously, *structurally* necessary. Once we *must* speak of *an* origin, we *cannot* speak of *the* origin. However one thinks, speaks, writes, textualizes, configures, or reconfigures *the* origin, it always comes to "The answer is difficult." Heraclitus and Nietzsche intimated as much. They said, "It's a game": this is perhaps still as far as we can go. At this moment in the history of theory, however, we do "know" or are compelled to conclude, first, that the play is of chance and necessity, and second, that the calculus of this play is interminable.

Heraclitus thus offers to Nietzsche the resources of the idea of play—his "rare invention"—however metaphysical these resources might be in Heraclitus or in the other theories and texts on which Nietzsche depends. There could have been no other resources for Nietzsche. For us perhaps there are, *now, critical* or *deconstructive* resources—the resources of transformed closure or closures of theory—such as Nietzschean or Derridean ones, among others. Even these might, and according to Derrida must, still remain, at least to a degree, within the closure of metaphysics. But the closure itself might have been transformed as a result, and the degree and the structure of our dependence on it are different as well. This transformation also concerns the very idea of metaphysical closure: one transforms the closure by introducing the very idea of the closure of metaphysics and philosophy. This idea in fact "creates" this closure as *closure*, insofar as it (re)configures the functioning of metaphysics via the economy of closure.

Heraclitus also offers Nietzsche the strategies—the "logic"—of thinking *play*, the ways of arriving at such a conception. Perhaps most powerfully, Nietzsche uses the idea of play in "guessing" Heraclitus' reply to Anaximander, if it can still be called a reply, for Heraclitus neither merely avoids nor exactly replies to the questions about the logic of becoming and the many. Instead Heraclitus replays them in a different—what?—"logic" or perhaps *play*, conceived as a limit of artistic philosophy. Nietzsche offers his great guess after exploring and perhaps exhausting the possibilities for "becoming" and "the many" that could be offered by metaphysics—"dialectical detective work . . . and calculations":

> These are un-Heraclitean loop-holes and aberrant paths: once again he proclaims, "The one is the many." The many perceptible qualities are neither eternal substances nor phantasms of our senses (Anaxagoras is later to imagine the former, Parmenides the latter); they are neither rigid autocratic Being nor fleeting semblance wandering through the human

mind. The third possibility, the only one remaining for Heraclitus, cannot be guessed by dialectic detective work or by quasi-calculations: for what he here invented is a rarity even in the sphere of mystic incredibilities and unexpected cosmic metaphors—The world is the *game* Zeus plays, or, expressed in the terms of physics, of the fire with itself, only in this sense is one at the same time the many. (Sec. 6, p. 58; *KSA* 1:827–28; translation modified)

Heraclitus' invention is the triumph of an artistic philosopher over a dialectician. In the end, it is a triumph over Socrates, as Nietzsche himself must have seen it. And if this is a tremendous achievement for Heraclitus, it is no less so for Nietzsche himself—"Nietzsche contra Socrates." For one does need an "intuitive" leap beyond classical logic toward a "logic" that for now cannot be sufficiently articulated. Like 'artistic,' 'intuitive,' under these conditions, is not an unconditional term. Its operation must be in turn recomprehended general economically and multiply complementarily with its various counterparts.

It is as if children were to play games without fully articulating their conceptions or rules before they could be sufficiently formalized—by them or by an outside observer—and made, for example, into a *game* for children. The conception of play must be itself configured through this law: one *plays* with "play." Placing Zeus in this position of a child playing games is itself a perception of great audacity on Heraclitus' part. In a profound and beautiful insight, Bataille says that "laughter, drunkenness, sacrifice and poetry, eroticism itself, subsist autonomously, in a reserve, inserted into a sphere, *like children in a house*. Within their limit they are minor sovereigns who cannot contest the empire of activity" (*L'Expérience intérieure*, 239).[36]

Games, however, including games for children, are also a serious matter. They are certainly "a matter very serious for children" themselves.[37] I refer, however, not so much to comprehending play, including children's games, by way of some "serious" category, such as "event" or "narrative," that is opposed to the conception of play. Rather, a reverse, or indeed double move is at issue: not only to introduce "seriousness" into play and our approach to the question of play, but also to introduce play, or chance, and related opposites or complements of the serious, into the serious—as a part of the general economic unconscious of the serious. Hence a broader role given to play at every level of theoretical analysis in no way precludes approaching "serious matters," a notion that, even within classical theories, is permeated with ambiguity. At the very least, the seriousness of philosophy—specifically in Kant, Hegel, and Heidegger—

and of other forms of theorizing continuously resorts to the metaphor of play; but many other theoretical and practical, including political, forms of dependence on play can be found there. Perhaps in part by way of repressing this dependence, philosophy rarely treats play seriously; nor are its serious treatments playful enough.

Freud, however, in one of his most famous *treatments*, takes his grandson's play most seriously in *Beyond the Pleasure Principle*. The game of *fort:da* (there:here)—of throwing and recovering, or "hunting for" small toys—has become perhaps the most famous child's play ever, and Freud's account the most famous narrative of child's play. The narrative and the *scene* of *fort:da* echo with the resonances of literary and theatrical prototypes. "Poets were there before me," Freud often said. The *scene* comes, and comes *as* a narrative, from Shakespeare's play, unlikely not to be known to Freud. In *Coriolanus* we encounter "the father's son" playing a kind of "hunting" *fort:da*: "O' my word, the father's son. I'll swear 'tis a very pretty boy. O' my troth, I looked upon o' Wednesday half an hour together. H' as such a confirm'd countenance! I saw him run after a gilded butterfly, and when he caught it, he let it go again, and after it again, and over and over he comes, and up again; catch'd it again. Or whether his fall enrag'd him, or how 'twas, he did so set his teeth and tear it—O, I warrant, how he mammock'd it!" (I.iii.57–65). Appearing early in the play, the game of "the father's son" "prefigures" the father's "game" with Rome no less than, as Derrida shows in his "To Speculate—on 'Freud,'" "the grandfather's grandson" mirrors the game Freud plays in the essay, and finally perhaps the politics of psychoanalysis as well. Certainly, a very serious politics, such as at stake in *Coriolanus*, may be "just gaming." "Just *gaming*," however, is also *"just* gaming," the play of justice.[38]

The economy of play so emerging—"the game of the world"—will thus acquire crucial political dimensions, specifically in the context of the question of narrative. As I discussed in the preceding chapter, this economy would thus have to be related to an economy of the political, although not as political economy in its traditional sense as a *restricted economy*. Instead, a general economy of the political is needed. The radical, irreducible multiplicity—which is *play* in the present sense—of the political or of the historical implies that the logic of the political cannot obey the logic of narrative or *only* the logic of the narrative. "Stories" are never enough to account for politics and its theater—its performance and its performative. If all history might or even must be seen as political, then it is not only that "history" can no longer be seen as history in the classical sense, but that it must also be replaced by a story—a pluralized and metaphorized narrative. A general economy of history, to be discussed in Chapter 6, can no longer see history only along narrative lines, however pluralized. It would have to be *played* out differently. This is why *différance* must also imply a radical undermining of Hegelian historicity and history, History with a capital *H*—Hegel's master narrative.

The "logic" of play therefore enables one to approach more effectively the problems of the historical, the political, and the narrative. The Nietzschean conception of play could be, and to an extent has been developed into, a different and more effective theoretical economy of all three. Let me recapitulate, briefly, why this may be the case.

First, rhetorically, given the history of the concept, the idea of play or game would render necessary a broader, perhaps even maximal "play" of different theoretical possibilities. The closure of its "openness" is a powerful instrument of theory.

Second, the concept of play offers analysis a fundamental or *structural* configuration—a *structure* or a set of structures, manifesting itself as a series of *effects*. Several economies accounting for such effects can be mentioned here, even though some of them are "reductions" of *radical* play, are restricted economies: mathematical game theory; Wittgenstein's language games; children's play; the play of chance and necessity in *différance*; and a variety of recent—and some old—aesthetic theories. The Democritean possibility of accounting for chance, or rather of *allowing* chance to enter the economy, is perhaps the major appeal of play or game as a theoretical paradigm manifesting itself in, among others, Nietzsche, Freud, Saussure, Bataille, Deleuze, Lyotard, and Derrida. Among other things, the "naive" logic of play, the "against-logic" and "against-dialectic" of play, may thus be set to deconstruct and recomprehend that the logical and dialectic *understanding* and *knowledge* of philosophy are not good enough. Hegel, according to Bataille, made himself "blind to chance"; this blindness is perhaps necessary for the existence of philosophy and determines its closure. It is a far more complex question whether this blindness is also responsible for philosophers' insights, specifically Hegel's. The best "logic" demands a 'naivete'—that is to say, a highly nontrivial way of thinking—of play. But it also—complementarily—demands all the power of classical logic.

One must stress, however, that even though we can meaningfully speak of a certain, indeed more comprehensive, *logic* or theory and an articulation achieved by its means, we *cannot* speak of a complete or full articulation. Otherwise we would not depart from classical and in particular Hegelian logic, arguably the most comprehensive classical logic, which may become necessary under the conditions of such an assumption. The belief in or an assumption of such a fullness—full presence—in articulation, actual and potential, human or divine, is among the major differences between the logic of restricted economy and the logic of general economy. The latter is "by definition" a logic of radical incompleteness, a radical loss in re-presentation. One might even describe this post-Gödelian incompleteness by borrowing an idea from Aristotle, the father of logic, although there are always Plato and Socrates, or Parmenides, before him. Aristotle's "Logic" was the model for Euclid and thus, in the end, for Gödel. The idea, however, comes, from the *Poetics* rather than the *Logic*. Such is "the tragic flaw" of logic—its overabundance: there is just too much of it; it is too rich.

"Play," then, is something that eventually might make sense, might acquire a "logic" or a "logical" and theoretical articulation. However strange it may be, however much of a rarity, or however naive or incredible, this logic is better and less contradictory than philosophical "logics," "dialectics," or other available metaphysical forms of "calculus." As the complementary logic of general economy, the logic of play is also more comprehensive in the sense that it differently *comprehends*, reinscribes, reconfigures classical logic and its major developments, such as dialectics, formal logic, the Oedipal logic of psychoanalysis, and other classical theories, or the major narrative repertoire of intellectual history.

This recomprehension or reconfiguration enacts, among other things, a certain *correspondence* principle, analogous to the relationships between classical and quantum physics introduced by Bohr: at moments or junctures when classical logic works, it is accommodated by the "logic" of play, or more generally a restricted economy, including dialectic, by a general economy.

The relations between the rules of a controlled or limited play and the rules—or un-rules—of unlimited—"limitless"—play could be considered from this perspective, for example, the rules of narrative as comprehended within a certain play, such as in Blanchot's narratives. This emphasis on play does not mean that an *unconditional* primacy of "play" over "rules," or any unconditional primacy, would be established or reestablished as a result. One must always confront a long and plural history, such as a history of play, or games defined by the rules emerging from some preceding game(s) or play without defined rules. Furthermore, such processes remain, as a *rule*, highly nonlinear. Relations of that kind become once again analogous to those between a restricted and a general economy in Bataille. A general economy, appearing, in the present context, as an economy of play, may in a given configuration be more comprehensive or possess a strategic privilege or priority; nevertheless, it cannot be absolutely primary, as it always depends on some restricted economy for its inscription.[39] This interaction leads to a configuration or economy, by definition general, of *mutual inhibition*, permeating all processes at issue here, which I shall consider in more detail in Chapter 5. It follows that narrative or narrative rules, dialectic or dialectical history, and other classical or restricted economies, do not disappear. To begin with, they all remain on the scene of our literary, theoretical, or political practice; and they will, in all likelihood, continue to remain there. Often enough, they are extremely effective. One needs, of course, to know how to use them well.

Given Derrida's analysis, one cannot speak of the *meaning* of the concept of play—of "neither a term nor a concept" of play. Such formations—"neither terms nor concepts"—are designed to undermine the concept of meaning, or the concept of concept, if at the same time to comprehend them. Thus they are also designed to expose a play within which both meaning and concepts become possible and at certain junctures necessary. Heraclitean, or Nietzschean, play *can* in fact be inscribed and articulated. As a general economy and in opposition to the restricted economies of the philosophical project, such a text would include and make possible specific inscriptions and articulations of what cannot be articulated or inscribed. At issue, once again, is a difference or alterity, more radical than any difference developed in the history of philosophy as the metaphysics of presence, including, for example, any absolute difference, idealist or materialist, or even Heideggerian difference, the most powerful philosophical attempt in this respect. This type of "project" plays a major role in both Bataille, specifically in *Inner Experience*,[40] and Derrida.

As it did for Heidegger, for these thinkers, particularly Bataille, this project relates to Nietzsche's project, although, as such, it receives less attention in Nietzsche's own text. If within a different form of "project," then, the play at issue can be articulated *logically* enough. Nietzsche does so on many occasions; Bataille, in speaking about the general economy; and Derrida, in inscribing *différance*. This play is articulated more logically than the logic of the classical "logical" texts; in fact, it is articulated so as to expose the logical problems of classical texts. The poststructuralist theory at issue in the present study offers powerful support for this claim. Given this new "logic" of play, both as already actual and as still potential, there are, however, and certainly will be other manifestations of its emerging theoretical and practical, including political, power. The latter is particularly the case if we assume, as I think we must, that an understanding of the political demands the complexity of such a logic.

I do not think that one should speak in this context of a *science* of play. Both 'play theory' by analogy with game theory, and 'play analysis,' by analogy with psychoanalysis, are tempting and potentially productive terms, for example, in relation to a possible deconstruction and recomprehension of game theory in its application to the social and the human sciences. Mathematics itself is a different case. The Greek word for play—*paideia*—offers some tempting possibilities as well, for example, by virtue of its relation to children's games and pedagogical practices.[41] All these, however, would remain Promethean gifts and, thus, the gift of *logos*, albeit as a *playful* logos of Heraclitus. We should at this point recall, with Nietzsche, that the Heraclitean logos is also a play of fire, perhaps the most precious of the Promethean gifts.[42]

Derrida's *grammatology* would still remain the gift of *logos* in this sense, a relation that is consistent with the idea of metaphysical closure, specifically in early Derrida. Derrida plays upon this possibility, particularly in relation to the concept of *grammē* (line) that enables him to inscribe nonlinear writing. He also carefully clarifies the status of grammatology: it cannot be "a positive science"; indeed, it is not a science at all in the classical sense of *epistēme*, *logos*, and so forth. To a certain extent, however, grammatology might be seen as having been abandoned in Derrida's later texts in favor of more plural—or more playful—textual possibilities, or *styles*.

The implications of the foregoing considerations for the question of narrative are multiple, some of them having been amply explored in recent years. They cannot all be pursued here, given the constraints of the present discussion—temporal, narrative, and performative. We have only so much time or space—pages, ideas, arguments, or examples—to be able to perform, to play out our possibilities and chances. I would argue, however, that throughout history the "event" of chance and the "event" of play persistently appear wherever an undermining of the "event" of narrative occurs; or, in theoretical terms, wherever an undermining of the category of narrative takes place. Play and chance are not the only such "events." I am purposely using the narrative category of "event" here: the events of chance and play may, and within the closure often must, be seen as events in the narrative sense. Indeed, there is more than one such sense to begin with. The point is that at times they cannot be seen as *events* in any conceivable sense. The very disseminating power of the conception of play already points toward other antinarrative "events," such as the performative of language and drama, the montage of cinema, the nonlinearity of music, and other possibilities. I would suggest that "play," owing to the disseminating power of its "events," "words," and "concepts," incorporates many such configurations and encompasses, via the general economy, theoretical economies emerging thereby.[43]

At this juncture, all such economies, whether undecidable or not, seem at the moment best to be seen as general economies in Bataille's and Derrida's sense. Nietzsche, however, might still be the best proper name or the best "signature," under*writing* the economies of play so emerging. The "event" of this signature, the "events" of all these "signatures" are bound to be events of enormous complexity—not that they, and the copyrights thereby entailed, are going to disappear. The economies themselves would remain, at least for now, the complementary "play of chance and necessity in calculations without end."

Storytellers

> —Und so erzähle ich mir mein Leben
> [and so I tell my life to myself].
>
> —Nietzsche, *Ecce Homo*

In his lectures on Paul de Man, Derrida offers a complaint: "I have never known how to tell a story. Why didn't I receive this gift from Mnemosyne? From this complaint, and probably to protect myself before it, a suspicion continually steals into my thinking: who can really tell a story? Is narrative possible? Who can claim to know what a narrative entails? Or, before that, the memory it lays claim to? What is memory?" (*Memoires: For Paul de Man*, 10). While the lectures are concerned with the *problem* of narrative in personal, theoretical, and political terms, the storytelling itself becomes immensely complicated. It could hardly be otherwise, given the sense—or even the vision—of *différance* emerging behind every "event," every beginning and every end, and every middle invading—"always already"—all alleged beginnings and ends.

One could say that Tristram Shandy does not know how to tell a story either, and for much the same reason. Or rather, such reasons should be seen as Laurence Sterne's rather than Shandy's. Perhaps Shandy plays it out more naively. It is not that one does not quite know how to tell a story. They all do, from Sterne on, including Derrida. According to Victor Shklovsky, *Tristram Shandy* becomes—or begins as—an exhaustive encyclopedia of storytelling techniques, analogous to, and perhaps a prototype for, Vladimir Propp's *Ur*-Tale, containing within itself all folk tales. One knows too much, as it were: in literature, one knows too much to be able to rely on stories alone; and in literary theory, one knows too much to be able to rely on the concept of narrative alone. Sterne plays with these impossible possibilities on both planes—literary and theoretical—as the Russian Formalists understood and themselves played out. To know or to see "too much" can paralyze even one's perception,[44] let alone storytelling. It can even make one go mad. In a certain sense, Tristram Shandy's is a mad narrative. But Sterne's narrative is hardly mad, even though, while he plays it out brilliantly, he cannot control all of it, either.

It is certainly not coincidental that Nietzsche speaks with such great admiration of both Stendhal and Sterne, two great dislocators of classical narrativity and temporality, and yet great masters of the rhetoric, or anti-rhetoric, of both. Thus, he describes Sterne as "the freest writer [der freieste Schriftsteller]," in *Human, All Too Human* (vol. 2, sec. 113, p. 238; *KSA* 2:424), a description that traverses many themes discussed here—seriousness and play, profundity and farce, parody, ambiguity—and, as Samuel Weber observes, "could be also read as a self-portrait" (*Institution and Interpretation*, 60). The same comment would be even more applicable to Nietzsche's various comments on Stendhal and several others. Nietzsche's portraiture as self-portraiture is an important part of his repertoire of telling his life to himself and others, even though, and indeed because, Nietzsche has understood perhaps more profoundly than anyone else that we are the most distant from "ourselves."[45] Not coincidentally, I think—not by chance—earlier Nietzsche speaks of Democritus, the grand philosopher of chance, "as the freest man [Demokrit der freieste Mensch]" (KSA 7: 546), which description could also be read as a self-portrait.

It is a precious gift, indeed, the gift of storytelling that enables one to play precariously: between story and nonstory, or between story and play, play as drama, or the play of chance and necessity. But then, although one might claim to, no one can tell stories only as stories. There is always—"always already"—a nonstory there of one kind or another. The question is rather how to do it well, whether under the guise of a story or of an antinarrative, or still otherwise. It might be the gift of Mnemosyne. I doubt that it can be only that. Derrida probably also alludes to the Heideggerian problematic of the gift (Gabe)—the gift of Being, of thinking, of poetizing, particularly, in Heidegger, in relation to Hölderlin. Maybe that gift is not Prometheus' gift, either. Memory is, by way of *writing*, one of Prometheus' gifts. Contrary to Heidegger, it may not be a "gift" at all. Are gifts gifts?

What does it mean to be or to give a gift? Bataille has much to say on gifts and their general economy of at once giving and not giving, or taking away—the general economy is the economy of (the impossibility) of gift.

Nietzsche, of course, *knows* how to tell a story, perhaps better than Derrida, even if it is, as Nietzsche claims, "to [him]self." Or is it a story? Is *Ecce Homo: How One Becomes What One Is (Wie man wird, was man ist)* quite storytelling? Certainly, it is not only that. Rather, it is a massive complementarity of narrative, play—including some theater, comedy, and tragedy—theory, and criticism. Among other things, it includes Nietzsche's reading of his own texts. In this sense, it is much more a history, or a story, of Nietzsche's writing, which he, *according* to Derrida, also understood in Derrida's sense.[46] Nietzsche, careful as ever, does not say that he is about to tell a "story," the story of his life, but instead writes: "I tell my *life* to myself [Und so erzähle ich mir mein Leben]" (*KSA* 6:263; emphasis added).[47] Perhaps, if one agrees that *différance* is the efficacity of "the history of life . . . as the history of *grammē* [dans l'histoire de la vie . . . comme histoire du gramme]" (*Of Grammatology*, 84; *De la grammatologie*, 125).

Nietzsche does not know how to tell a story, either, but rather how to tell one's *life*, which would be an even greater gift; or still more precisely, he *tells* his life to himself, for "knowledge," narrative or other—*all* knowledge—is radically put into question by Nietzsche, including by his "storytelling." Nietzsche tells the story of his life as, above all, the history of his writing; and the "story" of this writing cannot be contained *in* a narrative and *by* the narrative as a category, or as an allegory, including in de Man's sense, or as an irony—a much more playful, but also more serious, concept. Nietzsche's writing, "not originarily subordinate to the logos and the truth [(n'est) pas originairement assujettie au logos et à la vérité]" (*Of Grammatology*, 19; *De la grammatologie*, 33), is, by the same token, not originarily subordinate to any master narrative or master concept of narrative. As Keats once wrote: "Lord Byron cuts a figure—but he is not figurative—Shak[e]speare led a life of Allegory; his works are the comments on it" (*Letters of John Keats* 2:67). These are complex lives, works, allegories: they tell their "story" by continuously upsetting the allegory of the narrative. Nietzsche grasped this complexity and played it out with an extraordinary brilliance and power in *Ecce Homo*.

One could date the inception of narratology still differently—to Vladimir Propp's study of the folktale. That is a fairly acceptable story, a good narrative—or a "folktale"—of the modern history of narratology. One could then use a still different trope. One could move—narratology has already done so—from tale, "story," to *fairy*-tale, to its "magic," nonnarrative "events," and to its more complex economy—the economy of chance and play, of cinematic, musical, or even dancing "events" or "effects," particularly performative effects. Instead of the "folktale" of narratology—anthropological, nostalgic, structuralist, folkloristic, "guilty"—one moves then to the richness of a fairytale, more unconscious and more playful. One moves to movielike, cinematic "events" and "effects"—to *Last Year at Marienbad* and the mirrors of Jacques Lacan, displacing, curving and re-curving, the points and lines of the temporal; or again, to the still more complex economies of Hitchcock's films. Lacan once reread the story of a "purloined letter" as a *play* of a signifier, even the play of nothingness. The story does not disappear, but rather is reconceived or reconfigured by another means, bringing in something which stories cannot account for. Is Edgar Allan Poe best seen as a storyteller; and if so, through what play of chance and necessity are his stories told? Poe pays frequent tributes to Democritus and Epicurus, specifically in his Dupin stories; and the question plays a major role throughout Poe's writing, whether in his fiction, poetry, or theoretical essays.

Derrida's "My Chances/*Mes Chances*: A Rendezvous with Some Epicurean Stereophonies" is, among other things, (a story) about stories told by Freud about himself and by other figures or "proper names," including Democritus, Epicurus, Poe, Lacan, and Derrida himself, as he tells us how his analysis comes about—almost by chance. Nietzsche appears in a footnote, though it is a crucial one, I think. Derrida points out that "Nietzsche is also a name that Freud would have very much liked to forget," before concluding "Concerning chance and chaos there would be a great deal to say at this point in the name of Nietzsche" (31). Derrida *concludes* where he concludes for *three* reasons:

> Freud concludes, as you will see, by an allusion to the incalculable and the innumerable. This is the first reason to cite him. But it is precisely a question of the incalculability and the innumerability of the reasons or the causes (*ragione, causes, Ursachen*) that are in nature and that "never enter experience." Second reason: this allusion to nature as "full of countless causes (*ragione*) that never enter experience" is a quasi-citation and from an artist. Once again indebtedness and filiation. Freud cites Leonardo da Vinci, whom he had come to recognize as being out of the reach of analytical science by virtue of a certain random enigma. ("My Chances," 28)

The third reason has to do with Shakespeare, from whom the present analysis has never departed, and *King Lear*. As is any *closure*, then, or any opening, Derrida's conclusion in "My Chances" is an effect of what his subject is—"the *play* of chance and necessity in calculations without end."

Another proper name Derrida inserts in this Democritean chain and its "'literary' ascendance" is Sterne's, specifically in the context of Freud's substitution of names, such as Democritus and Protagoras, both of whom appear in *Tristram Shandy*. "The absolute precursor, the grandfather is the author of *Tristram Shandy*," Derrida even claims, citing "Freud citing somebody else citing Sterne" ("My Chances," 18). Sterne is "the absolute precursor, the ultimate grandfather" of many things. Shklovsky's famous "estrangement" (ostranenie) grafts—weaves—perhaps even intentionally, Tristram Shandy's name into its texture, making it a kind of "*otristra-menie*"—*tristramshandiness* as it were: something that Tristram Shandy does all the time. Since, furthermore, Sterne's own name is grafted in *ostranenie* as well (and it is grafted, perhaps intentionally, although only partially, into Tristram Shandy's name), one can read *ostranenie* as *osternenie* as well: Sterne's technique, *sternization*.[48]

It is worth expanding the intertextuality of the case, using *Tristram Shandy* in the context of Leonardo's "random enigma": "But may one not take objection to the finding of an inquiry which ascribes to accidental circumstances (Zufälligkeiten) of his parental constellation so decisive an influence on a person's fate (Schicksal)—which, for example, makes Leonardo's fate depend on his illegitimate birth and on the bareness of his stepmother Donna Albiera?" (*Standard Edition* 11:136–37; "My Chances," 30). The opening pages of *Tristram Shandy* are concerned precisely with the "random enigma" of one's birth as an un-*fortunate* accident of Nature. But, as Sterne implies, conception is never quite random, either, depending in the novel on a certain regularity of the clock that Shandy's father has to wind at a regular time. There are certainly other aspects of the notion and metaphor of clock, and of regularity in general, that are involved here, including as related to another natural enigma, the enigma of woman. But they in effect preclude an absolute randomness of this "monstrous"—enigmatic—"natural" event: birth.

These "regularities," of course, may also be seen as random effects of nature at a higher level; but that is one of the points of the play at issue here. As old Mr. Shandy puts it: "My Tristram's *misfortunes* began nine months before ever he came to the world" (*Tristram Shandy*, vol. 1, chap. 3, 6–7; emphasis added). The actual *calculations*—those given by Sterne—show Shandy to have been born *eight* months after the supposedly "certain" day of his conception, if one assumes, of course, that Mr. Shandy was indeed his father. As Shandy himself formulates the issue of what Freud calls "a person's fate": "[F]or I can truly say, that from the first hour I drew my breath in it, . . . —I have been the continual sport of what the world calls *fortune* . . . in every stage of my life, and at every turn and corner where she could get fairly at me, the ungracious Duchess has pelted me with a set of as pitiful *mis-adventures* and gross *accidents* as ever a small hero sustained" (vol. 1, chap. 5, p. 10; emphasis added).

Play, necessity, chance might still be "walled up within *closure*," but this is as far as we can go at this moment in the history of the closure of philosophy, and in transforming this closure. In this sense, we may be still interpreting—re-*producing*, re-*creating*, re-*configuring*, re-*figuring*—the Heraclitean text, although, given the radical reconfigurations at issue here, such a claim is no longer quite possible, either. On the scene of this theory and this theater, it is fitting to conclude by citing—*re*-citing, reciting (but is it a *récit?*)—Nietzsche. But Nietzsche is in turn citing, and perhaps also reciting, *spectacularly*—everything is still play and performance here—Heraclitus, the artistic philosopher. As Nietzsche tells us in *The Birth of Tragedy*, Socrates can only dream of becoming an artistic philosopher, as he dreams of playing the flute (*The Birth of Tragedy*, 92–93)—an instrument Shakespeare and Hamlet also make very good use of, and at the right moment. Nietzsche only cites Heraclitus, perhaps: "—*ein Spiel.*"

Chapter 4

Nietzsche's Revolutions

Difference and Authority

With virtually a single proposition in *Of Grammatology*, Derrida relates to Nietzsche's *writing* nearly his entire grammatological project, both in its deconstructive aspect—as a radical critique of the metaphysics of presence—and its constructive aspect—as the matrix of *writing, différance, trace,* and so forth, in short, as the grammatological general economy:

> Nietzsche *has written what he has written.* He has written that writing—and first of all his own—is not *originarily subordinate* to the logos and to truth. And that this subordination has *come into being* during an epoch whose meaning we must deconstruct. (*Of Grammatology*, 19; *De la grammatologie*, 32–33; some emphases added)

Nietzsche, actually, has not written that. Nowhere in his text does such a statement occur. One must take the term 'writing' here in Derrida's sense, however. Stating that "Nietzsche has *written* what he has *written*" suggests that such are the "effects"—"historical," "theoretical," "political," or other—of Nietzsche's writing, as all these denominations, including "effects" (*Positions*, 66–67) and above all *writing*, are put into question. Any given text is thus constituted supplementarily only by its effects, even though the very concept of effect, and thus also the concept of cause, must be subjected to the choreo*graphy* of *writing*.[1] Theoretically and strategically, the emphasis on "effects" has its place and significance (*Positions*, 66–67).[2] Any text, including Nietzsche's, and any of its meanings, or effects, are locally constituted. They are produced by reading-*writing* and *iterability* in Derrida's sense. "What I am referring to here is not richness of substance,

149

semantic fertility, but rather structure: the structure of remnant or of iteration. But I have given this structure many other names, . . ." ("Living On: Border Lines," in *Deconstruction and Criticism*, 81; "Survivre," in *Parages*, 125). It is never the same structure, either, however, even beyond the "iterability" of all Derrida's "structures," which are never quite identical to themselves. Derrida's *disseminating* structures relate to a broad front, although never an absolute horizon, of effects and efficacities.

The general economic textual production thus suggested is in fact what Derrida calls *writing*, among other names, or "neither words nor concepts." In distinguishing between *différance* and *writing*, one might suggest as a starting point that *writing* is a result, an effect of the transformation, the reconfiguration of language, *spoken or written*, under the conditions of *différance* and its satellites, such as *dissemination, trace, supplement*, and others; and, in terms of theoretical *writing*, under the conditions of general economy. Borrowing its name from the subordinate member of the classical oppositions such as speech and writing—usually subordinated in turn to the logos and to truth—*writing* thus emerges in the place to which classical theories and fields—such as philosophy, linguistics, anthropology, or literary criticism—would assign the denomination of language. Simultaneously, this distribution privileges speech over writing, in its conventional sense. If this conventional concept, or field of concepts, of writing emerges thereby as uncritical, the same is also true of the classical field of the concepts of speech. Derrida's economy of writing reconfigures and refigures, remetaphorizes both.

The general economy of writing so conceived acquires tremendous theoretical potential, allowing one to attach the *reconfigurative* operator *writing*, which is neither signifier nor signified, neither word nor concept, to many other classical denominations. It may be *writing*-speech, *writing*-writing, *writing*-thinking, *writing*-philosophy or, of course, *writing*-literature, *writing*-theory, or *writing*-criticism or *writing*-reading, and *writing*- practice and *writing*-painting, or even *writing*-dancing, as in Mallarmé, where according to Derrida's analysis, all these forms of *writing* participate and interact.[3]

In the end, by virtue of the general economic character of their inscription and interrelations, *writing* and *différance* can be neither unequivocally dissociated nor identified or unified within a single economy. Such an economy, by definition, would be a restricted economy, and in effect Hegelian economy. An absolute unity of writing and difference, which, as Derrida shows, defines Hegel's project, would indeed demand no less than Absolute Knowledge. In this sense, Hegel and Hegel's logic—his argument and the science of logic as conceived by Hegel—are irrefutable. "What is at stake here is [indeed] enormous [L'enjeu est ici énorme]," as Derrida says, in "defining" *différance*, "if there were a definition of *différance*, [as] . . . the limit, the interruption, the destruction, of the Hegelian *relève* [*Aufhebung*, in this reading] *wherever* it operates" (*Positions*, 40–41; *Positions*, 55).

Nietzsche profoundly understood these stakes and these implications. It is the power of this understanding that allows one to conclude with Derrida that "he has *written what* he has written," when "[h]e has written that writing—and first of all his own—is not *originarily subordinate* to the logos and to truth" (emphases altered). There are many other effects of Nietzsche's writing, in whichever sense—the effects of proximity and the effects of distance from Derrida and deconstruction, or those which may function outside the field of deconstruction. The proximity of major propositions in Nietzsche and Derrida is crucial. But there are also differences; and *writing* and what makes it writing in Derrida's sense are, after all, *Derrida's* "neither words nor concepts." The following passage of Nietzsche's, however, amply confirms Derrida's point:

> Out of being *used to unconditional authorities*, at last a strong need for *unconditional authorities* has developed:—this need is so strong that, even in a critical age such as Kant's, it proved itself superior to the need for criticism and was, in a certain sense, able to *subordinate* the *entire work* of critical reason and put it to its own uses.—It proved its superiority once again in the following generation, which was necessarily drawn by its historical instinct toward a relativity of all authority, by pressing into its service even the Hegelian philosophy of evolution, history rebaptized philosophy, and presenting history as the progressive self-revelation, self-surpassing of moral ideas. Since Plato, philosophy has been dominated by morality. Even in his predecessors, moral interpretations play a decisive role (with Anaximander, the perishing of all things as punishment for their emancipation from pure being; with Heraclitus, the regularity of phenomena as witness to the moral-legal character of the totality of becoming). (*The Will to Power*, sec. 412, p. 222; *KSA* 12:259; translation modifed)

The most immediate major *effect* of this extraordinary elaboration is a radical deconstruction of the conception of the *unconditional* authority and the historical and theoretical implications—effects—of the removal or erasure of any unconditional authority demanding originary subordination "to the logos and to truth," moral, philosophical, or other. Although Nietzsche's critique of morals is crucial, for the moment it may be seen as secondary to the general critique of ultimate authority as subordination to the logos and truth. Morality and ethics, however, have reciprocally conditioned the philosophical conceptions of the logos and truth as authority throughout their history. In addition, there are analogous effects of mutual complicity between philosophy and religion or theology—theo-*logy* and *theo*-logy—which Nietzsche exposes throughout his writing. Morality supplies the metaphor, without philosophers' realizing the metaphoricity involved.

"Authority" and "subordination" reduce the difference.[4] They also establish the profound—and profoundly *metaphysical*—complicity between metaphysics and empiricism: "thinking by metaphor without thinking metaphor as such [. . . la pensée *par* métaphore qui ne pense pas la métaphore comme telle]," as Derrida writes in his critique of Levinas ("Violence and Metaphysics," in *Writing and Difference*, 139; *L'Écriture et la différence*, 204).[5]

Philosophy's active forgetting (aktive Vergesslichkeit) of metaphoricity or Derrida's *writing*—whose "'proper' meaning" must also be "determin[ed] as metaphoricity itself [Il ne s'agirait donc pas d'inverser le sens propre et le sens figuré mais de déterminer le sens 'propre' de l'écriture comme la métaphoricité elle-même]" (*Of Grammatology*, 15; *De la grammatologie*, 27; translation modified)[6]—is crucial and perhaps necessary for the very existence of philosophy. In the wake of Nietzsche's text, the exploration of this forgetting has been one of the most prominent dimensions of deconstruction. A critical or deconstructive text also "forgets" in one way or another, including—*at times*—in the same ways a precritical or metaphysical text forgets. I would insist, however, against deconstruction, or certain forms of deconstruction, that one cannot quite identify either the degree or, importantly, the character—the *structure*—of such "forgetting" in the precritical and critical texts, specifically in cases like Nietzsche's and Derrida's. I shall consider this issue in more detail shortly.

Thus, more than criticizing morality, certainly more than *simply* doing so, Nietzsche exposes the philosophical, as well as the empiricist, conceptions of the logos and truth—unconditional authorities—as local effects of a particular system or a particular conception, or metaphor, of morality. These effects, however, also become "causes" of many other things and act over long historical intervals and across broad spaces—geographical, historical, political, or theoretical. They become globalized, hence the complexity and instability of all these denominations. As Nietzsche says elsewhere: "Fundamental insight [Grundeinsicht]: Kant as well as Hegel and Schopenhauer—the skeptical epochistic attitude, as well as the historicizing, as well as the pessimistic—are of *moral* origin" (*The Will to Power*, sec. 410, p. 221; *KSA* 12:144; translation modified).[7]

Once the local character of all philosophical authority and subordination is exposed, however, the ultimate or unconditional nature of authority, starting with *logos* and truth, is removed. All such authorities have to be reconfigured locally, historically, practically, including politically, but also psychoanalytically, extending this latter term beyond its Freudian, or conventionally Freudian sense, to the psycho-political for example, such as Oedipal politics. One might employ terms such as historico-analytically, politico-analytically, or socio-analytically. All authorities then become *conditional* authorities. It is this reconfiguration of authority and subordination as local and always conditional "determinations" and "effects" that I see here as the Nietzschean "revolution." Whenever history must be invoked, this "localization" must be seen as radically *historical*, but also *radically* historical. As will be seen in more detail in Chapter 6, such a radical historicity may, and at times must, imply a reconfiguration of the historical as nonhistorical—ahistorical or antihistorical. At issue is a reconfiguration even more radical than any historicization, however radical the economy itself of historicity *as* historicity may be. A radical expansion—*dissemination*—of all names and a radical suspension of all unique or final names, one of Derrida's major points, is a crucial aspect of this reconfiguration.

The implications, or consequences, of the transformations at issue are tremendous. "Tremendous implications [ungeheure Folgen]" is Nietzsche's own phrase, repeated several times in *Daybreak* [*Morgenröte*], which, along with and coming in the wake of *Human, All Too Human*, opens Nietzsche's mature period, when most of the conceptions involved in this reconfiguration and refiguration—rechoreographing—of history and theory, or in his famous phrase, his own "revaluation of all values [Umwerthung aller Werthe]" hitherto, began to crystallize and Nietzsche began to articulate some of the far-reaching implications of his insights.[8]

The removal of all ultimate authorities and of the subordination of "writing" to the logos and truth does not mean that authorities or acts of subordination do not exist, nor especially that historically there have been no authorities or instances of subordination. Rather, the opposite is the case: authorities and subordinations emerge and impose themselves all the time. We might say that much as "there are," according to Derrida, "everywhere only differences and traces of traces [Il n'y a, de part en part, que des différences et des traces de traces]" (*Positions*, 26; *Positions*, 38), there always are everywhere manifestations of authority and subordination; both economies demand and inhabit—and inhibit—each other. They are complementary features of the general economy. No other statement is perhaps more "faithful" to Nietzsche's analysis of history, for example, as the genealogy of morals; or to his analysis of theory, for example, philosophy, whose history is the history of the will to knowledge and—or as—the will to power.

The insistence on difference thus does not preclude an awareness of or an insistence on authority, but instead exposes historical "*subordination*" to the *difference* of all authority, including logos, truth, consciousness, and specifically self-consciousness, and presence. In this sense, the "and" in the title of this section is both an opposition and a conjunction; it is the opposition of *radical difference* to *ultimate authority* or *subordination to the logos and truth*, and the conjunction—or complementarity—of historical difference and historical authority and subordination. The suppression of difference is itself a local effect of the power—authority, violence, subordination, or at times the surrender of authority—of the historical difference of *writing* in Derrida's sense. "Writing," Derrida maintains, "cannot be thought of outside of the horizon of intersubjective violence" (*Of Grammatology*, 127; *De la grammatologie*, 185).[9] Derrida's critique and deconstruction of Lévi-Strauss' human science of anthropology—"nostalgic, Rousseauistic" science—hinges on a Nietzschean critical assessment and a Nietzschean recognition of the nonethical origin of the ethical model behind all human sciences. Thus Derrida invokes Nietzsche in concluding his analysis of Lévi-Strauss: "To recognize writing in speech, that is to say *différance* and the absence of speech, is to begin to think the lure. There is no ethics without the presence *of the other;* but also, and consequently, there is no ethics without absence, dissimulation, detour, *différance*, writing. The arche-writing is the origin of morality as of immorality. The nonethical opening of ethics. A violent opening. As in the case of the vulgar concept of writing, the ethical instance of violence must be rigorously suspended in order to repeat the genealogy of morals" (*Of Grammatology*, 139–40; *De la grammatologie*, 202; translation modified).[10]

"The ethical instance of violence must be rigorously suspended in order to repeat the *genealogy* of morals," but not in order to deny it in a theoretical or necessarily in a practical sense. As Nietzsche writes in *Daybreak*, again on the question of morality and the denial of morality:

> Thus I deny morality [Sittlichkeit] as I deny alchemy, that is, I deny their premises: but I do *not* deny that there have been alchemists who believed in these premises and acted in accordance with them.—I also deny immorality: *not* that countless people *feel* themselves to be immoral, but a foundation in *truth* so to feel. It goes without saying that I do not deny—unless I am a fool—that many actions called immoral are to be *avoided and resisted*, or that many actions called moral are to be done and encouraged—but I think the one [should be encouraged] and the other

[avoided] *for other reasons than hitherto.* (*Daybreak*, 60; *KSA* 3:91–92; translation modified)

This is a statement of extraordinary importance; moreover, given the history of reading Nietzsche, it is always necessary to insert it in one's reading of Nietzsche—his thinking or writing, and his life. "For other reasons than hitherto [aus anderen Gründen, als bisher]" could serve as a defining proposition of Nietzsche's life and thinking and *writing* "not *originarily subordinate* to the logos and to truth."

This suspension, radical but not absolute, of "the ground" does not imply that there is nothing left behind, that is, that there is no efficacity of our morals or actions, ethics or philosophies, or theories, all of which, of course, are also actions, or histories. There is a great deal left—authorities and subordinations, for example, or other constraining, as well as shaping or enabling, factors. One might say that when the ultimate authority of all transcendental signifieds, or signifiers, philosophical or political, is erased, everything is left; in other words, it is only then that such things as authorities and subordinations begin to make sense and open the possibility of rigorous analysis.

One can speak, as Derrida sometime does, of the efficacity at issue as "nothing" (*Of Grammatology*, 286) only in the sense that *nothing* in the history of the metaphysics of presence—no present being, neither presence nor being, nothing that *is* or can *be*—to which this efficacity could correspond; and this erasure of being should be distiguished from Heidegger's economy, finally restricted, placing Being under erasure in *The Question of Being*.

That one discovers in such deconstructions an abundance of efficacities, though not classical causes, rather than emptiness or absolute suspension of all connections, derivations—or again authorities and subordinations—is crucial, both in general and in the context of Nietzsche. The resistance to the idea that there is *nothing* left, a resistance to nothingness, is the point at which Nietzsche takes issue with the whole history of European nihilism, which he says would rather will "nothingness" than have nothing to will. Nihilism, "as the denial of a truthful world, of being," is to an extent necessary, even might be "a divine way of thinking [Insofern könnte Nihilism, als *Leugnung* einer wahrhaften Welt, eines Seins, eine göttliche Denkweise sein:]" (*Will to Power*, 15; *KSA* 12:354). It is, however, only a very preliminary phase and is never good enough for the Nietzschean active, affirmative way of thinking or writing. Nihilism itself requires the massive historico-theoretical analysis that Nietzsche undertakes throughout his works. The Nietzschean question is that of the conditions—historical, political, and theoretical—of the possibility and necessity of European nihilism. His question is "Why?" Along the way he exposes the fundamentally nihilistic nature of all desire for ultimate authority—not only the ultimate authority of nothingness—whether in Socrates, Saint Paul, Kant, or Schopenhauer, who were Nietzsche's most explicit targets, all of whom Nietzsche characterizes as nihilists—deniers of life. This is a crucial point. It implies that nihilism—or philosophy, religion, or ethics—is rooted in the complex, general economy of historical, social, political, psychological, even physiological, or other conditions of its emergence. Nietzsche writes:

> The nihilistic question *"for what?"* is rooted in the hitherto existing habit by force of which the goal seem to be put up, given, demanded *from outside*—that is to say, by some *superhuman authority*. Having unlearned faith in that, one still follows the old habit and seeks *another authority* would know how to *speak unconditionally* and could *command* goals and tasks. The authority of *conscience* now steps up front (the more emancipated one is from theology, the more imperativistic morality becomes) to compensate for the loss of a *personal* authority. Or the authority of *reason*. Or the *social instinct* (the herd). Or *history* with an immanent spirit and a goal within, so one can entrust oneself to it. One wants to *get around* the will, the willing of a goal, the risk of positing a goal for oneself; one wants to rid oneself of the responsibility (one would accept fatalism). Finally, *happiness*—and with a touch of Tartuffe, the *happiness of the greatest number*. (*Will to Power*, sec. 20, pp. 16–17; *KSA* 12:355–56; translation modified)

In the margins Nietzsche adds one of his most extraordinary insights: "Individual goals and their conflicts . . . collective goals versus individual ones. . . . *Everybody merely a partisan* [a party], *including the philosophers* [individuelle Ziele und deren Widerstreit . . . kollektive Ziele im Kampf mit individuellen. . . . Jedermann wird Partei dabei, auch die Philosophen]" (*Will to Power*, 17; *KSA* 12:356). This statement powerfully reconceives the conditions of philosophy, which in a certain sense are always already political. This proposition, however, may not be intended as an encouragement of "partisanship"—or party lines—in doing theory. To a degree, and with qualifications, it is actually the contrary. Politics and "partisanship" are, of course, impossible to avoid. In one way or another, one engages in politics all the time; sides or nonsides and positions or nonpositions have to be taken. Politics, however, entails stratifications of immense complexity, and, as with any other denomination, the denomination 'political' itself cannot be absolute, final, or always irreducible, for example, as opposed to being theoretical. The theoretical, then, while it may and often must be political, must under certain conditions be theoretical. The complexity of this economy, by definition general, may require not only being partisan in relation to a different economy of power, but also being sufficiently nonpartisan. Conversely, however, there may be conditions under which even the very best theory has to be suspended, "sacrificed," or diplomatically negotiated. Such negotiation actually goes on almost all the time, although at times it requires great skill. Obviously, the "promotion" of any given theory, good or bad, is similarly conditioned and constrained.[11]

Nietzsche's "historical" analysis of "the genealogy of morals" thus becomes a manifestation, perhaps even the most famous one, of a different model or a different choreography of the historical difference, which begins to emerge as one of the crucial consequences of Nietzsche's revolutions. It can be shown in detail that Nietzsche's analysis is in many ways already *textual* in the deconstructive or postdeconstructive sense of the term.[12] This textualization makes Nietzsche's genealogies at once more and less historical than history in the classical—Hegelian—sense.[13] In order to perceive this economy in Nietzsche, however, one must once again read Nietzsche's text following Nietzsche's style of writing, although, as I have pointed out in Chapter 1, in dealing with the *Genealogy*, this task is often difficult.[14] Nietzsche's style, however, points, at any point,[15] toward a potential and an actual reversal of moral or other values, such as aesthetic ones, or stratifications of perspective, within or outside a given "subject" or group. According to such a reading, for example, Nietzsche always begins *in medias res* in this sense and argues that things must always be engaged *in medias res* with provisional "primary" configurations. Specifically, in the book "good" and "bad" emerge "first" as active "morality," followed then by "good" and "evil," or rather "evil" and "good" as reactive, "*ressentiment*" morality. Reactive morality assigns "evil" to the "good" of active morality, and the oppositional values of "good" to itself. Reversed or re-reversed configurations, however, not only are possible but, as the *Genealogy* reiterates, continually occur.[16]

Nietzsche certainly does not claim that morality has an absolute origin. Rather, he suggests something like the following: "Let us consider a genealogy of morals different, even opposite to the traditional view of things. Is it not more likely that things *often* proceed in this way—from active to reactive—rather than in the ways priests and philosophers want us to believe. Then, once such a genealogy is also possible, let us see why and what would be the consequences." The consequences, it turns out, are tremendous.

Such a reading would naturally be opposed to any reading ascribing to Nietzsche a claim of offering a unique or original history of morals, or some form of primary and original morals. The latter reading is possible; and all the potential nuances and deviation notwithstanding, it would be analogous to, and often still more problematic than, Heidegger's reading of Nietzsche, against which Derrida's reading proceeds.[17] "To save Nietzsche from a reading of the Heideggerian type, it seems that we must, above all, not attempt to restore or make explicit a less naive 'ontology,' composed of profound ontological intuitions acceding to some originary truth, an entire fundamentality hidden under the appearance of an empiricist or metaphysical text. The virulence of Nietzschean thought could not be more completely misunderstood" (*Of Grammatology*, 19; *De la grammatologie*, 32).

What emerges thereby is rereading, also largely against Heidegger, or rewriting—making *written*—the Western philosophical tradition as the metaphysics of presence. At issue, is a reading, on the one hand, more rigorous and more nuanced, and on the other, following Nietzsche's plural, *written* style of inscription. In general, nearly everything depends on how one reads Nietzsche—this crucial margin of philosophy, even "central," to the extent that any centrality is possible. "Radicalizing the concepts of *interpretation, perspective, evaluation, difference,* and all the 'empiricist' or nonphilosophical motifs that have constantly tormented philosophy throughout the history of the West, and besides, have had nothing but the inevitable weakness of being produced in the field of philosophy, Nietzsche, far from remaining *simply* (with Hegel and as Heidegger wished) *within* metaphysics, contributed a great deal to the liberation of the signifier from its dependence or derivation with respect to the logos and the related concept of truth or the primary signified, in whatever sense that is understood" (*Of Grammatology*, 19; *De la grammatologie*, 31–32).

It may not necessarily follow, however, that as Derrida contends, "*therefore*, rather than protect Nietzsche from the Heideggerian reading, we should *perhaps* offer him up to it completely, underwriting that interpretation without reserve; in a *certain way* and up to a point where, the content of the Nietzschean discourse being almost lost for the question of being, its form regains its absolute strangeness, where his text finally invokes a different type of reading, more faithful to his type of writing" (*Of Grammatology*, 19; *De la grammatologie*, 32; emphasis added). Derrida does add a qualifying "perhaps," and his own reading is very effective.[18] Nietzsche's text appears to me to be "strange" enough in this sense, "rich and strange"; and it is curious that Derrida relies here on two classical, even formalist tropes—the difference between form and content, and defamiliarization or "estrangement" in Shklovsky's sense. Derrida makes significant references to Russian Formalism in this part of the book (9) and in *Positions* (70). Deploying these tropes is also a consistent strategy, however, given that one of the reasons for "*accentuat*[ing] the 'naiveté' of the [Nietzschean] breakthrough" is a necessary reliance on older concepts—the closure of concepts. These concepts, however, must be read by way of this closure in Nietzsche and Derrida, as opposed to attempting to make them fundamental structures—transcendental signifieds or signifiers—as is always the task of metaphysics, overt or hidden, from Socrates and before to Heidegger and after. As opposed to trying, as Heidegger does, to assign this task—whether as fulfilled or failed—to Nietzsche, "on the contrary, one must *accentuate* the 'naiveté' of a breakthrough which cannot attempt a step outside of metaphysics, which cannot *criticize* metaphysics radically without still utilizing in a certain way, in a certain type or a certain style of *text*, propositions that, read within the philosophic corpus (i.e., according to Nietzsche, ill-read or unread), have always been and will always be 'naivetés,' incoherent signs of an absolute appurtenance" (*Of Grammatology*, 19; *De la grammatologie*, 32).

Hardly anything is "naive" here, either in Derrida or in Nietzsche. One must relate one's reading, however, to Nietzsche's plural style. The latter, as Derrida shows, depends on the closure of metaphysics and operates within a metaphysical register, but at the same time uses this register to undermine metaphysics. As shall be seen in more detail later, the manifold of such registers—the plurality of style—in Nietzsche and elsewhere may be extended. The extension also poses the question of transformations of our theoretical closure(s) such as the closure of metaphysics in Derrida's sense. My point at the moment is that Nietzsche's plural style and his general economic matrix must be engaged in reading the *Genealogy* or in attempting to understand Nietzsche's economy of history.

The preceding analysis may seem to overstate the case for history and the historical and for their role in Nietzsche. Nietzsche, after all, does offer one of the most powerful critiques of historicism ever, again specifically in his comments on "modern historiography [moderne Geschichtsschreibung]" toward the end of *On the Genealogy of Morals* (157; *KSA* 5:405). One must be attentive, however, to what kind of history or historiography, "modern historiography," is being criticized here or elsewhere. The earlier essay "On the Usages and Disadvantages of History [Vom Nutzen und Nachteil der Historie für das Leben]" is a more complex and more problematic case; there Nietzsche's ideas of history are not as rich and effective as in his later works. Even so, I think, the essay would support the points I make here more than it would contradict them. The significance of historical determination, or efficacity, is crucial in *Human, All*

Too Human [*Menschliches, Allzumenschliches*], where Nietzsche begins by insisting on the necessity of "historical philosophy [historische Philosophie]," which he opposes to "metaphysical philosophy [metaphysische Philosophie]" (*Human, All Too Human*, sec. 1:1, p. 12; *KSA* 2:24). In *Daybreak*, the same question of the conditions of possibility and necessity is formulated explicitly in historical terms under the title "Historical Refutation as the Definitive Refutation [Die historische Widerlegung als die endgültige]." There belief in God is at issue rather than the truths of philosophy. That focus, however, is only that much more pertinent to the questions at issue. Nietzsche, as I have pointed out, has always viewed philosophy and its unconditional authorities as fashioned on the model of Christianity and the priesthood. In this case, too, Nietzsche most likely writes with Kant and Descartes in mind:

> *Historical refutation as the definitive refutation.* In former times, one sought to prove that there is no God—today one indicates how the belief that there is a God could *arise* and how this belief acquired its weight and importance: a counter-proof that there is no God thereby becomes superfluous.—When in former times one had refuted the "proofs of the existence of God" put forward, there always remained the doubt whether better proofs might not be adduced than those just refuted: in those days atheists did not know how to make a clean sweep. (*Daybreak*, sec. 95, p. 54; *KSA* 3:86–87)

A deeper consequence of this "historical refutation" of all theology and ontotheology is a radical—general economic—historicity of philosophy, or of all theory. Or, to be more precise, since nothing can be always historical or always conform to any given denomination, when and *to the extent* that theory must be historical, it will be more radically historical than is allowed either by classical, metaphysical ahistorical positions or by classical historicism, such as Hegelianism. *Nietzschean* historicity thus by no means reduces the force of Nietzsche's critique of history and historicism as a critique of classical or metaphysical concepts of history and historicism. Instead, Nietzsche's insistence on history reinforces this critique. It certainly problematizes radically the Hegelian relations between historical understanding and "historical" or political practice, or between understanding and practice, in general.[19] At issue is the concept or concepts, classical or metaphysical—*precritical*—concepts, of history and their critique by Nietzsche; the very notion of history undergoes a radical transformation in the process. Writing no longer "*originarily subordinate* to the logos and to truth" *often* emerges as historical. In fact, as shall be seen in Chapter 6, only thus does *writing* become meaningfully or productively historical, whenever history must be the issue; only thus can *writing* relate to the radical historical difference of *différance*, as opposed to the final repression of history and difference in the name of history and difference, characterizing various restricted economies of history, Hegelian or other.

This is perhaps the reason why Nietzsche, while criticizing *historicism*, in answering his own question "What do philosophers lack?" says first of all, "an historical sense" (*Will to Power*, 220; *KSA* 11:176). In *Twilight of the Idols*, although another question against "philosophers"—"You ask me which of the philosophers' traits are really idiosyncrasies?"—generates a multiplicity of answers, the first example will be "their lack of historical sense, their hatred of the very idea of becoming, their Egypticism. They think that they *honor* a cause when they de-historicize it *sub specie aeterni*— when they turn it into a mummy [Sie fragen mich, was Alles Idiosynkrasie bei den Philosophen ist? . . . Zum Beispiel ihr Mangel an historischem Sinn, ihr Hass gegen die Vorstellung selbst des Werdens, ihr Ägypticismus. Sie glauben einer Sache *Ehre* anzuthun, wenn sie dieselbe enthistorisiren, sub specie aeterni,—wenn sie aus ihr eine Mumie machen]" (*Portable Nietzsche*, 479; *KSA* 6:74; translation modified). In the very next section, Heraclitus is seen as an exception "with the highest respect [mit hoher Ehrerbietung]" (*Portable Nietzsche*, 480; *KSA* 6:75). In itself, the Heraclitian "becoming" is, of course, not history. Nietzsche does use the term "history" here, however. Furthermore, there can be neither "becoming" nor "history" by themselves and in themselves as philosophers' "concepts-mummies." But once nothing is absolutely general, nothing is in turn absolutely idiosyncratic, either. Not only are some of "the philosophers' traits idiosyncrasies," but also some idiosyncrasies are equally traits.

Nietzsche pursues a different, above all, a more unconscious economy—a general economy—of becoming and history. Such a different economy may in turn borrow from philosophy. It may borrow that which can be reinserted into a different chain and thus become a part of a different trait or even a different idiosyncrasy. Often, it is a matter of setting one idiosyncrasy against another or, depending on where one stands, originality against idiosyncrasy.

Hegel obviously plays a crucial role in the historical configuration under consideration here. If one were to characterize the theoretical revolution under discussion in terms of a history of proper names, one could say "Nietzsche" *after* "Hegel," and perhaps *after* Heidegger. For as soon as the ultimate authority of, or subordination "to the logos and to truth" is removed, it is "history" that often, although again *not* always, emerges as the *efficacity* of interpretive, theoretical, and political production. At issue is *history* against Hegel, to whom Nietzsche clearly refers when he speaks of "historicizing"— history as the unconscious against history as consciousness.

Whenever one must practice history, one must practice a different "history," *consciously*, by virtue of a different theory than one possesses, or otherwise. "Or otherwise"—or better, "*and* otherwise"—constitutes a crucial qualification here. First, there is no unique relationship between (the articulation of) a theory and a given practice of history or historical analysis. Nietzsche's plural style does not imply a fully conscious "calculus." The latter, as a full—or again, if you wish, Hegelian, or Leibnizian—calculus, is in fact impossible under all conditions; and in the end, such a Nietzschean style might even possess a more powerful *calculus* as well, along with a more effective "unconscious"—Dionysian—play. This style, however, can offer only a better practice of history or theory, not a full mastery of either. For example, the theoretical and the practical consequences and implications of what can be called Nietzsche's revolution are never determined solely by his own theories or ideologies, that is, by any given interpretation of Nietzsche's views as "his own." In general, no ideology or theory can ever fully determine its own effects or its theoretical or practical strategies, however much it shapes them; and to some extent it always does exert this shaping force. Nor are such or similar effects, theoretical or practical, always necessarily produced by Nietzsche's text. Their efficacity may emerge historically quite differently. In this sense, our accounts are always partial.

There will be, then, no unconditional authority or originary subordination to history, whether a classical, a deconstructive, or still another economy of history is at issue. This understanding, as was stated earlier, constitutes a part of Nietzsche's critique of historicism. Nor, once again, is Nietzsche's own analysis always historical in this or any given sense. Nietzsche also speaks of psychological, physiological, political, and many other namable and as yet unnamable effects and prejudices of philosophers. They cannot always be reassembled under the rubric of history, although they are often historical in various senses of the term. Nietzsche's critique of historicism is a critique not only of a particular metaphysical conception of history, but also of the unconditional authority of any history. My relative insistence on Nietzsche's relative insistence on history is not aimed at reducing the radical plurality of Nietzsche's theoretical and historical strategies, or the plurality of Nietzsche's styles. Nietzsche's is a general economy of difference, transformation, becoming. The general economy efficacity engaged by Nietzsche cannot, therefore, be reduced to history, particularly conscious and self-conscious—Hegelian—history. Nor, as we have seen, can the efficacity of this differential and transformational play be reduced to difference or play or to any single term or concept—the "proper word [mot propre]" and the "unique name [nom unique]"—the "quest [quête]" for which, according to Derrida, constitutes "Heideggerian *hope* [*l'espérance* heideggerienne]" (*Margins*, 27; *Marges*, 29).

By contrast, as Nietzsche understood, Hegel and Hegelian history are, above all, the ultimate or unconditional authority of and subordination to the logos and truth. Hegel's history itself is the authority now. As Nietzsche says in the passage cited earlier, this *is* "history with an immanent spirit and the goal within, so one can entrust oneself to it." Hegel's history is thus of a very specific, very determinate, and very philosophical type. This history is always the history of the conscious or of conceptual spirit, *Geist*; thus, in Hegel's philosophy of history, true historicity permits no unconscious. All history is eschatologically or teleologically the history of philosophy. Thus *Hegelian* history is *not historical* enough. It is the restricted economy of subordination to the logos, to truth, to philosophy and, above all, to consciousness; this economy must be deconstructed and, often, deconstructed *historically*. Hence Derrida says: ". . . all that Hegel thought within [the] horizon [of absolute knowledge], all, that is, except eschatology, may be reread as a meditation on writing" (*Of Grammatology*, 26; *De la grammatologie*, 41).

But then, "except eschatology" is almost "except everything" in Hegel, whom Derrida sees as the "last philosopher of the book and the first thinker of writing [. . . dernier philosophe du livre et premier penseur de l'écriture]" (*Of Grammatology*, 26; *De la grammatologie*, 41). Hegel's or any other eschatology rather *excepts* history in the general economy of *différance*, excepts *writing*. This eschatology—the eschatology of the Hegelian *Aufhebung*—is the eschatology of truth, consciousness, and presence. Derrida, we recall, insists that "if there were a definition of *différance*, it would be precisely the limit, the interruption, the destruction of Hegelian *relève* [*Aufhebung*] *wherever* it operates" (*Positions*, 40–41). If such is the case, however, Hegel may not have been a thinker of writing at all. Instead, we must "think"—or better, write—*writing* and a different, radically or structurally unconscious historicity—in short, a general economy of history. In this general economy we must reconfigure as *writing* that which Hegel thought, thinking—and *writing*—of this writing quite differently from the way Hegel thought and *wrote* about it. Thus one may recomprehend Hegelianism by way of this writing, a recomprehension that is quite a different matter, however, from claiming Hegel as a thinker of writing.

Why the first, then? Why not Rousseau, as would follow with just as much force from Derrida's own analysis? Or Socrates/Plato—Socrates who does not write, and Plato who does? It is true that Derrida in fact, or in effect, claims that they, too, were the first thinkers of writing, thus implying that there is no first thinker of writing.[20] Strictly, however, none of them may be seen as a thinker of *writing* in Derrida's sense. It may be Nietzsche, who is another "first," according to Derrida—Nietzsche *against* Hegel. The proximity between what Nietzsche has to offer and Derrida's *writing* is fundamental. In truth, however, the *first* thinker, or rather *writer*, of *writing* must be Derrida. Derrida's *writing* does of course have its continuities with, among others, Nietzsche, and indeed Hegel. Nevertheless, a structure—the effect—of break, or rupture, is no less decisive.

Nietzsche's history, or Nietzsche's genealogies, then, imply a radically new theory of history. In the first place, for Nietzsche, as later for Freud, the primary activity and thus the primary historical activity are always unconscious. As soon as the unconscious enters this economy, the historical heterogeneity can never be integrated or subsumed in a philosophical synthesis, whether the Hegelian *Aufhebung*, Marxist historical materialism, or another sort. In Hegel, history is eventually eschatologically and teleologically subsumed by the conceptuality and consciousness of philosophy, or a still higher form of (self-)consciousness and presence. In Nietzsche, all philosophy, all truth, all consciousness, and all presence are dissolved, or deconstructed so as to emerge as *local historical* "determinations" and "effects." This localization engages a more powerful theoretical economy than either Marx's or Hegel's. This perspectivization, however, precludes the possibility of subsuming all such "determinations" and "effects" under the rubric of historical—or local or perspectival determination, effects, or any other single rubric.

One cannot quite do without philosophy and its concepts, either, hence the closure of metaphysics in Derrida. For Nietzsche, however, whenever *theory* is needed, one needs a theory different from philosophy. Philosophy, much like religion, and simultaneously with it, remains interesting for Nietzsche mostly *as* the *history* of philosophy, not as the history of *philosophy*. Thus the Hegelian formula "history is the history of philosophy" is repeated—reiterated—against Hegelianism.[21]

It also follows, however, that no given articulation or inscription of history can account for or master the range of all possible "effects," or fully master any given theoretical or interpretive effect. In other words, whatever our historico-theoretical model or paradigm may be, neither can it fully account for any given configuration nor is it applicable to all configurations; "consequences," "implications," and "effects" appear within a far more complex and more radically mediated historical model. A mediation, but without the unconscious, is already at the center stage of Hegel's writing. The *Hegelian* conscious or conceptual *mediation*, however, is not radical enough, *not mediated* enough, nor in fact, in a certain sense, is it immediate enough; in many cases a more radical immediacy, a more radical *presence*, needs to be configured.

Nor, all his mastery of plural styles notwithstanding, can Nietzsche fully master all the difference or calculate all undecidables. As Derrida points out in *Spurs*:

> It is not that it is necessary to choose sides with the heterogeneous or the parody (which would only reduce them once again). Nor, given that the *master* sense, the sole inviolate sense, is irretrievable, does it necessarily follow that Nietzsche's mastery is infinite, his power impregnable, or his manipulation of the snare impeccable. One cannot conclude, in order to outmaneuver the hermeneutic hold, that his is an infinite calculus which is similar to Leibniz' God, but is the infinite calculus of the undecidable. Such a conclusion in its very attempt to elude the snare, succumbs all the more surely to it. (*Spurs*, 99; translation modified)[22]

The allusion to Gödel is very subtle and to the point.[23] "Writing . . . not *originarily subordinate* to the logos and to truth," by definition, cannot be originarily subordinate to a master calculus of undecidables, whether historical or theoretical.

The "historical"—genealogical—investigation demanded by Nietzsche always involves a "theoretical" investigation as well. "History" and "theory" develop a mutual complicity and complementarity of their own, without fully reducing or subsuming each other and without full mutual synthesis, as in Hegel—without the *Aufhebung*. One can continually adjust the balance of these elements, as Nietzsche does, to pursue a plural historico-theoretical style. Nietzsche's textual practice is no denial of theory—no theoretical nihilism, any more than it is a historical nihilism. It involves in the first place the theory of history as just indicated, and it leads to the general economy, that is, *theory*, of "history," which is a major issue in its own right and which I shall consider in Chapter 6. One needs, however, a considerable range of other theory as well, even in the practice of history.

From this perspective, Nietzsche's analysis—for example, in the *Genealogy*—might be said to be *theoretical*. It is an analysis of "causes" and "effects," simultaneously deconstructing classical concepts, such as cause, effect, or history, and classical history and historiography. It also thus has powerful historical and historiographical effects. To a degree, this kind of "program" and theoretico-historical practice begins with *The Birth of Tragedy*. The general economy of the unconscious as the Dionysian becomes the "efficacity" powerfully shaping the history—the birth and death—of tragedy as well as philosophy, such as in the problematic case of Socrates. As no other text before it does, *The Birth of Tragedy* "shows" that "the unconscious" leads above to—always already—mutual inhibitions of consciousness and the unconscious, or of the Apollinian and the Dionysian, or of many other such oppositions, which as oppositional pairs overlap and inhabit each other, disabling one from, for example, fully correlating the Apollinian with consciousness, or the Dionysian with the unconscious, and further fracturing all such relations. Nietzsche himself does not perhaps fully follow these implications in his first book, a text that requires a degree of deconstruction in order to derive these consequences and implications.[24] These implications form the tasks of Nietzsche's later works, and the *Genealogy* is fully in possession of these *theoretical* results.

Theory (*theoria*) is, we recall, also Greek for 'spectacle,' and *historia* also means 'inquiry,' 'investigation.' Nietzsche's play (*paideia*) is that of history and theory, theory and theater, of both, or all three, at once; and perhaps even more than it is Heraclitean, Nietzschean play is Dionysian, carried on in *Nietzsche*'s style of *writing* no longer "*originarily subordinate* to the logos and to truth."

Tragedies and Revolutions

The relationship between literature and truth—or philosophy—is one of the central "undecidables" in Derrida's analysis and deconstruction of Western metaphysics and its history. Derrida, we recall, introduces "undecidables," by analogy with Gödel, in this very context of literature and truth in his reading of Mallarmé in *Dissemination*. The undecidable of literature and truth is defined by way of what Derrida calls "*hymen*," actually a specific "*hymen*": "*L'hymen: ENTRE Platon et Mallarmé*" (*Dissemination*, 181). This *hymen* is introduced in juxtaposition to and is set to deconstruct the decidable, controlled ambiguity of the Hegelian *Aufhebung* and the whole dialectical, and thus restricted, economy of historical and interpretive transformations. This juxtaposition also defines, via both Hegel and Lacan, the difference between *dissemination* and polysemy. The economy, by definition general, of *dissemination* and its *différance* pertains, as we have seen, to the *dissemination* of Derrida's very terms—*différance, writing, general economy, dissemination*—is opposed to the organized and controlled, and thus restricted, economies of classical systems, such as, in particular, Hegel's dialectics or Heidegger's ontology. Derrida's analysis of the undecidable between literature and truth or philosophy—the "proof," as it

were, of undecidability—and his very inscription as *"hymen"* are prolonged, as they perhaps must be, given the complexity of the issue. The
"hymen" itself is "between" or *inter*, as Barbara Johnson translates it, many
things—and many an "inter": between Plato or Socrates/Plato and Mallarmé, or Hegel and Mallarmé (194), Latin as language between the Greeks
and Western philosophy or literature, particularly French literature. It
might even be an *inter* between Nietzsche—Nietzsche as Heraclitus—and
Derrida—Derrida as Heraclitus. Dionysus might be a more complex case.
It certainly is an *inter* between German and French, as Hegel stands between Plato and Mallarmé, and Nietzsche between Hegel—or indeed between everything from Heraclitus or even Anaximander and Thales—and
Derrida, via Freud and Heidegger.

Freud, as Derrida suggests in *The Post Card*, is a case of the repression
of Nietzsche and, perhaps inevitably, of the return of the repressed. But
then, the prolonged deliberate encounter notwithstanding, there is a strong
repressed element of Nietzsche in Heidegger, especially in a repression of
the (question of the) feminine. This "case," *treated* by Derrida in *Spurs*, is
also that of a *hymen*—between Nietzsche and Heidegger, between literature, here tragedy, and truth, between tragedy and philosophy. In "The
Double Session [La Double séance]," Derrida writes:

> *Inter Platonem et Mallarmatum*, between Plato and Mallarmé—whose
> proper names, it should be understood, are not real references but indi-
> cations for the sake of convenience and initial analysis—a whole history
> has taken place. This history was also a history of literature if one accepts
> the idea that literature was born of it and died of it, the certificate of its
> birth as such, the declaration of its name, having coincided with its dis-
> appearance, according to a logic that the hymen will help us define. And
> this history, if it has any meaning, is governed in its entirety by the value
> of truth and by a certain relation, inscribed in the hymen in question, *be-
> tween* literature and truth. In saying "this history, if it has any meaning,"
> one seems to be admitting that it might not. But if we were to go to the
> end of this analysis, we would see it confirmed not only that this history
> has a meaning, but that the very concept of history has lived only upon
> the possibility of meaning, upon the past, present, or promised presence
> of meaning and of truth. Outside this system, it is impossible to resort to
> the concept of history without reinscribing it elsewhere, according to
> some specific systematic strategy. (*Dissemination*, 183–84; *La Dissémina-
> tion*, 209)

Much is at stake or in play in this "systematic strategy," or this "'general economy,' a kind of *general strategy of deconstruction* [(une) 'économie
générale,' une sorte de *stratégie générale de la déconstruction*]" (*Positions*, 41;

Positions, 56). The historico-theoretical trajectory of this matrix proceeds from Nietzsche to Derrida via a complex chain, or rather network, involving many proper names, here most pertinently Freud, Heidegger, Bataille, Lacan, Althusser, and Deleuze, and many *texts* without "signatures."

Along and as part of this reinscription of history, the opposition between literature and truth or literature and philosophy becomes *undecidable*. In this new historico-theoretical regime of complementary interactions, it becomes impossible to decide upon any such relation once and for all, often even in a given case, such as Nietzsche's or Mallarmé's. In addition, this configuration also has to be played out differently at different moments of textual engagement. It may be either literature or philosophy, or neither of these. One must apply the logic of either/or that may or may not be simultaneously neither/nor, invoked by Derrida in *Positions* (43). Such an either/or or neither/nor, or both at once, may or may not be associated with truth, as the value of truth is played out between truth without value and value without truth. This play may be used in order to undermine the classical value of truth—the truth-value of philosophy in a critical or deconstructive text such as Nietzsche's or, as Derrida suggests, Mallarmé's, or more deliberately, Derrida's own, or in a critical and deconstructive stratum of another given text, whether it is under deconstruction or not. On the other hand, as happens in Heidegger, particularly in the case of his notion of thinking-poetizing (on the truth of Being) that is developed in his later works, this play, as we have seen, may and must be used in order to reinstate presence and the control of transformations by "the highest law and the hidden rule" (*The Question of Being*, 104–5).

Under these conditions, however, "names"—proper names—become important "signs" or rather specific cases and modes of *différance* that can be differently played out by a reading, in the deconstructive or postdeconstructive sense of the term. *The degree of claim* for the transformational potential of any given text remains an important issue, however, including specifically in the case of Derrida's reading of Mallarmé. While Derrida's reading does, I think, project a few things into "Mallarmé," Derrida's analysis of literature and the literary may be seen, or *read*, as shaped by Mallarmé's conceptions to a much greater degree than by other texts that might be invoked here. Derrida's general claims concerning Platonism would stand in any event: "'Platonism' here standing more or less immediately for the whole history of Western philosophy, including anti-Platonisms that regularly feed into it. . . . the presumed possibility of a discourse about what is, the deciding and decidable *logos* of or about the *on* (being-present)" (*Dissemination*, 191; *La Dissémination*, 217). Platonism is thus also a claim for the original object of imitation, while deconstruction shows that if one wants to or must speak about imitation (mimesis), and so forth, one cannot speak of the absolutely or unconditionally *original* object of imitation. Everything thus becomes precisely *written*, against the parallel Socratic hierarchies—the order of writing, speech, and thought, and "the clinical paradigm of *mimēsis*, the order of the three beds in the *Republic* (10.596a ff.): the painter's, the carpenter's, and God's" (*Dissemination*, 191–92; *La Dissémination*, 218). Every one of these beds is always already in the same—supplementary—position, being at least twice removed from the posited original in this philosophical bedroom—in the bedroom of the three beds.[25]

One of Derrida's major points in the passage cited and in "The Double Session" as a whole is that we cannot productively analyze the question of fiction or literature outside "this history" from which Nietzsche, Mallarmé, or others inherit the very terms of their overturnings. That would specifically refer to the configurations of reversal—reconfigurations by way of reversal—placing literature above philosophy, whether by way of truth, or against truth as in Nietzsche.[26] The analysis also raises and must deal with two further aspects of the question: whether such a reversal would finally reinstate the ground and hierarchy that it wants to subvert, and whether and to what degree it would manage to avoid such a reinstatement. In "White Mythology: Metaphor in the Text of Philosophy," Derrida makes a similar and equally convincing case for "metaphor" as the undecidable. Metaphor is surely a "between," too, *by definition*. It is another "*inter*," through which Nietzsche begins his assault on truth in an earlier essay, "On Truth and Falsity in the Extra-moral Sense," which has been, justly, so prominent in recent discussions. Metaphor, in *truth*, is itself an *undefinable* concept; for its definition always depends on another "undefined" metaphor such as "*inter*," or "between," or whatever inscribes the "relation"; and throughout "this history" metaphor, too, has lived between (*inter*) philosophy and literature.

Once a transformation—a reconfiguration and a *new* configuration—of, among other things, philosophy and literature take place, however, even though they may not take place at once, other—"new"—things become possible. In a certain sense, as Derrida says, "everything becomes possible, for example, 'literatures' and 'revolution,'" an issue that I shall consider later. On the other hand, some "old" things become impossible; even everything becomes impossible in the way it is configured by the old system. "That law [enacted by the text of *Mimique*] does not apply only to the text of 'Mallarmé,' even though he 'illustrates' it according to a 'historical' necessity whose entire field needs to be mapped out, and even though such an illustration *entails a general reinterpretation of everything*" (*Dissemination*, 245; *La Dissémination*, 276; emphasis added).

New constraints emerge, both as limiting and as productive forces, while many—*but not all*—old ones are removed. One is no longer constrained by, no longer subordinates one's writing, in whatever sense, to an *unconditional* authority, such as the authority of the logos and the truth. These authorities, though claimed to be unconditional, are in fact and can only be conditional; furthermore, they are always conditioned differently from the way they are claimed to be conditioned. Thus, for example, as Nietzsche states: "That which *enforces* it [asceticism], however, this unconditional will to truth, is *faith in the ascetic ideal itself*, even if as its unconscious imperative—don't be deceived about that—it is the faith in a *metaphysical* value, the value in itself of *truth*, sanctioned and guaranteed by this ideal alone (it stands or falls with this ideal) [Was aber zu ihm (dem Ascetismus der Tugend) *zwingt*, jener unbedingte Wille zur Wahrheit, das ist der *Glaube an das asketische Ideal selbst*, wenn auch als sein unbewusster Imperativ, man täusche sich hierüber nicht,—das ist der Glaube an einen *metaphysischen* Werth, einen Werth *an sich der Wahrheit*, wie er allein in jenem Ideal verbürgt und verbrieft ist (er steht und fällt mit jenem Ideal)]" (*Genealogy*, 151; *KSA* 5:400; translation modified).

Although succinct, this statement is brilliant and complex. Nietzsche *re-comprehends* the old forces and constraints *as* forces and constraints within a different, unconscious, and in effect general economy, introducing and producing *new* configurations of forces and constraints. These new constraints are then articulated and analyzed throughout the book, both as productive and enabling and as constraining and limiting. Derrida, too, in "The Double Session," speaks of the "constraint of differential-supplementary structure [la contrainte de la structure différential-supplémentaire]" (*Dissemination*, 270; *La Dissémination*, 301; translation modified).

While, however, this differential supplementary structure, or structures—*différance, dissemination, iterability*, and so on—do "entail a general reinterpretation of everything [donne tout à relire]" and an imposition of new *general* constraints, they do not entail a global or unified configuration of control. In the first place, while there may and must be sufficiently general traits and operation of *différance, dissemination*, or *iterability*, their functioning may need to be reconfigured differently each time. Second, the general economy does not offer a full mastery of any interpretive configuration. As we have seen, it relates to a radical difference that cannot be mastered either in actual articulation or in principle by any philosopheme or cluster of philosophemes, that cannot be *represented*. The "difference" at issue, as against philosophy—for example, the Heideggerian ontological difference or more complex, but still restricted economies of difference offered in his later works—is not subject to any *presence*—being-presence, becoming-presence, history-presence, multiplicity-presence. In Derrida, "presence" becomes a comprehensive general rubric relating to all such forms of the metaphysics of presence.

Nor, as a corollary, can such a difference—never one difference or one anything to begin with—be mastered by any configuration of critical, as opposed to classical, discourse, by any general economy such as Nietzsche's, Bataille's, Derrida's, or another. Otherwise, a theoretical economy would not be significantly different from classical forms of the "inaccessible" transcendental signified, such as Heidegger's Being. The "difference" to which one must refer does not exist "there"—in some transcendental space or nonspace—as a "thing" that commands everything and controls everything, particularly as postulated in the form of presence, but in fact in any form. All these configurations imply the possibility of mastering the difference of the transcendental—to "master" it as mastery that cannot be mastered—and thus imply one or another form of the metaphysics of presence. The transformations of the general economy are more radical in this sense. That which "ultimately" controls and constrains a given interpretive configuration at a given moment may not be any of the things just listed. It might be neither difference nor transformations nor constraints nor controls. One might claim that *at bottom* no interpretive or historical configuration can finally ever be sufficiently grasped by anything that is available within the theoretical closure or closures on which we must rely. The situation is always bottomless in this sense.

This abyssal economy—famous by now, although not always understood in its full implications—need not preclude the possibility of comprehensive interpretations, explanations, theories, or histories. Rather, one must reconceive such notions themselves. It is crucial to keep in mind, however, that bottomlessness also may be differently configured. The general economy of transformations implies that a bottomless economy has a different economy from a metaphysical one like Heidegger's. Hence, any form of articulation, configuration, inscription, or "approach," including *différance* or general economy, in turn can be replaced. None can be seen as fully governing a multiplicity, although some can be sufficiently comprehensive.

In this sense and with these qualifications, the new economy so emerging—the general economy—is not only less ordered, but is also more highly ordered in the sense of being able to *comprehend* things that

171

were incomprehensible within the old system, however systematic the latter might appear or might be claimed to be. The old system is restricted in every conceivable sense. Not only is it not unsystematic enough, but it is also not systematic enough. It has too little chaos and too little order. It has too little *play*. Perhaps, above all, it has too little interaction—inter-*play*—between them in the first place, for example, by way of complementary articulations, decidable or undecidable, between literature and theory, history and theory, or indeed restricted and general economies. A general economy is always by definition a complementary matrix in this sense; this fact, in Derrida, leads to the complementary economy between the inside and the outside of philosophy, as the metaphysics of presence, by way of the closure of philosophy.

At any given moment, of course, there may be no instance of untransformed closure anywhere; in addition, old systems are continually transforming themselves. Radical transformation in this sense, however, can be set against the type of transformation that continues to operate within an already established system. Such a distinction between the types of transformation would not necessarily imply that a radical transformation can be fundamentally determined by an "exterior" of a given system or field: one cannot be fully—absolutely—"outside" of what one wants to, or must, or does transform. The question is rather, on the one hand, that of the relative balance of the exterior and the interior of a system such as philosophy or a given canon of philosophy, and on the other, that of how far a closure of such a system, specifically the closure of metaphysics, extends in a critical text, for example, Nietzsche's. That relative balance or extension of closure would fundamentally affect how one defines—or refuses to define—one's field or one's position(s) between (*inter*) fields; or how one refuses to take a position, either once and for all, or locally. No given configuration of styles and positions can determine the effectiveness or success of a given text, or a given reading. That effectiveness will remain, *finally*, undecidable, to the point that no plurality of style, no strategic or tactical flexibility, helpful as it might be, can guarantee such effectiveness. The metaphysics of presence, even in its most naive or vulgar form, can be—and has been—successful, even though—*now*—such a success, *from the perspective of general economy*, can be explained only by way of a plural—*general*—economy.

Once, then, a general economy replaces and (re)comprehends the unconditional authorities of philosophy and once the philosopher is no longer "able to delimit the object-fiction . . . except by another counter-fiction" (*Limited Inc*, 100), the status of fiction or literature changes along with the status of truth, as unconditional authority. Literature and truth mutually define each other within the historical and conceptual closure of philosophy as the metaphysics of presence. Changing their relations by way of general economy, however, constitutes neither a simple reversal nor a simple elimination of the difference between literature or fiction and truth, although the ultimate unconditional difference, of course, is rigorously suspended. Only as a result of this transformation do both notions— truth and fictionality—acquire the theoretical rigor that their history demands, but they always need a plural—general—economy of truth*s* and fictionalitie*s*. As is the case with authority, there will always be truths everywhere, as well as fictions and literatures. They emerge and impose themselves all the time. But their operation must be conceived of differently, even though some of their effects in practice will retain their previous form.

At some point in "Limited Inc, abc. . . ," Derrida makes a famous remark on "literatures and revolutions." The essay itself is Derrida's response to John Searle and an extension of Derrida's critique of speech act theory in "Signature Event Context." Since speech act theory, as Derrida demonstrates, is a form of the unconditional authority of consciousness and presence, his statement has a far broader historical and political range; and Derrida invokes the attendant political implications throughout both texts. As I have indicated, the conjunction of "literature and revolution" actually emerges earlier in Derrida's reading of Bataille in "From Restricted to General Economy" (*Writing and Difference*, 261). Derrida may also be thinking of Trotsky's famous essay "Literature and Revolution" and a Marxist social and historical perspective. In "Signature Event Context," Derrida introduces "iterability" as another aspect of radical difference or another structure, since the plurality at issue cannot be integrated into a single conglomerate. These structures necessitate each other, however, and multiply and heterogenerously interact. *Writing* demands *différance*, and *différance* makes it necessary to speak of *trace* on the one hand and *supplement* on the other; writing demands *dissemination*, which in turn continuously enacts a powerful *différance*, and so on.

Inscribed or reinscribed via Mallarmé, the 'literary' is also necessarily l-*iterary*, the structure of iterability or, rather, carrying along with itself the necessity of iterability. Conversely, given the history at issue—Platonism— iterability is also "literability." They form, in short, a complementarity, which, though finally undecidable, is locally operative and effective. This complementarity is or involves something that iterates as it "literates," and even ob-l-iterates a few things along the way. *Iteration*, actually, appears or is already intimated in *Of Grammatology*, again in the context of art and imitation (209). In "Limited Inc" and "Signature Event Context," the question of theater and performance is as crucial as it is in *Mimique*, where the dance of the mime is also a choreography of writing. In "Limited Inc abc . . ." it is also a (con)juncture of "literature(s)" and "revolution(s)," their *inter*-play, their undecidable relationships. Derrida writes:

> . . . once this parasitism or fictionality can always add *another* parasitic or fictional structure to whatever has preceded it—everything becomes possible against the language-police; for example "literatures" or "revolutions" that as yet have no model. Everything is possible except for an exhaustive typology that would claim to limit the powers of graft or of fiction by and within an analytical logic of distinction, opposition, and classification in genus and species. The theoretician of speech acts [or any theoretician] will have to get used to the idea that, knowingly or not, willingly or not, both his treatment of things and the things themselves are marked in advance by the possibility of fiction, either as the iterability of acts or as the system of conventionality. He will therefore never be able to *de-limit* the object-fiction or the object-parasite except by another counter-fiction." (*Limited Inc*, 99–100)[27]

Elsewhere Derrida speaks of his own writing as operating in the double register of the literary and the philosophical. One cannot deny the significance of this stratification for the history of Western philosophy and the current scene of criticism and theory, which is the issue in *Dissemination*—"*inter Platonem et Mallarmatum*," "*inter Hegelem et Mallarmatum*," and thus *inter Platonem* or *Socratem, et Derridatum*, and *inter Hegelem et Derridatum*. Other names that Derrida invokes in that context, such as Artaud, Bataille, Mallarmé, or Sollers, have likewise had a profound influence upon this scene. By the same token, however, one must operate in the *multiple* register—*within* as well as between "literature*s*" and "revolution*s*." As is the case with authority and power, and involving powers and authorities—social, institutional, practical including political, or other—literatures and revolutions will be seen as emerging, interacting, and differentiating, conflictually or otherwise, in this complementary (inter)play—which is both inter*play* and *inter* play, the play of the *inter*. Indeed, both literatures and revolutions begin only now to emerge theoretically; but they will have no single model, no unique term or finally proper name will fully comprehend or govern such events—neither literature nor revolution, "not even the name Being, not even the name *différance*" (*Margins*, 27). There will be no name as a unique or final or finally proper name; in practice, in the history of short and long sessions of analysis of the cases of literature and revolution, they will have all these and many other names.

Within their closure, then—and, I would suggest, *transforming* it—and by way of this complementarity, Nietzsche perceives this differential play as an artistic rather than a philosophical phenomenon. The Dionysian is juxtaposed to the Socratean in the beginning of Nietzsche's career, and to Christianity at the end of it, to "Socrates [and Christ], who [do] not write"; and, as we have seen, Heraclitus, still earlier, is seen by Nietzsche as an artistic philosopher as contrasted to Anaximander or Parmenides. The terms Nietzsche uses are "*artistic [künstlich]*" and "*tragic [tragische]*," rather than "literature"—"*tragic artist [der tragische Künstler]*," "*tragic poet [der tragische Dichter]*." Derrida's "literature" finds its specificity between Plato and Mallarmé and in the context of *mimesis*, a rubric less central for Nietzsche. Derrida's register, however, remains broad enough to relate to Nietzsche's terms, which are in turn related to their history in a given culture. The problem of translation does arise here, in any language, including German in Nietzsche and French in Derrida. These terms can be managed within the textual economy, I think; and Nietzsche's conceptual and rhetorical chains substantially determine their functioning, or perhaps overdetermine it. In the end, making all absolute mastery impossible, Nietzsche's master rubric is perhaps the *tragic*, that joins the Dionysian, beginning with Nietzsche's earliest writing.[28]

Given the fundamentally, structurally perspectival conditions demanded by Nietzsche, an economy—tragic or Dionysian, qualities that may be indissociable but are not identical in Nietzsche—may only be one perspective, one vision among others. *From this perspective*, however, the tragic—the affirmation of life, even under the condition of the greatest tragedy—is also the *best* vision, artistic or theoretical, one can offer. Nietzsche is the great master of plural style, and he could have played in many registers, artistic or theoretical. Nevertheless, he *does* take strong positions, which is not to say that either these positions or their general economy is simple—quite the contrary. The style is plural and extraordinarily flexible. But the positions are affirmative: they are not only Yes!-saying positions—always saying Yes! to life—but also positions firmly taken. In this sense, one of the major questions—we might call this question politico-theoretical—posed by Derrida and deconstruction and the style it pursues is whether there can be an *affirmative* style that also refuses to take positions. Derrida and others do speak of the deconstructive style as affirmative. Derrida's own style can in turn be seen as oscillating between these two affirmative styles, between taking positions and refusing to take them; but, I think, it does so quite differently from Nietzsche's style. As Derrida writes, in a—*perhaps*—different context: "I say it *against* Nietzsche, *perhaps* [Je dis cela contre Nietzsche, peut-être]" ("Living On: Border Lines," 125; *Parages*, 169; emphasis added).[29] That is not to say that one style is always better than another: one should not *perhaps/of course* always be affirmative and one should *perhaps/of course* at times take positions, very firm positions. One might practice plural styles in this sense, too, between what might be termed the "of course" style and the "perhaps" style.

Nietzsche, let me reiterate, continuously uses transformations, reversal, and mutual contamination and inhibitions of terms and concepts; and utilizing immense resources of his plural style, he plays with many terms, concepts, and strategies, classical and critical, with great flexibility and richness. Most playful and often most unconscious in his play, Nietzsche, whenever necessary, is logical, often more logical than many philosophers before and after him, even though he often sees logic, especially dialectic, as "a symptom of decadence." Thus, in referring to writing *Daybreak*, Nietzsche says: "In the midst of the torments that go with uninterrupted three-day migraine [brain pain], accompanied by laborious vomiting of phlegm, possessed a *dialectician's clarity* par excellence and thought through with very cold blood matters for which under healthier circumstances I am not mountain-climber, not subtle, not *cold* enough." Nietzsche often relates these matters to physiological sickness, physiological decadence, in himself: "The perfect brightness and cheerfulness, even exuberance of spirit, reflected in this work, is compatible in my case not only with the most profound physiological weakness, but even with an excess of pain," and in general: "My readers perhaps know in what way I consider dialectic as a symptom of decadence; for example, in the most famous case, the case of Socrates" (*Ecce Homo*, 222–23; *KSA* 6:265; emphasis added).

Such a correlation between the mental and the physical may be problematic, including in Nietzsche's own case. It is, however, of secondary importance for the moment: whatever the conditions of Nietzsche's logical abilities and power—"a *dialectician's clarity* par excellence"—these abilities and this power are themselves hardly in question. Physical sickness is far from the only decadence that Nietzsche diagnoses in Socrates' case; and relations to logic, including dialectic, become increasingly complex, as one explores Nietzsche's styles further. Nietzsche's logical skills, however, remain exquisite under all conditions.

Correlations between physical and theoretical—or artistic—symptoms are by no means impossible, either, however. Such matters are far from discountable, either in Nietzsche's case or in general, although we are far from knowing how to account for them. While Nietzsche himself may at times rely on a dubious physiology, the relation itself of the *philosophical* spirit to the *body* is a crucial part of Nietzsche's *psychology*—and the *physiology*—of philosophy, as part of his critique of the *philosophy* of philosophy. The system of philosophy can no longer be contained within itself. Philosophy must depend on an exterior that it cannot master; and this mastery cannot extend to the mastery of inscribing that which cannot belong to or is absolutely outside of the concern and the text of philosophy. After "an historical sense," the second item on Nietzsche's list of "what philosophers lack" is actually "knowledge of physiology"—"Was *fehlte* den Philosophen a) historischer Sinn b) Kenntniß der Physiologie" (*Will to Power*, 220; *KSA* 11:176). Physiology, along with psychology, is for Nietzsche a crucial aspect of that *stratified* and radical—but again never absolute—"exterior" from which Nietzsche's critique and deconstruction proceed.

A plural style must always operate both from the inside and from the outside of the deconstructed field. This double strategy defines the *plural* style, according to Derrida, most specifically in relation to the philosophical register. Within this *différance* of the inside and the outside of philosophy, however, Nietzsche often and pointedly shifts the balance toward the exterior. He sees himself both as the first *tragic*—that is, Dionysian—"philosopher" and the first psychologist and physiologist of philosophy. More generally, as we have seen, the plurality of style in Nietzsche, or Bataille and several other practitioners of plural style, relates to other registers than those defined by the philosophical field, double and multiple, of even fractional complementarities, and configurations of closure. In the draft of a letter to Lou Andreas von Salomé, Nietzsche writes: "I was at once a philologist, a writer, a musician, a philosopher, a free-thinker, etc. (perhaps a poet, etc.)" (*Nietzsche Briefwechsel*, pt. 3, 1:282).

The *artistic* side—"play" as against "logic"—of Nietzsche's general economic and complementary practice is equally rich and complex, and, according to the complementary character of this economy as defined in Chapter 1, this *artistic* play, too, can at times employ powerful logic. Along with other things, perhaps subordinating his writing to the unconditional authority of Socrates and his truth, Plato—"the *artist* Plato"—is also condemned by Nietzsche as a decadent of style, even "the first decadent in style." Nietzsche, on this occasion, does not fail to put to use the very classical strategy of invoking "the authority of the ancients," moreover, without specifying which of the ancients, which is yet another very classical strategy: "In the end, the subtlest judges taste among the ancients themselves are here on my side" (*Twilight*, in *Portable Nietzsche*, 557; *KSA*

6:155). Plato is *not* a *tragic* artist, nor a *tragic* philosopher. He remains forever a disciple of Socrates, not of Dionysus; or else, seduced by Socrates, Plato abandons Dionysus for Socrates. But once it is not playful, not Dionysian enough, his logic, along with and following Socrates', becomes not logical enough, either.

Nietzsche's strategies thus may be complementary—theoretical or artistic, engaging multiple functioning of these terms themselves, and complementarizing them with other terms. They may be *tragic* as well as comic, often deliberately comic. There can be no Dionysian without comedy. This itself is a crucial part of Nietzsche's confrontation with Aristotle's *Poetics*. Nietzsche was doubtless well aware of Socrates' contentions in the end of *Symposium* "that the same man might be capable of writing both comedy and tragedy—that the tragic poet might be a comedian as well" (223d, in *The Collected Dialogues of Plato*, 574). At the level of theory, this dual capability is what Nietzsche himself practiced, holding Shakespeare in mind as the greatest example of the Dionysian artist—tragic and comic, narrative and dramatic, prosaic and poetic. Nietzsche not only told many a story but wrote many a poem as well, often to accompany his theoretical writing. This orientation is part of his *writing*, part of *theoria* as spectacle and performance; there is, as we recall, a collection of Nietzsche's poems called "*Dionysos-Dithyramben*."

That styles and strategies are many must always be taken into account. While it is not possible to dissociate strategies or styles and the propositions produced, however, or even less, to subtract style from propositions, neither can one simply or fully correlate them. Different things can be *written* in Derrida's sense of *writing* as "not *originarily subordinate* to the logos and to truth." There is, in fact, no other writing, despite philosophy's claims that such writing exists or is possible—along with the logos and truth. Nor, by the same token, can plural style be restricted to conscious, deliberate practice, specifically in Nietzsche, although there are many deliberate styles of all sorts and much consciousness and self-consciousness in Nietzsche.

Let us recall in this context that, as Derrida shows in *Spurs*, it is not only the "style" that Heidegger misses in Nietzsche, but also a proposition on "the idea becoming a woman." Heidegger misses the constative as well as the performative.[30] Derrida, of course, in a characteristic self-referential and quasipsychoanalytic fashion, thematizes Nietzsche's style via these propositions: Heidegger missed "style" in part because he missed the proposition on style. This meta-economy is, however, far from the only form of relationship between propositions and style that can emerge in a given textual economy, as must in fact follow from Derrida's broader analysis. There can be no unique or unconditionally privileged relationship—of proposition or of anything else—to "style," no more to style than to anything else. Style may be differently related as much to propositions as to (taken) positions; and the positions and propositions may in turn have different relations to each other. Neither "*inter*" can be decided once and for all. It may be undecidable in some cases; it certainly appears to be *finally* undecidable. In other cases, though, it may also be decidable—and decisive—enough. Positions and propositions may be affirmed and maintained in the absence of the logos and truth. While they may all be ultimately or finally undecidable, still they might be the best positions and propositions available within a given configuration, or the only propositions possible. One might also have a different attitude toward one's positions; and that attitude might in turn result in a difference in style, including a difference, possibly quite radical, in one's plural style.

From Nietzsche's first texts to his last, the *tragic* as Dionysian, as opposed to just about any other denomination, never surrenders its position as the highest value. At times by way of tragic art, at times by way of tragic philosophy, "tragic" remains the major name in the Nietzschean "reevaluation of all values" hitherto. Along with and alongside becoming, the *tragic* is the conjunction—the complementarity—of the Dionysian and the Heraclitean that defines the Nietzschean:

> In this sense I have the right to understand myself as the first *tragic philosopher*—that is, the most extreme opposite and antipode of a pessimistic philosopher. Before me this transposition of the Dionysian into a philosophical pathos did not exist: *tragic wisdom* is lacking; I have looked in vain for signs of it even among the *great* Greeks in philosophy, those of the two centuries *before* Socrates. I retained some doubt in the case of *Heraclitus*, in whose proximity I feel altogether warmer and better than anywhere else. The affirmation of fading *and destroying*, which is the decisive feature of a Dionysian philosophy; saying yes to opposition and war; *becoming*, along with a radical repudiation of the very concept of *being*—all this is clearly more closely related to me than anything else thought to date. The teaching of the "eternal recurrence," that is, of the unconditional and infinitely repeated circular course of all things—this teaching of Zarathustra *might* in the end have been taught already by Heraclitus. At least the Stoa has traces of it, and the Stoics inherited almost all their principal notions from Heraclitus. (*Ecce Homo*, 273–74; *KSA* 6:312–13; translation modified)

Derrida sees the Nietzschean affirmation as "the joyous affirmation of the play of the world and of the innocence of becoming." Against the "saddened *negative*, nostalgic, guilty, Rousseauistic," or structuralist, specifically in Lévi-Strauss, or modernist, "thematic of broken immediacy, . . . *this affirmation then determines the non-center otherwise than as loss of the center*" (*Writing and Difference*, 292; *L'Écriture et la différence*, 427). One of Derrida's points here and in *Of Grammatology* is that structuralism—say, from Rousseau to Lévi-Strauss and beyond—should have noticed that the loss of center—*the* center—is ineluctable. Perhaps structuralism did notice this fact, in spite of itself—saw it without seeing, as Derrida likes to have it. Psychologically and politically, this "thematic of broken immediacy" may even be seen, for example, in the context of postmodernism as considered earlier, as a nostalgia for the impossible—not only for that which, in fact, has never been and, in principle, is still possible, but also for that which *cannot* be, while it can still offer itself to nostalgia.

This point is rather Nietzschean, of course, as the passage just cited would also suggest; moreover, it is a crucial aspect of Nietzsche's conception of the *tragic*, which is always a joyous affirmation. Interestingly, the '*tragic*' itself, as a term and to its full or fuller extent as conception in Nietzsche, is not invoked by Derrida here or elsewhere, although it may be conceived of as implied here. Many reasons for this perspective are possible—theoretical, rhetorical, or political: the *affirmation of* tragedy, the tragedy of *life* and not theater alone, is a complex and perhaps not unproblematic concept even in Nietzsche—Should one, *can* one affirm everything, all tragedies? Also, Derrida's main concern here is the *structure* of the general economy as against the *structuralist* restricted economy of the sign. *Différance* as *structure* also becomes Derrida's interpretation of "the Heraclitean play of the *hen diapheron heautōi*, (of the one differing from itself, the one in difference with itself" (*Margins*, 22; *Marges*, 23). In the *structure* of becoming, Nietzsche's vision conforms to Derrida's formulation: it is a *general* economy of the Heraclitean. Nietzsche—"the third Heraclitean," as Heidegger calls him, after Hölderlin and Hegel (*Heraclitus Seminar*, 115)—grasps thereby, for the first time, a radical transformational play. This play must be opposed to Hegelian and Heideggerian becoming and to the interpretation of Heraclitus as "a play which, the more richly it unfolds, the more strictly it is held (within the domain governed) by a hidden rule," as discussed earlier.

Heidegger, then, customarily invokes the first Heraclitean, Hölderlin. The question of whether Hölderlin's text—or his style—conforms to the Heideggerian reading cannot be addressed here.[31] More relevant in the present context is that *The Question of Being* moves in the orbit of the question of nihilism and Nietzsche, "in whose light and shadow everyone today thinks and writes poetry with his 'for him' or 'against him' [in dessen Liht und Schatten jeder Heutige mit seinem 'für ihn' oder 'wider ihn' denkt und dichtet]" (*Question of Being*, 106–7; translation modified). The command [ein Geheiss], "the highest law" and "the hidden rule," which also "commands" Heidegger to place Being under erasure—in Heidegger's and not Derrida's sense—was, according to Heidegger, also "heard" by Nietzsche ("Nietzsche hörte ein Geheiss") (*Question of Being*, 106–7). As Derrida shows, it must always be heard, whether as the voice of Being or as that which places Being under erasure: the metaphysics of presence is, we recall, always the metaphysics of voice, *phonē*, from Socrates to Heidegger. Heidegger does not so much claim that Nietzsche's text, as such, speaks of hearing this command. He "subordinates" Nietzsche's discourse to this law. Nietzsche's text, *in this reading*, conforms to the law by revealing and forgetting the highest law, which is always hidden.

Heidegger's erasure differs from Derrida's precisely because it erases Being in the name of a still higher form of presence, *logos*, truth, and so on, governing all historical and interpretive transformations. It is the unnamable that cannot be accessed by any form of human signified or signifier—a transcendental signified—but which nevertheless controls all economies of signification, interpretation, or history. The transcendental signified itself and the relations between the transcendental and the human are assigned a form of presence, specifically as the (process of) "presencing" what is present. The general economy of *différance* reconfigures these Heideggerian structures, thus opening a possibility for conceiving of "difference" that no economy of presence can master. Nor can any other economy fully *master* it, including the general economy of *différance*. This is also the reason why *différance* cannot be a unique or final name, as opposed to Being or a still higher unnamable that erases Being in later Heidegger.

Différance, as we have seen, "governs nothing, reigns over nothing, and nowhere exercises any authority." This claim, while it is in fact very precise, is perhaps not fully qualified and elaborated by Derrida at this specific textual juncture. In the deconstructed and reconfigured field, *différance* becomes a very powerful constraint. Or rather, as it is disseminated, it imposes a general-economic manifold of constraints that operate differently each time, without a unified or integrated—global—configuration of control. *Différance*, specifically via *writing*, *generates* powerful constraints. In itself—though it does not exist in itself and by itself—it indeed "governs nothing, rules over nothing . . . ." In general, as we have seen, *différance* relates to an alterity more radical, if again never absolute, than can be *governed* or mastered by these terms of authority or indeed any other terms available within the closure of metaphysics of presence. This difference is obviously a part of its radical difference and undermining of the Hegelian restricted economy, where *Geist* "governs everything, reigns over everything, and everywhere exercises its authority," or any other ontotheological economy of Spirit, Matter, Subject, Object, Being, Capital, or (Self-)Consciousness, or the Unconscious.

Even further qualifications are necessary, however. As I have stressed throughout, neither *différance*, the extended chain in which it is included, any cluster of terms and concepts, nor "neither terms nor concepts," can ever fully master "the unconscious," which, to reiterate, is not a master term, either, and the unconscious "difference" whose possibility it opens. "[*Différance*] is not announced by any capital letter. Not only is there no kingdom of *différance*, but *différance* instigates the subversion of every kingdom [(La différance) ne s'annonce par aucune majuscule. Non seulement il n'y a pas de royaume de la différance mais celle-ci fomente la subversion de tout royaume]" (*Margins*, 22; *Marges*, 22). Nor, by the same token, can there be any given operation, such as the radical metaphoric or catachrestic qualities of Derrida's writing, that would always, or "always already," *operate* at any given point. Undoubtedly, in *most* cases where metaphysics and philosophy see an unadulterated "presence," *writing* in any of its definitions or functions "is" always already in play. *Différance* itself is *not*, not *present* or "there." One cannot say, however, that such is *always* the case, perhaps even in accounting for the efficacy of configurations of presence where the descriptive or inscriptive power of various general economies of *différance, dissemination, writing*, and so forth is tremendous. Nor, by the same token, can one ascribe to any of these names or to "all" of these names— they cannot constitute a set—a wholeness, one multiplicity, contained or uncontained. Such a view would reinstate a transcendental or ontotheological, or let us say, a "quasitranscendental" or quasi-ontotheological, and therefore a restricted, economy.[32] Therefore, Derrida must maintain that "the efficacy of the thematic of *différance* may very well, indeed must, one day, be superseded lending itself if not to its own replacement, at least to enmeshing itself in a chain that in truth it never will have governed, whereby once again it is not theological [including negative theology]" (*Margins*, 7; *Marges*, 7) or ontotheological. "If not to its own replacement" means perhaps that whatever is that which will have replaced *différance* will be, or will be produced by, a reconfiguring, "replacement" of the very "place" where *différance* is produced as *différance*.

It is in fact at the point of "*différance* instigat[ing] subversion of every kingdom," that Derrida considers the question of Heideggerian difference as the ontico-ontological difference in early Heidegger and its relation to *différance*. The question becomes whether *différance* can "settle down into the division of the ontico-ontological difference, such as it is thought, such as its 'epoch' is thought, 'through,' if it may still be expressed such, Heidegger's uncircumventable meditation." While, "there is no simple answer to this question" (*Margins*, 22; *Marges*, 22), Derrida argues correctly in "Différance" and elsewhere that it is rather *différance* that is "older"—not ontologically, but prelogically—and that its general economy precomprehends the Heideggerian restricted ontological economy in *Being and Time* and various configurations that emerge in later works, from Heidegger's lectures on Nietzsche all the way to *Time and Being* and the *Heraclitus Seminar*.

Two different economies of transformation are thus at stake—two different readings of the "Heraclitean"—as well as the economy of their difference, which itself becomes a general economy. At least two are involved, since Nietzsche also introduces a Dionysian—*tragic*—supplement of the Heraclitean, a supplement that is perhaps more original than the Heraclitean "origin" of his vision. The Dionysian becomes the affirmation of becoming even under conditions of the greatest tragedy, and in this sense in radical opposition to all nihilism. Among at least three general economies that might be invoked here—Nietzsche's, Bataille's, and Derrida's—Bataille's might be seen as more Dionysian than Heraclitean, precariously situated between Nietzsche's—the Heraclitean-Dionysian—and Derrida's, the latter being more Heraclitean in this sense than Dionysian. In *Ecce Homo*, immediately before the passage just cited, Nietzsche cites, modifying somewhat his original text, the anti-Aristotelian passage from *Twilight of the Idols*:

> Saying Yes to life even in its strangest and hardest problems; the will to life rejoicing over its own inexhaustibility in the *sacrifice* of its highest types—that is what I called Dionysian, that is what I understood as the bridge to the psychology of the *tragic* poet. *Not* in order to get rid of terror and pity, not in order to purge oneself of a dangerous affect by its vehement discharge—Aristotle misunderstood it in this way—but in order to *be oneself* the eternal joy of becoming, beyond all terror and pity—that joy which includes even joy in destroying. (In *Portable Nietzsche*, 273; *KSA* 6:312; translation modified)

Here, actually, Hölderlin, on Sophocles, may be a source, or at the very least a point of interesting and important proximity, even if simultaneously a point of difference as well:

Viele versuchten umsonst, das Freudigste freudig zu sagen,
Hier spricht endlich es mir, hier in der Trauer sich aus.
[Many sought in vain to say the most joyful joyfully.
Here it speaks, finally, to me, here in mourning speaks out itself.]
(*Sämtliche Werke* 1:i:305)[33]

As we have seen, this affirmation of life, while not always unproblematic and certainly always a complex position, by no means amounts—
"unless [one is] a fool"—to condoning anything or to eliminating the
differences between good and bad in their conventional sense. Instead one
needs a different and more complex understanding—"for other reasons
than hitherto"—of "beyond good and evil" in "the great economy of the
whole" as the economy of the *tragic*. In this economy "the terrible aspects
of reality (in affects, in desires, in the will to power) are to an incalculable
degree more necessary than that form of petty happiness which people call
'goodness'; one actually has to be lenient to accord the latter any place at
all considering that it is based on the instinct—mendaciousness" (*Ecce
Homo*, 329; *KSA* 6:368; translation modified).

One of the last manifestations of the Dionysian spirit, both historically
for Nietzsche and in Nietzsche's text is "Goethe—not a German event, but
a European one [*Goethe*—kein deutsches Ereigniss, sondern ein europäis-
ches]," who is viewed as an affirmative spirit—"*he does not negate any more* [*er
verneint nicht mehr*]"—against, incidentally, Kant, "the antipode of Goethe"
(*Twilight*, in *Portable Nietzsche*, 553–54; *KSA* 6:151–52). If Kant, in this juxtaposition, is still seen as a philosopher—but not "a disciple of the philosopher Dionysus"[34] and certainly not a philosopher with a hammer, as
Nietzsche sees himself, or "the artistic philosopher" of *The Birth of Tragedy*—
Goethe is once again an "event," a rich event of *difference*. This would be the
case not only for the obvious reasons of the enormous diversity of his talents
and interests—his plural style—but also by virtue of a more profound,
Dionysian diversity that is at issue here: the difference of spirit and of affirmation, the affirmation of life, even under the conditions of tragedy.

Finally, however, the final manifestation of the Dionysian spirit is
Nietzsche himself, certainly in *Twilight of the Idols*, *The Antichrist* and *Ecce
Homo*. I would not necessarily say that Nietzsche identifies himself with
Goethe on that or any score, or identifies much with anybody: this is not
Nietzsche's style, as Bataille astutely grasped.[35] "And herewith I again
touch that point from which I once went forth: *The Birth of Tragedy* was
my first reevaluation of all values. Herewith I position myself on the
ground out of which my intention, my *ability* grows—I, the last disciple of
the philosopher Dionysus—I, the teacher of the eternal recurrence" (*Twi-*

light, 563; *KSA* 6:160; translation modified). Or: "Have I been understood?—*Dionysus versus the Crucified* . . . [Hat man mich verstanden?—*Dionysos gegen den Gekreuzigten* . . .]" (*Ecce Homo,* 335; *KSA* 6:374; translation modified). This may be the final sentence, possibly in every sense conceivable of both words; but it is also the entire closing section of *Ecce Homo.* It is the shortest section—or shortest *session*—of all, even though it encompasses the whole history of Christianity and a great deal of philosophy and other "nihilisms."

The insistence itself on the artistic, the tragic, or the Dionysian, or any given clustering of these, may not be always equally effective; at times or at different levels, it can be problematic. Nietzsche suggests as much himself in his brilliant later "Attempt at a Self-Criticism," in which he speaks of *The Birth of Tragedy* as "an *impossible* book" [ein *unmögliches* Buch] (18; *KSA* 1:13; Nietzsche's emphasis). It is "impossible" partly in virtue of presenting the problem in "the context of *art* [(hingestellt) auf den Boden der *Kunst*]" (18; *KSA* 1:13; Nietzsche's emphasis). And if Nietzsche's notion of the artistic or the Dionysian is not problem-free, it is worth considering how tremendous the *problems* are—"grave questions [(ein ganzes Bündel) schwerer Fragen]" (22; *KSA* 1:17)—that Nietzsche approaches via the Dionysian and how *new* their very positing and the way they are posited *as* problems are. As Nietzsche writes:

> What I then got hold of, something frightful and dangerous, a problem with horns, not necessarily a bull, but in any case a *new* problem—today I should say that it was *the problem of science* [*Wissenschaft*] *itself,* science considered for the first time as problematic, as questionable. . . . presented in the realm of *art*—for the problem of science cannot be recognized in the realm of science— . . . however disagreeable it now seems to me, however strange it appears now, after sixteen years—before a much older, a hundred times more demanding, but by no means colder eye which has not become a stranger to the task itself which this audacious book dared to tackle for the first time: *to look at science through the optics of the artist, but at art in that of life.*" (*Birth of Tragedy,* 19; *KSA* 1:13–14; translation modified)

It is worth noting, briefly, that it may well be the *case* of Socrates, the man of science and logic, "that despotic logician" (*Birth of Tragedy,* 92; *KSA* 1:96), that emerges as the main problem in the book, along with a very different question—the question of the *possibility* of "an 'artistic Socrates,'" that is, an *artistic* philosopher, a possibility that in the end may not be an altogether contradictory one, perhaps to "the Socratic impulse": "And though there can be no doubt that the most immediate effect of the

Socratic impulse tended to the dissolution of Dionysian tragedy, yet a profound experience in Socrates's own life impels us to ask whether there is *necessarily* only an antipodal relation between Socratism and art, and whether the birth of an 'artistic Socrates' is altogether a contradiction in terms" (*Birth of Tragedy*, 92; *KSA* 1:96). From this perspective, Nietzsche's section, or session—another short session—on "What One Should Learn from Artists" in *The Gay Science* (sec. 299) is of great interest:

> What means do we have to make things beautiful, attractive, and desirable for us even when they are not? And I rather think that in themselves they never are. Here we could learn something from the physicians, when for example they dilute what is bitter or add wine and sugar to a mixture—but even more from the artists who are really continually trying to bring off such inventions and feats. Moving away from things until there is much that one no longer sees and there is much that our eye has to add if we are still to see them at all; or seeing things around a corner and as cut out and framed; or to place them so that they partially conceal each other and grant us only glimpses or perspectival vistas [oder sie so stellen, dass sie sich teilweise verstellen und nur perspectivische Durchblicke gestatten]; or looking at them through tinted glass or in the light of the sunset; or giving them a surface and skin that is not fully transparent—all this we should learn from artists while being wiser than they are in other matters. For with them this subtle power usually comes to an end where art ends and life begins; but we want to be the poets of our life—and first of all in the smallest, most everyday matters. (*Gay Science*, 239–40; *KSA* 3:538; translation modified)

In so describing art, Nietzsche relies here, and elsewhere, on several classical strategies of Western aesthetics. These classical strategies and classical propositions themselves are by no means discountable, and Nietzsche uses them with great effectiveness in the deconstructed and reconfigured field. Nietzsche's conclusion, however, is of greatest interest, as it indicates the necessity of exceeding the economy of art in his own enterprise. There is, clearly, a more general programmatic import in the passage as part of Nietzsche's overall "reevaluation of all values" and different vision of life. As in logic, also in life, we need art "as a protection and remedy [als Schutz und Heilmittel" (*The Birth of Tragedy*, 98; *KSA* 15:101), even though in the end it may always turn out to be a *pharmakon*, a remedy and poison at once, which in turn needs to be diluted and mixed, for example, with logic or philosophy—a touch of Socrates, as it were. The excess or, perhaps better, the difference from art invoked by Nietzsche also suggests the difference between art and Nietzsche's own writing or style. The passage thus returns us to the problem of "the artistic Socrates," on the one hand, that was posed at the end of the first version of *The Birth of Tragedy* (secs. 14–15), and that of the tragic or Dionysian philosopher or thinker, although neither word may be finally suitable here, that was posed more radically in Nietzsche's later texts. These two cases are clearly related, although perhaps not identical, and by implication, engage related but not identical styles of thinking or writing. I would suggest that Nietzsche would see himself as closer to the Dionysian, or tragic, or artistic philosopher, such as (Nietzsche's) Heraclitus, as considered earlier, than to "the artistic Socrates," although other readings are possible, including identifying both with each other. Both figures, however, may be juxtaposed to the tragic artist. It is obviously not a question of priority. In Nietzsche, it appears, a true tragic artist, such as Sophocles and Shakespeare, will always take priority.[36]

Obviously, this issue has a direct bearing on the question of plural style or the massively complementary style of theory—and, if you wish, life—as considered at the end of the preceding chapter. Nietzsche's invocation of "mixture" is hardly accidental here; and the metaphor of mixing or diluting, for example, the doses of his own writing—this great *pharmakon*—often recurs in his work. It is clearly not only a question of mixing textual strategies and styles among literature, philosophy, criticism, literary theory, psychoanalysis, or still other fields—an important and relevant issue that has been given much well-deserved attention in, and in the wake of, Derrida's discourse, particularly *Glas*, and deconstruction in general. A more complex economy of "life" may well be at stake; and, in this context, too, such figures or cases as Nietzsche, Bataille, Blanchot, or Oscar Wilde, acquire a particular significance. In truth, of course, one cannot separate the question of narrative from that of mixing textual strategies and styles. Moreover, at its best, the deconstructive analysis of this situation, specifically in Derrida, would never claim such a separation. The point that needs to be made is rather the complexity, and *plurality*, of relationships between plural styles and plural texts, together with the resulting difference between different plural styles, such as Nietzsche's, Bataille's, Blanchot's, Derrida's, or that of recent feminist discourse. Nietzsche's "narrative" in *Ecce Homo*, as considered earlier, is positioned, fundamentally, in relation to this general economy of "life."

Perhaps, accordingly, a totally different relation between art and science is at stake, *new* problems, "things unattempted yet in Prose or Rhyme" (*Paradise Lost* 1:16), in the rhyme of literature or the prose of philosophy—the *true* prose of which Hegel speaks. Whether inscribed as "artistic"—*tragic*—"historical," or "theoretical," these "things" make all classical concepts tremble. They make the whole closure of all our concepts tremble. In addition, they *transform* this closure, which is perhaps the hardest task of all and, when it works, the rarest of all achievements.

"I am not a human being, I am dynamite [Ich bin kein Mensch, ich bin Dynamit]," Nietzsche says in one of his final Dionysian self-evaluations (*Ecce Homo*, 326; *KSA* 6:365), which is undoubtedly a part of his "reevaluation of all values," by way of a very extraordinary economy. Naturally, one should take into account the multiple and multidirectional ironies of this and many other self-evaluations; still, one should not be deceived too much by these ironies, either. Nietzsche is, often enough, no more ironic in evaluating himself—as a "new" value—than he is in evaluating and reevaluating "old" values. The characterization itself is actually not Nietzsche's, although one doubts that the original author (J. V. Widmann) could give it quite the sense Nietzsche did. It must also, I think, be seen as referring to the *dynamic* quality of Nietzsche's analytical, theoretical, but also performative, style. Above all, however, it refers to that trembling—the tremor—of all reason (Vernunft) and reasons hitherto. Nietzsche—"the philosopher Dionysus," "the philosopher with a hammer"—is also "a European event, not a German one." He is an explosive event—"dynamite."

Dynamite, it must not be forgotten, is a weapon of revolution, a destructive weapon of revolutionary politics. In this sense and within the power of this metaphor, Nietzsche's lack or contempt—*in a certain sense*—for *political* commitment and programs or practical political action itself becomes interesting. "I, the last *anti-political* German [ich, der letzte *antipolitische* Deutsche]"—Nietzsche says in one of the versions of *Ecce Homo* (*Ecce Homo*, 225; *KSA* 14 [*Kommentar*]:484).[37] It is so only "in a certain sense," however, and specifically in contrast, for example, to Marx. For much of Nietzsche can and has been *read* in either direction—from left to right, or from right to left—as a "political program." Along with and alongside the grand style and grand or great economy (grosse Ökonomie), Nietzsche speaks of "great politics," and in no uncertain terms, even though, as always, multiple ironies and parodies come into play.

As Deleuze and Guattari point out, "Zarathustra [cannot] be separated from the 'grand politics'" (*Anti-Oedipus*, 86), although one must, I think, read Nietzsche, including "the political Nietzsche," as much against Deleuze and Guattari as with them. But, at certain points, Nietzsche does indeed make a move toward the political, from a theoretical revolution—war with "the lies of millennia"—to a political one:

I contradict as has never been contradicted before and am nevertheless the opposite of a No-saying spirit. I am a bringer of glad tidings like no one before me; I know tasks of such elevation that any concept of them has been lacking hitherto; only beginning with me are there hopes again. For all that, I am necessarily also the man of calamity. For when truth enters into a fight with the lies of millennia, we shall have upheavals, a convulsion of earthquakes, a moving of mountains and valleys, the like of which has never been dreamed of. The concept of politics will have dissolved entirely into a war of spirits/ghosts; all power structures of the old society will have been exploded—all of them rest on the lie: there will be wars the like of which have never yet been on earth. It is only beginning with me that the earth knows *great politics* [*grosse Politik*]. (*Ecce Homo*, 327; *KSA* 6:366; translation modified)

Nietzsche's invocation of truth—his own truth—against "the lies of millennia" does not contradict the radical undermining of *the* "truth" of metaphysics and philosophy, which is one of the lies at issue. If one wants to or does speak in terms of truth, as philosophers do, for example, what Nietzsche says would be truths, against the truths of philosophy—"the lies of millennia." I shall consider this issue further in the next chapter, concentrating for the moment on the question of politics in Nietzsche, great politics or, conversely, small politics. A bit earlier, in the context of Wagner, Nietzsche does speak of "small [petty] politics [die kleine Politik]" and "this most *anti-cultural* sickness and unreason there is, i.e., nationalism, this *névrose nationale* with which Europe is sick, this perpetuation of European particularism" (*Ecce Homo*, 321; *KSA* 6:360).

The *great politics* [*grosse Politik*] of the concluding section ("Why I am a Destiny"), however, should not be seen as corresponding to what would oppose this *kleine Politik* here. However, the "political and *economic* unity [eine politische *und wirtschaftliche* Einheit]" of Europe (*Ecce Homo*, 321; *KSA* 6:360)—*great politics* "in the great economy of the whole [der grosse Ökonomie des Ganzen]" (*Ecce Homo*, 329; *KSA* 6:368)—could well have been conceived by Nietzsche as a consequence, albeit highly mediated one, of a kind of vision, affirmative and tragic at once, of the political very much akin to his own.[38]

Crucially, it follows again that localization, or perspectivization, by no means precludes global or even maximally extended perspectives—"the great economy of the whole." But these will still be seen only as perspectives. "Great politics" refers, then, more broadly and more profoundly, to the vision of the play of forces resulting from Nietzsche's "reevaluation of all values." This *great politics* is radically different from what Marx would have in mind. It may be even more revolutionary, however, perhaps too revolutionary in the sense that it cannot be made into an ideology that could then lead, or at least claim to do so, to a practically/politically viable program for revolutionary practice, such as is found in Marx. But then the *great politics* announced by Marx does not lack its own practical complexities; and only some of these upheavals and revolutions might be seen as practice predicated—still via many mediations—on the Marxist politico-economic model. It may be, on the other hand, that the upheaval that Nietzsche invokes in this rather prophetic pronouncement has as its efficacity, at least in part, the kind of political dynamics Nietzsche exposes. This efficacity, in other words, could be a result of Nietzsche's "perspectival optics," for example, as opposed to Marx's.

It may be that one might need a fusion—a complementarity—of some form of "Nietzschean" matrix and some form of "Marxist" matrix, at the very least for political theory, but perhaps for political practice as well. To some extent, this fusion already characterizes the gradient of most recent intellectual history. Such a fusion or complementarity, needless to say, is bound to be an extremely complex and difficult task, proceeding, as concerns its Nietzschean counterpart, via Freud, Bataille, Lacan, Deleuze, and Derrida—via the unconscious. The dialectical—Hegelian—counterpart, including the grounding in *consciousness* of the Marxist model, is a major problem. The fusion in question here certainly cannot be dialectical and thus, as I shall suggest in Chapter 6, cannot perhaps finally retain its Marxist counterpart. An equally important and indissociable point, depending on this nondialectical fusion, is that "material" history cannot be dialectical. On the other hand, some "political economy"—a kind of analysis Nietzsche does not pursue—might be just as indispensable for a kind of *general* political economy that one needs as *theory*. *Reading* "war and peace," or *writing*—including as offering such a reading—as Tolstoy attempted, is an extraordinarily complex task. Such a reading or such writing cannot be contained in a book, which is one of Derrida's major propositions against the task and ambition of philosophy. Among other things— things possible and impossible—it is also this impossibility that both Hegel's *Phenomenology* and Tolstoy's *War and Peace* demonstrate so magnificently, even if in spite of themselves. The political *practice*—*great politics*— is undoubtedly an even more complex issue.

At the very least, Nietzsche's revolutions—his "reevaluations of all values" and his "reasons other than hitherto"—can serve and have served as a "model," interactively, for theoretical and political subversions, for a complex and exuberant, and at times dangerous, play. The "model," however tentative and preliminary, is also powerful and productive. At the intersection of Nietzsche and Marx, Bataille's vision remains perhaps the greatest, if in turn a not always unproblematic example of a theory—general economy—of the intersection of the political and the theoretical, and the artistic or Dionysian.

It is worth noting that, while in many ways a reversal and, to a very limited degree, a re-reversal—going back to the Greeks, the Dionysians—of a Socratic, or Christian, system of values, the move or strategy itself aiming at radical reevaluation of all values, is not without similarity to the Socratic agenda as both a radical critique of "all value hitherto" and as an introduction of new values. From his earliest writings, particularly *Philosophy in the Tragic Age of the Greeks*, Nietzsche refers to Socrates in these terms, as he does to Christian values in the *Genealogy* and other later works. There are, of course, immense differences between the two systems of values—Christian and Socratic—both in the values themselves and in the way they are introduced; and Nietzsche powerfully explores and utilizes both proximities and differences between Socratism and—in turn as and as not Platonism—or Christianity, "Platonism for 'the people' [Platonismus für's 'Volk']" (*Beyond Good and Evil*, 3; *Jenseits von Gut und Böse*, in *KSA* 5:12). Thus Socrates is an important model, but many differences—*in style and substance*—between Socratism and Dionysianism are much more decisive than the necessity of "reevaluation of all values hitherto."

As was discussed earlier, Nietzsche cannot calculate all the effects, theoretical or political, of his explosive actions even in his own text, let alone elsewhere, nor of his constructive, architectural, acts. Often these are both at once in antinihilistic Nietzsche: nihilism—absolute destruction—must be destroyed first. As a result, some of the effects—the (re)appropriations or derived consequences—of Nietzsche's strategies and terms can be quite different and even contrary or antagonistic to the effects that I suggest here. And while Nietzsche anticipated some of these appropriating effects and warned against them on many occasions, he naturally could not anticipate *all* such effects, nor could he prevent any appropriation of that type. Admittedly, Nietzsche's text will always be problematic in some respects, even considered under the best conditions. The implication of that fact is that, *from the perspective of the present analysis*, there may be no effective reading—or appropriation—of Nietzsche that would be free of problems, even though Nietzsche remains vastly superior to most of his critics. And, as Nietzsche says in the draft of *Ecce Homo*: "Finally, I speak only of what is experienced, not merely of what is; the opposition of thinking and life is lacking in my case. My 'theory' grows from my 'practice'—oh, from a practice that is not by any means harmless or unproblematic" (*Ecce Homo*, 340; *KSA* 14:485; translation modified).

Thus, to give an example of great importance, I would suggest, although I cannot consider the issue here in detail, that "the question of woman," the question of gender and gender difference and, to some extent the related but different question, of sexual difference, remains a fundamental problem of Nietzsche's text. Such is the case, I think, in spite of recent, at times brilliant, efforts to save Nietzsche's text in this respect, including not only deconstructive but also, perhaps more importantly, feminist readings, deconstructive or other. There are undoubtedly many readings Nietzsche should be saved from, for example, as was considered earlier, some readings of the Heideggerian type. One way to accomplish this project is by way of the question of woman, as Derrida does in *Spurs*. Still, it would not follow, as is sometimes claimed, including to some extent by Derrida, specifically in "Choreographies," that Nietzsche's "position" or "positions," however plural, would cease being problematic as a result.

There is no doubt that the case is complex; Nietzsche's text elicits a great deal of critique that seems immediately to offer itself, but ends by being more problematic in its turn than Nietzsche. The "positions" are numerous, and "each" is in turn stratified; furthermore, some of the positions and layers of stratifications will offer theoretically, and at times even politically, effective formulations, strategies, and styles. Nietzsche might be bad on feminism or gender; but he is still Nietzsche and thus usually "better" than many of his readers or nonreaders on either side, or indeed many sides of these issues. Nor can one claim that there are no propositions or strategies of style in Nietzsche, even when he speaks on women—let alone in general—that can be productively utilized by a feminist text. Indeed, Nietzschean propositions or strategies have been powerfully explored by feminist texts throughout the recent history of feminist studies, particularly in the wake of and anticipating deconstruction in France. In general, Nietzsche certainly does attack and destroy much of what needs to be demolished along the lines of feminist critique as well. In this sense, feminism can utilize Nietzsche with great effectiveness, at the same time that equally there can be a feminist critique of Nietzsche. Importantly, the latter is the case not only, and perhaps not so much, because Nietzsche may often, but not always, be "bad" in this respect, but also because the issues and the problems have been and still remain "bad"—that is, extraordinarily difficult, both theoretically and politically. This problem in Nietzsche's text must be addressed *under the conditions of a rigorous reading of this text* and the complexity of the relations between "style" and "positions." Certainly Nietzsche's plural style, and much else in his Dionysian *Wissenschaft*, tragic and joyful at once, may be used to establish other "positions," as has been brilliantly done in a number of feminist readings. But these are *not* Nietzsche's "positions" or positional play on the question of woman, gender, gender difference, or sexual difference. Not inconceivably, a still different style may be needed, one more Nietzschean than deconstructive, for example, or more deconstructive as opposed to Nietzschean, or an entirely different type, including possibly a more *radically feminist* style. Such a style may lead, in general, to reconfigurations that are more radical than hitherto, or are at least more radical than anything for quite some time— let us say, since Nietzsche.

The problems I am referring to are not the "mistakes" or "miscalculations" that, in principle, can be corrected within Nietzsche's text, although those, too, can be found; but the ones for which no such corrective procedure can be established within Nietzsche's text. Such claims remain subject, of course, to the conditions of (re)appropriation, the irreducible inhibition of reading; but no other conditions of reading are possible or accessible, at least for now. Such are the consequences and implications of what Nietzsche has *written*, and some of them are profoundly political. Their consequences, too, cannot be calculated in advance or once and for all.

I shall not pursue any further the question of revolution and revolutions as a political question, even though, as follows from the analysis just given, politics of one type or another is never fully reducible, whatever revolution is at stake. I do not think that there is as yet a model for the politics of revolution, for instance, for political revolutions at stake in Marxism. We know, however, something about their practical—*political*—effects. Derrida's matrix is a profound contribution to the understanding of historical, theoretical, and interpretive transformations and thus of "literatures" and "revolutions." Whether it will prove to be rich enough even for a theoretical model or nonmodel of the political still remains to be seen. The question of political, including revolutionary, practice is even more complex, even though Bataille in introducing general economy definitely had revolution in mind. All of Bataille's economies are always the economies of at least both (the practice of) "literature" or "theory" and "revolution." I shall consider, however, via the question of closure, the implications of the general economy of transformations for the *theoretical* revolution enacted by Nietzsche, or by what "Nietzsche *has written*."

Closures and Transformations of Theory

For better or worse, to one degree or another, "we," *now*, inherit terms and concepts such as language, literature, philosophy, or history, together with logic, strategies, or rhetoric, from "the history of philosophy" or from *the historical closure* into which, by way of the general economy of *différance*, *dissemination*, *writing*, Derrida transforms—reconfigures—this history. There are, however, on the one hand, new terms—either new in a given field or more general—such as Derrida's *différance*, and on the other, the transformation or *sliding* of old terms in such a way as radically to alter or affect their functioning. This transformation or sliding certainly occurs in both Nietzsche and Bataille, who along with introducing new names, transform old names and concepts by their textual work, or play. For Nietzsche, the question of the radical difference of his style, text, and language from the language of philosophy or even German itself—a certain German that served as the language of philosophy—is a major issue and a crucial point of transgression. In addressing the question of the necessity of new styles and languages, Nietzsche, at one point, refers to Ural-Altaic languages (*Beyond Good and Evil*, 15). The distance from German and philosophy appears to be always at issue in Nietzsche, even though he writes in German—a radically different, *new*, German, as he often claims. Thus he cannot avoid the proximities—at times, but again not always, infinitesimal—to the language and concepts that he transforms, "slides," and makes tremble, along with the very agenda of philosophical language, and German as *the* philosophical language, as in Hegel, or later, together with Greek, in Heidegger. The term *sliding* [glissement] is powerfully used in this sense in Derrida's reading of Bataille, from whom Derrida borrows the term itself (*Writing and Difference*, 262–63).

The closure (clôture) of metaphysics in Derrida designates our dependence on the language and concepts developed throughout the history of philosophy, but operative elsewhere as well. This closure thus also implies a dependence—in Derrida, a fundamental one—on classical metaphysical oppositions and strategies in the very undermining of metaphysics, which Derrida continuously detects in all deconstructive or proto-deconstructive texts as well, and specifically in Nietzsche. In many ways, Derrida's deconstruction might be seen as the investigation of this closure, which may well be an interminable project, for indeed "what is held within the delimited closure may continue indefinitely [Ce qui est pris dans la clôture dé-limitée peut continuer indéfiniment]" (*Positions*, 13; *Positions*, 22; translation modified). Defining the "historical and systematic unity" of this closure, Derrida further writes in *Positions*:

> Don't you see, what has seemed necessary and urgent to me, in the historical situation which is our own, is a general determination of the conditions for the emergence and the limits of philosophy, of metaphysics, of everything that carries it on and that it carries on. In *Of Grammatology* I simultaneously proposed everything that can be reassembled under the rubric of *logocentrism*—and I cannot pursue this any further here—along with the project of *deconstruction*. Here, there is a powerful historical and systematic unity that must be determined first if one is not to take dross for gold every time that an emergence, rupture, break, mutation, etc. is allegedly delineated. (*Positions*, 51; *Positions*, 69)

Thus one of Derrida's major points regarding this "historical and systematic unity," the point defining the closure, is that, operating at "the limits of philosophy," *deconstruction* does not imply an absolute and unconditional break with the language and concepts of philosophy, and the structures, such as *différance*, can only be inscribed or obliquely related to *within* this closure. An absolute break is in fact impossible, and often particularly when such a break is claimed. Deconstruction, therefore, must take place, utilizing the *resources* of philosophy. "And this in no way minimizes the necessity and relative importance of certain breaks, of the appearance and definition of new structures" (*Positions*, 24; *Positions*, 35). The problematics of closure and the fundamental engagement with the major philosophical texts that shape this closure and are shaped by it permeate Derrida's analyses throughout, from his earliest to his most recent works.[39]

One cannot deny the possibility and the necessity of this dependence on philosophy and its closure in a critical text. The *degree* of this dependence is a more complex issue, particularly in cases like Nietzsche. At issue, therefore, is instead a stratification of the history of a given theoretical transformation. For, on the one hand, a transformation must have a history, indeed always more than one; but on the other, that which makes a transformation possible might come from a stratum of history that would not be subsumed by a history of metaphysics or philosophy. A transformation might even transform the very closure of philosophy, if one assumes that there can be *one* closure to begin with, which, I think, one cannot do. As I suggested earlier, one can even define *radical* transformations as transformations of the closure of a given theory or field. Such transformations cannot come from nowhere; they must have another *history* or *histories*, and other *closures*. I use these terms of the closure constraining the present analysis, the closure perhaps already *transformed*, as against the pre-Nietzschean tradition. Both "history" and "the closure" so configured lead to a reconfiguration of the preceding system and its closure, if "system" is the term, given the transformations at issue, the structure of the transformational field where they take place, and the plurality of styles and genres that must be engaged.

The closure, as conceived by Derrida, also relates to the necessity —psychological, social, cultural, historical, perhaps even political—of what Derrida calls broadly "presence," of which metaphysics, as the metaphysics of presence, becomes in turn an effect, or rather a diversified field of theoretical effects. Thus, the closure of metaphysics may be related to, but may also be differentiated from, a broader interpretive closure or economy of closures, specifically the closure of "presence" itself. As I have indicated, the latter economy may in turn be traced to Nietzsche, particularly to the passage on forgetting that opens "The Second Essay" of the *Genealogy*. The closure of difference, exteriority, or transformation is no less at issue, however, particularly in relation to the question of history and temporality, even though, as both Heidegger and, still more critically, Derrida demonstrate, both temporality and historicity have been grounded in the notion of presence or continuum throughout their history.

More generally, difference, exteriority, transformability, discontinuity—or of course, continuity—and other major philosophical rubrics of that type may variously overlap with various configurations assembled under the rubric of presence. It would be therefore more effective in turn to complementarize such closures and constraints rather than to summarize them under any given rubric. One can suggest, however, a more general and stable, if complementarized, *interpretive* closure as opposed to a more differentiated or disseminated and more transformable *theoretical* closure. "Presence" is, for powerful reasons, a notion and rubric of central significance for Derrida. Metaphysics itself, as Derrida argues, is always—wherever it operates, inside or outside philosophy—the metaphysics of presence, even if that of difference and becoming. Indeed, philosophy as the metaphysics of presence is often, and certainly in Hegel and Heidegger, the metaphysics of difference and exteriority, but *as* the metaphysics of presence or continuum, spatial, temporal, or other.

The closure of *presence* or, more generally, the interpretive closure or closures, accounting for the effects of presence and absence, identity and difference, interiority and exteriority, continuity and rupture may, perhaps must, be differentiated from the closure of philosophy, even though no such description or concept can be seen as existing in itself and by itself, specifically as fully outside the history and text of philosophy. The history of these concepts cannot be dissociated from the history and the closure of philosophy, although it cannot be contained thereby, either. Instead one should see the closure of philosophy as the effect of the closure of presence, difference, and other interpretive closures. The question of the closure of discourse—at least of theoretical discourse, but perhaps of all discourse— thus becomes suspended between this necessity of presence, or difference and other interpretive forces, on the one hand, and the necessity of philosophy and our engagement with the text of philosophy, on the other.

The interpretive closures at issue, then—the closures of presence, difference, exteriority, continuity, rupture, and so forth—often operating jointly or again complementarily, would be a kind of "psychological" or even "biological" conglomerate of constraints, always differentiated in practice, affecting all our interpretive processes. To a degree, it may be permissible to see this economy as that of one closure; but even in this case, a complementary economy of closures is more effective. For the sake of convenience, I shall use here mostly the rubrics of presence and difference, although other constraining or en-closing forces just mentioned will be implied as well. There are more natural correspondences between them— such as presence and continuity, or difference and rupture; but they are not aligned in any unique or fixed manner. The closure of philosophy itself, though it must once again not be seen as a fully homogeneous field, remains everywhere irreducible. As Derrida writes in "The *Retrait* of Metaphor":

> for me it was not a question of taking "metaphysics" ("la" métaphysique) as the homogeneous unity of an ensemble. I have never believed in the existence or in the consistency of something like metaphysics *itself* (la *métaphysique*). . . . Keeping in account such and such a demonstrative sentence or such a contextual constraints, if I happened to say 'metaphysics' or 'the' closure of 'metaphysics' (an expression which is the target of [Ricoeur's] *Life Metaphor*), very often, elsewhere, but also in "White Mythology," I have put forward the proposition according to which there would never be 'metaphysics,' 'closure' not being here a circular limit bordering a homogeneous field but a more twisted structure which today, according to another figure, I would be tempted to call: 'invaginated.' Representation of a linear and circular closure surrounding a homogeneous space is, precisely, the theme of my greatest emphasis, an auto-representation of philosophy in its onto-encyclopedic logic. ("The *Retrait* of Metaphor," 14; "Le Retrait de la métaphore," 72)

Derrida's difference, or *différance*, from ontotheology remains decisive, and Ricoeur indeed misses the point of Derrida's analysis in this and many other respects. The difference and proximities at issue, specifically between Derrida and Heidegger, as I have stressed throughout, form a complex play and make the question—the question of Derrida and the philosophy of closure versus the metaphysics of presence—all the more interesting and important.[40] Derrida suggests at the beginning of *Of Grammatology*: "Hegel was already caught up in this game. . . . he undoubtedly *summed up* the entire philosophy of the logos. He determined ontology as absolute logic; he assembled all the delimitations of being as presence [Hegel, déjà, était pris à ce jeu. . . . il a sans doute *résumé* la totalité de la philosophie du logos. Il a déterminé l'ontologie comme logique absolue; il a rassemblé toutes les délimitations de l'être comme présence. . . .]" (*Of Grammatology*, 24; *De la grammatologie*, 39; translation modified).[41] That philosophy, also *presented* as the philosophy, becomes "the philosophy of the *logos*"; and "presence" is, of course, crucial to it. By the same token, the closure of difference and of the metaphysics of difference is at issue; and philosophy as the metaphysics of presence is always the metaphysics of difference—*as*, however, "the metaphysics of presence"—the restricted as opposed to the general economy. This difference defines the difference between a critical and a precritical or deconstructive perspective, and the difference between, or *différance* of, *différance* and *dialectics*, Marx's as well as Hegel's, between general and restricted economy.

One must keep in mind that the terms and concepts of both presence and difference do belong to the closure of philosophy; but the closure, if it is the closure, of general economy exceeds this closure, and perhaps not only by virtue of its oblique inscription *within* the preceding closure, but—as is my point here—by transforming this closure, even if only by way of offering a possibility and establishing the necessity of oblique inscriptions.

There are differences between these general economies, as of course between different restricted economies, such as Hegel's or Marx's; and a general economy, as against restricted economies, is never practiced as one economy. It demands, by definition, plural style and multiple genres. Insofar as I speak of *the* general economy I refer, as stated, to their major traits, such as the irreducible loss in presence, representation, meaning, or consciousness or the impossibility of the unified control of historical and interpretive transformations characterizing all general economies, and specifically Nietzsche's, Bataille's, and Derrida's.

The metaphysics of *presence*, or difference may then emerge and be practiced as the economy—by definition *restricted*—of and in the name of difference, such as "the self-proximity" and "eschatology" or "teleology," that, however differently, characterize Hegel's or Marx's dialectic. Marx would certainly follow Hegel in "determin[ing] ontology as absolute logic," even as he redetermines the Hegelian subjectivist, idealist logic and ontology by giving both a material base and thus making them into dialectical and historical materialism. This determination is clearly the core of Heidegger's positive assessment of Marx in "The Principles of Thinking"; throughout the essay and elsewhere Heidegger always emphasizes this necessity of ontological and historical expansion of "logic" in Hegel ("The Principles of Thinking," in *Piety of Thinking*, 57).

Much of what constitutes the closure of metaphysics in Derrida's sense thus intersects with the "logic" of philosophy, consciousness and self-consciousness, and even the most self-conscious usage of philosophical concepts, along with the most nonphilosophical concepts, including those upon which all dialectic is based. Against Hegel, or Heidegger, this closure can never absolutely "determine ontology," of any kind or with any base, idealist or materialist, Spirit or Matter, historical or ahistorical, conscious or unconscious. Nor can it determine, absolutely or unconditionally, logic of any kind, formal or transcendental, or some deconstructive logic. It cannot determine logic as "absolute logic," although it certainly demands and determines a great deal of the most logical, or most rigorous, logic, along with and alongside the most playful play. The ontological determination remains fully in place in Marx as well. It controls the theory and the very question of political economy, such as with respect to determining all ideology as superstructure by way of a material or materialist, historico-politico-economic base.

Reversing Hegel, Marx's dialectic retains Hegel's dialectical logic. This remains the case even though Marx understands very well that many of his concepts, such as the "proletariat," are determined by ideologies that can—should, must, and in the end will—be changed along with their material politico-economic base. The proletariat, in the first place, must radically transform its self-consciousness, by reversing it from that of the slave to that of the master, which is once again in accord with Hegel. This reversal is another crucial aspect of the "determination of [materialist] ontology as absolute logic" in Marx and Marxism. The play or, from the perspective of dialectic, the labor of historical transformation remains unified and controlled by the single law—*the* law—the law of dialectic.

The closure at issue in Derrida must be seen *as* closure, that is, as a different type of theoretical and perhaps political constraint or economy of constraints, set against philosophy as the metaphysics of presence. Neither

Hegel nor Marx nor—at least not quite—Heidegger offers such an economy. Not even Nietzsche quite offers it, although, like Bataille, he comes close when he speaks of (philosophy's) truth as a necessary error. What would emerge, by way of "the question of method,"[42] is the difference, and *différance*, of two "necessities" and the resulting economies, again restricted and general: on the one hand, the economy of the conscious, and the dialectical determination of all *theory* and practice—political economy in the broadest sense; and, on the other hand, the economy of a certain, perhaps unavoidable theoretical and historical closure of "the metaphysics of presence." A theory so conditioned, here Derrida's general economy, does not prescribe *the* method, for example the dialectical method, that Marx claimed as indispensable to his project. But such a general economy does not discount or depreciate methods, either, including logical or dialectical methods. It offers a different "estimate" of their "value," a different theoretical "economics"—except that a general economy would also have a calculus different from only "evaluation," "transaction," or "economic," or any single determination or countable or calculable set of determinations.[43]

By the same token, this general economic calculus suggests a certain difference between the closure of philosophy and the closure of presence, or difference, as described earlier. While they intersect and interact or are in fact indissociable, I would hesitate to identify them. To recapitulate briefly, the closure of *presence* is a kind of "psychological" or even "biological" constraint or a conglomerate of constraints, always differentiated in practice. The closure of *philosophy* is an effect of the closure of presence, producing the history of philosophy *as* the metaphysics of presence. "Our" discourse depends on this history; and one of Derrida's central points is that we can no more be only philosophical than only nonphilosophical. Often the first is the case, particularly when we *want to* be philosophical, even as philosophical as possible; and the second, particularly when we want to be nonphilosophical, even as nonphilosophical as possible. There may be effects of (the closure of) *presence* and difference, however, that cannot be contained within the history of philosophy or to which, since we depend on the closure of *presence*—or difference—we cannot assign the capacity to contain them and thus to contain the closure of *presence* within the closure of *philosophy*.

It may be that Derrida sees as the closure of *philosophy* as the metaphysics of *presence* those interpretive and conceptual structures that share this—differentiated—efficacity and that manifest themselves as the "effects" of that type.[44] In other words, such "effects" emerge in an analogous way in all theoretical structures, wherever *presence* enters—and, at one point or another, *presence* enters everywhere, no less than difference, or traces of difference. So the difference between the closure of *presence* and difference—the *interpretive* closure—and the closure of *philosophy* becomes reduced a great deal. But then one *cannot* perhaps speak of the closure of *metaphysics*, nor of one closure of any type, not perhaps even of the closure of *presence* and *difference*, powerful and extensive as its operation is. Derrida's historical analysis of our dependence on such concepts is impeccable. *Theoretical* closure, however, may differentiate itself and, historically, transform itself more radically. The *transformation* of closure is never invoked by Derrida, and "the closure" never occurs in plural form in his text. If, for example, the phrase "the reduction of difference in presence" is a good example of the working of the closure of philosophy, it is also a good example of a transformed closure. For it is a conceptual configuration not found in the history of philosophy up to a certain point. In fact, one might question whether and to what extent the very economy of presence and difference as inscribed by Derrida, belongs to the closure of metaphysics or philosophy or what constitutes that closure, *prior* to Derrida's and other contemporary texts. In addition, the closure(s) of *philosophy*, as opposed to the closure of *presence* or difference, may be seen as referring to specific historical configurations, including "our own," in which "our" dependence on philosophy exceeds the question of presence, or difference. More generally, we cannot, under the constraints of general economy, relate everything to presence or difference, either. One is compelled, therefore, to consider the "difference" between the closure of philosophy and the closure of presence and difference, and then the differentiation—*dissemination*—and transformations of the closure of interpretation and theory. It may indeed be necessary, at some point, to suspend the very economy of closure, whether interpretive or theoretical.

By way of the Freudian analogy that persists in Derrida, the closure of metaphysics can be compared to or metaphorized as a kind of theoretical neurosis that is never completely curable—it just has to be lived with—and that demands an interminable analysis. Perhaps the closure of *presence* may be seen along similar lines, too: to be neurotic simply means to be human, according to Freud; and presence and difference, as we have seen, constrain all human, and perhaps not only human, functioning. I do think, however, that the psychoanalytic analogy or metaphor at issue is much stronger in the case of the closure of *metaphysics*. According to Derrida's argument in *Positions* and elsewhere, one may theoretically advance perhaps only by way of interminable engagement with that closure, and this "interminability is not an accident and contingency" but "is essential, systematic, and theoretical" (*Positions*, 24; *Positions*, 34).[45]

That may be, although one might want to speak of the inevitability of engaging some old structures in one way or another and along one history or another, rather than of a theoretical strategy of *deliberate* interminable engagement with old concepts, such as those developed by the philosophical tradition at issue in Derrida. Of this latter type of analysis Derrida is, of course, as great a practitioner as Freud is of interminable analyses. As was indicated earlier, while Nietzsche's *theoretical—performative—*practice is not independent of some old concepts and theories, it may be juxtaposed to a *therapeutic* one, which, however, is also a *performance*. It is much different in this respect and is much more radically antiphilosophical, but as *theory* it is no less effective.

For Nietzsche, too, philosophy is a kind of case study, a *sick* or *decadent* phenomenon. In opposition to Derrida, via Freud, Nietzsche's practice is not "therapeutic" in this sense. Nietzsche does not believe that we must live with such a "disease"—the interminable neurosis of philosophy—and in turn interminably investigate its symptoms and its closure, although philosophy remains a useful case and the pleasure—and pain—of the analyst. For Derrida, "By means of this simultaneously faithful and violent circulation between the inside and outside of philosophy—that is of the West— there is produced a certain textual work that gives great pleasure" (*Positions*, 6–7; *Positions*, 15). Even when Nietzsche must engage such circulations, he is hardly faithful, although "*philosophizing* with a hammer," he is always violent in this sense. It should be pointed out that the term "violent," used by Derrida here and on several other occasions, must be treated with caution; and in general, the term would demand a further analysis.[46] I use it here, consistently with Derrida's usage, in the sense of subjecting the edifices of philosophy to a radical dislocation (ébranlement), which may be accompanied by different forms of distancing and proximity, or approximation, to the field of philosophy. Even when it is a theory and a *criticism*, to oppose this term to a philosophical "critique," is Nietzsche's "philosophizing" finally philosophy? Can it finally be philosophy? Violent or faithful, how much circulation is still necessary? Nietzsche's analysis appears thus to have a different gradient of direction— toward different, "healthy," theories and attitudes, which Nietzsche opposes to decadent, "sick," philosophy—"a [case] history of an error."

The sessions themselves are the "short sessions," as in Lacan's analytical practice, to follow here perhaps the *letter* rather than the spirit of Lacan's theory and practice.[47] It is true, of course, that Nietzsche is never quite finished with his cases, either, such as the case of Socrates. From *The Birth of Tragedy* to *Twilight of the Idols* and *The Antichrist*, his patients return for more sessions, as Freud was to recommend. Yet there is a difference in balance and attitudes. The procedure is radical—surgical—rather than therapeutic. By itself it cannot always guarantee critical or theoretical success. No procedure can. Nietzsche, however, perhaps the first theorist of interminability—*before* Freud, although read as such *after* Freud—was a great master of the short session. Breaking new grounds with extraordinary speed, Nietzsche's style continuously subjects interminable problems to the brisk attacks of his writing—to coups, and "coup" also means "revolution," or to attacks of his foil or sting, stiletto. Let us take up the metaphor of fencing here, this the most dancing of sports; and fencing, as Derrida implies in *Spurs*, is not only the most dancing but also the most writing, at any rate the most graphic of all sports. *On the Genealogy of Morals* is subtitled "An Attack," "*Eine Streitschrift*"—"an attack writing," perhaps even an attack by writing "not originally subordinate to the logos and the truth." It is arche-texture that is also architecture, a point that I will discuss in the next chapter. At some point, in fact, Nietzsche says, "I approach deep problems like cold baths: quickly into them and quickly out again [schnell hinein, schnell hinaus]" (*The Gay Science*, sec. 381, p. 343; *KSA* 3:634).

In this sense, Nietzsche is different from Derrida's interminable sessions—Wagnerian in duration, as it were. I refer here to the opposition "short session/long session" rather than to that of terminable and interminable analysis. Derrida plays upon the necessary and self-imposed constraints of terminability in "Limited Inc, abc. . . ." The issue is also related to, although somewhat different from, the question of continuities and breaks in a given theoretical style. Wagner was also a kind of psychoanalyst, another proto-psychoanalyst; and in this sense, too, Nietzsche's style is "contra Wagner," contra interminable sessions of interminable analysis. The treatment of Nietzsche's coups or, as metaphorized by Derrida in *Spurs*, "Nietzsche's coup sur coup," is much more like that of Lacan's short sessions. Nietzsche does engage other strategies and approaches, of course.

A complex balance within Nietzsche's plural style is at issue, and therefore a complex difference in balance between different plural styles and different general economies, such as Nietzsche's, Bataille's, or Derrida's. Derrida's *reading* of Nietzsche in *Spurs: Nietzsche's Styles* is in fact also a *stylization* of Nietzsche's style: a sequence of short—Nietzsche-style—sessions. There is "thinking" and textual work in Nietzsche, proceeding with extraordinary speed, condensing, or changing the scales of, the interminable. There might also be intervals of "slow" thinking or prolonged textual work that are concealed by a short session. And then Nietzsche has a great many short sessions. As "brief" and "abbreviated" a writer as Nietzsche is and sees himself (*Ecce Homo*, 340), he is also quite extended. His total output is enormous, given that he stopped writing at forty-four; and the subsequent silence was long, too—a case in turn of great complexity. At stake is a complex balance of reading—on Nietzsche's part and in reading Nietzsche.

Configuring the closure or closures at issue as *closure* is crucial for Derrida; he uses the economy of closure brilliantly throughout his discourse and in relation to many difficult theoretical tasks. For example, by using closure, Derrida shows that Hegelianism, or idealism in general, can be dislocated only in a complex and mutually inhibiting interaction between the outside and inside of dialectics. This mutual inhibition and *différance* is powerfully opposed to most reversals of *dialectics*, such as Marx's, that move outside idealism, but remain within *dialectic*. Dialectic thus must be undermined, once again, "*wherever* it operates" (*Positions*, 41; *Positions*, 55). A reversal may be possible and even necessary, as a first stage—the phase of reversal—but it must be followed by a reinscription in a general economy (*Positions*, 41–42). Using a similar procedure or as part of the same procedure, metaphysical materialism—the idealism of matter—will be dislocated as well; for the metaphysics of presence or logocentrism, which is Derrida's other major name, is, ". . . of course, a larger concept that idealism, for which it serves as a kind of overflowing foundation [il sert d'assise débordante]" (*Positions*, 51; *Positions*, 70). Once dialectic—materialist *and* idealist—is deconstructed, however, the engagement with Hegel's text may no longer be necessary; it may be *terminated*.

Nor is it impossible that a similar economy of history can be produced outside, or at least by way of a much less intense engagement with Hegel's text, as is perhaps the case in Nietzsche. A reconfiguration of presence and difference, on the one hand, and of philosophy, on the other, by way of the closure of presence and difference and the closure of philosophy, followed by a perhaps necessary reconfiguration of either closure, certainly entails a much more complex equilibrium. One tries to stay on one's feet, to dance with Zarathustra and Nietzsche, or, as Derrida suggests in his reading of Freud in *The Post Card*, to leap with Oedipus and Freud. But then again, walking or staying on one's feet is a complex equilibrium. We might do it easily, but it is not easy to explain fully, or at least well enough, how it is possible and indeed necessary to manage. Such is perhaps the problem of philosophy and, and *as*, the problem of the closure of metaphysics and—*as* or as *not*, or both at once—the closure of presence and difference.

The issue is the degree of operation and the power of the conceptual and rhetorical "forces" of metaphysics and philosophy in a given text, specifically a theoretical text. That difference in degree, however, suggests the possibility of transforming—reconfiguring—radically, such as happens in Nietzsche, the conceptual and rhetorical closure of a given theory, such as that of literature and revolution.

While one cannot overemphasize the highly original and the radically revolutionary nature of Nietzsche's role on the scene of modern theory, the revolution at issue did not and could not happen one single time. Such a transformation cannot be contained within Nietzsche's text. Nietzsche's text, to begin with, itself cannot be constituted as a single text; and the revolution did not happen there one single time, either. Nor can this revolution be an absolutely discontinuous event. It enacts a radical discontinuity along some lines—histories, theories, politics—and *continues* along other lines—histories, theories, politics. These continuities, or evolutions, enable the breaks with the chains with which they are connected, producing the effects of revolution. Such would in fact appear to be a general structure, a general economy—in either sense, for it must be configured by way of a general economy—of at least theoretical revolution. Such, one might say, is "the structure of scientific revolution."

Nietzsche's revolutions belong therefore to the dance of heterogeneous yet interactive—historical-ahistorical—rhythms. No "event," from the perspective of this general economy, can escape this double structure, but it may have a different balance of continuities and breaks, making it possible, from different perspectives, to configure and reconfigure such events as conforming to different economies, restricted or general.

Derrida often, and quite strongly, warns against radical breaks: "Breaks are always, and fatally, reinscribed in an old cloth that must interminably be undone. This interminability is not an accident or contingency; it is essential, systematic, and theoretical. And this in no way minimizes the necessity and relative importance of certain breaks, of the appearance and definition of new structures . . ." (*Positions*, 24; *Positions*, 35). The statement is careful, and the warning, as Derrida shows—interminably, systematically, theoretically—is well worth repeating. But it also reflects a certain style of theory and a certain *positioning*, specifically in its relation to philosophy and a discourse on the margins of philosophy.

For Nietzsche, however, "break" is often just about the only possible strategy and a profound theoretical necessity; and it is, again, specifically the case in relation to philosophy and even its margins with which Nietzsche appears to aim at breaking as well. Such breaks may relate to both a radical abandonment of the previous historico-theoretical configuration or field, such as philosophy and its margins, or to radical transformations of a given configuration or field from its exterior. As indicated earlier, such an exterior may not be absolute; but it may be exterior enough to be able to, indeed to be constrained, to speak of it as an exterior. It may never be absolute, but it may at times be radical, even more radical than an absolute exterior, which once again seems never to be able to be radical enough.

At issue, thus, is not a claim of absolute departures and breaks, but rather a relative positioning and balance between philosophy, its margins, and its others in Hegel, or Kant, Husserl, Heidegger, and finally, Derrida, on the one hand, and Nietzsche, on the other. Nor, as I have stressed, is it ever a question of suspending *theoretical* rigor in Nietzsche and Bataille, however differently they play rigor out under the condition of play.[48]

Nietzsche's breaks do often emerge as creations of new centers, even and precisely under the conditions of *abandoning* the—absolute or unconditional—centrality of all centers. These noncenters may, under certain conditions, be quite central, because "*this affirmation then determines the noncenter otherwise than as loss of the center [Cette affirmation détermine alors le noncentre autrement que comme perte du centre]*" (*Writing and Differance*, 292; *L'Écriture et la différence*, 427).

A break cannot come from nowhere, of course—differences do not fall from the sky, as Derrida often says. Nor can one, by abandoning an "old" configuration or field, begin the "new" one from nothing. Continuities, therefore, must be engaged and constructed, but new and different continuities. This play is complex; it can, and often must, be multiply perspectivized, reinscribing continuities into what appear as breaks. The effects of breaks, however, are equally necessary insofar as transformations must be configured. These effects are radical in Nietzsche's case, both in his theoretical practice—departures and abandonments on the one hand, and moves to new territories on the other—and in the theories themselves that are produced as a result. Of course, in general these two aspects do not always accompany each other; but in Nietzsche they do. In other words, there may be a different practice—but also a different ideology—of transformations, including between Nietzsche and Derrida. Nietzsche does not always escape "reinscribing his breaks in an old cloth," and such reinscription must be undone whenever necessary.

No strategy of continuity and interminability in itself can protect one in this respect, however. One can think of many examples of deliberate attempts to adhere to Derrida's proscriptions to that effect, that retain or reinstate metaphysics to a degree far greater than Nietzsche does. According to Derrida himself, Nietzsche's record is in fact extraordinary in this respect. Much depends on where and how one is positioned in relation to or in the margins of philosophy—its texts, its institutional matrix, its politics, its history, and its geography—or what one's agendas—theoretical or political, conscious or unconscious, subliminal—are. Much also depends on which texts, which circulations and transformations, what *work* or *play*, gives one "great *pleasure*"—or *pain*.

It must be kept in mind, that from this perspective—which perspective is a part of Nietzsche's revolution—no "event" may be claimed to have a given economy, historical or other, or to be an event, to begin with, outside perspectival inscriptions or configurations. But in turn, no configuration can offer an absolutely exhaustive configuring of anything. The *writing* of this *writing*, therefore, must obey the *laws* of *writing* as *différance* in the general economy: ". . . it can only be marked in what I would call a *grouped* textual field: in the last analysis it is impossible to *point* it out, for a unilinear text, or a punctual *position*, an operation signed by a single author, are all by definition incapable of practicing this interval" (*Positions*, 42; *Positions*, 58).

The revolution at issue is thus not only Nietzsche's or Derrida's, although one must always discriminate to the extent possible as to the originality of each contribution. The "composition"—or juncture—of Derrida's *différance* in "Différance" relates, in addition to Nietzsche, to conceptions of difference in—and to varying degrees, against—Saussure, Freud, Levinas, Heidegger, Husserl, Bataille, and, of course, Hegel. But, as this juncture necessarily expands, there is also Mallarmé, whose proximity to Nietzsche is so important for Derrida, or Deleuze. There is Deleuze, but then there are also Foucault and, as shall be seen, Althusser and Marxism in general. On the psychoanalytic side of this landscape, Lacan remains an irreducible proper name; and the scene of French feminism—including Simone de Beauvoir, Irigaray, Cixous, and many others—powerfully affects these developments.

One must immediately move outside this double register of philosophy and literature, however, *to the extent* that this register can be perceived as such—as double in this sense or only as double in general. The expansion at issue is in fact inevitable. It has already—always already—occurred and has powerfully affected modern intellectual history, at least since Freud and psychoanalysis, or Nietzsche to begin with. One has no choice but to divide—"always already"—both inside and outside of either philosophy or literature or the *inter*—*hymen*, *différance*—of philosophy and literature, and—"always already"—to convert each register into a multiple one, and indeed simultaneously multiple and partial or fractured. The extent of the possibility of ever being double is vanishing quickly, which is the most immediate—that is, the most speedily *mediated*—effect of everything being "always already" double.

As we have seen, already to a degree in Mallarmé and in a more complex way in Nietzsche, the multiple register characterizes a literary—Mallarmé's—or tragic—Nietzsche's—style. Both denominations relate to other things as well. Both, however—Nietzsche's "tragic" and Mallarme's "literary"—must be seen as operating against the philosophical register, specifically, which is Derrida's major point, as *dissemination* against polysemy—a controlled multiplicity, by way of *Aufhebung*, Heideggerian Being or of thinking-poetizing in later works, or Lacanian economy.

In this history, too, or this a-history, inheres many a history, such as the histories of science—thermodynamics and quantum physics and relativity and a great deal of classical physics and some modern mathematics and logic as well, biology, the theory of evolution, and genetics—and the history and philosophy of science, such as in Thomas S. Kuhn, Feyerabend, and Michel Serres, among others. They all interactively and heterogeneously produce the "effect(s)" and "cause(s)" of the "Nietzschean" revolutions. But no enrichment or stratification in the articulation of historical events, historical contexts, or historical signatures can ever enable us to totalize, to have any *Aufhebung* of this history and this nonhistory. Some proper names, mediating the effects of Nietzsche's transformation, are bound to be lost here; and by no account nor under any rubric can they ever be fully reassembled. There also other histories and nonhistories, possible ensembles and configurations, that might in turn emerge so as to (re)configure the "Nietzschean" reconfiguration, as Nietzschean or otherwise, or conversely bypassing its possibility, necessity, or importance. A general economy of reconfiguration must be heterogeneous enough to admit these too—a strictly Nietzschean position, in fact. This heterogeneity does not mean, of course, that all such reconfigurations will be equally acceptable from such a position. This position appears—to some of us—to be the best available at the moment. But it can, and at some point must, either be transformed by a reconfiguration or abandoned, radically displaced with a different chain so that one day it may disappear without a trace and may never be recovered again. Such a disappearance, however, will remain undetermined; for anything might reappear and reenter the scene, although some things must disappear—as some already have—without a trace or possibility of return. But what will reappear or when it will reappear can never be determined once and for all.

Nietzsche's writings are difficult, he claims, in a draft for the chapter "Why I Write Such Good Books":

My writings are difficult; I hope this is not considered an objection? To understand the most *abbreviated* language ever spoken by a philosopher—and also, the one poorest in formulas, most alive, most artistic—one must follow the *opposite* procedure of that generally required by philosophical literature. Usually, one must *condense*, or upset one's stomach; I have to be diluted, liquefied, mixed with water, else one upsets one's stomach, too.

Silence is as much of an instinct with me as is garrulity with the messieurs philosophers. I am *brief*: my readers themselves must become long and comprehensive in order to bring up and together all that has been thought, and thought after by me [hinterdacht: thought through].

On the other hand, there are prerequisites for "understanding" here, which very few can satisfy: one must be able to put a problem in its proper place—that is, in the context of the other problems that *belong with it*; and for this one must have at one's finger tips the topography of various nooks and the difficult areas of whole sciences and above all philosophy. (*Ecce Homo*, 340; *KSA* 14:484–85; translation modified)[49]

Now, how much or how little does Nietzsche *read* and how much must one read in order to read Nietzsche? In the first section of the chapter itself Nietzsche says: "My triumph is precisely the opposite of Schopenhauer: I say, '*non* legor, *non* legar [I am not read, I *will* not be read]' [Mein Triumph ist gerade der umgekehrte, als der Schopenhauer's war,—ich sage '*non* legor, *non* legar']" (*Ecce Homo*, 259; *KSA* 6:299). Among other things, that statement demands a reconfiguration of the whole economy of reading, perhaps even beyond what has emerged in deconstruction, particularly once again in the context of de Manian and post-de Manian agendas of reading, a major development as it is. One might need a different theory and practice of reading, however, to approach the "eloquence of power in forms [Machtberedsamkeit in Formen]" that defines architecture for Nietzsche (*Twilight*, 521; *KSA* 6:118), but also, I think, his own writing. It no longer even requires any proof—"What does it matter if *I* remain right [Was liegt daran, dass *ich* Recht behalte!]" (*Twilight*, 473; *KSA* 6:66). Yet its "brief" and "abbreviated" language and style, as against the language and style of proof, its architecture, might still "conceal" an immense texture—the arche-texture of writing. Nietzsche still adds, however: "I *am* much too right [Ich *habe* zu viel Recht]" (*Twilight*, 473; *KSA* 6:66).

Like Lacan's, Nietzsche's short sessions may not be the cure either. "And that must end us, that must be our cure, / To be no more," Milton's Belial says (*Paradise Lost* 2:145–46). Geoffrey Hartman cites these very lines in his *Saving the Text*, a book mainly on Derrida's *Glas* (66). Belial, however, may be seen as a naive—nihilistic—Nietzschean—at best, for after all:

> A fairer person lost not Heav'n; he seem'd
> For dignity compos'd and high exploit
> But all was false and hollow; though his Tongue
> Dropt Manna, and could make the worse appear
> The better reason, to perplex and dash
> Maturest Counsels: for his thoughts were low;
> To vice industrious, but to Nobler deeds
> Timorous and slothful: *yet he pleas'd the ear* (110–18; emphasis added)

Belial actually continues [Hartman cuts the passage]:

> . . . sad cure; for who would lose,
> Though full of pain, this intellectual being,
> Those thoughts that wander through Eternity,
> To perish rather, swallow'd up and lost
> In the wide womb of uncreated night,
> Devoid of sense and motion? (146–51)

Nietzsche's affirmation, however, is a Yes!-saying affirmation. It does not much please the ear, particularly the ear of philosophy, "the ear of the other."[50] Derrida, one of whose texts on Nietzsche is entitled "The Ear of the Other," does not miss this moment in "Tympan": "To philosophize with a hammer. Zarathustra begins by asking himself if he will have to puncture them, batter their ears (Muss man ihnen erst die Ohren zerschlagen), with the sound of cymbals or tympani, the instrument, always, of some Dionysianism. In order to teach them to hear with their eyes too" (*Margins*, xii–xiii; *Marges*, iii–iv). Derrida, however, offers a different "project": "But we will analyze the metaphysical exchange, the circular complicity of the metaphor of the eye and the ear [Mais nous analyserons l'échange métaphysique, la complicité circulaire des métaphores de l'oeil et de l'ouïe]" (*Margins*, xiii; *Marges*, iv). At issue in Derrida, in the margins of *philosophy*, will also be a circular complicity of philosophy and nonphilosophy, a very different project. That project is not necessarily pleasing to many philosophical ears, either. Other ears are a different story; and Nietzsche has pleased some ears after all, he has even opened some ears, and eyes, too—"the ears of those whose ears are related to ours":

> One does not only wish to be understood when one writes; one wishes just as surely *not* to be understood. It is not by any means necessarily an objection to a book when anybody finds it impossible to understand: perhaps that was part of the author's intention—he did not want to be understood just by "anybody." All the nobler spirits and tastes also select their audience when they wish to communicate; and choosing them,

they at the same time erect barriers against "the others." All the more subtle laws of any style have their origin at this point: they at the same time keep away, create a distance, forbid "entrance," understanding, as said above—while they open the ears of those who can relate to us through ears. (*The Gay Science*, sec. 381, p. 343; *KSA* 3:633–34; translation modified)

There are, then, ears for the strange music of Nietzsche's Dionysianism. The flute, we recall, is its instrument, too.

Part II

Implications

Chapter 5

Theoria

Contaminations

One of the major implications of poststructuralist theory, especially deconstruction, is the irreducibility of the double binds, blind spots, undecidables, and related complications, or contaminations, emerging in any general, and indeed already some restricted economies. This irreducibility often leads to a kind of theoretical schizophrenia, when one is unable to linearize one's logic and to separate the logical levels—such as levels from metalevels—of one's discourse. In the final account, the radical nonlinearity of the general economy makes theoretical linearization not only difficult but also, in strict terms, impossible at certain points. The general economy does not preclude linear effects. It enables one to account more rigorously as much for the efficacity of the linear as for the efficacity of the nonlinear, and it demands accounting for both. I use the terms "linear" and "linearity" here as general rubrics, analogous and related to the rubric of presence as considered in the preceding chapter. There are many classical configurations that can also be seen as—*classically*—nonlinear, at times approaching, even infinitesimally approaching, but never quite reaching the radical nonlinearity and double binds of the general economic theories.

The association itself of the double bind and schizophrenia follows Gregory Bateson's theories, where it is also related to the question of logic and, by implication, to undecidables.[1] 'Double bind' has been an often used—indeed overused and at times abused—term in the history of deconstruction and related developments, perhaps most prominently in Deleuze, although various forms of double bind had been practiced well before deconstruction, in connection with Bateson's theories and independently of

215

them. Certainly, double binds were practiced, with both great playfulness and great theoretical rigor, by Nietzsche and Bataille.

Double binds or other forms of undecidability do not preclude the possibility of theory; in fact, often, if imperceptibly, they enhance it. Nor, as I have indicated, do the relevant theoretical economies—general economies—preclude one from accounting for linearities. Strictly speaking, all theory, including philosophy, has always been, throughout its history, under the condition of schizophrenia, no matter how hard it has tried to purify itself from it. Double binds are, by definition, inhibitions or contaminations. Still, they may often be productive, even extraordinarily so. In effect, it appears that all theory depends on the schizophrenia of its double binds, even though, like all schizophrenias, it does at times force theory—*theoria*—to make a spectacle of itself. And if we do not always have to be theoretical, often we must be, however irreducible are other—for example, political—dimensions of our endeavors. Yet one cannot say "always." That prohibition on "always" is a major, perhaps the only, unconditional prohibition of general economy and its irreducible double binds.

Along with a recomprehension of linearity, a theory as general economy demands a recomprehension, not a dismissal of classical theory. The irreducibility of double binds and undecidability does not imply that theory is in practice always schizophrenic. It implies only that the play of double binds, which is also the double bind of play, in the sense developed earlier, is *irreducible* in principle: a double bind can always be found that is (re)produced by a theory, and at certain moments it can take the center stage of theory. But such is not always the case in practice. In practice, there are moments when we must be logical and check our logic, separate double binds, and be as "conscious" and self-conscious as possible.

A separation of the levels of description may play a decisive role in a system's own accounts of itself. Gödel's theorem is a major, and most formal, example of such a system, relating to the system of propositions of a given calculus—*containing* numbers. In general, however, such accounts, which may be historical, theoretical or political, are often necessary. They are in fact more necessary under the conditions of general economy and its contaminations, undecidabilities, and double binds than under the classical conditions, specifically under the conditions of theory and history as self-knowledge and self-consciousness, which as Hegel—and in great measure already Descartes, or indeed Socrates and Plato—profoundly understood, may be demanded by all classical theory, from Socrates to Heidegger.

The possibility and necessity of a system's fully conscious historical account of itself—its full, absolute historical self-consciousness—defines the Hegelian economy. This is how *Geist* or, later, the Idea is configured in Hegel. The enormous undecidability of such a system becomes clear when one considers it or analogous economies rigorously—*systematically*. In fact, Hegel brilliantly grasped some of these complexities. It is, in Hegel's resolution of this immense problem, only *Geist*'s equally enormous power of linearization that enables it to manage this complexity and de facto undecidability, or, to be more precise, to manage that which no human science can articulate otherwise than by resorting to undecidability. Hegel's appeal to self-consciousness is understandable and indeed logical, in general and specifically given the historical character of the Hegelian economy. A system may well need to account for itself in order to maintain itself, or even to survive, and often in order to *transform* itself. Furthermore, some aspects of classical systems, including their conceptual and self-reflecting character, make a great deal of sense as "structural" or "organizing" memory, or history, since they suggest richer configurations than more direct and linear structures of record keeping. The necessity of this expansion and enrichment, in part, led Hegel to *Geist*.

As Derrida shows throughout his analysis of Freud and in many of his general elaborations from *Of Grammatology*[2] on, this necessity also structures the economy of memory in Freud, and indeed all of record keeping, and demands the general economy of *writing* in Derrida's sense. Such a writing demands, of course, much beyond the classical modes and theories of record keeping. But one cannot simply dispense with them, either. Nor would one want to. More complex organizations are often necessary, however; one needs *more* organization along with—and at times *as*—*less* organization. One needs more order along with more chaos. Derrida's *writing* is in part a response to this profound theoretical and practical, and perhaps political, necessity.

As one of the consequences of this reconfiguration of memory and history by way of writing, a rigorous critique and deconstruction of *metaphysical* historicism, such as Hegelianism, become possible and necessary. When *history*, Hegel's great discovery, is reconfigured in the deconstructed field, it becomes all the more important to the structure and the functioning of theory. Hegel's system remains a great and, in great degree, still paradigmatic economy of the self-reflexive. Hegel brilliantly understood that the core of Descartes' *cogito*, particularly the philosophical *cogito*, was that it was reflecting upon and was conscious of itself as *cogito*. Insofar as self-consciousness and self-definition are at issue, it is difficult and in many ways impossible to do better than Hegel; and the general economy and deconstruction, which operate against dialectic and the *Aufhebung* wherever they operate, are always a deconstruction and a recomprehension of self-reflexivity.[3]

Thus self-consciousness retains its significance, whether one speaks of an individual or of a collective theoretical consciousness, or of any form of interaction between them. For we often need to know how we can or cannot speak about history or theory, or how we can or cannot define a given field in relation to other fields, or see it as undefinable. There are fields, such as philosophy or literature, that often, although not always, define themselves as concerned with their own nature, or structure. Such economies of self-definition or, more generally, self-referentiality need to be considered within the context of their specific fields, as well as in the context of the difference between more self-referential fields, such as philosophy, literature, literary criticism and theory, and less self-referential fields, such as the natural and exact sciences.

By the same token, however, some of the things that are reduced or suspended by philosophy should, or must, be reduced and suspended, or have already been reduced and suspended in practice, but, to return to Nietzsche's formulation, if such is the case, it is *"for other reasons than hitherto."* According to Nietzsche, philosophy and the "asceticism" of philosophy—which might be seen as a will to reduce—are not without value: ". . . a certain asceticism, a severe and cheerful continence with the best, will belong to the most favorable conditions of supreme spirituality, and is also among its more natural consequences" (*On the Genealogy of Morals*, 112; *KSA* 5:356).

Nietzsche also speaks about the necessity of developing tremendous consciousness and self-consciousness—tremendous concentration. Thus, he makes a very strong statement to that effect in *Twilight of the Idols*:

> I put forward at once—lest I break with my style, which is *affirmative* and deals with contradiction and criticism only indirectly, only involuntarily—the three tasks for which educators are required. One must learn to *see*, one must learn to *think*, one must learn to *speak* and to *write*: the goal in all three is a noble culture. Learning to *see*—accustoming the eye to calmness, to patience, to letting things come up to it; postponing judgment, learning to go around and grasp each individual case from all sides. (*Portable Nietzsche*, 511; *KSA* 6:108; translation modified)

This statement needs to be read with care and with respect to Nietzsche's broader argument and his overall style, which he invokes here, for it does not exclude the unconscious and play. Nietzsche's demands, however, are *in part* what philosophy wants from knowledge and what it urges us to do. Certainly quite similar demands would be made by Hegel, who is inescapable whenever any consciousness, particularly self-consciousness, is concerned. Nietzsche may have grasped Hegel extremely well in this respect. In general, against the claims made by Nietzsche's critics and even by some admirers, including Bataille, it appears that Nietzsche knew and understood Hegel quite well—exceedingly well, I think. Nietzsche's attitude toward Hegel was *ambivalent*, it is true; but this ambivalence is often a result of his profound understanding of Hegel. One should also give the term 'ambivalent' its Freudian sense here, with all the implications of this sense, such as the anxiety of influence. Nietzsche saw Hegel, often against Kant, as a more *affirmative* thinker, even though *Nietzschean* affirmation itself remains as anti-Hegelian as it is anti-Kantian. The passage just cited clearly reflects an "active"—*affirmative*—psychology as against a "reactive" or negative one. This distinction serves Nietzsche as a major theoretical instrument throughout his later writing. *On the Genealogy of Morals* is the most pointed case in this respect. As he writes, again showing himself, simultaneously, a most astute "historical" thinker and a most astute critic of metaphysical historicism: "The Hegelian way out, following Plato, a piece of romanticism and reaction, at the same time a symptom of the historical sense, of a new *strength*: the 'spirit' itself is the 'self-revealing and self-realizing ideal': in 'process' and 'becoming' more . . . more of this ideal in which we believe manifests itself—thus the ideal realizes itself; faith is directed into the *future* when, in accordance with its noble requirements, it can worship" (*Will to Power*, sec. 253, p. 147; *KSA* 12:148; translation modified).

One might say that the tremendous concentration of consciousness invoked by Nietzsche was what Hegel "actually" had in mind throughout his writing. Such is not always or not only the case, however, given Hegel's central presupposition—*Geist*, or the Idea, to which all Hegel's major conclusions, and all his other presuppositions, must be related. *Geist is* Hegel's central presupposition, even if it might well have been arrived at at a certain point of his textual process—as thinking and as writing—by way of conclusion. *This Geist* is, naturally, quite absent in Nietzsche, and is antithetical without a possibility of synthesis between them to the "supreme spirituality [höchster Geistigkeit]" invoked in the *Genealogy*, even if, in some measure, it is still a product of this "supreme spirituality."

Hegel, at the very least, believed in something that we cannot believe, or that we can no longer afford to believe at whatever level. Hegel, too, "*has written* what he has written." He has written that a self-consciousness, namely Absolute Knowledge, can exist—a system that is, *first*, concerned with itself alone—the first impossibility, and that is, *second*, concerned only with knowledge—the second impossibility. He has also written that all human knowledge—*consciousness*—is part of and is governed by this absolute machinery. Hegel would never accord the unconscious the name 'knowledge.' But, as Nietzsche was first to understand in full measure, "our apparatus for acquiring knowledge is not *designed* for knowledge [Unser Erkenntniß-Apparat nicht auf 'Erkenntniß' *eingerichtet*]" (*Will to Power*, sec. 496, p. 273; *KSA* 11:184), or more precisely, this apparatus may not have been designed for knowledge or for knowledge alone. It is certainly never fully governed by consciousness or self-consciousness, in whatever form the latter is conceived, whether the Hegelian *Geist* or some human economy of self-consciousness, such as Marx's political economy. Any cognitive economy, whether individual or collective, becomes irreducibly unconscious—and, of course, irreducibly political—once it becomes concerned with itself as a cognitive structure. As a result, it becomes concerned with a great many things beyond knowledge, even supposing that we could rigorously conceive of or articulate knowledge as economy. We now "know" very well what such concerns imply; and this knowledge makes the whole Hegelian machinery and, in Hegel's mighty shadow, many other machineries of knowledge tremble.

As we have seen, it does not follow, however, that one can simply say that everything is political, or psychological, or social. The political and the theoretical, for example, are always interactive. But they can never be fully unified; and, contrary to Hegel, their balance can never be fully determined by consciousness and knowledge. No dialectic and *Aufhebung* can achieve that. Along with other inhibitions and contaminations that will impose themselves, the theoretical unconscious of the political, and perhaps even more so the political unconscious of the theoretical, cannot be reduced. There are always a *différance* and a complementarity between them, a certain difference and a certain common ground, as these relations continuously reconfigure themselves, but never either an absolute difference or an absolute unification. This fact is what enables a radical interruption of the *Aufhebung* and a deconstruction of Hegel. One must rigorously stratify different levels and domains, such as the theoretical and political. One must analyze both their difference and their interaction—their mutual contamination and inhibition, and possibly their undecidability, on the one hand, and their complementarity, on the other.

One must develop a powerful "*consciousness*" of the unconscious, which Hegel—or Kant, or Descartes—perceived, but which they wanted to overcome. To a considerable degree, the confrontation with, and the desire to erase, the unconscious may be seen as defining philosophy and its history. In Hegel this economy takes its ultimate form, as history becomes the history whose necessary aim is Absolute (Self-)Consciousness—Absolute Knowledge (das absolute Wissen). In this sense, when Bataille says that Hegel did not know to what extent he was right, he may also be saying that Hegel's idea of knowledge—that is, Absolute Knowledge and all that it implies—fails as *theory*. It is indeed *restricted*, and the question is not only whether we can erase the unconscious—we cannot—but also whether we *need* to do so. A different logic, the logic of the unconscious and of play—Nietzschean, Dionysian logic—is demanded by theory; and, as we have seen, one cannot fully calculate and control the effects and consequences of one's text and one's theoretical or political actions.

For example, one often *forgets*, sometimes forgetting very important things, and always forgetting something. While at times one might *simply* forget, forgetting itself is, of course, never a simple matter, as both Nietzsche and Freud have taught us. Thus one might and often must practice the "active forgetfulness [aktive Vergesslichkeit]" that Nietzsche discovers and that he even ascribes, to a degree, to consciousness (*Genealogy*, 57–58; *KSA* 5:291). Active forgetfulness cannot be configured without inhibition, however; and its general economy demands the complementarity existing between the terms one engages. As a result of this forgetting, one may end up employing, even naively, naive metaphysics. One may also do so on purpose, of course, either as play or parody, or in order to use metaphysics against itself. When this strategy works, as in Nietzsche, it also radically problematizes the whole concept of naivete. As we have seen, however, much depends on how one *reads* the metaphysics employed by a critical text such as Nietzsche's. How naive could Nietzsche have been, after all, given what "he has written"? Still, however admirable—or detestable—one's control of one's text might be, no text can ever be fully controlled. This, too, is what Nietzsche has written—Nietzsche who controls his text perhaps better than Hegel.

A "loss of consciousness" is ineluctable even in the most affirmative style. Yet the Nietzschean style remains an "*affirmative* style." Whatever the differences between different authors involved, a critical or deconstructive style—a plural style—is, as we have seen, affirmative, indeed too much so for the taste of many critics of Nietzsche, Bataille, Derrida, and other practitioners of plural style. Against Hegel, "loss of consciousness" refers, on the one hand, to the necessary *consciousness* of the unconscious, and on the other, to the mastery of a more unconscious theoretical play to the extent that such a mastery is possible. The latter, once again, does not exclude the necessity and mastery of classical logic. While different from and under-mining the Hegelian *Aufhebung*, a general economy must function so as not to dismiss restricted economies, but rather to comprehend them and often to give them broader theoretical scope. There are situations in which Hegel's logic or other restricted economies become extremely effective. At issue are the relative distribution and the relative effectiveness of various theoretical and political economies—their interaction, balance, mutual in-hibitions, undecidability, or complementarity—but never the absolute mastery achieved by any given structure or arrangement. The relative power of unconscious play, however, must be seen as a fundamental aspect of all knowledge. While the word 'knowledge' itself loses a great deal of its Hegelian power as a result of this proposition, it does not lose all of it. Sup-plemented in this way, it might even acquire new power. In spite of phi-losophy's many claims to the contrary, there may never have been a rigorous concept of *knowledge*. In order to give the word 'knowledge' ef-fectiveness and power, one must practice a general economy of (un)knowledge.

Nietzsche sees or metaphorizes such theory as dream in partial recog-nition of its dreaming.[4] At issue is a fundamental reconsideration of the structure of knowledge, particularly in relation to the unconscious, to which Nietzsche's and then Freud's contributions were so revolutionary.[5] Strange as it may be to philosophy, this consciousness is—for some of "us"—*better* knowledge and even better *logic*. It is, if you like, both a progress of knowledge and a power and triumph of logic, although it cannot be seen as complete—absolute—knowledge and all sorts of losses are incurred in the process. For Hegel, losses of that type would be inad-missible even for proper human knowledge, certainly for philosophy. Ab-solute Knowledge loses or wastes nothing. Knowledge that the unconscious cannot be excluded enables one to set into operation a better understanding of what counts and what does not count, of what can and cannot be excluded—consciousness and the unconscious, history and theory, and, as theory, logic and play, argument and spectacle, or perfor-mance—and of how such exclusion can proceed.

That a general economy as theory or history is always an economy of distribution, as opposed to an economy of exclusion, is therefore of crucial importance, even though there may and must be configurations of radical exclusion as well. The latter may also be radical incisions—surgical proce-dures as opposed to therapeutic ones. Under the conditions of general economy, however, destroying the *unity* of consciousness or the unity of unity (and throughout the history of philosophy they often go together) is never simply a destruction of *consciousness* or the *effects* of (self-)consciousness, including *theoretical* (self-)consciousness. Such would not be the case whether one refers to Nietzsche—who often practices radical surgery—or Freud and Derrida—who are more therapeutic practitioners—or Lacan—who may be closer to Nietzsche in his theoretical and even his practical style, in the style of his practice, as a theorist and as a therapist.

One must comprehend consciousness of whatever type by other means, including by means of "the unconscious," whether Freudian, theoretical, or political. One must account for the psychological or even the biological necessity of presence—a crucial issue and one of the main points in both Nietzsche and Derrida. Historico-political factors are equally indispensable to such recomprehensions. Along with all these, there are powerful *theoretical* considerations of great interest and significance—the irreducible effects of consciousness and theory—offered by the text of philosophy, from Socrates to—most directly—Plato, and then from Socrates and Plato to Aristotle, to Descartes, to Leibniz, to Spinoza, to Kant, to Hegel, to Husserl, to Heidegger. These considerations are *theoretical* very much in the classical sense of their *conscious* comprehensiveness. They are classical instruments and strategies of theoretical thinking as theory and as practice, including political practice. We need all their power, along with all other powers and along with much that cannot be assembled under the heading of power. Whatever else philosophical endeavors are and however multiply they are motivated and determined, or overdetermined, they, from Socrates' and Plato's projects, or before, to Heidegger's "uncircumventable meditation," are also attempts to understand the facts and effects of consciousness and self-consciousness.

Consciousness, knowledge, understanding are, as both Nietzsche and Freud—the great thinkers of the unconscious—pointed out, deeply enigmatic things, more enigmatic perhaps than the unconscious. This enigma of consciousness, like Derrida's "post card," has been circulating "from Socrates to Freud and beyond," via Descartes, Kant, Hegel, Husserl, and Heidegger. It has been detoured via the postal routes of the thinkers of "the unconscious"—most specifically, Nietzsche, Freud, Bataille, Lacan, Deleuze, and Derrida—who by now, to a degree, have taken it over. There are other figures and important earlier precursors; and the two routes at issue are far from always distinct or separable, as cases like Rousseau would easily demonstrate. The differences emerging at certain, often crucial points of these two trajectories are decisive, nonetheless. For Socrates, the greatest enigma was perhaps not the *impossibility* for human beings to attain full or clear understanding, consciousness, or communication; this he could *understand* quite well. The enigma was rather the *possibility* of even a relative, and at times a relatively stable, consciousness or understanding. How is it possible? How is it all possible? Such is the question confronted by all the figures just listed, asked and circulated quite differently along the two routes just indicated, but not without many connections between them.

Truths

The problem, then—a very difficult problem—is how to account for conditions of stabilization, unification, understanding, communication, and consciousness, specifically theoretical consciousness, rather than merely to recognize the undecidability, plurality, heterogeneity, and relativity of meaning or value pervading all these processes. The last could be seen as obvious, were it not for the fact that such pronouncements as "All things are relative" or even "radically relative," or "Everything is undecidable" may still be accompanied by the metaphysics or ideology of consciousness and thus by a restricted economy of one kind or another. Nor is it easy to understand the emergence of decidable propositions under the condition of undecidability, or of the unities under the conditions of plurality, particularly the radical plurality of the general economy. But it must be done whenever necessary, which is often, and in a certain sense always, for we can no more speak of absolute or unconditional undecidability, or plurality and heterogeneity, than of decidability or unity and homogeneity. This necessity, as opposed to rejecting, for whatever reasons, the undecidability and heterogeneity, marks the difference between a critical and a metaphysical text, the general and a restricted economy.

Although, as I have indicated, this history is long, Descartes obviously holds a particular significance in this context and in the sequence of proper names marking this history. Descartes might be seen as the name of the problem *consciousness*. In *Of Grammatology*, Derrida inserts ("the name of the problem") Rousseau into this sequence, "between Descartes and Hegel" (98). This is a powerful and effective placement. In invoking this sequence, however, one must not repress (the name of the problem) Leibniz, either. "Why are there things rather than nothingness?"—which Heidegger proclaims as "the fundamental question of metaphysics" in *An Introduction to Metaphysics*[6]—is specifically Leibniz' question, although it had been asked, to be sure, many times before and many times after.

To Descartes, however, without suspending "origin," there has been no answer given in either the classical text or the critical text. Even assuming, as some recent cosmological theories do, that "all" has begun with "nothingness,"[7] one can always ask, as Descartes no doubt did as well, who or what put the nothingness there, or some analogous question of that type. This possibility leads to a certain closure of theory, and of interpretation in general. On that score, this closure is perhaps irreducible as the closure of difference and presence, considered in the preceding chapter. The same configuration, however, also forces one to ask whether one *can* always ask this question, as a question of theory under given conditions. From this perspective, the difference between the classical and the critical or general economic theory is the difference in the economy of suspension. A general economy, as we have seen, demands a rigorous, recomprehending, suspension of *all* "alls," all absolute origins, centers, or wholes. Such a theory may replace these absolutes with the closure of metaphysics, as in Derrida, or with a still more complex and more transformational economy of closures. Such a closure would manifest itself in the form of questions—such as "What was there before?"—that, in principle, can be asked and answers that, in principle, can or cannot be given.

It cannot be overemphasized that there are other questions asked or not asked, forgotten or repressed, and other answers that may be given or contemplated. There are other reasons for philosophy or knowledge. For these other reasons, "reasons other than hitherto," *the unconscious* of the text of philosophy and the general economy of this text becomes, or remains, *our* question. Is this question central? Perhaps, but there will also always be other reasons, questions, or answers—concealed, avoided, repressed, or forgotten—even for "us," and certainly for others. "Our" reasons and questions, however, and our against-methods, cannot be pursued and explored without "their" reasons and questions, "their" methods, and at times "their" answers. Valéry brilliantly, in a grand, Nietzschean style of his own, comments on the grand style of Descartes, that "truth is Descartes's last concern"—his first is rather style. Derrida comments, closer to Nietzsche, perhaps, than to Valéry:

> What is the operation of the I in the Cogito? To assure itself of the source in the certitude of an invincible self-presence, even in the figure—always paternal, Freud tells us—of the devil. This time a *power* is gained in the course of a movement in grand style which takes the risk of enunciating and writing itself. Valéry very quickly suggests that truth is Descartes's last concern. The words "truth" and "reality" are once again in quotation marks, advanced as effects of language and as simple citations. But if the "I think therefore I am" "has no meaning whatever," and a fortiori no truth, it has "a very great value," and like the style is "entirely characteristic of the man himself." This value is that of a shattering blow,

> a quasi-arbitrary affirmation of mastery by means of the exercise of a style, the egotistic impression of a form, the stratagem of a mise en scène powerful enough to do without truth, a mise en scène keeping that much less to truth in its laying of truth as a trap, a trap into which generations of servile fetishists will come to be caught, thereby acknowledging the law of the master, of I, René Descartes. (*Margins*, 294–95; *Marges*, 351)

Descartes' "truths" survive, in spite of their impossibility, because of his style; and they are impossible not only because style, rather than truth, might be his main concern. It becomes possible to indicate the performative—or a certain performative, including theatrical—aspect and model of the Cartesian *cogito*. "I perform, therefore I am," "*even if I am mad*," and even if "philosophy is perhaps the reassurance given against the anguish of being mad at the point of the greatest proximity to madness [la philosophie, c'est peut-être cette assurance prise au plus proche de la folie contre l'angoisse d'être fou]" ("Cogito and the History of Madness," in *Writing and Difference*, 59; *L'Écriture et la différence*, 92). This proximity may also be seen as proximity to what de Man sees as absolute—and thus impossible—irony, whose limit is madness. Nietzsche was the first to make, in a grand style, the general point asserted by Valéry in relation to Descartes—that value and style take preeminence over truth as the main concern of philosophy. It must be easily apparent from the preceding discussion and from the passages cited earlier. There are, however, several specific references and allusions in Valéry and Derrida that are worth pointing out.

One may begin with *The Birth of Tragedy*, the birth that, as the book proceeds, becomes "the death of tragedy." But toward the very end of the first version, the death of tragedy also becomes the birth of philosophy—out of and as the death of tragedy—which in turn finally becomes the death of philosophy. Paradoxically but inevitably, philosophy dies back into tragedy, or at least art. At the limit of science (Wissenschaft) " . . . the new form of insight breaks through, the *tragic insight* [*die tragische Erkenntniß*] which merely to be endured, needs art as a protection and remedy" (*The Birth of Tragedy*, 98; *KSA* 1:101). In fact, everything returns to music—returns to where it all begins—as "the artistic Socrates" appears, practicing music in his dreams, "the only sign of any misgivings about the limits of logical nature [Jenes Wort der sokratischen Traumerscheinung ist das einzige Zeichen einer Bedenklichkeit über die Grenzen der logischen Natur]" (*Birth of Tragedy*, 93; *KSA* 1:96; translation modified). Or perhaps it returns to dance, the Dionysian dance, for instance, where music and tragedy begin, or . . . here again we, with Heraclitus and Nietzsche, reach our limits and perhaps need art "as protection and remedy." The passage that concerns me at the moment, however, belongs to the movement in the section of *The Birth of Tragedy* preceding the sections on Wagner, where Nietzsche's initial version ends. Nietzsche mentions "exuberance" as well, when he invokes "a profound *illusion* [Wahnvorstellung: delusion, hallucination] that first saw the light of the world in the person of Socrates: the unshakable faith that thought, using the thread of causality, reaches into the deepest abysses of being, and that thought is capable not only of knowing [erkennen] being but even of *correcting* it. This sublime metaphysical illusion accompanies science as an instinct and leads science again and again to its limits at which it must turn into *art—which is really the aim of this mechanism [auf welche es eigentlich, bei diesem Mechanismus, abgesehn ist]*" (*Birth of Tragedy*, 96–95; *KSA* 1:99; translation modified).

Nietzsche's analysis becomes much more nuanced and general economic in later works. His point, however, is interesting enough here, too, both in supporting and in questioning Valéry. There are other reasons for style. Thus, in the end, and *against* Nietzsche here, there are reasons other than art, which is perhaps not, or not always, the aim of or is proper to the mechanism at issue. There are in fact always other reasons for anything, as Nietzsche says in his later works. Perhaps, however, the reason here is the exuberance of Descartes, who, along with Hegel and Kant, must have been on Nietzsche's mind. At least, he should have been, for "a profound delusion" at issue is certainly Descartes' delusion as well. "Lessing, the most honest theoretical man, dared to announce that he cared more for the search after truth than for truth itself—and thus revealed the fundamental secret of science, to the astonishment, and indeed the anger, of the scientific community. . . . [an] isolated insight, born of an excess of honesty if not of *exuberance* [Uebermuth]" (*Birth of Tragedy*, 95; *KSA* 1:99; emphasis added). This is the exuberance of Descartes, and even more so of Nietzsche himself, who does not care to search for truth, even though he might have discovered more truth than many of those who did. Nietzsche, who said many times that "truth is a kind of error," also said many times that the truths of philosophy are *not* true. While one must accept the necessity of lies in this sense, *not all of philosophy's truths are necessary lies*. At least some of these truths are no longer necessary to "us" as truths or as lies, although they must have been necessary to those who advanced them as truths.[8]

Another inescapable point on the Nietzschean trajectory of Valéry's assessment of Descartes is "The History of an Error" in *Twilight of the Idols*: "'I, Plato, *am* the truth' ['ich, Plato, *bin* die Wahrheit']" (*Portable Nietzsche*, 485; *KSA* 6:80). In fact, this is what Descartes says, too, leading to Valéry and to Derrida's "the law of the master, of I, René Descartes." This is the point that Nietzsche clearly makes here as well in relation to Plato or Socrates. The point emerges with particular power in the textual chain of the book that begins, after the prelude of "Maxims and Arrows," with "The Problem of Socrates," and then moves to "'Reason' in Philosophy," with all-important quotation marks around "reason," where "The History of an Error" is in fact placed, very well placed indeed.

My last reference also comes from *Twilight of the Idols*, when Nietzsche speaks of the "grand style" and things "powerful enough to do without truth." The latter is a proposition that neither Valéry nor Derrida, nor indeed Nietzsche, could *in truth* do without. Nietzsche's elaboration is also on "the law of the master." In this case it is the artist, and specifically the architect, who "represents neither [the] Dionysian nor Apollinian state," but a *"grand style"*: "The power that no longer needs any proof . . . a law among laws, *that* speaks of itself as a grand style [Die Macht, die keinen Beweis mehr nöthig hat . . . ein Gesetz unter Gesetzen: *Das* redet als grosser Stil von sich]" (*Twilight of the Idols*, 520–21; *KSA* 6:118–19). There is a much richer content in, and a much greater complexity to these Nietzschean elaborations, from which I extract my quotations. Much there is brilliant; some of it is not entirely unproblematic: everything demands a careful and prolonged analysis. I must restrict myself, however, to what is most relevant to the question of style—style against truth.

This point is made, by the "texts" at issue here, with a lot of power and with a lot of style—grand style; and, in many ways, this point is *profoundly true*. Above all, there are profound truths in these propositions about many of the "profound *delusions*" of philosophy; and I retain *Nietzsche's* emphasis. And yet this is also not altogether *true*. I am *not* referring to the irreducible illusion of every "truth," or every proposition, however powerful or effective, or in however grand a style. My point is rather that *Truth* may very well have been Descartes' *concern*, however performative his philosophical or theoretical *cogito* was. Perhaps it was even his *first* concern, particularly given the context of mathematics and mathematical truth, which cannot be disregarded. Descartes may have wanted to *understand* understanding, may have tried to *think* "thinking" through.

My point is directed, perhaps, more against Valéry, and to some extent Nietzsche, than against Derrida; and perhaps neither one of them would necessarily deny the point as such. Derrida wants to argue, correctly, by way of Descartes and Valéry, and Nietzsche and Freud, that philosophy and the truth of philosophy, are *written* (*Margins*, 294) in Derrida's sense, and "this subordination [of *writing*] to the logos and truth has *come into being* during the epoch whose meaning we must deconstruct" (*Of Grammatology*, 19; *De la grammatologie*, 33).[9]

Without question, there is no such thing as truth in the way metaphysics wants to have it. There is no absolutely conscious truth or truth in the presence of, or in the immediate—and thus present—proximity to the logos. There can be no question, either, that such concerns for truth, including mathematical truth, are never simple, fully innocent or sincere, although at times they are innocent and sincere enough.[10] This is *true*, or if it is not true—since nothing may be, in all truth—it is true enough.

It must not be forgotten that Descartes may have been ironic and self-conscious—and ironically self-conscious—in his statement. For him "thinking" must have had "existence," particularly given how exceedingly well he thought, and he was certainly quite aware of that. Descartes' mind is a kind of machine upon which God, as a grand thinking *machine*, could indeed be modeled or supplemented. Many of Descartes' ideas about consciousness and thinking were indebted, of course, to preceding theological and philosophical notions.

We may not think in the way that we think we think. Thinking as a term and concept is itself a product of the history of philosophy and thus a part of its closure of our discourse; and, in a certain sense, we may not think at all. As Derrida suggests against Heidegger (*Of Grammatology*, 93), one would not want to assign a special priority to the term 'thinking,' even leaving aside the particular mode of thinking that Heidegger speaks or "thinks" about. It is, in principle, not inconceivable that the term 'thinking' will be given up, at least by theory. To a degree, it has in fact already lost much of its scope and effectiveness as a theoretical term. The model of *cogito* is iterable—iterable well beyond *cogito*. For example, it is iterable to Derrida's iterability and its *différance*, which thus becomes the efficacity of "thinking" *cogito*.

These qualifications are crucial. Descartes, or Socrates, or Kant, or Hegel, however, may very well, *for whatever reasons*, have been concerned with truth, with trying to understand, in one way or another, understanding and consciousness. Their accounts are often extraordinary even by modern standards, let alone for their respective times; and we cannot quite do without some of their answers, let alone without their questions. This is so, in part, because "we" are also created by their questions and answers, but only in part, for we are also created by many other questions and answers. In part, we also created them by our many forces of resistance to their great questions, above all their grand question—*Who are we?* Will we have to give up the question itself? It is quite possible. Even though he repeats the question, Nietzsche to a degree has already suggested as much. They, however, have survived enormous forces of resistance. There are, of course, also many stratifications of forces in "their" texts—against each other and within any given text—in part conditioning a deconstruction of the text of philosophy as a reading of one stratum of a given text against another. But there are also forces more exterior to their texts, and a deconstruction can only be produced by such an exteriority. They—their names—are our names and (the names of) *our* problems.

We may indeed now know, after Nietzsche,[11] that "our apparatus for acquiring knowledge is not *designed* for 'knowledge'"—a proposition perhaps unthinkable—*un-thinkable*—to Descartes, or Hegel, against whom it might be advanced more specifically, particularly as a radical a-teleology of knowledge. Hegel, however, offers the first radically *historical*, although not quite *radically* historical, response to Descartes, alongside Leibniz, Spinoza, and Kant. Hegel's proposition would be "I think, therefore I am history" or "I think, therefore I am the product of the history of *Geist*." In Lacan's transition, via Freud and in some measure Hegel,[12] from Cartesian *cogito* to the unconscious and language, the logical consequence of "I think" is becoming the language that one speaks. The question of language inevitably engages the whole question of structural, or structuralist and historical linguistics, leading to the deconstruction of all classical semiology—before and after Hegel's and Saussure's, which two semiologies are powerfully joined by Derrida—to the *general* economy of Derrida's *writing*, by way of Nietzsche, Freud, and Lacan—the thinkers of the unconscious.

Of Grammatology opens with the announcement, somewhat teleological, that—in 1967—"as if in spite of itself, . . . a historico-metaphysical epoch *must* finally determine as language the totality of its problematic horizon" (6; *De la grammatologie*, 15). Derrida could have said, "I think, therefore I *write*," but he does *not*; and that fact cannot be ignored, either. This radical insertion of language and then of *writing*—or of metaphor, since writing must also be seen as "metaphoricity itself [la métaphoricité elle-même]" (*Of Grammatology*, 15; *De la grammatologie*, 27)—into "thinking" has had momentous consequences for the recent history of theory. But this insertion must not be understood as the subsuming of "thought"—or *theory*—by language, or writing, or metaphor in a simple, unproblematized fashion. The relations at issue are determined, at times determined as undetermined, by a radical mutual insufficiency— "thought" is always less than "language"; language is in turn less than "thought"; "theory" is less than "history"; "history" is less than "theory"; and so forth. *Writing* is Derrida's name for this mutual inhibition and radical insufficiency or incompleteness. As such, it is opposed to the omnipotent power of any one of these metaphysical oppositions, or, against Hegel, to their full synthesis.

There are further complexities. As I indicated earlier, one should say, modifying Nietzsche, that "our apparatus for acquiring knowledge *may not* be designed for knowledge." Yet, it may also be, or at some point of its long history become, designed for knowledge along certain lines. The latter remains a radically and profoundly non- or anti-Hegelian proposition, however much Darwin's conception, clearly at work here, might depend historically on Hegel. Nietzsche's main aim, I think, is to indicate that "our apparatus" cannot be seen as specifically designed, once and for all, for anything at all. The "history" of knowledge is both too *long* (Darwin) and "*too* historical" in the sense of not being unconditionally— absolutely—subject to any form of historicity or historicism, or a-historicity and a-historicism. We know now that a different history and a different structure, a different—*general*—economy of knowledge and consciousness are possible. But we must still account for the Hegelian, Kantian, or Cartesian dimensions of this economy; and in many ways we would have to do so using Descartes, Kant, or Hegel. Certainly some of us may even want to understand these things *consciously*, even though, contrary to Hegel or Descartes, such an understanding can never be seen as fully conscious. The very economy of consciousness must be submitted to a massive reconfiguration as a general economy. By the same token, we might want to understand the issue at stake with a degree of consciousness that Descartes and Hegel could at best only *dream* of.

It may be true that it is only by insisting on the necessity of lies and laughter that real seriousness often begins. Often such indeed may be the case—often but, as always, *not* always, even though the economy itself of chance, play, laughter, and their relation to all forms of seriousness must always be taken into account. There is never one way to seriousness or to truth, or to anything, for example, to laughter and to the lie.

We must have the unconscious and *we must have* theory or science, as Bataille insists when speaking of general economy. We must have history, too, but again in a general economy. It was Hegel, of course, who had first attempted to account and to understand, rigorously, history and the unity of history, along with—and *as*—history of (the) unity. From where we stand now, Hegel's flaws and at times even follies are undeniable. But even from where we stand now, much of Hegel retains its power and value. There is certainly enough unity and historical unity to be accounted for. Once absolute unity is abandoned by theory, more unity may emerge than philosophy ever wanted or could account for, and perhaps even more than we can in principle account for in whatever style of theory. There is equally more diversity, more difference than philosophy could and wanted to account for, and perhaps again more than we can in principle account for. Both unity and diversity have to be played out together as the effects of a play that might be neither. They must be played out by a theory, more playful and "unconscious," but also more theoretical and more conscious and self-conscious than ever before.

One might be somewhat hesitant to say that "*we must have* [*il faut*] truth," although we must have theoretical effects that function analogously to the truth in classical discourse. Or must we? Could not a different operation of theory be possible in the radical absence of truth, for example, as a strictly performative operation? It is possible, to be sure, under certain conditions; *theoria*, once again, may always appear and function as spectacle, performance, or still otherwise.[13] But do we want such conditions, and if so, to what degree? Do we want, for example, to give up theoretical rigor, and how much of it do we want to give up? On the scene of modern theory, can a good performative be achieved without it? Or, assuming that such may be the case, would we want to, or can we in the first place, transform the scene of modern theory, make theory into theater? But is theater ever fully theatrical? And there is still the question of the performative or theatrical rigor. In the end, we might want more, let us say in the absence of—for now, a better name—*truth* than all philosophy and its reasons have hitherto been able to give us.

Derrida in fact does say at one point: "*We must have* [*il faut*] truth," echoing, and perhaps alluding to, Heidegger's equally strong claim in *Being and Time*: "We *must* presuppose truth [Wir *müssen* die Wahrheit voraussetzen]" (271). It is worth noting perhaps that no other "name" has elicited a stronger and more decisive—if not necessarily *decidable*—affirmation from Derrida, even though there is throughout an equally powerful erasure of all unique or final names, even the name 'Being' or the name '*différance*.' The same therefore must be the case, must be true, for *truth*—as a *unique* or *final* name. And yet Derrida does say: "I repeat, then, leaving all their disseminating powers to the proposition and the form of the verb: *we must have* [*il faut*] truth. For those who mystify (themselves) to have it trippingly on the tongue. Such is the law [C'est la loi] [Je répéterai donc, laissant à cette proposition et à la forme de ce verbe tous leurs pouvoirs disséminateurs: il *faut* la vérité. A ceux qui (se) mystifient pour l'avoir facilement à la bouche ou à la boutonnière. C'est la loi]" (*Positions*, 105 n. 32; *Positions*, 80 n. 23).

Derrida, it is true, says this in a footnote; and perhaps he does so not, or not only, because he wants, as deconstruction commands, to play upon the idea of the "truth" in the margins of the text. But he does say so, and the footnote is in *Positions*. Such is then his *position*. It is equally important to bear in mind that this is only *one* of his positions, hence disseminating the power of the proposition and the many ironies involved in it. Still the (pro)position might be a bit too strong, given much of Derrida's analysis elsewhere, specifically of Nietzsche in *Spurs*, and even more so given Nietzsche's analysis. It is also bound to be misconstrued, all of its massive ironies and qualifications notwithstanding, by "those who have it trippingly on their tongue," with statements such as "even Derrida admits . . . ," "as Derrida himself acknowledges," and so forth.[14] Before—and after—his "*il faut*," Derrida, *comme il faut*, has a few more things to say in his footnote. This footnote is in many ways extraordinary, gathering many of Derrida's concerns and "proper names" from Hegel or, if you wish Descartes, to Heidegger and Freud, who appears in the text right after "the law of truth." First, however, let me cite the preceding passage:

> In my improvised response, I had forgotten that Scarpetta's question also named *historicism*. Of course, the critique of historicism in all its forms seems to me indispensable. What I first learned about this critique in Husserl (from *Philosophy as a Rigorous Science* to the *Origin of Geometry*: Hegel is always the target of this critique, whether directly or whether through Dilthey), who, to my knowledge, was the first to formulate it under this heading and from the point of view of theoretical and scientific (especially mathematical) rigor, seems valid to me in its argumentative framework, even if in the last analysis it is based on a historical teleology of truth. On this last question the issue is to be reopened. The issue would be: can one criticize historicism in the name of something other than *truth and science* (the value of universality, omnitemporality, the infinity of value, etc.), and what happens to science when the *metaphysical* value of *truth* has been put into question, etc.? How are the effects of science and of truth to be reinscribed? This brief reminder in order to mention that during the course of our interview Nietzsche's name was not pronounced. By chance? On what we are speaking about at this very moment, as on everything else, Nietzsche is for me, as you know, a very important reference. Finally it goes without saying that in no case is it a question of a *discourse against truth* or against science. (This is impossible and absurd, as is every heated accusation on this subject.) And when one analyzes systematically the value of truth as *homoiosis* or *adequatio*, as a certitude of the *cogito* (Descartes, Husserl), or as a certitude opposed to truth in the horizon of absolute knowledge (*Phenomenology of the Mind*), or finally as *alētheia*, unveiling or presence (the Heideggerian repetition), it is not in order to return naively to a relativist or skeptical empiricism. (See, notably, *De la grammatologie*, p. 232, and "*La Différance*" in *Marges*, p. 7.) I repeat, then, ... (*Positions*, 104–5; *Positions*, 79–80 n. 23)

"In no case it is a *discourse against truth* or against science." Perhaps, however, *it is*. At least, this must be a discourse against some sciences and certain truths, as Derrida himself in effect says here. *In truth*, the latter may even be, or should have been, one of his points. Therefore, it does not really "go without saying"—not *in truth*. "A relativist or skeptical empiricism" needs far more qualification as well; and neither Derrida's adverb "naively" nor his references to his other texts, where the references are equally cryptic, quite suffice. These are, comparatively speaking, small qualifications; and they are made *in general agreement with*, and *not against* Derrida's point, and with the "disseminating power of the proposition and the form of the verb" in mind. Clearly, Derrida would not want to suggest that there is some unique form of truth whose law we must obey, but rather that there always appear to be constraints that function in a certain sense—but only in a certain sense— analogously to the functioning of "the *metaphysical* value of *truth*."[15] I want primarily to stress that without propositions against *(the)* truth, *contra* truth, the present discussion—*pro* truth or *pro* theory—becomes just about meaningless. The discussion at the moment must be seen as proceeding under the conditions of the radical dismantlement of "the *metaphysical* value of *truth*." The question of history and of the historicization of theory also becomes crucial in this context, along with and as part of the radical critique of *historicism* and of "the *metaphysical* value of *history*"—an entry, if not a starting point, of Derrida's footnote.

One might speak, therefore, of the difference between Nietzsche's and Derrida's *theoretical* or *performative* practices, or as a rule, interactively both, as considered in the preceding chapter. That "Nietzsche's name was not pronounced in the course of [the] interview" itself may not be "by chance." As I have argued, Derrida's *positions* and *style* are not always Nietzsche's. There are other reasons why Nietzsche's names, or other names, may or may not be pronounced; and for that matter, the reasons why certain names are always already *written* or others always already omitted in a given text are always complex.

In *Positions*, there is also a very long footnote on Lacan that is of considerable interest in the present context. Lacan, in general, looms large over this and many other Derridean texts; he casts a huge shadow in Derrida, almost as large as Hegel's. Lacan's may be the darker shadow and, in Derrida's case, the more menacing; and the question of these relations and related texts and statements of both authors would demand a long and painstaking analysis that cannot be pursued here. Lacan (one must not repress this) offered some of his most famous pronouncements, including on Descartes, *in the Descartes* Amphitheater ("amphi*theater*") of the Sorbonne.

Lacan no doubt knew Valéry's statement on Descartes: "The law of the master, of I, René Descartes"—or of I, Jacques Lacan. The discussion of Descartes, *cogito,* and of the question of certainty in Lacan's seminars assembled in *The Four Fundamental Concepts of Psycho-analysis* would perhaps be most pertinent here. Lacan powerfully reinscribes and interlaces the "I's" (and the "eyes")—in (and of) Descartes and Freud, and of course in and of his own discourse. The gaze is one of the primary themes of these seminars; and the English pun on *I/eye* could not have been missed by Lacan. Many other textual junctures, however, could be invoked in the present context.

All these things are never—or almost never—"by chance." Derrida's mentioning of Freud at the end of the footnote may itself have a metonymic relation to the *question of chance* rather than appearing as a *chance* analogy. Derrida's much later essay, "My Chances," discussed in Chapter 3, on Freud, along with Lacan, Heidegger, and others, treats of his own chances and the question of chance. There the *positioning* of Derrida's footnote to Nietzsche is analogous to that of the reference in *Positions* just considered. It is by chance? Once again, hardly so, or only, even leaving aside the question of chance itself. Derrida does end his note by "paraphrasing" Freud: "*We must have [il faut]* truth. . . . Such is the law. Paraphrasing Freud, speaking of the present/absent penis (but it is the same thing), we must recognize in truth 'the normal prototype of the fetish.' How can we do without it? [C'est la loi. Paraphrasant Freud, qui le dit du pénis présent/absent (mais c'est la même chose), il faut reconnaître das la vérité 'le prototype normal di fétiche.' Comment s'en passer?]" (*Positions,* 105; *Positions,* 80).

Leaving aside for the moment the question of the effectiveness of Derrida's analogy, namely, the relative functioning of two "prototypes," which must again be considered as much in the context of Lacan as of Freud, one could still ask, "Whose truth then?" "Who must have what?" "What is, and what should be, or can be, the *normal*—normal?—prototype of truth, theory, play, performance, or spectacle?" Further, Derrida, in the essay on Valéry cited earlier, likens the interpreters of (the truth of) Descartes' "I think therefore I am" to "servile fetishists." The very question "How [or when and where] can we do without it?"—How can we do without "the normal prototype of the fetish"?—acquires other dimensions, and is put into other play, assuming, of course, that the question could originally be outside these dimensions. As I indicated earlier, it is quite likely that Derrida plays all this out, for the footnote was published, and possibly written, after *Spurs* where Derrida offers his analysis—via Nietzsche and Heidegger—of the question of truth-woman.[16] Among other things, then, the question of truth and science appears in Derrida's footnote between the (question of) performance and the (question of) woman. That *la loi* or *la vérité* is feminine in French could well have been part of Derrida's textual play even here: "The Law of Genre," where Derrida engages such a play directly, is a later text. It must certainly be taken into account in reading all French texts at issue here. But the woman's "prototypes" and "fetishes," assuming that these terms apply, might transform—refigure and reconfigure—the theory of truth, theory and truth.

As in Descartes or Hegel, in a critical, general economic text, the question of truth remains a major *theoretical* and historical concern, notwithstanding all its other concerns—or displacements, repressions, or avoidances—however irreducible they must be. Theory is not reducible to such concerns, although one cannot, of course, say that it is *never* reducible to them; at times it very well may be. In fact, theory for the sake of theory may rarely be possible. Politics is often conducted for the sake of politics, including as the politics of theory. But no *specific form* of politics can be an irreducible factor, either. Nothing can. And there is no politics in general, any more than theory, or indeed anything else.

Nietzsche points out in the end of "The History of an Error" that once the true world is abandoned, so must be the apparent world—the world of appearances. Earlier, in *The Gay Science*, he writes:

> *The Consciousness of Appearance* [Schein]. . . . What is "appearance" to me now! Certainly not the opposite of some essence: what could I say about any essence except to name the attributes of its appearance! Certainly not a dead mask that one could place on an unknown *x* or remove from it! Appearance is for me that which lives and is effective itself, that which goes so far in its self-mockery that it makes me feel that this is appearance and will-o'-the-wisp and a dance of spirits and nothing more—that among all these dreamers, I, too, the "knower," am dancing my dance; that the knower is a means for prolonging the earthly dance and thus belongs to the masters of ceremony of existence; and that the sublime consistency and interrelatedness of all knowledge perhaps is and will be the highest means to *preserve* the universality of dreaming and the mutual comprehension of all dreamers and thus also *the duration of the dream*. (116; *KSA* 3:416; translation modified)

Any truth, then, including Nietzsche's truth, is only an appearance—if once again this is the word, in the absence of the true world—a fiction, or an error necessary for the continuation of a dream. This position, however, does not prevent Nietzsche from insisting that theoretical arguments should be rich—if at times also strange—and that scholarship, which includes the historical and the philological, should be nuanced and rigorous. As I have stressed from the outset of this study, Nietzsche always insists on historical, philological, and theoretical rigor. This rigor becomes even more necessary, and indeed at a certain point it becomes possible, only in the absence of truth as an unconditional authority. This insistence need not signal a return to a form of metaphysical truth or an unconditional authority in the practice of theory, philology, or history. It does have to do with the question of the historical closure of all our discourse, including in relation to "the mutual comprehension of all dreamers." As we have seen, along with "only, everywhere differences and traces of traces," there are also everywhere—conditional—authorities and indeed "truths" constraining us, but also enabling us to get where we want to be or to protect us. Nietzsche knows very well among what dreamers he dreams his own dream. He also knows that his interaction—whether as an attack or a defense or otherwise—with the philologist and the historian demands a better, more rigorous history and philology, or philosophy for that matter. As he says in *On the Genealogy of Morals*, "I made opportune and inopportune references to the propositions of that book [by Paul Ree] not in order to refute them—what have I to do with refutations?—but, as becomes a positive spirit, to replace the improbable with the more probable, possibly one error with another" (*Genealogy of Morals*, 18; *KSA* 5:250–51).[17] As becomes positive, and affirmative, spirits, we must have [*il faut*] error, and certainly the possibility of error, in order to have the possibility or necessity—the "*il faut*"—of truth. We must *build* theory under these conditions.

Architectures

To accept the Nietzschean economy as irreducible in one's theoretical practice will frustrate the great desire of theory, to offer proof, or in terms of a more Nietzschean "grand ambition," to make one's statements "become logical, simple, unambiguous, mathematics, laws [logisch, einfach, unzweideutig, Mathematik werden; *Gesetz* werden]" (*The Will to Power*, 444; *KSA* 13:247). Such, however, would be the case only at a certain level and in relation to the classical or restricted economy of proof, logic, simplicity, (un)ambiguity, mathematics, or law. In fact, "the grand ambition" can still be maintained, perhaps more than ever, under the conditions of general economy, in particular Nietzsche's general economy. Under these conditions, it may also retain some of its politically problematic consequences and implications, as Nietzsche, Bataille, and Derrida understood very well, although with differences in their own political attitudes. All these terms, however—logical, simple, unambiguous, mathematics, laws—will have to be reconfigured in turn.[18]

Nietzsche's "logical, simple, unambiguous, mathematics, laws" by no means exclude complexity, subtlety, richness. Mathematics and science can be extraordinarily complex, a point that Nietzsche could hardly have missed. One of his "maxims and arrows" in *Twilight of the Idols, in* the twilight of the idols, is "'All truth is simple.' Is that not doubly a lie? ['Alle Wahrheit ist einfach.'—Ist das nicht zwiefach eine Lüge?]" (*Portable Nietzsche*, 467; *KSA* 6:59; translation modified). Nietzsche hardly demanded any naive simplicity from music, poetry, or architecture. It is difficult—although, of course, not impossible—to see Nietzsche's central example of "the grand style," the Palazzo Pitti in Florence, as a simple building. This example, like many others in Nietzsche, represents simplicity in a different sense, which demands a radical transformation of all the concepts involved and of the very difference between the simple and the complex.

Nietzsche's simplicity is "the highest feeling of power and sureness" (*Twilight*, 521). On the one hand, this feeling is produced by the power of *appropriation*—not in, but against Heidegger's sense of appropriation: the creator overcomes the constraints in order to produce value, and then imposes value on individuals and society or even on nature, the universe. On the other hand, it is produced by the power of appropriation as value by a recipient of art, or theory. The latter process is, importantly, *active* in Nietzsche. It is interpretation as active appropriation.

As far as theory, argument, or proof is concerned, Nietzsche's "simplicity" and "mathematics" suggest something like an irrefutable "theory" or "art." At the same time, however, such a "theory" or "art" may be extremely complex and place unsurmountable constraints upon, for example, some recipients of *a* specific theory or art. Irrefutability, therefore, may require considerable or even enormous power and the will to power. The very difference between simplicity and complexity demands a differently structured and differently stratified reconfiguration; it demands a general economy. Quantum mechanics or the theory of relativity is theoretically more complex and, which is perhaps the same, a great deal less accessible than classical physics. And yet, as far as modern physicists are concerned, these theories are also more simple in the sense of their *fittingness* to experimental data and to the theoretico-experimental ensemble of physics as a whole, which classical physics can no longer offer. They make things previously in conflict cohere, fit together, operate, and thus enable the theory and the institution of physics to sustain themselves and to move ahead. Thus, both "physics" and the "world"—nature, matter, universe—reconfigured by modern physics become more accessible, particularly to physicists. Such theories indeed become laws, for the reasons just indicated. They reshape (our interpretation of) the world and impose this shape on all, or at least on some, of us. It is thus the question of the conditions of the possibility or necessity of art or theory, specifically as law and in general.

Would, for example, Ockham's principle, the principle of parsimony or the economy of *restriction*—"It is vain to do with more what can be done with fewer," or "Entities should not be multiplied without necessity"—be *simply* dismissed as a result? Certainly not—nothing can be simply dismissed. It is certainly a very powerful principle, a powerful law, although by no means universal; and it will have to be reconceived, reconfigured, as a law. Moreover, while Ockham's razor is an important example of an economy of the simple, it is not the only such example. We would have to ask where the necessity of forbidding the multiplication of essences comes from. The whole economy—and the term acquires additional pertinence here—of Ockham's principle must be related to that which, in the wake of Nietzsche's, Freud's, Lacan's, and Derrida's analysis, may be seen as a complex that prelogically, but not necessarily ontologically, precedes the simple, or rather a "neither" that precedes both.

The conditions under which a theorist, or an artist, does not want or cannot afford to multiply entities are both complex and fascinating. They might include, for instance, the economy of time required in operating reduced configurations such as calculations in physics or, interactively, the psychological constraints imposed upon any creation or reception. The question of why or when a simplicity of configuration is preferable, including aesthetically, is by no means an easy one. Various historically diverse configurations that are traditionally or conventionally termed 'aesthetic' are themselves local effects that have emerged from corresponding general economies. To put the question somewhat differently: Why does simplicity make it easier for a configuration to become law? For another "logic"—that which would demand an accumulation of entities—is always and often simultaneously possible. The very plurality of these conditions needs to be analyzed.

In sum, we must analyze the conditions that locally eliminate some entities, whether psychologically or even biologically, theoretically, historically, socially, politically, while at the same time analyzing the conditions that necessarily multiply them. Instead of Ockham's razor, one might introduce a different, more *general*-economic, principle, the double economy principle. But is the appropriate word here really "instead": has the operation of Ockham's razor ever been, could it ever be, anything else? Such a principle can be formulated as follows: Entities should not be multiplied or should be further multiplied insofar as their multiplication or reduction ensures conditions under which they become "law." These conditions may be logical—theoretical— psychological, or physiological,[19] or political, or may involve the complementary relations among them.

The following moral of proof in mathematics has been offered: "The moral: a good proof is one which makes us wiser" (Y. I. Manin, *Course in Mathematical Logic*, 51). One should not, I think, take "wise" for granted here. It has been understood as a most complex term by mathematicians, physicists, and other scientists who have thought the issue through carefully.[20] The complex dynamics of the constitution of this term require analysis along the lines just indicated. "The will to knowledge is the will to power," Nietzsche maintains; and no word can be taken for granted in this sentence, either. Speaking about the artist and the grand style, he invokes "the power which no longer needs any proof." This is not an easy task, however; and it makes one "play a dangerous game":

> It might even be possible that what constitutes the value of these good and revered things [the true, the truthful, the selfless] is precisely that they are insidiously related, tied to and involved with these wicked, seemingly opposite things [appearance, the will to deceive, selfishness, lust]—may be even one with them in essence. Maybe.
>
> But who is willing to concern himself with such dangerous maybes? For that, one really has to wait for the advent of a new species of philosophers, such as have somehow different and converse taste and propensity than those we have known so far—philosophers of the dangerous "maybe" in every sense.
>
> And in all seriousness: I see such new philosophers coming up. . . .
>
> . . . but the genuine philosopher—as it seems to *us*, my friends?— "lives 'unphilosophically' and 'unwisely,' above all *imprudently*, and feels the burden and the duty of a hundred attempts and temptations of life— he risks *himself* constantly, he plays *the* wicked game." (*Beyond Good and Evil*, sec. 2, pp. 10–11; sec. 205, p. 125; *KSA* 5, 17, 133; translation modified)

In invoking "this power which no longer needs any proof" in *Twilight of the Idols*, Nietzsche, however, speaks not of a philosopher or even of a musician. "No musician has yet built as that architect did who created the Palazzo Pitti" (*Will to Power*, 444; *KSA* 13:247). Nietzsche speaks of the architect, who represents perhaps the culmination of the "psychology of the artist" in *Twilight* (*Portable Nietzsche*, 518). It might also be seen as an equal component in a classification—actually dubious enough, if taken strictly—of different arts in terms of the Apollinian and the Dionysian. Dionysian frenzy, including as sexual frenzy, is a central concept for Nietzsche here as "saying Yes" and "doing Yes," and "the power which no longer requires any proof." Raphael, a major presence in the Palazzo Pitti, is Nietzsche's major example of "saying Yes" and "doing Yes." Raphael often serves an exemplification of Nietzsche's major ideas, throughout his writing, beginning with *The Birth of Tragedy*, where Raphael's "Transfiguration" is seen as a great example of the interplay of the Apollinian and the Dionysian. In *Twilight*, however, Nietzsche's hierarchy culminates in the art of the architect:

> The *architect* represents neither a Dionysian nor an Apollinian state; here it is the great act of will, the will that moves mountains, the ecstasy [Rausch] of the great will which aspires to art. The most powerful human beings have always inspired architects; the architect has always been under the spell of power. In the building, the pride, the victory over gravity, the will to power shall be rendered visible. Architecture is a kind of eloquence of power in forms—now persuading, even flattering, now only commanding. The highest feeling of power and sureness finds expression in a *grand style*. The power which no longer needs any proof, which spurns pleasing, which does not answer lightly, which feels no witness near, which lives without consciousness of opposition against itself, which rests within *itself*, fatalistically, a law among laws—*that* speaks of itself as a grand style. (*Twilight of the Idols*, 520–21; *KSA* 6:118–19; translation modified)

The passage again points to a difference, perhaps profound, between Derrida's and Nietzsche's style, including in relation to and on the subject of architecture. The same may well be the case, although different respectively, for Nietzsche and Bataille. In many ways, Bataille's thinking is "against architecture,"[21] or against *some* architecture, often by way of another architecture—the architecture of, and as, labyrinths against the architecture of dialectical corridors and pyramids.[22]

In one of Derrida's more recent texts, "architectural *thinking*" is analyzed, again perhaps in a manner closer to Heidegger than to Nietzsche ("Architettura ove il desiderio pou abitare"). It has been suggested that "Derrida's use of the term 'architectural thinking'—as that which is (always already) thought before the ground is broken—seems to mute the aggressive tendencies of architecture in general. When he speaks of architectural thinking, he is suggesting that a certain idea of space must be thought prior to ground breaking, in order for the ground to be split, broken in a certain way. This idea is of the same order as his discussion of the arche-violence, arche-writing that belong always and already to culture."[23] The issue is more complex; and one would be hesitant to accept this characterization, particularly the usage of the term 'idea,' even if one sees it as of the same order as *writing*, and an unequivocal claim that Derrida's *writing* "always, and already, belongs to culture," or "belongs" in the first place. It is, again, the question of relative balance and emphasis—whether in architecture or thinking—between (the delay of) "thinking" and "breaking the ground," and the complex, nonlinear economies of interaction between them. It is quite possible and in fact necessary that there is "architectural thinking" in Nietzsche, too, prior to "breaking the ground." It may involve, for example, thinking at an extraordinary speed, or concealed periods of prolonged "slow" thinking—the multiple effects of deferral. Their manifestations in Nietzsche's "short" sessions are in turn quite complex, but this complexity would not contradict the present point.

The difference at issue, again, would concern primarily the style of breaking *new* ground, against which—as radical breaks—Derrida, as we have seen, persistently warns and which Nietzsche persistently practices in his equally plural but, in this sense, more architectural style. This style is not Apollinian and—an interesting nuance—perhaps finally not even Dionysian. To a degree it might be seen as theory as architecture, as opposed to theory as arche-texture, a prolonged textualization, extremely effective in Derrida, of theoretical *arche*-textual thinking—*arche*-trace, *arche*-writing, and so on. In this sense, too, Bataille would be closer to Nietzsche than to Derrida. This difference would have also to be related to the question of the closure of philosophy, as considered earlier. Although, as I have indicated, Derrida's most recent texts indicate some movement toward Heidegger in contrast to his early texts, one should not identify Derrida's arche-textures with a Heideggerian economy of thinking. The differences remain profound, including, and perhaps always, via Nietzsche. By the same token, Nietzsche's "architecture" must still be seen as writing—as arche-texture—but as differently grained, differently textualized, differently styled.

Much of Derrida's own "architectural thinking"—his thinking about and by way of architecture, its concepts and metaphors—is permeated by Nietzschean "architectural thinking," often in conjunction with Nietzsche's "musical thinking." These interactions and perhaps anxieties might be traced from "Tympan" to "The Ear of the Other" to, most overtly and deliberately, "Why Peter Eisenman Writes Such Good

Books?" Perhaps it is, in fact, "architectural thinking" that best reflects the oscillation between Nietzsche's *writing*, "not subordinate to the logos and the truth," and Heidegger's thinking that characterizes much of Derrida's deconstruction, both in its theoretical, constructive—architectural— thinking and its arche-textual style, naturally using this distinction in a very provisional way. Still, Derrida's "architectural style" may again be seen as "against Nietzsche, perhaps" ("Living On: Border Lines," in *Deconstruction and Criticism*, 125).

The "simplicity" of the "eloquence of power" of which Nietzsche speaks thus demands an immense "complexity." Nor can one take for granted (the metaphor of) power or (the power of) metaphor either, or any of the metaphors constituting its chain, including architecture or the metaphor constituted by this seductive proper name Nietzsche—more se-ductive than truth perhaps. A rigorous, minute, and nuanced analysis of power must be undertaken and, no less so, an analysis of the theoretical question of power and of the question of Nietzsche. For does not Nietzsche also deceive himself a bit here? How far does the power of this law among laws extend? Perhaps Nietzsche did not think of the question of these limits or forgot it for a moment. Yet perhaps only for a moment. As soon as Nietzsche awakens from the dream of power, awakens to an-other theoretical or artistic dream, he "knows" that the great power of art is only another trick with mirrors. There are many mirrors in the Palazzo Pitti, and some of Raphael's paintings are very beautifully reflected there. So one sometimes does not quite know the painting from the reflection, the truth from metaphor, one figure from another.

Chapter 6

Radical Alterity: Materialism, History, and the Unconscious

Effects of Différance

The question of alterity has played a crucial role both in the history of the concept of the unconscious and in the history of the idea of history itself. More generally, alongside and interacting with the problematics of difference, the problematics of alterity, exteriority, and otherness are central both in the history of philosophy and in the history of general economy, leading to the general economy, or general economies, of history and of the unconscious, or, complementarily, both. The unconscious may well be the most counter-philosophical idea ever. The history of the idea of the unconscious, however, especially insofar as it relates to the history of the idea of history, cannot be thought of as being *outside*—as absolutely *exterior* to—the history of philosophy. As I have argued earlier, our theoretical closure has been transformed, and various fields have been reconfigured and new fields configured, quite radically. This closure, however, may not have been transformed radically enough to enable us to leave philosophy and the history of philosophy behind altogether, even assuming that we would want to do so. The significance of the relations among alterity, history, and the unconscious can be traced in all the figures discussed in this study, from Kant, to Hegel, to Marx, to Nietzsche, to Freud, to Bataille, to Lacan, to Althusser, to Deleuze, to Derrida.

In this chapter, I shall consider first some major implications of the general economy, particularly in Derrida and deconstruction, for the question of history and matter. The first section offers, as it were, an outline of the general economy of matter, history, and the unconscious, and their complementarity; the radical alterity at issue is in fact defined by the radical loss in representation to which the general economy relates. Then, en route to

Althusser, I consider a case of "late Marxism" in Fredric Jameson's writing and related Marxist political economies, by juxtaposing them, as restricted economies, to the general economy of history and culture. The final section offers, first, some general considerations on the general economy of history. I then proceed to a discussion of Althusser, whose reading of Marx suggests a theoretical trajectory proceeding closer to the general economic and, as such, may be contrasted with Jameson, or classical Marxism in general. I also consider Althusser's connections to Derrida.

The goal of this chapter is not solely, and not so much, a discussion of relations—theoretical, historical, or political—between materialism and deconstruction, or Marxism and deconstruction, an issue that has been amply discussed in recent years, as a delineation of major features of the general economy of matter and history, via the general economy of the unconscious—and a kind of triple conjunction or complementarity between them. Althusser's analysis, specifically as mediated by deconstruction, plays a major role in the history of these issues. My discussion will proceed mostly along theoretical lines. Neither history nor politics can ever be avoided; they are inescapably involved in any given account of whatever kind. As I have maintained from the outset of this study, however, in themselves they are never quite sufficient, either, and always demand something else—for example, theory. At issue in this chapter are the very complexities of this mutual or complementary general economy and the limits it imposes on historical, theoretical, or political analysis or denominations themselves.

As we have seen, in "Différance" and throughout his works, Derrida fundamentally—*structurally*—relates the unconscious to "a certain alterity [une certain altérité]," a radical exteriority, or otherness, characterizing *différance* and related structures in their general economy. This general economy demands a reinscription of the unconscious or what has been given, in the wake of Freud, the metaphysical name "the unconscious." While it remains inscribed within, among other closures, the closure of presence and difference, the resulting *différance* inhibits every process of (re)presentation, of an appearance of *presence*, and of anything in its *presence*. This inhibition affects representation of "presence" and all concepts of presence—or difference. But it also affects representation of "the unconscious," both in any of its classical forms, *as "metaphysical* names" and concepts, and as a radical alterity, whereby it becomes "neither a name nor a concept." Hence, according to Derrida: "In this context, and beneath this guise, the unconscious is not, as we know, a hidden, virtual, or potential self-presence. It differs from, and defers, itself; which doubtless means that it is woven of differences, and also that it sends out delegates, representatives, proxies; but without any chance that the giver of proxies might 'exist,' might be present, be 'itself' somewhere, and with even less chance that it might become conscious" (*Margins*, 20–21; *Marges*, 21).[1] Thus, as we have seen, one also confronts a fundamental inhibition in inscribing or relating to "*différance itself*"—already an impossible denomination.

Différance continuously inserts, *inscribes*, the irreducible exterior into the emergence of *presence*, consciousness, self-consciousness and so forth, specifically at the level of history, such as in the movement of the Hegelian *Geist* or Idea (Idee), or in the historical process implied by the Heideggerian economy of Being or, in later works, thinking, and then appropriation. *Différance*, however, relates to the efficacity of presence and difference, or complementarily both, even though in order to do so Derrida must extend his analysis, interminably, to other terms and structures—trace, supplement, dissemination, iterability, and so on. The efficacity of (metaphysical) presence and (metaphysical) difference thus becomes a radical alterity or difference, radical but not absolute. For, as we have seen, an absolute difference or alterity is always governed by one economy of presence or another, by a restricted economy. Accordingly, as Derrida writes:

> Thus one comes to posit presence—and specifically consciousness, the being beside itself of consciousness—no longer as the absolutely central form of Being but as a 'determination' and as an 'effect.' A determination or an effect within a system which is no longer that of presence but of *différance*, a system that no longer tolerates the opposition of activity and passivity, nor that of cause and effect, or of indetermination and determination, etc., such that in designating consciousness as an effect or as a determination, one continues—for strategic reasons that can be more or less lucidly deliberated and systematically calculated—to operate according to the lexicon of that which one is delimiting. (*Margins*, 16–17; *Marges*, 17–18)

It is important to keep in mind, that both concepts—difference and exteriority—appear jointly; they jointly play a crucial role in Hegel or Heidegger as well. One may even speak of an irreducible difference and an irreducible exteriority in Hegel. But *in Hegel*, they are also not radical enough. In this sense the movements of Mallarmé's mime followed, or (re)inscribed, by Derrida in "The Double Session," graphically signal—*graph* and *graft*—a decisive difference between two economies of difference and transformation, restricted and general, in the latter case as the complementarity of free and controlled play. Difference and exteriority always appear in Hegel in the form of becoming-presence, that is, in the form of historicity defined by way of and dominated by the concept of presence, or a linear or quasi-linear model of becoming, and further, via the concept of meaning and the concept of concept. Both difference and exteriority, and thereby history, are governed by the *conceptual* consciousness as self-consciousness that controls the totality of the play of historical transformations.

One might utilize "an empty form" of this Hegelian exteriority, however, as to a degree Bataille does, along with "an *empty* form of *Aufhebung* [la forme *vide* de l'*Aufhebung*]" ("From Restricted to General Economy," in *Writing and Difference*, 275; *L'Écriture et la différence*, 406). "Through such a relating of a restricted and a general economy the very project of philosophy, under the privileged heading of Hegelianism, is displaced and reinscribed. The *Aufhebung*—*la relève*—is constrained writing itself otherwise. Or perhaps simply into writing itself. Or, better, into taking account of its consumption of writing" (*Margins*, 19; *Marges*, 21). By displacing Hegel in this fashion, one is able to engage a very different—general—economy of exteriority.

Derrida incessantly inserts and reinserts—and reiterates—the operators of difference, exteriority, and alterity throughout his text. In addition to *différance*, *dissemination*, *iterability*, they include "interval" as radical temporalization, "spacing" as a radical spatialization, and many others, including the reversal, transpositions, and superpositions of "interval" and "spacing." Often, and often necessarily, implying each other, these operators are never identical to each other. Their *dissemination*, in turn, is irreducible. More conventional spatial and temporal effects, or spatiotemporal effects— spatiality of space, temporality of time, spatiality of time, temporality of space—are themselves the products of this play. As neither terms nor concepts, such structures "designate" different and continuously differentiating and disseminating effects of the field to which they relate, collectively or complementarily, but never exhaustively or by way of synthesis.

This "field" is itself irreducibly multiple. It cannot be constituted as a single or unitary field or as a set, although the corresponding effects of field, sets, concepts, and the effects of these very nominations are continually produced. That which is itself at issue here cannot be *constituted*, above all, not by itself or in itself, such as a thing-in-itself (Kant) or by itself or for itself—*für sich*, as in Hegel's self-consciousness, for example. It does not have a *constitution*—a master law or set of laws—whether theoretical, psychological, political, legal, or other. Or rather, it does not have *the* constitution governing the field as a whole, since the laws, rules, constitutive effects, and so on are also produced all the time. The *dissemination* at issue cannot therefore be *constituted* merely by a lack of *constitution*, or by any form of absolute or unconditional lack, such as Lacanian lack, to which Derrida's *dissemination* is opposed by definition. As Derrida comments in *Positions*: "In effect, these two concepts [*alterity* and *spacing*] *do not signify exactly* the same thing; that being said, I believe that they are absolutely indissociable. . . . *Spacing* designates *nothing*, nothing that is, no presence at a distance; it is the index of an irreducible exterior, and at the same time of a *movement*, a displacement that indicates an irreducible alterity. I do not see how one could dissociate the two concepts of spacing and alterity" (*Positions*, 81; *Positions*, 107–8).

Like most of Derrida's works, *Positions* presents, or rather *positions*, the economy of spacing and alterity as the *general* economy of the unconscious, thus engaging Nietzsche's, Freud's, Bataille's, and Lacan's frameworks. Elsewhere in *Positions*, however, approaching the question of matter and materialism and the proper names that, in the shadow of Hegel, define it— Marx, Engels, Lenin, and Althusser—Derrida speaks of *matter* in terms exactly parallel to his description of the unconscious. The description again proceeds via Bataille and the general economy: "Above all [these questions] refer to the general economy whose traits I attempted to outline based on a reading of Bataille. It follows that if, and in the extent to which, *matter* in this general economy designates, as you said, radical alterity (I will specify: in relation to philosophical oppositions), then what I write can be considered 'materialist'" (*Positions*, 64; *Positions*, 87).

Derrida's qualifications and quotation marks are crucial. He says, as it were: "If 'matter' is *différance*, then what I write can be considered 'materialist.'" In "Différance," again in the context of Nietzsche and the unconscious, Derrida invokes *physis* in *différance*: "In this way, we may see the site of reinterpretation of *mimēsis* in its alleged opposition to *physis* [Ici s'indique le lieu d'une réinterprétation de la mimésis, dans sa prétendue opposition à la *physis*]" (*Margins*, 17; *Marges*, 18). More, however, is at stake, for "as you can imagine, things are not so simple. It is not always in *the* materialist text (is there such a thing as the materialist text?) nor in *every* materialist text that the concept of matter has been defined as absolute exterior or radical heterogeneity. I am not even sure that there can be a 'concept' of an absolute exterior" (*Positions*, 64; *Positions*, 87).[2]

As I have emphasized throughout, the radical exteriority at issue here cannot be absolute, which is one of the reasons why it must be "the site of reinterpretation of *mimēsis* in its alleged opposition to *physis*"—some absolute form of *physis* such as in Lenin's—restricted—economy of matter as objective reality independent of the economy of its interpretation or inscription. Lenin, to be more precise, refers to consciousness, but takes the concept uncritically, thus making his economy of matter even more problematic. In effect, in whatever form and however materialist in its inscription, the "absolute" will always remain the form of idealism. In other words, at issue is a problematic transcendental signified of, or behind, matter and a "metaphysical materialism," which requires, therefore, a deconstruction of the ensuing politico-theoretical economy as a restricted economy. One might speak in this sense of the "idealism of matter." At issue in such a deconstruction may also be a transcendental signifier: "matter" or, of course, "the unconscious." Such a transcendental signifier may in effect function as a transcendental signified, which, as Derrida argues in "The Purveyor of Truth" (*The Post Card*) takes place in Lacan. In *Positions*, Derrida sums up as follows:

> In short, the signifier "matter" appears to me problematical only at the moment when its reinscription cannot avoid making of it a new fundamental principle which, by means of theoretical regression, would be reconstituted into a "transcendental signified." It is not only idealism in the narrow sense that falls back upon the transcendental signified. It can always come to reassure a metaphysical materialism. It then becomes an ultimate referent, according to the classical logic implied by the value of referent, or it becomes an "objective reality" absolutely "anterior" to any work of the mark, the semantic content of a form of presence which guarantees the movement of the text in general [i.e., movement of *writing* in Derrida's sense] from the outside. (I am not sure that Lenin's analysis, for example, does not always give in to this opposition: and if it does so strategically, we must first reelaborate—in a transformational writing— the rules of this strategy. Then there would be no reservations to be made.) This is why I will not say that the concept of matter is in and of itself either metaphysical or non-metaphysical. This depends upon the work to which it yields, and you know that I have unceasingly insisted, as concerns the non-ideal exteriority of writing, the gram, the trace, the text, etc. upon the necessity of never separating them from *work*, a value itself to be rethought outside of its Hegelian affiliation. . . .
>
> Rigorously reinscribed in the general economy (Bataille) and in the double writing of which we were just speaking, the insistence on matter as the absolute exterior of opposition, the materialist insistence (in contact with what "materialism" has represented as a force of resistance in the history of philosophy) seems to me necessary. (*Positions*, 65–66; *Positions*, 88–89)

In this sense, reinscribing "matter" as "a radical alterity" and deferring it to difference, and in the end to *différance*, is crucial if deconstruction is to operate effectively against the *materialist* metaphysics as a form of metaphysics of presence. For, much as in the case of Heidegger's [reinstatement of an] "instance of the logos and of the truth" as a transcendental signified (*Of Grammatology*, 20; *De la grammatologie*, 33), it is only through delay and difference that the signifier of matter can be reinserted into a textual chain; and, at the level of classical oppositions of philosophy, it can take place only through its difference from other philosophemes. This process, however, cannot be described and analyzed by means of restricted economies and demands structures such as *différance* and general economic matrices of analysis.

Such general economic reinscriptions and reconfigurations of "matter" do not lead, then, to the absolute primacy of "difference." A general economy announced by the propositions just considered would obviously prohibit that. Derrida's *différance*, let me reiterate, is not simple difference, any more than it is simple identity or presence, but a certain efficacity of inscription of specific differences, including general—but always *theoretically*, *historically*, and *politically* specific—differences. Nor, therfore, can it be restricted to the joint economy of differing-deferring connoted by its name, although this aspect of its calculus is important. Rather, the transformational play of *différance* is a condition of possibility of reinserting the signifier of matter into any discursive chain. One can inscribe or relate to this play, according to Derrida, only within the closure of classical concepts and thus the closure of the metaphysics of presence and difference. Such is the limit for now, or so it seems: no other articulation of matter is available in or within this closure, although, as I suggested in Chapter 4, one can perhaps push the economy of closure and of dissemination and transformation of closure beyond the limits suggested by and operative in Derrida's analysis.

It may be useful at this point to restate the question of radical alterity by separating, provisionally, the thematics of interpretation in general and the thematics of theoretical analysis:

First, since one speaks, as Derrida does, of inhibiting *every* process of (re)*presentation*, the inhibition of *différance* affects all interpretive situations. In other words, a theory at issue, a *general* economy, offers "an interpretation of interpretation" as a process of production and dislocation of presence and representation.

Second, however, Derrida's qualification "in relation to philosophical oppositions" poses this problem of radical inhibition at the level of *theoretical* inscription, relating to theorizing the efficacity of this inhibition itself. The question, perhaps for the first time asked in this form by Althusser, is how to produce a theoretical articulation or how one can relate theoretically to that which cannot be grounded in meaning or concept, or conversely, some fundamental signifying structure, as in Lacan, or a certain Derridean reading of Lacan. Such a general economy must thereby relate to that which cannot obey the law of the restricted Hegelian economy as the economy of consciousness and knowledge—in Hegel, ultimately as Absolute Consciousness and Absolute Knowledge—even though the latter is also a transformational economy. One must produce an economy of *material temporality*—with both terms reconfigured in the deconstructed field—that is responsible for dislocating and producing the specific effects of presence, difference, exteriority, alterity, transformations.[3]

As I have emphasized, while engaging similar strategies earlier in this study, one cannot speak of any full or unconditional separation here. But one cannot fully unify them, either, as Hegel would want to do by mastering alterity through absolute consciousness and its self-reflection. One must continuously confront complementary interaction, mutual inhibitions, and double binds, as considered in the preceding chapter. In general, whether alterity and difference are seen as absolute difference, which is roughly a Kantian position,[4] or as overcome by the power of absolute consciousness, as in Hegel, or still other absolutes—for example, an absolute or otherwise metaphysical form of the unconscious—such unification of philosophical and general interpretation will retain the same metaphysical ground and as such will reinforce the power of metaphysics.

The power of Hegel's analysis is in suggesting, in part against himself, that general representation or language can be no more simply separated from the philosophical than the philosophical can be made absolutely free of the general. But then, can there be such a thing as representation, or memory, language, metaphor, and so forth, in *general?* The issue is instead the closure of theory and of the oppositions that thus emerge, as considered earlier. Although we cannot do without them, neither can we fully maintain them—in any domain. This closure relates to the irreducible interaction and mutual inhibition of the philosophical and the nonphilosophical. It reconfigures these interactions as a closure, as against a claim for the necessity of philosophy or a philosophical position of one kind or another. As we have seen, it is also the question of relations and inhibitions between (the closure of) presence and difference, and (the closure of) metaphysics and then of the *transformations* of closure, assuming that there is only one such closure, as opposed to a configuration or interplay of closures in any given case.

When Derrida speaks of materialism as "a force of resistance in the history of philosophy," in question is primarily the critical or deconstructive potential of materialist discourse to undermine the institutional and conceptual power of metaphysics. Such undermining, however, is impossible without the concept of matter developed throughout Western history—from Democritus, perhaps even from Thales, on—which is also the history of interaction between materialism and metaphysics. This idea of *matter* as a *hard* structure—we might even call it, with certain precautions, the "experimental" structure—resists both philosophical and "general" representation. That does not mean that nothing has changed since Democritus, or Marx, or even Nietzsche, although Nietzsche might yet prove to be ahead of some of the changes. On the contrary, it is precisely a question of the historical, that is to say transformational, force of resistance to metaphysics, and therefore the question of the critical or deconstructive reinscription of matter, history, and the unconscious. At stake is the reconfiguration of matter *and* materialism as a transformational structure inscribed, *written* in Derrida's sense, in a transformational general economy. For, if *matter, history*, and *the unconscious* resist idealism, they must also resist metaphysical materialism—the *idealism* of matter.

Untranscendable Horizons, Transcendental Horizons: On the Logic of Early and Late Marxism

The political impact of Marxism goes almost without saying, although much has been, is, will be, and needs to be said in order to understand this impact. In addition, however, throughout its evolution, and some revolutions, Marxist *theory* has made many contributions to modern intellectual history. It may or may not be seen as "an immense theoretical revolution," as Althusser described Marx's political economy, but it has certainly had a major influence upon modern theory. Recent developments in Marxist theory have been important as well; and they have affected, and have been affected by a broad spectrum of theories, within the interactions between theoretical, historical, political, and some geopolitical concerns and agendas characterizing the last decade. First, following classical Marxism and related social theories, from Auguste Comte to Max Weber to contemporary sociology, contemporary Marxism contributed to establishing the significance of the historical and the political on the contemporary scene of criticism and theory, developing in particular the relations of Marxism to feminist and gender studies, and race and colonial or postcolonial studies.[5] Second, recent Marxist discourse operates using psychoanalytic frameworks, again specifically in the areas just indicated. The interactions between Marxism and deconstruction and poststructuralism, or postmodernism, have been extensive as well. Conversely, all these interactions have affected the revisions and expansions of the standard Marxist model that characterize the recent history of Marxism.

The standard model itself, if there is indeed one such standard model even in a given author such as Marx, has by no means lost all of its political, theoretical, or critical force. Engaging multiple models at each point, Marx's many analyses retain their historical, political or politico-economic, theoretical, and cultural import.

Naturally, the economy of this import in recent discussions, or of Marx's text, to begin with, demands a complex—general economic—analysis, which exceeds "Marx" while not simply going beyond it. Lenin's concept of unequal development has enunciated an important heterogeneity in the historical process.[6] As the present analysis suggests, however, one needs a much more radical, more general economic, theoretical and historical, or political matrix, at once, or complementarily, more global and more heterogeneous. Various unequal developments are important effects of the general economy of history, for example, as manifesting itself in spatiotemporal, psychological, social, cultural, or political aspects of Nietzsche's, Bataille's and Derrida's works. But such a general economy also demands a much richer interplay of forces than in more classical or restricted economies of unequal historical development, which must therefore be placed and reconfigured within this general economy. One needs, at the very least, that rich a mapping or antimapping, or complementarily both, in order to approach modern or postmodern geopolitical history, or indeed any history. The whole Marxist or post-Marxist geopolitical economy may well have to be reconfigured yet again, given the most recent developments on the geopolitical or geopolitico-economic scene, simultaneously post-Marxist and poststructuralist or postmodernist.

In the context of Marxism and critical theory, Jameson's work, in particular *The Political Unconscious: Narrative as a Socially Symbolic Act* and subsequent essays, especially the first, title essay, collected in *Postmodernism, or, the Cultural Logic of Late Capitalism*, has been a subject of many recent discussions, especially those concerning the politics of modern criticism and theory and their relations to politics at large.[7] The present discussion is motivated by exploring a different theoretical trajectory, closer to general economy, suggested by Althusser's analysis, if at times against its grain, to which Jameson's post-Althusserian, although more classically Marxist, economy of history offers a useful contrast. The present analysis, therefore, is shaped in accordance with these goals and proceeds by way of a general economic critique of major theoretical problems emerging in Jameson, some of them more or less transparent and better known, others less familiar. Many of these problems persist in various forms, including in the works of authors critical of Jameson; and these problems are, I shall argue here, irreducible, unless all determinations defining the Marxist matrix as Marxist are critically suspended. In short, I shall argue that there can be no Marxist general economy, insofar as the denomination 'Marxist' can be rigorously retained. *Theoretical* problems of Marxism are, in this sense, irreducible, and it may, as *Marxism*, be given up; and whatever theoretical issue it can usefully address can always be more effectively approached otherwise. Politics, as always, is a more complex question; and in this sense whatever political, or geopolitical, transformations, along or against Marxist gradients, take place, they by no means necessarily undermine Marxist political and ideological agendas.

I shall argue this *general* case, let me stress, by *using* Jameson's case and not seeing the latter as either uniquely representative or, conversely, exemplary of "late Marxism," even though it may manifest a variety of trends and problems that can be assembled under this rubric. In this sense, the present discusion is not really a reading of Jameson, either. I would stand by my claims here, however, were I to offer such a reading, where Jameson's more recent work could be engaged still more actively, particularly *Postmodernism* and *Late Marxism: Adorno, or, The Persistence of the Dialectic*. These works, however, do not deviate from the theoretical framework and political agendas of *The Political Unconscious*, as Jameson himself points out,[8] and do not mitigate and may even exacerbate the problems at issue here. The second part of the subtitle of the book on Adorno is quite indicative in this respect, reflecting the agenda of the book throughout. In either case, capitalism or Marxism, ostensibly "late," are not as decisive as "early" determinations that control Jameson's analysis and make it problematic, as I have already indicated earlier in the context of postmodernism.

In the context of postmodernism,[9] the question of Marxism retains or reacquires its significance, in spite of or because of the problems of Marxist analysis as just indicated. It is indeed the question of the political, theoretical, and cultural logic of late Marxism, or the function of Marxism at the present time, to paraphrase Arnold's famous title. As the discussion in Chapter 1 would suggest, it is to this Arnoldian rubric of "the function of criticism at the present time" that most discussions of postmodernism always refer, however they disseminate or attempt to encompass the term and the manifold of related phenomena themselves. The function of Marxism at the present time is by no means easily dissociable from "the function of criticism at the present time"; and the literary, cultural, and political agendas of many critics, including Marxist-oriented critics, are often not so different from Arnold's.[10]

It is true, of course, that the "present time" and the "past time" cannot be unequivocally differentiated, which is one of the major lessons of recent intellectual history, in part against Marxism, or some Marxisms, or Hegelianisms. Whichever matrix is applied, an analysis of any historico-theoretical or historico-cultural configuration is affected. One cannot unequivocally distinguish different historical points or intervals, via some economy of progress, in a dialectical law relating quantity and quality, or any other restricted economy. Yet new theoretical and practical, including political, effects emerge and transform our view of the past, or future, and demand a different history. These dynamics may be illustrated by Nietzsche's analysis, or Marx's analysis of "always already late capitalism," Freud's psychoanalysis of "late capitalist" neurosis, Deleuze's analysis of the age of schizo-technology, Foucault's historical analysis after the age of the prison, Derrida's analysis of writing emerging in the age of electronic reproduction, techno- or telegrammatology, or by many other examples.

Although the authors' own views of the dynamics at issue may differ, in all of these cases one finds a depiction of the difference offered by, and often defining, the present, along with the transformation of the past in view of a new theoretical and historical matrix. Such a matrix is often produced in part by reacting to the present, but by virtue of its overall comprehensiveness it must lead to a reinterpretation of everything, including the past. At best such an analysis would not erase, although it would necessarily reconfigure, the economy of difference between past and present. Moreover, as I have stressed from the outset, the transformational laws of restricted economies do in fact apply within reconfigured and localized limits, although the historical transformation must be seen as general economic and cannot be contained by these laws.

Marxism, as I have said, loses the theoretical battle. This battle may have been lost, as a *theoretical* battle, with Marx's insistence on a dialectical and thus restricted political economy, all its "immense theoretical revolution" and political impact notwithstanding. It was lost specifically against Nietzsche's general economy; but one can point to other forces in play already at the time, and in subsequent history in the wake of Nietzsche, such as in Freud, for example, or Foucault, Deleuze, or Derrida and deconstruction. The play of these forces is multiply stratified; it is itself general economic. As I have suggested, however, it is difficult—I think, impossible—to transform Marxism, given its positions and history, so as to compensate for such losses. Although it is indeed quite possible to attach the name 'Marxism' itself to some compensated matrix, I do not think it can be done in rigorous terms, historically or theoretically.[11] That does not mean that Nietzsche, for example, or any theory, is invulnerable—quite the contrary, as I have stressed throughout. It is even possible that a new effective theory may emerge that would be closer to Marx than to Nietzsche, or even closer to Marx than to anything else. The latter prospect seems unlikely to me; but there is no way to be sure what will be lost or gained, will die or survive, or will be resurrected in the general economy of any such development.

For the moment, the understanding of the political and cultural landscape of postmodernism demands a general economy. Postmodernism may indeed demand it as "the cultural logic of late capitalism," to use Jameson's subtitle, or late socialism, or indeed late communism, postcommunism even—postcapitalism, postsocialism, and postcommunism. Against Jameson's logic, however, all these appear to coexist, or rather, in the mode of a general economy, are all simultaneously in play, the play that can never be quite simultaneous, although not without simultaneities, either. Obviously, such terms, and specifically "late capitalism," have complex relations to the cultural logic of the modern, or the postmodern, or any period.

An important qualification is due here. As I have already indicated, most Marxist authors, beginning with Marx and Lenin, would not deny a degree of heterogeneity of the historical process and the complexity of interactions at issue. This understanding, then, cannot be ignored in either early or late Marxism, or post-Marxism or pre-Marxism—for example, in Hegel's text, which Kojève understood and amplified, if also exaggerated. In accord with this tradition, Jameson, too, insists on such interrelations, or "interrelationships" and "feedback loops" between "culture and the economic," in part via Lenin's notion of unequal development and the ideas of poststructuralist authors, such as Lacan, Althusser, Deleuze, and Foucault, throughout *The Political Unconscious* and even more so in *Postmodernism*.[12] As always, however, the question is within what economy such terms and interactions are inscribed. One must also differentiate such economies as general economies of inscriptions from many restricted economic strategies, propositions, and claims, such as those found in Jameson or Althusser, or Marx and Hegel, to begin with.[13] Connecting, finally in the Hegelian—although not necessarily Hegel's—way, early and later Marxism, heterogeneity in Jameson is always predicated upon and purposely "presuppose[s] . . . a certain unifying and totalizing force" (410), and thus a control of transformational play as discussed earlier; this control is, in fact, more rigid than in his predecessors, specifically in Althusser. As a result, Jameson's analysis, from *The Political Unconscious* to *Postmodernism*, which is also a progression of a sort, becomes problematic, or to make a stronger and perhaps harsh claim, theoretically deficient, whatever one's political agenda is. While restricted economies retain their role under the conditions of general economy, they do so only within reconfigured limits and in reconfigured modes of functioning. Such a reconfiguration does not take place in Jameson, or in many related or analogous frameworks developed in early and later Marxism.

Althusser is, I shall argue, a very different case in this respect, given that his critical and theoretical results, especially his methods, remain powerful, in spite of their problems. At a certain level, *dialectical* Marxism becomes nearly subtractable from or is exceeded along more general economic gradients of Althusser's analysis.

Once again, I am not saying that politics and theory may simply be disconnected. On the contrary, as I pointed out throughout this study, they may well be connected. In one way or another, they are always connected, as Althusser's case shows, for example. They are also often connected, however, in such a way that political practice operates against the best theory. Nor is the economy of theoretical appeal a simple matter. Like that of ideological or political appeal, it is also a general economy. Thus it is also an economy of radical losses, some of them, but not all, for political reasons, yielding all the consequences of such losses for the appeal or success of theory, whether a given theory or theoretical practice in general. My point is that theoretically a given analysis, such as Jameson's, or a given form or spectrum of analysis, such as a Marxist one, may be problematic under all conditions, whatever one wants to achieve practically or politically. Of course, all such conditions and positions are themselves always interpreted from a given perspective, here the perspective of general economy, which is always local, but also simultaneously or complementarily, multihistorical, multicultural, multitheoretical, and multipolitical. But one must also understand the functioning of this localization, given the general economic condition of this multiplicity, interactively heterogeneous and heterogeneously interactive; and it is this understanding that is at issue here. One can achieve this understanding, I think, only against the theoretical structures and economies—the restricted economies—of Marxism, which control, among others, Jameson's analysis.

In assessing these problems, one can begin with the following formulations, "revising" Althusser, in Jameson's *The Political Unconscious*, prominent in recent discussions:

> . . . history is *not* a text, not a narrative, master or otherwise, but that, as an absent cause, it is inaccessible to us except in textual form, and that our approach to it and to the Real itself necessarily passes through its prior textualization, its narrativisation in the political unconscious (35).
>
> . . .
>
> History is . . . the experience of Necessity, and it is this alone which can forestall its thematization or reification as a mere object of representation or as one master code among many others. Necessity is not in that sense a type of content, but rather the inexorable *form* of events; it is therefore a narrative category in the enlarged sense of some properly narrative political unconscious which has been argued here, a retextualization of History which does not propose the latter as some new representation or "vision," some new content, but as the formal effects of what Althusser, following Spinoza, calls an "absent cause." Conceived in this sense, History is what hurts, it is what refuses desire and sets inexorable limits to individual as well as collective praxis, which its "ruses" turn into grisly and ironic reversals of their overt intention. But this History can be apprehended only through its effects, and never directly through some reified force. This is indeed the ultimate sense in which History as ground and untranscendable horizon needs no particular theoretical justification: we may be sure that its alienating necessities will not forget us, however much we might prefer to ignore them. (102)

While, as I shall argue, the propositions themselves are problematic, the operation of the economies "beyond the pleasure principle of history" reflected in Jameson's formulation is important, particularly in relation to exteriority and the unconscious as considered in the preceding section; so is the trope of irony invoked by Jameson here.[14] Nor can one deny the complexity of the Althusserian conception of history and the importance of the issues to which Jameson's formulations respond. Given this complexity, a great deal will depend on (re)figuring Spinoza's brilliant concept of "absent cause" and thus on the conceptual chain in which such a refiguration takes place. Roughly, one can see it either as an "absent *cause*"—and thus as a transcendental signified, however materialist in its conception it might become—or an "*absent* cause"—an absence of the transcendental signified. This difference may be seen as defining, or structuring, the difference or *différance* between a general economy—such as that of Derrida's *différance*—and a restricted economy—such as implied by Althusser's notion of "Lacanian or metonymic causality."

Indeed, the first and perhaps most decisive problem of Jameson's analysis here and elsewhere is a reinstatement of the transcendental signifier/signified in relation to Spinoza's notion of "absent cause." Both the transcendental signified and the transcendental signifier, as in Lacan,[15] are involved in Jameson's model, although one should not identify the latter either with Lacan or Althusser. The spectrum of possibilities is large: Jameson's is a different case from, and in my view, one that is weaker than, Lacan's or Althusser's restricted economy. It is true that Jameson does offer a renunciation of "the transcendental signified" in relation to the question of interpretation in general, which would include, one would suppose, literary interpretation (58). Such a renunciation is an almost obligatory gesture after Derrida and de Man, to whom Jameson is generally more sympathetic. The reinstatement occurs at the level of Jameson's main concepts themselves and the logic that connects them. Both lend power to the resulting repression of difference in the name of difference and history, or difference as history. His conceptions are at once too historical, capitalizing and idealizing his materialist history, and not sufficiently historical, repressing difference in the name of history.

The latter, according to Derrida, often characterizes the insistence on history. As he writes: "If the word 'history' did not in and of itself convey the motif of a final repression of difference, one could say that only difference can be 'historical' from the outset and in each of their aspects" (*Margins*, 11; *Marges*, 12). The "historical" possibilities offered by *différance* are crucial, however; and contrary to some, particularly earlier, assessments, Derrida insists on, not minimizes, history, although he pays much attention to the limits of historical analysis and offers a critique of classical historicism.[16] These "historical" possibilities in fact allow one to inscribe the very movement of *différance*: ". . . we will designate as *différance* the movement according to which language, or any code, or any system of referral in general, is constituted 'historically' as a weave of differences. Here 'is constituted,' 'is produced,' 'is created,' 'movement,' 'historically,' etc., are necessarily understood beyond the metaphysical language in which they are retained, along with all their implications. We ought to demonstrate why concepts like *production*, constitution, and history remain in complicity with what is at issue here" (*Margins*, 12; *Marges*, 12–13).

Among such forces of the repression of difference and history in Jameson, I have already pointed out his unequivocal and thus restricted economic reliance on the concepts of cause, totality, and in particular, dialectic.

The economy of *absolute* alterity is immediately apparent in the passage from *The Political Unconscious* cited above and throughout Jameson's texts, with some nuances, on which I shall comment later. Any economy of absolute alterity, always *restricted*, must be distinguished from the radical alterity in *general* economy. Equally problematic is the configuration of the ultimate horizon of history, determined via the "modes of production." History, according to Jameson, progresses from more to less and less diachronic and more and more universal levels: ". . . through the notions, first, of political history, in the narrow sense of the punctual event and the chroniclelike sequence of happenings in time; then of society, in the now already less diachronic and time-bound sense of a constitutive tension and struggle between social classes; and, ultimately, of history now conceived in its vastest sense of the sequence of modes of production and the succession and destiny of the various human social formations, from prehistoric life to whatever far future history has in store for us" (*The Political Unconscious*, 75).

In *Postmodernism* this logic demands less and less diachronic and more and more "spatial logic" (25), first in relation to culture (53–54), and then in accord with the program just indicated, with very broad—global—political implications as well (409–11). To a degree, a repression of history here, finally, gives up the name history itself, or perhaps rather temporality, so that the resulting spatiality supports, rather than undermines, as temporality and history could, the model announced earlier by way of "the political unconscious."[17] As Jameson tries to show "how mapping has ceased to be achievable by means of maps themselves" (410), the still mapped space of postmodernism and late capitalism becomes the postmodernism and capitalism of space, conceptually and geopolitically. The radical heterogeneity becomes repressed so that a restricted economy of the current moment and, teleologically, of history, can become possible.[18]

The geopolitical transformations addressed by Jameson need to be taken into account, whether theory, history, politics, or culture is at issue. But one needs a very different economy in order to do so—a general economy, or possibly a still more radical theory. Jameson's approach is far short of these limits. The utopian dimensions of Jameson's program further manifest these problems. In most passages cited or referred to in the present discussion, "hope" is an ever-present signifier—and signified, even a transcendental signified—throughout these texts, reinforcing a massive repression of history and difference in the name of history, or geography, particularly postmodern geography—local or global, or globalized, economic, political, or cultural—enacted by Jameson's program. The structure and economy, a restricted economy, of this hope is itself predicated on this repression, as in Marx's, or Hegel's, utopia, or in Heideggerian hope, invoked by Derrida at the end of "Différance."

The role of the political or other unconscious in his theory notwithstanding, the economy offered by Jameson is, then, always a *restricted economy*. This economy also falls short of the historico-political frameworks developed both in the work of his allies, particularly Althusser, and in the work of his opponents, or one might say, "opposition," specifically Deleuze and Derrida. It is true that Jameson qualifies his opposition and credits his opponents. Deleuze's and Derrida's theories and positions are *not actually argued* against or presented at any length, either in *The Political Unconscious* or in later books at issue, nor, in truth, with any rigor elsewhere in Jameson. In *The Political Unconscious* Jameson merely says that they "come to mind" as an example in which "the concept of 'totality' may also be shown at work in those very post-structural philosophies which explicitly repudiate such 'totalization' in the name of difference, flux, dissemination, and heterogeneity" (53).[19] The repeated invocations of Nietzsche and Lacan are actually more self-serving than rigorous and, particularly with respect to Nietzsche, are often the result of misunderstanding.

I would not want to repeat Jameson's gesture here, and not to argue my own points. What does Jameson think he is doing, to begin with, when he concludes his theoretical chapter with the just-cited "History [that] can be apprehended only through its effects, and never directly as some *reified* force? This is indeed the *ultimate* sense in which History as *ground* and *untranscendable horizon* needs no particular theoretical justification" (102; emphasis added)? How much more "reification" does one need? Is it not a transcendental signified as the ultimate control of "historical" transformations, albeit without ever presenting itself directly, similar to that directed by Derrida in Heidegger (*Of Grammatology*, 20)? Heidegger at least refuses to name it, although, as we have seen, this refusal and the great subtlety and rigor of Heidegger's analysis are not enough to avoid a reinstatement of metaphysics. It is imperative to maintain the difference of such conceptions from the general economic "efficacities" and "effects," such as those of Derrida's *différance*. *Différance* also never quite "appears"; but it is never capitalized, or is absolutely necessary, or marks an untranscendable horizon, or the ultimate sense or ground.

One will need a "history" that is at once more historical and less historical than in Jameson, and even Althusser. It follows, among other things, that history cannot be capitalized, cannot be made, as in Jameson, a "unique word, finally proper name."[20] It must be a "history" that is never one thing, not always historical—not always "history"—and certainly does not always obey any given economy of the historical. Things cannot always be historical. Strictly speaking, one cannot say that such a *history* is not always historical. Nor would the quotation marks suffice, as any denomination can always be suspended; and one would also need an analogous general economy of "geography." This radical historicity, the historicity without a capital *H*—History without *Hegel*—at times, more than historical, at times less than historical, at times not historical at all—and forces, historical and other, of its repression are not taken into account by Jameson, and other Marxist economies, perhaps once again, all Marxism hitherto. Instead, in the end, the force of repression and even "Hegel" take over, overtaking the materialist force of resistance to metaphysics. It is always, in the end, "Hegel," whenever dialectic reigns. The differences are repressed; and a certain teleology, or at least a certain teleological horizon, of history is restored.

Jameson's "political unconscious" likewise retains too much consciousness and self-consciousness, as it must, given the Marxist appurtenance of Jameson's program. This claim can be made, I think, even though one does find various "unconscious" agendas and questionings of consciousness and self-consciousness in Jameson. Jameson, however, never questions dialectic, which severely diminishes any critique of consciousness. Thus he writes in *Postmodernism*: "Whether or not the impact of psychoanalysis and linguistics, on the one hand, or the end of individualism, on the other, are satisfactory explanations, it is certain that the notion of 'self-consciousness' is today in crisis and no longer seems to do the work it was thought able to perform in the past; it no longer strikes people as an adequate foundation for what it used to ground or complete. Whether the dialectic is itself inextricably bound up with this now traditional valorization of self-consciousness (something often meant by loose repudiations of Hegel, which ignore passages where something very different seems to be going on) must remain an open question; nor is the loss of the concept of self-consciousness (or indeed that of consciousness either) necessarily fatal to the very conception of agency itself" (244–45).

It is a very big question, indeed. Dialectics itself does not appear to be in question, nor, obviously, the search for adequate—dialectically adequate—foundations, grounds, and completions. Jameson does not specify which passages in Hegel he has in mind. I do not think one can *rigorously* suspend self-consciousness from the Hegelian dialectic, although the relations in many of Hegel's passages show a great complexity in this respect—for example, an analysis of the dialectic of master and slave or the dialectic of desire opening the chapter "Self-consciousness" in the

Phenomenology. These complexities have been amply explored in recent deconstructive and postdeconstructive readings of Hegel, some of them referred to in this study. If anything, more recent discussions would appear to pursue deconstructive, antidialectical reinterpretations and revisions of Hegel. At their best, however—for example, in Derrida—they never simply suspend the role of consciousness in Hegel.[21] At the very least, there are numerous other passages in which self-consciousness conditions and grounds Hegel's dialectical logic. They can no more be ignored than the passages that undermine Hegel's own logic, which, I would argue, always is or aspires to be the logic of self-consciousness, which is not always necessarily a bad thing. Insofar as general economies—in particular, that of Derrida's *différance*—undermine the *Aufhebung* and dialectic, "wherever it operates," they always offer a radical, although rigorous, critique of self-consciousness.

Hegel profoundly understood that dialectic and reflexivity demand self-consciousness and, at a certain level—unavailable, it is true, to the human mind—absolute self-consciousness, which is absolute knowledge. Jameson does not say what he means by "the dialectic" or "reflexivity," "about which," as he indeed says parenthetically, he "begged the question . . . by neutrally designating it as mechanism" (244). The rather Hegelian formulations he offers in the book—for example, on what he calls "dialectical narratives" in the passage at issue (244) and elsewhere—may not name "self-consciousness," but they are precisely "inextricably bound with it," albeit at times, to paraphrase Valéry, as the unconscious self-consciousness. So are, and must be, following both Hegel and Marx, the theoretical, cultural, and political logic of early or late Marxism, such as Jameson, particularly insofar as their untranscendable and transcendental horizon is delimited by—or limited to—and is controlled by the history and geography of the modes of production.

It cannot be otherwise. There can be, by definition, no Marxism without self-consciousness, specifically as class consciousness. The metaphysics of self-consciousness cannot be contained within Marxism, of course, or even within Hegelianism, however encompassing the latter rubric and the power of Hegel's logic of self-consciousness. Jameson's "political unconscious" is and can only be "political self-consciousness," even if unconscious political self-consciousness. Thus it is fully in place in his "aesthetic and cognitive mapping—*a pedagogical political culture which seeks to endow the individual subject with some new heightened sense of its place in the global system*—even though "it will necessarily have to respect this now enormously complex representational *dialectic* and to invent radically new forms in order to do it justice" (54; emphasis added). Can one claim greater self-consciousness than that? Can one surrender more to Hegel, who demands hardly a less, indeed more, complex representational dialectic and cognitive mapping from human knowledge, individual or collective?

As I have stressed throughout, neither consciousness nor self-consciousness can be simply, uncritically or unrigorously suspended; nor, on the other hand, can the complexity of all representational or nonrepresentational engagements. At issue is how consciousness is recomprehended, specifically but not exclusively, via or in relation to the unconscious of one type or another. This relation, too, cannot be dialectical, except within reconfigured limits where dialectic may still function, theoretically, culturally, pedagogically, or politically. In this sense, while not quite radical enough, the Althusserian trajectory of refiguring and reconfiguring Marx via Lacan, remetaphorizing Marx by way of metonymic causality, remains, perhaps, the most effective Marxist theory available.

In fact, Jameson's attempt to depart from "the sweeping negativity of the Althusserian formula" furthers the repression of difference, alterity, transformation, and history in his text. If Althusser's matrix allows for a "formula" of that type and if it can be seen as "sweepingly negative"— neither of which, I think, is the case—Jameson takes the formula outside of the rigorous chain of its inscription in Althusser. This "formula," according to Jameson, becomes "misleading insofar as it can readily be assimilated to the polemic themes of a host of contemporary poststructuralism and post-Marxisms, for which History in the bad sense—the reference to a 'context' or a 'ground,' an external world of some kind, or the reference, in other words, to the much maligned 'referent' itself—is simply one more text among others, something found in history manuals and that chronological presentation of historical sequences so often called 'linear history.' What Althusser's own insistence on history as an absent cause makes clear, but what is missing from the formula, as it is canonically worded, is that he does not at all draw the fashionable conclusion that because history is a text, the 'referent' itself does not exist" (*The Political Unconscious*, 35).

Jameson ends here, as in his subsequent works, by over-"correcting" Althusser. Jameson, as we have seen, also insists on and idealizes, transcendentalizes, History with a capital "H" and, all quotation marks notwithstanding, a "referent." This capitalization and transcendentalization is not inconsistent with repression of radical historicity or with a restricted economy of spatialization. On the contrary, as must be apparent from the analysis given here and throughout this study, all these are consonant and indeed mutually enhancing. Nor, as we have seen, does Jameson's determination of history avoid "an external real world of some kind," indeed of a rather definite kind of reality unrepresentable and independent of representation, but, as will be seen later, not "unknowable" in a certain sense. Their "unconscious" dimensions notwithstanding, all Jameson's theoretical and political economies are thus determined by a set of metaphysical strategies that he shares with classical dialectical materialism—"early Marxism"—and the metaphysics of presence in general. Althusser's understanding of the "absent cause" is far more subtle in this respect; his notion is closer to Derrida and has quite probably influenced some of Derrida's most important formulations. Although Althusser's propositions are, finally, not unproblematic either, they can more effectively deal with the radical difference that a general economy of history requires than can Jameson's. As would follow from the analysis offered in the next section, Jameson's differentiation of the historical horizons referred to earlier, while clearly dependent on Althusser, also displaces them.

Concomitantly, perhaps for the same reasons, Jameson uses uncritically, and again displaces the concept of text borrowed from deconstruction.[22] The question itself of the textuality of history has, of course, a major significance in the present context, or in general. In pursuing the general economy of the historical, one must relate to a difference and to *an* outside more radical than *the* outside, to a difference—such as *différance*, or perhaps a still more radical one—and an outside that are neither outside nor inside, yet simultaneously both, according to the logic described by Derrida in *Positions* (43). Such an economy of history must therefore take into account the inscription of the *textuality* of the textual in Derrida. Derrida's *text* as *writing, trace, différance*, and so on is never *the* text. But it has no absolute outside, either, as one of Derrida's most famous propositions states: "*There is nothing outside the text* [there is no outside-text: *il n'y a pas de hors-texte*]" (*Of Grammatology*, 158). That also means, however, that there is no all-encompassing—absolute—text inside which everything can be contained. Such a possibility would always amount to a Hegelian economy, however much one endows textuality with matter, history, or the unconscious. There can be no textuality or nontextuality in itself and by itself, unconditionally; nor are "history," "matter," and "exteriority" always "textual," or conversely, nontextual.[23]

What is lacking in Jameson, partly as a result of the absence of a critical analysis of the (non)concept of text, is *dissemination*—and the radical *différance* it enacts—of the historical. Jameson writes: ". . . history—Althusser's 'absent cause,' Lacan's 'Real'—is *not* a text, for it is *fundamentally* non-narrative and non representational; what can be added, however, is the proviso that history is inaccessible to us except in textual form, or in other words, that it can be approached only by way of prior (re)textualization" (*The Political Unconscious*, 82; emphasis added). This logic, theoretical, historical, political, or cultural, is repeated by Jameson throughout his later works, although at times moving closer to both Marx and Hegel, and away from more Kantian, or more unconscious economies of difference. In *Postmodernism*, several commentaries in the conclusion of the first, title essay (53–54) and the last, very long chapter of the book, "Conclusion" (411) are indicative in this respect.

Jameson's economy of difference there is closer to Hegel than, for example, to Kant in his more radical conceptions of difference, or to the various unconscious economies that may be invoked here. Thus, "Marxian 'science' provides just such a way of knowing and conceptualizing the world abstractly, in the sense in which, for example, [Ernest] Mandel's great book [*Late Capitalism*] offers a rich and elaborate *knowledge* of that global world system, of which it has never been said here that it was unknowable but merely that it was unrepresentable, which is a very different matter" (53; Jameson's emphasis). No departure from Hegel is achieved here. In order to do so, one needs instead a general economic logic as just indicated. Within the economy suggested by Jameson, or Mandel, one may even fall short of Hegel, or indeed Kant, who, of course, analyzed this problem throughout his life, offering different, or differently nuanced, answers, or forms of questioning, in different texts.[24] Let me stress that what is at issue is not a denial of various claims of that type—unknowability and knowability, unrepresentability and representability, accessibility and inaccessibility, and so forth—but delimiting them general economically, as opposed to dialectically, and indeed re-delimiting dialectic itself.

In general, to claim history, or anything, as *fundamentally* nontextual, or by inversion as *fundamentally* textual, would be precisely to reinstate an instance of metaphysics—the metaphysics of historical materialism as the materialist idealism of history. In a general economy, history or rather the efficacity of "historical" effects is as knowable as it is unknowable, as textual as it is nontextual, as narrative as it is nonnarrative, as global as it is local, to the extent that these terms may apply. At different points, it is also differently—and in terms of the present study, complementarily—balanced in relation to all these denominations. At certain points this efficacity may not be related to any of these terms—historical or nonhistorical, to begin with, textual or nontextual, representational or nonrepresentational, narrative or nonnarrative—or these terms may not be related to history; once again, history may, and at times must, itself be suspended as term or concept.

But to speak simultaneously of both textual and nontextual, neither textual nor nontextual, both history and nonhistory, neither history nor nonhistory, is quite different from saying, as Jameson does, that history is "*fundamentally* non-narrative and non-representational." Here, Jameson's is a logic of "the outside" *only*, rather than the logic of "neither/either" outside "nor/or" inside needed here. In fact, however, here and in the subsequent works, particularly in *Postmodernism*, oscillating between Kant and Hegel, Jameson, as I have indicated, simultaneously claims a metaphysical access to this difference—"unrepresentable," but not "unknowable" (*Postmodernism*, 53). In effect, he already makes such a claim by assigning this difference the name of history or necessity, indeed *History* and *Necessity*. Once again both *dissemination* of difference, or *dissemination* of *différance* and *différance* of *dissemination* are lacking, along with the economy of closure as described earlier, which becomes necessary under these conditions, the conditions of general economic "difference" as considered in this study, via Nietzsche, Bataille, and Derrida.

The considerations just offered are decisive, if one is to establish the difference between a general economic unconscious of history suggested by the present analysis and Jameson's political unconscious—or analogous Marxist and post-Marxist economies and, with important nuances to be considered later, Althusser's structural causality. It is worth reiterating, however, that such overtly differentiating propositions and the general economy they imply will *not*—and *cannot*—directly describe, fully articulate, "map," or claim, or name, the structure of the radical unconscious, alterity, exteriority, difference, and multiplicity: there is no such single structure, or no set of structures. As was considered earlier, a general economy does not fully configure—represent—these "structures," including as absolutely absent or absolutely other. Insofar as such terms apply, one deals with neither unknowable or unrepresentable, or both, nor knowable or representable, or both; and one must engage other oppositional or more multiple complementary clusters and the closures that they generate.

This logic makes the very term 'structure' quite provisional, implying a new set of constraints, often productive, rather than an edifice or a figure of some sort. Thus one can indeed relate only *obliquely* to "the unconscious" as an efficacity of certain effects and only in a certain form—style—

of discourse, whereby the term "unconscious" must in turn undergo a transformational reinscription. But this "obliqueness" and this style must be rigorously differentiated from, at times similar but never identical, restricted economic operations, even though such differences may not always be readily apparent.[25] These differences can be always practiced and often directly articulated, however, thus allowing one to establish the difference between the general economy of history at issue here and the restricted economy of history in Jameson and elsewhere. Although in a more subtle fashion, the same, as will be seen, can be achieved in relation to Althusser's economy of history and, I would maintain, in any Marxist discourse hitherto.

In broader terms, the question is one of relating to the unconscious and a kind of historicity it implies, along the lines of Nietzsche-Freud-Derrida as opposed to, let us say, Marx-Lacan-Althusser. One of the central issues in this context is the economy of the unconscious in a kind of deconstructed Freudian field of *writing* in Derrida's sense as contrasted to the Lacanian or Saussurean field of *speech*. Derrida appears, in this sense, to use Freud against Lacan. The question of the relations between speech and writing in Lacan remains complex, however; Derrida does not really address it. The question of Nietzsche remains crucial, too; and to say that there is not enough difference, or that the difference as configured in the Marxist economies of difference is not radical enough, is perhaps to say that there is not enough Nietzsche there.

One of the main reasons why I earlier invoked the *idealism* of matter is precisely this presence of Hegel in all Marxist discourses hitherto, all their materialism and historicism notwithstanding, and thus the presence of Hegelian presence—becoming-presence, history-presence, dialectic-presence. This inability to avoid Hegel is as pronounced in Jameson as in most Marxist texts, beginning with Marx. In the purported absence, and often under the name of critique, of *Geist* as the ideal Subject, everything that *constitutes Geist* in Hegel, makes it possible, is retained—at times in a more uncritical, even dogmatic form than in Hegel himself. In fact, in *The Political Unconscious* (49–50), Jameson correctly indicates this residual of Hegelianism in the context of the history of Marxist thought, together with a similar point concerning Marx and Hegelian Marxism in Lukács, Marcuse, Sartre and their relation to Althusser and structural Marxism. According to Jameson, Hegel can be only as good as Marx: "Rather than diagnosing some irremediable vice of 'idealism' in Hegel's thought, we more modestly accuse him of not having been able, in his historical moment to become Marx" (51); and this view governs Jameson's analysis of Adorno in

Late Marxism and in much of *Postmodernism*. Even if such were the case, however, one would come short of a kind of historical, and indeed *political*, unconscious that one needs under the rigorous conditions of material history and the unconscious. One might even use some Hegel against Marx in this respect. In *Late Marxism*, Jameson offers, against Jürgen Habermas, the following assessment or prognosis:

> . . . any number of straws in the wind point out to an impending Hegel revival, of a new kind, likely to draw a revival of Capital-logic with it, and not only in those fields (essentially political theory of the so-called state-derivation type) where it still flourishes. But the Hegel who emerges from this rereading will be the unfamiliar materialist-mathematical Hegel, one who comes *after* the *Grundrisse*; quite unlike the idealist conservative Hegel who *preceded* the writing of Marx's first great work, the unpublished commentary of the *Philosophy of Right*. (241)

The notion of "the materialist-mathematical Hegel" is intriguing in suggesting some connections with modern science on which I shall comment in Chapter 7. It may well be, however, that, contrary to either Jameson's or Habermas' sense, this Hegel will be much closer to Nietzsche[26]—Hegel against Marx, and against himself, against all dialectic, materialist and idealist, left and right, positive and negative. Whether in *The Political Unconscious*, *Late Marxism* or *Postmodernism*, Jameson's logic—theoretical, historical, political, ideological, and cultural—as the logic of late, or belated, Marxism, never exceeds, if anything falls well short of, Hegel's logic. For the Hegelian problem always finds, as a problem, its extension in all claims of fundamentally *ideological* determination, from Marx up to the present, however differentiated the determining ideologies themselves might become, however implicit their function is, or however much they are under*written* by other determinations, material, economic, or political. Insofar as it fully or unequivocally determines whatever it is called upon to determine, "ideology" becomes remnants of *Geist*, and more directly, etymologically or otherwise, of the Idea. Obviously, Hegel's terms and concepts have their history, too, and their political economy.[27]

I return, by way of conclusion, to the title of this section. Inescapably, definitionally even, a reinstatement of the *"ultimate"*—"the *least* diachronic"—horizon of history controls or (en)closes Jameson's economy of the political unconscious, and then of late capitalism, as a restricted economy. The specific form of this horizon as determined through the means of production is understandable and in fact inevitable. Jameson's "untranscendable horizon" of history is the transcendental horizon established by means of the *materialist* idealism and *materialist* history. It makes Jameson's analysis Marxist, providing a firm link—for Jameson, a necessary one—between early and late Marxism. This link is maintained throughout Jameson's program, perhaps in more dimensions and in relation to more names than he wants or expects, particularly to Heidegger, the distance from whom may also be seen among the gauges measuring a proximity to Adorno in *Late Capitalism*.[28] Jameson's horizon economy returns one to Heidegger's analysis of temporality and history in *Being and Time*, through establishing time as "the ultimate horizon of the question of Being." This is a part of the fundamental and profound link—a kind of axis—of Hegel, Marx, and Heidegger on the question of history established by Heidegger himself in "The Principles of Thinking" (*The Piety of Thinking*, 57). But Heidegger, even the early Heidegger of *Being and Time*, offers an analysis that, in spite of its problems, can be used against, among others, Jameson and much of late Marxism.

Derrida, in 1967, as contrasted to Jameson in 1981 or in 1990, in *Of Grammatology* (6), also invokes the notion of horizon and the determination of horizon. These propositions must be taken into account as affecting other propositions of Derrida's text, just as the propositions being debated here affect Jameson's or Althusser's text. It is always a question of how different or conflicting propositions affect each other and a given textual chain or network. I shall not consider the question of horizon in Derrida and the transformation of the concept of horizon in its reinscription through the question of play and language, which already indicates a crucial difference in the respective determinations involved. The analysis given in preceding chapters in fact makes this difference irreducible.

One must also note here that, as this analysis suggests, for Derrida the question of the horizon will be related to the question of the closure of metaphysics. Derrida's reference to Heidegger on time, together with Saussure, as the horizon of the question of Being, is inescapable, however.[29] This relation, too, suggests a radical difference from, it appears, any Marxist text so far. That difference will relate both to the very introduction of the—new—concept of the closure of metaphysics, not found in Marxism or any philosophy up to Heidegger, and to the transformation of the concept of horizon, or indeed of all concepts at issue. This transformation may extend to the concept of closure, whereby, as I suggested earlier, a displacement of Derrida's economy may in turn become necessary, but within a matrix very different from any Marxist theoretical economy, at least among those produced so far.

In the proposition referred to earlier, defining the programmatic, theoretical, and political closure of Jameson's *Postmodernism*, or *Jameson's* postmodernism, Jameson says: "A certain unifying and totalizing force is presupposed here—not the Hegelian Absolute Spirit, nor the Party, nor Stalin, but simply capital itself; and it is at least certain that the notion of capital stands or falls with the notion of some unified logic of this social system itself" (410).

Leaving aside "simply capital itself," which notion is no longer possible in this form even in a Marxist text, and certainly not for Marx, the notion—or let us say, the *economy*—of capital more likely demands a rigorous suspension of precisely such logic—unless of course this notion is taken here, as it appears to be, in Marx's sense, as defined by such a logic to begin with. Still, let me stress that in Marx what would be involved would not and cannot be "simply capital itself." I say "most likely," for I cannot offer here and do not possess a political economy of modern or postmodern capital, which would be required to support such a claim. Jameson, incidentally, unlike Marx, does not offer such an economic or a politico-economic analysis, either in general or in support of his claims. The economic problems of that type are immense, as Jameson points out at the outset in his remarks and qualifications on the notion of late capitalism; in addition, he pointedly varies the terms throughout the book (xviii).

The problem here is that since, for Jameson, as for Marx, capital and the means of production define and limit the horizon of history, or geography, the contemporary or the postmodern economy of capital, of late capitalism, must be rigorously engaged, analogously to the way in which Marx engages capital.[30] Marx does not quite offer an analysis of art, or as it has been put, never writes his *Aesthetics*; he offers us *Capital* without aesthetics. Culture, though, is a more complex issue. Jameson, in a way, attempts to offer in *Postmodernism* an "Aesthetics" without a "Capital." All economic parameters of postmodernism as the cultural, or political, logic of late capitalism in Jameson's "late Marxism" are in fact derived from and are announced to be those of, or consistent with, old Marxism, and specifically Lenin and Marx, and, in addition, against the intervening usages (xviii–xix). According to Jameson, as Marxism, *late* Marxism is and, by definition, must be *old* enough; or only now, in or after, postmodernism, the old Marxism, and particularly Marx, acquires its full force. The latter may be not a fully discountable claim, once one engages a rigorous analysis of modern or postmodern, or after-postmodern, capital. Given Marxism's other determinations as considered here, however, the theoretical potential of the matrix is questionable. To the extent that Jameson does address specific features of the *cultural* landscapes of postmodernism, he always reinscribes them within the classical, and in the end Hegelian, if not necessarily Hegel's, logic of old Marxism. It may not be Stalin, it may not be the Party, although one is not quite sure, it may not be the Hegelian Absolute *Spirit*,[31] but once it becomes "certain that the notion of capital [or any notion, *Begriff*, to use one of Hegel's big words] stands or falls with the *notion* [*Begriff*] of some unified *logic* of this social system itself," or again any unified logic, it surely is a *Hegelian Absolute*. In some of its aspects, it is well short of *Hegel's* Absolutes. One might even say that it is an absolute idealism, albeit an idealism of matter—the idealism and ideology, of the metaphysical, totalizing materialism of history and culture.

The Parts and their Wholes: Althusser's Reading [of] Capital *and History in General Economy*

The general economic calculus of history resulting from the present analysis as a whole, to continue with the mathematical metaphor, is both differential and integral, or local and global. It is the calculus of both continuous and discontinuous, infinite and finite, decidable and undecidable, of interminability and termination, and of other complementary relations of that type, multiple and double. In short, it is the calculus and economy, a general economy, of the complementary, produced by an efficacity that itself may not be assigned the name history or any other name, such as the name and concept of absolute difference, or even neither a name nor a concept such as Derrida's *différance*. As a calculus of history, it may be characterized by the following major traits:

First, every local historical perspective is figured as already—"always already"—multiplied and thus further localized. This process corresponds to *dissemination* in Derrida's sense, including in its opposition to polysemy as a containable plurality, in fact or in effect, and in principle. That is, all local boundaries and local unifications are always provisional and may always be differently reinscribed, further localized and further differentiated, or, conversely, or simultaneously, further integrated or unified. An absolute localization or absolute fragmentation is just as impossible as an absolute unification. Broader structures continuously emerging in all such processes must always be taken into account, specifically the effects of permanence or extended stability, often introduced by radical transformations, revolutions—political, theoretical, artistic, or other.

Second, every local historical account, including all global accounts, which are always locally produced, appears at the site—and as an *effect*—of an interplay of heterogeneous histories and concepts of history. The latter, furthermore, may always take the form of an irreducible theoretical or practical, for example, political, conflict, analogous to what Jean-François Lyotard calls the *differend*.[32] The potential, not to mention any "actual," conflicts involved must be taken into *account* within a general economy and complementarity of the historical and, whenever necessary, described by historical accounts conditioned by such a theory of history. Conversely, or complementarily, such an economy must also account for the effects of joined historical forces. In this sense, historical, or political, difference is a rhetorically useful, but not quite precise term. One has to conceive of rich and multiple efficacities and complementarities of differences, similarities, and their interplay, such as of continuities and breaks or proximities and distances within a given history. Nor would such other perspectives necessarily be recognized as equally valid. They are, of course, recognized as true or valid by those who have them. Here as elsewhere, we are at the site of a potential, and potentially irreducible, conflict or *differend*. Such a conflict or *differend* is not inevitable, however—and an indeterminacy always exists, both with respect to a possible emergence of possible resolution of such conflicts, or conversely with respect to at what point and how forces may be joined. In Nietzsche's terms, these are the conditions of perspectivism, which, as we have seen, is a complex economy in Nietzsche, even in nature, let alone history: "Perspectivism is only a complex form of specificity. My idea is that every specific body strives to become master over all space and to extend its force (—its will to power:) and to thrust back all that resists its extension. But it continually encounters similar efforts on the part of other bodies and ends by coming to an arrangement ("union") with those of them that are sufficiently related to it; thus they then conspire together for power. And the process goes on—" (*Will to Power*, sec. 636, p. 340; *KSA* 13:373–74).

As opposed to Hegel and his World History, or Heidegger, and many others in their many shadows, nothing can ever be unequivocally or unconditionally, once and for all, discounted or delegated to some India, Africa, or Siberia. These names have proved to have a powerful "unconscious" historical potential in relation to *Hegel's* World History. As Foucault's analysis shows—at times in spite of Foucault himself—these Indias, Africas, and Siberias can be found right in the center of Paris, perhaps the most central center ever (pro)claimed as such—from the Indians, or the American Indians, Africans, and Siberians on the streets to the metaphors of the vast expanses of mind, nature, or culture that these names offer. This aspect is crucial. Hegel, aware of the multitude of contemporaneous events elsewhere, would not deny the possibility that some of these exterior regions and forces may hold the potential of becoming historical; and he offers an extremely complex, if still restricted, economy of historical difference. Rather, his claims concern the possibility of becoming or not becoming historical *within the scheme of history*, which scheme, however, collapses precisely as a result of the potentiality of such exterior forces to become historical. The question is what can be discounted, when and how. In a general economy of history, this distribution must be determined to be *finally* undetermined, or at once both, determined and undetermined; and it certainly can never be determined once and for all, thus demanding ever more complex complementarities of accounts.

Third—particularly in relation to the history of theory, but with potentially important extensions elsewhere—a general economy of history must consider, or "calculate," the effects, and the diversity of the effects, of *presence* and the *closure* of presence, and the closure or closures of *theory*. Philosophy, specifically as the metaphysics of presence, plays a crucial role in this respect, but the economy of closure at issue cannot be restricted thereby, nor can it be a restricted economy; and one must engage complementary relations to other theoretical fields, such as both the natural or exact and the human sciences, psychoanalysis, or literary criticism and theory. The investigation of the interplay and transformations of different closures that might function in any given case is itself an important potential theoretical, historical, or critical project. The closure of presence, difference, and other interpretive forces involved appears to be much more stable. It, too, however, may at some point be reconfigured differently, neither via closure nor even via presence and difference.

Fourth, this global calculus—"all history is like that"—of history and, at times *as*, the unconscious, together with whatever unifications may emerge there, is itself subject to the structural loss defining the general economy. This loss further differentiates the calculus at issue, so that it becomes impossible always to use history—or *any* terms or names—in all cases, in practice and in principle. This impossibility exceeds simply allowing other local or global perspectives on history.

Even the perspective of radical differentiation must continue to be seen as incurring a certain ineluctable loss of presentation, and this perspective may eventually prove to be just another theoretical "error." In the history of theory, which always has a huge unconscious in this sense—its Indias, Africas, and Siberias—there may always be something else going on, just as in any other history. Most crucially, however, what makes "historicity" complex and irreducible, *in those cases where configurations and economies will be configured as historical,* is also that which—never the same—demands that there will be configurations and economies in which history and historicity will be reducible or, in Derrida's terms, differently *iterable.* To engage such an economy is quite different from suggesting that any *historicity as historicity,* named as such, is not always historical, even if the latter becomes nonsimple, nonlinear, heterogeneous, disseminated and differentiated through and through, without a single or undivided origin. A far more radical plurality is at stake that allows for no absolutely indispensable economy, concept or name. Otherwise, after the metaphysics of history has been deconstructed, the metaphysics of historicity emerges. As the transcendental signified or signifier of history is erased, that of historicity appears.

History and historicity can be inscribed only as complementary in relation to other names and economies. This complementarity is necessary for history and historicity, but neither history nor historicity can encompass all possibilities. The closure of history and historicity is powerful, but it cannot close everything. It interacts with different closures and thus always has the potential to be taken over by any of them. Against Hegel and Hegel's *Geist* that can only negate *itself*—ultimately, a weakness, a disability—a general economy demands the possibility of ever-new exteriority. It demands radical exteriority; but, as we have seen, this radical exteriority cannot be absolute. It follows that any exterior may always be suspended, or differently appropriated or reappropriated; and it can never be determined once and for all which, when, or how.

Under these general economic conditions, or constraints, then history and the so-called "whole" of history, whether in Hegel's, Heidegger's, Marx's, or Freud's sense, or any other sense, *cannot* be a "whole," or always constitute a history. One must remain cautious, for it is *perhaps* possible that at some point a concept of wholeness will be introduced that will render this statement obsolete or at least theoretically problematic. History can never be fully or unconditionally integrated into one history, *the* history, not even, as we have seen, for a single fact or event at any given moment. By the same token, various local historical perspectives cannot always be correlated, nor can they perhaps ever be fully correlated. Moreover, given the impossibility of always or fully correlating "all" perspectives, the very notion of "all perspectives" is equally impossible. Different and conflicting perspectives, *under certain conditions*—but again, *not always*—can be *negotiated* as "errors." They can also be practiced or imposed, of course, or self-imposed, as "truth"—by power, seduction, or still otherwise.

Histories, then, cannot be correlated or integrated, assembled or re-assembled together into one history, whether by way of form or by way of content. Such correlation of histories or such integration of history may not be needed, however. We may be much better off without them. One can actually question the theoretical as well as the practical, including the political, necessity of the universal, let us say, Hegelian, projects as well as the necessity of bringing perspectival diversity to a common denominator. Perhaps globalization is too heavy a burden for theory and practice alike. Hegel had to pay an enormous price for his absolute conceptions and the picture of history they entail, as well as for the consequences of the logic of the universal and absolute. In the end, Hegel had to sacrifice, to use this word also in the sense of that term in the end of the *Phenomenology*, just about the whole world—the "whole" world history.[33] Beyond Hegel, one can offer a long list of problematic—often more problematic than in Hegel himself, and at times disastrous—theoretical, political, and other consequences of global ideologies.

The economy of any set of theoretical, ideological, or political preferences, obviously, is complex—irreducibly nonsimple. It amounts to the very general economy at issue in the present study. According to Derrida, "in the region of historicity . . . the category of choice seems particularly trivial [dans une région . . . de l'historicité—où la catégorie de choix paraît bien légère]" (*Writing and Difference*, 293; *L'Écriture et la différence*, 428). Under the constraints of general economy, we should naturally hesitate to speak of necessity, an equally trivial category in the same domain. The historical divergence at issue is structural, ineluctable. Our "global" historical perspective forbids any unconditional totalization of history. It will not forbid, however, the conditional formation of broader comprehensive historical projects, accounts, or political programs. How can it forbid them? How can it forbid anything at all, given the triviality of the category of necessity, particularly in a metaphysical opposition to the equally trivial category of choice? Rather, it will compel us to account, *in a general economy*, for such conceptions, reconfiguring and comprehending them as local "historical" effects, specifically those relating to the unconscious. This general economy is itself historically constituted as necessarily heterogeneous—in the radical, general economic sense.

At this point, in considering the question of totalization and history, one may, and perhaps must, return to Althusser, arguably the most powerful theoretical presence on the scene of modern Marxism. Among other possibilities, the scene of return may be chapter 9 of *Reading Capital*, "Marx's Immense Theoretical Revolution." As the title suggests, the analysis in this chapter is of paramount significance in the Althusserian theoretical program. Historically, it "marks" for Althusser "a decisive punctuation, a revolution in the history of the Theoretical" (186); although one cannot overlook the political force of the metaphor either. What Althusser sees as "Marx's immense theoretical revolution" consists of two stages.

First, this revolution undermines the classical principle of causality and thus of totalization—for we are here in the domain of historical and therefore causal totalization. Althusser considers these issues in earlier chapters, as well as in other works. Second, Marx's is a theoretical revolution proper, an introduction of a new principle of totalization—"structural causality." Structural causality is the third, perhaps most radical consequence of "Marx's fundamental theoretical concept" (183), although Lacan and Althusser might be more suitable signatures underneath this concept, albeit, for Althusser, *via* Marx and Spinoza: "The only theoretician who had the unprecedented daring to pose this problem and outline a first solution of it was Spinoza" (187). As Althusser writes,

> *Third*: if the field of economic phenomena is no longer this planar space but a deep and complex one, if economic phenomena are determined by their *complexity* (i.e., their structure), the concept of linear causality can no longer be applied to them as it has been hitherto. A different concept is required in order to account for the new form of causality required by the new definition of the object of Political Economy, by its "complexity," i.e., by its peculiar determination: *the determination by a structure.* (184)
>
> But our third conclusion is quite different, and so is the requirement it imposes on us to think the economic phenomena as *determined by a (regional) structure* of the mode of production, itself determined by *the (global) structure* of the mode of production. This requirement poses Marx a problem which is not only a *scientific* problem, i.e., one that arises from the theoretical practice of a definite science (Political Economy or History), but a theoretical, or philosophical problem, since it concerns precisely the production of a concept or set of concepts which necessarily affect the forms of existing scientificity or (theoretical) rationality themselves, the forms which, at a given moment, define the *Theoretical* as such, i.e., the object of philosophy. This problem certainly does involve the production of a theoretical (philosophical) concept which is absolutely indispensable to the constitution of a rigorous discourse in the theory of history and the theory of political economy: the production of an indispensable philosophical concept *which does not exist in the form of a concept.* (185) . . .
>
> The epistemological problem posed by Marx's radical modification

of Political Economy can be expressed as follows: *by means of what concept is it possible to think the new type of determination which has just been identified as the determination of the phenomena of a given region by the structure of that region?* More generally, *by means of what concept, or what set of concepts, is it possible to think the determination of the elements of a structure, and the structural relation between those elements, and all the effects of those relations, by the effectivity of that structure? And a fortiori, by means of what concept or what set of concepts is it possible to think the determination of a subordinate structure by a dominant structure? In other words, how is it possible to define the concept of a structural causality?*

This simple theoretical question sums up Marx's extraordinary scientific discovery: the discovery of the theory of history and political economy, the discovery of *Capital*. But it sums it up as an extraordinary theoretical question *contained* "in the practical state" in Marx's scientific discovery, the question Marx "practiced" in his work, in answer to which he gave his scientific work, without producing *the concept* of it in a philosophical *opus* of the same rigor. (186)[34]

Perhaps such a concept or network of concepts can in fact only be practiced rather than "produced in the philosophical *opus* [contained in a book, as Hegel wanted] of the same rigor."[35] That much, at least, would be suggested by the development of a more radical general economic "concept." Such would be the theoretical or *analytical*—psycho-analytical, socio-analytical, politico-analytical—general economic practice.

Analogously, can the major concepts of Freudian practice be "produced in a philosophical *opus*," contained in a book, and so on? Can they not be *written* in Derrida's sense? Here lies another immense question, namely, the question of the difference in practice and theory—in the theory of practice and the practice of theory—between Freudian analysis and Marxist analysis.[36] That, again, is not to say that more comprehensive concepts and sets of concepts would not be *produced* along the way or that some of them would not be articulated in more classical terms, or that books would not be written. One would have to reconsider, however, the structure of their functioning and would have to engage in a different, more plural practice of theory.

By translating Marx's economical, political and historical economy into the economy of structural causality, Althusser, then, opens the way to translating it into Freudian terms. This translation—as a structural transformation—is supplemented by one of the key terms—*Darstellung*—as used in Marx:

'*Darstellung*' means in German, among other things, *theatrical representation*, but the figure of theatrical representation immediately participates in the full sense conveyed by the word, which means 'presentation,' 'exposition/exhibition' and, at the level of its deepest etymological root, *'positioning,* or putting into place, of presence'—given and visible presence. For the purpose of expressing its particular nuance, it may be instructive to contrast *Darstellung* to *Vorstellung.* In the case of *Vorstellung,* there is indeed a positioning (a putting into place), but it involves an emplacement *in front,* which supposes that there is something held *behind* this foregrounded position, something *represented* by that which is held in front of it, by its emissary: Vorstellung. *With Darstellung, on the other hand, there is nothing behind*: the thing itself is there, *'da,'* given and put into place as presence. The entire text of a play is there in this way, given in the presence of the representation (Darstellung), but the presence of the play in its entirety is not exhaustively manifested in the immediacy of the gestures or the utterances of such and such a character: we 'know' that it is the presence of a completed whole, which inhabits each instant and each character, and all the relationships between the given characters within their personal presence; however, it can *only* be apprehended as the very presence of the whole, as the latent structure of the whole, *within the whole,* and is merely adumbrated in each particular element and role. This is why, *depending on the level on which one places oneself,* it can be said that '*Darstellung*' is the concept of *the presence of the structure in its effects,* of the modification of effects by the efficacy of the structure which is present in its effects. Or, on the contrary, that '*Darstellung*' is the concept of the *efficacity of an absence.* It is in this second sense that Rancière used the decisive concept of '*metonymic causality,*' more fully elaborated by Miller last year during the course of our seminar on Lacan. I believe that this concept, when understood as *the efficacity of an absent cause,* is an admirably fitting one by which to designate the absence in person of the structure in its effects, considered from the flattening perspective of their existence. However, the other aspect of the phenomenon must be emphasized: that of presence, of the immanence of the cause in its effects or, in other words, of the *existence of the structure* in its effects. (*Lire le Capital* 2:170–71)[37]

The configuring of a certain relation between micro- and macroeconomic structures occurs in a manner rather similar to general system science. Althusser may have been influenced as much by cybernetics and systems theories prominent at the time as by the Lacanian and Saussurean structuralist matrix. The relations between both frameworks and between the history of science and mathematics on the one hand, and psychoanalysis and linguistics on the other, are clearly relevant in this context. Such relations would include the question of the form and genre of analysis in various theoretical fields, specifically the question of "the *Theoretical* as such" posed by Althusser. That question is certainly a central one for the structure of the theoretical revolution enacted by both Marx and Freud and, I think, inescapably by Nietzsche, at the very least as a crucial anticipation of and influence on Freud.

A broader historical and political unconscious and a corresponding calculus or economy are thus implied by Althusser, although, finally, still a restricted economy. Inserting first *Darstellung* and then Lacan into his logic, Althusser writes:

> This text ["Introduction" to *Capital*] is discussing the determination of certain structures of production which are subordinate to a dominant structure of production, i.e., the determination of one structure by another and of the elements of a subordinate structure by the dominant, and therefore determinant structure. I have previously attempted to account for this phenomenon with the concept of *overdetermination*, which I borrowed from psycho-analysis: as one might suppose, this transfer of an analytical concept to Marxist theory was not an arbitrary borrowing, but a necessary one, *for the same theoretical problem is at stake in both cases: with what concept are we to think the determination of either an element or a structure by a structure?* It is the same problem that Marx has in view and which he is trying to focus by introducing the metaphor of a variation in the *general illumination*, of the *ether* in which the bodies are immersed, and of the subsequent alterations produced by the domination of one particular structure in the localization, function, and relations (in his own words: the relations, their rank, and influence), in the original color and the specific weight of the object. The constant and real presence of this problem in Marx has been demonstrated by the rigorous analysis of his expressions and forms of reasoning in the preceding papers. It can be entirely summed up in the concept of "*Darstellung*," the key epistemological concept of the whole Marxist theory of value, the concept whose object is precisely to designate the mode of *presence* of the structure in its *effects*, and therefore to designate structural causality itself.
>
> The fact that we have isolated the concept of "*Darstellung*" does not mean that it is the only one which Marx uses in order to think the effectivity of the structure: a reading of the first thirty pages of *Capital* shows that he uses at least a dozen different expressions of a metaphorical kind in order to deal with this specific reality, *unthought before him*. If we have retained it [the concept of *Darstellung*], it is because that term is both the least metaphorical and, at the same time, the closest to Marx's conceptual aims [when he wants to designate at once both absence and presence, i.e., *the existence of the structure in its effects*].

This is an extremely important point if we are to avoid even the slightest, in the sense of inadvertent, relapse into the diversions of *the clas-*

sical conception of the economic object, if we are to avoid saying that the Marxist conception of the economic object is, for Marx, determined *from the outside by a non-economic structure*. The structure is not an essence *outside* the economic phenomena which comes and alters their aspect, forms and relations and which is effective on them as an absent cause, *absent because it is outside them. The absence of the cause in the structure's "metonymic causality"* [an expression Jacques-Alain Miller introduced to characterize a form of structural causality registered in Freud by Jacques Lacan] *on its effects is not the fault of the exteriority of the structure with respect to the economic phenomena; on the contrary, it is the very form of the interiority of the structure, as a structure, in its effects.* This implies therefore that the effects are not outside the structure, are not a pre-existing object, element or space in which the structure arrives to *imprint its mark*: on the contrary, it implies that the structure is immanent in its effects, a cause immanent in its effects in the Spinozist sense of the term, that *the whole existence of the structure consists of its effects*, in short that the structure, which is merely a specific combination of its peculiar elements, is nothing outside its effects. (*Reading Capital*, 188–89; *Lire le Capital* 2:169–71)[38]

Many of these are admirable formulations. They pose fundamental and often pioneering questions, most importantly perhaps the question of "the production of an indispensable philosophical concept *which does not exist in the form of a concept*" and of "*the existence of the structure in its effects*." Derrida, it may be suggested, repeats—"iterates," but with some crucial differences—some of Althusser's formulations in inscribing—a *dispensable*—*différance*. The whole of Althusser's analysis certainly had a major impact and influence on Derrida's discourse and much else in recent history; and I have cited it at some length here partly in order to make this latter point. This formulation and a number of others in *Reading Capital, For Marx*, and elsewhere, have a clear proximity to some of Derrida's most famous formulations. Derrida's introduction of *différance* as "neither a term nor a concept" is a rather immediate response to this problem—in 1967 or thereabouts. Derrida proceeds, however, against dialectic and against Marx, and finally against Althusser. Among the major reasons why "in delineation [dans le tracé] of *différance* everything is strategic and adventurous" (*Margins*, 7; *Marges*, 7) is certainly that it cannot be practiced in the form of a philosophical concept or indeed in the form of logico-philosophical discourse. But, different from and operating against Hegel's *dialectical* style, the style of practicing the theory—the general economy—of *différance* is also different from Marx's—*dialectical*—style and from Althusser's own style of theory. This general economic style moves, if you wish, from *Darstellung* to *Entstellung* on all fronts, but without discounting the former. Such a *writing* comes before the book, as the first part of *Of Grammatology* announces.[39]

As we have seen, "before" here does not have ontological meaning, for at stake is also a radical deconstruction of all ontology, along with the classical logic, formal or transcendental. It has instead "(pre-)logical," *theoretical*, meaning. One must relate to *différance* and *writing* that is always already "there"—that is, *operative* but never *present*—before the book. The movement of *writing-difference*—and of *writing-différance*—makes concepts, their chains, logic, and the book possible and under certain conditions necessary. But, at the same time, this movement reconfigures them by exposing their character as "effects," a reconfiguration that, again, implies a deconstruction of the classical concept of "effect" (*Positions*, 66). This general economy thus makes impossible all such concepts in their classical sense and rigorously suspends the claims that philosophy makes on behalf of these concepts: "Différance produces what it forbids, makes possible the very thing that it makes impossible" (*Of Grammatology*, 143; *De la grammatologie*, 206).

The "existence" of *différance* as *différance* also "consists in," or rather manifests itself by, "its effects," just as in Althusser. A further deconstruction of structuralist thematics is in order, however, along with, and *as*, metonymic or Lacanian causality controlled by a transcendental signifier, or an array of such signifiers. They in turn become the effects of *différance* as *structure*. The relations that lead to metonymic causality—whether in Althusser or Lacan—demand *différance*. They may actually demand more, but they cannot demand less, as Derrida shows in his analysis of Lacan's seminar on Poe's *The Purloined Letter* in "The Purveyor of Truth." A very different postal circulation is at stake, a very different history, whose always—always already—delayed letters may never finally arrive at their destination, although, importantly, at times they do arrive "properly," to the extent it can be possible in the deconstructed—and thus general—economy of the proper and of arrival. They may—or again also may not—arrive at a very different destination, often more than one. But this general economy implies a different, above all, a more *dynamic*, sense of the term "structure" as constraint, something akin, to cite a pertinent economic example, to "structural unemployment":

> Differences are the effects of transformations, and from this vantage the theme of *différance* is incompatible with the static, synchronic, taxonomic, ahistoric motifs in the concept of *structure*. But it goes without saying that this motif is not the only one that defines structure, and that production of differences, *différance*, is not astructural: it produces systematic and

regulated transformations which are able, at a certain point, to leave room for a structural science. The concept of *différance* even develops the most legitimate principled exigencies of "structuralism." (*Positions*, 27–28; *Positions*, 39)

While in a more limited fashion—still as *causality, not complementarity*—Althusser's, or Lacan's, economy also injects a dynamic motif into the notion of "structure," as does in fact Hegel, well before Marx, and Heidegger, all of whom influence Lacan. Althusser also engages a critique and, to a degree, a deconstruction of the concept and model of presence and linearity, in particular, of history. Althusser defines this model as that of "the homogeneous continuity of time":

(1) The homogeneous continuity of time. The homogeneous continuity of time is the reflection in existence of the continuity of the dialectical development of the Idea. Time can thus be treated as a continuum *in which* the dialectical continuity of the process of the development of the Idea is manifest. On this level, then, the whole problem of the science of history would consist of the division of this continuum according to a *periodization* corresponding to the succession of one dialectical totality after another. The moments of the Idea exist in the number of historical *periods* into which the time continuum is to be accurately divided. In this Hegel was merely thinking in his own theoretical problematic the number one problem of the historian's practice, the problem Voltaire, for example, expressed when he distinguished between the age of Louis XIV and the age of Louis XV; it is still the major problem of modern historiography.

(2) The contemporaneity of time, or the category of the historical *present*. This second category is the condition of the possibility of the first one, and in it we find Hegel's central thought. If historical time is the existence of the social totality, we must be precise about the structure of this existence. The fact that the relation between the social totality and its historical existence is a relation with an *immediate* existence implies that this relation is itself *immediate*. In other words: the structure of historical existence is such that all the elements of the whole always co-exist in one and the same time, one and the same present, and are therefore contemporaneous with one another in one and the same present. (*Reading Capital*, 94; *Lire le Capital* 2:39)

Althusser's analysis is powerful, particularly in seeing the category of historical *present*, and by implication, *presence*, in general as determining the whole framework. This framework is, of course, also the framework of the whole, the Whole which is the True, of which Hegel speaks in the Preface to the *Phenomenology* (11). The continuum of time, furthermore, is also shown, correctly, to be only a "reflection in existence" of the continuum of the Idea (Idee). The statement also proves the enormous significance of the model itself as permeating our thinking about history throughout the history of this thinking. In the end, it will be returned to its classical functioning and status by Althusser's reading of Marx and the politico-historical matrix that followed from Marx. This "return" will take place at a different level, the difference being important, but it will take place, nonetheless. Althusser also correctly points to "the whole problem of the science of history," on the one hand, and "the major problem of modern historiography," on the other. In fact, one would have to speak of politics, rhetoric, ethics, poetics and so on, moving via Aristotle's titles, which still shape the structure and politics of our institutions of knowledge and name, for example, university departments. Aristotle may still have more claims than anyone else on the model itself at issue. Althusser then proceeds to juxtapose the Hegelian totality, "the metaphoric causality," to the Marxian totality defined, via Jakobson and Lacan, as "metonymic" or "structural" causality. The question of presence and continuum, however, or of "homogeneous continuity," is crucial in its own terms. While Althusser speaks of the "historical time," general considerations of temporality are also clearly implied: first, given the broader post-Husserlian and post-Heideggerian scene against which Althusser reads Marx; and second, given the general model on which such historical considerations are predicated. The differences in the levels and domains of the model's functioning are important. For, problematic as the model is at the level of historical or psychological time, it has been extremely effective elsewhere. Within limits, it is also in fact effective in the theory and practice of history and politics.

At issue in Althusser is not a dismissal of the classical models, even in their most Hegelian aspects, but the understanding of the limits of their functioning and applicability. "Continuums" do work as models, for example, in mathematics, although, strictly speaking, their functioning in the mathematical realm is virtually ungrounded in classical logic. How then are the conditions of the possibility and the necessity of mathematical continuums to be reconfigured? Or from another vantage point, why and how does mathematics or do the exact—more or less mathematical—sciences work? This problem cannot be addressed here. As I have indicated, one can trace these connections to the "formal" and mathematical aspects of the model in Althusser by way of information theory, cybernetics, and related developments; in vogue at the time, all these developments inescapably influenced not only Althusser directly but also the structuralism on which Althusser depends. Koyré's studies of both Hegel and Newton, including the problematic of the continuum, are another major part of the landscape at issue here, which, in general, has long-standing relations to the history of mathematics and science. In addition, the general question of the foundations of mathematics and of modern physics continues to be an important feature of this scene.

As was suggested earlier, Derrida's *différance*, at the juncture of its general economy, exceeds Althusser, along with Hegel and Heidegger. This is in accord with Derrida's strategy of simultaneously engaging close proximity and radical difference, whether in relation to Hegel, or Heidegger, or Althusser, whose "entire, and necessary, critique of the 'Hegelian' concept of history" is invoked in *Positions*. Perhaps, however, it is invoked in order to move away from it, specifically to "the concept of history that Sollers calls 'monumental'" (*Positions*, 57; *Positions*, 79). Derrida is careful to use quotation marks. "Hegelian" is a complex term; and so is "monumental history," a phrase Nietzsche also used in his early *Vom Nutzen und Nachtheil der Historie für das Leben* in *Untimely Mediations* [*Unzeitgemässe Betrachtungen*]. In Althusser, presence is reinstated at the level of historical *totality*, a move that is unacceptable in a general economy. Althusser radically questions "the homogeneous continuity of historical time," while, as the passages cited earlier clearly point out, nevertheless maintaining the presence of the parts to the whole, which entails the (self-)presence of the totality to itself. Such a claim already presupposes continuum, which, though acceptable and indeed necessary in *Reading Capital*, is problematic as a general theoretical and historical matrix. As was discussed earlier, one needs to depart from Marx in this respect.

The economy of history in Derrida is more radically differentiated, more radically transformational, than in Althusser. Nor, under the same constraints, can *différance* be seen as an "indispensable concept." Some of the "only, everywhere, differences and traces of traces" (*Positions*, 26; *Positions*, 38) are such that it becomes impossible for the "term" and "concept," or "neither term nor concept," of "differences and traces of traces" to control a configuration, thus continuously forcing Derrida to introduce new names and structures. More generally, as we have seen, *différance* enacts many fundamental differences between general economies and restricted economies, and thus all Marxist economies, although, given Nietzsche's case, not all materialist economies. There can be no overt or hidden "presence" of *différance*, always and everywhere, in the theoretical economy, such as the Lacanian hidden presence of absence, which structures Lacanian metonymic causality and perhaps also its reconfiguration in Althusser.

One cannot then deny the positive and critical value and the "revolutionary" significance of Althusser's formulations for modern theory. Althusser's essay on Freud and Lacan takes on a specific importance in this sense; it clearly can be incorporated into the present analysis (in *Lenin and Philosophy and Other Essays*, 195–219), as also "Ideology and Ideological State Apparatuses," where Althusser indirectly but powerfully engages Lacanian ideas. The analysis of Hegel and of the whole problem of historicism in *Reading Capital* is equally important and redefines the whole problem and the concept of historicity. One must also point out Althusser's critique of the "outside" as metaphysical exteriority. It must be seen as the critique of the metaphysics of the *essence* and of the *outside*, somewhat along lines considered earlier. At issue is the necessity of *thinking* a radical difference and the structure of transformations rather than a simple or unproblematic negation of the role of the noneconomic in the constitution of the economic. Althusser's formulations, however, are also problematic in a number of respects; and the proximity of Althusser's propositions to Derrida's should not prevent one from accentuating the differences between them. It also allows one to expose and articulate the metaphysical appurtenance of Althusser's conceptions, specifically totality.

Althusser's formulations reflect an interactive complexity, "a relational richness," of the French scene, where one finds all these figures—Althusser, Lacan, Sartre, Levinas, Blanchot, Deleuze, Foucault, Derrida, and quite a number of others—acting against the background of the older proper names, from Hegel to Marx, to Nietzsche, to Freud, to Heidegger, to Bataille, and a great many literary figures as well. This scene itself has therefore a structural complexity. It has, if you wish, the complexity of *structure*, in both Althusser-Lacan's and Derrida's senses of the term; and these are in turn multiply interactive. This complexity is structured by a metonymic causality translating itself into *différance* in the general economy.

The main problem in Althusser is, then, a reintroduction of and, as the passages cited here suggest, an insistence on *totality*, defining Althusserian *Darstellung* and structural causality; and I shall deal with this question in concluding this essay. The problem of totality may be considered sufficiently self-evident at this point in the history of theory. It is, however, a complex conception in Althusser, as is Althusser's strategy of introducing it. In general, Althusser's text demands much theoretical rigor, much respect for his own rigor; and once the workings of his conceptual chain are given their due, Althusser, like Hegel and Marx, is a great deal superior to most of his critics and admirers alike. The question of totality, in Althusser and in general, acquires interesting new dimensions from the perspective developed in the present analysis. We are by no means finished with totalities. They are powerful beasts—monsters in the labyrinths—and we can never quite escape them.

Althusser's reintroduction of totality is a reintroduction of an instance of *presence*, albeit the presence of structure—the presence of all parts to the whole. This configuration of "structure" *as* presence has had a major significance in the whole history of structuralism and then deconstruction. Althusser's gesture is not dissimilar to determining an interpretive and historical configuration on the model of presence and presencing in Heidegger, throughout his career from *Being and Time* to *Time and Being*. Heidegger, as was indicated earlier, reads Marx via this economy of presence and history and totality as presence—becoming-presence. Moreover, this reading is effective, in contrast to the case of Nietzsche, whom Heidegger reads in this way as well.[40] Althusser, we recall, speaks of a "relative independence." It is, however, "totality" rather than "*relative* independence" that requires quotation marks in Althusser's proposition. One is much better off speaking of a "*relative* totality" rather than of "relative independence." Or rather, one must speak of a totality that is no more and no less relative than independence or locality. One must consider what I call here the complementarity of both as the economy—the general economy—of the interactively heterogeneous and heterogeneously interactive interplay of totalization and localization.

As must follow from the present discussion, a different logic of theory or a different logic—a different *law*—of logic is in order; and, as must follow from Derrida's analysis of Lacan, it must be specifically different from the Lacanian configuration of metonymic or structural causality. The latter does not allow us to move beyond the restricted economy of the transcendental signifier or other transcendental structure; in this case, it does so again in a fundamental proximity to Heidegger, even while possibly reversing him. As Derrida argues in "The Purveyor of Truth," it is the impossibility of *fragmenting*, of dividing, of disseminating the signifier—"letter," "phallus," or whatever—that leads at a certain point to a transcendental signifier. It makes it into a transcendental signified as well "underneath" all other signifiers and signifieds, analogues to Heidegger's Being or other configurations of that type emerging in later Heidegger, even under the conditions of the Heideggerian—as opposed to Derridean—erasure of Being. Althusser inherits this problem from Lacan, once again confirming profound complicity—in the metaphysics of presence they share—between structuralism and phenomenological thematics, in Husserl, or phenomenological-ontological thematics in Heidegger.[41] The understanding of this complicity is one of Derrida's main achievements.

All this is, once again, not to deny the fundamental significance of Althusser's propositions as an analysis of what we might see as the *local* structures of totalization. This question is certainly crucial in both Marx and Freud. In Freud, it appears as the question of memory and the unconscious, but also consciousness, in relation to the question of language or *writing* opened by Lacan's analysis and then developed by Derrida's. It is the *theoretical* question, the question of a rigorous theory of structural relations, in the multiple senses of both terms, 'structure' and 'rigor,' that have emerged throughout the present analysis. This theory must proceed through the general economy of the unconscious, dislocating—and relating to the *structural* loss in—both representation or, if you wish, *Darstellung*, and totalization. For totalization constitutes one form, one of the most fundamental ones, of presence and re-presentation, or *Dar-stellung*. Indeed, one might say that, by reading Marx, Althusser poses a kind of question that requires a *general*—more unconscious, more radically unconscious—political economy.

Marx's *organization* of the system of transformations does open the possibility of a structuralist reading of "determination" in his political economy, which has had some crucial consequences and implications for modern theory, and specifically for deconstruction. Althusser's emphasis on the theoretical character of Marx's revolution was as important as it was original, and it retains its significance to this day. For at issue is the *structure*—the formal configuration—of relating the elements within the system, rather than the specificity of the politico-economic grounding of history. Politico-economic considerations remain important to Althusser. In reading Marx and interactively in his own theoretical and political program, Althusser was clearly motivated by the political concerns of the period as well as his own. His insisting on the totalization of history within the plurality of the historical and the political does reflect both contemporary and broader political constraints. Nevertheless, the theoretical question retains its importance, beyond its debts to structuralism. We are far from being finished with formal or *theoretical* considerations on this and other issues, perhaps *all issues*, notwithstanding many tempting "trends" away from the "theoretical" and toward the ideological and political. We might in fact need theory, and perhaps particularly political theory, that is more theoretical than ever. "Immense theoretical revolutions" may be needed.

It may be shown that one cannot ascribe only metaphoric causality to Hegel. Althusser's analysis is not fully rigorous in this respect, even though there is indeed a great degree of metaphoric causality in Hegel—many isomorphisms, to use a formal term, between *Geist* and its various subsystems, including individual and collective human economies. Various forms of metaphoric causality, in fact, are found in Marx, too. The Hegelian system also has crucial structural or metonymic dimensions, just as Marx's does; and one might even speak of "Hegel's immense theoretical revolution"—History. Both Jakobson and Lacan may well have borrowed, and Marx certainly did borrow, a few things from Hegel in this respect.[42]

Hegel, it is true, does not rigorously produce his metonymic causality to the degree that Marx does by way of the political economy within actual—"material"—history (wirkliche Geschichte). At this point, "formulas," or rather *names*, alone—metaphoric, metonymic, or whatever—will not do. One needs specificity of connection; thus Marx's immense theoretical revolution may consist, after all, in its *politico-economic specificity*, which rigorously provides necessary formulas or formalisms. Hegel's—"metonymic"—connections remain from this point of view "mystical" enough, as Marx said. One—although not Hegel, perhaps—needs a *material* metonymic economy. One may well speak of a tremendous revolution, theoretical *and* political, in Marx's economy, in which the relations between consciousnesses and self-consciousnesses are organized metonymically—structurally—by way of (the difference) of class and relation to the means of production as opposed to the Hegelian ideology of consciousness and self-consciousness. The latter, at the human level, is defined by Hegel as consciousness of the historical self-consciousness of *Geist*, or later, the Idea. But then, Marx's configuration cannot be sustained as a model of material "metonymic causality," either. *Material* history, economic and political, cannot fully obey Marx's again *deliberately dialectical*—Hegelian—model; and in Hegel, too, this model, as I indicated at the outset of this study, has powerful, in many ways decisive, politico-economic genealogies. Neither economy can obey history without "the unconscious," that is, be subject to a historical economy that will sum up and control the wholeness of the whole, the behavior of the elements within the system.

In this sense, with all due credit to Marx, what is perhaps most decisive is Althusser's own fusion of a Lacanian—or fundamentally unconscious and, in the deep sense, *material*—economy with Marx's political economy. Despite its problems, this fusion contributes within a broader textual field to the immense theoretical revolution in the theory of social, economic, and political formations—in short, *the theory* of *history*.

It could be suggested that Althusser introduces the totalization of history for political reasons, and that possibility cannot be discounted. Besides, the complexity of the political configuration in France that would necessitate such an insistence on Althusser's part must be considered. Possibly even more important is the general problem of the constitution and stratification of the political and its specific manifestation in France at the moment of Althusser's writing—the politics of state and class, the politics of the institutions of theory and education, for example, at the École Normale where the course was given (an institution that has a bearing on Derrida's case, too); family politics; and the complex, often incalculable, relations among all these and still other political levels.

Yet, granting these determinations, or overdeterminations—or indeterminations—and *within their network*, and thus without claiming at any point an unconditional separation between the political and the theoretical, I would suggest that Althusser's insistence on totality and totalization has a fundamental *theoretical* significance, particularly given his reliance on Spinoza. Marx, of course, also functions as a crucial theoretical background; nevertheless, all theoretical revolutions notwithstanding, Marx remains a "more political" case, even though Spinoza—the practical philosopher, according to Deleuze—is far from free of politics, and from practice and politics. All these politics, once again, are irreducible. Such, however, were Althusser's *theoretical* conclusions, insofar as one can speak and insofar as one must—and one often must—speak of *theory*. Althusser speaks, after all, of "Marx's immense *theoretical* revolutions." I insist on this point, even in view of the irreducible nature of the political, because it is crucial—historically and theoretically—to maintain the difference, often in fact a radical one, between apparently proximate *theoretical* propositions without uncritically explaining away this difference by *delegating* it, to use a useful political metaphor here, to some naively conceived political necessity. The latter "necessity" can in fact never be absolutely necessary. Is the theoretical in turn reducible? Can opposition be simply dissolved here? I would even risk the assertion that the difference between the propositions at issue is irreducible at any level of the political that one can conceive of at the moment. Thus, it would be hard, perhaps impossible, to reduce the "totality" in Althusser.

At the most formal level of our calculus, then, any "whole" can only be—"always already"—a *part*. In their own calculus of disjunction, Deleuze and Guattari reinscribe this configuration through Proust's and

291

Blanchot's texts—or rather, thematize them accordingly. They write in *Anti-Oedipus*:

> Maurice Blanchot has found a way to pose the problem in the most rigorous terms, at the level of the literary machine: how to produce, how to think about fragments whose sole relationship is sheer difference—fragments that are related to one another only in that each of them is different—without having recourse either to any sort of original totality (not even one that has been lost), or to a subsequent totality that may not yet have come about? It is only the category of multiplicity, used as a substantive and going beyond the One and the many, beyond the predicative relation of the One and the many, that can account for desiring-production: desiring-production is pure multiplicity, that is to say, an affirmation that is irreducible to any sort of unity.
>
> We live today in the age of partial objects, bricks that have shattered to bits, and leftovers. We no longer believe in the myth of the existence of fragments that, like pieces of an antique statue, are merely waiting for the last one to be turned up, so that they may all be glued back together to create a unity that is precisely the same as the original unity. We no longer believe in a primordial totality that once existed, or in a final totality that awaits us in some future date. We no longer believe in the dull grey outlines of a dreary, colorless dialectic of evolution, aimed at forming the harmonious whole out of heterogeneous bits by rounding off their rough edges. We believe only in totalities that are peripheral. And if we discover such a totality alongside various separate parts, it is a whole *of* these particular parts but does not totalize them; rather it is added to them as a new part fabricated separately.
> . . . .
> Hence Proust maintained that the Whole itself is a product, produced as nothing more than a part alongside other parts, which it neither unifies nor totalizes, though it has an effect on these other parts simply because it establishes aberrant paths of communication between noncommunicating vessels, transverse unities between elements that retain all their differences within their own particular boundaries. Thus in the trip on the train in *In Search for Lost Time*, there is never a totality of what is seen nor a unity of the points of view, except along the transversal that the frantic passenger traces from one window to the other, "in order to draw together, in order to reweave intermittent and opposite fragments." This drawing together, this reweaving is what Joyce called *reembodying*. (*Anti-Oedipus*, 42–43; *L'Anti-Oedipe: Capitalisme et schizophrénie*, 50–51).[43]

Proust's perhaps most explicit and most powerful statement to that effect, also relating to his own work as a *whole*, occurs in *The Captive*:

L'univers est vrai pour nous tous et dissemblable pour chacun. Si nous n'étions pas pour l'ordre du récit obligé de nous borner à des raisons frivoles, combien de plus sérieuses nous permettraient de montrer la minceur menteuse du début de ce volume où, de mon lit, j'entends le monde s'éveiller, tantôt par un temps, tantôt par un autre. Oui, j'ai été forcé d'amincir la chose et d'être mensonger, mais ce n'est pas un univers, c'est des millions, presque autant qu'il existe de prunelles et d'intelligences humaines, qui s'éveillent tous les matins.

[The universe is real for us all and dissimilar to each one of us. If we were not obliged, in the interests of narrative tidiness, to confine ourselves to frivolous reasons, how many more serious reasons would enable us to demonstrate the mendacious flimsiness of the opening pages of this volume in which, from my bed, I hear the world awake, now to one sort of weather, now to another! Yes, I have been forced to whittle down the facts, and to be a liar, but it is not one universe, but millions, almost as many as the number of human eyes and brains in existence, that awake every morning.] (*La Prisonnière*, 290; *The Captive*, in *Remembrance of Things Past*, 189–90).

Proust's "*almost* as many" is extraordinary. Everything depends on the "almost," *almost* everything. Reasons are most serious; and "the narrative tidiness" is a very serious reason, too, or "whittling down the facts," or "being a liar," or—or as—"telling the truth." The last one would force one to reconceive, but not eliminate, the difference between the two, making truth into "a *kind* of error," as Nietzsche says. But errors may be of a different kind, and different each time, whenever both truth and error may or must appear. It is also significant that in the next paragraph Proust returns to Albertine—the Goddess of time, the Goddess of the lie, the woman: "Pour revenir à Albertine, je n'ai jamais connu de femmes douées plus qu'elle d'heureuse aptitude au mensonge animé, coloré des teintes mêmes de la vie, si ce n'est une de ses amies—une de mes jeunes filles en fleurs aussi, rose comme Albertine . . . [To return to Albertine, I have never known any woman more amply endowed than herself with the happy aptitude for a lie that is animated, with the very hues of life, unless it be one of her friends—one of my blossoming girls also, rose-pink as Albertine . . .]" (*La Prisonnière*, 290; *The Captive*, 190).

The logic of "neither . . . nor/either . . . or," and then the logic of complementarity that emerges in the case of continuity and rupture, are fundamentally related to the history of temporality. The relativization of temporality in the theory of relativity played a role, metaphorically and otherwise, in the modern part of this history. Both Husserl and Heidegger have actually dismissed these discoveries as irrelevant to "authentic," *proper* (*eigentlich*) temporality. They, it is worth noting, never dismissed their importance for modern science. Relevance of that type is a highly complex issue. It is more complex perhaps than the question of "authentic," that is to say, *impossible*, temporality.[44] Henri Bergson is another important reference, particularly for and in the context of Proust. Derrida also invokes Bergson in the context of the question of time, and at one of the crucial moments in *Of Grammatology* (67), when the radical dislocation of classical temporality, the breakdown of the continuum at every conceivable level, is at stake.[45]

We may not be able quite to conceive of either one or the other—of absolute continuity or absolute rupture—but we need to, and seem to be able to, re-*present* the *effects* of both. There are representations in various domains that function as continuums and ruptures or complementary configurations of both, while they both might be the effects of a play which is neither, and relate to what is never either fully a continuum or fully a break. These observations can be referred to the related and possibly still more complex case of finitude and infinity or, as Derrida shows, more generally to all oppositions of that type on which philosophy has depended throughout its history. In the wake of Derrida's analysis, the logic itself of "neither . . . nor/either . . . or," in *this form*, the logic of undecidability has been practiced extensively by deconstructive criticism and theory. According to Derrida himself, however, it was Nietzsche who *for the first time*, or at least to an unprecedented, revolutionary degree, grasped the necessity of this logic and *practiced* it most deliberately, *consciously*, although not without the unconscious or a deliberate, *conscious* unconscious.

Although it may be true that, after Nietzsche, "we live today in [among other things] the age of partial objects . . ." and "no longer believe in" any form of absolute totality, the grand Nietzschean question "Who are we?" is still to be asked here. There are those, at least some, who still "today do *not* live in . . ." and "still believe in . . ."; and their assumptions, conceptions, and beliefs do require handling in a far more delicate and complex manner than by an unconditional dismissal or denial, or indeed by postulating *any given mode or model of interaction between the whole and its parts*. The analysis in *Anti-Oedipus* and the subsequent *A Thousand Plateaus*, where the question and economy of history is at issue, is not unproblematic in this respect. At a certain level, one might speak of a reinstatement of totality there as well, often along with an unproblematized—or insufficiently problematized—economy of partiality. Deleuze and Guattari's "rhizome" economy of history in *A Thousand Plateaus* offers a brilliant and rich conceptual and metaphoric play; nevertheless, it remains finally a restricted economy. "We" who, after Nietzsche, must think this loss of wholeness and center, this loss of presence, "without *nostalgia*, that is outside of the myth of a purely maternal, or paternal, language, a loss of native country of thought" and "on the contrary, . . . must affirm this, in the sense in which Nietzsche put affirmation into play, in a certain laughter and a certain step of a dance" (*Margins*, 27; *Marges*, 29). We, however, are still "human, all too human," always destroying, always rebuilding our household economy (*oikonomia*), which we still "live in" and which, at times, we "still believe in." It is not impossible, however, that at some point we shall transform our closures to the point of no longer requiring the whole and its parts.

For now, that economy powerfully shapes and constrains our theoretical environment and its ecology. The whole must still be comprehended in one way or another, even if *as a part*. Given the history in question, the insistence on "parts" is strategically effective. As Bataille suggests in *Guilty*, "the 'lack of wholeness' is *only* real at a profound level (because it is perceived by means of an imperfection in what is arbitrary) . . . [. . . le 'defaut d'ensemble' n'est réel que *profondément* puisqu'il est perçu par le moyen d'une imperfection de l'arbitraire . . .]" (*Le Coupable*, 36; *Guilty*, 30; translation modified).[46] "We live today in the age of partial objects, bricks that have shattered to bits, and leftovers." We live in the age and in the house (*oikos*) and economy (*oikonomia*) of fragments, "bricks that have shattered to bits." An unconditional fragmentation, however, the Many, in an absolute and capitalized sense—"the truth is the part," a reversal of Hegel's famous "The True is the Whole [Das Wahre ist das Ganze]" (*Phenomenology*, "Preface," 11; *Werke* 3:24)—is just as impossible as an absolute wholeness—the One.

Chapter 7

Machines

Demokrit als Resultat von Maschinen.
Die secundären Eigenschaften der
materie *nomo*, nicht an sich.
— Nietzsche[1]

Entropies

Among other possibilities that may offer themselves and that have been explored in recent history, the Hegelian system—the system of *Geist*, or in later works, of the Idea—may be metaphorized as a machine of history—a *perpetuum mobile* of the *Aufhebung*, reiterating itself from stage to stage, finally to the point of absolute self-consciousness as the full presence of all its parts to its whole. The metaphor is capacious, and Hegel's equally capacious text engages and enacts many a perpetuum mobile and many a machine. In a perhaps more restricted context of mathematical and scientific metaphors, one can actually speak, interactively or complementarily, of two kinds of machines that are at work in the technologies of Hegel's text, or that these technologies are never quite able to set to work: a physical—energy-entropy—machine and a mathematical—calculation—machine. "Hardware" and "software" immediately invite themselves as further metaphors; and at one level or another one always needs both in any machine, whether it is a mathematical calculating machine, which must still work and waste energy, or a machine that is designed for physical work,

297

which always employs a program of one kind or another. But this is not the only mode of operation or of connections, metaphorical or other, between physical and mathematical machines, whether those functioning— or not functioning—in, or *as*, Hegel's text or found elsewhere. My discussion here will proceed along these two lines of metaphorization, organizing the division of this chapter into two sections, "Entropies" and "Calculations." Inevitably, however, these metaphorizations, general economic to begin with, become complementary in their functioning. They connect as much as separate, divide as much from within as from without, generate undecidables and double binds. But, as we have seen, beyond being the only available economy and economics of the theoretical, these schizophrenias may not be such a bad option.

The metaphorization at issue does not make a strong claim on an *interpretation* of Hegel's *Geist* itself—a claim, let us say, on the design of this perpetuum mobile. Who would risk making such a claim? Not even Hegel makes such claims. Hegel is quite careful in what he claims concerning *Geist* and how he claims it, or what in general can and cannot be known to a human mind, however profoundly or properly philosophical it is— that is, however attuned to *Geist*. Given the immensity and complexity of Hegel's text, it is difficult to make definite claims even on the structure of whatever Hegel claims concerning various aspects of *Geist*, such as history, consciousness, self-consciousness, mediation, or becoming. We can deal only with spirits of Hegel's Spirit, with Ghosts of *Geist*.

The latter is the most prominent metaphor in what may be seen as late deconstruction, specifically in Derrida's readings of Heidegger on *Geist* in *Of Spirit* and Kafka. These ghosts or shadows emerge and move either along more classical or along more deconstructive lines of reading and more or less classical interpretation or reinterpretations and revisions— ghosts and shadows, or ghosts of ghosts and shadows of shadows—of whatever Hegel or *Geist* emerges as a result. Against Hegel, these metaphorics or schizophrenics—"only, everywhere," the spirits of spirits, ghosts of ghosts, shadows of shadows, traces of traces—powerfully constrain, although not absolutely or unconditionally determine, any reading or writing. Hegel, as Derrida does not fail to point out, already knew this, but not quite to the degree that we demand now. These claims do count; and there is much else in Hegel's text that must count, too. For one thing, Hegel still thought that there was *that* which—*Geist* or other ghosts—escapes the ghostly necessities of writing, or reading.

The perpetuum mobile is one of the spirits of Hegel's Spirit, one of the ghosts shadowing Hegel's systems. There are only ghosts everywhere, but there are at times also unavoidable, inescapable ghosts. As in the case of any other perpetuum mobile, Hegel can only offer or imply a project, a design of such a perpetuum mobile of *Geist*, or again rather claim a possibility and some attributes, ghosts, of *Geist*. He offers his own ghosts of *Geist*. *Geist* itself is Hegel's greatest ghost, in either sense of this double genitive, insofar as Hegel tries to shadow it and insofar as it still shadows us, even though, while history no doubt moves, it does not conform to most of Hegel's designs. Hegel's *text* is a kind of machine, too; and it does move, even if not quite or no longer in the direction that Hegel envisioned for it and for History that it was supposed to follow.

As Hegel's *Geist* and Hegel's text move forward, however, they continually come back, or eternally return, to the point of Bataille's laughter; and they come to the highest point of Bataille's laughter at their highest point—the point of Absolute Knowledge. Bataille can only laugh at this machine of perfect nourishment and absolute consumption, the machine that wastes nothing, loses nothing that can be utilized by its perfect organism—a self-consuming and self-engendering artifact. Continuously "reinstated [herstellen]" in the economy of Hegelian "sacrifice" by "the movement of Nature" (*Phenomenology*, 492) and by the death—finitude—of *human* subjects, *its* human subjects, the Subject-*Geist* discards and sacrifices much; but it never wastes anything, even at the moment of death and consumption—self-consumption—by fire, like the phoenix, that consummately Hegelian image. According to Derrida, "Hegel . . . situated the passage from the philosophy of nature to the philosophy of spirit in the combustion from which, like the sublime effluvia of a fermentation, *Geist*—the gas—rises up or rises up again above the decomposing dead, to interiorize itself in the *Aufhebung*" (*Of Spirit: Heidegger and the Question*, 99; *De l'esprit: Heidegger et la question*, 161—62).[2]

The process is fully in place already in the *Phenomenology*, particularly in its concluding elaborations on the economy of sacrifice, which is the Hegelian economy—a restricted economy—of history. It is a kind of process that would be precisely prohibited—*in nature*—by the second law of thermodynamics. For Bataille, conversely, the economy of death and particularly the economy of sacrifice—seen, however, as a *human* economy as against the ideal and superhuman *Geist*—are indissociable from waste, that often deliberate and deliberately senseless waste, which offers a very different model of consumption. Bataille's "thermodynamics"—the general economy—of psyche, nature, history, and sacrifice, is much closer, although not identical, to the metaphoric economy of thermodynamics and subsequent modern theories in physics, such as quantum mechanics, specifically complementarity, understood as a general matrix around quantum principles and the uncertainty relations.

While no machine and no consumption is possible without waste, however, a *machine* or an economy of absolute waste would be just as impossible, since it would require resources as infinite as those of the Hegelian *Geist*. A corresponding metaphor and the theoretical economy conditioned by it would quickly *run* into all the Hegelian problems. Bataille, as we have seen, pursued a complex "thermodynamics" of expenditures, productive and unproductive, reserved and unreserved. All "absolute" economies are restricted economies. If such a machine were possible, even as it created waste, it would have to maintain itself, at least for a while. In practice, it might eventually be fully dissipated; and in practice, any machine or system, that of wasting energy or that of consuming energy, must be so dissipated by the force of entropy. With enough energy, this entropy can be enhanced to the point of an apocalyptic event, as it were, of the absolute destruction of a system, its software or its hardware, at which point the *extent* of the system and the degree of its wholeness become important.

Bataille always deconstructs even *local*, let alone global, dialectic, a local *Aufhebung* of one kind or another, individual or collective. Hegel does not maintain *absolute* consumption or presence at such *local* levels, either. Hegel, however, does maintain, even in becoming, the underlying *restricted* economy of presence, (self-)consciousness, meaning, and concept, even at local levels—by virtue of his global economy or machinery. Hegel and Hegelianism always operate within the theoretical and political model of presence—being presence and becoming-presence, history. By virtue of this model, they claim a gradient of history—which history refutes—and ideology of theoretical and political practice—which theory and politics no longer want or can afford.

Whether "matter" itself—Nature, the Universe—can be seen as constituting a whole—by way of modern physics and cosmology, for example—is a complex and problematic question. It is extremely, perhaps intractably, complex even in the field of science, where it has its own distinguished history, such as in relation to the question of entropy, the arrow of time, and related issues. All these things have been discussed extensively in the ever-proliferating literature of science, philosophy, and other fields. The question of entropy does have a profound relation to the possibility of partitioning or containing the system and its exterior, and thus to general cognitive models. *At this level*, however, the question is not really a question of general economy, which, as has been discussed throughout this study, cannot fully be an economy of wholeness. Alongside the economy of radical alterity of matter in relation to the classical oppositions or larger clusters of philosophemes considered in the preceding chapter, a general economy demands radically *disseminating* efficacities—always multiple and capable of transformation at each point. This economy of *dissemination* and accompanying *différance* must be maintained, whatever the structure of matter at global, cosmic—*universal*—scales may be. A very small portion of *this* matter—a very local entropy or very local apocalypse—could suffice to destroy "all" history.

That is not to say that the question itself of the wholeness of matter and the universe, along with a great deal of physics, from Galileo and Newton, or indeed Aristotle, to modern physics, has not affected, metaphorically or otherwise, the history of thinking on the issues to which the general economy, whether in Nietzsche, Bataille, or Derrida, relates in the most fundamental way. Along with much else in thermodynamics, atomic theory and quantum physics, and the mathematics of continuum, Bataille thought about these matters; and they affected his conceptions: "*In truth, if I envisage the universe, it is, as one will affirm, constituted by a great number of* galaxies (*of nebulous spirals*). *The galaxies constitute clouds of stars, but does the universe constitute the galaxies?* (*Is it the organized sum of the galaxies?*) *The question which surpasses understanding leaves a comical bitterness. It affects the universe, its totality. . . .*" Referring to Paul Langevin's *La Notion de corpuscules et d'atomes*, Bataille writes this in relation to the conception of "a man [as] a particle inserted in unstable and tangled groups," conditioned and metaphorized simultaneously by a micro- and macrophysics of matter: "Being is always a group of particles whose relative anatomies are maintained. These principles—constitution transcending the constituent parts, relative anatomy of the constituent parts—order the existence of each 'being'" (*Inner Experience*, 84–85; *L'Expérience intérieure*, 132–33).[3]

Bataille's anti-phoenix vision of the physical universe, which permeates his *La Somme athéthéologie*—*Inner Experience*, *Guilty*, and *Sur Nietzsche*—is both a metaphor and an example of a general economy, clearly provoked by modern physics. Developed and nuanced throughout Bataille's work, the anti-Hegelian *structure* of the process and hence of metaphor is important. While ultimately any star, for example, will be annihilated, it also *consumes* itself: consumption is always a part of a general economy, although, importantly, it may always operate on a different plane than does waste. This disjoined, de-synchronized—anti-dialectical, anti-Hegelian—economy is itself a defining aspect of Bataille's matrix. This economy, to put it strongly, *is* the general economy, making all "is," such as Heideggerian Being, impossible. At a certain point, annihilation may take place very rapidly, indeed; the explosion of a supernova in the vicinity of the solar system, which is undergoing its own self-annihilation, would easily destroy the whole of history, all its profits, presence, and records. *Inner Experience* and most of Bataille's major works utilize the conceptual and metaphorical richness of modern mathematics and science, particularly in combining the micro- and macrocosmic—descriptions—"moving universes" (95) in his description of "inner experience."

Obviously, as I have pointed out from the outset of this study, in Bataille, or Nietzsche and Derrida—in the general economy—a much more complex and incalculable—indeterminate and undecidable—economics, or "thermodynamics," of forces is involved than in science, even in quantum physics. The latter is also the case in Hegel, or Marx and Heidegger, among others. The difference is a gradient of increased richness and complexity; and the general economy may—perhaps must—use, metaphorically and otherwise, modern scientific theories—from thermodynamics on—and their increasing complexity against, and in order to deconstruct, restricted economies. In this sense, one would proceed from Newtonian models of forces and the play of forces to Hegel, as opposed to Newton, for example, in Hegel's "Force and the Understanding" in the *Phenomenology* or in the many powerful and beautiful elaborations in the *Logic*; to a more complex statistical play of forces of thermodynamics, against Newton and Hegel, although there are important earlier related developments in science, some preceding Hegel; to Nietzsche, against a still statistical dream of thermodynamics, perhaps still using some Hegel; to a still more complex determination of modern quantum theories and the irreducible complexity—a radical nonsimplicity—of the general economy in Bataille and Derrida.[4] As Lyotard points out,

> Einstein balked at the idea that "God plays with dice."
> Yet dice is precisely a game for which this kind of "sufficient" statistical regularities can be established (so much for the old image of the supreme Determinant). If God played bridge, then the level of "primary chance" encountered by science could no longer be imputed to the indifference of the die toward which face is up, but would have to be attributed to cunning—in other words, to a choice, itself left up to chance, between a number of possible, pure strategies (*The Postmodern Condition*, 57; *La Condition postmoderne*, 93).

Bridge, which is governed by von Neumann's mathematical game theory, may still be too simple a game for the general economy, although bridge effects, or dice effects, or the Newtonian, or Hegelian—that is, the nonstatistical—effects retain their powerful *force*; and a general economy must take them into account. Bohr's reply to Einstein is quite interesting in its language and rich in implications: "On his side, Einstein mockingly asked us whether we could really believe that the providential authorities took recourse to dice-playing (". . . ob der liebe Gott würfelt"), to which I replied by pointing at the great caution, already called for by ancient thinkers, in ascribing attributes to Providence in everyday language" ("Discussion with Einstein on Epistemological Problems in Atomic Physics," in *Atomic Physics and Human Knowledge*, 47).

Loss—depreciation—is inevitable for any "machine," any theoretical system that always depends on material resources, whether a system of production and consumption of meaning or something else, or a nonsystem, contrasystem, or any combination of these. In a general economy, there can be only such combinations, whatever the overt aims or claims. Losses of "energy" are irreducible but never absolute. Nor, while gains can never be absolute, are they reducible, either. No given combination determines once and for all the entropy or energy potential of a given theory, field, rhetoric, metaphoric, and so on, or their ability to survive. In a general economy, which must always be the economy of *matter* and, and *as*, the unconscious—the materialist, although nondialectical, economy—one thing appears to be *determined*: everything will have to be *finally* destroyed. Economy is a metaphor of energy; but all economies, theoretical, political, or other, are subject to entropy or that which necessitates the metaphor of entropy. It is never absolutely determined, however, *when* or *how* things will be destroyed. Their destruction is just like any other death, that is to say, like the metaphor(s) characterizing many things that may be called "death"—an event always random and necessary at once, although its random effects, as a rule, are more powerful.[5]

This finitude, as structure, is important if one deals with becoming and transformations in either a restricted or a general economy; in both types, nothing remains the same, everything is always life-death. Finitude in a general economy, however, prohibits the global control of transformations.[6] What destroys a given system is always some other system; in addition, all systems are always controlled, at least partially, by something else. In such an economy, "matter"—its energy and entropy—or what is thus conceptualized or metaphorized, plays a crucial role. "Time" and "history" create and maintain—conserve—at times over very broad historical intervals: "Hegel" would be impossible otherwise. But they always destroy in the end.

Most "theories," it is true, die well before their "material" carriers are destroyed, although—insofar as any carrier exists, however mediated—they can be "resurrected" as well. As George Herbert wrote, however, "What shall point out to them, / When they [marbles with inscriptions] shall bow, and kneel, and fall down flat / To kisse those heaps, which now they have in trust?" ("Church-monuments," ll. 14–16). The "death" of a theory cannot be determined and proclaimed in advance, or once and for all. For this case, too, Nietzsche's "God is dead" is still the best example. The way Nietzsche introduces it in *Zarathustra* plays out this very situation: "'Could it be possible? This old saint in the forest has not yet heard anything of this, that *God is dead*?' ['Sollte es denn möglich sein! Dieser alte Heilige hat in seinem Walde noch Nichts dann gehört, dass *Gott todt* ist!'" (*Thus Spoke Zarathustra*, 12; *KSA* 4:14). The news of the death of an idea, however great, does not make it die elsewhere or be, at some point, resurrected anywhere.

The problematics of the perpetuum mobile of both the first kind—the energy conservation law—and the second kind—the entropy law—have developed historically in proximity to Hegel. Actually, Sadi Carnot (1796–1832) discovered the second and possibly the first law of thermodynamics around 1820—a remarkable achievement, although a logical one. The logic of connecting both may in fact be Carnot's greatest achievement in the sense that he proceeds by putting the whole configuration together by way of the deconstruction—the first deconstruction?—of the perpetuum mobile or better, the grounds—conceptual *and* experimental—on which such a machine of either the first or the second kind would be possible. The whole history of this question, however, is profoundly related to Hegel. In a famous decision of 1775, the Royal Academy of Sciences "resolved, this year to examine no longer any solution to problems on the following subjects: the duplication of the cube, the trisection of the angle; and quadrature of the circle, or any machine claiming to be a perpetuum mobile."[7]

The relations among Hegel, the Enlightenment, and science, along with, or between, mathematics and technology, are rich and well known, although they may not as yet have been explored to the degree their richness demands. From this perspective, metaphorizing *Geist* as a machine is not only theoretically useful, but also historically pertinent. The question of the machine, "the question concerning technology," is irreducible in the text of Hegel, from Newton's universe as a machine to the perpetuum mobile, to calculating machines for numbers or thoughts, as in Leibniz.[8]

Geist is Hegel's "solution," as it were, to the problem of perpetuum mobile. This solution would by no means contradict scientific findings or the opinion of the French Royal Academy of Sciences. For, while always in motion, in the perpetual motion of its becoming, *Geist*, according to Hegel, cannot—*absolutely*—be seen as a machine. *Geist* and, by virtue of its proximity to it, philosophical thinking, often served Hegel to criticize mathematico-technological thinking. The latter phrase is actually Heidegger's characterization of modern science. The characterization is *correct*, I think, even as it serves Heidegger to pursue a critique similar but not identical to Hegel's, and similarly *untenable*, in "The Question Concerning Technology" and related essays.[9] I shall comment on this critique shortly. For the moment, I will consider the conceptions of the machine and the perpetuum mobile and their powerful effects in Nietzsche and Bataille, who both depend on thermodynamics and entropy as theory and metaphor. Demonstrably, the question of entropy in physics and elsewhere has a profound relation to the question of temporality and presence, in addition to the question of wholeness. These issues are complex and cannot be pursued here; maybe in general they cannot be pursued aside from their rigorous physical and mathematical content.[10] It is remarkable that both continuum and entropy should be major concepts for Bataille.

Entropy also has a significant, if mediated, effect in the question of political economy in Marx, in such "material" issues as amortization of the means of production. Hegel's "standpoint" of labor—the labor of *Geist* and History—which Marx justifiably, if somewhat reductively, sees as "the standpoint of modern political economy," already belongs to this conceptual and metaphoric traffic (*Economic and Philosophical Manuscripts of 1844*, in *The Marx-Engels Reader*, 112). These connections are crucial for the history of the question of the movement from the restricted economy—manifesting itself at the level of political economy—to the general economy as the economy of irreducible entropy at every level of production—economic, theoretical, artistic, or political. The whole problematic, *processed* via Marx, Nietzsche, and Freud, is also a major conceptual and metaphoric aspect of Deleuze's work, from his analysis of Nietzsche in *Nietzsche and Philosophy*, to the vision of technological schizophrenia, techno-schizo-analysis, in Deleuze and Guattari. *Anti-Oedipus: Capitalism and Schizophrenia* is a theory of and a program for "the desiring-machines." The shadow of Hegel over this vision is immense, too—both over the powerful critical or deconstructive dimensions of the project, using machines and (schizo-)technology against Hegel, and over its problematic utopian aspects and, finally, its outcome.

Nietzsche's reading list included books on thermodynamics as well as books depending on or related to these conceptions in biology and the social sciences. Of obvious significance are, even as titles, J. R. Mayer's

Thermal Mechanics (1874) and Wilhelm Roux's *The Struggle of Parts in the Organism* (1881).[11] It is curious, although logical, that Nietzsche would think, specifically in relation to the question of "eternal recurrence," of the World as an "organism" that "lives on itself: its excrements are its food." With this conception Nietzsche opens one of his later notes, though its exact date may not be certain: "*The new world conception.*—The world exists; it is not something that becomes, not something that passes away. Or rather: it becomes, it passes away, but it has never begun to become and never ceased from passing away—it *maintains* itself in both.—It lives on itself: its excrements are its food" (*Will to Power*, sec. 1066 [March-June 1888], p. 548; *KSA* 13:374). It would thus still be a perpetuum mobile, albeit of a very different kind from Hegel's. In a related note (sec. 1067), Nietzsche compares "the world" to "a household"—economy (*oikonomia*)—"without expenses or losses, but likewise without increase or income" (p. 550).

In Hegel, by contrast, in the absence of loss, the *increase* of *Geist* never stops: hence *Geist's infinite* excess over everything else, the nonwaste surplus. The dream of this excess may well be only a *human* desire, although perhaps one of the fundamental ones. "From fairest creatures we desire increase, / That thereby beauty's rose might never die," Shakespeare says in the first lines of the first of his *Sonnets*; and Shakespeare might indeed be closer to Nietzsche than anyone else, than to anyone else. For Hegel, there is no beauty at stake, or not quite the same beauty, as philosophy takes over from both nature and art: there is truth and knowledge, knowledge that knows all it has to know because it knows all. It is a very different form of relation between beauty, truth, and knowledge than in the famous lines of the "Ode on a Grecian Urn" (49–50) or Keats's economy of negative capability, which is a kind of general economy, or Shakespeare, who is Keats's chief example of negative capability (*Letters of John Keats* 1:193–94). In Shakespeare—who does seem to know all, much more than one has to know, or, as Nietzsche noticed, more than one wants to know—time and the great machine of entropy take over in the next line: " . . . the riper should by time decease."

Infinite resources of presence are needed to maintain any presence. As Derrida writes, "Only infinite being can reduce the difference in presence [Seul l'être infini peut réduire la différence dans la présence]" (*Of Grammatology*, 71; *De la grammatologie*, 104). This is how *Geist* is conceived by Hegel, as a being—being-becoming—that possesses the infinite resource or excess of presence in order to maintain the economy of (becoming as) presence. This necessity of the infinite present in order to have any presence at all—in truth, not as an illusion or active forgetfulness—is perhaps Hegel's greatest theoretical insight, even if it must be used against him, leading for example to Nietzsche's "active forgetfulness," an even greater insight.

Nietzsche's "world" is thus very different from Hegel's and is conceived, among other things—and other *against*'s or *contra*'s—against Hegel and others in Hegel's shadow. To begin with, this world is nonteleological, also antiteleological, replacing the progress of *Geist* with "eternal recurrence." Nietzsche's is also a materialist vision—the play of matter, not the work of spirit. That distinction makes an immense difference in all ensuing claims. Becoming is never given up. Nietzsche is the most Heraclitean of all the Heracliteans on this scene: "the high point of meditation" is "that *everything recurs* is the most extreme *approximation of a world of becoming to a world of being* [*Das Alles wiederkehrt, ist die extremste Annäherung einer Welt des Werdens an die des Seins*]" (*The Will to Power*, sec. 617, p. 330; *KSA* 12:312; translation modified).

Teleology and archaeology, however, *are* given up. The differences from Hegel become even more pronounced once one moves from "matter" to "history." For, whatever the problems of Nietzsche's logic of "matter" and eternal recurrence *here*—and some of his claims simply do not follow—eternal recurrence and the infinitude of the world are powerful weapons against the logic, far more untenable than Nietzsche's, that Nietzsche invokes in the note under consideration: the logic of origin, creation, or conversely teleology, including entropic—mechanistic—teleology. Lord Kelvin is mentioned a bit later. Nietzsche's "world" is also used against nihilism, specifically against teleological nihilism: "[L]et us think this thought in its most terrible form: existence as it is, without meaning or aim, yet recurring inevitably without any finale of nothingness: '*the eternal recurrence.*' This is the most extreme form of nihilism: the nothing (the 'meaningless'), eternally" (*Will to Power*, sec. 55, pp. 35–36; *KSA* 12:213). Against Nietzsche's contention, *here*, "eternal" recurrence, and indeed the infinity of the world, do not necessarily *follow* from the absence of origin or—according to another of Nietzsche's contentions—the absence of a final state, although, as we have seen, a certain perceptual and conceptual closure would emerge. Understanding of the global economy of the universe would demand a great deal of physics—and some metaphysics or indeed deconstruction—and immensely complex interpretive and conceptual closures or openings, that were unknown, and one may even risk saying "unimaginable," in Nietzsche's time. The issues are far from, and may never be, settled; and further complexities—and simplicities—continue to be discovered all the time.

Nietzsche's "infinitist," but "materialist," metaphysics is—or certainly was at the moment—a much better alternative to what he dismisses here as "a rudimentary survival from the ages of superstition [rudimentär aus Zeiten des Aberglaubens]" (*Will to Power*, sec. 1066, p. 548; *KSA* 13:374). It also seems that he has in mind a number of specific conceptions, only some of which are indicated and none of which is sufficiently elaborated. I mention this because in his earlier analysis in *Philosophy in the Tragic Age of the Greeks*, Nietzsche offers an extraordinarily sophisticated analysis of the general logic of the possibility of origin, creation, chance, and so on, to which he cryptically refers in the passage: "I have come across this idea in early thinkers" (*Will to Power*, sec. 1066, p. 548; *KSA* 13:375). Even in the case of the will to power, however, which affects and *connects* everything in Nietzsche—his vision of the material or spiritual world—and which might be seen on a number of occasions as a kind of transcendental signified in Derrida's sense, Nietzsche *never* translates the wholeness of the material world into a Hegelian wholeness of history.

As we have seen, in Nietzsche, history cannot be an absolute or unconditional whole of any kind, or based on presence and consciousness and selfconsciousness. That deconstruction leads to an enormous difference from the unity of *Geist*—"*Geist*, inc.," "*Geist*-body," which *incorporates* Nature or matter—or from the unity and teleology of history in dialectical materialism, the materialism of consciousness. Furthermore, Nietzsche is greatly aware, certainly more than anyone before him, of the metaphoricity of his discourse and the metaphoric traffic that he engages as he moves from one "world" to another. Nietzsche *knows* the *perspectival* nature of his or anybody's interpretation of the world and of interpretation itself, "the perspectival evaluation." Hence both perspectivization and quotation marks are found in this case, too: "And do you know what 'the world' is *to me*? Shall I show it to you *in my mirror*?" (*Will to Power*, sec. 1066, pp. 549–50; *KSA* 11:610; emphasis added).[12]

It is important, nonetheless, to point out the problematic nature of Nietzsche's conceptions whenever they become problematic, as they do here. Admittedly, in this case one is dealing with Nietzsche's unpublished and unfinished notes. For this and other reasons, some of his conceptions, particularly the "eternal recurrence," may be said to be more enigmatic than problematic; also, they may be read so as to reduce their problematic aspects. There are other notes in which some of these conceptions, including the "eternal recurrence," are treated more skeptically. Nor, as Deleuze correctly argues in *Nietzsche and Philosophy*, should one reduce the richness of the question of relations between Nietzsche's thinking and science to the question of eternal recurrence (44–46). Conversely, the economy of eternal recurrence is played out on many other levels in

Nietzsche, specifically in *Zarathustra*. It demands a long and complex analysis; and it has elicited such analysis, for example, and specifically in the case of *Zarathustra*, from Heidegger (*Nietzsche*, vol. 2, *The Eternal Recurrence of the Same*).[13]

Nothing is ever simple in Nietzsche. Nevertheless, this point would not be enough to explain away the problems in Nietzsche. Nietzsche is not a god. He does not *know* everything. Nor can he master, calculate, or anticipate everything, either consciously or in the unconscious style of his "*fröhliche Wissenschaft*"—not even always to the extent of "possible" anticipation or mastery. Nietzsche can be problematic and even—why not?—wrong; undoubtedly one must be as critical with respect to Nietzsche as to anyone else, however powerful his insights and conceptions are. One must also *account for* the problematic theoretical and political effects of his text, including when these effects are produced by what is not problematic in his text. One must stratify perspectives in accord with Nietzsche's sense of reading or *writing* an "original" text. Thus, given the "empirical" and "theoretical" constraints of general economy, the "best" local perspective may not allow the wholeness of "matter" either. Whatever the structure of "matter," however, be it global or local, it would not affect the radical difference of interpretation and history in Nietzsche. As a result, while the problems of Nietzsche's text should not be ignored, one can still use it effectively, subtracting or decoupling the problematic strata. Nietzsche's description of his "world"—"a monster of force [Kraft]" (*Will to Power*, sec. 1067, p. 550)—actually strikes one more as a picture of diversity—a kind of Maxwellian vision of field—than one of unity, save for the claims of wholeness of "the household [*oikonomia*] without expenses or losses" and the eternal return to the same "global" states. The interval of such recurrences can be immense, of course, on a cosmic scale well beyond the scale of human history. Naturally, there may be many local effects of recurrence at the level of matter, psychology, or history. These are important, crucial effects, as both Nietzsche and Freud understood; and one would not want to suspend them. The effects of repetition and recurrence, including the compulsion to repeat—one of Freud's great ideas—are irreducible aspects of any general economy, such as that of *différance* in Derrida—the economy of both difference and repetition simultaneously. As Nietzsche writes, then:

> And do you know what "the world" is to me? Shall I show it to you in my mirror? This world: a monster of force, without beginning, without end; a firm iron magnitude of force that does not grow bigger or smaller, that does not expend itself but only transforms itself; as a whole of unal-

terable size, a household without expenses or losses, but likewise without increase or income; enclosed by "nothingness" as by its boundary; not something blurry or wasted, not something endlessly extended, but set in a definite space as definite force; not in a space that would be "empty" anywhere, rather as force throughout; as a play of forces and waves of forces, at the same time one and "many," increasing here and the same time decreasing there; a sea of forces flowing and rushing together, eternally changing, eternally flooding back, with tremendous years of recurrence, with an ebb and a flood of its forms; out of the simplest forms floating out toward the most complex, out of the stillest, most rigid, coldest forms toward the hottest, wildest, most self-contradictory, and then again returning home to the simple out of abundance, out of the play of contradiction back to the lust of concord, still affirming itself in this uniformity of its courses and its years, blessing itself as that which must return eternally, as becoming that knows no satiety, no ennui, no weariness—this my *Dionysian* world of the eternally self-creating, the eternally self-destroying, this mystery world of the twofold voluptuous delight, this my "beyond good and evil," without goal, unless the joy of the circle is itself a goal; without will, unless a ring feels good will toward itself—do you want a *name* for this world? A *solution* for all its riddles? A *light* for you, too, you best-concealed, strongest, most intrepid, most midnightly men?—*This world is the will to power—and nothing besides!* And you yourselves are also this will to power—and nothing besides! (*Will to Power*, sec. 1067, pp. 549–50; *KSA* 11:610; translation modified)

The anthropomorphic projections here are undeniable. The world *is* Nietzsche—the philosopher Dionysus. Nietzsche's text is full of self-mirrors and self-portraits—Dionysus, Democritus, Heraclitus, Sterne, Stendhal, . . . finally the world itself. The general problem that this self-mirroring poses and other problems of this picture—which Nietzsche himself called "*my* Dionysian world"—should not be overlooked, even given the radically perspectival and perspectivized framework of this vision, this specific mirror. "*Nothing besides!*" cannot be "salvaged" under any conditions. It implies a restricted economy of the will to power, which cannot be compatible with any writing, first of all Nietzsche's own, as "not *originarily subordinate* to the logos and to truth." The metaphor of the "monster," however, positively used, should be seen as an antiphilosophical strategy. It recalls Voltaire's "Un monstre gai vaut mieux/ Qu'un sentimental ennuyeux [A gay monster is worth more/ than a sentimental bore]," to which Nietzsche's refers (*Will to Power*, sec. 91, p. 56; KSA 11:571).

"Monsters" are something that philosophy always turns away from, just as it does from difference, that is, the difference—such as in

Nietzsche—that it cannot appropriate to its controlled play, whether Kantian, Hegelian, Heideggerian, or to its properly philosophical taste, whether by way of consuming or by way of rejecting—"vomiting"—it. Whenever there is too much of it, it always becomes a monstrosity for philosophy, as much of the Nietzschean difference has become for philosophy.[14] But there seems never to be too little of it.

The wholeness of matter, or its view as objective reality independent of a given inscription, can serve to maintain the unity of interpretation and history, as happens to some extent in Marxist discourse. "Matter," as we have seen, no less than Spirit, will have to be deconstructed and reinscribed—reconfigured—in a general economy. That will demand an entirely different logic of "non"-origin, along with a closure of both "origin" and "infinitude." This logic is consistent with much and depends on much in Nietzsche. It is certainly most consistent with and depends on Nietzsche's style of *writing*, on the "logic" of Nietzsche's—plural—style. Nietzsche, on different occasions, offers a powerful critique of the—*metaphysical*—concept of "matter," along with spirit, subject, object, and everything else that "tormented philosophy" (*Of Grammatology*, 19; *De la grammatologie*, 31). Such Nietzschean propositions or positions concerning "the subject" would be impossible, unimaginable in Hegel, as those concerning "matter" would be in Marx. The absence of such critical propositions in Hegel, Marx, or elsewhere makes an enormous difference, even though Nietzsche's propositions on wholeness are not always discountable, either.

One must therefore proceed by way of a mutual deconstruction: deconstructing idealism by using matter, and deconstructing metaphysical materialism—for example, dialectical materialism, the idealism of matter—by using subjectivity. Nietzsche anticipates, prepares, and often engages many such moves: "If we give up the concept 'subject' and 'object,' and then also the concept of 'substance'—and as a consequence also various modifications of it, e.g., 'matter,' 'spirit,' and other hypothetical entities, 'the eternity and immutability of matter,' etc. We have got rid of *materiality*" (*Will to Power*, sec. 552, p. 298; *KSA* 12:384). In *Positions* (65), Derrida cites this note specifically, commenting on deconstruction and, through Bataille, the general economy of "matter." Many other statements Nietzsche made to that effect could be cited, however. Once a radical difference such as *différance* affects all interpretation, there is no guarantee of the unity of matter, either; nor is there the security of dialectic—idealist, as in Hegel, or materialist, as in Marx. There is no machine of history without entropy, which will destroy everything that history creates.

Calculations

Hegel would no doubt have resisted, in the strongest terms, conceiving of *Geist* as a machine, let alone as a monster—and not without reason. One needs an excess of "the machine" in the economy of matter, interpretation, memory, consciousness and the unconscious, theory, history, or politics. But, as against the Hegelian excess conceived in the form of superior, indeed absolute presence, even if as the economy of becoming or—*controlled*—transformations, one must inscribe or relate to a certain "unconscious" excess by way of general economy. Among other things, it means, against Hegel, that the "machine" cannot be exceeded absolutely. A general economy does "exceed" the "machine"—*technology*—but it cannot and does not aim to reduce it absolutely. The indeterminacy of a general economy prohibits anything from being absolutely and once and for all determined as a nonmachine. Nor, conversely, does it allow one to determine, unconditionally and once and for all, any machine as only a machine. As in the related case of logic and formal logic—the logic of the machine, computer logic—absolute excess is not radical enough. Formal logic must be exceeded, but it cannot be exceeded absolutely; the machine, including the machine of logic—the computer—must be exceeded, but it cannot be exceeded absolutely. Contrary to both Hegel and Heidegger, this point would also refer to technology, adding it to the list of things that need to be exceeded but cannot be exceeded or reduced absolutely and that make the *absolute* reduction of difference in presence—a grand dream of philosophy—impossible, except as a dream.

In "The Question Concerning Technology" and accompanying essays, Heidegger advances his famous and much discussed claims concerning a secondary, derivative nature of scientific—in the sense of the modern exact sciences—and technological "thinking" as against the primordial nature of true thinking—thinking on the truth of Being. If scientific and technological thinking is derivative, it also "deviates" in relation to the truthfulness of the truth, the essentiality of the essence, and so forth. It depends and deviates at the same time. In this manner it participates in the concealment and revealing of Being, its sense, its voice, its truth—a process controlled by the highest law of (the truth of) Being. Hence arise the famous pronouncements to the effect that "the essence of science has nothing to do with science," "the essence of technology is nothing technological," and other propositions to that effect—often profoundly *problematic*, even if at times also *profoundly* and interestingly problematic.

As in all other cases, proximity to philosophical thinking is at issue; this is thereby also the closest proximity, or the best proximity-distance, to the truth of Being.[15] This proximity ensures true science (Wissenschaft) or knowledge as opposed to mere *technical* achievement in mathematics and the exact sciences. The latter are not dismissed as such but are depreciated hierarchically in relation to the—*true*—truth. In *What is a Thing?*, his analysis of Kant, Heidegger makes the point most emphatically in the case of modern—experimental and, and *as*, mathematical—physics, from Newton to Bohr and Heisenberg. Heidegger's characterization of the modern scientific project of Newtonian or Galilean, as opposed to Aristotelian, physics is profound, suggesting fundamental connections between science, mathematics, and technology: "Modern science is experimental on the ground of the mathematical project [Die neuzeitliche Wissenschaft ist experimentierend auf Grund des mathematischen Entwurfs]" (*What is a Thing?* 93; *Die Frage nach dem Ding*, 72; translation modified). The assessment of modern scientific *thinking*, to use this term not in, but against Heidegger's sense, however, is neither rigorous nor tenable, specifically as concerns the opposition between technical and nontechnical scientific thinking and in general.

Within his general *program*, from *Of Grammatology* on, and within a very broad conceptual and historical matrix, Derrida relates the question of *technē* to the question of *writing*. But well before he introduced *writing*, Derrida makes the point, or much of his point, in his analysis of Husserl's "The Origin of Geometry." Husserl pursues a scheme analogous to Heidegger's. The origin of geometry is *not* geometry; it is "philosophy" in the general sense of that which thinks on the essentiality of essences, and not all philosophy is truly philosophical in this sense. All other thinking, including that of mathematics and science, may and often does deviate from, or even betray the true —proper, authentic (eigentlich)—thinking; it can only be the effect of the process that makes true thinking possible. As in Heidegger, it simultaneously conceals and reveals the authentic (eigentlich) process of thinking, or Being. What Husserl sees as "the crisis of European science" would then belong to this betrayal of true thinking, a perhaps inevitable betrayal.[16]

This is the process that must be deconstructed, along with all other forms of originary subordination to the meaning and the truth: "This subordination has *come into being* during an epoch whose meaning we must deconstruct" (*Of Grammatology*, 19; *De la grammatologie*, 33). Derrida clearly also plays here both upon Heidegger's Being and Husserl's conception of *epochē* as "phenomenological reduction." The reduction of difference and *writing*, including as *technē*—technology—is part of the history of philosophy and is the condition of the possibility of this history, even though it is *writing*, including as *technē*, that makes this history possible. In simultaneously repeating or parodying and displacing the Heideggerian scheme, philosophy is a concealment—repression—of *writing*, but it also "reveals" it. What is crucial, however, is that, against Heidegger's Being, Hegel's *Geist*, and many other restricted economies or philosophical machines, *writing*, including by virtue of its relation to *technē*—as technique and as technology— is not a superior form of presence, authentic or proper (eigentlich) thinking. Nor is *writing*, or *différance*, or *dissemination*, or any other of Derrida's names a unique or final or finally proper name, including, but not exclusively, by virtue of this multiplicity of names. This possibility of *one*—proper, unique, or final—name would, as we have seen, constitute "Heideggerian *hope*"— the hope characterized by "the quest for the proper word and the unique name" (*Margins*, 27; *Marges,* 29).

"Technological" considerations in general play an important role in (Derrida's) deconstruction, from his introduction to Husserl's *The Origin of Geometry* to *The Post Card* and his most recent texts. Technology has been one of the most persistent themes "after deconstruction" and on the postmodern and postmodernist scene in general, or after postmodernism.[17] In *Of Grammatology* and "Freud and the Scene of Writing," "the liberation of memory," as a radical expansion of exteriority involves an irreducible technological remainder. Derrida's main point, among other things, against Heidegger's critique of technology, is that the technological and the mathematical-technological have always already begun—from "the amoeba and the annelid" (*Of Grammatology*, 84; *De la grammatologie*, 125)— just as writing has always already begun. Both in fact occur in the same movement, introducing the irreducible complication, the "complexification" of the simple, thus offering Derrida a possibility of parallel or joined deconstructive strategies. Derrida's quasi-cybernetic inscriptions in these early texts (1967) might also be seen as set against the background of Heidegger's critique of cybernetics and information theory as an aspect of the epoch of the mathematico-technological forgetting of Being.

The analysis in "Freud and the Scene of Writing" yields similar conclusions concerning both subjectivity and "the question concerning technology." The technological exterior is irreducible in this economy of the efficacity of both the writing machines suggested by Freud's metaphorical models and the general machine of *writing*, and this technological exterior participates in their mutual complicity and determination (*Writing and Difference*, 227–28; *L'Écriture et la différence*, 336–37). Somewhere between matter and the unconscious, between metaphor and technology, between history and play, *writing* becomes possible; and it becomes possible to inscribe, obliquely, some of the more complex effects of this expanded *différance*.

Once *writing*, condemned throughout the history of philosophy as *technē*—an auxiliary technique, becomes irreducible, so does technology. Hence, this perspective generates a very different view of technology—as *writing* programs, hardware and software. Technology—as *writing*—poses a very different question, the question of *writing* or records that come "before" the "originals." Or there emerges a play where all "befores" and "afters" must be re-played, re-inscribed, although, in certain sequences, the classical forms of "origin" will have to be preserved; but in a different type of efficacity and *"for other reasons than hitherto."*

If one recalls that entropy is fundamentally related to information, then profound and fundamental relations emerge between the question of machine as perpetuum mobile, the question of entropy and "record keeping" and thus of *writing*. These *relations* will have to be configured and reconfigured not only or simply by way of metaphoric analogy, but also by way of extremely complex and richly mediated metaphoric fields and clusters. The energy-entropy of *différance* and *writing* both makes all records possible and forbids absolute retention of presence. It thus connects entropy and presence, records and machines. It would therefore imply an irreducible insufficiency—incompleteness—of technology and indeed of any machine, physical or mathematical. (Mathematical machines, as Alan Turing and Kurt Gödel demonstrated, are never sufficient even for mathematics.)

The general economic entropy of *différance* is very different from Heidegger's—restricted—anti-technological economy, suggesting a kind of radical incompleteness "theorem" for both technical-mathematical and ontological-phenomenological knowledge. Difficult but potentially extremely important questions remain to be asked along these lines. Metaphorically and otherwise, they will relate writing and machines, *indeterminability*—a statistical and thus entropic conception—and mathematical undecidability, computer logic and computer memories, including by way of the statistical undecidability of quantum mechanics, which is another powerful and apparently irreducible constraint, and other related matters. These issues are of great importance and may have a powerful role to play in theoretical discussions in modern criticism and theory, specifically but not exclusively by way of offering rich metaphoric models. In great measure, they define modern—or postmodern—thinking and intellectual history.

Against Hegel's protestations, Hegelian logic, above all as the logic of consciousness, becomes helpless against, if not its identification with, at least its very powerful similarity to a machine; and, as was indicated in Chapter 3, in spite of, or because of, being a transcendental, rather formal logic, this logic is finally too much of a machine and not enough *of* the machine, not *formal* enough. Certainly, metaphorically, conceptually, or otherwise, it cannot do without machines. Descartes, Leibniz, Spinoza, Kant, Hegel, Husserl, Heidegger—indeed, philosophy—cannot do without a technical and technological exterior of one kind or another, any more than without metaphor or *writing*. Philosophy can avoid neither, either in its thinking or its writing, even as it seeks other names and concepts—or interiorization, appropriation, or mastery—for this exteriority, such as *Geist*, or sign (Saussure), or Being (Heidegger). This inability to escape technology enables Derrida to maintain that even *thinking* is already—always already—writing, let alone speech, whose value, as opposed to writing, is determined in philosophy by its immediate proximity to thinking. But by virtue of this irreducibility of writing and within the same general economy, Derrida shows the irreducibility of "the machine" in Hegel or anywhere:

> Would it suffice then silently to set some apparatus in place? No. We must still *machinate* its presentation. For example, through the reading proposed here, now, of the following Hegelian statement, whose severe irony belongs, unwittingly, to the very old procedure. . . .
>
> "Calculation [*Rechnen*] being so much an external and therefore mechanical business, it has been possible to construct machines [*Maschinen*] which perform arithmetical operations with complete accuracy. A knowledge of just this one fact about the nature of calculation is sufficient for an appraisal of the idea of making calculation the principal means for educating the mind and stretching it on the rack in order to perfect it as a machine." (*Logic*, 216–17) (*Margins*, 107–8; *Marges*, 126–27)[18]

Hegel's remark also suggests another important aspect of the difference between the human mind and *Geist*—a major issue in Hegel. In this case, however, it would not prevent linking Hegel's *Geist* as well to the machine, the—impossible, unthinkable—"machine that runs by itself." Calculations and mathematical knowledge in general—which, as Hegel never fails to understand, are not the same thing—are too formal; but they might be used for training a philosophical "machine." Again, Descartes might have been the best example in this respect; Hegel could well have had him in mind here. There is also Pascal, a mathematical genius and the inventor of one of the first calculating machines; and then, both Newton and Leibniz.

Leibniz plays a major role in this context, specifically in relation to the question of Chinese writing as a model of formalization of logic and philosophical thinking. The same general economy, and thus the entropy producing the unutilizable excesses of intellectual energy—an irreducible intellectual waste—of which Bataille speaks, may in the end be at issue in these questions. That entropy of excess makes Leibniz' project impossible, too.[19] This unconscious excess, in fact, makes Hegel's critique of Leibniz possible. This critique is at times astute and effective, although it remains inescapably limited, sometimes proving inadequate to Leibniz' project. Hegel's logic, as Derrida shows, has its own problems with Chinese writing and culture, in fact, with the whole Chinese civilization, which, we recall, can never quite make it into the Hegelian World History. Leibniz' "relation" of ideas to writing can in fact be used, up to a point, against Hegel, specifically against privileging phonetic writing. "Chinese culture and writing are reproached simultaneously for their empiricism (naturalism, historicism) and their formalism (mathematizing abstraction)" (*Margins*, 102; *Marges*, 120). A number of other "contradictions" may be added to this list.

Naturally, given the logic of *Geist*, most of these contradictions would not appear to Hegel himself as contradictions at all. To "us," however, much of this logic appears as what Freud calls "kettle logic"—a set of logical or factual inconsistencies, unperceived by the subject but perfectly justified by the "logic"—by the desires and constraints—of the unconscious. Hegel's logic would be problematic even leaving aside his treatment, if such can be the word, of Chinese writing, let alone culture. Certainly, many of the differences between the Occident and Orient that either Leibniz or Hegel wants to claim, cannot be sustained at all. But then at issue is not so much Chinese writing itself, but the model or the set of models which Chinese writing serves and according to which it is *constructed*—positively, as in Leibniz, or critically, as in Hegel—in order to justify the general—that is to say, *restricted*—economy grounding all such models. Various Occidental, most specifically alphabetical, forms of *writing* serve the same function as well. That does not justify the claims made about Chinese writing and culture; nor, in fact, against writing in general. Derrida demonstrates that point with great persuasiveness, both in general and specifically in his analysis of Leibniz and Hegel in *Of Grammatology* and

"The Pit and the Pyramid." The relevant section of *Of Grammatology* has an interesting title in the context of mathematical formalism, "Algebra: Arcanum and Transparence"; and it proceeds historically from Descartes. Derrida's argument relates to both Occidental and "Oriental" writing; for *writing* itself is at issue, particularly within the Western tradition, which would use the various conceptions of Oriental writing against *writing*. In this sense, the criticism that can be used against Leibniz or Hegel cannot apply to Derrida's analysis. These considerations, however, do pose a general question of the determination of the metaphysics of presence *as Western* metaphysics—admittedly a very complex issue.

One could add, via Freud and Harold Bloom, that "the unconscious" behind Hegel's "kettle logic" on mathematical knowledge or, for they are considered next to each other in the Preface to the *Phenomenology*, historical knowledge and Chinese writing, might to a great extent be determined by Leibniz—the father of the question of writing as representation of ideas—along with Descartes, and perhaps Pascal, all brilliant mathematicians as well as brilliant philosophers. Even for thinkers of the stature of Hegel, or Kant, a confrontation with any of these is difficult, when and to the extent it should arise. The configuration itself—of relations between philosophy and mathematics—would have to be extended all the way into the twentieth century, to Bertrand Russell and Wittgenstein, for example, and Husserl and Heidegger, and perhaps Derrida as well, as well as all the way back to Socrates, if not earlier to Anaximander or Thales—the "first" philosopher-scientists.[20] Following Hegel, both Husserl and Heidegger argue against the tradition that sees mathematics, though not as philosophy, as *the* model for philosophy. In this tradition Descartes may again be seen as the central figure. The relations between modern mathematics and science and modern philosophy thus acquire an additional chain that shapes the continuities and breaks between them, or the desire for continuities and breaks, proximities and distances. Like *Geist*, for example, poetry and mathematics are the closest to and the most distant from philosophy.[21]

Newton seems to occupy a somewhat different position in this respect, for he can at least be seen, by a philosopher like Hegel or Kant, as a lesser philosopher than, say, Descartes or Leibniz; but he produces hardly any less anxiety. Even leaving aside the question and the model of differential calculus, uncircumventable throughout Hegel, Hegel's metaphoric and conceptual dependence on Newton's physics is enormous, for example, via such central concepts as force and gravitation.

In *Inner Experience*, which, as we have seen, begins with Kant in parentheses, Bataille, in "Post-Scriptum to the Torment," offers a list of titles, via proper names: God, Descartes, Hegel, Nietzsche. This is quite an inner experience of quite a subject. Should one see it as a post-scriptum, or rather as many supplements, a strange structure that produces that—here torment—to which it is supposed to be added? These are no doubt most tormenting names, which come, furthermore, with a post-scriptum to "Nietzsche," "Digression on Poetry and Marcel Proust." In an inescapable intertextual *connection*, Bataille's post-scriptum also comes by way of post—almost a postcard, *la carte postale*, or if you wish, *Descartes postal*, as it must go by the philosophical post into Derrida's famous text that likewise includes, in relation to Edgar Allan Poe and Lacan, the question of relations among poetry, mathematics, and philosophy. Several of Descartes' own statements on these relations may be suggested as a context or, better, intertext. That Descartes' name is inscribed in Derrida's title is surely too obvious a point to escape Derrida's "consciousness," particularly in view of the discussion in the preceding chapter.

The difference between "formal" and "philosophical" thinking—"formal" and "transcendental" logic—such as in Hegel, Heidegger, Husserl, and many others, cannot be rigorously maintained. In this context, Husserl's whole project may be seen as suspended between—via *Formal and Transcendental Logic*—two of his works and titles, *Philosophy as Rigorous Science* and *The Origin of Geometry*. Derrida in fact refers to both in *Positions* in the context of the question of truth and science, and the question of rigor: "from the point of view of theoretical and scientific, especially mathematical, rigor" (*Positions*, 105 n. 32; *Positions*, 79 n. 23).

The question of theoretical and, or as against, scientific, and again especially mathematical, rigor has been, of course, one of the central issues of modern intellectual history, from Husserl and Heidegger—and in a certain sense again from Nietzsche—to Bataille, Gaston Bachelard, Serres, and others. The question of Freud, Lacan, and psychoanalysis also relates importantly to this thematics. These statements assume, of course, that there is such a thing as rigorously "formal logic" of any kind to begin with. Since Gödel this possibility is an immensely complex, indeed ultimately an undecidable, issue. It is worth recalling here that Gödel's proof itself might be seen as proceeding from Leibniz' idea of mapping all the necessary propositions, all *ideas* in the manner of the hiero*glyphs*—*glyphs* and *graphs*—of Chinese writing, or again, what Leibniz believed Chinese *writing* to be. Gödel, as we have seen, shows that numbers would suffice. Gödel's *results*, however, proved to be unexpected and, along with quantum mechanics, radically transformed the modern intellectual landscape.

The *idea* of mapping has to be mapped as well; one thus encounters the problematics of the levels of logical analysis, and the problematic of the double bind and *writing* as double bind, or the problematic of maps, that was discussed earlier. In fact, one can see the Hegelian system or Hegel's text as a kind of "machine"—a conscious machine—or a *program*, a software—Leibniz' dream—the machine of the philosophical consciousness or all forms of knowledge, from which the configurations, or "plot-lines," of philosophy can be generated, as in a kind of subprogram. It would be similar to Vladimir Propp's *Ur*-tale assembled via the morphology of the folktale, which actually has sources in common with Hegel and Marx, such as Leibniz and Goethe. Any actual folktale can then be generated as a subplot of the *Ur*-tale.[22]

This idea suggests another interesting and important relation between narrative and the text of philosophy. What the developments in modern mathematics and science and modern intellectual history as a whole unquestionably suggest is that such concepts as 'formal' or 'rigorous' must be reconsidered in the first place, although certainly not by way of fully suspending logic in a theoretical argument. Logic can be suspended only as the unconditional ground of argumentation in mathematics and philosophy, or anywhere; but, in one way or another, it also *must* be so suspended on certain occasions.

Connections to mathematical formalism and symbolism are important in Derrida. One of the earliest footnotes in *Of Grammatology* (323 n. 1) relates the question of mathematical symbolism as *writing* to the question of secondary elaboration in Freud's theory of the interpretation of dreams—a crucial juncture for the whole grammatological project as well as much else in Derrida. First of all, mathematical symbolism offers an example of non-phonetic writing, which as non*phonetic* helps to undermine the metaphysics of presence, which, as Derrida shows, is profoundly related to *phonē*. From Socrates to Saussure, logocentrism is always, or almost always, phonocentrism. To a degree this undermining, resulting from his insistence on mathematical writing, does in fact take place in Leibniz, thus creating a deconstructive stratum of his text. In the same movement, however, Leibniz reinstates the *logos*, presence, truth, proximity to thinking, even a closer proximity than that of speech in this case, and thus to the—silent, as it were—voice of God inside one's consciousness—and to conscience. Leibniz, thus, reinstates or rather never gives up everything that is in question in the question of *writing*, according to Derrida.

Derrida's most important treatment of these issues remains his analysis of Husserl, although the related discussion of Leibniz and Hegel concerning formalism remains important, along with more general elaborations on mathematical discourse in "White Mythology." That priority is natural, for the question of philosophical rigor as against mathematical rigor may be seen as defining the whole Husserlian project. It may even be suggested that mathematics or mathematical logic is more rigorous than any other form of logic; but it may not be claimed to be fully, absolutely rigorous, either. Unlike the logic of philosophy, however, perhaps the logic of mathematics *is* rigorous enough for its purpose. In the end, that may have been Husserl's overriding anxiety as a philosopher.

Mathematics, one might observe, encounters some of these problems—the problems of the possibility, or necessity of rigor—when it tries to define and understand, *in full rigor*, its rules and procedures, when it attempts to define what it is—in other words, at its moments of *self-consciousness*. More or less "unself-conscious" mathematicians meanwhile continue their work unperturbed by such considerations, although it is far from inconceivable that these considerations may come into play at a certain point and shake the foundations of mathematics—the very conditions of its possibility—as much as its practice. The suspension of self-consciousness is not absent in the field of philosophy, either: philosophy is not *always* the only, or even the main concern of philosophy. The history of the two fields—of modern exact and natural sciences and philosophy—may be seen as rather different, however. As Hegel grasped, it seems that in this respect it is *more* different, rather than more or less different; this insight may have conditioned many of Hegel's claims on the role of self-consciousness. Thus, clearly and predictably, from a 'short session' on mathematics in the Preface to the *Phenomenology*, the main difference between mathematical and philosophical thinking is the degree of the presence, in every sense conceivable, of self-consciousness both in the process and the truth of thinking. From the opposite pole, the same applies to historical thinking. The self-consciousness of philosophy is defined, in addition, as its consciousness of (the Self-Consciousness of) *Geist*; but that is of less importance at the moment than "self-consciousness" as such.

Hegel positions Science (Wissenschaft), *Geist*'s "philosophy," and thereby human *philosophy*, in juxtaposition, on the one hand, to mathematical knowledge, and on the other, to historical knowledge. Thus mathematical knowledge is formal and abstract—in Hegel, even too formal and too abstract, while historical knowledge is concrete and specific—again, in Hegel, too concrete and too specific. But he also positions philosophy between them, thus giving it—and himself having—the best of both worlds and conserving, through the *Aufhebung*, what is best in both mathematical and historical knowledge. Science (Wissenschaft) exceeds both mathematical and historical knowledge in just about everything: it is less formal, but also in a certain sense more formal, less specific but also more specific, whenever it needs to be either one or the other. Above all, however, it exceeds them in self-consciousness. In the end, nothing would be possible without *Geist*, neither mathematics nor any form of history, just as is the case with Being in Heidegger. This economy then serves to ground both the critique of, and the insistence on reforming, mathematical, scientific, or historical thinking. Nothing is meaningful outside history in Hegel; but outside (self-)consciousness, history is meaningless.

Reflexivity, however, does remain an important, indeed indispensable, configuration that has historically shaped, as fields, much of philosophy, literature, and literary criticism and theory. Reflexivity has also played a crucial role in determining the difference between these fields and mathematics and the natural sciences. In that respect, Hegel's perception retains its force, however much one must question his relative evaluation of the two types of thinking. The point is not that mathematics and the exact sciences are unconcerned with defining themselves or with hosts of other questions—theoretical, cultural, or political—about themselves. In the quest for definition and this questioning, they encounter many of the problems of the foundations of formal logic and mathematics as a whole. Nevertheless, the distribution of these concerns differs in mathematics and the exact sciences, as distinguished from other tasks and problems, from the distribution found in what are commonly termed the human sciences.

This difference of distribution, in fact, seems to be the only difference there is between just about anything. The exact—mathematical—sciences may "succeed," and they often do, without self-consciousness; or rather, successful practice in these fields does not seem to be determined by self-consciousness. Nor do effectiveness and success there appear to depend on a general philosophy or ideology of mathematical knowledge. The practice of both modern philosophy and modern history is a much more complicated case, in part because it is extraordinarily diverse in this respect. Overall, however, philosophy would seem to be characterized by a much greater degree of self-consciousness than are mathematics and the exact sciences.

To a degree, then, Hegel's, Husserl's, or Heidegger's claims concerning the excess of formal, such as mathematical, thinking, would be justified and consistent with these considerations, particularly since their claims often are actually claims against the claims that would deny such an excess. There is always an excess of the formal. If anything, what can be suspended absolutely would apparently be *transcendental* logic, not formal logic—from which transcendental logic can never rigorously distinguish itself. While transcendental logic is a historically important step in this direction, it does not offer enough excess of formal logic, or rather the kind of excess that a general economy can offer here. The central problem remains the claim that, in all these cases, assigns a fundamental, grounding structure to philosophy, theory, knowledge, and thinking and, to a degree, defines the history of these terms themselves. This fundamental, absolute ground may be, and often is, *philosophical* thinking itself or the transcendentals in proximity or complicity with it. The claim of the ground itself, however, is more decisive; it must be deconstructed first, although without in any way reducing the specificity of a given conceptualization or inscription. Indeed, such a deconstruction must always *depend* on this specificity. Although by now this has become a standard deconstructive moment and procedure, it is still powerfully significant. The "machine" of transcendental logic refuses, perhaps must refuse, both machines *and* the unconscious, or matter, and in its radical form, history.

The reconfigured—general economic—unconscious becomes a crucial juncture in this respect, leading to a different configuration, a reconfiguration, of the mathematico-technological and to a very different "question concerning technology." Like all machines, the (pro)claimed antimachine of transcendental logic—Hegel's, Husserl's, Heidegger's, or many others in their mighty shadows—cannot run by itself: either without one or another form of machine—as mathematics or technology—or without one or another form of the unconscious. As Derrida argues in "Tympan," ". . . the text—Hegel's, for example—functions as a writing machine in which a certain number of *typed* and systematically enmeshed propositions (one has to be able to recognize and isolate them) represent the 'conscious intention' of the author as a reader of his 'own' text, in the sense we speak today of a mechanical reader. Here, the lesson of the finite reader called a philosophical author is but one piece, occasionally and incidentally interesting, of the machine" (*Margins*, xi; *Marges*, ii).

Hegel's "thinking" machine cannot run by itself, not without certain un-thinking, or as Bataille calls it with Hegel in mind, un-Knowledge—un-consciousness. Derrida invokes Hegel's machines again in "The Pit and the Pyramid," clearly with Bataille in mind:

If we consider the machine along with the entire system of equivalences just recalled, we may risk the following proposition: what Hegel, the *relevant* interpreter of the entire history of philosophy, *could never think* is a machine that would work. That would work without, to this extent, being governed by an order of reappropriation. Such a functioning would be unthinkable in that it inscribes within itself an effect of pure loss. It would be unthinkable as a nonthought that no thought could *relever*, could constitute as its proper opposite, as *its* other. Doubtless philosophy would see in this a nonfunctioning, a nonwork; and thereby philosophy would miss that which, in such a machine works. By itself. Outside. (*Margins*, 107; *Marges*, 126)

Like every perpetuum mobile, Absolute Knowledge must stop at some point, as its first—and last—book the *Phenomenology* stops; and like every perpetuum mobile, it cannot run by itself. One must waste in order to consume and produce; an economy of gain is always an economy of loss, although losses themselves are not always gains, or gains losses. These *complementary* relations cannot be, in any given form, decided once and for all; in many given cases, they are undecidable. "The general economy," however, "in the first place, makes apparent that excesses of energy are *produced*, and that by definition these excesses cannot be utilized. The excessive energy can only be lost without the slightest aim, consequently without any meaning" (emphasis added). But we can continue to maintain and produce, for a while, the energies, and technologies, of our writing, speech, thinking; and under these irreducibly, but not absolutely, technological conditions, our writing, speech, thinking—and all our technologies—are never fully technical or technological either, but "for other reasons than hitherto." Many things become no longer possible, but at the same time new possibilities arise, some of them possibly "insurmountable possibilities."

Notes

Chapter 1   General Economy

1. Both are of major importance for Jean-François Lyotard in *La Condition postmoderne: Rapport sur le savoir*, translated as *The Postmodern Condition: A Report on Knowledge*, but their role can be easily demonstrated throughout the scene of poststructuralism and modern intellectual history in general.

2. The literature on the issues and their implications for modern science and modern intellectual history is by now enormous. A brief bibliographical survey up to 1985 can be found in Jonathan Powers' *Philosophy and the New Physics*, 189–94. Bohr's two great collections, *Atomic Physics and Human Knowledge* and *Atomic Theory and the Description of Nature*, are, in my view, among the greatest documents, not only of modern science but also of modern intellectual history, indeed all intellectual history. Beyond the works by the founders of quantum mechanics—Einstein, Bohr, Born, Heisenberg, Pauli, and Dirac—including their extremely important correspondence and some classical works, such as Max Jammer's *The Philosophy of Quantum Mechanics*, several recent books may be mentioned here, all of which contain extensive bibliographies: Henry J. Folse, *The Philosophy of Niels Bohr: The Framework of Complementarity*, and Dugald Murdoch, *Niels Bohr's Philosophy of Physics*. For a more technical discussion, see the excellent books by Abraham Pais, *"Subtle is the Lord . . .": The Science and the Life of Albert Einstein*, *Inward Bound: Of Matter and Forces in the Physical World*, and most recently, *Niels Bohr's Times: In Physics, Philosophy, and Polity*.

3. See Folse, *The Philosophy of Niels Bohr*, 168–93.

4. See most specifically the reading of Freud in "Spéculer-Sur 'Freud,'" in *La Carte postale: De Socrate à Freud et au-delà*, translated as "To Speculate—On 'Freud,'" in *The Post Card: From Socrates to Freud and Beyond*.

5. There are, we recall, "less rich" systems to which Gödel's results do not apply.

325

6. Now, in contrast to the earlier stages of this history, such negative possibilities are sometimes seen as necessary and effective, while the constructive possibilities of such radical theories, or general economies, are often still denied.

7. This part of the *Phenomenology*, especially Hegel's dialectic of desire, has played a crucial role in modern intellectual history, and especially in France, from Kojève on, particularly in Bataille and Lacan.

8. Many of Kant's elaborations on the sublime may be cited, however, indicating the richness of Kant's analysis and its relations and proximities to Hegel's analysis, specifically in "Self-consciousness" in the *Phenomenology*.

9. For Lyotard's exploration of the Kantian sublime in political context, see, beyond the better-known works *The Postmodern Condition* and *The Differend*, his *La Faculté de Juger* and a number of essays (particularly secs. 16–20) collected in *The Lyotard Reader*. The issue, however, is addressed throughout Lyotard's writing. The relationships among the aesthetic, the political, and the ideological extend and multiply, and invade each other, proceeding in various directions. Thus, to use de Man's phrase, one must consider a broad spectrum of "aesthetic ideologies." De Man himself pursued various dimensions of such ideologies in his later works on Kant, Schiller, and Hegel. The question is considered, from the Marxist, or a certain Marxist, ideological position, in Terry Eagleton's *Ideology of the Aesthetic*. The issue is indeed of great importance; but it deserves, and demands, a much more rigorous treatment than the one offered by Eagleton on virtually all the figures considered in the book, and particularly Nietzsche.

10. For Nancy's encounter with Kant, see his *Le Discours de la syncope* and *L'Impérative catégorique*, but also his subsequent works expanding the political dimensions of the Kantian and post-Kantian landscape—from Hegel, to Nietzsche, to Heidegger, to the current debates—most recently *L'Expérience de la liberté*.

In general, Kant and the complexities of his text have been the subject of many interesting and productive investigations—most pertinently, for this study, in Deleuze, Lyotard, Derrida, de Man, Nancy, and commentaries on these authors. These and related works have complex intellectual and institutional—political—relations to the classical commentaries on Kant, both Anglo-American and Continental. It is remarkable, however, even astonishing, that the two arguably most representative collections of essays on Kant produced within Anglo-American institutional philosophy, *Essays in Kant's Aesthetics*, edited by Ted Cohen and Paul Guyer, and most recently *The Cambridge Companion to Kant*, edited by Paul Guyer, neither include any of the works representing the massive reengagement of Kant on the French scene, nor, still more remarkably, contain a single reference to these works, most of them preceding the publication of both volumes. Not unpredictably, one finds a similar omission of Heidegger's lifelong encounter with Kant. Paul Guyer's two earlier full-length studies, *Kant and the Claims of Taste* and the more recent *Kant and the Claims of Knowledge* are equally uninformed in this respect. There are obvious, although by no means discountable, questions of institutional and intellectual politics involved here; and it is worth pointing out that many French works at issue are produced by professional philosophers, albeit mostly, almost exclusively, studied in departments other than philosophy in the United States. I shall comment further on this issue more generally later in this chapter. Beyond these political and institutional considerations, both facts—the lack of representation of and particularly the lack of engagement with these authors—represent, in my view, an unfortunate and often detrimental narrowing of intellectual horizons, whether what is at issue is Kant's works themselves or their role in modern intellectual history. But then, of course, thus to go "beyond" the political and the institutional is impossible, although, as will be seen, the problems at issue are never simply reducible to politics, whether institutional or other. It is, conversely, unfortunate that, partly on account of considerations of space, this study cannot engage some of the more traditional commentaries mentioned here, although I must admit that such an engagement could be critical, in part because many such studies often take, in my view, an uncritical attitude toward Kant. In the absence of a sustained engagement, I would, however, be hesitant to insist on this latter claim or any negative assessment. My subject here is primarily the contemporary, and mostly French, poststructuralist landscape; accordingly, in the next chapter, I consider the question of Kant only in the context of the juncture of Bataille and Derrida. In fact, I wish I could give more space to Deleuze's, de Man's, Nancy's, and related works on Kant here. I shall offer a broader engagement of recent literature on Nietzsche, however, crossing institutional boundaries more actively, even though I do recognize that other fields and institutions, such as philosophy (whose field and institutions are, again, not homogeneous), have their own specific forms and norms, theoretical or again political, for conducting research and judging professional work in these fields.

11. This aspect of Saussure's theory was correctly emphasized by Gregory S. Jay in the context of the question of economy and Marx in Derrida in his recent *America the Scrivener: Deconstruction and the Subject of Literary History*. Jay's emphasis is finally too strong, I think, subordinating the play of forces in Saussure to politico-economic thematics and agendas (see 51–54). This approach is consistent with the theoretical and political agenda of Jay's book itself. In general, while arguing against several theoretical and political misconceptions concerning deconstruction and related texts, Jay's study remains well within the limits of restricted economy, specifically in relation to the question of history. While Jay insists on historical locality and diversity, the notion of history itself is not taken critically and is never diversified or problematized with respect to the limitations of the denomination "historical" itself.

12. Derrida explores some of these possibilities in his essay "Fors: The Anglish Words of Nicolas Abraham and Maria Torok," reprinted in *The Wolf Man's Magic Word*. The title is a pun on "force." See Barbara Johnson's remarks in her *Georgia Review* translation (64 n.).

13. Both essays are included in *L'Écriture et la différence*, translated by Alan Bass as *Writing and Difference*. On the economic thematic in Derrida's analysis of Husserl and in Husserl's own text, see John D. Caputo's "The Economy of Signs in

Husserl and Derrida: From Uselessness to Full Employment," in *Deconstruction and Philosophy: The Texts of Jacques Derrida.*

14. Bataille pursues this idea throughout his life, and I shall refer to various related texts as this analysis proceeds. The major text, the one that Bataille himself considered his central theoretical work, is *La Part maudite, La Part maudite précédé de La Notion de dépense*; *The Accursed Share*, vol. 1.

15. The English translation here is taken from *Writing and Difference.*

16. As will be seen, proceeding in the opposite direction, the general economy has a similar relation to Kantian absolute difference, although the configuration is complex, and more than two directions are involved (not all of which are opposite), even in juxtaposing Kant and Hegel by means of classical or restricted economies, let alone in the general economy.

17. Derrida supplies an important footnote to this statement, containing one of his rare references to Sartre, of which this essay contains several. Derrida there speaks of "the weak moments of Bataille's discourse," specifically concerning Heidegger; in this assessment he agrees with Sartre, although he also shows that Sartre's own interpretation of Heidegger is problematic (*Writing and Difference*, 338 n. 42). Derrida develops this critique in "The Ends of Man," in *Margins.*

18. Melville does not discuss Derrida's matrix as a general economy, although he correctly stresses the role of the unconscious and psychoanalysis, which are crucial dimensions of Derrida's text and style and which, in part, lead Derrida from restricted to general economy. Melville also does not consider the economy of multiplicity, plurality, and dissemination as part of the general economy in either Derrida or Bataille; and *dissemination* is not given much, if any, space in his book. His concerns are elsewhere, along the Derrida-de Man axis and a certain program of criticism—of literature, theory, or culture—as what Melville defines as self-criticism. Melville's main emphasis is on the movement of the "a-thesis," particularly as elaborated in Derrida's reading of Freud in *The Post Card*. Important commentary on the a-thesis is found in Philippe Lacoue-Labarthe, *La Fiction du politique: Heidegger, l'art et la politique*; *Heidegger, Art and Politics: The Fiction of the Political*, 8–15. The relations between the economy of the a-thesis and the economy of the thesis are analogous, but not identical, to and are a part of the relationship between the general and the restricted economy. Melville's subtitle, "*On Deconstruction and Modernism*," is significant in this respect, in contrast, for example, to "postmodernism"; it suggests an interesting difference in emphasis, including with respect to radical plurality or *dissemination*, which, as shall be seen below, is crucial to the postmodern. Melville's major theme is the proximity between deconstruction and Clement Greenberg and Stanley Cavell, via Michael Fried, as opposed to the proximity between deconstruction and Nietzsche at issue in the present study. Nietzsche is mentioned by Melville only in passing and usually in conjunction with other authors. Nietzsche, however, is a decisive difference here—perhaps *the* difference between modernism and postmodernism, to the degree that any given factor can play such a role. We must grant, of course, all the necessary complexity

to either term or to divisions and demarcations either suggests. Moreover, the post-modern is related, perhaps irreducibly, to the modern, not unlike the way in which the general economy is related to the restricted economy. In the end, Melville's agenda brings deconstruction closer to de Man than to Derrida, even though Melville correctly stresses several specifically Derridean aspects of deconstruction, such as relations to Bataille and psychoanalysis. At the same time, however, de Man's project, in my view, is also subordinated too much to Melville's "modernist" agenda. More generally, whatever de Man's specific aims or tasks of reading, de Man's writing offers a very interesting case of the complementary interaction of criticism and theory, specifically philosophy. Melville is actually somewhat uneasy with respect to his reappropriation of Derrida via his "modernism/self-criticism" agenda and invokes Derrida's own related warnings (4–5). One would have to be quite uneasy, I would think, about claiming proximity between Derrida, or de Man, and Greenberg or particularly Cavell. At the very least, in this case the differences, which Melville does not really consider, are just as crucial as—I think, more crucial than—the proximities. Within the same agenda, Melville offers some general claims concerning the demarcation of the domains or economies of literature, criticism, deconstruction, and so forth, toward the end of the book (152–54); in my view, these general claims are untenable or, at the very least, insufficiently qualified. Nor do I see them as compatible either with de Man's or Derrida's work. That is not to say that the relations and the proximities between modernism, or various modernisms, and deconstruction, or postmodernism, are not significant. The differences, however, remain decisive and need to be considered.

19. In the case of Mallarmé, for example, where a similar configuration emerges, I would, against Derrida, read Mallarmé as closer to Hegel than to *différance*, in spite of Derrida's claims in "The Double Session."

20. Derrida has a text entitled "Ellipsis" ("L'Ellipse"), a reading of Edmond Jabès that closes *Writing and Difference*. Indeed, like Nietzsche's and Bataille's texts, much of Derrida's text is about, let us say, general "ellipsisity," to which, as we have seen, every general economy must relate.

21. See, for example, Rorty's *Contingency, Irony, and Solidarity* and also *Objectivity, Relativism, and Truth*.

22. See, in particular, his "Introduction," 1–9.

23. Nietzsche's insistence on "philology" may have been one of the sources of de Man's late essays such as "Against Theory" and "The Return to Philology" (in *The Resistance to Theory*). All these are complex, and at times questionable, denominations in de Man. As has been pointed out by the better commentators, however, including some otherwise critical of de Man, he is neither against theory nor even against history, although the latter claim has been advanced commonly enough, and certainly not against the rigor of criticism or, or "as," reading. By now the literature on these issues in de Man is extensive. See, for example, the essays assembled in *Reading de Man Reading*, edited by Lindsay Waters and Wlad Godzich. For an extensive discussion of de Man's essays "resisting theory," see

Peggy Kamuf's *Signature Pieces: On the Institution of Authorship*, 201–27. I think that the problem in de Man may lie elsewhere, namely, in a certain privileging of criticism—"reading"—and a specific type of reading of literary, philosophical, theoretical, or critical texts, including as a prerequisite for theory or history. This agenda characterizes, in particular, his later essays, such as those assembled in *Resistance to Theory*. The question of the role and the possible privileging of literature is more complex; it, too, has been extensively discussed in recent studies, such as in Melville's *Philosophy Beside Itself*. I do not think that de Man privileges literature, as against reading—at least not radically or unconditionally, even though, as in Derrida, "the space of literature," to use Blanchot's phrase, has a specific and interesting role in either case, including in relation to various deconstructive procedures. In de Man, it appears, theory must proceed *necessarily* by way of such a reading; which claim may be seen as problematic. To this claim, Nietzsche's practices of theory and reading offer perhaps the most powerful counterexample. The case is very complex, however; it would demand an analysis of de Man's economy of reading and textuality and the differences in this respect between de Man and Derrida, or de Man and Nietzsche. This analysis cannot be undertaken here; and I would be hesitant to make a strong claim in the absence of such an analysis. De Man's work certainly offers a specific and very interesting case of the complementary economy of reading and theory.

The question of philology in Nietzsche is extensively considered by Eric Blondel in his *Nietzsche, The Body and Culture: Philosophy as a Philological Genealogy*. On the question of reading, see in particular his discussion in Chapter 7, "Nietzsche and Genealogical Philology" (88–93). While massively engaging Nietzsche's text and suggesting many important textual knots and connections, Blondel's treatment of the issue and of Nietzsche's case in general never exceeds the classical limits—the limits of restricted economy.

24. Nietzsche grasped well that the core of ontotheology is the metaphysics of presence, as Derrida argues. See specifically the discussion in *De la grammatologie*, 31–33; *Of Grammatology*, 19–20. I shall discuss this issue in detail in Chapter 4.

25. See again Philippe Lacoue-Labarthe's discussion opening his *Heidegger, Art and Politics* (1–7) and Jean-Luc Nancy's introduction to *Who Comes After the Subject?*.

26. Compare the opening of Derrida's essay on Levinas, "Violence and Metaphysics" (*Writing and Difference*, 79–80). This issue is addressed by Derrida throughout his writings, and I refer to the relevant passages throughout the present study. See, in particular, Derrida's essay "Of an Apocalyptic Tone Recently Adopted in Philosophy," in which he pertinently invokes Kant and his idea of "mystagogues." In this essay and elsewhere, specifically in *Positions*, it is not simply a matter of refusing to take a position on the issue once and for all, but rather, of complicating the positions, the complexity of relations within and between philosophy and its others.

27. Derrida, "The *Retrait* of Metaphor," 14. This essay is published in French as "Le Retrait de la métaphore," in *Psyché: Inventions de l'autre*, 72. See also the remarks in *Margins*, 72.

28. It is not, of course, that Nietzsche's impact in these texts is particularly hidden. At issue are more subtle but powerful influences, which, it can be argued, rival even those of Heidegger.

29. Gary Shapiro's *Nietzschean Narratives* argues for the extraordinary richness of Nietzsche's narrative strategies and styles, as well as Nietzsche's own deep understanding of the operation of narrative or, interactively and I would say complementarily, of history. Shapiro correctly warns against seeing Nietzsche's major ideas as "an antihistorical or antinarrative thought[s]" (10), a question I shall consider more specifically in Chapter 4. The book thereby demonstrates Nietzsche's "most multifarious art of style" [vielfachste Kunst des Stils], here of narrative style. It proceeds closer to Lyotard than Derrida, whose analysis of Nietzsche, however, remains a crucial background. Shapiro's analysis suggests, at least de facto, that Nietzsche's narrative style may be seen as a kind of model for Lyotard's economy of the postmodern as the economy of multinarrative and anti-metanarrative, or anti-grand-narratives, as Lyotard calls them. The point can in fact be amplified by referring, in part against Lyotard, to a general economy and a more broadly plural and complementary style of practice. Shapiro does not consider general economic aspects of Nietzsche's styles. At certain moments he tends, actually, to repress the latter somewhat. Thus, even within the proposed framework of the book, the *narratives* engaging the economies of expenditure would need to be considered in one way or another, along with related, more undecidable narrative configurations, on which I shall comment further in Chapter 3. Some of the dimensions of Bataille's general economic ideas, specifically the significance of expenditure—"squandering"—are addressed, mostly in the context of *Zarathustra*, in Shapiro's more recent *Alcyone: Nietzsche on Gifts, Noise and Women*. The book offers a suggestive analysis, once again illustrating the power and effectiveness of Bataille's ideas. It does not consider the question of general economy as "science"—thus in fact centering on sovereignty. This emphasis is understandable and to a degree justified in view of the book's topic and aims, although it does lead at certain points to overemphasizing the role of expenditure in Nietzschean, and indeed Zarathustrian, economies; and one must, of course, be aware of an immensely complex play—*différance* and complementarity—of differences and proximities between Zarathustra and Nietzsche. In short, this case, too, demands both a general and a complementary economy of analysis.

Nietzschean Narratives, similarly, does not consider various complements of narrative in Nietzsche, such as "play," whether as narrative play or as a complement of narrative. This bracketing is again understandable, given Shapiro's context. Such complementarities, however, particularly with play as one of Nietzsche's key economies, do affect Nietzsche's narrative strategies. Shapiro cogently suggests "Nietzsche's own hermeneutic strategies in the *The Antichrist*" as a specific model of Derrida's reading, via "I have forgotten my umbrella," in *Spurs* "of *all* Nietzsche's writing in its ambiguity and undecidability of meaning and its systematic evasion of contextual explication" (124). Nietzsche employs this strategy throughout, which, I think, is also one of Derrida's points. At stake are much broader interpretive, theoretical, historical, and political models and economies. I would agree with Shapiro's suggestion, or implication, that it is Nietzsche's thinking and "textualization" of the thinking on eternal recurrence—thinking "decenter[ing] the self who thinks it"—that was most revolutionary, rather than "the thought of eternal recurrence" itself: "Yet if the thought of eternal recurrence could not inaugurate a tradition in this way, Nietzsche does at times contemplate a historical watershed, a new definitive marking of time that would be associated with this thought and *his textualization of it*" (37, emphasis added). Thus, one might add, what is most crucial and most revolutionary in Nietzsche's thinking is textualization in general. This thinking might indeed have led Nietzsche to the thought of eternal recurrence—a very complex and in my view not always unproblematic thought in Nietzsche. But, then, Nietzsche has many great thoughts, and one might see several of them as similar watersheds—the Dionysian, the death of God, Zarathustra, *Übermensch*, the will to power. These thoughts, or graphemes, continuously relate to each other, but cannot be synthesized in Hegelian fashion; the general economic interplay so enacted is itself a great watershed.

30. *KSA* gives the chronological arrangement of, among Nietzsche's other notes, the notes assembled in and arranged as *The Will to Power*. The question of this arrangement is a part of a long and well-known debate. The term, as will be seen, is also used elsewhere in Nietzsche, specifically in *Ecce Homo*, 329; *KSA* 6:368. The note at issue itself is one of Nietzsche's magnificent "short sessions," enacting a radical deconstruction of consciousness and knowledge, but also a general economy as, clearly, both the interplay of conservations, or profits, and an expenditure of meaning and value at all levels—theoretical, psychological, cultural, or political.

31. Henry Staten's *Nietzsche's Voice* points out the general significance of the notion and metaphor of economy in Nietzsche. It also considers Nietzsche's own discourse or style as situated at the level of, in Nietzsche's terms "grand" or "great" economy (grosse Ökonomie) (*The Will to Power*, sec. 291), which he sees as "a spendthrift or potlatch economy, what Bataille calls a 'general' economy" (10). Beginning with its initial elaborations, however, the book displaces general economy toward expenditure and misses the complexity of the interplay, or in present terms, the complementary—heterogeneously interactive and interactively heterogeneous—interplay and the plural style demanded by the general economy, whether in Bataille or Derrida, or Nietzsche—the interplay of production, conservation, and expenditure; the general economy as science and the "economy" as a practice of life and style, including science; and so forth—and thus the plurality of Nietzsche's strategies based on this interplay of different economies, which characterizes Nietzsche's "grand economy," a notion that is undoubtedly one of Bataille's major sources. While, as I have indicated, Shapiro's *Alcyone* does not consider some of these issues, particularly the question of Nietzsche's own practice as general economy, the book offers a vastly more rigorous and effective treatment of the question of expenditure in Nietzsche's texts than Staten provides.

Staten defines his approach as "psychodialectic" (1), a term that, while he does avoid speaking of the Hegelian synthesis in Nietzsche, enacts a register that is too oppositional and too dialectical, rather than general economic. In effect, Staten's analysis does not really develop the metaphoric, theoretical, or political possibilities of the economic matrix in Nietzsche, even at the level of restricted economy—the questions of play of forces, or play to begin with, the economy of exchanges, value, and other questions at issue in the present study. In his book, the scope of "economy" is *restricted*, in either sense. What is missing most in the book, however, is the richness of the complementary interplay, and in particular the mutual interpenetration of accumulation, or conservation, and expenditure, and many other pairs and clusters—in short, the general economy in the present sense, first, I suggest, introduced precisely by Nietzsche.

I find many of Staten's claims and analyses problematic in relation to all the major Nietzschean questions, such as the Dionysian, Christianity, and pity and love, on which Staten particularly concentrates. The most problematic, perhaps, is Staten's analysis of *On the Genealogy of Morals* and *ressentiment* in particular. It severely diminishes both the power of Nietzsche's concepts and Nietzsche's style. In particular, concerning masters and slaves, the active and the reactive, and above all *ressentiment*, Nietzsche's nuanced stratifications certainly deserve much more care and attention than Staten gives them. Staten's reading is, I would say, remarkably *literal*. He pays virtually no attention to Nietzsche's own statements concerning the book in his preface, or in his comments on it in *Ecce Homo*. The status of Nietzsche's great fable on the lambs and the birds of prey *as a fable* is not considered, and Nietzsche appears to be assigned an unimaginable naivete at this point of Staten's reading (105-7): ". . . when Nietzsche affirms cruelty, the urge to dominate, acquisitiveness, and so forth, he slides insensibly into a nostalgic naturalism which he erects as a normative model" (105). Even leaving aside a misuse, if not abuse, of Nietzsche's "affirmation"—joyful, but also and even more so tragic, on which more in Chapter 4—and Staten's assigning to Nietzsche a sympathy so unqualified with the birds of prey, to speak of "nostalgic naturalism" or, even more so, of "normative models" of any kind in Nietzsche, is very strange and misleading. Such a view is inattentive to so much in Nietzsche, whatever, or however different from Nietzsche's, one's interpretive, ethical, or political stance may be. Nietzsche offers a powerful critique, in many ways still unsurpassed, of all naturalism and all normativity. While he cannot fully control his own text or interpretive process, for Nietzsche "to forget himself" to such a degree would be simply impossible at any point in his text, and particularly in a very carefully thought through and finished book. Throughout, Staten tends to identify Nietzsche's analysis with his positions and misses the general economic, plural style of Nietzsche's text at the most crucial junctures.

32. Staten comments on the issues (155). The analysis itself, however, is one of the most problematic parts of Staten's book, notably Chapter 8, "Pity and Love," which is partly controlled by the set of ethical and political agendas that

Nietzsche in fact criticizes or "attacks," perhaps most specifically in the *Genealogy* and *The Antichrist*, but in truth throughout his text. That need not mean that all elements of such agendas disappear, but that they operate, as Nietzsche says, "for reasons other than hitherto [aus anderen Gründen, als bisher]" (*KSA* 3:92; *Daybreak*, sec. 103, p. 60). I do not think that "*it is clear* that Dionysus and the Crucified are uncomfortably close *in significance*, and Nietzsche must struggle to drive a wedge between them" (*Nietzsche's Voice*, 147, emphasis added). They may even be closer than Staten suggests—*as the figures interpreted by Nietzsche*—but are also simultaneously more distanced, along very different lines of proximities and distances and with a very different perspectival evaluation than in Staten, and "for reasons other than hitherto." The analysis of these different reasons is most markedly missing in Staten, although the fact that Staten ignores Nietzsche's analysis of Saint Paul, which is central to *The Antichrist*, does pose a problem, irrespective of one's theoretical, ethical, or political position.

The issue is complex, particularly given political *differends* these texts are bound to generate, and it may not have received a necessary or effective treatment as yet. Luce Irigaray's concluding discussion in *Amante marine* (*Marine Lover*, 164–90), offers an extraordinarily interesting treatment of the relationships between Dionysus and Christ in Nietzsche, and of the question of Christianity in the poststructuralist context.

In Robert J. Ackermann's *Nietzsche: A Frenzied Look*, the analysis of the *Genealogy* and the question of morality in Nietzsche (89–105) shares some of the problems, as well as many agendas, with Staten's book, although Ackermann has different priorities with respect to Nietzsche's major themes. See Staten's opening remarks in *Nietzsche's Voice* (1). In particular, and again pertinently to the *Genealogy*, this point concerns the question of pity, Ackermann remarks in concluding his book: "Pity, unlike ressentiment, connotes social bonds that Nietzsche fails to theorize" (167). This statement is hardly correct, particularly in relation to *ressentiment* and ascetic ideals. To be sure, Nietzsche's is a very different set of attitudes and modes of theorizing. With respect to Nietzsche's style and strategies, Ackermann's differentiation between history and general maps of morality particularly misses both Nietzsche's style and argument. See specifically remarks on Nietzsche's discussion in section 13 of "The First Essay" as "hopelessly abstract" (94), in which the word "abstract" is itself rather suspect. It is there that Nietzsche offers the fable on lambs and the birds of prey, followed by a very powerful theoretical discussion on "force," both of which effectively supplement his genealogical—historical, cultural, anthropological—argument. Insofar as the word "abstract" can be used, for example, to connote theory, Nietzsche is indeed at times abstract, necessarily abstract. It may well be that, like almost anything in Zarathustra, with his many deep abysses, the question of pity requires as much theory—"abstraction"—as one can master, and, as Hegel grasped, complementarily, a great deal of history.

33. I refer here, in particular, to the elaborations on death and sacrifice concluding the *Phenomenology*, crucial for both Bataille and Derrida, and possibly also for Nietzsche.

34. At issue in Derrida's reading of Nietzsche in *Spurs* is also, of course, a radical plurality, a *dissemination* of Nietzsche's *writing* or, interactively, *writing* itself in Derrida's sense—all of which demand a general economy. The reception of and attitude toward Derrida's reading of Nietzsche or, again interactively, of his theories has changed somewhat by now. Some of his major points on Nietzsche and in general, however, are rarely fully understood or rigorously argued—for or against—particularly on the institutionally philosophical side of the issues and readings of Nietzsche in this country, proceeding in part from Walter Kaufmann's and Arthur Danto's readings of Nietzsche. The case is different with what can be seen as more deconstructive philosophical approaches, closer to Heidegger and then Derrida, that have emerged more recently. For the moment, I refer to a very different intellectual tradition. Thus, for example, while Ackerman's *Nietzsche: A Frenzied Look* offers a sympathetic view of Nietzsche's theories, strategies, and attitudes, it is far from rendering the plural and general economic character of Nietzsche's writing. Ackerman's analysis of Heidegger and Derrida in chapter 8, "Women," is a standard (mis)understanding and reduction of Derrida's analysis. According to Ackerman, Derrida "in producing an attack on the metaphysics of mastery, produces an open conception of reading that makes the life-enhancing aspect of Nietzsche wither into complete hermeneutical freedom of intepretation" (137), a claim that Derrida, of course, never makes. If anything, "the life-enhancing aspect of Nietzsche" may be seen as beyond, not short of Derrida's multiplicity, although in either case, there is no complete freedom of any kind either presupposed or derived. It is true, of course, that Derrida in *Spurs* "produces no reading of will to power and the Eternal Return" (137), an omission that may even be prudent. One finds similar problems in Tracy B. Strong's reading of Derrida on Nietzsche in "The Deconstruction of the Tradition: Nietzsche and the Greeks," in *Nietzsche and the Rhetoric of Nihilism*, 64–66; or in Maudemarie Clark's commentary on Derrida and de Man in *Nietzsche on Truth and Philosophy*. Even more problematic in this respect is Mark Warren's *Nietzsche and Political Thought*. Such statements as "[Derrida and de Man] accept the popular notion that Nietzsche lacked a theory of truth, that Nietzsche believed all truth claims to be interpretations without foundations" (15), "on Derrida's account all meaning is style," or "Derrida must confuse the world with a text" (182) are indeed "interpretations without foundations," accompanied by a massive confusion in relation to such notions as text, world, and the work of art, in Derrida, de Man, and other poststructuralist authors, whose treatment in Warren is equally problematic, and ultimately, or to begin with, in Nietzsche as well. They are certainly not helpful, whether in reading Nietzsche or in our understanding of various aspects of poststructuralist theories. Both of these, of course, may be critical. But they require a

very different approach, however, and a different form of theoretical analysis and rigor, including with respect to the question of the political. I do not find Warren's analysis rigorous in either its reading of Nietzsche or political theory.

35. For Derrida's views of the recent scene of theory and pseudo-theory in this context, see "Some Statements and Truisms about Neologisms, Newisms, Postisms, Parasitisms, and Other Small Seismisms" (in *The States of "Theory"*).

36. Lyotard may be credited with the introduction of the thematics of the map on the scene—the drama, the landscape, and the map—of postmodernism in *The Postmodern Condition*, via Jorge Luis Borges' text "Del Rigor en la ciencia," which illustrates Gödel's theorem. The preceding or contemporary developments of various "cartographic" economies in Foucault, Deleuze, Guattari, and several other authors have been equally influential, however. The topic enjoyed great prominence in recent discussions, in a variety of fields and contexts, such as in addition to, and in interaction with, postmodernism itself, modern cartography, cognitive or mental maps, and psychogeography. A few recent references reflect this prominence in their very titles—such as Antoine Compagnon, "Mapping the European Mind"; David Harvey, *The Condition of Postmodernity*; Andreas Huyssen, "Mapping the Postmodern"; *After the Future: Postmodern Times and Spaces*, edited by Gary Shapiro; and Edward Soja, *Postmodern Geographies: The Reassertion of Space in Critical Social Theory*—and there have been many more works in various fields. Fredric Jameson addresses these thematics in "Cognitive Mapping," in *Marxism and the Interpretation of Culture*, and in the chapter "Postmodernism, or, the Cultural Logic of Late Capitalism" (originally published in 1984 in *New Left Review* 146 [1984]) in *Postmodernism, or, the Cultural Logic of Late Capitalism*, which I shall discuss further in Chapter 6. "Cartographic" economies are, as I have stated, of major importance in both Foucault and Deleuze. In Deleuze's *Foucault*, Foucault's work of the late, or a middle, period is defined as a project of "new cartography." Related ideas permeate much of Deleuze's work, specifically his collaborations with Guattari, as well as Guattari's own work. Derrida addresses, critically and deconstructively, this thematic in "*Géopsychoanalysis 'and the rest of the world'*," in *Psyché: Inventions de l'autre*. Umberto Eco's recent work engages the thematics of the map as well; see, for example, "Map of the Empire," *The Literary Review* 28 (1985).

37. For his more recent nuancings of the theme of the postmodern, see his "*Réécrire la modernité*," in *L'Inhumain: Causeries sur le temps*.

38. See Meaghan Morris' discussion in "Postmodernity and Lyotard's Sublime."

39. In Gilles Deleuze and Claire Parnet, *Dialogues*, translated by Hugh Tomlinson and Barbara Habberjam as *Dialogues*, Deleuze has a chapter entitled "On the Superiority of Anglo-American Literature."

40. Bataille introduces "the heterogeneous" in "La Structure psychologique du Fascisme," *La Critique sociale* 10, 11 (1933, 1934); *Oeuvres Complètes* 1:339–71; "The Psychological Structure of Fascism," in *Visions of Excess*, edited by Alan Stoekl. Gasché's analysis in the chapter "Beyond Reflection: The Interlacings of

Heterology" in *The Tain of the Mirror* is clearly indebted to Bataille, although Bataille himself surfaces only at the end of the chapter (103) by way of quotation from Derrida's "From Restricted to General Economy." As I shall suggest, this "avoidance" of Bataille may be determined, or overdetermined, by certain agendas of the book. Gasché has written on Bataille previously in *System und Metaphorik in der Philosophie von Georges Bataille*, "L'Almanach hétérologique," and "L'Échange héliocentrique."

41. See his scattered remarks throughout *Dialogues* and, for Deleuze's more extensive analysis, *Spinoza: Philosophie pratique*, translated as *Spinoza: Practical Philosophy*, and *Spinoza et le problème de l' expression*, translated as *Expressionism in Philosophy: Spinoza*.

42. As far as the question of modern science is concerned, Paul Feyerabend's analysis in *Against Method* and related works is another crucial point or trajectory of proximity to Lyotard and Deleuze, in both their positive and their problematic, particularly their utopian, aspects.

43. The title of this section of the chapter is actually an allusion to William James's essay "On Some Hegelisms," in *The Will to Believe*. "On Some Poststructuralisms" may be more precise, although one can also speak here of many "post-Hegelisms."

44. Lyotard juxtaposes the Kant of the third critique, and specifically "The Analytic of the Sublime," to the Kant of the first critique in the context of Heidegger. See, for example, *Peregrinations: Law, Form, Event*, 32. It may be suggested that in the case of, or by way of Habermas, one can see a similar juxtaposition, in Lyotard, between Kant on the sublime and *The Critique of Practical Reason*.

45. See Derrida's remarks on the notion of experience in *Of Grammatology*, 60.

46. This juncture of Kant and Freud is particularly pronounced in Lyotard's *Heidegger et "les juifs,"* translated as *Heidegger and "the jews."*

47. There are, naturally, "earlier modulation[s]" of various Nietzschean themes in Kant and Hegel, as well as other authors. Beyond obvious cases, which Nietzsche often points out himself, such as Hume, Heine, or Stendhal, or some Romantics, German or English, they may be found in some rather anti-Nietzschean authors, even among Nietzsche's great enemies, such as Rousseau, along with Kant and Hegel.

48. See Gasché's discussion in "Deconstruction as Criticism," in *Glyph 6*, 177–215.

49. See Derrida's "Différance" (*Margins*, 6–7) and Lacoue-Labarthe's opening elaborations in *Heidegger, Art and Politics*. Lyotard offers separate, very appealing, remarks on his "style" and "genre" in *The Differend* (xiv), and related remarks are scattered, and relevant practices engaged, throughout his recent works, both specifically in the context of postmodernism and in general. Thus the question of the essay, in the tradition of Montaigne, as a postmodern genre, as opposed to, for example, the fragment, as in *The Athaeneum* (see "What is Postmodernism?" in *The Postmodern Condition*, 81) is of particular interest here, specifically in the con-

text of Nietzsche's style. All these issues, however, belong to the ensemble defined by the question of theoretical style and its relation to the question of philosophy, its language, its text, its institution, and its closure.

50. The conjunction of Heidegger and Freud obviously defines much of Derrida's texts, and not only by way of overt mutual engagements that are persistent. This conjunction may well be one of Lyotard's frames of reference and is an interesting intertext here. But then it is one of the most pronounced features of the French landscape of the modern and postmodern, rivaled only by the conjunction of Marx and Freud, which is an old theme of Lyotard's work, such as in particular the essays collected in *Dérive à partir de Marx et Freud* and *Économie libidinale*. See Geoffrey Bennington's discussion of *Économie libidinale* in *Lyotard*, 10–51.

51. I use this term also in Freud's sense of "pathbreaking," defining the structure and economy of memory, which Derrida considered in "Freud and the Scene of Writing." Here, however, I use the notion particularly in relation to powerful new ("first") impressions, establishing new trajectories and possibilities of thinking, and demanding radical changes in our maps, or possibly the changes that cannot be covered by maps. One cannot avoid here the significance of the sea and "sea" voyage themes in Nietzsche's own writing, specifically in the context of "the question of woman" and thus the question of Nietzsche's style. See, for example, great passages in *Zarathustra* (*Thus Spoke Zarathustra*, 246; *KSA* 4:290), or section 70, "*Die Frauen und ihre Wirkung in die Ferne* [Women and their Effects in the Distance]" of *The Gay Science*, and Derrida's discussion of it in *Spurs*. Another major text to be mentioned in this context of Nietzsche's seas and storms is Luce Irigaray's *Amante marine de Friedrich Nietzsche* (*Marine Lover of Friedrich Nietzsche*). Shapiro pertinently comments on these themes in Nietzsche in the context of Derrida and the question of woman (*Nietzschean Narratives*, 95) and more generally. Shapiro also offers suggestive related elaborations, in the context of the eternal recurrence and *Ecce Homo*, on Nietzsche as a "halcyon figure [Halkyoner]" and the myth of Alcyone (the daughter of Aeolus), whose husband, Ceyx, was drowned on a sea voyage and subsequently transformed into a sea-bird (164–66). These issues are further developed in his *Alcyone*.

52. As will be seen in Chapter 6, Deleuze's work with Guattari, in particular, poses problems in this respect. Guattari, in fact, offers an extremely problematic treatment of the postmodern in "The Postmodern Dead End," although he is more effective on Baudrillard than on Lyotard. But then, Baudrillard, in general, is much more problematic than Lyotard. The figures and postmodernisms and poststructuralisms at issue here have been the subject of many recent discussions, in Habermas, to begin with, or in many studies referred to in the present discussion, or in such studies as Vincent Descombes, *Le Même et L'Autre*, translated as *Modern French Philosophy*; Alan Megill, *Prophets of Extremity: Nietzsche, Heidegger, Foucault, Derrida*; and along Marxist lines, in Perry Anderson, *In the Tracks of Historical Materialism*. While these works survey the landscape(s) that relate, in particular via the question of Hegel and Hegelianism, to the problematic at issue here, they do not rigorously engage it, offering more of an analysis along the lines of tra-

ditional intellectual history. I do find problematic the models of history they engage, especially in the case of Megill's book, even though it does attempt a critique of *some forms* of classical historicism. As part of the same problem, one can point out that most of Megill's working concepts and categories operate in a classical, metaphysical mode, and that the analysis as a whole relies on uncritically used classical models of representing the texts at issue. Megill offers a very limited and often reductive depiction of, in particular, Nietzsche's critique and deconstruction in Derrida, and of analogous forms of disassemblage in Heidegger and Foucault.

53. Benjamin occupies an important place in Derrida's most recent works. On the other hand, the appearance of Adorno's *Negative Dialektik* in 1966, along with Derrida's *La Voix et la Phénomème, De la grammatologie*, and *L'Écriture et la différence* (1967), and Deleuze's *La différence et la répétition* (1968), may be seen as signaling the beginning of the poststructuralist period.

54. The statement concerning "lay[ing] claims to a unique kind of knowledge" is simply absurd, whether one speaks of Heidegger or Derrida or Nietzsche, except, of course, insofar as one finds in these thinkers original and often unique insights and developments of new theories and insofar as they, particularly Nietzsche, have awareness of this novelty. Derrida's project and other related endeavors, and again specifically Heidegger's, have nothing to do with "lay[ing] claims to a unique kind of knowledge." Such a claim is never made or implied by Heidegger, Deleuze, Lyotard, Derrida, or others involved, Hegel in particular. Conversely, "pursu[ing] the rise of the philosophy of the subject," including "back to its pre-Socratic beginnings," may well be a necessary and important part of such a project. Indeed, rigorously undertaken, the latter project makes "pretending to a unique kind of knowledge" rather difficult.

In general, as has been pointed out by many commentators, the rigor of Habermas' treatment remains problematic, at the very least. The statement that "[Nietzsche] proclaims Dionysus a philosopher and himself the last disciple and initiate of this god who does philosophy" (97), in which the general assessment at issue is grounded, is based on his complete disregard, first, of the allegorical or ironic—in whatever sense, including de Man's—fablelike quality of Nietzsche's concluding elaborations in *Beyond Good and Evil*. Nietzsche tells a great many fables throughout his works, including a fair number about Dionysus. Nietzsche's conception of the Dionysian is extremely complex, from *The Birth of Tragedy* to some of Nietzsche's last statements; and Habermas pays no attention to this complexity.

Habermas' discussion of Derrida relies on—in truth, *is*—a discussion of Jonathan Culler's summary of a very limited portion of Derrida's text; neither is it a very accurate discussion of Culler. For Derrida's comments, understandably harsh, see *Limited Inc*, 157–58 n. 9). Specifically, as Derrida points out, Habermas and several other critics, such as John Searle, *consistently*, and much more casually than their opponents, violate what they demand in a scholarly discussion and what, as they claim in a wholesale manner, the poststructuralist writers declared to be abolished. If anything, poststructuralist writings have been characterized by an extraordinary theoretical and textual rigor, however radically they question the classical accounts of theoretical or general articulation, interpretation, or communication—partly, in fact, because of this questioning. Naturally, one can always find examples to the contrary. But it is hardly rigorous, by any set of rules, to judge by such examples, which can be found in any field.

Habermas' analysis of Bataille poses equally severe problems, in my view. Although I would be inclined to be critical concerning Habermas' analysis of Heidegger, Adorno, and Horkheimer, and of Foucault as well, I shall reserve a more definitive assessment since I cannot pursue a more extensive textual discussion of Habermas' lectures and since I do not discuss these authors in detail in the present study.

55. "Heidegger a toujours été pour moi le philosophe essentiel. . . . Tout mon devenir philosophique a été déterminé par ma lecture de Heidegger" ("Le retour de la morale," 40; "Final Interview: Michel Foucault," 8–9). The English translators have used the title appearing on the *cover* but not accompanying the interview itself: "Dernier entretien: Michel Foucault." The interviewers were Gilles Barbedette and André Scala.

56. See Derrida's comment in "From Restricted to General Economy," in *Writing and Difference*, 338 n. 42.

57. One might suggest that, of all the figures at issue, to which one can add Blanchot, and in some measure in juxtaposition to them, Deleuze may be seen as a radically non-Heideggerian philosopher, in part via Marx, Nietzsche, Freud, and Bataille. In this sense, he may be juxtaposed to Derrida, whose text maintains a much closer interactive proximity or proximity-distance between Heidegger and these figures, Marx excepted.

58. Several commentators have commented on these problems in Habermas, particularly in relation to deconstruction. Beyond the authors more customarily associated with deconstruction, one can point out Jonathan Arac's discussion in *Critical Genealogies: Historical Situations for Postmodern Literary Studies*, 281–316. Arac also edited an influential volume *Postmodernism and Politics*. Jay discusses the issue in some detail in *America the Scrivener* (42–48), and while his discussion of Habermas on deconstruction is critical, the proximity of several of Jay's own theoretical positions to Habermas' and his reading of Derrida are in turn problematic. I cannot agree with Jay that "Habermas makes the best case for a fundamental complicity between Heidegger's philosophical principles and his endorsement of National Socialism" (36 n. 10), particularly in the chapter of *The Philosophical Discourse of Modernity* to which Jay refers. Many of Habermas' statements are irresponsible, including those cited by Jay (37–38 n. 11), no matter how much one sympathizes with someone's feelings in this respect. Nor can I agree with Jay's own treatment of the issue, which remains at best an oversimplification. His discussion of philosophical proximity between Heidegger and Habermas is even more problematic. I myself find it problematic to see such a complicity as *fundamental*, specifically to "Heidegger's endorsement of National Socialism." Certainly, this *fundamentality* as *fundamentality* needs a much more complex analysis

than has ever been offered by Habermas. The *complexity* of these relations in Heidegger's text has been explored in several recent works, some of which Jay cites. Beyond Derrida's work on Heidegger, see specifically Lacoue-Labarthe's *Heidegger, Art and Politics*; "Symposium on Heidegger and Nazism," *Critical Inquiry* 15 (Winter 1989); and a special issue of *Diacritics* (Summer 1990).

59. For the most recent encounter, in an interesting conjunction with Levinas, see "'Eating Well,' or the Calculation of the Subject: An Interview with Jacques Derrida," in *Who Comes After the Subject?* 96–119.

60. The relationships between Heidegger and Derrida are considered in Herman Rapaport's *Heidegger and Derrida: Reflections on Time and Language*, which examines these relationships by perusing virtually the totality of Derrida's text—not, however, without some interesting exceptions, such as *Spurs* in particular. The book in fact closes with a cogent critical discussion of Habermas on Derrida (259–64). Rapaport does point out the significance of Heidegger on the French scene, where Derrida's discourse on Heidegger must be situated (110–11). Rapaport rightly resists establishing an unequivocal pattern of development—either continuous or discontinuous—in either case, although it is the later Derrida and the later Heidegger that are crucial to his case. In this sense, Rapaport's comments on Gasché (6) are not without grounds, although Gasché is, I think, correct in stressing the difference between Derrida and Heidegger, whichever of their texts may be at issue. In my view, Rapaport's book suffers from its marginalization, even repression of the distances from Heidegger—such as Nietzsche, or Bataille, and to a lesser degree, Freud—and of non-Heideggerian aspects of Derrida's texts, especially Derrida's *analysis* of "the unconscious" and of general economic dimensions of Derrida's texts—and style, the issue suspended by Rapaport. Perhaps the most curious and most revealing feature of Rapaport's book in this sense is its completely ignoring—forgetting? repressing?—*Spurs: Nietzsche's Styles*—a text no less uncircumventable in Derrida on Heidegger, or on Nietzsche, than "Heidegger's uncircumventable meditation" itself (*Margins*, 22). Unless I am mistaken, *Spurs* (*Éperons*) is mentioned only once in the book, in the general bibliography of Derrida's works (280), interestingly omitting the subtitle: *Les Styles de Nietzsche*. Naturally, it is impossible to take everything into consideration; and the goal is not to reconstitute some wholeness of either Derrida's or Heidegger's text, or a decidable difference between them. But Nietzsche, Freud, Bataille, the feminine, the unconscious, general economy, plural style, or closure, which is not addressed by Rapaport either in Heidegger or in Derrida, are the issues that, in *Spurs* and elsewhere, irreducibly affect the relationships between Derrida and Heidegger, or Blanchot and Levinas, all crucial figures for Rapaport. In this sense, another essay by Derrida on the question of the feminine and the sexual and gender difference, "Choreographies"—also not considered by Rapaport—is of some interest since he comments there on both Heidegger and Levinas. Also of considerable interest in this respect is Derrida's first *Geschlecht* essay on Heidegger, which Rapaport again only mentions (20, 114, 164) in conjunction with the second one, which is discussed extensively in the book. See "Geschlecht: Différence sexuelle, différence

ontologique," in *Psyché*, translated as "*Geschlecht*: Sexual difference, ontological difference"; and "*La Main de Heidegger (Geschlecht II)*," in *Psyché*, translated as "*Geschlecht* II: Heidegger's Hand" in *Deconstruction and Philosophy*, edited by John Sallis.

The Nietzschean margin is also diminished in Gasché's works cited earlier, athough Gasché, once again, draws more sharply the difference between Derrida and Heidegger within the philosophical register in which he operates. On the difference between Heidegger and Derrida, see also Gasché's "Joining the Text: From Heidegger to Derrida," in *The Yale Critics: Deconstruction in America*, and in his *The Tain of the Mirror*. Among the recent books that attempt to engage the Nietzschean-Freudian axis alongside the philosophical register in Derrida is David Farrell Krell's *Of Memory, Reminiscence and Writing: On the Verge*. Krell's analysis, too, proceeds outside the register of general economy, although there are some insubstantial references to Bataille and "Derrida's . . . debt to Bataille" (335 n. 19). The trajectories of the book finally lead, I think, to a reduction—forgetting, or repressing—of the radical unconscious in the economy of memory, of the radical difference of writing in Derrida's sense. Krell does point out, correctly, the role of inhibition in Freudian economies (105–62), which were elegantly and more general economically—and more *economically*—analyzed in Samuel Weber's *The Legend of Freud*, 32–60.

61. The question of Wittgenstein and his differences from and proximities to Heidegger, Derrida, Deleuze, and Lyotard is an important feature of the postmodernist landscape. However much he may be on the *margins* of philosophy, Wittgenstein would remain, in my view, the major *philosophical* margin of the postmodern.

62. The question of general economy is never mentioned in Staten's book, although, as we have seen, it becomes important in his *Nietzsche's Voice*, or, as I have indicated, in Rapaport's. Gasché, as I pointed out, pertinently invokes Bataille on several occasions, although he does not engage general economy. Irene E. Harvey's *Derrida and the Economy of Différance*, while usefully stressing the economic thematics in Derrida, and de facto deriving some general economic implications, similarly to Gasché's book, bypasses the thematics of general economy, which diminishes the effectiveness of the analysis she offers. Stephen Melville's *Philosophy Beside Itself* is somewhat of an exception in this respect, although during the last five years Bataille has acquired a much greater significance in Anglo-American discussions, to a degree as part of the rearticulations, after deconstruction, of the French pre-deconstructive landscape and the resulting repositioning or "re-genealogizing" of Derrida and deconstruction. The number of Bataille's works that has appeared in translation since the mid-1980s is nothing short of remarkable. Julian Pefanis' recent *Heterology and the Postmodern: Bataille, Baudrillard, and Lyotard* positions Bataille as nearly the central figure in his genealogy of the postmodern, offering a reasonably extensive survey of the postmodernist scene. As a reading of Bataille, Pefanis' book, in my view, diminishes the richness of the general economy, displacing the latter too much toward privileging the expendi-

ture—"the destructive *consumption*"—while at the same time relating the latter to "a *positive* economic principle" (29, emphasis added). The book does not sufficiently consider the theoretical stratifications of the general economy in Bataille, perhaps in accord with its more historical or "genealogical," rather than theoretical, goal. For an earlier account of Bataille, see Michèle Richman, *Reading Georges Bataille: Beyond the Gift.* The French debate surrounding Bataille is, of course, a separate and larger issue; and the literature on or related to Bataille is extensive. Virtually every major author has been affected by Bataille, and most have commented on him.

63. One can thus consider specifically the difference between Derrida and Lyotard and, in this context, Lyotard's reliance on Wittgenstein, on the one hand, and Kant, on the other. As we have seen, the issue actually does take a somewhat different shape in *The Differend* from its treatment in *The Postmodern Condition.* See, however, the discussion of Derrida and Lyotard, along different and more philosophical lines, in Gasché's essay "Deconstruction as Criticism." Interestingly, Staten, in *Wittgenstein and Derrida*, does not offer an analysis of language games in Wittgenstein. The phrase itself, I believe, occurs in Staten's books only once (88), by way of quotation from Wittgenstein. Nor does he consider the role of the concept of play in Derrida or, perhaps more importantly, in Nietzsche in *Nietzsche's Voice.* In citing Derrida's passage on the strategic character of his inscription of *différance* in "Différance," Staten abbreviates it so as to exclude the term 'play'—and the economy of the play of chance and necessity—that closes Derrida's paragraph. The repression or suspension of play is everywhere apparent in the book or, in Nietzsche's case, in *Nietzsche's Voice.* The repression of play-game is one of the most customary repressions of philosophy, and is crucial in both Nietzsche and Derrida. Staten does mention Freud occasionally, in the context of deconstructing metaphysics in Freud.

64. There has been a growing literature along these lines of more "philosophical" engagement of and with deconstruction during the last decade. Several recent books and collections of essays may be specifically mentioned here, such as *Deconstruction and Philosophy*, edited by John Sallis; *Derrida and Différance*, edited by David Wood and Robert Bernasconi; *Derrida and Deconstruction*, edited by Hugh J. Silverman; and *Dialogue and Deconstruction: The Gadamer-Derrida Encounter*, edited by Diane P. Michelfelder and Richard E. Palmer; *The Textual Sublime: Deconstruction and its Differences*, edited by Hugh Silverman and Gary E. Aylesworth; *Postmodernism and Continental Philosophy*, edited by Hugh J. Silverman and Donn Welton. One of the most sustained and well-balanced examples of treatment of Derrida, as well as Nietzsche, by way of engaging the philosophical register, but rigorously treating the remainder of the philosophical, is David B. Allison's work, beginning with his translation of and introduction to *Speech and Phenomena.* This development has been accompanied by a rapidly growing literature on Heidegger, in relation to Derrida and deconstruction and more generally, often by the authors represented in the collections just cited. One can mention specifically John D. Caputo's *Radical Hermeneutics: Repetition, Deconstruction and the Hermeneutic Project*;

and several studies by John Sallis, most recently *Echoes: After Heidegger*. Since the mid-1980s or so, there has been an expansion of the philosophical, or philosophically influenced, literature on Nietzsche that is, I think, a partly interactive development; and this literature, too, at times, *but far from always*, engages both Heidegger and deconstruction and other related French authors. I have referred to some of this literature earlier. Other works and collections of essays that may be mentioned in this context are *Why Nietzsche Now?*, edited by Daniel O'Hara, and *Nietzsche's New Seas*, edited by Tracy B. Strong and Michael Allen Gillespie; *Exceedingly Nietzsche: Aspects of Contemporary Nietzsche-Interpretation*, edited by David Farrell Krell and David Wood; David Farrell Krell, *Postponements: Sensuality and Death in Nietzsche*; and John Sallis, *Crossings: Nietzsche and the Space of Tragedy*. Naturally, there has been a longer history of the reception of Nietzsche on the Anglo-American philosophical scene, but nothing comparable to the profusion of the last few years, clearly in great measure in response to the "New French Nietzsche" and poststructuralist developments.

65. As I have indicated, the point may be made in relation to Rapaport's book as well. In Staten's *Wittgenstein and Derrida* the problem is apparent. The textual and theoretical losses in his analysis are particularly unfortunate; in my view, it is a displacement, even a misunderstanding, of Derrida's analysis of temporality, specifically in relation to Heidegger and Husserl. See in particular the preface (19–26), which suspends, even undermines, the deconstructive potential of Derrida's text by suggesting too close a proximity—without simultaneous difference—among Derrida's and Husserl's and Heidegger's, or indeed Hegel's, economy of the temporal.

66. A similar deconstruction is, of course, what Habermas, or John Searle before him, completely misses in Derrida's analysis of J. L. Austin in "Signature Event Context" and related essays, where an analogous economy applies; Derrida indicates the connection to Husserl in the essay itself.

67. I allude to "*Hegel, la mort et le sacrifice*," 23–43.

68. Thus, as was suggested earlier, while Melville's *Philosophy Beside Itself* pertinently considers Bataille's works, it does not rigorously relate Derrida's and Bataille's analysis, either textually or conceptually, in general economic terms. Nor does it fully consider the general economy—whether as the economy of loss or as the economy of multiplicity, particularly in Derrida. The very term 'general economy' is not considered by Melville in relation to Derrida's matrix. Nor is this problematics sufficiently elaborated in Pefanis' book. It is not only and not so much the question of a given term, although the role of the terms themselves cannot be discounted. Thus Steven Shaviro's reading of Bataille in *Passion and Excess: Bataille, Blanchot, and Literary Theory* pursues the question of loss in Bataille without much discussion of general economy as such. As with several other studies discussed earlier, the problem in Shaviro's book is, conversely, a suspension of productive dimensions of the general economy in Bataille. While understandable given the gradient of Shaviro's analysis, this suspension is not justifiable.

69. Conversely, of course, a degree of literary (re)orientation may be found among the institutional philosophers, reflecting the play of proximities and differences and their reconfiguration at issue at the moment. The reconfigurations of the philosophical project and its discursive, institutional, and political margins are also at stake here, perhaps most specifically, but certainly not exclusively in Derrida's enterprise. More specifically in relation to the French scene, compare, again, Lacoue-Labarthe's discussion in *Heidegger, Art and Politics*, and Jean-Luc Nancy's introduction to *Who Comes After the Subject?* These transformations of philosophy, however, do not suspend the differences between attitudes and positions in this respect, for example, in Nietzsche and Derrida, or in the institutional demarcations that continue to operate and exercise their power.

70. As indicated earlier, in addition to, and in interaction with the institutional issues involved, the Yale critics' works, particularly de Man's, together with related developments in literary studies, pose an important theoretical question concerning the interaction and complementarity—the general economy and plural style—of criticism, or in de Man's terms, reading and theory or history. In this case, too, the framework of general economy is extremely effective, although it has hardly been utilized in relevant literature, particularly by de Man. The literature on Yale criticism in general and on de Man in particular is voluminous by now, and the most relevant works and collections are well known. See specifically *The Yale Critics: Deconstruction in America*, edited by Jonathan Arac, Wlad Godzich, and Wallace Martin. Derrida's *Memoires: For Paul de Man* is perhaps the most important, if uneasily situated, text on de Man in this context.

71. This question, too, is rarely addressed, as is quite clear from most of the studies already cited here, to which many others may be added. An exception is Eugenio Donato's "Ending/Closure: On Derrida's Edging of Heidegger." The essay, however, does not address the problematic of closure as posed by this study.

72. As I have said, the unconscious, in the deconstructed field, is a decisive structure of any general economy; and all these questions—the unconscious, the general economy, closure, and plural style are suspended or diminished by Gasché's, Rapaport's, and most other studies.

73. In this context, one can also point out the prominence of Pierre Bourdieu in recent discussions in the field of critical theory, as well as a somewhat more extended history of engagements with Jean Baudrillard's writings.

74. Fredric Jameson, in *The Political Unconscious*, speaks of "mov[ing] from Derrida to Nietzsche" (114). The suggestion itself is interesting both in the very possibility that it posits and in its offering a relatively rare sympathetic view of Nietzsche in a relatively orthodox Marxist text like Jameson's. Nowhere is this suggestion supported, however, by a rigorous theoretical elaboration or textual analysis of either Nietzsche or Derrida. See Jonathan Arac's discussion in *Critical Genealogies*, 263–71. Arac, while sympathetic, is also pertinently critical of Jameson on Nietzsche. He does not consider Nietzsche's case in sufficient detail to enable one to derive more definite implications concerning the relationships between Nietzsche and Marxism—admittedly a difficult issue.

75. See Foucault's remark invoking Nietzsche, Artaud, Bataille, Freud, Hegel, and Marx, in *Les Mots et les choses*; *The Order of Things: An Archeology of the Human Sciences*, 328.

76. Stanley Fish's argument, elaborated at great length in *Doing What Comes Naturally*, that "theory has no consequences" is made possible by this mediation, although the analysis itself is not as rigorous and nuanced as it should have been. One should speak of the *mediation* of consequences; one would need, against both Hegel and Kierkegaard, a general economy of such mediation, accounting, let us say, for the *différance* of consequences. See also Barbara Herrnstein Smith's discussion in the last chapter, "Matter of Consequences," the title possibly alluding to Fish, of *Contingencies of Value: Alternative Perspectives for Critical Theory*, 150–84. See also the discussions in the essays assembled in *Consequences of Theory*, edited by Jonathan Arac and Barbara Johnson, which pursue the question in a variety of recently prominent contexts. While the analyses offered there are concerned with the consequences and implications of theory in contemporary literary and historical studies, however, their theoretical scope is, in fact, somewhat limited. In the context of the Anglo-American scene of criticism and theory, the questions at issue demand an extensive historico-political analysis both of the recent scene and over longer historical intervals.

77. I cannot offer a discussion of all of these studies here. I would suggest, however, that, whether sympathetic or critical or both, with respect to Derrida and deconstruction, or Nietzsche, or Bataille, most recent studies maintaining strong affinities with Marxism theoretically remain restricted economies—a characteristic shared by their many counterparts. I refer specifically to authors and commentators such as Jameson, Jay, Frow, Ryan, and several others.

78. Such studies continue to proliferate. In addition to the works already cited, including extensive literature in France, one can cite Gayatri C. Spivak's many works, in particular, *In Other Worlds: Essays in Cultural Politics*; Samuel Weber, *Institution and Interpretation*; John Frow, *Marxism and Literary History*; Barbara Johnson, *A World of Difference*; Robert Con Davis and Ronald Schleifer, eds., *Rhetoric and Form: Deconstruction at Yale*; Lindsay Waters and Wlad Godzich, eds., *Reading de Man Reading*; Jonathan Arac, ed., *Postmodernism and Politics*; and the special issue "Marx after Derrida," *Diacritics* 15 (Winter 1985). Among earlier works on Marxism and deconstruction, Michael Ryan's *Marxism and Deconstruction: A Critical Articulation* is customarily cited. I find this book problematic, however, both in its theoretical analysis and in its utopian reappropriations of deconstruction.

79. Walter A. Davis' recent *Inwardness and Existence: Subjectivity in/and Hegel, Heidegger, Marx and Freud* would be a characteristic example, as is Jay's *America the Scrivener*. A rigorous application of deconstruction would make the political implications suggested by Jay problematic, in part because they are based on the utopian possibilities of difference and otherness, which on that occasion are seen to imply political responsibility—as "styles of civil disobedience." Similar problems arise with Jay's understanding of play and "theory [as] the space of play" (15), as the latter is in turn related to the opposition of theory and practice—again uncritically

rendered by Jay—in relation to both theory and practice, and the interaction between them (15). In spite of Jay's contention that theory and practice are separate matters, theory, namely deconstruction, here as a theory promoting respect for difference and otherness, is *directly* related to politics (79–81). From this perspective, allying Derrida with such thinkers as Thoreau or Melville, the strategy that controls Jay's book throughout becomes extremely problematic. Davis' book is different in this respect. Via Hegel, Marx, and Freud, and a certain existential thematics, it attempts to pursue an economy of the subject as an alternative to Derrida's matrix. This economy, however, is a restricted economy; as such, it offers no alternative to the Derridean matrix, but indeed reinstates many dimensions of subjectivity deconstructable by standard Derridean techniques.

The list of studies, both articles and books, that analogously reinstate metaphysical subjectivity—qualifications and equivocations, often quite subtle, notwithstanding—would be long. Other recent examples include Paul Smith's *Discerning the Subject* and, along post-Lacanian feminist lines, Judith Butler's *Gender Trouble: Feminism and the Subversion of Identity*.

80. For Derrida's most recent statement on the issue, again see his "'Eating Well,' or the Calculation of the Subject: An Interview with Jacques Derrida," in *Who Comes After the Subject?*

81. See, for example, *Of Grammatology*, 68–69; but many other passages could be cited.

82. Of the latter, Frank Lentricchia's *Criticism and Social Change* has often been cited as a paradigmatic case, which it may well be; but the front of this attack has been and still remains massive, as we have seen earlier in the context of Habermas. A recent example is John M. Ellis' *Against Deconstruction*, where the treatment of this issue is particularly problematic and misleading. At times, however, one has to worry just as much, perhaps more, about one's so-called friends as one's enemies. It would not be difficult to cite overly sympathetic commentators on Derrida, de Man, or on deconstruction in general, whom deconstruction would, or should, rather want to avoid.

83. See, for example, Derrida's powerful critique and deconstruction of Lévi-Strauss in *Of Grammatology* (101–40), where the point is made with great clarity and force.

Chapter 2   The Maze of Taste

1. "My room connects with a decrepit sitting room full of rapidly disintegrating furniture from the beginning of the last century. In the midst of the fracas in the sky I thought I heard the sound of a sneeze. I got up to put out the light; I was naked and I stopped before opening the door . . .

". . . I was sure I was going to find Immanuel Kant waiting for me behind the door. He didn't have the diaphanous face that distinguished him during his lifetime: he had the hirsute mien of a bushy-haired man wearing a three-cornered hat. I opened the door and, to my surprise, found nothing. I was alone; I was naked in the midst of the biggest thunderstorm I had ever heard.

"I said to myself rather softly:

'You're a fool!'

"I turned out the light and went back toward my bed, guiding myself by the duplicitous light of the flashes of lightning" (Georges Bataille, *L'Abbé C*, 134-35; *L'Abbé C.*, *Oeuvres complètes* 3:343; translation modified).

2. The work, of course, is not among the best known, but the passage has been circulated widely enough in modern intellectual history to have been known to Bataille, even if he did not read the book. Specifically, it is cited and discussed by Heidegger in *Being and Time*, 143–44.

3. It is far from self-evident that this closure can be subsumed under the rubric of the Occident, however convenient or comfortable this demarcation might appear. I shall continue throughout this analysis to use the notion of closure in Derrida's sense, although, as Lacoue-Labarthe does in *Heidegger, Art, and Politics*, one can speak of an analogous, but not identical, economy of closure in Heidegger.

4. The latter is also a crucial metaphor for Derrida's view of deconstruction and the closure of metaphysics, specifically in the conclusion of "The Ends of Man" (*Margins of Philosophy*, 135–36), which I shall discuss at the end of this chapter.

5. While one can suggest some proximity to and possibly some influence of Heidegger in Bataille's formulations, I would see them as closer to Derrida than to Heidegger, if, for both Bataille and Derrida, within a certain Heideggerian *closure*.

6. I shall not engage here the question of Derrida's relations to Kant, although it may be more significant than the somewhat sparse attention that it has received in comparison to his relation to Hegel or Heidegger. See, however, Irene Harvey's discussion in *Derrida and the Economy of Différance* (1–22). For her somewhat oversystematizing and, as a result, limiting account of the question of "parergon" in Derrida, see "Derrida, Kant, and the Performance of Parergonality" (in *Derrida and Deconstruction*, 59–76).

7. The term "parerga" first appears in the second edition (1793).

8. See Derrida's discussion in "Signature Event Context" and his subsequent reply to John Searle, "Limited Inc abc...." "Signature Event Context" was originally published in French in 1972 and then in English translation in *Glyph 1* (1976), 172–97. Both essays are reprinted in Jacques Derrida, *Limited Inc.*

9. The translation is modified, and the parentheses at the end of the passage, in the English translation, are removed in accordance with the second edition, which Kant supervised. The German text reads: "*Der Redner* also kündigt ein Geschäft an und führt es so aus, als ob es bloß ein *Spiel* mit Ideen sei, um die Zuschauer zu unterhalten. Der *Dichter* kündigt bloß ein unterhaltendes *Spiel* mit Ideen an, und es kommt doch so viel für den Verstand heraus, als ob er bloß dessen Geschäft zu treiben die Absicht gehabt hätte. Die Verbindung und Harmonie beider Erkenntnisvermögen, der Sinnlichkeit und des Verstandes, die einander

zwar nicht entbehren Konnen, aber doch auch ohne Zwang und wechselseitigen Abbruch sich nicht wohl vereinigen lassen, muß unabsichtlich zu sein, und sich von selbst so zu fügen scheinen; sonst ist es nicht *schöne* Kunst. Daher alles Gesuchte und Peinliche darin vermieden werden muß; denn schöne Kunst muß in doppelter Bedeutung freie Kunst sein: sowohl daß sie nicht, als Lohngeschäft, eine Arbeit sei, deren Größe sich nach einem bestimmten Maßstabe beurteilen, erzwingen oder bezahlen läßt; sondern auch, daß das Gemüt sich zwar beschäftigt, aber dabei doch, ohne auf einen andern Zweck hinauszusehen (unabhängig vom Lohne), befriedigt und erweckt fühlt.

Der Redner gibt also zwar etwas, was er nicht verspricht, nämlich ein unterhaltendes Spiel der Einbildungskraft; aber er bricht auch dem etwas ab, was er verspricht, und was doch sein angekündigtes Geschäft ist, nämlich den Verstand zweckmäßig zu beschäftigen. Der Dichter dagegen verspricht wenig und kündigt ein bloßes Spiel mit Ideen an, leistet aber etwas, was eines Geschäftes würdig ist, nämlich dem Verstande spielend Nahrung zu verschaffen, und seinen Begriffen durch Einbildungskraft Leben zu geben: mithin jener im Grunde weniger, dieser mehr, als er verspricht" (*KdU*, 258–59).

10. See Derrida's analysis in "From Restricted to General Economy" (*Writing and Difference*, 274–75). On *Aufhebung*, see in particular Hegel's remark in the first *Logic* (*Hegel's Science of Logic*, 106–8).

11. It is worth pointing out that, as follows from the analysis given earlier, complementarity in quantum mechanics relates precisely to this type of problem. In fact, in his attempts to extend or generalize, and simultaneously historically to position complementarity as a theoretical matrix, Bohr often invokes this and related analogies. Indeed, more than analogies is at issue here; for the interactive general economy just described is always, necessarily, involved in every process of observation and measurement, and, as opposed to classical physics, is not reducible in obtaining and theorizing any quantum mechanical data.

12. It might in fact be seen as the major theme of Derrida's reading of both Bataille and Kant in "Economimesis."

13. These considerations also pose the question, crucial from Socrates and Plato on, of the relations between philosophy—the work of logic and reason, and the production of concepts—and *mimesis*, in juxtaposition between philosophy and art, specifically literature, and in general.

14. I refer in particular to the first chapter of *Capital*, but, of course, this *economy* must be kept in mind throughout Marx.

15. The control of transformations is understood here in the sense of a corresponding restricted theoretical economy. As shall be seen below, Heidegger, in his later works, defines such an economy of controlled transformations in an arguably encompassing way. As we have seen in Chapter 1, in a number of recent approaches interpretive and historical transformations emerge as directed—toward positive social changes, for example—in the absence of direct political control or enforcement. They proceed in the correct direction under the condition of play, such as—or so it is claimed—that of Derrida's matrix. As a rendition of the Der-

ridean matrix, such a position is *theoretically* and *textually* problematic. Rigorously read, *différance*, to contain Derrida's framework within its most famous rubric, is also a play where differences are, at certain moments, repressed or politically suppressed, leading to various forms of oppression. See, for example, "Différance" (in *Margins*, 17–19). The latter point is obviously even more pronounced in Nietzsche; in Freud, it is, of course, decisive as well.

16. One can see relevant and interesting intimations to that effect, emerging by way of exploring various dimensions of Derrida's matrix, in Marxist or post-Marxist encounters with deconstruction, or deconstructive or post-deconstructive encounters with Marx, in many recent critics and commentators. The subject enjoyed considerable prominence during the last decade; and the list of relevant books and articles is quite long by now, including a fair number of works referred to in this study. As I have indicated earlier, however, the question and the implications of general economy have not been sufficiently addressed in this context, even though Derrida specifically invokes it at a very important point in his discussion of materialism and Marxism in *Positions* (64). This omission has not been beneficial from a theoretical standpoint.

17. Barbara Herrnstein Smith, in *Contingencies of Value,* offers an economy of value that accounts for the globalization of value, along with the relativization of value. Strictly considered, value can never be absolutely *contingent*, or rather any given contingency is always an interplay—a complementarity—of chance and necessity, even though, under certain conditions one encounters radically random configurations.

18. I have considered these issues and the question of the general economy of value, via Nietzsche, Freud, Heidegger, Bataille, and Derrida, in greater detail in "Interpretation, Interminability, Evaluation: From Nietzsche to General Economy," in *Life after Postmodernism*, edited by John Fekete. On Nietzsche and value, see also Shapiro's *Alcyone*, 13–51. Gayatri C. Spivak offers an intriguing, although tentative, approach to the issue from the jointly Marxist and deconstructive perspective in her essay "Scattered Speculations on the Question of Value," in *In Other Worlds: Essays in Cultural Politics*, 154–79. See also her related essay "Speculations on Reading Marx: After Reading Derrida," in *Post-structuralism and the Question of History*, edited by Derek Attridge, Geoff Bennington, and Robert Young. Fredric Jameson comments on the question of value in attempting to relate, in part via Adorno, de Man's *"Allegories of Reading* and the Marxist problematic" in *Postmodernism, or, the Cultural Logic of Late Capitalism*, 237–38. Finally, however, Jameson ends up with Lukács and Antonio Gramsci: "The notion of value, however, usefully ceases to imply and entail any of these issues of error and truth [in Adorno, Derrida, and de Man]: its instances may be judged in other ways (thus both Lukács and Gramsci saw the central purpose of revolution at the very abolition of the law of value), but its abstractions are objective, historical and institutional, and thus they redirect our critique of abstraction in new directions" (237–38). The claim that "the notion of value [as presented by Jameson] ceases to

imply or entail these issues of truth and error" is extremely problematic. Nor does Jameson critically consider the notion of value, referring mostly to Marx's analysis of the concept in *Capital*, which, in fact, makes the claim at issue even more problematic. I do not think that such a notion as "objective abstractions" can redirect "our critique in new directions." Nor can it cease to imply or detail the notion of error and truth, in particular, of truth—the truth of matter, the truth of history, the truth of capital, the truth of truth.

There has been, of course, a fair amount of literature, dealing more specifically with the question of literary value, in a variety of contexts, including Marxism or socially oriented criticism and theory, most recently Barbara Herrnstein Smith's *Contingencies of Value* (see Chapter 1, n. 77). See also John Fekete, "Introductory Notes for a Postmodern Value Agenda," in *Life After Postmodernism*. Specifically in the context of Kant and in relation to the general problematic at issue in the moment, one must also refer to Pierre Bourdieu's many important and influential studies and Jean Baudrillard's works. Baudrillard's analysis is marked by a decisive connection to Bataille but never exceeds the limits of restricted economy. While Bourdieu's analysis is problematic in this and several other respects, it is much more effective than Baudrillard's.

The question of "value and deconstruction" is addressed by Gregory Jay in the first chapter of *America the Scrivener* (31–80). Although Jay indicates some of the implications of Derrida's matrix for the question of value, his analysis does not approach the radical implications of the general economy for the problematic of value. Nor does Jay's discussion of Heidegger's critique of Nietzsche's analysis of value pursue the radical implications of Nietzsche's and Derrida's positions. Jay mentions only "On Truth and Falsity" and *The Birth of Tragedy*—two early texts. Also, while the book contains a chapter on Freud, neither the question of the unconscious nor relevant dimensions of Nietzsche's thought are considered in the context of the question of value. Jay does not really address the question of general economy, most specifically in Bataille, which is a necessary connection in the context of relationships between political economy and deconstruction. The question of loss and resulting radical conceptions of difference (*différance*) and multiplicity (*dissemination*) are not considered, while the separation between the restricted and general economy is all too rigidly maintained, as illustrated by Jay's remark in this regard on page 54, but sustained throughout. The economy of value in Jay is in fact a restricted economy, even classical political economy. Jay does mention the general economy in Derrida, largely bypassing—even repressing, or avoiding—Bataille, mostly in order to suggest "that Marx plays an important part in Derrida" (55). This discussion appears to be part of the general theoretico-political agenda of Jay's study, resulting, among other things, in a displacement of Bataille, Nietzsche, and Derrida. The strategy becomes a classical move from Nietzsche and Freud toward Marx, and along the way a displacement of deconstruction into a restricted economy subordinated to the Marxist—or a certain Marxist—political and ethical agenda.

351

19. Marx refers to thought-value in this way, or, to be more precise, to Hegel's logic which defines it, in pointing out its economic nature, via Adam Smith (*The Marx-Engels Reader*, 110).

20. See Smith's analysis of the exchange and marketplace framework in *Contingencies of Value* and, to a degree, in *On the Margins of Discourse*.

21. This interplay is engaged throughout Bataille and specifically throughout *The Accursed Share*. See, for example, his most *interesting* "thermodynamical" remarks on "interest" in relation to "loss" and "excess energy" (30–31), although once again, they *gain* by being placed in the book's broader conceptual and terminological network.

22. The French reads: "Sans doute, être négocié n'est pas, pour un sujet humain, une situation rare, contrairement au verbiage qui concerne la dignité humaine, voire les Droits de l'Homme. Chacun, à tout instant et à tous les niveaux, est négociable, puisque ce que nous livre toute appréhension un peu sérieuse de la structure sociale est l'échange."

23. One might speak of the instances in which the metaphysics of proximity, and by implication of consumption, reemerges in their texts.

24. The full sentence reads: "Eben dadurch wird aber das ästhetische Urteil selbst subjektiv-zweckmäßig für die Vernunft, als Quell der Ideen, d.i. einer solchen intellektuellen Zusammenfassung, für die alle ästhetische klein ist; und der Gegenstand wird als erhaben mit einer Lust aufgenommen, die nur vermittelst einer Unlust möglich ist" (*KdU*, 184).

25. The full sentence thus reads: "Allein es sind auch namhafte Unterschiede zwischen beiden in die Augen fallend. Das Schöne der Natur betrifft die Form des Gegenstandes, die in der Begrenzung besteht; das Erhabene ist dagegen auch an einem formlosen Gegenstande zu finden, sofern *Unbegrenztheit* an ihm, oder durch dessen Veranlassung, vorgestellt und doch Totalität derselben hinzugedacht wird" (*KdU*, 165).

26. On the significance of the sublime and Kant in *The Birth of Tragedy*, see John Sallis, *Crossings: Nietzsche and the Space of Tragedy*, 91–101.

27. See, in addition to the texts cited earlier, Lyotard's remarks in *Peregrinations: Law, Form, Event* (32) and the discussion throughout the lectures. The point can be made, however, with respect to most of his recent and many earlier works. It is interesting that, while the question of narrative and of the deconstruction of metanarratives is central to many of Lyotard's works, he does not discuss the implications of Kant's analysis, specifically of the sublime, for the question of narrative. For an extended discussion of Kant and narrative see Claudia J. Brodsky, *The Imposition of Form: Studies in Narrative Representation and Knowledge*, particularly Chapter 2 (21–87).

28. See in particular section 27, in which Kant considers the interaction of pleasure and pain, or unpleasure (Unlust).

29. Importantly, the question of the body is also addressed by Kant in this part of the book in his analysis of humor and gratification ("Remark," 175–81). While

remaining within a restricted economy, governed by consumption throughout, the concluding sections of "The Analytic of the Sublime" and "Dialectic of the Aesthetical Judgement" offer powerful possibilities of problematizing the restricted economy of taste.

30. See Derrida's discussion of "The Colossal" in *The Truth in Painting* (119–48).

31. See, for example, Heidegger's remarks in "What is Metaphysics?" in *Existence and Being* (360–61) and in *Wegmarken* (107).

32. De Man does not comment on self-reflexivity in his discussion of the *Aesthetics* in "Hegel and the Sublime," in *Displacement*, edited by Mark Krupnick. This absence is perhaps understandable, given de Man's topic and contexts there. In general, however, while self-consciousness itself has been a very prominent issue in deconstruction, the question of self-consciousness in Hegel receives little comment in either Derrida or de Man. The reason may be that the question is too central, or not *marginal* enough for Hegel, as opposed to things that hide in and invade from the margins.

33. On these issues, see Philippe Lacoue-Labarthe and Jean-Luc Nancy, *The Literary Absolute: The Theory of Literature in German Romanticism*. These topics may also be related to Mikhail Bakhtin's writings, specifically in the context of Hegel— a major confrontation for Bakhtin, from his earliest writing on—and Romanticism. Bakhtin juxtaposes both, as *monological* theory and discourse, to the *dialogical* theory and art of the novel, most specifically Dostoevsky's art. The juxtaposition is perhaps not as successful as Bakhtin wants it to be or thinks it is.

34. This theme is central in *Inner Experience*, *Guilty*, and *Sur Nietzsche*—"la somme athéologique," or "anti-onto-théologique."

35. Marx's personal history and the history of his "discovery" and encounter with Hegel are interesting in this respect. Young Marx, describing his initial encounter in the letter to his father, first compares Hegel's style to "grotesque craggy melody." Then, however, he moves from poetry to writing a philosophical *dialogue* on "the *necessary* continuation of philosophy," as he discovers the "*last* proposition" of "[Hegel's] philosophical-dialectical account of divinity" (on the divinity "as *history*") to be "the *beginning* of the Hegelian system" (*The Marx-Engels Reader*, 7–8, emphasis added).

36. In Hegel, Absolute Knowledge is never quite attained. I refer here to the *Phenomenology*, but the economy itself can be adjusted without major difference in relation to Hegel's later works, including the *Encyclopedia* and the *Aesthetics*.

37. That economy can in turn be related to Heidegger's notion of gift (Gabe), crucial in his later works and in recent discussions of Heidegger. The juxtaposition of Bataille and Heidegger along these lines is an interesting and important issue in its own right, but it cannot be considered here.

38. De Sade and Nietzsche are notable exceptions, of course, in the history of the issues themselves; but their texts operate precisely *against*, even more than on the margins of, philosophy. One of Bataille's life projects is tracing different

economies of expenditure in the history of art, anthropological history of different cultures, or indeed animal life, and even in the economy of matter itself, that philosophy has not accounted for and cannot account for.

39. See his frequently cited remarks in *Limited Inc* (100). I shall consider the question of literature and revolution in Chapter 4.

40. This relation, too, is simultaneously that of an infinitesimal proximity and a radical difference—a kind of *différance*. See *Glas*, 124–32.

41. In *The Truth in Painting* (1978), Bataille appears only marginally in the context of Van Gogh (265). In general, as I indicated, in Derrida's later work, the thematics of general economy recedes into the background, giving space to a more Heideggerian approach, although, again, it is not Heidegger's. *The Truth in Painting* may even be seen, to a degree, as one of the transitions from "Nietzsche" and "Bataille" to "Heidegger" in Derrida, although parts of the book were developed as early as 1972, and "Economimesis" is a later essay.

42. See in particular a very important remark in the Introduction on "the marked pleasure in the comprehensibility of nature and in the unity of its division into genera and species" (24)—a nonaesthetic pleasure, the pleasure of conceptualization.

43. See Derrida's discussion in "From Restricted to General Economy" (*Writing and Difference*, 264–69).

44. I shall consider Nietzsche's plural style and the diversity of his discursive practices in detail in Chapter 4.

45. Derrida's discussion of Nietzsche's styles in *Spurs* several years later did not change Derrida's positions on the questions at issue here.

46. I shall consider the question of architecture and its metaphors in Nietzsche, Bataille, and Derrida in Chapter 5.

47. Here a certain shift in Derrida's "positions" in later texts becomes interesting. See, for example, his remarks on deconstruction made in 1983 in *Derrida and Différance*, edited by David Wood and Robert Bernasconi (1–2), as compared with the original text (1968) and other relevant elaborations throughout earlier texts. Indeed, in contrast to his practice in his earlier works, specifically *Of Grammatology*, in his later works, such as *Of Spirit: Heidegger and the Question* (*De l'esprit: Heidegger et la question*), Derrida uses the term 'deconstruction' to translate *Destruktion* (16), and the whole Heideggerian program of *Destruktion* is now seen under the rubric of deconstruction. Heidegger's other term is *Abbau*. It may be in this sense even closer to de-construction, although it is often translated as 'dismantlement' and as such may again be juxtaposed to deconstruction. On these issues see again Herman Rapaport, *Heidegger and Derrida: Reflections on Time and Language*, and also Rodolphe Gasché's discussion of *Abbau*, *Destruktion*, and deconstruction in Husserl, Heidegger, and Derrida in *The Tain of the Mirror* (109–20, and in much of the remainder of the book). Similar considerations may be invoked in relation to the question of the closure of metaphysics, which I shall consider in more detail below. See again Lacoue-Labarthe's discussion on both subjects (*Heidegger, Art and Politics*, 3–10). Derrida continues to maintain a measure

of difference between Derrida's deconstruction and Heideggerian "uncircumventable meditation" (*Margins*, 22), in the early or later Heidegger. In Derrida's later works, however, especially those on Heidegger, the difference from Heidegger becomes at times almost nonexistent. See in particular the closing discussion in *Of Spirit*. That "infinitesimal proximity" does not yet exclude a "radical difference"; indeed, according to Derrida, in relation specifically to Heidegger and Hegel, and deconstruction, both must be maintained simultaneously. The question, therefore, may become whether this difference is finally radical enough, suggesting that perhaps a more Nietzschean program is necessary. But then, necessary for what, and for whom? I shall address these questions in more detail in Chapter 4 in the context of the question of closure.

48. The style of the feminist encounters with Nietzsche is itself one of the most interesting manifestations of the radical plurality of style at issue, both, to distinguish them provisionally, "within" such texts as Irigaray's *Marine Lover* and in relation to the plurality of practice as just discussed.

Chapter 3   Rich and Strange

1. I am grateful to Ralph Rosen for retranslating this passage for me.

2. See, for example, Derrida's remarks in "To Speculate—On 'Freud'" (in *The Post Card*, 287–90).

3. This and related propositions in "Différance" reveal, or perhaps conceal, a rather close proximity to Lacan's propositions on the unconscious, specifically in *The Four Fundamental Concepts of Psycho-Analysis*, thus making Lacan a name conspicuous by its absence in "Différance."

4. Bataille's discussion of Proust in *Inner Experience* is particularly relevant, in the context of temporality or narrative. Bataille is not strictly concerned with, and devotes a very limited space to, narrative thematics. Bataille's reading may even be seen as illustrating primarily that, as the general economy of "inner experience" would demand, a general economy of narrative—or by implication, of history—cannot be restricted to narrative or history alone, even if one takes into account undecidable narratives, or the narratives of loss. The relation to "the unknown" forms a kind of decentered focus, or unfocused center, of Bataille's discussion of Proust, particularly in relation to the question of temporality. A "loss," inscribed in the process, enacts a kind of general economic "unconscious" or *différance* of narrative that itself is not narrative or anything else—no single thing of any kind, not even "nothing," and by the same token, is not in itself and by itself. Thereby this general economy demands multiple complements of narrative and complementary clusters that are not narrative. The question of narrative, however, in relation to Proust's major themes and his textual strategies, is essential to Bataille's discussion, especially since the question of temporality permeates Bataille's elaborations, not to mention Proust's text itself. The latter is is many ways the founding text of modern narratology, beginning, let us say, with Gérard Genette, although

many other genealogies and narratives of narratology could be engaged. Proust's text, however, relates to a long and well-known sequence of narratologists and narratologies or antinarratologies—modern, postmodern, poststructuralist, Freudian, Lacanian, and still others. Perhaps most pertinent in the present context are de Man's readings of Proust in *Allegories of Reading: Figural Language in Rousseau, Nietzsche, Rilke, and Proust* and Barthes' many direct and indirect encounters with Proust. It may well be that Barthes' *La Chambre claire (Camera Lucida)* is an essential text in this respect, and is most relevant to the present discussion as a whole, particularly Barthes' understanding of the relationships between the temporal and the real, to use this term in its Lacanian or post-Lacanian sense. See also Michael Riffaterre's discussion of Proust's textual consciousness and the unconscious in the chapter "The Unconscious of Fiction" in *Fictional Truth* (84–111). Claudia Brodsky's *The Imposition of Form: Studies in Narrative Representation and Knowledge* offers an interesting placement of Proust in a Kantian context.

5. Stendhal may already have sensed this radical complexity of temporal displacements and deferrals; and one can read Proust's text, via Harold Bloom, as the antithetical displacement of Stendhal's rhetoric of temporality—and historicity. The latter, as de Man aptly points out, is both allegorical and ironic at once, finally proving to be "the allegory of irony" ("The Rhetoric of Temporality," in *Blindness and Insight*, 228). De Man concludes the essay on that phrase, via "Schlegel's definition of irony as a "permanent parabasis" (228); and Schlegel's definition, extended—"slightly"—by de Man to allegory, also closes *Allegories of Reading* (301). One can risk an assertion that Stendhal's temporality and historicity—and narrativity—and his epistemology, particularly in the *Chartreuse de Parme*, is neither Hegelian nor Kantian. One may be tempted to think of this giant shadow, Hölderlin, over the *history* at issue, after Hegel and up to Heidegger, or even Derrida. As many "readings of de Man's readings" indicate, including by Derrida, Hölderlin is arguably the single most important force behind all de Man's thinking on temporality. Via Hölderlin or otherwise, at issue is the possibility of a certain antidialectical (anti)temporality. It brings us close to the general economic temporality at issue at the moment, although what is at stake may be a still different and possibly more radical conception.

6. Compare also Derrida's remarks in *Of Grammatology* (93).

7. This radical *dissemination* also conditions the difference between Derridean and Heideggerian placing of concepts under erasure. Placing "Being" under erasure in *The Question of Being*, in the name of a still higher command, does not sufficiently transform the economy at issue and does not make it into a general economy. In relation to Derrida's erasure, see Spivak's discussion in "Translator's Preface" (*Of Grammatology*, xiii–xx). Nietzsche's destruction of the philosophical concepts and systems of concepts is more radical but by no means absolute. I shall consider this difference more specifically in Chapter 4. As I have indicated, several recent studies, and to a degree Derrida's own texts, suggest a closer proximity of some of Heidegger's elaborations to Derrida. Once again, I do not think that, at any point of Heidegger's text, the difference between Heidegger and the general

economy, whether as found in Nietzsche, Bataille, or Derrida, may be fully reduced. Whether in his earlier or in his later works, even when the proximities become infinitesimal, the differences remain radical.

8. In speaking of Shakespeare as "the Hitchcock of the Renaissance," I refer both to the cultural economy within which Shakespeare functions as a text and to the multiple—rich and strange—conjunction of the popular or mass cultural and the high cultural appeal—the conjunction that in turn problematizes the possibility of all distinctions of that type. I reverse here Tom Cohen's formulation in "Hyperscript: Hitchcock's *Secret Agent* and the Death of (Mr.) Memory," where he speaks of Hitchcock as "almost the postmodern Shakespeare" on partially similar grounds. Proceeding along more Nietzschean and de Manian lines, Cohen's essay offers an interesting and effective non-Lacanian reading of Hitchcock, although, in my view, as Cohen explores Hitchcock's deconstruction of the visual, he in turn diminishes the deconstructive potential of Hitchcock's visual economy. In my view, Hitchcock's film-writing enacts a more complementary productive-deconstructive economy along all lines involved.

9. The prominence of film studies in recent feminist and gender criticism and theory is of considerable interest here, and many of these works specifically address Hitchcock's films.

The work of such critics as Laura Mulvey, Tania Modleski, Kaja Silverman, and Teresa de Lauretis in the context of feminist studies, and of many other recent authors, suggests the significance of the interactions between various narrative and nonnarrative economies of cinematic production, reception, and criticism and theory. To extend Bataille's general insight to the question of gender, the gender economy of film, specifically as political economy, may perhaps be understood only in relation to its general economy. More generally, the economy of gender demands a general economy. A more limited point at the moment is that cinema tells us something about any economy of narrative as demanding a general economy and, thereby, multiple complements of narrative in order to account for narratives and the concept, or nonconcept of narrative. Both the gender economy of film and the general economy of film make the case more powerfully by introducing stratifications which, it appears, cannot otherwise be accounted for.

Much of the recent work in film theory proceed via Lacan, most recently in Slavoj Žižek's work, again with Hitchcock as the central case. Žižek's work has played a prominent role in recent discussions and debates in film studies, Lacanian studies, and gender studies. Although I cannot discuss the issue here, the theoretical economy offered by Žižek is, in my view, a restricted economy. In fact, I find his reading of Lacan, and even more so of Hitchcock, too restricted (in either sense). The problem particularly concerns the Lacanian register of the Real, which is central for Žižek. While I agree that the question of the Real in Lacan may indeed hold crucial, perhaps central significance, I would tend to read the Lacanian Real as closer to Derrida, particularly in Lacan's later works, pre-Derridean or post-Derridean. In his approaches to the Real, Lacan may well come the closest to a general economy, although perhaps never quite reaching it.

The literature on these issues is very extensive. For an engaging recent commentary of Lacanian and post-Lacanian film theory, see Craig Saper, "A Nervous Theory: The Troubling Gaze of Psychoanalysis in Media Studies." For a more Derridean approach see Peter Brunette and Davis Wills, *Screen/Play: Derrida and Film Theory*.

10. On expansions of the narrative and narratological horizon in this sense, see Gerald Prince, "Narrative Pragmatics, Message, and Point." His earlier *Narratology: The Form and the Function of the Narrative* offers an open-minded account and exploration of the "logic" of narrative, that, even in some of its most classical aspects, is far from being exhausted. See also the discussion of narrative in Jonathan Culler's *The Pursuit of Signs* and Wallace Martin's later *Recent Theories of Narrative*. There have been other, equally important developments during the last decade or so, leading to productive contributions to the question of narrative. Didier Coste's recent *Narrative as Communication* offers a comprehensive "neostructuralist" matrix of narrative as communication, to borrow—and somewhat displace—a term from Manfred Frank. The title already suggests the rubric "neostructuralist" rather than poststructuralist; for while the book is clearly written in the wake of poststructuralism, its roots and agendas have a much closer proximity to structuralist than to poststructuralist developments, specifically those at issue here—via Nietzsche, Bataille, and Derrida. This statement is not offered as an evaluative assessment, especially given the great effectiveness, even now, of the work of such structuralist or neostructuralist authors as Barthes, or even earlier, Roman Jakobson. The book has a suggestive chapter, "Narrative Economy: A Dissident Approach to Logic and Necessity" (239–51), relevant to the main themes of the present study, in which "general economy" is invoked, without mentioning Bataille, however (241), although Coste does not develop the radical, general economic implications of these ideas. See also Wlad Godzich's foreword to *Narrative as Communication*, "The Time Machine," particularly his remarks on temporality and perspectivism (xv–xvi).

11. I do not mean to imply etymological connections, but rather alliterative ones. *Rhythmos* derives etymologically from *rhein*, 'to flow'—a conception not unrelated to the whole problematics of (the continuum) of presence. It is worth pointing out at this juncture, however, that "musicological" thematics play an interesting and important role in Derrida's analysis and deconstruction of linearity. Throughout the history of metaphysics, linearity has always been associated with sound; it has always been a "phono-logical" linearity and linearization—that is, a repression of difference and multiplicity—for example, that of writing. Derrida specifically refers to Jakobson's critique of Saussure in the context of musical structures (*Of Grammatology*, 72). This problematic is then related by Derrida to Rousseau's musicological investigations, and, along different lines, to the question of rhythms and pleasure in "To Speculate—on 'Freud'" (in *The Post Card*).

12. These considerations of Derrida's most widely known texts are by now familiar. On writing as drawing lines, see Derrida's analysis of Lévi-Strauss in *Of*

Grammatology (101–40). Both Derrida and Lévi-Strauss also offer an analysis of children's games, on which I shall comment later.

13. The essays by Derrida on Blanchot's fiction to which I refer are "The Law of Genre," "Living On: Border Lines," and "Title (to be specified)." Derrida's writings on Blanchot are now assembled in *Parages*.

14. See Derrida's "Signature Event Context" in *Margins*. Actually, the essay ineluctably engages narratological problematics as well, once the question of "event" is at issue. There Derrida's specific example is the "event"—and the law, and perhaps the genre—of "signature." Derrida's reading of Poe and—and against—Lacan in "The Purveyor of Truth" (in *The Post Card*) pursues these thematics as well.

15. See specifically "Living On: Border Lines" (87–89); but these economies are explored and played on by Derrida throughout his readings of Blanchot, as well as his reading of Mallarmé's *Mimique* in "The Double Session."

16. On "a-thesis," see again Derrida's "To Speculate—On 'Freud'" and Lacoue-Labarthe's opening elaborations in *Heidegger, Art and Politics*. Let me stress here, however, that while the general economy of the a-thetic drift demands a deconstruction of the classical or restricted economy of thesis, it does not mean that theses are no longer produced. It does mean that the functioning of any thesis—classical or deconstructive, restricted or general economic—is recomprehended. Both the point and the production of theses themselves are evident throughout Derrida's writing, including in "To Speculate—On 'Freud.'" See also Derrida's essay "The Time of the Thesis: Punctuation," in *Philosophy in France Today*.

17. Derrida's discussion thus indicates further connections, in part via Kant, between the question of narrative and the question of parergon as discussed in Chapter 2, and between the respective general economies.

18. In this sense, the computerization of the hypertext—another recent trend—while useful and perhaps now even indispensable, will be unable to disentangle the logical and topological, or tropological, narrative knots.

19. In this sense, contrary to Rapaport's analysis in *Heidegger and Derrida*, one may suggest that a certain distance from Heidegger is still at issue. Blanchot's fiction suggests or demands a radical departure from Aristotelean temporality, while Heidegger's, in spite of his claims, remains within the same metaphysical—ontotheological—limits.

Rapaport specifically locates Derrida's "turn" closer to Heidegger in Derrida's encounters with Blanchot (16, 104–48), beginning in 1970. The book explores at length the interface between Derrida and Blanchot, which makes considerable sense in the context of Heidegger, to whom Blanchot is very close, but is also important in general. On the other hand, Rapaport does not consider in any detail Derrida's readings, as such, of Blanchot's fiction. The latter, in general, receive little attention (102, 119, 140) and then mainly in the context of the Apocalypse, which is, of course, a pertinent issue. As a consequence, however, the radical potential of Blanchot's fiction, as opposed to his theoretical ideas, in Derrida and in general is diminished. Such a reading of Blanchot's fiction, which depends on and engages his ideas no less than his theoretical texts, together with a separation of that type, may perhaps be contested. The point is, however, that Derrida does consider these more radical dimensions of Blanchot, as well as more Heideggerian ones, and that both aspects must be taken into account. In these essays, along with various proximities, which Rapaport does examine, the distances at issue reemerge, via Derrida's analysis in "The Double Session" and *Spurs*—a general economic conjunction of the question of Nietzsche, the question of woman, and the questions of style, play, undecidability, and the unconscious. All these themes, especially play, as will be seen later in this chapter, have important connections to the problematic of narrative. The question of play in Derrida is also not discussed by Rapaport; and the term and the notion are important in both Heidegger and Blanchot. The discussion of "chances" in Derrida (127–29) leads to a (re)determination of Derrida's economy of "this writerly canon, which is both determined/undetermined by chance, [via] 'other' time . . . , a late Heideggerian notion of time, as mediated by Blanchot" (129). But this discussion hardly does justice to the complexity of this economy as the (inter)play of chance and necessity in Derrida, or indeed in Blanchot.

20. See Rapaport's comments in *Heidegger and Derrida* (129–33).

21. One would have to add here "in the present reading of Derrida"; and in this case I would make a much stronger claim concerning this reading as offered here than with respect to either Blanchot's theory or his fiction, a reading of which I do not claim to offer here. I do find Derrida's reading of Blanchot's fiction quite effective; and I do suggest that this reading and the economy of narrative that emerges through it—which is the main point—are to some extent in conflict with Blanchot's theories of narrative. It may be pointed out, in addition, that in most readings of Derrida, including those cited here—Gasché's, Rapaport's, Weber's, Spivak's, Melville's, and others—the difference between the economy of *différance*, at least in "Différance" and related earlier texts, and Heidegger's would be maintained, even though there would still be differences and nuances of reading among them. Closer proximities, where they are argued, are drawn along different *lines*, in whatever sense of this most suggestive term, than the *lines* of general economy.

22. Hayden White's books are perhaps best known in this respect, although in my view the most rigorous and most powerful applications—and implications—of undermining the classical ideologies of history are to be found in more radical treatments of that type, mostly outside institutionalized historical studies. Beyond the deconstructive and postdeconstructive approaches at issue at the moment, I refer here to Lyotard's work and related discussions of multinarrative economies, as also to recent studies of these issues along both Marxist and Foucauldian lines.

23. It is interesting that Lyotard does not engage the undecidable narratives, given the significance he assigns to Gödel's theorem in *The Postmodern Condition*. In this context, Blanchot's fiction acquires major importance as a text positioned

between modernism and postmodernism in terms of Lyotard's distinction considered earlier.

24. As I have already indicated, an important figure and one of the most significant precursors of Nietzsche in this respect is Schiller, whose aesthetics is based, in an unprecedented fashion, on the idea of play (Spiel). It is true that Schiller takes the idea of play from Kant. But Schiller has many other sources for all his terms and ideas, including play—the Greeks and theater, for example, which are also a very important reference for Nietzsche in *The Birth of Tragedy*, where Nietzsche engages in a discussion of Schiller. More significantly, Schiller radically transforms the idea of play against Kant, even if he does not transform it as radically as Nietzsche does. The relations among Kant, Schiller, and Nietzsche are touched on in Martin Heidegger, *Nietzsche*, vol. 1, *The Will to Power as Art*. In spite of the rigor that Heidegger exhibits there, I cannot agree with Heidegger's sense of a proximity between Kant and Nietzsche on the question of art.

25. The notion of play is analyzed, in several contexts that are relevant here—namely, Nietzsche, Heidegger, Deleuze, and Derrida—by Mihai I. Spariosu in his *Dionysus Reborn: Play and the Aesthetic Dimension in Modern Philosophical and Scientific Discourse* and *God of Many Names: Play, Poetry, and Power in Hellenic Thought from Homer to Aristotle*. Both of these books, particularly the first, offer a comprehensive discussion of historical connections regarding the idea of play. The author's qualifications notwithstanding (*Dionysus Reborn*, x–xii, 3), I find the basic theoretical framework of *Dionysus Reborn*, and to a degree, its historical framework, often problematic, frequently missing the radical implications of the idea of play, both in "modern philosophical discourse" and "modern scientific discourse." The book certainly never considers a general economy of play. One of the major problems of the book is its reliance throughout on the classical concepts and oppositions that are not developed or examined even within the classical limits—such as 'mentality' in the first place, 'aesthetic,' 'rational' and 'pre-rational.' Equally questionable is Spariosu's combining Heidegger, Fink, Hans-Georg Gadamer, Deleuze, and Derrida under the rubric of "the Artist-Metaphysicians." The analysis, instead of reducing, reinforces the problematic nature of this rubric, whether in historical or theoretical terms, consequently posing difficulties even in the case of classical figures such as Kant and Schiller, although the book correctly emphasizes the significance of play in Kant and the importance of Schiller's ideas on play in modern intellectual history. Spariosu's analysis becomes far more problematic in the case of later figures, beginning with Nietzsche, most notably in the case of Derrida and Deleuze. In the last two cases, he offers a very limited, rather cursory summary, and some of his conclusions are hardly tenable or even possible. To cite just two examples, he states, "Derrida conceives of deconstruction as a violent subversive movement within what he calls 'Western metaphysics' (meaning, of course, only the metaphysics of Being or presence)" (159–61), and "Deleuze and Derrida place the *simulacre* squarely in the service of the French leftist movement" (161). His analysis of Nietzsche offers several useful discussions of

Nietzsche's various economies, specifically of perspectivism, as well as pertinent criticism of an uncritical understanding of Nietzsche's perspectivism, his economy of power, or his insistence on the artistic (68–99). The principal general problem of the book is the lack of the unconscious, even in the classical sense of the term, in the analysis of play, although the book does consider the role of the concept of play in Freud, psychoanalysis, modern psychology, and related developments (176–204). Play is crucial to the economy of the unconscious. But, if anything could *define* play, it would be the unconscious—the radical unconscious, which connotes the impossibility of all such definitions, classical or general economic, as *definable* or decidable definitions.

26. Along with other possibilities suggested earlier, one may see the question of difference and relations between Heidegger and Derrida, via the economy of play, specifically in relation to the question of general economy. The question of Nietzsche remains decisive in this context.

27. Derrida, it should be pointed out, insists not on the choice —"trivial category"—between two "interpretations of interpretation" thus emerging but on the difference and *différance* that are also "the common ground" of both. In my view, however, such a *différance* is best understood precisely through the resources of Nietzschean play, and I would see *this différance*, perhaps to a degree against Derrida, as shifted more radically toward Nietzsche.

28. The passage does not appear in the version published in *Margins*.

29. Bataille opens *Inner Experience* by citing this passage. The interaction, the inter*play*—or inter-*seriousness*—of seriousness and play is a theme found in different configurations and reconfigurations in other works by Nietzsche, or Nietzschean "moments." See, for example, his elaboration in *Human, All Too Human: A Book for Free Spirits* (sec. 628, p. 198; *KSA* 2:354).

30. As I shall discuss in Chapter 4, the 'artistic' emerges in turn as a highly complex denomination in Nietzsche.

31. Nietzsche's attack on Wagner, to whom he opposes a more *playful* Bizet, might be seen in this context, although there are, of course, many other games, politics, histories, and stories played out in this attack and this juxtaposition.

32. The question of the metaphysics of the *proper* (eigentlich) as the metaphysics of *presence*, is, of course, crucial throughout Derrida's analysis, in particular as it relates to Heidegger and Nietzsche. See specifically the discussion throughout *Spurs*.

33. The entire section, which deals more with Schopenhauer than with Kant, is of great interest in the present context.

34. See Derrida's analysis in *Spurs* (99–100) and the analysis in Chapter 4 of this study.

35. Derrida makes this remark during the discussion after the original presentation of "Différance" (in *Derrida and Différance*, edited by David Wood and Robert Bernasconi, 93). See also *Margins*, 22.

36. Quoted by Derrida in *Writing and Difference* (260).

37. See Barbara Herrnstein Smith's discussion in *On the Margins of Discourse* (125). One of the major, if not the major, contexts of Smith's analysis of children, and in general, is the question of narrative. These ideas are elaborated in a subsequent essay "Narrative Version, Narrative Theories," in *On Narrative*, edited by W. J. T. Mitchell, mainly devoted to the social conditions of narrative.

38. In this sense, as I have indicated, Lyotard's conjunction, via Wittgenstein's language games, of game playing and the political is a theoretical—and political—strategy of great importance, even if it is not developed radically enough *in theoretical terms*. Possibly for this reason, it leads to some problematics, specifically a utopian, political claim. Of course, one has here to negotiate a most difficult set of *differends*, which may ultimately prove nonnegotiable—such as those between theory and politics, or aesthetics and politics, the necessity and the impossibility of justice, power, and consensus, and still others. Not all of them are, as I have said, only double—for example, theory, art, and politics—making both practical negotiations and a theoretical calculus all the more complex.

39. Schiller's remains a powerful early attempt at comprehending, if still within a restricted economy, this interaction or inter*play* of limited and limitless play. In effect, the most rigid systems of rules can be generated, and their economy thereby comprehended, within an economy of play—aesthetic, theoretical, or political. Artaud's texts and stage practice, insisting on a certain, and even, at certain points, an absolute, *formality* of dramatic configuration, remain perhaps the most interesting and instructive examples in this respect.

40. In *Inner Experience*, as well as in its sequels, *Guilty* and *Sur Nietzsche*, the project is also, and perhaps above all, that of the impossibility of project as understood by philosophy, most specifically Hegel: "Nevertheless inner experience is project, no matter what" (*Inner Experience*, 22; *L'Expérience intérieure*, 44).

41. Compare again Derrida's remarks in *Of Grammatology* (50). This argument is an old one, and it has been used throughout the history of the issues, beginning with Aristotle's *Poetics*: we master play prior to and as a prerequisite for mastering logic, or we also master stories before logic. That claim would be hard to support rigorously, however. Much more complex, and irreducible, mutual complicities or complementarities and inhibitions are at stake.

42. The metaphorics become important in relation to Heidegger's reading of Heraclitus in "Logos," in *Early Greek Thinkers*, and thus in relation to the difference between Heideggerian and Nietzschean, or Derridean, play as considered here. Kant, too, closes the "Analytic of the Beautiful" with a Heraclitean passage on the "changing shapes" of fire and of water—"a rippling brook"—(*Critique of Judgement*, 81), whose "charm" he juxtaposes to the beautiful, but, imperceptibly to his own argument, offering a picture through which the scheme of the beautiful, or of taste and judgment, can be deconstructed.

43. This play-full dissemination also demands complementarity. As applied to the thematics of play and narrative, the idea might be seen as originating in Aristotle's idea of "complex plot," although in this case, the second, *complementary*

counterpart of a given plot need not necessarily be a plot; it may be, for example, a play, or a character, or a chorus. Chorus is a repressed complement, or supplement—or both at once—of tragedy that is brilliantly utilized, in part against Aristotle, by Nietzsche in *The Birth of Tragedy*. In relation to the problematic of narrative, the difference, considered in Chapter 1, between complementarity and deconstruction as undecidability will suggest the difference between undecidable narratives, such as those in Blanchot, as indicated earlier, and complementary narratives, or complementarities between narratives, decidable or undecidable, and nonnarratives, as for example, narrative and play. Complementarities of that type may be explored particularly, but not exclusively, in the texts that explore dislocation of narrative, which, as any dislocation, must come, at least in part, from something other than narrative.

44. This "overabundance" was, of course, a major point for both Nietzsche (specifically in the passage opening "The Second Essay" of *On the Genealogy of Morals*) and Freud.

45. See, among many other passages, his opening remarks in the preface to the *Genealogy* (15).

46. Compare Derrida's reading of Nietzsche, against Heidegger and Heidegger's reading of Nietzsche, in *Of Grammatology* (19–20) and in *Spurs*. I shall consider this question in detail in Chapter 4.

47. Friedrich Nietzsche, *Ecce Homo*, 221. Here, in particular, while Shapiro's analysis in *Nietzschean Narratives* of Nietzsche's many narrative strategies, specifically in *Ecce Homo*, remains suggestive, one may also need the interactively heterogeneous complements of the narrative in order to approach both Nietzsche's narratives and his nonnarratives or antinarratives, among which his "telling his life" must be positioned. The question of Nietzsche's telling his life would demand a massive engagement of his many texts and their positioning—and self-positioning—especially his prefaces, his correspondence, in particular his famous last letter, as well as much of the secondary literature. My point here is only to indicate Nietzsche's approach as a manifestation of his plural style, by which Nietzsche confronts both the possibilities and the constraints, including the impossibilities, of telling a story or his own life. Among the works that are relevant in the context of the present discussion, on the question of Nietzsche's "autobiographies," see Pierre Klossowski's classic *Nietzsche et le cercle vicieux*, and Philippe Lacoue-Labarthe's "*L'Écho du sujet*," in *Le Sujet de la philosophie*, reprinted in *Typography: Mimesis, Philosophy, Politics*, edited by Christopher Fynsk. Derrida's continuous and complex encounter with Nietzsche, engages the question of the autobiographical in the essays collected in *L'Oreille de l'autre*, edited by Claude Lévesque and Christie V. McDonald, translated as *The Ear of the Other: Otobiography, Transference, Translation*. The question of the autobiographical has been extensively commented upon in recent literature, beginning with the discussion published in the volume. See, specifically, Rodolphe Gasché, "Autobiography as Gestalt," in *Why Nietzsche Now?* edited by Daniel O'Hara; David Farrell Krell, "Consultations with the Paternal Shadow: Gasché, Derrida and Klossowski on

Ecce Homo," in *Exceedingly Nietzsche,* which contains important juxtapositions of different textual versions of the relevant passages in *Ecce Homo*; and Ruben Berezdevin, "Drawing: (An) Affecting Nietzsche: With Derrida," in *Derrida and Deconstruction,* edited by Hugh J. Silverman. Irigaray's *Marine Lover* offers most interesting possibilities of reading, in some proximities to, but also with many distances from, in addition to Nietzsche himself, Bataille's, Deleuze's, and Derrida's general approaches to Nietzsche. All these readings suggest that the economy, the general economy, of the biographical is distributed in the most complex fashion across Nietzsche's texts and styles.

48. The significance of Sterne in Russian literary history, from Pushkin on, is overwhelming. The title of one of Shklovsky's early novels is, we recall, *Sentimental Journey.*

Chapter 4 Nietzsche's Revolutions

1. It is fitting to invoke here the title—"Choreographies"—of Derrida's discussion on the question of women, Nietzsche, and history. The thematics and metaphorics of dance are equally evident in *Spurs,* and in Derrida's reading of Mallarmé in "The Double Session."

2. As will be seen in Chapter 6, this emphasis on effects and the general economy of "effects" emerging thereby has an important relation to Althusser's reading of Marx. Derrida's remark in *Positions* occurs in the context of the question of materialism and history, via Althusser.

3. On the field of writing as a refiguration of the field of language, see specifically *Of Grammatology* (8–9), although one can refer here to numerous passages throughout Derrida's writing. *Writing*-criticism as *writing*-reading, interacting with or complementarizing *writing*-theory, was explored in and by the practice of de Man's deconstructive and postdeconstructive *writing* (in either sense), at times with some important differences from Derrida, for whom *writing*-reading is likewise a crucial economy. Derrida's reading of Mallarmé, in fact, thematizes it. Among, and interacting with, many other "writings" played out by Mallarmé's *Mimique, writing*-reading, or reading-*writing,* plays an important role ("The Double Session," in *Dissemination,* 223).

4. This reduction was profoundly understood by Foucault.

5. On the question of the complicity between empiricism and metaphysics, see also the discussion later in the essay (151–52); and on the related question of the metaphor as the philosophical detour to philosophical truth, see "White Mythology: Metaphor in the Text of Philosophy" in *Margins of Philosophy* (particularly 270). Hegel, who, as Derrida points out, justly criticizes "empiricism"— "Empiricism always forgets, at the very least, that it employs the word to be" (*Writing and Difference,* 139; *L'Écriture et la différence,* 204)—does not escape this forgetting of metaphor.

6. Spivak's translation of *propre* as "literal" misses Derrida's play on *propre*— and thereby a deconstruction of the metaphysics of the *proper* (authentic,

eigentlich)—which is engaged and remains crucial throughout his writing, especially in the context of Nietzsche and Heidegger.

7. See also *The Will to Power*, sec. 415, p. 223; *KSA* 12:162–63.

8. One should not miss Nietzsche's grand historical positioning of this recomprehension of all reasons and revaluation of all values hitherto. Christianity and Socratism are described in the same terms of "revaluation of all values" See, for instance, *On the Genealogy of Morals*, "First Essay," sec. 8, p. 35. The *new* revaluation and recomprehension at issue here are, of course, Nietzsche's own. It is quite clear throughout his writing, however, that Nietzsche does not see them exclusively in the personal sense (although Nietzsche's sense of his own contribution remains important) but also as a general—but not universal—development grasped earlier by his writing. The economy of this anticipation should not be identified with the Hegelian economy of historical *Geist* but should be seen instead in general economic terms. I shall comment further on this positioning later in this chapter.

9. *Différance*, as indicated, is a more complex matter; for "it governs nothing, reigns over nothing, and nowhere exercises any authority" (*Margins*, 22; *Marges*, 22). The "difference" of *différance* is too radical to be assigned "violence," or indeed anything, although, among other things, by way of writing, violence must be seen as the effect of *différance*.

10. Nietzsche's margin is, of course, equally crucial in "Structure, Sign, and Play in the Discourse of the Human Sciences," in *Writing and Difference*. The Nietzschean themes and connections of writing, power, history, morality, priesthood, and so on are also developed in Derrida's lesser known but important essay on Warburton, "Scribble (writing-power)." The passage just cited also alludes to and implies a deconstruction of Levinas' economy of the ethical.

11. Here one might refer to Paul Feyerabend's powerful analysis of Galileo in *Against Method*.

12. Compare Gayatri C. Spivak's discussion in her "Translator's Preface" (*Of Grammatology*, xxiii–xxvii).

13. In this sense, Nietzsche's economy of history is, as a general economy, more radical than Foucault's archaeology, which, even according to Foucault himself, owes much to Nietzsche, but in the end does not borrow enough from him. Foucault's "archaeologies," particularly in his later and more Nietzschean works may be seen as specific historical—"archaeological"—stratifications worked by way of the Nietzschean "play of forces." The *Genealogy*, particularly the first essay, offers the main model. I use the term 'model,' for, while the book, like other works by Nietzsche, does contain the elements of historical analysis, often precise and penetrating, it is not and does not offer itself as strictly a historical analysis. It offers instead a general matrix of historical analysis. Foucault still restricts its potential, also in the sense of the restricted economy of historical analysis.

14. *On the Genealogy of Morals* may be the most difficult text in Nietzsche's canon. The complexity of forces and economies, restricted and general, addressed by and producing the text, is great; it is much more tempting to use the book than

to analyze it. Of all the works by Nietzsche on which Bataille comments, he is least successful with this one, although he wisely offers only very partial treatments; actually, most other figures on the poststructuralist landscape at issue in the present study also restrict their discussions to limited aspects of this text. Deleuze's extensive analysis of it in *Nietzsche and Philosophy* is an exception; and while it is not unproblematic and by now is somewhat dated, it is preferable to many more recent approaches. Foucault considers the book in the context of history in his essay "Nietzsche, Genealogy, History" (in *Language, Counter-Memory, Practice*). Derrida offers only several scattered remarks. A relevant and important discussion, in the Kantian context, by Jean-Luc Nancy in *L' Impérative catégorique* (63–86) concentrates on earlier texts, and does not address the book. Earlier French encounters with Nietzsche, such as Blanchot's and Klossowski's, and, overshadowing the whole landscape at issue, Heidegger's readings of Nietzsche, must be kept in mind, of course.

In *Nietzschean Narratives*, Shapiro makes a cogent remark on one of the aspects of Nietzsche's style in this text in saying that "in *The Genealogy of Morals*, as we shall see in the next chapter, Nietzsche makes the spectacle into an important structural principle for the understanding of history" (108). Shapiro makes several pertinent comments on the book and uses it effectively in his critique of Habermas on Nietzsche. The *Genealogy* is given extensive attention in Alexander Nehamas' *Nietzsche: Life as Literature*. Nehamas' work could have benefited by engaging Nietzsche's style more plurally and more general economically. However, both in the case of the *Genealogy*, where he is closer to Foucault, and in general, Nehamas' approach and intepretation are more cogent than that of Staten in *Nietzsche's Voice* or Ackerman in *Nietzsche*, on which I have commented earlier. Another recent book, Alan White's *Within Nietzsche's Labyrinth*, gives considerable space to the *Genealogy* and correctly suggests its significance to Nietzsche. In my view, however, it does not pay enough attention to the complexity and plurality of Nietzsche's style, both in the *Genealogy* and in general. More generally, the concept of Nietzsche's hermeneutic that White offers is too confined and is problematic, in spite of some valid points made, such as those concerning the affirmative dimensions of ascetic ideals (49–55). The book interprets Nietzsche in rather rigidly classical terms and assigns Nietzsche himself a classical hermeneutics, *restricting* Nietzsche's style and the general economy of his analysis, and *repressing* in particular the radically "unconscious" aspect of Nietzsche's (anti)interpretations. Bruce Detwiler, in *Nietzsche and the Politics of Aristocratic Radicalism*, emphasizes the political aspects and their impact in the *Genealogy* (115–43) and on Nietzsche's writing in general, also connecting them correctly with Nietzsche's anticipations of Freud (129). He, too, however, misses the complexities and the impact of Nietzsche's plural, general economic style, leading to several ineffective interpretations, such as seeing Dionysian affirmation in Nietzsche as "nihilistic affirmation" (142). Partly for the same reasons, the book oscillates too unequivocally between both conceptual and political oppositions and polarities, such as between the radical left and the far right. Both political orientations, of course, may find appealing elements in Nietzsche, but the most *radical* dimensions of Nietzsche's writing fundamentally lie elsewhere. The political dimensions of Nietzsche's text and, in some measure, the *Genealogy* are also addressed in Mark Warren's *Nietzsche and Political Thought.* As I indicated in Chapter 1, however, I find unrigorous and problematic Warren's treatment both of Nietzsche and, in particular, of poststructuralist or postmodernist readings of Nietzsche, such as those by Heidegger, Derrida, Deleuze, de Man, and others. One of the agendas—perhaps the main agenda—of the book is to locate in Nietzsche's text the implications for "liberal democratic culture" (218–19), which, as Warren acknowledges, Nietzsche opposes and criticizes. Warren does not see, however, that Nietzsche offers a devastating critique of all his major ideological and theoretical premises as well as of "self-reflective rationality" in particular. Beyond displacing Nietzsche's text, this oversight produces an untenable matrix of the political, whatever one's political agendas or whatever the problems of Nietzsche's political theory—or the absence of one—in Nietzsche may be.

15. Derrida, we recall, metaphorically relates Nietzsche's style to *stylus*, or 'quill,' 'stiletto,' 'rapier,' but also simultaneously dissociates it from unequivocal metaphorizations of that type, by way of "feminine" styles (*Spurs*, 37–47).

16. See, for example, the opening of section 7 of "The First Essay" (*Genealogy*, 33).

17. To a degree, Foucault's and Foucauldian readings of Nietzsche, from Foucault's "Nietzsche, Genealogy, History" to the present, would also operate against the metaphysics of history and a metaphysical reading of Nietzsche, although, as I have indicated, they would do so less radically than the reading just suggested and with certain problems of their own.

18. It may be suggested that Derrida follows Heidegger's general program of reading, specifically as it is applied to Hegel's *Phenomenology* (*Hegel's Phenomenology of Spirit*, 42). Derrida, as it were, re-iterates this program in applying it to Heidegger's reading of Nietzsche. This program can, to a degree, be juxtaposed to Nietzsche's encounters—or Nietzsche's style of encounter, as different from either Heidegger's or Derrida's. One would be hesitant to claim that Nietzsche does not read anything carefully, as one would be equally hesitant to separate the form and content of Nietzsche's text. The proximities and distances, and the reiterations, or iterability, of style, including the styles of proximity or distance, or both at once, or of reiteration, emerge and reiterate themselves quite differently. Derrida's rigorous suspension of all Heideggerian grounds of reading—in Hegel, Nietzsche, or others—and thinking remains crucial under all conditions and is, in my view, decisively closer to Nietzsche than to Heidegger, at the very least in Derrida's earlier writing. As I have argued earlier, however, a certain Nietzschean difference from Heidegger can be traced in all Derrida's texts, although, as we have seen, other, less Nietzschean, readings of both Derrida and Heidegger are possible, either bringing them closer, as in Rapaport, or distancing them, as in Gasché. At the

same time, one may need to maintain the differences between Nietzsche and Derrida, possibly simultaneously positioning Derrida, particularly in his later works, closer to Heidegger.

19. As Nietzsche points out throughout his writing, this belief in the possibility of linking and the desire finally to link understanding and consciousness and practice is a crucial part of Socratism or Socratism/Platonism.

20. Compare *Positions*, 13–14.

21. See also Derrida's elaborations in *Of Grammatology*, 285–87.

22. The French reads: "Non qu'il faille passivement prendre son parti de l'hétérogène ou du parodique (ce serait encore les réduire). Non qu'il faille conclure, de ce que le maître sens, le sens unique et hors greffe est introuvable, à la maîtrise infinie de Nietzsche, à son pouvoir imprenable, à son impeccable manipulation du piège, à une sorte de calcul infini, quasiment celui du Dieu de Leibniz, mais calcul infini de l'indécidable cette fois, pour déjouer la prise herméneutique. Ce serait, pour l'éviter à coup sûr, retomber aussi sûrement dans le piège" (*Spurs*, 98).

23. It is curious that Gödel arrives at his proof of "undecidability"—a central context and analogy for Derrida here and throughout—via exploring what is in many ways, and perhaps fundamentally, Leibniz' procedure for labeling—"hieroglyphically," as it were—all logical or philosophical propositions. Gödel's "hieroglyphs" are, finally, natural numbers: 1, 2, 3, ... Numbers, to simplify, are enough to calculate everything, but lead finally to irreducible undecidability. I shall comment further on this issue in Chapter 7.

24. How much deconstruction the text requires, or how much it already performs, including of itself, is a different and complex question. See the essays on Nietzsche in Paul de Man, *Allegories of Reading*; Sarah Kofman, *Nietzsche et la scène philosophique*; and Andrzej Warminski, *Readings in Interpretation: Hölderlin, Hegel, Heidegger* (xxxv–lxi). See also David Allison's interesting essay "Nietzsche Knows No Noumenon," in *Why Nietzsche Now?* In *Crossings: Nietzsche and the Space of Tragedy*, John Sallis offers an extensive analysis of the book and other early works by Nietzsche and argues for many important continuities with Nietzsche's later works and ideas. Sallis' analysis, proceeding closer to Heideggerian lines, does not consider the unconscious or the general economic dimensions of early Nietzsche, such as those suggested by the analysis given in Chapter 3 of this study.

25. On the question of mimesis in its post-Nietzschean and post-Heideggerian context, see also Philippe Lacoue-Labarthe's numerous texts, some of which are assembled in *Typography*, which contains an introductory essay by Derrida.

26. Oscar Wilde also comes to mind, particularly his extraordinary and quite Nietzschean essay, "The Truth of Masks," one of the four great essays in "Intentions," in *The Artist as Critic*, edited by Richard Ellmann (408–32). See Derrida's remark on Wilde in *The Post Card* (32).

27. The French version is in "Limited Inc," *Glyph* 2 (Supplement), 72.

28. On various dimensions and "crossings" of the tragic and the Dionysian in early Nietzsche, see Sallis' *Crossings*, although, as I indicated, even in the earlier works a more radical—aesthetically, theoretically, psychologically, or politically—reading of the Nietzschean tragic is possible and indeed necessary.

29. See also "Tympan" (*Margins*, xii–xiii) and the conclusion of "Structure, Sign and Play" (*Writing and Difference*, 292–93), where the difference between Derrida and Nietzsche reemerges. I shall comment on these passages later in this chapter.

30. I use these terms of J. L. Austin a bit loosely here. But the issue can be related to Derrida's, or de Man's, various discussions of the problematics of speech act theory.

31. This issue, as I indicated earlier, is important in the context of de Man and of the intertextuality of Derrida's and de Man's work. It has occupied a number of recent commentators, including some of those cited earlier. Specifically, on the de Manian, or, perhaps better, post-deManian *reading* of Hölderlin and the post-de-Manian problematic of reading, see Warminski's *Readings in Interpretation* and Gasché's introduction to that book. Both authors bypass the thematics of the unconscious or general economy, as in great measure does de Man. The place—or the absence, perhaps avoidance—of this thematics in de Man is an interesting question; but it cannot be considered here. On the unconscious in de Man and on de Man and psychoanalysis, see Kamuf's discussion of de Man in *Signature Pieces*.

32. This latter possibility transpires at the end of Gasché's analysis in *The Tain of the Mirror* (271–318), from which I borrow the term "*quasitranscendental*" (316). Gasché has some hesitations in using it, and for good reasons, I think. To a degree, Gasché thereby returns Derrida to Heidegger, or positions him closer to Heidegger and metaphysics, or let us say, "*quasimetaphysics*" than one might want to, even though, as I have pointed out, Gasché, in contrast with other recent studies, maintains many differences between Heidegger and Derrida. I am afraid that the *quasi*transcendental, finally, is, or is too close to, the *transcendental*; and leads to the emergence of a position or economy—a *restricted* economy—that can be deconstructed by way of what which this "quasitranscendentality" wants to explain, namely, Derrida's *différance*. For if *différance* does relate to that which itself cannot be represented, it, by the same token, cannot *transcend*. Nor can I quite agree with Gasche's claim, made at the same juncture, that "metaphoricity has a structure and a function similar to transcendental without actually being one" (316). At the very least, the differences, on which Gasché does not comment, are just as or even more radical than the proximities are close. It is also strange that Gasché wants to contain the diversity of *différance* within one operation, or a limited set of operations. He does not, in short, address a radical *dissemination* of *différance* itself, nor a radical *dissemination* enacted by *différance*, to begin with. The economy of *dissemination* receives no attention in the book. Nor, as I pointed out earlier, do the questions of the unconscious and general economy, an omission that reduces the

nonphilosophical space—Nietzsche, Freud, Bataille, Lacan—of the margins of philosophy in Derrida, but also insufficiently renders the philosophical register of Derrida's text. Gasché does extensively and effectively consider the economy of "undecidability" in Derrida, which is an important aspect of Derrida's general economic ensemble, if perhaps more containable within the philosophical register. It may be true that the subject of Gasché's study is "Derrida and the Philosophy of Reflection," and thus primarily the philosophical register in Derrida. In *The Tain of the Mirror*, however, particularly its conclusion, and his other essays, where a similar set of positions and agendas emerges, Gasché makes much broader claims concerning the positioning of Derrida and deconstruction, specifically in relation to literature, literary criticism, and theory—the claims that are sometimes characteristically un-Derridean and problematic in general; and the issue obviously extends beyond the problems of demarcating and stratifying Derrida's texts in this way. It may be that, specifically toward the end of *The Tain of the Mirror* (318), Gasché refers to what may be seen as "classical" modes, or earlier stages, of literary criticism and theory, as opposed, for example, to deconstructive or postdeconstructive criticism and theory. Still, Gasché's claims there (318) would require considerable qualification, particularly, but not exclusively, given the state of criticism and theory at that moment (1986)—in view of de Man's work, for example. It is interesting in itself that Gasché should close the book with the statement on literary criticism and theory, juxtaposing them to philosophy, "very specific philosophical problems to which [Derrida's theory of metaphoricity] responds," which thereby "cannot be of any *immediate* concern to literary theory" (318). Nothing, in truth, can be of *immediate* concern to anything, as Derrida's analysis demonstrates. If anything, in historical and theoretical terms, literary criticism and theory have responded to and concerned themselves with this theory far more immediately than did most philosophy. Several similarly problematic or insufficiently discriminating claims open the book as well (3). Gasché's analysis is in fact *framed* by what he wants to bracket, but in all rigor cannot, and should not—at least not in the way he attempts to do—however understandable and justified some of his reasons may be (3). *Within these limits*, Gasché's analysis is superior to most other recent treatments; and he, as I have said, is aware of the exterior of philosophy in Derrida. The question is whether this demarcation is possible even locally, in Derrida's case, or—this is why the question has a more general importance—the similar and related, if of course also different, cases of Nietzsche, Bataille, Blanchot, and other practitioners of the plural style, or even classical cases, where such demarcations are indeed attempted—in short, in the case of philosophy itself. The question is whether and to what degree one can contain deconstruction at issue in Gasché's book within the register practiced by this book; or whether—which I think is the case—this register is itself deconstructable in this sense or, if one assumes that there are no undeconstructable registers, whether this register is sufficiently effective. See also Derrida's own, rather strong qualifications of, or dissociations from, Gasché in *Acts of Literature* (70–72).

33. I am grateful to Silke Weineck for suggesting this translation to me.

34. One should of course keep in mind the complexity and multifacetedness of, say, the structure and economy of the Dionysian in Nietzsche, starting with the *The Birth of Tragedy*, where it is related to the complexity and historical development of the Greeks' sense of Dionysus, and continuing throughout Nietzsche's works.

35. Bataille juxtaposes Nietzsche and fascism precisely by way of *nonidentification*, in which essays, as we have seen, Bataille also introduces the heterological as a general structure, or a general economy. Dionysian spirits, such as Goethe and Nietzsche, would always remain far apart, as much apart from one another as from everybody and everything else, even and above all when they admire one another: ". . . love of the neighbor [the near] I do not recommend to you: I recommend to you the love of the farthest," Zarathustra says [(Meine Brüder,) zur Nächstenliebe rathe ich euch nicht: ich rathe euch zur Fernsten–Liebe]" (*Thus Spoke Zarathustra*, 62; *Also sprach Zarathustra, KSA* 4:79).

36. This priority, as indicated in Chapter 3, is a classical gesture, too, although, from pre-Socratics and Socrates and Plato—all the banishments of poets notwithstanding—to Freud and Heidegger, or Derrida, it can be played out diversely. And, of course, it can be and is played out deconstructively as well, in Nietzsche or Derrida, and again differently, in Heidegger.

37. Nietzsche rewrote this section of the book rather radically; the final version does not mention the political, or rather "the anti-political," which is perhaps more significant.

38. "The whole," of course, is always a problematic term, even in Nietzsche, as will be seen in the final chapter of this study. Nietzsche knows very well that wholeness never possesses its wholeness absolutely. His point here is the necessity of expanded perspectives; that necessity, needless to say, also indicates the general complexity of Nietzschean perspectivism.

39. Compare another set of remarks in *Positions* (6–7).

40. In addition Derrida's own many texts and several other commentaries cited earlier, on the questions of the relationships, always complex, between metaphysics and philosophy, the end of metaphysics and the end of philosophy, and surrounding problematics in Heidegger, see John Sallis' *Echoes: After Heidegger*. Sallis' analysis proceeds within the philosophical, or at least Heideggerian, register, which is understandable given his subject. Let me reiterate, in this context, that at issue at the moment and in the present study as a whole is not the philosophical register of theory, but the question of dependence of other theoretical registers on philosophy (understood in historico-institutional terms) and its closure. To deny the possibility of such alternative registers, if at times—but again not always—interactive with philosophy, would be to reinstate a totalizing, and in the end Hegelian, instance of the historical economy of theory.

41. The English translation substitutes "philosophy" for 'being' (*l'être*). The term *'jeu'* (game or play) that Derrida uses to describe Hegel's engagement with philosophy, is far more than a casual metaphor; it can be seen, first, as problema-

tizing the opposition of work—labor—and play, that affects and often structures much of philosophy of *logos* as the metaphysics of presence and that is one of the questions at issue in the present analysis as well. Second, as we have seen, the very difference between restricted and general economy, as the general economy of *différance*, is conceived of by Derrida, via Nietzsche and referring to Heidegger and Heidegger's engagement with Nietzsche, by way of play as "the absence of the transcendental signified as limitlessness of play, that is to say as the deconstruction [ébranlement: trembling] of ontotheology and metaphysics of presence [l'absence du signifié transcendantal comme illimitation du *jeu*, c'est-à-dire comme ébranlement de l'onto-théologie et de la métaphysique de la présence" (*Of Grammatology*, 50; *De la grammatologie*, 73). *Writing* and *différance*, grammatology or pragrammatology—"the intersection of a pragmatics and a grammatology" ("*My Chances*," 27)—all will be related to the concept and metaphor of 'play' along various lines considered earlier. While he never dismisses labor or some more playful dialectics, actually or potentially, such as Adorno's "negative dialectics," Derrida, importantly, never privileges labor, either, a move that would be *forbidden under the constraints of the general economy*, by way of which grammatology as the "science" of *différance* is practiced, as an always rigorous treatment, however nonscientific in the classical sense it may be. If, and to the extent that, a concept or theory, economy, political or other, that "does not have a form of a concept" is *practiced* by (Althusser's) Marx or by deconstruction—in Derrida, Bataille, or Nietzsche—these are certainly two very different economies of practice, one restricted and another general, even though both operate against Hegel. But then, they operate against— or at times together with—different "Hegels," too. Thus, a general economy may utilize Hegel against Marx as much as Marx against Hegel, in a general economy of matter and history as radically nondialectical. Importantly, the opposition of play and labor, or pleasure and pain, can always be reversed—replayed or relabored—for example, in relation to reading a "philosophical" text such as Kant's, specifically on play and pleasure in his third critique. The products of Kant's philosophical labors can be pleasurably consumed. They have already been so consumed—at least to a degree, they must have been, including in the course of their very production, by Kant himself, all overt or implicit argument to the contrary notwithstanding. Yet, as we have seen, a text can never be only "consumed," either, or ever altogether digested. Nothing can be; some waste is always and everywhere necessary, for example, the waste in and of taste. But taste is only one example, and the critique of taste but another.

42. Deconstruction is, of course, always a deconstruction of the classical concepts of method and of the classical claims for methods. But, as we have seen, whether in Nietzsche, Bataille, or Derrida, it is never an absolute suspension of methods or rigor. "Against method," to borrow Paul Feyerabend's title, is also, under certain conditions, the necessity of methods.

43. Thus, while there may be other reasons—psychological or political, or psycho-political, as it were—for Derrida to minimize the Marxist sources of deconstruction, perhaps most specifically Althusser, there are powerful *theoretical*

reasons as well. They are bound to have political implications too, as we have seen, but I want for the moment to stress their theoretical force. Above all, these reasons concern the difference of the unconscious, or in terms of proper names, the difference of Nietzsche and Freud. The latter are themselves proper names in juxtaposition to Marx and, as Derrida acknowledges in *Of Grammatology*, in the context of Lévi-Strauss, "to reconcile . . . Marx and Freud is a difficult task [accorder . . . Marx et Freud est une tâche difficile]" (*Of Grammatology*, 118; *De la grammatologie*, 173). I subtract Rousseau from Derrida's formulation. In terms of proper names, such may well be *the* question of modern intellectual history, the question of Marx and Freud, or—a more hidden, but perhaps more powerful possibility—of Marx and Nietzsche as the question of history and the unconscious. It is a question of their (im)possible reconciliations, or of their difference and common ground in *différance* or general economy, as against the (self-)consciousness and synthesis (*Aufhebung*) of dialectics, materialist, as in Marx, or idealist, as in Hegel. The unconscious is a crucial and in the end perhaps irreducible difference between Marx and Freud. This is not to say that the various strata of the two texts cannot be reconciled, partially integrated, or otherwise utilized, including in a general economy. Still, it is always "a difficult task." The closure configured by Derrida is the effect of profound theoretical necessities, but it also reflects the difficulty of the task.

44. Compare, however, Gayatri C. Spivak's comment to that effect ("Translator's Preface," in *Of Grammatology*, xxi). Spivak's point that "Derrida uses the word 'metaphysics' very simply as shorthand for any science of presence" is not wrong, but perhaps a degree of further discrimination and analysis is required. For while it is true that identical or analogous metaphysical economies operate across different fields within and outside the history and institution of philosophy, the name "metaphysics" has its own historical and strategic appurtenance. These operational crossings of boundaries, therefore, would precisely prevent us from speaking without further qualification or, above all, differentiation, about *the* closure of metaphysics.

45. It can be suggested, briefly, that for de Man "literature" plays a similar role; and one can speak, by analogy, of the closure of literature, as opposed to simply or unequivocally privileging literature in de Man, particularly as a homogeneous or undifferentiated field.

46. See Derrida's "Force of Law: The "Mystical Foundation of Authority" and other articles in this issue of *Cardozo Law Review* and in the sequel (*Cardozo Law Review* 11 [1990] and 13 [1991]).

47. This point is still in the spirit of Lacan, who insists on following the *letter*, not the spirit of Freud, although, as Derrida argues in "The Purveyor of Truth" (in *The Post Card*), Lacan never quite departs from the Spirit—*Geist*—of Freud, Heidegger, Hegel: the Spirit of philosophy as the metaphysics of presence and truth.

48. In this context, Gasché's juxtaposition of Nietzsche and Derrida and deconstruction becomes interesting (*The Tain of the Mirror*, 125). Gasché's insistence

on rigor is a well-taken point. But, as I have indicated, I find somewhat problematic, and again rather anti-Derridean, Gasché's strict—"rigorous"—association of rigor with philosophy, albeit deconstructive philosophy, in the book and throughout much of his writing. See, in particular, the "Introduction" (8). The question of theoretical and critical rigor in Derrida, or in Nietzsche and Bataille, is crucial. It may be that in this context, too, Gasché, aware of Derrida's "transgression" of the philosophical, primarily responds to the lack of rigor elsewhere and to a reverse "forgetting" or repression of the significance of the philosophical register in Derrida (8). Gasché's analysis of de Man in "In-Difference to Philosophy: De Man on Kant, Hegel, and Nietzsche" (in *Reading de Man Reading*, 259–94) is in fact suggestive in this sense, showing, *rigorously*, the difference between de Man's project and rigor and the project and rigor of the classical philosophy, specifically with respect to de Man's reading of philosophy itself. Again, however, Gasché's demarcation becomes too rigid, as becomes particularly problematic in Nietzsche's case. I mean Nietzsche's own text, rather than de Man's essays on Nietzsche, although Nietzsche, it is true, is not really Gasché's subject here. He does speak problematically, however, of Nietzsche's texts as philosophical, alongside Hegel's and Kant's (262). It is most interesting that Derrida is never mentioned in this essay. While one must indeed rigorously differentiate between Derrida's and de Man's projects and styles of reading, as Gasché in fact does in his other works, there is a complex economy of differences and proximities between them. This economy suggests that a general economy of Derrida's text and style, the economy of *rigor* of Derrida's analysis, is irreducibly complementary in relation to literature, criticism, and philosophy, or what can or must be so seen under given conditions.

49. Nietzsche also refers here to a Greek custom in wine drinking, of diluting wine with water. This reference is of great interest in the context of the Dionysian on one hand, and of Plato's *Symposium* and Socrates, on the other. Socrates, the *Symposium* tells, was careful never to become intoxicated, always keeping his faculties of dialectical reasoning intact. At the same time, however, this reason and its text are not as clearly juxtaposed to the Dionysian, or Nietzschean, language that Nietzsche invokes here.

50. Nietzsche has many interesting and important elaborations on the subject of ears, many ears—even, as is well known, on "a *third* ear" in *Beyond Good and Evil* (sec. 246, p. 182), which has been the subject of many recent discussions in Derrida, Irigaray, Lacoue-Labarthe, and other commentators. I shall further comment on the question of the ear in Nietzsche in the context of architecture in Chapter 5.

Chapter 5 Theoria

1. See "Toward a Theory of Schizophrenia," "Double Bind, 1969," and accompanying essays in *Steps to an Ecology of Mind*.

2. See, for example, Derrida's elaborations in chapter 3 of *Of Grammatology* (84–87) and his analysis there of Lévi-Strauss, as well as his analysis throughout "Freud and the Scene of Writing."

3. In *The Tain of the Mirror*, Gasché correctly emphasizes this aspect of deconstruction, although he perhaps does not develop fully its radical implications. In this context, Derrida's analysis of Descartes, via a deconstruction of Foucault, in "Cogito and the History of Madness" (in *Writing and Difference*) represents a powerful and important early approach (1963) to the problem.

4. A number of Nietzsche's passages may be cited here, most specifically perhaps his great elaboration on "The Consciousness of Appearance" in *The Gay Science* (116), to which I shall return later. Nietzsche's passage is cited by Bataille in *Inner Experience* (28), and may in fact be seen as the central point of departure for the book. Somewhat less critically than in his later texts, Nietzsche conceives of a similar economy in *The Birth of Tragedy* as the Apollinian, or at least as a major aspect of the Apollinian. The Dionysian connotes a more complete oblivion, a more radical loss of consciousness. In truth, however, the economy of the interaction between the Apollinian and the Dionysian implies a mutual inhibition rather than a strict demarcation or, conversely, a Hegelian synthesis of the two. The latter permeates, for example, Kaufmann's reading, and to a degree his translation, of *The Birth of Tragedy*. In the light of the recent history of reading Nietzsche, such a view would be difficult to accept. Giving a certain priority to the unconscious, Nietzsche marks this *inhibition* with the conception of the Dionysian that emerges more fully in his later writings.

5. One might suggest, however, that the issue in this form was perhaps first decisively, if predictably antagonistically, addressed by Plato in *Ion*.

6. "Die dem Range nach erste, weil weiteste, tiefste und ursprünglichste Frage: 'Warum ist überhaupt Seiendes und nicht vielmehr Nichts?'" (*Einführung in die Metaphysik*, in *Gesamtausgabe*, pt. 2, 40:3; *An Introduction to Metaphysics*, 1).

7. I refer here to modern physics; for such an assumption had been made in previous *meta*physical and theological cosmologies many times, and it must have been known to Descartes. In modern cosmology the idea is usually credited to the physicist Alexander Vilenkin. See Stephen W. Hawking's remarks on "the origin and fate of the universe," closing with Saint Augustine, in "Quantum Cosmology" (in *Three Hundred Years of Gravitation*, 650–51) or his *Brief History of Time* (115–41). Currently there are, it should be pointed out, many competing physical theories in this domain, with a variety of "metaphysics"—of beginnings and ends, or their absence—or by now conceivably, of deconstructions, attached to them.

8. See again Nietzsche's remarks on Kant in *Beyond Good and Evil* (sec. 11, p. 19).

9. See also Derrida's analysis of Descartes in "Languages and Institutions of Philosophy."

10. Obviously, all such determinations as 'innocent' or 'sincere' are themselves complex and problematic.

11. One may also say "after Darwin," whom Nietzsche must be following—and attacking—here.

12. I refer, again, especially to the dialectic of desire in the *Phenomenology*.

13. Derrida plays on this possibility in his analysis of J. L. Austin in "Signature Event Context." While insisting upon the performative, Austin marginalizes the theatrical.

14. Such phrases pervade numerous papers and books on related—and unrelated—issues, whatever their degree of agreement or disagreement with and whatever their understanding of, or unwillingness to understand, Derrida and deconstruction.

15. See also Derrida's discussion in the section "The Invention of Truth" of his essay "Psyche: Inventions of the Other" (in *Reading de Man Reading*, 48–53).

16. Derrida's reading of Lacan—of Lacan's reading of Poe—comes later.

17. These propositions already acquire a different and complex significance, an appurtenance to a general economy of discourse and style, in "On Truth and Lie in Their Extra-Moral Sense."

18. Nietzsche, as I have indicated, often speaks of value rather than truth, of value without truth or without truth-value. According to Heidegger's reading, most specifically toward the end of *An Introduction to Metaphysics* and in scattered remarks throughout his encounters with Nietzsche, for Nietzsche truth is a value, particularly as the condition of the preservation of power. Heidegger's point is correct. He is mistaken, however, in claiming the metaphysical nature of Nietzsche's economy of value, because he misses the Nietzschean economy of evaluation and interpretation as, in present terms, a general economy. I shall not discuss at the moment what happens to "value" in Nietzsche as a result, although a number of studies and collections dealing with Heidegger, Nietzsche, Derrida, and poststructuralism in general, cited earlier, may be engaged here. The considerations offered in Chapter 2 also remain relevant here. I have considered the question of Heidegger and Nietzsche on value in the context of general economy more specifically in "Interpretation, Interminability, Evaluation: From Nietzsche toward a General Economy" (in *Life After Postmodernism*, 120–41). "Value" is one of many words found in the noncentered sheaf of disseminating theoretical terms; no more than any other name can it be unique or final. In Nietzsche, value has a local and strategic function, as but one name among others. Truth is *a* value among others, never a 'truth-value' in the classical sense of the term developed by philosophical tradition. As a value, truth must be and is analyzed by Nietzsche in relation to the psychological, social, and historical conditions of its possibility or necessity, including the conditions of the preservation of power of which Heidegger speaks. Nietzsche reconceives truth in terms of "value"—a strategically useful shift—while Heidegger wants instead to reinscribe value and, crucially, history in terms of truth. Heidegger, then, reads Nietzsche according to this scheme. Nietzsche's theory of value, however, is a *general* economy of "value," which radically transforms evaluation itself. Some of these implications are readily apparent

from earlier discussions in Chapters 2 and 4. The most crucial and most affirmative aspects of Nietzsche's grand style—the affirmation of play without truth, origin, or center—will therefore remain inaccessible to the Heideggerian interpretation of Nietzsche and of interpretation itself.

19. Nietzsche speaks of aesthetics as applied physiology.

20. On some of these issues, see Roger Penrose, *The Emperor's New Mind*, which explores a broad field of interaction among modern physics, mathematics, computer science, and biology. Extraordinary earlier perceptions (around 1830) on both psychology and sociology, and indeed politics, of mathematics and its truth, are those of Evariste Galois—one could have no better credentials as a mathematician. A summary account and further references are given in Leopold Infeld, *Whom the Gods Love* (170–71).

21. See Denis Hollier, *Against Architecture: The Writings of Georges Bataille*, originally published as *La Prise de la Concorde*.

22. All these structures and metaphors are clearly of major significance throughout Derrida's texts.

23. Marco Diani and Catherine Ingraham, "Introduction" (in *Restructuring Architectural Theory*, 2). This volume contains an essay by Derrida, "Why Peter Eisenman Writes Such Good Books?" The French version is contained in *Psyché*, together with another relevant essay by Derrida, "Point de Folie—maintenant l'architecture." The essay on Peter Eisenman, as its title suggests, again alludes multiply to Nietzsche. Derrida's main reference, however, is the theme of labyrinth in Nietzsche rather than Nietzsche's sense of architecture at issue in the present discussion. Indeed, the "architecture" that emerges in Derrida's essay by way of Plato's notion of *chora* (in *Timaeus*) is, "perhaps," not Nietzschean, as Derrida himself suggests (99). Rather, it may again be closer to Heidegger, in part by virtue of its relation to Plato and *chora*.

Chapter 6 Radical Alterity

1. The political metaphor employed by Derrida is not accidental and not without consequences for the questions at issue in this chapter.

2. Derrida offers several important further elaborations, again in the context of Bataille, in his response to a letter from Jean-Louis Houdebine (*Positions*, 91–96).

3. It is important that, from Nietzsche and Freud on, the unconscious is materialist; that is, it is figured in relation to the economy of *matter*. This materialist economy also relates to the question of the body, which is an important dimension both of the question of matter and of the deconstruction of philosophy. As we have seen, the problematic of the body is central to the question of general economy; and it played a crucial role in Nietzsche's, Bataille's, Derrida's, and other "deconstructions" of classical philosophy, more recently, particularly in feminist theory. This continuous inscription of the *material* body into all fields of

discourse and analysis is also a crucial part of Foucault's and Deleuze's projects; but, as I have pointed out, these do not produce a general economy. While an idealism of the body is possible, to parallel an idealism of matter, the body may be an even greater enemy of idealism than matter is. But the question of matter must always be reinserted in turn into the chain where the question of the body is engaged.

4. Once again, this is not to say that such is, *simply*, Kant's own position or to deny the complexity and rigor of Kant's analysis of the ensuing economy.

5. In this sense, whatever criticism one advances against the "race, class, and gender" cliché, it reflects the continuing powerful impact of Marxist theory and ideology; and the economy—and especially, the general economy—of cliché is a very interesting question in its own right, far from being adequately developed. More generally, postcolonial, race, and gender studies, or more recently gay and lesbian studies, and other inquiries developing previously marginal or marginalized areas do open fields controlled neither by a single determination nor by a given determined opposition or relational cluster, but by engaging fluid multiplicities or, in present terms, dynamic complementarities—interactively heterogeneous and heterogeneously interactive relations. Such interactions do engage more or less stable denominations, oppositions, or interactions, whether determined by classical oppositional pairs or clusters—such as the global and the local, difference and identity, continuity and rupture, and so forth—or more recently developed historico- or politico-theoretical determinations—such as race, class, and gender. But these interactions also continuously, dynamically redefine such terms and rearrange their interactions, and introduce new denominations and clusters. In short, these interactions very much reflect and demand the economies at issue in the present study—general economies. In recent history, the fields at issue have developed by using Deleuze, Foucault, Derrida, Lacan, modern feminist theory, and other authors and frameworks defining the poststructuralist landscape, in short, by not only massively engaging but also powerfully affecting contemporary criticism and theory. The literature is growing, and in some areas exploding. The works of such scholars as Anthony Appiah, Houston Baker, Henry Louis Gates, Gayatri Spivak, and many others can be mentioned here. I have indicated some relevant studies in Chapter 1. The most recent interactive explorations include *Afro-American Literary Study in the 1990s*, edited by Houston A. Baker, Jr., and Patricia Redmond; Houston A. Baker, Jr., *Workings of the Spirit: The Poetics of Afro-American Women's Writing*; *Reading Black, Reading Feminist: A Critical Anthology*, edited by Henry Louis Gates, Jr.; *Inside/Out: Lesbian Theories, Gay Theories*, edited by Diana Fuss; *The Nature and Context of Minority Discourse*, edited by Abdul R. JanMohamed and David Lloyd; and Héctor Calderón and José David Saldívar, *Criticism in the Borderlands: Studies in Chicano Literature, Culture and Ideology*.

6. The notion of unequal development has a complex genealogy within the history of Marxism and in general. Lenin, however, developed it directly and made it into a powerful rhetorical and political tool. Its effectiveness in political practice is a complex issue, which may in turn need to be considered in the general

economy of historical and political interactions, as opposed to Lenin's restricted economy.

7. Among the more sympathetic studies or those generally following the Marxist orbit, one might point out two studies cited earlier: Jonathan Arac, *Critical Genealogies: Historical Situations for Postmodern Literary Studies*, and John Frow, *Marxism and Literary History*. See also Cornel West's "Ethics and Action in Fredric Jameson's Marxist Hermeneutic," in *Postmodernism and Politics*, edited by Jonathan Arac. Samuel Weber's discussion of *The Political Unconscious* in *Institution and Interpretation* is a strong critique, but one that is, in my view, justified. Weber's, actually, is a joint critique of Jameson's positions and of the institution where it emerges and operates. See also J. A. Berthoud, "Narrative and Ideology: A Critique of Fredric Jameson's *The Political Unconscious*," in *Narrative: From Malory to Motion Pictures*," edited by Jeremy Hawthorn. On the critique of Jameson in the context of narrative, see Didier Coste, *Narrative as Communication* (25–32).

8. See, in particular, a comment in *Late Marxism* (8), and a footnote at the outset of *Postmodernism* (xix n. 5), which persistently returns to the formulations of *The Political Unconscious*. See especially *Postmodernism* (53–54, 411).

9. We might now want to keep the term 'postmodernism' despite its perhaps all too great disseminating potential and the potential problems of using it. For Jameson's own attitude to the term, see his "Introduction" to *Postmodernism* (xxii).

10. One may even suggest cautiously that such agendas of criticism, so different in many ways, as the deconstructive, particularly the Yale school; the Foucauldian, such as the New Historicism; or some Marxism—for example, in Jameson and specifically *Postmodernism*—have and at times do in fact claim Arnoldian genealogies. While strategically and tactically disseminating itself, Arnold's strategy of moving from criticism of literature to criticism of culture governs, strategically and ideologically, much of the recent scene of literary studies.

11. Bataille's affinities with Marxism, specifically via Kojève, which Bataille persistently affirms, are of course relevant here, particularly given his simultaneous proximity to Nietzsche, also persistently claimed by him. They reflect both the capacious nature or the reappropriative economy of the Marxist matrix itself and even more the complexity and uneasiness of Bataille's balancing, or conflictualizing, his multiple theoretical, political, and aesthetic concerns. Given the analysis developed earlier, I think that Bataille's case, particularly in view of its close proximity to Nietzsche, finally confirms rather than undermines the point at issue.

12. See in particular the remarks respectively opening and closing *Postmodernism* (xiv–xv, 410).

13. There are a few things in both Marx and Hegel, or Heidegger and Althusser, that are more subtle and powerful than in Jameson's late Marxism. Recent readings of Hegel, particularly but not exclusively in and concerning deconstruction, and the exploration of related historical, political, cultural, or aesthetic logic, are indicative in this respect. Moreover, this "revival of Hegel" proceeds along lines quite different, more radically antidialectical, from the dialectical ones sug-

gested by Jameson himself in *Late Marxism* (241) and elsewhere. The analysis of Althusser below is offered here as an example that Marx, too, can be read more subtly in this respect and also as closer to the general economy, specifically concerning the notion of *Darstellung*, which Jameson engages in *Late Marxism* in the context of Adorno. Adorno himself is another interesting example in this respect but remains outside the scope of this study. I do think that both Adorno's and de Man's texts resist Jameson's analysis, such as with respect to the question of value in *Postmodernism* (237–38) or elsewhere in the chapter (217–59) that deals mainly with de Man.

14. One detects echoes of de Man here and elsewhere in the book, as well as in *Late Marxism* and *Postmodernism*. The latter contains a lengthy sympathetic discussion of de Man, often contrasting him with Derrida. De Man is obviously a part of the general landscape of modern criticism and theory. The significance of his ideas in some recent Marxist texts, such as Terry Eagleton's *Ideology of the Aesthetic* and Jameson's work is, however, notable and interesting. De Man's radically discontinuous economy of history may in fact be juxtaposed to the more continuous, more Hegelian economies of Marxism, such as the one described here in Jameson. Or, to be more precise, since, beginning with Hegel, the theories and rhetoric of temporality and historicity may involve both continuous and discontinuous economies, one should speak of the difference in distribution and functioning of the continuous and the discontinuous. In this respect, de Man's distances from all forms of dialectic, Hegelian or especially Marxist, far exceed his proximities to them. De Man's proximities to Hegel emerge along different lines in Hegel's own text, closer to Bataille or Derrida—along the lines of the economy of death, sacrifice, or loss of meaning.

15. See Derrida's analysis in "The Purveyor of Truth," where he shows that in Lacan, at least in the seminar on Poe, the transcendental signifier is the transcendental signified, always concealed by all other signifiers and signifieds.

16. The same, as we have seen, is also the case in Nietzsche, as also in de Man, although, in my attempts to trace de Man's concept of history across his various texts, I find his concept of history more problematic than either in Nietzsche, particularly later Nietzsche, or Derrida. In any event, de Man's historical concerns permeate most of his text, more so than they were given credit for in this respect, at least until the most recent, usually sympathetic readings of de Man, often "defending" him. One must perhaps add the qualification that de Man's historical vision or *Weltanschauung*, or a reading of it, is at issue here; for de Man throughout his readings engages many analyses and deconstructions of very diverse and multiply balanced historical economies.

17. Jameson actually invokes "genealogy" at this point (410) in a quasi-Nietzschean fashion, although the economy itself could hardly be more different.

18. One should not, of course, simply identify "spatial" and "synchronic," or historical, or temporal, and diachronic; and they often function differently in Jameson as well. These qualifications, however, would not undermine my point here.

19. The displacements, however, are persistent in this book and elsewhere, often by using terms that Derrida, in particular, never used. In *Postmodernism* and particularly in *Late Capitalism*, such displacements, at times quite significant, take place on just about every occasion, as in *Late Capitalism* (58, 235, 241, 244).

20. My reference here is to Derrida's remarks on Heidegger at the end of "*Différance*," by which I also want to indicate a certain proximity between the Marxist and the Heideggerian economy, on which I shall comment later. Several aspects of this point and the consequences of "capitalizing history" in Jameson are discussed in Samuel Weber's critique of Jameson, referred to earlier.

21. The opening analysis in Gasché's book is a fine example in this respect, offering a rigorous deconstructive questioning of self-consciousness in Hegel.

22. There is, of course, no such thing as a *general* deconstructive concept of 'text.' I refer to Jameson's specific remarks on Derrida's *différance* and *writing* and on some of de Man's tropes, which Jameson similarly displaces in *The Political Unconscious* and elsewhere. The essay "Deconstruction as Nominalism" in *Postmodernism* is particularly problematic in relation to Derrida and to the proximities and differences between Derrida and de Man. In Derrida's case, Jameson, it is true, only summarizes some ideas—"overhastily," as he admits (226). He does correctly point out, however, the significance of Althusser in Derrida and de Man, via Rousseau (231).

23. A critical understanding, definition, and analysis of the concept of text, or rather a lack of these and of a developed theory of the text, is in my view one of the problems of the New Historicism. This problem, let me note, does not disappear, but takes a different and more complex shape in Foucault, a major figure behind the New Historicism. See Paul Bové's discussion of Jameson, Foucault, Heidegger, and Deleuze and Guattari, in "The Foucault Phenomenon: The Problematics of Style," the foreword to Deleuze's *Foucault* (vii–lx). Jameson discusses New Historicism, more specifically Walter Benn Michaels' work, sympathetically in "Immanence and the New Historicism," the first part of his analysis of "postmodern theoretical discourse" in *Postmodernism* (181–216). Michaels' work is a relatively limited and special case of New Historicism, which, while found in other fields, has been most prominent in Renaissance studies. Jameson also discusses at length Stephen Knapp and Walter Benn Michaels' collaboration in "Against Theory," in *Against Theory*, edited by W. J. T. Mitchell, and "Against Theory 2," which, alongside his analysis of de Man in "Deconstruction as Nominalism," reflects clearly defined and delimited—and in some measure limited—theoretical and political choices. Jameson's pairing of "Against Theory" and de Man parallels Peggy Kamuf's much more cogent and rigorous discussion of both in *Signature Pieces* (177–228). Given the present study, Knapp and Michaels' analysis would have to be seen as extremely problematic. De Man's "resistance to theory" offers a far more complex case. The question of New Historicism is extensively discussed, including specifically in the contexts just indicated, in several essays assembled in *Consequences of Theory*, edited by Jonathan Arac and Barbara Johnson.

24. Jameson, on this occasion, opposes Lacan's symbolic register to Althusserian economy: "But the Lacanian system is threefold, and not dualistic. To the Marxian-Althusserian opposition of ideology and science correspond only two of Lacan's tripartite functions: the Imaginary and the Real, respectively. Our digression on cartography, however, with its final revelation of a properly representational dialectic of the codes and capacities of individual languages or media, reminds us that what has until now been omitted was the dimension of the Lacanian Symbolic itself" (53–54). I leave aside many problematic general points here that confirm the analysis given earlier. The point at the moment is that the Symbolic is crucial in Althusser. Lacanian or metonymic causality, so central to *Reading Capital* and structuring Marx's "immense theoretical revolution" as presented in that work, must engage the Symbolic Order. It may be that Jameson refers here mainly to "Ideology and Ideological and State Apparatuses," where Althusser seems to engage the Imaginary more actively and does not speak of the Symbolic. But that excuse is weak and would not sustain a strong argument. One can in fact argue, *strongly*, for the role of the Symbolic in the later essay, if one rigorously considers the economy of reproduction there, which Jameson does not do. The power of Althusser's analysis arises from its interactive engagement with all Lacanian registers, which may be engaged still more effectively against each other, particularly in deconstructing the Symbolic, as, to a degree, Irigaray does. That Jameson needs or privileges the Symbolic is understandable, for it is the most dialectical, the most Hegelian, of Lacanian or Althusserian registers, although it is in fact less Hegelian than in Jameson.

25. See again Derrida's remarks, in the context of Husserl, on the complexity of differentiating between the "pre-critical" and the "ultra-transcendental" text (*Of Grammatology*, 60–62).

26. The invocation of Nietzsche in *The Political Unconscious*, including against Derrida, is not accidental in this respect, as is also clear in the next section of *Late Marxism* (243–44).

27. Grouping various Marxist determinations—material, economic, political, or ideological—under the heading of "ideology" is "determined" by my "context" at the moment, the context of "late Marxism." Although much history and many recent works, some considered in this study, could be used to support my argument, the claim just made concerning my own "determination" at the moment cannot be strictly true. There are always other determinations or overdeterminations, or nondeterminations; and, as Derrida argues, no context or set of contexts can encompass them. As he points out in "Signature Event Context," "a context is never absolutely determinable, or rather . . . its determination is never certain or saturated" ("Signature Event Context," in *Margins*, 310; *Marges*, 369). This economy of interpretive determination—of whatever is to be determined— can thus be related fundamentally to context and ideology. A little later in the essay, Derrida defines Condillac's analysis, which he deconstructs, as "ideological." Derrida does so with qualifications and in quotation marks, and "not primarily in order to contrast its notions to 'scientific' concepts, or in order to refer

to the often dogmatic—one could also say 'ideological'—use made of the word ideology, which today [1972] is so rarely examined for its possibility and history. If I define notions of Condillac's kind as ideological, it is that against the background of a vast, powerful, and systematic philosophical tradition dominated by the self-evidence of the *idea* (*eidos, idea*) . . . " (*Margins*, 314; *Marges*, 374). For these very reasons, however, the term "ideological" is crucial. Perhaps not as much has changed since 1972 as could or should have. Also, some changes have in fact proceeded in the opposite—metaphysical, "ideological"—direction, even though, as is clear from the present analysis and many of the works referred to here, "Ideology," with a capital "I," as it must be seen from, and before, *Capital* throughout late Marxism, retains much of its power. The question may well be whether ideology can be made something else than this "self-evidence of the *idea*"—onto-ideo-theology. The analysis of the question of ideology in Althusser, including in its relation to Freud and Lacan there, is an important historico-theoretical juncture in this respect; but it would demand an extensive, separate treatment.

28. Jameson's comments on Heidegger throughout *Postmodernism* are also of great interest in this respect.

29. He may also be referring to Ludwig Wittgenstein's famous propositions on language at the end of the *Tractatus*.

30. It is interesting that Jameson's qualifications of late capitalism respond, as it were, to Derrida's remark: "Each time I fall upon this expression 'late capitalism' in texts dealing with literature and philosophy, it is clear to me that a dogmatic or stereotyped statement has replaced analytic demonstration" ("Some Questions and Responses," in *The Linguistics of Writing*, 254; *Postmodernism*, 419 n. 6). This statement is curiously framed by Jameson: "In particular people have begun to notice that it functions as a sign of some kind and seems to carry a burden of intent and consequence not clear to noninitiates" (xviii). In fact, Derrida's comment may actually be in need of further qualification, although it is understandable given the difficulties just indicated. One can and must establish historical connections, as well as some theoretical ones; in point of fact, such connections or possibilities are to be found in Jameson's book. One can—and within certain limits, must—speak of late, or later, capitalism and the specificity of its cultural logic.

31. Jameson's specific choice of examples is of interest as well.

32. I say "analogous," because such *differends*, when they occur, are only one type of effect of the general economy, which itself can never be a single or unitary economy. The latter may not be Lyotard's understanding of the economy of history in general. The "vision" of the historical and political as heterogeneous that emerges in *The Differend* has considerable critical potential, however, even if Lyotard himself does not always utilize it. One might also want to account for multiple *differends*, even within a given perspective.

33. I do not want to oversimpify the complexities of the Hegelian economy. Nevertheless, this complexity does not suspend the problematic dimensions of

Hegel, in particular various Hegelianisms. This point will be sustained, I think, however much Hegel's text becomes open to reinterpretations and revisions in the wake of recent developments, such as deconstruction. The very question of such "reinterpretations and revisions in the wake of" is a complex issue, and one must be careful as to the degree of claims made about "old" texts in the wake of "new" developments.

34. For the French version, see Louis Althusser, Étienne Balibar, and Roger Establet, *Lire le Capital* 2:164, 165, 167.

35. Althusser's recourse here, undoubtedly deliberate, to the notion of production should not be overlooked, however.

36. Here one might also refer to Foucault's analysis of the specificity of Marxist and Freudian discourse and their juxtaposition to scientific discourse in "What Is an Author?" (1969) (in *Language, Counter-Memory, Practice*, 113–38).

37. This passage is absent from the abridged edition of 1968 and from the English translation. Both in its own specificity, or more precisely, many of its own specificities in the texts that employ it, and as part of the general problems of representation, *Darstellung* is, of course, a crucial concept across a very broad spectrum. Walter Benjamin opens his *Ursprung des deutschen Trauerspiels* by pointing out the necessity for philosophy continually to confront the question of *Darstellung*. In the context of Marxism and particularly Marx's "immense theoretical revolution," a rigorous analysis of the history of the concept of *Darstellung* would have to begin with its role in Hegel. This analysis cannot be undertaken here. See Warminski's discussion of Hegel, particularly "Pre-positional By-play" (in *Readings in Interpretation: Hölderlin, Hegel, Heidegger*, 95–111). Here I refer to it only in the context of Althusser's using it; even there, he deploys it still in a limited fashion, and one would in fact have to nuance the difference between *Vorstellung* and *Darstellung* further. In *The Eighteenth Brumaire* Marx uses still another word for (and thus the concept of) representation—*Vertretung*—a kind of substitutive representation or substitution. From a certain perspective, the economy of Derrida's *différance* is a necessary pre-comprehension or reconfiguration of the restricted economy of *Darstellung*—or the interplay of *Darstellung* and *Vorstellung*, or again *Vertretung*—or the spectrum of such economies operative in the history of Western metaphysics. In this economy as a general economy, more radical displacing possibilities (*Entstellung*) are taken into account both in order to deconstruct and precomprehend *Darstellung*—or again *Vorstellung*—and the restricted metaphysical economies organized around it. In Althusser, these problems specifically concern the question of totality, an issue that I shall consider later. On *Entstellung*, see also Weber's discussion of Freud in *The Legend of Freud* (20–31).

38. The English translation is modified in accord with the French edition.

39. See also *Positions*, 13–14.

40. Nothing, in fact, is or can be read otherwise according to Heidegger, which is not to say that the economy of such a reading is not complex—quite the contrary.

41. I apply this rubric 'phenomenological-ontological' to Heidegger while retaining his own numerous qualifications, beginning with *Being and Time*, as to his proximities to and distances from Husserlian phenomenology.

42. Lacan's dependence on Hegel's dialectic of desire in the analysis of self-consciousness in the *Phenomenology* becomes important in the present context. One can even say that Hegel's dialectic of desire already offers an economy of structural or metonymic causality, analogous and possibly equivalent to the one Althusser develops in his reading of Marx.

43. The invocation of a train ride is singularly appropriate here. Einstein's famous popular exposition of relativity begins with an example of trains. See Albert Einstein, *Relativity: The Special and General Theory*.

44. Herman Weyl, in *Space—Time—Matter*, one of the major works in the history of modern science, begins with a reference to Brentano's phenomenology, which could be replaced by Husserl's without significantly altering Weyl's point. Brentano's conceptions are more "psychological"; and Husserl's "phenomenological reduction," specifically to "authentic temporality," is accompanied by a critique of psychologism in Brentano, whose student Husserl was. Freud would have had to have been familiar with Brentano's ideas; thus Brentano is doubtless a "source" of a few things in Freud as well. Brentano's legacy—the estate of "psychological phenomenology"—became, as it were, divided between Freud and Husserl, between psychoanalysis and phenomenology; it was then transmitted and transformed, disseminated, perhaps most importantly, as concerns its phenomenological capital, via Heidegger, to most figures on the modern scene at issue here.

45. Bergson, we recall, had a keen interest in Einstein's theory from very early on. Einstein himself, while he is reported to have come "to know, like, and respect Bergson, . . . of Bergson's philosophy used to say, 'Gott verzeih ihm,' God forgive him" (quoted by Abraham Pais, "*Subtle is the Lord . . . ,*" 510). Bergson, of course, is a crucial reference throughout Deleuze's work, and specifically in the context of Einstein's general relativity and Riemann's manifold as its mathematical model in Deleuze and Guattari's *A Thousand Plateaus* (32–33, 482–488). See also Deleuze's *Foucault* (13–14). These connections are also important in the context of spatialization and cartographic economies as discussed earlier. Riemann's theory offers a possibility of mapping complex, such as non-Euclidean, geometrical structures. In a way, it is a very general mathematical, and specifically topological, theory of heterogeneous but sufficiently continuous mapping.

46. Bataille offers some extraordinary elaborations on the topic at issue in this part of the book.

Chapter 7 Machines

1. "Democritus as the result of machines. . . . The secondary properties of matter, *nomo*, not of Matter-In-Itself" (*KSA* 7: 555–56).

2. The thematics and metaphorics themselves, with their multiple applications and implications, are elaborated by Derrida in relation to Hegel—and the ghost of *Geist*—in *Glas*; then in more general terms, in *The Post Card*, with its apocalypse of letters; and in relation to Heideggerian problematics, in Derrida's recent works on Heidegger, Blanchot, and other authors, together with *Of Spirit*. The economy of death and its relation to the question of writing, technology, and related issues in Heidegger's own works, would require a separate treatment. I can address these questions here only in a limited way.

3. In this case, Bataille proceeds by a rather direct metaphoric transfer. The relations between Bataille's ideas concerning general economy and modern physics, specifically quantum mechanics, are more profound, fundamentally shaping Bataille's thinking on the issue. Conversely, it may be argued that quantum mechanics, at least complementarity as Bohr's interpretation of quantum physics is general economic.

4. In this context, too, Deleuze's analysis of the question of difference and force in *Nietzsche and Philosophy* is important; and as we have seen, it has influenced many subsequent discussions. More recent scientific theories, such as theories of dark matter—black holes and the like—combining gravity and general relativity, thermodynamics, and quantum mechanics may offer an extraordinary metaphoric potential in this respect. They are themselves the products of very complex and, I would say, general economic metaphoric configurations and reconfigurations. My main sources here are texts assembled in *Three Hundred Years of Gravitation*, edited by Werner Israel and Stephen W. Hawking, and *Complexity, Entropy, and the Physics of Information*, edited by Wojciech H. Zurek; but the literature on the issues—scientific, semipopular, and popular—is extensive.

5. De Man, in "Shelley Disfigured," says that "the power of death is due to the randomness of its occurrence" (in *The Rhetoric of Romanticism*, 122)—often, perhaps even mostly, but not always.

6. As such, it must be opposed to Heideggerian finitude, which is not to say that the latter or the opposition at issue is a simple matter. See Derrida's remark on *différance* as "something other than finitude" (*Of Grammatology*, 68), again indicating a very complex engagement between Heideggerian and Derridean economies of difference. At issue is the relation to a "difference" that is neither finite nor infinite, but within the closure of, among others, the opposition between the finite and the infinite—to the extent that, in particular, the latter notion can be rigorously, or indeed in any way, conceived of.

7. *Historie de l'Academy Royale des Sciences, Année 1775* (Paris: Imprimérie Royale, 1778), 61–66; cited in Pais, *Inward Bound*, 105.

8. Newton's own conceptions concerning the Universe as a whole are far more subtle and nuanced, displaying a great awareness of the problems—of (human) perception and consciousness, conceptions of wholeness, or physics itself, in the first place—than what is conventionally invoked as the *Newtonian* universe tends to suggest. See, for example, Koyré, *Newtonian Studies*. See also Roger Pen-

rose, "Newton, Quantum Theory and Reality" (in *Three Hundred Years of Gravitation*, 17–49).

9. Some of them are assembled in *The Question Concerning Technology*.

10. For a recent historical exposition, mostly within the fields of modern physics, see, for example, Abraham Pais' discussions of the issue in *"Subtle Is the Lord..."* (55–110, 357–434) and *Inward Bound*. An enormous amount of literature has accrued on the issues, including in relation to quantum mechanics, in the history of science, popular and semipopular expositions, and so on. The most ambitious and best-known attempt to address these issues in general terms, from the perspective of science, is Ilya Prigogine and Isabelle Stengers, *Order out of Chaos*, which invokes many of the figures in the landscape of this discussion—Hegel (there is a section on Hegel and Bergson [89–93]), Nietzsche, Heidegger, Deleuze, and many others.

11. See David Farrell Krell, "Analysis," in Martin Heidegger, *Nietzsche*, vol. 2, *The Eternal Recurrence of the Same*, 261.

12. See also his powerful remarks on physics itself in section 636.

13. A number of recent studies cited earlier and many others throughout the history of reading Nietzsche could be mentioned here. The only other notion generating an actual and potential range of interpretation that is comparable to that of Nietzsche's eternal recurrence may be Heraclitean flux. Both notions—along with, among others, Heidegger's Being or Time or Hegel's *Geist* or Derrida's *différance*—might still be interpreting each other, or interpreting the "same" thing—or the (im)possibility of the "same" as identical to itself in being or becoming, and thus the (im)possibility of interpreting the same thing. As I have stressed throughout, however, we must rigorously maintain the differences between different economies emerging as a result, most importantly, between restricted and general economies.

14. See Derrida's conclusion to "Structure, Sign, and Play" (in *Writing and Difference*, 293).

15. As I have indicated earlier, however, the term 'philosophical' must be used with caution in relation to all Heidegger's ideas, particularly in his later essays.

16. See Edmund Husserl, *The Crisis of European Sciences and Transcendental Phenomenology*.

17. In addition to Derrida's own many recent works (from *The Post Card* on, most recently, in "Circumfession," in Geoffrey Bennington and Jacques Derrida, *Jacques Derrida*) where the questions of technology are extensively engaged, and Lacoue-Labarthe's *Heidegger, Art and Politics*, see, for example, on Heidegger, Samuel Weber's discussion in "The Debts of Deconstruction," in *Institution and Interpretation*; and more directly "technologically," Avital Ronell's recent *The Telephone Book: Technology—Schizophrenia—Electric Speech*. Gregory Ulmer, in *Applied Grammatology* and *Teletheory: Grammatology in the Age of Video*, explores the technological thematics as well.

18. See also Derrida's analysis of Joyce's *Ulysses* in *Ulysse grammaphone: Deux mots pour Joyce* and his "Psyche: Inventions of the Other," in *Reading de Man*

Reading (originally published as the title essay of *Psyché: Inventions de l'autre*). See, in addition, Geoffrey Bennington's essay on de Man and Pascal "Aberrations: De Man (and) the Machine," in *Reading de Man Reading*. In *The Differend*, Lyotard comments on the issue in the context of both Hegel and Derrida's statement just cited (96). One can also refer to Deleuze and Guattari's notion of the 'literary machine,' in relation to Blanchot, Proust, and Joyce (*Anti-Oedipus*, 42–43), which I have mentioned in Chapter 6; Deleuze and Guattari's discussion there may be one of Derrida's sources on Joyce.

19. This point again suggests the conceptual and metaphoric relations between undecidables and incompleteness in Gödel's sense and entropy.

20. A collection of Einstein's writing was published entitled *Albert Einstein: Philosopher-Scientist*, edited by P. A. Schilpp. As I have suggested at the outset of this study, however, Bohr may actually be the most radical physicist-philosopher in this century.

21. The issue of these relations between poetry and mathematics (re)emerges in Poe's *The Purloined Letter* and then is played out both in Lacan's seminar on the story and Derrida's reading of Lacan—and Poe—in "The Purveyor of Truth."

22. See Vladimir I. Propp, *Morphology of the Folktale*. See again Derrida's discussion in *Ulysse grammaphone* and Deleuze and Guattari's comments on Blanchot (*Anti-Oedipus*, 42–43).

Bibliography

Ackermann, Robert John. *Nietzsche: A Frenzied Look*. Amherst: University of Massachusetts Press, 1990.

Aeschylus. *Prometheus Bound*. Bilingual ed. Translated by H. W. Smyth. Cambridge, Mass.: Harvard University Press, 1922.

Adorno, Theodor W. *Negative Dialektik*. Frankfurt am Main: Suhrkamp Verlag, 1966. Translated by E. B. Ashton as *Negative Dialectics*. London: Routledge & Kegan Paul, 1973; New York: Seabury Press, 1973.

Allison, David B. Introduction to *Speech and Phenomena*, by Jacques Derrida. Translated by David Allison. Evanston, Ill.: Northwestern University Press, 1972.

―――. "Nietzsche Knows No Noumenon." In *Why Nietzsche Now?* ed. Daniel O'Hara. Bloomington: Indiana University Press, 1985.

Althusser, Louis. *Lenin and Philosophy and Other Essays*. Translated by Ben Brewster. New York: Monthly Review Press, 1971.

―――, Étienne Balibar, and Roger Establet. *Lire le Capital*. Paris: François Maspero, 1965. Translated by Ben Brewster as *Reading Capital*. London: Verso, 1983.

Anderson, Perry. *In the Tracks of Historical Materialism*. London: Verso, 1983.

Arac, Jonathan. *Critical Genealogies: Historical Situations for Postmodern Literary Studies*. New York: Columbia University Press, 1987.

―――, ed. *Postmodernism and Politics: New Directions*. Minneapolis: University of Minnesota Press, 1986.

―――, and Barbara Johnson, eds. *Consequences of Theory*. Baltimore: Johns Hopkins University Press, 1991.

Arac, Jonathan, Wlad Godzich, and Wallace Martin, eds. *The Yale Critics: Deconstruction in America*. Minneapolis: University of Minnesota Press, 1983.

Bachelard, Gaston. *L'Air et les songes*. Paris: Corty, 1943. Translated by Edith R. Farrell and C. Frederick Farrell as *Air and Dreams: An Essay on the Imagination of Movements*. Dallas: Dallas Institute Publications, 1988.

Baker, Houston A., Jr. *Workings of the Spirit: The Poetics of Afro-American Women's Writing.* Phototext by Elizabeth Alexander and Patricia Redmond. Chicago: University of Chicago Press, 1991.

——, and Patricia Redmond, eds. *Afro-American Literary Study in the 1990s.* Chicago: University of Chicago Press, 1989.

Barthes, Roland. *La Chambre claire.* Paris: Éditions du Seuil, 1980. Translated by Richard Howard as *Camera Lucida: Reflections on Photography.* New York: Hill and Wang, 1981.

Bataille, Georges. *L'Abbé C.* In *Oeuvres complètes,* vol. 3. Translated by Philip A. Facey as *L'Abbé C.* London and New York: Marion Boyars, 1988.

——. *Le Coupable.* Paris: Gallimard, 1944. Translated by Bruce Boone as *Guilty.* New York: Lapis Press, 1988.

——. *L'Erotisme.* Paris: Éditions de Minuit, 1957. Translated by Mary Dalwood as *Erotism: Death and Sensuality.* San Francisco: City Lights Books, 1986.

——. *L'Expérience intérieure.* Paris: Gallimard, 1954. Translated by Leslie Anne Boldt as *Inner Experience.* Albany: State University of New York Press, 1980.

——. "Hegel, la mort et le sacrifice." *Decaulion* 5 (1955):23–43.

——. "*La Part maudite*" *précédé de* "*La Notion de dépense.*" Paris: Éditions de Minuit, 1967. Translated by Robert Hurley as *The Accursed Share: An Essay on General Economy.* Vol. 1. New York: Zone, 1988.

——. *Oeuvres Complètes.* Paris: Gallimard, 1970– .

——. *Visions of Excess: Selected Writings, 1927–1939.* Edited by Alan Stoekl. Minneapolis: University of Minnesota Press, 1985.

Bateson, Gregory. *Steps to an Ecology of Mind.* New York: Ballantine, 1972.

Benjamin, Walter. *Ursprung des deutschen Trauerspiels.* Vol. 1, pt. 1 of *Gesammelte Schriften.* Frankfurt am Main: Suhrkamp Verlag, 1980. Translated by John Osborne as *The Origin of German Tragic Drama.* London: Verso, 1985.

Bennington, Geoffrey. "Aberrations: De Man (and) the Machine." In *Reading de Man Reading,* edited by Lindsay Waters and Wlad Godzich. Minneapolis: University of Minnesota Press, 1989.

——. *Lyotard: Writing the Event.* New York: Columbia University Press, 1988.

——, and Jacques Derrida. *Jacques Derrida.* Paris: Éditions du Seuil, 1991.

Berezdevin, Ruben. "Drawing: (An) Affecting Nietzsche: With Derrida." In *Derrida and Deconstruction,* edited by Hugh J. Silverman. New York: Routledge, 1989.

Bernstein, Richard J., ed. *Habermas and Modernity.* Cambridge, Mass.: MIT Press, 1985.

Berthoud, J. A. "Narrative and Ideology: A Critique of Fredric Jameson's *The Political Unconscious.*" In *Narrative: From Malory to Motion Pictures,* edited by Jeremy Hawthorn. London: Edward Arnold, 1985.

Blanchot, Maurice. *L'Entretien infini.* Paris: Gallimard, 1969.

Blondel, Eric. *Nietzsche, le corps and la culture: La Philosophie comme généalogie philologique.* Paris: Presses Universitaires de France, 1986. Translated by Seán

Hand as *Nietzsche, The Body and Culture: Philosophy as a Philological Genealogy.* Stanford, Calif.: Stanford University Press, 1991.

Bloom, Harold, ed. *Friedrich Nietzsche.* New York: Chelsea House Publishers, 1987.

Bohr, Niels. *Atomic Physics and Human Knowledge.* New York: Wiley, 1958.

————. *Atomic Theory and the Description of Nature.* Cambridge: Cambridge University Press, 1961.

————. *The Philosophical Writings of Niels Bohr.* 3 vols. Woodbridge, Conn.: Ox Bow Press, 1987.

————. "The Quantum Postulate and the Recent Development of Atomic Theory." *Nature* 121 (1928).

Bové, Paul. "The Foucault Phenomenon: The Problematics of Style." Foreword to Gilles Deleuze, *Foucault.* Translated by Seán Hand. Minneapolis: University of Minnesota Press, 1988.

Brodsky, Claudia. *The Imposition of Form: Studies in Narrative Representation and Knowledge.* Princeton, N.J.: Princeton University Press, 1987.

Brunette, Peter, and David Wills. *Screen/Play: Derrida and Film Theory.* Princeton, N.J.: Princeton University Press, 1989.

Butler, Judith. *Gender Trouble: Feminism and the Subversion of Identity.* New York: Routledge, 1990.

Calderón, Héctor, and José David Saldívar. *Criticism in the Borderlands: Studies in Chicano Literature, Culture and Ideology.* Durham, N.C.: Duke University Press, 1991.

Caputo, John D. "The Economy of Signs in Husserl and Derrida: From Uselessness to Full Employment." In *Deconstruction and Philosophy: The Texts of Jacques Derrida,* edited by John Sallis. Chicago: University of Chicago Press, 1986.

————. *Radical Hermeneutics: Repetition, Deconstruction and the Hermeneutic Project.* Bloomington: Indiana University Press, 1987.

Clark, Maudemarie. *Nietzsche on Truth and Philosophy.* Cambridge: Cambridge University Press, 1990.

Cohen, Tom. "Hyperscript: Hitchcock's *Secret Agent* and the Death of (Mr.) Memory." Paper presented at the International Narrative Conference, Nashville, Tennessee, April 1992.

Compagnon, Antoine. "Mapping the European Mind." *Critical Quarterly* 32, no. 2 (1990):1–7.

Coste, Didier. *Narrative as Communication.* Minneapolis: University of Minnesota Press, 1989.

Culler, Jonathan. *The Pursuit of Signs—Semiotics, Literature, Deconstruction.* Ithaca, N.Y.: Cornell University Press, 1981.

Davis, Robert Con, and Ronald Schleifer, eds. *Rhetoric and Form: Deconstruction at Yale.* Norman: University of Oklahoma Press, 1985.

Davis, Walter A. *Inwardness and Existence: Subjectivity in/and Hegel, Heidegger, Marx, and Freud.* Madison: University of Wisconsin Press, 1989.

Deleuze, Gilles. Différence et Répétition. Paris: Presses Universitaires de France, 1968.

———. *Foucault*. Paris: Éditions de Minuit, 1986. Translated by Seán Hand as *Foucault*. Minneapolis: University of Minnesota Press, 1988.

———. *Nietzsche et la philosophie*. Paris: Presses Universitaires de France, 1962. Translated by Hugh Tomlinson as *Nietzsche and Philosophy*. London: Athlone Press, 1983.

———. *Spinoza, Philosophie pratique*. Paris: Éditions de Minuit, 1981. Translated by Robert Hurley as *Spinoza: Practical Philosophy*. San Francisco: City Lights Books, 1988.

———. *Spinoza et le problème de l'expression*. Paris: Les Editions de Minuit, 1968. Translated by Martin Joughin as *Expressionism in Philosophy: Spinoza*. New York: Zone Books, 1990.

———, and Félix Guattari. *L'Anti-Oedipe: Capitalisme et schizophrénie*. Paris: Éditions de Minuit, 1972. Translated by Robert Hurley, Mark Seem, and Helen R. Lane as *Anti-Oedipus: Capitalism and Schizophrenia*. Minneapolis: University of Minnesota Press, 1983.

———. *A Thousand Plateaus: Capitalism and Schizophrenia*. Translated by Brian Massumi. Minneapolis: University of Minnesota Press, 1987.

———, and Claire Parnet. *Dialogues*. Paris: Flammarion, 1977. Translated by Hugh Tomlinson and Barbara Habberjam as *Dialogues*. New York: Columbia University Press, 1987.

De Man, Paul. *Allegories of Reading: Figural Language in Rousseau, Nietzsche, Rilke, and Proust*. New Haven: Yale University Press, 1979.

———. *Blindness and Insight: Essays in the Rhetoric of Contemporary Criticism*. Minneapolis: University of Minnesota Press, 1983.

———. "Hegel and the Sublime." In *Displacement: Derrida and After*, edited by Mark Krupnick. Bloomington: Indiana University Press, 1987.

———. *The Resistance to Theory*. Minneapolis: University of Minnesota Press, 1986.

———. *The Rhetoric of Romanticism*. New York: Columbia University Press, 1984.

Derrida, Jacques. *Acts of Literature*. Edited by Derek Attridge. New York: Routledge, 1992.

———. "Architettura ove il desiderio pou abitare." *Domus* 24 (April 1986): 17–24.

———. *La Carte postale: De Socrate à Freud et au-delà*. Paris: Flammarion, 1980. Translated by Alan Bass as *The Post Card: From Socrates to Freud and Beyond*. Chicago: University of Chicago Press, 1987.

———. "Choreographies." *Diacritics* 12 (1982).

———. *De la grammatologie*. Paris: Éditions de Minuit, 1967. Translated by Gayatri C. Spivak as *Of Grammatology*. Baltimore: Johns Hopkins University Press, 1976.

———. *De l'esprit: Heidegger et la question*. Paris: Éditions Galilée, 1987; Coll. La Philosophie en Effet. Translated by Geoffrey Bennington and Rachel Bowlby as *Of Spirit: Heidegger and the Question.* Chicago: University of Chicago Press, 1989.

▬▬▬. "La 'Différance.'" *Bulletin de la Société Française de la Philosophie* 62, no. 3 (July–September 1968):73–101.

▬▬▬. *La Dissémination.* Paris: Éditions du Seuil, 1972. Translated by Barbara Johnson as *Dissemination.* Chicago: University of Chicago Press, 1981.

▬▬▬. "'Eating Well,' or the Calculation of the Subject: An Interview with Jacques Derrida." In *Who Comes After the Subject?,* edited by Eduardo Cadava, Peter Connor, and Jean-Luc Nancy. New York: Routledge, 1991.

▬▬▬. "Economimesis." In Sylviane Agacinski et al., *Mimesis des articulations.* Paris: Aubier-Flammarion, 1975. Translated by R. Klein as "Economimesis." *Diacritics* 11, no. 3 (1981):3–25.

▬▬▬. *L'Écriture et la différence.* Paris: Éditions du Seuil, 1967. Translated by Alan Bass as *Writing and Difference.* Chicago: University of Chicago Press, 1978.

▬▬▬, trans. and intro. *Edmund Husserl, L'Origine de la géométrie.* Paris: Presses Universitaires de France, 1962. Translated by John P. Leavey, Jr., as *Edmund Husserl's Origin of Geometry: An Introduction,* by Jacques Derrida. Edited by David B. Allison. Stony Brook, N.Y.: Nicolas Hays, 1978.

▬▬▬. *Éperons: Les Styles de Nietzsche.* Paris: Flammarion, 1976. Translated by Barbara Harlow as *Spurs: Nietzsche's Styles.* Bilingual ed. Chicago: University of Chicago Press, 1979.

▬▬▬. "Force de loi: Le 'Fondement mystique de l'autorité.'" Translated by Mary Quintaine as "Force of Law: The 'Mystical Foundation of Authority.'" *Cardozo Law Review* 11, nos. 5–6 (July–August 1990):919–1045.

▬▬▬. "Fors: The Anglish Words of Nicolas Abraham and Maria Torok." Preface to Nicolas Abraham and Maria Torok, *Le Verbier de l'homme aux loups.* Paris: Flammarion, 1976. Translated by Barbara Johnson as "Fors." *Georgia Review* 31 (Spring 1977):64–116. Reprinted in *The Wolf Man's Magic Word: A Cryptonomy,* edited by Nicolas Abraham and Maria Torok, xi–xlviii. Minneapolis: University of Minnesota Press, 1986.

▬▬▬. "*Geschlecht:* Différence sexuelle, différence ontologique." In *Psyché: Inventions de l'autre.* Paris: Éditions Galilée, 1987. Translated as "*Geschlecht:* sexual difference, ontological difference." *Research in Phenomenology* 13 (1983):65–83.

▬▬▬. *Glas.* Paris: Galilée, 1974. Translated by John P. Leavey, Jr., and Richard Rand as *Glas.* Lincoln: University of Nebraska Press, 1986.

▬▬▬. "Languages and Institutions of Philosophy." *Récherches Sémiotiques/Semiotic Inquiry* 4 (1984):91–154.

▬▬▬. *Limited Inc.* Evanston, Ill.: Northwestern University Press, 1988.

▬▬▬. "Living On: Border Lines." Translated by James Hulbert. In Harold Bloom et al., *Deconstruction and Criticism,* 75–176. New York: Seabury Press, 1979.

▬▬▬. "La Loi du genre/The Law of Genre." Translated by Avital Ronnell. In *Glyph* 7, 176–232. Baltimore: Johns Hopkins University Press, 1980.

———. "La Main de Heidegger (*Geschlecht II*)." In *Psyché: Inventions de l'autre.* Paris: Éditions Galilée, 1987. Translated as "*Geschlecht* II: Heidegger's Hand." In *Deconstruction and Philosophy*, edited by John Sallis. Chicago: University of Chicago Press, 1987.

———. *Marges de la philosophie.* Paris: Éditions de Minuit, 1972. Translated by Alan Bass as *Margins of Philosophy.* Chicago: University of Chicago Press, 1982.

———. *Memoires: For Paul de Man.* Translated by Cecile Lindsay, Jonathan Culler, and Eduardo Cadava. New York: Columbia University Press, 1986.

———. "My Chances/*Mes Chances:* A Rendezvous with Some Epicurean Stereophones." In *Taking Chances: Derrida, Psychoanalysis, and Literature,* edited by Joseph H. Smith and William Kerrigan. Baltimore: Johns Hopkins University Press, 1989.

———. "Of an Apocalyptic Tone Recently Adopted in Philosophy." *Oxford Literary Review* 6, no. 2 (1984):3–37.

———. *L'Oreille de l'autre: Otobiographies, transferts, traductions.* Edited by Claude Lévesque and Christie V. McDonald. Montreal: VLB, 1982. Translated by Peggy Kamuf as *The Ear of the Other: Otobiography, Transference, Translation.* New York: Schocken Books, 1985.

———. *Parages.* Paris: Éditions Galilée, 1986.

———. "Point de folie—maintenant l'architecture." In *Psyché: Inventions de l'autre.* Paris: Éditions Galilée, 1987.

———. *Positions.* Paris: Éditions de Minuit, 1972. Translated by Alan Bass as *Positions.* Chicago: University of Chicago Press, 1981.

———. *Psyché: Inventions de l'autre.* Paris: Éditions Galilée, 1987.

———. "The *Retrait* of Metaphor." *Enclitic* 2 (Fall 1978): 5–33. Originally published as "Le Retrait de la métaphore." In *Psyché: Inventions de l'autre.* Paris: Éditions Galilée, 1987.

———. "Scribble (writing-power)." *Yale French Studies* 58 (1979):115–47.

———. "Some Statements and Truisms about Neologisms, Newisms, Postisms, Parasitisms, and Other Small Seismisms." In *The States of "Theory": History, Art, and Other Critical Discourse,* edited by David Carroll. New York: Columbia University Press, 1990.

———. "The Time of the Thesis: Punctuation." In *Philosophy in France Today,* edited by Alan Montefiore. Cambridge: Cambridge University Press, 1983.

———. "Title (to be specified)." *Sub-Stance* 2 (1981):5–22.

———. *Ulysse grammaphone: Deux mots pour Joyce.* Paris: Éditions Galilée, 1987.

———. *La Vérité en peinture.* Paris: Flammarion, 1978. Translated by Geoff Bennington and Ian Mcleod as *The Truth in Painting.* Chicago: University of Chicago Press, 1987.

———. *La Voix et le phénomène.* Paris: Presses Universitaires de France, 1967. Translated by David B. Allison as *Speech and Phenomena, and Other Essays on Husserl's Theory of Signs.* Evanston, Ill.: Northwestern University Press, 1973.

————. "Why Peter Eisenman Writes Such Good Books?" In *Restructuring Architectural Theory*, edited by Marco Diani and Catherine Ingraham. Evanston, Ill.: Northwestern University Press, 1989.

Descombes, Vincent. *Le Même et L'Autre*. Paris: Éditions de Minuit, 1979. Translated by L. Scott-Fox and J. M. Harding as *Modern French Philosophy*. Cambridge: Cambridge University Press, 1980.

Detwiler, Bruce. *Nietzsche and the Politics of Aristocratic Radicalism*. Chicago: University of Chicago Press, 1990.

Diani, Marco, and Catherine Ingraham. Introduction to *Restructuring Architectural Theory*, edited by Marco Diani and Catherine Ingraham. Evanston, Ill.: Northwestern University Press, 1989.

Donato, Eugenio. "Ending/Closure: On Derrida's Edging of Heidegger." *Yale French Studies* 67 (1984):3–22.

Eagleton, Terry. *Ideology of the Aesthetic*. Oxford: Basil Blackwell, 1990.

Eco, Umberto. "Map of the Empire." Translated by S. Eugene Scalin. *The Literary Review* 28 (1985): 233–38.

Einstein, Albert. *Relativity: The Special and General Theory*. Translated by Robert W. Lawson. New York: Crown, 1961.

Ellis, John M. *Against Deconstruction*. Princeton, N.J.: Princeton University Press, 1989.

Fekete, John, ed. *Life after Postmodernism: Essays on Value and Culture*. New York: St. Martin's Press, 1987.

Feyerabend, Paul K. *Against Method: Outline of an Anarchistic Theory of Knowledge*. London: Verso, 1975.

————. "Problem of Microphysics." In *Frontiers of Science and Philosophy*, edited by Robert G. Colodny. London: Allen & Unwin, 1962.

————. *Science in a Free Society*. London: NLB, 1978.

Fish, Stanley. *Doing What Comes Naturally: Change, Rhetoric, and the Practice of Theory in Literary and Legal Studies*. Durham, N.C.: Duke University Press, 1989.

Folse, Henry J. *The Philosophy of Niels Bohr: The Framework of Complementarity*. Amsterdam: North-Holland, 1985.

Foucault, Michel. "Dernier entretien." / "Le retour de la morale." Interview with Gilles Barbedette and André Scala. *Les Nouvelles* (28 June–5 July 1984). Translated by Thomas Levin and Isabelle Lorenz as "Final Interview: Michel Foucault." *Raritan* 5, no. 1 (1985):1–13.

————. *Language, Counter-Memory, Practice*. Edited by Donald F. Bouchard. Ithaca, N.Y.: Cornell University Press, 1977.

————. *Les Mots et les choses*. Paris: Gallimard, 1966. Translated as *The Order of Things: An Archeology of the Human Sciences*. 1971; New York: Vintage, 1973.

Frow, John. *Marxism and Literary History*. Cambridge, Mass.: Harvard University Press, 1986.

Fuss, Diana, ed. *Inside/Out: Lesbian Theories, Gay Theories*. New York: Routledge, 1991.

Gasché, Rodolphe. "L'Almanach hétérologique." *Nuovo Corrente* (Milan), no. 66 (1975):3–60.

———. "Autobiography as Gestalt." In *Why Nietzsche Now?*, edited by Daniel O'Hara. Bloomington: Indiana University Press, 1985.

———. "Deconstruction as Criticism." In *Glyph 6*, 177–215. Baltimore: Johns Hopkins University Press, 1979.

———. "L'Échange héliocentrique." *L'Arc*, no. 48 (1972):73–84.

———. "In-difference to Philosophy: De Man on Kant, Hegel, and Nietzsche." In *Reading de Man Reading*, edited by Lindsay Waters and Wlad Godzich, 259–94. Minneapolis: University of Minnesota Press, 1989.

———. "Joining the Text: From Heidegger to Derrida." In *The Yale Critics: Deconstruction in America*, edited by Jonathan Arac, Wlad Godzich, and Wallace Martin. Minneapolis: University of Minnesota Press, 1983.

———. *System und Metaphorik in der Philosophie von Georges Bataille.* Bern: Peter Lang, 1978.

———. *The Tain of The Mirror: Derrida and the Philosophy of Reflection.* Cambridge, Mass.: Harvard University Press, 1986.

Gates, Henry Louis, Jr. *Reading Black, Reading Feminist: A Critical Anthology.* New York: Meridian, 1990.

Godzich, Wlad. "The Time Machine." Foreword to Didier Coste, *Narrative as Communication.* Minneapolis: University of Minnesota Press, 1989.

Graff, Gerald. *Professing Literature: An Institutional History.* Chicago: University of Chicago Press, 1987.

Guattari, Félix. "The Postmodern Dead End." *Flash Art* 128 (May/June 1986):40–41. Originally published as "L'Impasse post-moderne." *La Quinzaine Littéraire* 456 (February 1986):1–15.

Guyer, Paul, ed. *The Cambridge Companion to Kant.* Cambridge: Cambridge University Press, 1992.

———. *Kant and the Claims of Knowledge.* Cambridge: Cambridge University Press, 1987.

———. *Kant and the Claims of Taste.* Cambridge, Mass.: Harvard University Press, 1979.

———, and Ted Cohen, eds. *Essays in Kant's Aesthetics.* Chicago: University of Chicago Press, 1982.

Habermas, Jürgen. *Der philosophische Diskurs der Moderne: Zwölf Vorlesungen.* Frankfurt am Main: Suhrkamp, 1988. Translated by Frederic Lawrence as *The Philosophical Discourse of Modernity.* Cambridge, Mass.: MIT Press, 1987.

Hartman, Geoffrey. *Saving the Text.* Baltimore: Johns Hopkins University Press, 1981.

Harvey, David. *The Condition of Postmodernity: An Enquiry into the Origins of Cultural Change.* Oxford: Basil Blackwell, 1989.

Harvey, Irene E. *Derrida and the Economy of Différance.* Bloomington: Indiana University Press, 1986.

————. "Derrida, Kant, and the Performance of Parergonality." In *Derrida and Deconstruction*, edited by Hugh J. Silverman, 59–76. New York: Routledge, 1989.

Hawking, Stephen W. *A Brief History of Time*. New York: Bantam, 1988.

————. "Quantum Cosmology." In *Three Hundred Years of Gravitation*, edited by Stephen W. Hawking and Werner Israel, 631–51. Cambridge: Cambridge University Press, 1987.

Hawking, Stephen W., and Werner Israel, eds. *Three Hundred Years of Gravitation*. Cambridge: Cambridge University Press, 1987.

Hegel, Georg Wilhelm Friedrich. *Enzyklopädie der philosophischen Wissenschaften im Grundrisse*. Vol. 19 of *Gesammelte Werke*. Hamburg: Felix Meiner, 1989.

————. *Gesammelte Werke*. Hamburg: Felix Meiner, 1968– .

————. *Hegel's Science of Logic*. Translated by A. V. Miller. Atlantic Highlands, N.J.: Humanities Press International, 1990.

————. *Phänomenologie des Geistes*. Vol. 3 of *Werke in 20 Bänden*. Frankfurt am Main: Suhrkamp, 1986. Translated by A. V. Miller as *Phenomenology of Spirit*. Oxford: Oxford University Press, 1977.

————. *Werke in 20 Bänden*. Frankfurt am Main: Suhrkamp, 1971.

Heidegger, Martin. *Early Greek Thinking*. Translated by David Farrell Krell and Frank A. Capuzzi. San Francisco: Harper & Row, 1984.

————. *Einführung in die Metaphysik*. Vol. 40, pt. 2 of *Gesamtausgabe*. Translated by Ralph Manheim as *An Introduction to Metaphysics*. New Haven: Yale University Press, 1959.

————. *Die Frage nach dem Ding*. Tübingen: Max Niemeyer Verlag, 1962. Translated by W. B. Barton, Jr., and Vera Deutsch as *What Is a Thing?* South Bend, Ind.: Gateway, 1967.

————. *Gesamtaufgabe*. Frankfurt am Main: Vittorio Klostermann, 1975– .

————. *Hegels Phänomenologie des Geistes*. Frankfurt am Main: Klostermann, 1980. Translated by Parvis Emad and Kenneth Maly as *Hegel's Phenomenology of Spirit*. Bloomington: Indiana University Press, 1988.

————. *Nietzsche*. 2 vols. Pfullingen: Günter Neske, 1961. Translated by Donald Farrell Krell as *Nietzsche*. 4 vols. in 2. Vol. 1, *The Will to Power as Art*. Vol. 2, *The Eternal Recurrence of the Same*. Vol. 3, *The Will to Power as Knowledge and Metaphysics*. Vol. 4, *Nihilism*. New York: Harper & Row, 1979.

————. *The Piety of Thinking: Essays*. Translated by James G. Hart and John C. Moraldo. Bloomington: Indiana University Press, 1976.

————. *The Question Concerning Technology, and Other Essays*. Translated by William Lovitt. New York: Harper & Row, 1977.

————. *On Time and Being*. Translated by Joan Stambaugh. New York: Harper & Row, 1969.

————. *Sein und Zeit*. Tübingen: Max Niemeyer, 1979. Translated by John Macquarrie and Edward Robinson as *Being and Time*. New York: Harper & Row, 1962.

————. "Die Ursprung des Kunstwerks." In *Holzwege*, pt. 1, vol. 5 of *Gesamtausgabe*. Frankfurt am Main: Klostermann, 1977. Translated by Albert Hofstadter as *Poetry, Language, Thought*. New York: Harper & Row, 1971.

————. "What is Metaphysics?" in *Existence and Being*. Chicago: Gateway, 1949.

————. *Wegmarken*. Frankfurt am Main: Klostermann, 1967.

————. *Zur Seinsfrage*. Frankfurt am Main: Klostermann, 1956. Translated by J. Wilde and W. Kluback as *The Question of Being*. New York: College and University Press, 1958.

————, and Eugen Fink. *Heraklit: Seminar Wintersemester 1966/67*. Frankfurt am Main: Klostermann, 1970. Translated by Charles A. Seibert as *Heraclitus Seminar*. University: University of Alabama Press, 1979.

Heisenberg, Werner. "Remarks on the Origin of the Relations of Uncertainty." In *The Uncertainty Principle and the Foundation of Quantum Mechanics*, edited by William C. Price and Seymour S. Chissick. London: John Wiley & Sons, 1977.

Heller, Erich. *The Importance of Nietzsche*. Chicago: University of Chicago Press, 1988.

Hilbert, David. *Grundlagen der Geometrie*. Leipzig and Berlin: B. G. Teubner, 1899.

Hölderlin, Friedrich. *Sämtliche Werke*. 6 vols. Stuttgart: W. Kohlhammer, 1966–. Reprint of *Sämtliche Werke*. 8 vols. in 15. Stuttgart: Cotta, 1946–1985.

Hollier, Denis. *Against Architecture: The Writings of Georges Bataille*. Translated by Betsy Wing. Cambridge, Mass.: MIT Press, 1989. Originally published as *La Prise de la Concorde: Essais sur Georges Bataille*. Paris: Éditions Gallimard, 1974.

Husserl, Edmund. *Ideen zu einer reinen Phänomenologie und phänomenologischen Philosophie*. Vol. 3 of *Gesammelte Werke (Husserliana)*. Edited by Walter Biemel. The Hague: Martinus Nijhof, 1950. Translated by W. R. Boyce Gibson as *Ideas: General Introduction to Pure Phenomenology*. 1931; rpt. New York: Collier Books, 1972.

————. *Die Krisis der europäischen Wissenschaften und die transzendentale Phänomenologie: Einer Einleitung in die phänomenologische Philosophie*. Vol. 6 of *Gesammelte Werke (Husserliana)*. Edited by Walter Biemel. The Hague: Martinus Nijhof, 1950. Translated by David Carr as *The Crisis of European Sciences and Transcendental Phenomenology: An Introduction to Phenomenological Philosophy*. Evanston, Ill.: Northwestern University Press, 1970.

Huyssen, Andreas. "Mapping the Postmodern." *New German Critique* 33 (1984):5–52.

Infeld, Leopold. *Whom the Gods Love*. New York: McGraw-Hill, 1948.

Irigaray, Luce. *Amante marine de Friedrich Nietzsche*. Paris: Éditions de Minuit, 1980. Translated by Gillian C. Gill as *Marine Lover of Friedrich Nietzsche*. New York: Columbia University Press, 1991.

James, William. "On Some Hegelisms." In *The Will to Believe*. 1898; rpt. Cambridge, Mass.: Harvard University Press, 1979.

Jameson, Fredric. "Cognitive Mapping." In *Marxism and the Interpretation of Culture*, edited by Cary Nelson and Lawrence Grossberg. Urbana: University of Illinois Press, 1988.

———. *Late Marxism: Adorno, or, The Persistence of the Dialectic*. London: Verso, 1990.

———. *The Political Unconscious: Narrative as a Socially Symbolic Act*. Ithaca, N.Y.: Cornell University Press, 1981.

———. *Postmodernism, or, the Cultural Logic of Late Capitalism*. Durham, N.C.: Duke University Press, 1991.

———. "Some Questions and Responses." In *The Linguistics of Writing: Arguments between Language and Literature*, edited by Nigel Fabb, Derek Attridge, Alan Durant, and Colin MacCabe. New York: Methuen, 1987.

Jammer, Max. *The Philosophy of Quantum Mechanics: The Interpretations of Quantum Mechanics in Historical Perspective*. New York: Wiley, 1974.

JanMohamed, Abdul R., and David Lloyd, eds. *The Nature and Context of Minority Discourse*. New York: Oxford University Press, 1991.

Jay, Gregory S. *America the Scrivener: Deconstruction and the Subject of Literary History*. Ithaca, N.Y.: Cornell University Press, 1990.

Johnson, Barbara. *A World of Difference*. Baltimore: Johns Hopkins University Press, 1987.

Kamuf, Peggy. *Signature Pieces: On the Institution of Authorship*. Ithaca, N.Y.: Cornell University Press, 1988.

Kant, Immanuel. *Critique of Practical Reason*. Translated by Lewis White Beck. Chicago: University of Chicago Press, 1949.

———. *Kritik der Urteilskraft*. Vol. 10 of *Werkausgabe in 12 Bänden*. Frankfurt am Main: Suhrkamp, 1974. Translated by J. H. Bernard as *The Critique of Judgement*. New York: Hafner Press, 1951.

———. *Was heißt: sich in Denken orientiern, Sämtliche Werke*, hg. p. Gedan et al. Leipsig: Verlag der Dürr'schen Buchhandlung, 1905. v. 466. Translated by Lewis White Beck as "What is Orientation in Thinking." In *Critique of Practical Reason*, edited and translated by Lewis White Beck. Chicago: University of Chicago Press, 1949, 293–305.

Keats, John. *The Letters of John Keats*. Edited by Hyder Edward Rollins. 2 vols. Cambridge, Mass.: Harvard University Press, 1958.

Kierkegaard, Søren. *Kierkegaard's Concluding Unscientific Postscript*. Translated by David F. Swenson. Princeton, N.J.: Princeton University Press, 1968.

Klossowski, Pierre. *Nietzsche et le cercle vicieux*. Paris: Mercure de France, 1969.

Knapp, Steven, and Walter Benn Michaels. "Against Theory 2: Hermeneutics and Deconstruction." *Critical Inquiry* 14 (Autumn 1987):49–68.

Kofman, Sarah. *Nietzsche et la scène philosophique*. Paris: Union Générale d'Éditions, 1979.

Koyré, Alexander. *Newtonian Studies*. Chicago: University of Chicago Press, 1965.

Krell, David Farrell. "Analysis." In Martin Heidegger, *Nietzsche*, vol. 2, *The Eternal Recurrence of the Same*. Translated by David Farrell Krell. San Francisco: Harper & Row, 1984.

————. "Consultations with the Paternal Shadow: Gasché, Derrida and Klossowski on *Ecce Homo*." In *Exceedingly Nietzsche: Aspects of Contemporary Nietzsche-Interpretation*, edited by David Farrell Krell and David Wood. London: Routledge, 1988.

————. *Of Memory, Reminiscence, and Writing: On the Verge*. Bloomington: Indiana University Press, 1990.

————. *Postponements: Woman, Sensuality and Death in Nietzsche*. Bloomington: Indiana University Press, 1986.

————, and David Wood, eds. *Exceedingly Nietzsche: Aspects of Contemporary Nietzsche-Interpretation*. London: Routledge, 1988.

Lacan, Jacques. "L'Excommunication" (1964). Reprinted in *Le Seminaire de Jacques Lacan XI*, edited by Jacques-Alain Miller. Paris: Éditions du Seuil, 1973. Translated by Alan Sheridan as "Excommunication." In *The Four Fundamental Concepts of Psycho-Analysis*. New York: W. W. Norton, 1978.

————. *Le Seminaire de Jacques Lacan XI: Les Quatre concepts fondamentaux de la psychanalyse*. Edited by Jacques-Alain Miller. Paris: Éditions du Seuil, 1973. Translated by Alan Sheridan as *The Four Fundamental Concepts of Psycho-Analysis*. New York: W. W. Norton, 1978.

Lacoue-Labarthe, Philippe. "L'Echo du sujet." In *Le Sujet de la philosophie*. Paris: Flammarion, 1979.

————. *La Fiction du politique: Heidegger, l'art et la politique*. Paris: Christian Bourgois Editeur, 1987; Coll. Détroits. Translated by Chris Turner as *Heidegger, Art and Politics: The Fiction of the Political*. Oxford: Basil Blackwell, 1990.

————. *Typography: Mimesis, Philosophy, Politics*. Edited by Christopher Fynsk. Cambridge, Mass.: Harvard University Press, 1989.

————, and Jean-Luc Nancy. *The Literary Absolute: The Theory of Literature in German Romanticism*. Translated by Philip Barnard and Cheryl Lester. Albany: State University of New York Press, 1988.

Lentricchia, Frank. *Criticism and Social Change*. Chicago: University of Chicago Press, 1983.

Lyotard, Jean-François. *La Condition postmoderne: Rapport sur le savoir*. Paris: Éditions de Minuit, 1979. Translated by Geoffrey Bennington and Brian Massumi as *The Postmodern Condition: A Report on Knowledge*. Minneapolis: University of Minnesota Press, 1984.

————. *Dérive à partir de Marx et Freud*. Paris: Union générale d'éditions, 1973.

————. *Le Différend*. Paris: Éditions de Minuit, 1983; Coll. Critique. Translated by Georges Van Den Abbeele as *The Differend: Phrases in Dispute*. Minneapolis: University of Minnesota Press, 1988.

————. *Économie libidinale*. Paris: Éditions de Minuit, 1974.

————. *Heidegger et "les juifs."* Paris: Galilée, 1988. Translated by Andreas Michel and Mark S. Roberts as *Heidegger and "the jews."* Minneapolis: University of Minnesota Press, 1990.

————. "Judicieux dans le différend." In Jacques Derrida et al., *La Faculté de Juger.* Paris: Éditions de Minuit, 1985.

————. *The Lyotard Reader.* Edited by Andrew Benjamin. Oxford: Basil Blackwell, 1989.

————. *Peregrinations: Law, Form, Event.* New York: Columbia University Press, 1988.

————. "Réécrire la modernité." In *L'Inhumain: Causeries sur le temps.* Paris: Galilée, 1988.

————. "Réponse à la question: Qu'est-ce que le postmoderne?" *Critique* 419 (April 1982).

Mandel, Ernest. *Late Capitalism.* London: NLB, 1975.

Manin, Y. I. *Course in Mathematical Logic.* Translated by Neal Koblitz. New York: Springer Verlag, 1977.

Martin, Wallace. *Recent Theories of Narrative.* Ithaca, N.Y.: Cornell University Press, 1986.

Marx, Karl, and Friedrich Engels. *Marx/Engels Gesamtausgabe.* Part 1. Berlin: Marx-Engels Verlag, 1932.

————. "Ökonomisch-philosophische Manuskripte (1844)." Vol. 3 of *Marx/Engels Gesamtausgabe,* pt. 1. Berlin: Marx-Engels Verlag, 1932. Translated as "Economic and Philosophical Manuscripts of 1844" in *The Marx-Engels Reader.* Edited by Robert C. Tucker. New York: Norton, 1978.

————. *The Marx-Engels Reader.* Edited by Robert C. Tucker. New York: Norton, 1978.

Megill, Alan. *Prophets of Extremity: Nietzsche, Heidegger, Foucault, Derrida.* Berkeley and Los Angeles: University of California Press, 1985.

Melville, Stephen. *Philosophy Beside Itself: On Deconstruction and Modernism.* Minneapolis: University of Minnesota Press, 1986.

Michelfelder, Diane P., and Richard E. Palmer, eds. *Dialogue and Deconstruction: The Gadamer-Derrida Encounter.* Albany: State University of New York Press, 1989.

Mitchell, W.J.T., ed. *Against Theory.* Chicago: University of Chicago Press, 1987.

————. *On Narrative.* Chicago: University of Chicago Press, 1981.

Morris, Meaghan. "Postmodernity and Lyotard's Sublime." *Art and Text* 16 (Summer 1984/85).

Murdoch, Dugald. *Niels Bohr's Philosophy of Physics.* Cambridge: Cambridge University Press, 1987.

Nancy, Jean-Luc. *Le Discours de la syncope.* Paris: Flammarion, 1976.

————. *L'Expérience de la liberté.* Paris: Galilée, 1988.

————. *L'Impérative catégorique.* Paris: Flammarion, 1983.

————. Introduction to *Who Comes After the Subject?*, edited by Eduardo Cadava, Peter Connor, and Jean-Luc Nancy. New York: Routledge, 1991.

Nehamas, Alexander. *Nietzsche: Life as Literature*. Cambridge, Mass.: Harvard University Press, 1985.

Nietzsche, Friedrich. *The Antichrist*. In *The Portable Nietzsche*. Translated by Walter Kaufmann. New York: Viking, 1954.

————. *Beyond Good and Evil*. Translated by Walter Kaufmann. New York: Vintage, 1966.

————. *The Birth of Tragedy and The Case of Wagner*. Translated by Walter Kaufmann. New York: Vintage, 1966.

————. *Daybreak*. Translated by R. J. Hollingdale. Cambridge: Cambridge University Press, 1982.

————. *The Gay Science*. Translated by Walter Kaufmann. New York: Vintage, 1974.

————. *Human, All Too Human: A Book for Free Spirits*. Translated by R. J. Hollingdale. Cambridge: Cambridge University Press, 1986.

————. *Nietzsche Briefwechsel: Kritische Gesamtausgabe*. Edited by Giorgio Colli und Mazzino Montinari. Berlin: Walter de Gruyter, 1981.

————. *On the Genealogy of Morals and Ecce Homo*. Translated by Walter Kaufmann. New York: Vintage, 1969.

————. *Philosophy in the Tragic Age of the Greeks*. Translated by Marianne Cowan. Chicago: Gateway, 1962.

————. *The Portable Nietzsche*. Translated by Walter Kaufmann. New York: Viking, 1954.

————. *Sämtliche Werke: Kritische Studienausgabe*. 15 vols. Edited by Giorgio Colli und Mazzino Montinari. 2nd ed. Munich: Deutscher Taschenbuch Verlag; Berlin and New York: Walter de Gruyter, 1988.

————. *Thus Spoke Zarathustra*. Translated by Walter Kaufmann. In *The Portable Nietzsche*, edited by Walter Kaufmann. New York: Viking Press, 1955.

————. *Twilight of the Idols*. In *The Portable Nietzsche*. Translated by Walter Kaufmann. New York: Viking, 1954.

————. *Untimely Meditations*. Translated by R. J. Hollingdale. Cambridge: Cambridge University Press, 1983.

————. *The Will to Power*. Translated by Walter Kaufmann and R. J. Hollingdale. New York: Vintage, 1968.

O'Hara, Daniel, ed. *Why Nietzsche Now?* Bloomington: Indiana University Press, 1984.

Pais, Abraham. *Inward Bound: Of Matter and Forces in the Physical World*. Oxford: Oxford University Press, 1986.

————. *Niels Bohr's Times, in Physics, Philosophy, and Polity*. New York: Oxford University Press, 1991.

————. *"Subtle is the Lord...": The Science and the Life of Albert Einstein*. Oxford: Oxford University Press, 1982.

Pefanis, Julian. *Heterology and the Postmodern: Bataille, Baudrillard, and Lyotard.* Durham, N.C.: Duke University Press, 1991.

Penrose, Roger. *The Emperor's New Mind: Concerning Computers, Minds, and the Laws of Physics.* Oxford: Oxford University Press, 1989.

Plato. *The Collected Dialogues of Plato.* Edited by Edith Hamilton and Huntington Cairns. Princeton, N.J.: Princeton University Press, 1961.

Powers, Jonathan. *Philosophy and the New Physics.* London: Methuen, 1982.

Prigogine, Ilya, and Isabelle Stengers. *Order out of Chaos: Man's New Dialogue with Nature.* New York: Bantam Books, 1984.

Prince, Gerald. "Narrative Pragmatics, Message, and Point." *Poetics* 12 (1983):527–36.

———. *Narratology: The Form and the Function of the Narrative.* Berlin and New York: Mouton, 1982.

Propp, Vladimir. *Morphology of the Folktale.* 2nd rev. ed. Translated by Laurence Scott. Austin: University of Texas Press, 1968.

Proust, Marcel. *La Prisonnière.* Paris: Flammarion, 1984. Translated by C. K. Scott-Moncrieff and Terence Kilmartin as *The Captive.* Vol. 3 of *The Remembrance of Things Past.* New York: Vintage, 1982.

Rapaport, Herman. *Heidegger and Derrida: Reflections on Time and Language.* Lincoln: University of Nebraska Press, 1989.

Richman, Michèle. *Reading Georges Bataille: Beyond the Gift.* Baltimore: Johns Hopkins University Press, 1982.

Riffaterre, Michael. *Fictional Truth.* Baltimore: Johns Hopkins University Press, 1990.

Ronell, Avital. *The Telephone Book: Technology—Schizophrenia—Electric Speech.* Lincoln: University of Nebraska Press, 1989.

Rorty, Richard. *The Consequences of Pragmatism: Essays, 1972–1980.* Minneapolis: University of Minnesota Press, 1982.

———. *Contingency, Irony, and Solidarity.* Cambridge: Cambridge University Press, 1989.

———. "Habermas and Lyotard on Postmodernity." In *Habermas and Modernity,* edited by Richard J. Bernstein, 161–75. Cambridge, Mass.: MIT Press, 1985.

———. *Objectivity, Relativism, and Truth.* Cambridge: Cambridge University Press, 1991.

Ryan, Michael. *Marxism and Deconstruction: A Critical Articulation.* Baltimore: Johns Hopkins University Press, 1982.

Sallis, John. *Crossings: Nietzsche and the Space of Tragedy.* Chicago: University of Chicago Press, 1991.

———. *Echoes: After Heidegger.* Bloomington: Indiana University Press, 1990.

———, ed. *Deconstruction and Philosophy: The Texts of Jacques Derrida.* Chicago: University of Chicago Press, 1987.

Saper, Craig. "A Nervous Theory: The Troubling Gaze of Psychoanalysis in Media Studies." *Diacritics,* forthcoming.

Schilpp, P. A., ed. *Albert Einstein: Philosopher-Scientist*. New York: Tudor, 1949.

Shapiro, Gary. *Alcyone: Nietzsche on Gifts, Noise, and Women*. Albany: State University of New York Press, 1991.

———. *Nietzschean Narratives*. Bloomington: Indiana University Press, 1989.

———, ed. *After the Future: Postmodern Times and Places*. Albany: State University of New York Press, 1990.

Shaviro, Steven. *Passion and Excess: Bataille, Blanchot, and Literary Theory*. Tallahassee: Florida State University Press, 1990.

Shutte, Ofelia. *Beyond Nihilism: Nietzsche without Masks*. Chicago: University of Chicago Press, 1984.

Silverman, Hugh J., ed. *Derrida and Deconstruction*. New York: Routledge, 1989.

———, and Gary E. Aylesworth, eds. *The Textual Sublime: Deconstruction and its Differences*. Albany: State University of New York Press, 1990.

Silverman, Hugh J., and Donn Welton, eds. *Postmodernism and Continental Philosophy*. Albany: State University of New York Press, 1988.

Smith, Barbara Herrnstein. *Contingencies of Value: Alternative Perspectives for Critical Theory*. Cambridge, Mass.: Harvard University Press, 1988.

———. *On the Margins of Discourse: The Relation of Literature to Language*. Chicago: University of Chicago Press, 1978.

Smith, Paul. *Discerning the Subject*. Minneapolis: University of Minnesota Press, 1988.

Soja, Edward W. *Postmodern Geographies: The Reassertion of Space in Critical Social Theory*. London and New York: Verso, 1989.

Spariosu, Mihai I. *Dionysus Reborn: Play and the Aesthetic Dimension in Modern Philosophical and Scientific Discourse*. Ithaca, N.Y.: Cornell University Press, 1989.

———. *God of Many Names: Play, Poetry, and Power in Hellenic Thought from Homer to Aristotle*. Durham, N.C.: Duke University Press, 1991.

Spivak, Gayatri Chakravorty. *In Other Worlds: Essays in Cultural Politics*. New York: Methuen, 1987.

———. "Speculations on Reading Marx: After Derrida." In *Post-Structuralism and the Question of History*, edited by Derek Attridge, Geoff Bennington, and Robert Young. Cambridge: Cambridge University Press, 1987.

———. "Translator's Preface." In *Of Grammatology*, translated by Gayatri C. Spivak. Baltimore: Johns Hopkins University Press, 1975.

Staten, Henry. *Nietzsche's Voice*. Ithaca, N.Y.: Cornell University Press, 1990.

———. *Wittgenstein and Derrida*. Lincoln: University of Nebraska Press, 1984.

Sterne, Laurence. *Tristram Shandy*. Indianapolis, Ind., and New York: Odyssey Press, 1940.

Strong, Tracy B. "The Deconstruction of the Tradition: Nietzsche and the Greeks." In *Nietzsche and the Rhetoric of Nihilism: Essays on Interpretation, Language and Politics*, edited by Tom Darby, Béla Egyed, and Ben Jones. Ottawa: Carleton University Press, 1989.

————, and Michael Allen Gillespie, eds. *Nietzsche's New Seas: Explorations in Philosophy, Aesthetics, and Politics.* Chicago: University of Chicago Press, 1988.

Ulmer, Gregory. *Applied Grammatology: Post(e)-pedagogy from Jacques Derrida to Joseph Beuys.* Baltimore: Johns Hopkins University Press, 1985.

————. *Teletheory: Grammatology in the Age of Video.* New York: Routledge, 1989.

Warminski, Andrzej. *Readings in Interpretation: Hölderlin, Hegel, Heidegger.* Minneapolis: University of Minnesota Press, 1987.

Warren, Mark. *Nietzsche and Political Thought.* Cambridge, Mass.: MIT Press, 1988.

Waters, Lindsay, and Wlad Godzich, eds. *Reading de Man Reading.* Minneapolis: University of Minnesota Press, 1989.

Weber, Samuel. *Institution and Interpretation.* Minneapolis: University of Minnesota Press, 1987.

————. *The Legend of Freud.* Minneapolis: University of Minnesota Press, 1982.

West, Cornel. "Ethics and Action in Fredric Jameson's Marxist Hermeneutic." In *Postmodernism and Politics,* edited by Jonathan Arac. Minneapolis: University of Minnesota Press, 1986.

Weyl, Herman. *Space—Time—Matter.* Translated by Henry L. Brose. New York: Dover, 1950.

White, Alan. *Within Nietzsche's Labyrinth.* New York: Routledge, 1990.

Wilde, Oscar. *Artist as Critic.* Edited by Richard Ellman. Chicago: University of Chicago Press, 1982.

Wood, David, and Robert Bernasconi, eds. *Derrida and Différance.* Evanston, Ill.: Northwestern University Press, 1988.

Žižek, Slavoj. *Looking Awry: An Introduction to Jacques Lacan through Popular Culture.* Cambridge, Mass.: MIT Press, 1991.

————. *The Sublime Object of Ideology.* London: Verso, 1989.

Zurek, Wojciech H., ed. *Complexity, Entropy, and the Physics of Information.* Redwood City, Calif.: Addison-Wesley, 1991.

Index

Note: Extensive discussions of major figures and topics are indexed under the heading "*key discussions*," with corresponding chapters indicated in parentheses. All works discussed and referred to are listed in the bibliography (391–407); the index contains only selected titles, listed under author's name at the end of the entry.

Reconfigurations

was composed in 11 on 13 Monotype Bembo
with display type in Adobe Centaur by
OCTAVO DESIGN AND PRODUCTION,
under the production supervision of
LYNN WERTS,
printed by sheet-fed offset on 55# Sebago Antique Cream,
Smyth-sewn and bound over 88 pt. binder's boards in
Holliston Roxite B, and perfect-bound with paper covers by
MAPLE VAIL BOOK MANUFACTURING GROUP;
with dust jackets and paper covers designed by
LARRY LESHAN
and printed in 4-color process by
JOHNSON CITY PUBLISHING;
and published by
UNIVERSITY PRESS OF FLORIDA.

∾